Praise for *Advanced Google AdWords*

Most books about search advertising show you how to do it. In Advanced Google AdWords, *paid search expert Brad Geddes takes it to the next level, showing you not only how to get the most from your search advertising campaigns, but more importantly why you should use specific features and techniques, who you should be targeting with your creative, and when to use the scores of advanced tactics he describes for maximum impact and profitability. I'd advise buying more than one copy of this book because you'll wear one out from constant use.*

　　—CHRIS SHERMAN, Executive Editor, Search Engine Land

The thing that differentiates this book from other AdWords guides is that it takes you inside the mind of a successful paid search advertiser and walks you through each and every step of the auction and advertising process. The two consistent strengths of the book are its ability to ground the reader in the core goals of their advertising program (generating leads and sales through effective targeting and messaging) and its relentless attention to detail. That perspective and thoroughness mean that the book is accessible to less sophisticated advertisers, and ensure that there are a series of valuable nuggets for intermediate and even expert AdWords users.

　　—TOM DEMERS, Director of Marketing with WordStream

Brad is the go-to guru for AdWords. Advanced Google AdWords *is actionable, readable, and has tons of handy tips that any online advertiser can try immediately. Even if you think you know everything about Quality Score or the Google content network, you'll find things you haven't thought about that can boost your sales right away.*

　　—RON DRABKIN, VP Business Development, JustAnswer.com

Brad has made a lot of people a lot of money in some of the most competitive markets of PPC marketing. Now he's put all his knowledge into one book. Buy and read this book before your competitors do!

　　—ADRIAN BYE, Founder, MeetInnovators.com

Ironically, it's hard to find complete, accurate, and intelligent information about how to build and manage paid search campaigns. Brad Geddes is one of the few people in the PPC world that I trust to deeply know the facts, communicate them clearly, and add value with insights that save time and/or money. This book is perfect for anyone who wants to really learn paid search and discover the best ways to improve their results.

　　—CRAIG DANULOFF, President, ClickEquations

Brad's book is the most comprehensive compilation of Google AdWords tools and how-to advice I've seen in some time. He gives a thorough explanation of the theory and history of search, and provides detailed, specific instructions on execution of strategies & tactics covering every possible facet of Google AdWords. Every online marketer, from novice to expert, will find this an invaluable resource in getting the most out of their AdWords campaigns.

—MELISSA MACKEY, Online Marketing Manager, Fluency Media; Search Engine Watch Expert Author, Search Advertising

Brad Geddes knows marketing, and he understands the inscrutable mind of Google—a killer combination when it comes to explaining AdWords. His book is a powerful combination of deep insight and simple prescriptions that will help anyone, from AdWords novice to seasoned pro, get more clicks and make more sales. I've never seen a clearer discussion of the buying funnel as it relates to choosing keywords and writing ads. And you ignore the chapter on Quality Score at your own risk. This book raised my game—and I'm sure it'll do the same with yours.

—HOWIE JACOBSON, Ph.D., author of Google AdWords For Dummies

There are many paid search experts out there, but Brad is unique in that he is not just an expert, but is able to effectively communicate his knowledge to those who are new to the field. It is rare to find someone in the industry that has such a deep understanding of a topic that can teach both the basics and the robust features of paid search.

—BARRY SCHWARTZ, CEO of RustyBrick, Editor at Search Engine Land & Search Engine Roundtable

Brad Geddes is one of the few AdWords experts I always pay attention to. He's one of the best in the field. This book is incredibly comprehensive, illustrative, and readable. Both beginners and experienced pay-per-click marketers will find invaluable insights here. Brad fills in a lot of gaps that the AdWords Help screens don't cover. Otherwise, you'd have to get the info from an AdWords rep, and only the biggest spenders get the best attention from these reps. Heeding this book's advice from the start will save you a lot of money and get you much better results. Highly recommended.

—BRIAN CARTER, Director of PPC, SEO, Social Media at Fuel Interactive

If Google set out to make AdWords simple—they failed. Brad steps into the breach and makes things clear, understandable, and profitable for us mere mortals with a marketing background.

—ANDY ATKINS-KRÜGER, CEO WebCertain

Successful PPC campaign organization and management is more complex than one would originally think. Thankfully, the author has provided us with a highly practical, easy-to-understand guide to launching and managing PPC campaigns that will simplify the process and increase the likelihood of great results. Brad really opens your eyes to not only how, but to why things should be done. For instance, in the chapter on ad writing you are given proven best practices, but also taught how to get into the minds of the search prospects and meet them where they are at in the sales funnel. Awesome! Whether you're a beginner or have been running PPC campaigns for a while now, you can be sure your head will be exploding with new ways to make your campaigns more effective and profitable.

—STONEY G DEGEYTER, CEO, Pole Position Marketing

Brad gets it! He has a wealth of hands-on experience and shares it freely. If you want to drive and convert Google AdWords traffic, you need to read this book—now!

—TIM ASH, CEO, SiteTuners.com; author of *Landing Page Optimization;* chairperson, ConversionConference.com

I'm not going to lie. I'm jealous. This is the AdWords book I wish I had written. I've been following and learning from Brad Geddes for years and without a doubt, this is the single most useful, detailed, and comprehensive book on AdWords available.

Who is this book for? Absolutely everyone who uses Google AdWords. Not only will beginners get a lot from this book, but seasoned professionals with years of experience will pick up a lot more than a few nuggets.

This is it. This is the AdWords book that others will try to match. This is the only book about AdWords you will ever need. Brad has brought something truly useful to the advertising community.

—DALE DAVIS, Managing Director, RedFly Limited

This book translates years of successful experience into language anyone can learn from to improve their skill level and understand paid search at a higher level. For years Brad has been my go-to source for the hardest of AdWords questions no one else could answer. Understanding the evolution of paid search is key to taking advantage of the nuances and complexities of current search algorithms. Brad does the impossible by teaching you high-level skills that will equate to actionable strategies you can apply immediately. He describes the lifecycle of paid search, and most importantly how to create a strategy from this understanding that applies to you. Brad has stayed fresh and documented his decade of experience and teaches people with a patience level acquired from years of teaching in person that results in an attention to detail that will be hard to find in any other book on the subject. The money you will save on understanding quality score alone makes buying this book a no-brainer.

—TODD MALICOAT, SEO Faculty at Market Motive

This is a book you'll keep on your desk, not your bookshelf.

Brad Geddes explains advanced optimization in plain, simple language. You read it and it makes sense, so you trust it. You read it and you understand it, and so you can put it to work on your own campaigns. He makes it seem easy, and that's the brilliance

of this book. Even as Google continues to expand and evolve, the techniques shown in the book will still be perfectly valid—they are built on a very sold technical foundation. I highly recommend it to any serious PPC campaign manager. Well done, Brad!
—Matt Van Wagner, President, Find Me Faster

Brad Geddes is the clearest voice on Advanced AdWords teachings, tactics, and strategies. I'm constantly referring to Brad's articles and sharing them with others to help our clients make tens of thousands of dollars in their PPC campaigns—so be sure to grab a copy of Brad's new book.

One of the best things I like about Brad's knowledge is that he is constantly sharpening his blade by teaching (Google's Seminar for Success, AdWords advanced courses) and doing (running his own campaigns) so his writing reflects his deep knowledge of the intricacies and details which, when followed, lead to improved campaign results.

There are a handful of books on the market which give you a broad understanding of the psychology behind how to advertise on Google; in Advanced Google AdWords *Brad gives you that plus a practical, step by step plan to leverage what you've learned by including the technical details you need to turn your knowledge into action.*
—Timothy Seward, Founder, ROI Revolution, Inc.

Brad has been the authority on Google AdWords for years, and this book is the best training tool I have seen since Google's own training on their program. Brad goes a step further by explaining everything from where PPC advertising got started to advanced optimization techniques. If there is one part that I focused in on the most, it was keyword and ad group organization. As Brad says, it is the most time consuming but most rewarding tactic you can use in PPC marketing. If you want to learn AdWords, this is a fantastic book to read to get the whole picture.
—Kate Morris, Search Engine Marketing Consultant, KateMorris.com

Very few people have the grasp and understanding of Google's content network or the ability to use words and illustrations to make it look so easy. From best practices to organizing your campaigns to the importance of placement performance reports, you'll find it step by step in Advanced Google AdWords.
—Shelley Ellis, CEO, Shelley Ellis Consulting

Brad Geddes is the quintessential AdWords authority.

His love of sharing information and his deep knowledge of pay-per-click systems makes this book a compelling read.

This book hits the mark by blending practical with creative strategies to help me organize, quantify, and present ads for the most effective return on investment.
—Brett Tabke, CEO, WebmasterWorld

For years, I've been recommending Brad Geddes to people who ask me for AdWords resources. I'm thrilled to now have Brad's book *Advanced Google AdWords* to recommend as well. This book clearly walks through every step of the paid search process in accessible, relatable language. Just as importantly, Brad keeps the focus on the audience. He understands that it's not enough to know how to create and buy ads and ensure they are visible in Google search results. The real goal is to connect your business to the right searchers, engage them, and turn them into paying customers. That's what this book will help you do.

—VANESSA FOX, author, *Marketing In The Age Of Google*

Many AdWords advertisers realize that the search and content network need different approaches. The problem is that most don't know how to handle the difference so they just ignore the content network. Big mistake. The content network has the potential to deliver more visitors with lower CPC's. Brad does a great job in breaking down, with a flowchart no less, how the approach to the content network differs and how to implement a winning content network strategy. Brad even goes a step further by showing you how to put a laser focus on certain content network sites to get the most out of what is available. If you want to boost your content performance you need to listen to what Brad has to say and follow in his steps.

—ROB LENDERMAN, Founder, Boost CTR

Brad Geddes takes the reader by the hand, starting with the basics of search engine marketing, and then steadily introduces more advanced concepts and more powerful tools. I really appreciate his consistent focus on maximizing conversion rates. All the traffic in the world won't help us unless it generates leads and sales. As a primer, a field guide, and a reference, this book will be a constant companion for online marketers at all levels of experience.

—BRIAN MASSEY, The Conversion Scientist

This book is a must-read for anyone working with AdWords! Whether you only have a basic understanding of AdWords or if you are AdWords certified, this book will give you insight from someone that continues to see success within the industry. This book will take your understanding of AdWords to the next level. In this book Brad's advanced knowledge in optimizing accounts for top performance is displayed. There are plenty of golden nuggets in this book that will surely help you optimize your accounts for top performance!

—TROY STOCKINGER, Senior Account Manager, Findability Group

For years I have been seeking out the one book that I can turn to when I need both a basic refresher and when I tackle more advanced AdWords tactics. Brad Geddes has finally provided me with such a resource. In Advanced Google AdWords, Geddes demonstrates his years of expert experience in paid search marketing as he demystifies the many components involved with AdWords and shares valuable secrets of those successfully dominating the AdWords platform. I can officially say my search is over—if you are looking for the one book that will help you drive qualified traffic to your site and increase ROI, you just found it!

—JOANNA LORD, Director of Customer Acquisition & Engagement, SEOmoz

What separates *Advanced Google AdWords* from the others on the bookshelf is the brilliance of the author and the wealth of experience he has in the search industry. Brad Geddes is well known amongst other leaders in search and is often sought for his expert opinion on AdWords campaigns and optimizing campaign performance by decreasing spend while increasing overall ROI. He has consulted online advertising agencies on setting up keyword taxonomies, written articles for major search news websites, and has collaborated with Fortune 500 companies on the implementation and performance of their PPC initiatives. Frankly stated, Brad is frequently sought for his insights on all areas of search because he knows what works and more importantly, he knows how to explain paid search strategies to any audience regardless of level of experience. I am thrilled that Brad has written this book as I, as well as you, will use this tool frequently.

—MICHAEL MARTIN, Director of Search Platform, AT&T Interactive

Brad has been the #1 resource on AdWords for many years and getting some of his insights has been priceless to many in the past. Now that he finally released his book I have to admit that this is probably the best book on the market for advanced AdWords topics. If you're serious about using paid search, this book is a must-buy. Not only does Brad share tips that were never published before, but also gives help on how to use your time as efficiently as possible.

—THOMAS BINDL, Founder/CEO Refined Labs

The word "expert" gets thrown out there a lot in the digital marketing industry, but Brad Geddes is FOR SURE one of our top experts in search engine marketing. I've had the pleasure to learn from Brad through the years through his various writings and speaking engagements. Bottom line, do you want to know how to win at paid search? Do you want to become an advanced AdWords user and make your organization successful at using PPC? Then read this book. Brad has compiled into one resource what it would take you a decade to learn yourself.

—JOSHUA DRELLER, Vice President, Media Technology and Analytics at Fuor Digital

Advanced
Google
AdWords™

Advanced Google AdWords™

Brad Geddes

Wiley Publishing, Inc.

Senior Acquisitions Editor: WILLEM KNIBBE
Development Editor: TOM CIRTIN
Technical Editor: PATRICK MCLAUGHLIN
Production Editor: RACHEL MCCONLOGUE
Copy Editor: LUNAEA HOUGLAND
Editorial Manager: PETE GAUGHAN
Production Manager: TIM TATE
Vice President and Executive Group Publisher: RICHARD SWADLEY
Vice President and Publisher: NEIL EDDE
Book Designer: FRANZ BAUMHACKL
Compositor: MAUREEN FORYS, HAPPENSTANCE TYPE-O-RAMA
Proofreader: REBECCA RIDER
Indexer: NANCY GUENTHER
Project Coordinator, Cover: LYNSEY STANFORD
Cover Designer: RYAN SNEED

Dear Reader,

Thank you for choosing *Advanced Google AdWords*. This book is part of a family of premium-quality Sybex books, all of which are written by outstanding authors who combine practical experience with a gift for teaching.

Sybex was founded in 1976. More than 30 years later, we're still committed to producing consistently exceptional books. With each of our titles, we're working hard to set a new standard for the industry. From the paper we print on to the authors we work with, our goal is to bring you the best books available.

I hope you see all that reflected in these pages. I'd be very interested to hear your comments and get your feedback on how we're doing. Feel free to let me know what you think about this or any other Sybex book by sending me an email at nedde@wiley.com. If you think you've found a technical error in this book, please visit http://sybex.custhelp.com. Customer feedback is critical to our efforts at Sybex.

Best regards,

Neil Edde
Vice President and Publisher
Sybex, an imprint of Wiley

To Lilith Rose for bringing joy and wonder to our lives.

Acknowledgments

Writing this book has been an amazing journey, and there are many who deserve a heartfelt thank you for contributing to this quest being completed.

I must first thank Sharon, my wife, who has supported my various adventures over the years no matter how crazy they sounded. During the creation of this book, our first child, Lilith Rose, was born. Lilith made it difficult for me to tear myself away from her to finish this book, and therefore, many pages were written with her sitting in my lap giving her interpretation of marketing.

Thank you to my business partner, Leslie Clark, who tirelessly read every single word. Her ideas helped shape this book. I must also thank her for keeping the company running while I was off writing and regularly ignoring emails and phone calls.

I was impressed with the team at Wiley. Willem Kibble not only had the idea of writing a book on advanced AdWords, but even after we worked through the details, he continuously provided input and assistance whenever necessary. Tom Cirtin was a great asset in many ways, and I truly appreciated his work in structuring every chapter to be a logical progression of comprehendible thoughts. Thank you to Rachel McConlogue and all the others who worked in the background to produce the final product.

Patrick McLaughlin checked my facts. Michael Martin checked my ideas. They are both good friends.

The teams at Google have not just given me support for the writing of this book, they have been giving me support for almost a decade, and for that I thank them. A special thank you goes to AdWords Advisor (who wishes to remain anonymous), who has been a customer advocate and a tremendous resource for several years. No one cares more about AdWords than Fred Vallaeys, who is constantly striving to improve the product and is willing to listen to my rants and feedback about Google.

Finally, I must thank the Internet marketing community. I have been writing, speaking, and blogging about online marketing for many years. During that time, I have been an active participant in forums, blogs, and conferences. My interaction with the community, made up of significantly more people than I could ever acknowledge on paper, has helped to increase everyone's understanding and success with Google AdWords.

About the Author

Brad Geddes has been involved in online marketing for more than a decade. Over the years, he has provided a variety of consulting services, including usability, conversion optimization, product development, product positioning, and agency consulting. He has managed SEO, PPC, and affiliate marketing campaigns for both himself and others.

One of his trademarks has been demystifying the more complicated aspects of SEO, PPC, and Internet advertising through writing, speaking, and training. Brad does not withhold secrets as he prefers to educate readers on the various aspects of crafting marketing campaigns to ensure the success for all parties involved.

Brad is not one to call himself an expert or guru. He prefers to train marketers and let the results speak for themselves. Therefore, instead of writing paragraphs that use the words "master," "wizard," or "thought-leader," and name-dropping companies he has worked with such as Amazon, Yahoo!, and Google, he prefers a simple bullet point list of facts to let intelligent readers make up their own minds.

As a Speaker:
- Spoke at more than 30 conferences and 50 sessions in many countries.
  - Such notable conferences as AdWords Days (Germany), Search Engine Strategies (SES), SES Local, SMX, SMX Local, Kelsey, PubCon, SuperZoo, Marketing 2.0 Bootcamp, SEO Class, and ad:tech.
- Spoke at events at both Google and Microsoft.

As a Trainer:
- Is one of only two Google-approved AdWords Seminar Leaders.
- Conducted more than 55 officially Google-supported AdWords Seminars for Success, attended by more than 3,500 marketing professionals. AdWords Seminars for Success are two days of intensive training on Google AdWords.
- Worked with Google in implementing their reseller training program at R.H. Donnelley.
- Helped institute a training program for LocalLaunch! that managed more than 40,000 PPC accounts.
- Conducted training days in multiple countries for conferences such as SEO Class, Search Engine Strategies (in New York, Toronto, and Chicago), Refined Labs, and PubCon.

As an Internet Marketer:
- Built first website in 1998.

- Started SEOing websites in 1998.
- Started affiliate marketing in 1999.
- Opened first PPC account in 1999.
- Formed first agency, iDjinni Consulting, in 2002, providing usability, PPC, SEO, and affiliate marketing services.
- Joined LocalLaunch! in 2004:
  - LocalLaunch! began as a boutique agency, and then built a marketing platform that empowered sales forces to sell marketing products to their customer bases while it did all of the product's management behind the scenes.
  - Helped grow the LocalLaunch! agency that provided PPC services to companies such as Red Lobster, Encyclopedia Britannica, YellowPages.com, and Yahoo!.
  - Helped build marketing products that were used by more than 100,000 businesses.
  - Helped build a system that managed more than 40,000 PPC accounts.
  - Worked with companies such as Amazon, World Directories, DEX Media, and Local.com.
- Continued managing vendor relations when LocalLaunch! was sold to R.H. Donnelley in 2006.
  - Guided R.H. Donnelley to become one of the few Google and Yahoo! resellers in the world.
  - LocalLaunch! was sold to R.H. Donnelley in 2006.
  - Formed bg Theory in 2008
- bg Theory is a company dedicated to consulting, educating, and training businesses on Internet marketing theory and best practices.

Even More Stuff:
- Author of *Advanced Google AdWords*.
- Co-moderated AdWords forum on WebmasterWorld since 2004.
- Has written a Search Engine Land column since 2007.
- Is a board member for Boost Media.
- Active blogger about PPC and marketing since 2001.
- Conducted the technical editing for *Winning Results with Google AdWords*, by Andrew Goodman.
- Participated in the beta test for Microsoft and became one of the first Microsoft adExcellence Members
- One of the first 100 Google Advertising Professionals.
- Worked with a range of companies that have spent from as little as $17.50 per month to millions per year.

Contents

Foreword

The need for advertisers to find customers—and vice versa—is an age-old marketing conundrum. With varying degrees of effectiveness, solutions have included phone solicitation, email outreach, print advertising, and more—all designed to connect consumers and advertisers at the right moment. I first got involved with pay-per-click advertising over a decade ago as a student at Stanford University. Using keyword buys on Goto.com, I started selling movies out of my dorm room, but my ads quickly lost effectiveness when I was outbid by advertisers with deeper pockets. There wasn't a book like this one to teach me the tricks of the trade and soon, I gave up. Then a few years later in 2002, I started buying keywords for my photography business, but this time on Google's brand new AdWords system. AdWords was revolutionary because it rewarded relevance as much as the maximum cost per click, making it a great fit for those who took the time to create more targeted ads. Like many other advertisers, I saw great success with my campaigns and I was so excited by this revolutionary new way of advertising that when the opportunity presented itself, I signed on to join the AdWords team to work directly on this ground-breaking new product.

During my many years at Google, I have been involved in countless product decisions in the development and decision-making process for tools like the AdWords API, the AdWords Editor, Conversion Tracking, Google Analytics, and many others that have helped shape AdWords into the advertising solution it is today. Nowadays, my role consists of helping AdWords users stay abreast of all our latest changes and working closely with our product development teams to relay feedback from our advertisers and ensure we continue building the best advertising solutions possible.

It's all about results...That was the slogan of AdWords when I joined Google. My role has changed over the years but there's always been a focus on making sure AdWords delivers the best results for advertisers and users of Google. Building a system that works well for a wide range of advertisers means adding many layers of sophisticated functionality and while AdWords is easy enough to use for novice advertisers, there are many advanced techniques for those who want more control. This excellent book will help you make the transition from novice to expert AdWords user and will give you a leg up in discovering some of the best ways to use AdWords to its fullest.

It is amazing how quickly search engine marketing has evolved into a key component of any successful marketing effort. This evolution continues today with new ad formats that combine the simplicity and relevance of text ads with new formats that make information more useful. We also continue to see new places where advertisers can connect with their target audience, such as on the Google Content Network, on mobile devices, and on television. The one constant thread amongst these many changes is our focus on delivering measurability and targetability. Regardless of where online advertising goes next, the expertise you gain in AdWords' advanced features today will help you become a savvier marketer in the future.

From the very start when AdWords became available as a self-service product, we were fortunate to have an active community of users who were ready to share their expertise with others. Brad was one of the very first community members who stood out as a trusted authority on all things related to AdWords, not an easy feat considering the rapid pace at which AdWords evolved. When I first heard about Brad, he was a top contributor in the AdWords forums, helping anyone who asked. To this day, he remains one of the leading experts on AdWords and I regularly see him continuing to share his knowledge and insight with others at industry conferences.

In this book, advertisers looking to get more out of AdWords will learn from one of the leading experts on the topic and someone who has used the system himself to build a very successful business. Once you get the basics of AdWords, there are a lot of sophisticated approaches to drive additional results—and this book will show you how.

Best of luck with your campaigns and please let me know what you think about our program and how it's working for you when you see me at a conference.

—FREDERICK VALLAEYS
Product Evangelist, Google AdWords

Introduction

The first dollar spent on pay-per-click (PPC) advertising occurred in 1998. The medium had just been invented, and like all new projects, no one knew if PPC advertising would succeed or fail.

Looking back on those early years, it is now obvious that early-adopter advertisers enjoyed this medium. The returns were fantastic, and advertisers kept pouring money into PPC campaigns.

By 2009, barely a decade after the first dollar was spent, it is estimated that more than $15 billion has been spent on PPC. Not only did the industry succeed, it far exceeded anyone's expectations, and it shows no signs of slowing down. Forrester Research estimates that more than $31 billion will be spent on PPC in 2014. In the same article, Forrester goes on to estimate that by 2014, search marketing will command 21 percent of all advertising spend (http://blogs.forrester.com/marketing/2009/07/interactive-marketing-nears-55-billion-advertising-overall-declines.html).

The biggest beneficiary of the search marketing boom has been Google, the company with the largest share of searches.

I once worked for a company that managed more than 40,000 PPC accounts and spent millions of dollars each month with Google. There are towns with both smaller populations and budgets. The amazing part is that there were other companies with larger portfolios than ours.

No longer is PPC dominated by the realm of Internet companies or early adopters. PPC does not care if you are a small local business or a large global enterprise. The rules are the same for everyone. The medium has brought equality to advertising for companies of any size or budget. Today, PPC should be a part of every company's marketing mix.

However, PPC has brought its own set of demands that have never been seen before. Once upon a time, marketing for a small business meant a two-hour yearly meeting with a yellow pages rep, and maybe an hour a month with the local newspaper or radio rep. In a total of 14 hours over the course of a year, most small businesses had completed their annual marketing.

Then along comes PPC, where bid prices are constantly in flux, advertisers can start and stop campaigns within minutes, companies are visible one moment and then gone the next. No longer does advertising take 14 hours a year—for many companies it's more than 14 hours every single week, or worse, every single day.

Along with the demands on time, PPC brings levels of transparency and control never before seen in any advertising medium. An advertiser can choose under exactly what conditions an ad will be displayed. The advertiser will then get a plethora of metrics where they can determine the success or failure for every click. More metrics, control, and transparency beg for even more hours of analysis and campaign tweaking.

Search marketing is still in its infancy. There are many more advances in targeting, tracking, analysis, and optimization still to come. Advertisers will demand even more controls. Search marketing will continue to add more features. Analytics will continue to bring new levels of analysis. Consumers will increase the time and money spent online.

To take advantage of these trends, advertisers have to become even more sophisticated so they can take advantage of the technology today and be ready for the advances yet to come.

Who Should Read This Book

Advanced Google AdWords is written for marketers who have a solid understanding of AdWords and have opened and managed their own account. What you will not find is information on how to open an account or navigate through the interface, or introductory material on keywords. These basics can be found in the AdWords Learning Center for free. This book begins where most blogs and training leaves off—optimization for intermediate and expert users.

What Is Covered in This Book

There are so many options with AdWords that it can be difficult to determine where to start or to understand what is possible. For instance, you could create an ad for a Google Android-powered phone that is only shown to a consumer if:

- The consumer is in the business section of the *New York Times* website.
- The article being read is about the iPhone.
- The consumer is on a mobile phone.
- The consumer is located in Minneapolis.
- The day is Monday.
- The time is between 6:00 a.m. and 8:00 a.m.

While rarely will you want an ad shown under such stringent conditions, choosing one or two of those options to constrain your ad serving so that you reach your ideal customer will help you save marketing dollars while putting the correct ad in front of your target market.

Of course, there is more to AdWords than image ads and the content network. We start with search and end with step-by-step instructions. We will dive into detailed ad copy and landing page testing, account organization, ad copy writing, and even multiple strategies for setting bids.

Inside, you will find one of the most comprehensive sections ever written on quality score. If you have been advertising with Google for a while and either do not know what quality score is or have had problems with high first page bids or low quality scores, this book is definitely for you.

If you are an advanced user and are wondering if you can learn from this book, just flip to the last chapter. There you will find a step-by-step guide for creating and optimizing AdWords accounts. Every single section in that chapter is a reflection of what you will learn throughout this book.

INTRODUCTION ■

This book's two mantra words are **creativity** and **profits**. To be creative with AdWords, you need to understand your options and how various settings influence other settings. To increase profits, you need to understand testing, conversions, and bidding strategies. When you combine creativity and profits, you will stop just advertising and spending money. Instead, you will put the correct ad in front of your ideal customer at the time when they are most likely to convert so that your company can increase their overall profits.

What You Will Learn

This book does not just tell you how a feature works, it gives you strategies for using that feature. For instance, most national companies ignore location targeting. This is a mistake. Did you know you can buy a diet beer in Japan? Try selling a diet beer to Americans. You cannot buy Coke Lite in the United States or Diet Coke in Europe. Why? The words "diet" and "lite" invoke different feelings in different geographies. This book will give you strategies to determine your conversion rate and spend for different geographies, how to test different ads by geography, and how to maximize your returns in each geography where you are advertising.

Not everything is about location. This book examines how to find, measure, change, test, and implement *strategies* for a variety of topics, including:

- Keywords
- Ad copy
- Quality score
- Time-of-day targeting
- Testing ad copy
- Testing landing pages
- Profit by impression testing
- Account organization

We will go through the steps of helping you learn where to best spend your time. With so many options, it can be difficult to determine where to start. We will help by not just showing you where to spend your initial time, but also how to set up reporting schedules so you can continue to grow and optimize your account.

By reading this book, you will learn step-by-step strategies that will increase your company's profits through using Google AdWords.

How to Use This Book

Since Google AdWords is so complex, this book is intended to be used in two ways. First, read it straight through to learn about the different strategies possible. After you have read it once, this book is intended to be a reference you can refer back to as you are optimizing your account. Each chapter ends with a Best Practices section that contains easy-to-comprehend points about the subject material to quickly refresh your memory.

The last chapter of this book is a step-by-step guide to getting things done. Refer to that chapter when you are opening or optimizing accounts and follow along. If there is a step where you need more information, simply refer back to the chapter where that topic is covered in detail.

By reading and then referring back to this book, implementing new AdWords strategies to optimize your account will save you time and money.

Chapter 1: Understanding Search Theory: Learn about the history of PPC advertising and the psychology of search.

Chapter 2: Keyword Research: How the buying funnel and your keywords work together. Control when your ad is displayed by using a combination of both positive and negative keywords.

Chapter 3: Keyword Tools: Extracting Valuable Data from Google: Learn how to combine Google's spiders with a dictionary to improve your keyword research. Learn how to use other Google and Microsoft free tools to improve your account.

Chapter 4: Writing Compelling Ads: From benefits to features to trademarks to unique selling propositions, learn to write ads that connect with the searcher.

Chapter 5: Landing Pages That Convert Searchers into Buyers: Learn how to choose the best page on your site for every keyword. Then ensure the proper elements of usability, trust, and option control exist on the page to convert the searcher into a buyer.

Chapter 6: Advanced Optimization Techniques: Learn strategies for increasing conversion rates, click-through rate, traffic, and ad impressions.

Chapter 7: Demystifying Quality Score: Each quality score factor is torn apart, examined, and put back together so you can see exactly how your quality score is determined. Then learn strategies for managing and increasing quality scores.

Chapter 8: Beyond Text: Image, Video, and Mobile Ads: There is more to Google than text ads. Dive into the best uses of video, image, and mobile ads.

Chapter 9: Understanding the Content Network: The content network may be the most misunderstood and least optimized part of AdWords. Understand how the content network really works and how to start taking advantage of it.

Chapter 10: Advanced Content Network Techniques: The content network's reach is significantly larger than Google's search reach. The techniques you will learn in this chapter will help you find new customers who have never searched for your products.

Chapter 11: Advanced Geographic Targeting: Control exactly where your ad is shown. Understand the technology so you can avoid pitfalls and take advantage of displaying unique messages through location targeting.

Chapter 12: Save Time and Scale Accounts with the AdWords Editor: When accounts include hundreds of thousands of keywords, and tens of thousands of pieces of ad copy, they can be difficult to create and optimize. This chapter will examine how to save you time in creating and managing small to enormous accounts through the AdWords Editor.

Chapter 13: Profitable Bid Strategies: Examine your business model so you can set and measure your marketing goals to ensure your company is profitable. Then learn how to set and manage bids by ROI, profit, position, day of the week, and time of day. Formulas and Excel walkthroughs are included so no one gets lost in the math and calculations.

Chapter 14: Successful Account Organization Strategies: Success starts with account organization. Read tips, tricks, and strategies that will help you find the correct organization for your AdWords account.

Chapter 15: Testing Techniques That Will Increase Profits: Testing ad copy and landing pages is essential to continuously increasing profits. Learn not just how to create and measure a test, but also how to determine how much money you make every single time an ad is displayed.

Chapter 16: AdWords Reports: How to Extract Actionable Information: Learn how to create and use all the valuable data that your AdWords account accumulates. Create a reporting schedule so you always have access to the data necessary to improve your account.

Chapter 17: Step by Step: Create and Monitor Your AdWords Account: After 16 chapters packed with information, it is time for a step-by-step walkthrough of how to create and optimize each campaign type based upon what you have learned. Refer back to this chapter every time you are working in AdWords to see what to do next.

Glossary: If you do not recognize an acronym or piece of jargon, refer to this handy reference guide to look up the term.

The Companion Website

Google AdWords adds or tweaks features over time. Therefore, we have created a companion website with additional links and features to help you through your AdWords optimization journey. The website can be accessed at http://AdvancedAdWordsBook.com.

How to Contact the Author

I welcome feedback from you about this book or about books you'd like to see from me in the future. You can contact me at www.bgtheory.com/contact/. For more information about my work, please visit our other sites:

- www.bgTheory.com
- www.AdvancedAdWordsBook.com
- www.CertifiedKnowledge.org

Understanding
Search Theory

very important simple

The search process itself may seem simple: A searcher visits a search engine, enters a search query, and receives results. Every step of the search process, however, is accompanied by the searcher's thoughts and expectations. Understanding how your keyword and ads align themselves with the search process can help bring more visitors to your site and achieve more conversions from those visitors.

Pay-per-click (PPC) advertising is effective because it mirrors the search process, and the two work seamlessly with each other. Understanding the origins and evolution of PPC advertising will also give you a glimpse into its future, so you can continue to take advantage of this ever-expanding form of advertising.

1

1

Chapter Contents

The Origins of Google AdWords

In 1996, a small company was formed that would forever change the world of Internet marketing. This company was called Idealab. It took two years of hard work and creative ideas before Bill Gross's company would launch GoTo.com with a simple business model: Advertisers could choose to display their ads based on what a searcher was trying to find. A searcher would type a query into the search box (Figure 1.1), and if advertisers chose to advertise on that word, their ad would show in the search results. There were four simple concepts that made this business model revolutionary.

Figure 1.1 GoTo.com's search page, circa 1998

The first was relevance, a word later adopted by Google throughout their AdWords program. Showing ads based on what someone was actively seeking made these new search ads more relevant than anything previous displayed on the Internet.

Note: AdWords is Google's pay-per-click program where an advertiser chooses words that will trigger their ad. The advertiser is charged only if their ad is displayed and clicked by a searcher. This unique pricing model ensures that an advertiser's message is not only seen, but that the advertiser only pays when someone arrives at their website.

Advertisers would only choose to display their ads on Keyword searches that were related to their products or services. Since their ads would then only be shown when someone was searching for related information, these ads would help the searchers find what they were seeking.

Before the days of PPC, the ads alongside a search results page were often banner ads that had nothing to do with the search query. While these ads did gather many impressions (an impression is when an ad is shown on a page), they were not relevant to the user and thus were rarely clicked. Advertisers were paying for exposure but were not receiving much traffic for their ad dollars.

In the early days of Google, before AdWords launched, the founders of Google had been questioned many times by their investors about how they would eventually monetize their search engine. At that time, the founders did not have an answer; however, they held steadfast to the belief that at the moment someone was shown a page of search results, Google had their undivided attention. It would be in that moment of someone scanning a page of search results that Google would make its money. It turned out to be an accurate observation by the early Googlers.

By displaying ads based on what someone was actively seeking, GoTo.com formed a synergy between searchers and advertisers that helped both reach their goals on a single search page. Advertisers would receive visitors who were actively seeking their products, and searchers would find products that were related to what they were seeking. This was a win for both searchers and advertisers.

The second concept was the pricing model. Previously, almost all advertisements were based on paying for impressions. A company would decide how many impressions they would like to buy for their banner ads, and then they would pay on a cost per thousand impressions (CPM) basis. This created a scenario where you had to have a large advertising budget to even sign an initial contract. In addition, you had no idea how many visitors or sales those ads would bring to your site. The world of Internet advertising was mostly formed of larger companies or companies with venture capital backing.

By changing to a PPC pricing model, advertisers only paid when they received traffic. This shift to performance-based advertising allowed companies to try out a fledgling business model with very little monetary commitment. The minimum monthly spend was roughly one dollar per day, a big change from minimums that were often several thousand dollars a month.

Because search engines were paid only when a click occurred, it also forced search engines to show only relevant ads. If an ad did not get clicked, the search engine did not make money. The pricing model helped reinforce that only relevant ads should be shown on a search results page. This forced advertisers and search engines to work together to create a better search page for the consumer.

The third concept—and how both Yahoo! and Google have built a base of hundreds of thousands of advertisers—was the signup process. GoTo.com removed the barrier of a salesperson between the advertiser and the inventory. Using a self-serve ad model, any advertiser could sign up for a PPC account and start selecting keywords and creating ad copy within minutes (Figure 1.2).

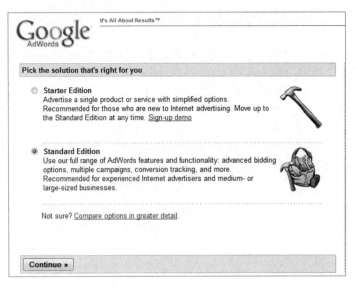

Figure 1.2 AdWords signup process is a simple wizard influenced by GoTo.com.

By choosing a self-serve model, a search engine did not have to pay commission to a salesperson. There were no contracts to sign, no insertion orders (IOs) to fax, and no phone calls had to be made before you could start advertising on the Web. This very straightforward approach allowed anyone from a small business to a Fortune 500 company to quickly experiment with Internet advertising.

The Internet was still a new concept to most people, and both companies and consumers were unsure how widely adopted the Web would become. Thus, having the ability to commit a few dollars and experiment with the new medium was paramount to introducing thousands of new companies to the concept that they could make money on the Web.

It also allowed the search engines to scale their advertiser base very quickly. People often slow down the advertising process, and by allowing a self-serve model, the only barrier to advertising was a little bit of time and a credit card.

The last concept is what has allowed Yahoo! and Google to make billions of dollars from their advertisers—the auction process. GoTo.com did not have a set price for what you needed to pay when a keyword was clicked in a search result. Advertisers set a price of what they were willing to pay, and the company willing to pay the most showed up highest in the search results.

If you were willing to pay more than your competitors, then your ad would show higher in the search results, which would gather more clicks and bring more visitors to your website. It is easy to see how the top positions were highly coveted.

The process has become much more complex over the years as search engines, users, and advertisers have become savvier.

In October 2001, GoTo.com, Inc., renamed itself Overture Services. In 2003, Overture was acquired by Yahoo! for $1.63 billion. Today, GoTo.com is an unknown name to most people as the service is now called Yahoo! Search Marketing. GoTo.com is no longer owned or operated by Yahoo! and now redirects to a site unrelated to PPC advertising.

As described earlier, GoTo.com's four founding concepts were quite simple: relevance, pay-per-click pricing, self-service, and auction-based pricing. However, these principles were combined to not only quickly gain advertiser adoption, but to also reap the monetary benefits of advertiser competition for the top ad positions.

Google Enters the Arena

Back in 1998, when GoTo.com was first launching, Google's search engine was named BackRub and was running on Stanford University servers. Creators Larry Page and Sergey Brin were more concerned with moving their operations into Susan Wojcicki's garage than making money.

Note: Susan Wojcicki's garage served as Google's first workspace away from Stanford's campus. Wojcicki was instrumental in Google's growth when she became one of their early employees and is often referred to as the "Mother of AdSense." (AdSense is Google's contextual advertising program.)

Over the next two years, Google moved to Mountain View, accepted $25 million in funding, and hired key employees to help in their evolution. Their early hires revolved around scaling their search technology. Craig Silverstein was their very first employee and served as the director of technology. Much of his early work helped scale the IT operations that would allow Google to grow. The next step was finding a way to start making money.

Google's first offering was an uninspired CPM program. To advertise with Google, you had to talk to a sales rep and sign a contract for a fairly high minimum spend. While advertisers could choose to show an ad based on a searcher's query, the four concepts that had made GoTo.com a success were not to be found.

The high barrier to advertising with Google was lowered in October 2000 when Google launched their first self-serve advertising program. The simply named Google AdWords started with 350 customers. However, AdWords was still bought on a CPM basis.

Google AdWords Select Revolutionizes PPC

February 2002 will always be remembered as the time when Google forever changed pay-per-click advertising. Google launched AdWords Select, which incorporated all of GoTo.com's founding principles; however, in typical Google fashion, they added their own twist to the auction model.

On GoTo.com, the more you paid, the higher your ad appeared in search results. That essentially made it so the company willing to pay the most had the highest visibility. Google's main advertising word was relevance, and they changed the PPC auction model to both increase relevance for a searcher and to maximize how much money Google made on a search results page.

Their twist was to incorporate click-through rates (CTR) in determining where an ad showed up in the results. They used a very simple formula to determine ad position: Maximum CPC (cost per click) multiplied by CTR.

Note: Search engines protect their most important metric, revenue per search (RPS), from public consumption. However, with some rough math the numbers can be approximated. In 2004, Google made around $0.10 per search, which increased to $0.19 in 2006, and finally surpassed $0.25 in 2007. Conversely, Yahoo's revenue per visitor was roughly only $0.16 in 2007. As the economy dipped in 2009, so did Google's RPS, to approximately $0.095, which was still higher than Yahoo.

However, it is difficult to blame the entire dip on the economy. As more information is integrated into the search results, there is less of a need for the consumer to always leave the search results. For instance, a search for "Chicago weather" will show the five day forecast within the search results, which results in less people clicking away from the page to find the weather forecast.

The logic was that if an ad was clicked more often, it was more relevant to the searcher, and the advertiser should be rewarded for showing an ad aligned with the searcher's query.

This simple formula also maximized the dollars Google made on every single search engine results page (SERP). In the PPC model, a search engine is only paid when a click occurs.

On GoTo.com, if advertisers were willing to bid more than everyone else for a click, their ads would show up at the top of the search pages. If those same ads did not receive clicks, the engines did not actually make money from displaying those ads.

Therefore, a search engine should not want to display the highest-bidded ads the most if they were not clicked. A search engine would make more money by displaying lower-bidded ads that gathered clicks than high cost ads that received few clicks.

By incorporating a combination of both bid prices and how many clicks those ads received, Google managed to maximize how much they made on any single search results page. This simple change also created an environment where a small company with a more compelling offer could have its ad displayed higher in a SERP than a large national company who did not take the time to create relevant ads. Price no longer trumped relevancy. Having the most money did not ensure the most clicks or visibility. Advertisers had to choose keywords that were more relevant to their products and create ads to match.

This level playing field helped spur advertiser adoption to the point that Google eventually dropped their CPM program completely and renamed the AdWords Select program to the name used today: Google AdWords.

Over the years, Google has become much more sophisticated and has revamped their formulas for displaying ads on search pages. However, throughout the growing complexities of AdWords, Google has always kept their ad serving synergistic with the search process. To understand how to take advantage of aligning your advertising efforts with Google's ad serving, it is important to understand the psychology of search.

The Psychology of Search

One of the advantages of online advertising is transparency of data to the advertiser. It is easy to track click-through rate, conversion rates, cost per conversions, total conversions, bounce rates, and more data points than anyone could ever analyze. The numbers can be overwhelming. Between the reports you can run in AdWords, some simple Excel formulas, and your analytics program, you can get buried in meaningless data.

It is essential to look beyond the numbers and consider the individuals sitting at their anonymous keyboards conducting the searches. While numbers tell the story of your marketing, it is the actual people who can make your advertising profitable.

Since search marketing—and Google AdWords in particular—is based around people using search engines, you must also think about how search engines are used in everyday life. Understanding not only how people use search engines, but how they decide to click on an ad from the search page will help align your marketing efforts with the searchers. Having someone arrive at your site is just one step in the equation. Your website must also be aligned with the searcher's interest so the searcher does not just browse your website but also becomes a new customer.

Search engines are not used to browse the Web. That is the domain of properties such as iGoogle, StumbleUpon, and Digg. There is more information on the Web than anyone could read in dozens of lifetimes, and most of that information is of no interest to the searcher. Therefore, people do not just read search engines attempting to absorb all of the information that has been discovered around the Web. Search engines are used when they want to find a specific piece of information. More importantly, people use search engines to find the answer to a question.

We all think differently. We all ask questions differently. Delving into the various ways that people think and ask questions can assist you in choosing keywords that will make sure your ad appears in front of someone searching with questions your site can answer.

Turning Concepts into Words

The majority of people do not think in words. Words are conventions to relay the thoughts that are present in our minds. While words are how we communicate in daily life, they are just a vehicle to help us express the concept of our thought to others.

People are not mind readers. You cannot think at a person and have them understand your thoughts. You have to take the concepts present in your brain and transform them into words so that another person can understand you. The translation that occurs from concept to word is different for each person. This is why you might readily understand one person and not understand another person who is trying to express the exact same idea.

This same process of putting our thoughts into words is also how we communicate with a search engine. Google has not yet developed the technology where you can telepathically receive your answer. Therefore, you need to express yourself in the typed word to receive a response.

To further the process of examining how people translate their thoughts into words, we will use the following scenario and examine some of the ways in which this scenario can be typed into a search engine.

Chicago is brutally cold in the winter. Imagine sitting in your suburban house watching a movie on a Saturday evening. Suddenly, your spouse tells you that there is water flooding the basement. Upon examination, you discover that a pipe has frozen, causing it to break, and now you need a plumber to come out to your house to fix the problem.

This is a very common winter scenario in Chicago. However, the ways in which people will attempt to solve this problem are very different.

Some people are very direct in their thinking. They will go to Google and type in the actual question they need to find an answer to, such as "Where do I find a Chicago plumber?" Many people, instead of typing out the entire question, will shorten the query to just "Chicago plumber" or maybe more precisely "Schaumberg plumber," or "emergency plumbing services Schaumberg."

Others will have a preconceived notion about what they wish to find, and their query will be more aligned with the answer they wish to receive. For example, the query might be "A site about Chicago plumbers."

If you are the do-it-yourself type, you might first want to turn off the water to stop the initial problem before contacting a plumber. A search for "How to turn off the water in my basement" would be more appropriate.

What is the root cause of the problem? If you searched for the root cause, the site that held the answer could also help you fix the broken pipes. Queries such as "broken pipes" or "frozen pipes" could lead you to your answer. You could also search for the actual problem, such as "flooded basement."

It can be a useful exercise to walk into the office tomorrow and describe this scenario to your coworkers. Then ask each of them what they would type in the search box. If you ask them one by one, instead of in a group, you are sure to receive a slightly different answer from almost everyone you ask. There will be some repetition, but concentrate on the different types of answers.

In fact, there are thousands of ways that someone could search for the answer to the above scenario. In later chapters, we will dive more into keyword research. Most queries usually fall into one of a few categories:

- The actual question, or a shortened version of the question

- The answer to the question

- A description of the problem

- A symptom of the problem

- A description of the cause

- Product parts or brand names

It is essential that you consider all of the ways someone can search for your products. Search queries are thought processes. Understanding someone's query can give you insight into what question they want answered.

Understanding Search Results

Once the thought has been translated into words, it is time to find the answer to the question. You go to Google, type in your words, and before you click the Search button, something psychological happens—expectation setting.

As a human, every time you conduct any action, you have an expectation of results. When you first looked at the spine of this book on the shelf, you had a notion of what it contained. Before you bought the book, you had an expectation of what you would learn by reading it. Every event also changes and refines those expectations. As you read this chapter, you have a different expectation of what you will find later in the book than when you first bought it.

This series of ongoing expectation setting also affects how you view search engines. When you input a query, you expect to see certain ads and websites displayed that will help you find the answer to your question.

This same expectation setting happens for every person using a search engine. Everyone expects to find websites that will help them answer their question. Therefore, before you ever click the Search button, you have already built an idea of what the act of typing your query into a search box will bring to your computer screen.

Within the search process, your ad has a specific role. Having your ad appear on that search page is not your endgame. Your ad must be relevant to the search result. You do not want everyone who sees your ad to come to your website. You only want those who are going to engage your company to click on your ads and cost you money.

The Purpose of Ad Copy

Once the Search button is clicked, Google displays a set of ads and websites (Figure 1.3). A quick scan of the page will tell the searcher if the results are in line with their expectations. If they are not, the searcher is likely to stop reading the results and change the search query.

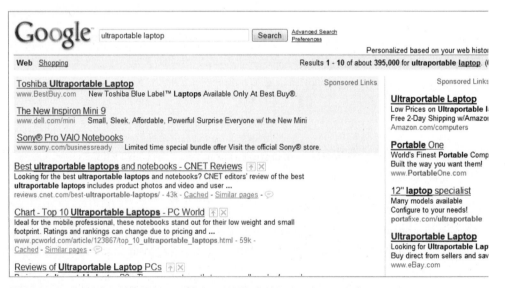

Figure 1.3 Google search result for "ultraportable laptops." Which ad answers the question?

As an advertiser, this brief moment is your chance to connect with the searcher. These few seconds can make the difference between the searcher visiting your site, your competitor's site, or just searching again for the answer and completely ignoring your ad.

At this moment, your ad needs to stand up, jump around, wave its arms, grab the searcher's attention, and shout, "I have the answer to your question! Come click on me and I'll show you the answer."

Attempting to create ads that both stand out from the crowd to gain initial attention and are compelling enough to entice someone to click is a difficult proposition. As a marketer, your job is to write ads that meet the expectations of the searcher, and yet can communicate to that same person that your website can deliver the answer to their question.

AdWords ads are only 95 characters in length, and they have a tremendous amount to accomplish in just a few scant words.

An ad needs to have a headline that draws attention. It needs to stand out from other ads on a page that are clamoring for attention. The ad copy needs to tell a visitor why you have the answer to their question. And yet, the ad also needs to be faithful to your products or services. You can never lose sight of what makes your company money; otherwise, you will be paying for clicks that do not help you reach your goals.

Ads should not be written to please the advertiser. They should not be written to make the CEO smile. Ads should be written to convey to the searcher that you hold the key to their question, and they must first walk through your ad copy to your website before they can find out the answer. We will spend time in later chapters discussing how to create these ads and even how to test them against each other.

Hopefully your ad has caught the searcher's eye. They think your ad can lead them to information that will help them complete their quest. And just before the searcher clicks on your ad, something else happens—another expectation is being set.

When a person does a search on Google, they have a preconceived notion of what they will see on a search results page based on what words they choose to search. Your ad copy is the only thing a user knows about your website, therefore those few characters are setting the user's expectations about what they will find. Your landing page needs to meet those expectations.

Landing Pages Lead to New Customers

When someone clicks on your ad, they are taken to your website. Usually this is the first brand interaction someone has with your company. It's your first chance to showcase your offer to that searcher.

"Landing page" is industry jargon for the first page a searcher views after clicking on your ad. It is rarely the home page of your site. It is usually the page within your website that is most logically connected to the search query.

For instance, if someone conducted a search for "Sony digital cameras," they would not want to be taken to Amazon.com's home page. The home page does not have information about Sony digital cameras. At best, the searcher will search again at Amazon's site. At worst, they will go back to the search results. A much better search experience would have the searcher taken to a page about Sony digital cameras within Amazon's website.

Remember, most searchers do not know your website. The searcher does not have prior knowledge about your company. They arrived at your site after clicking on just 95 characters of ad copy. That small amount of text is all the information they have about your site before first visiting it. In fact, your ad copy is the only thing within your entire AdWords account that a searcher can see. Therefore, that ad copy is crucial in setting the proper expectation for what the searcher will find after the click.

In order to continue meeting the searcher's expectations, your landing page must be an extension of your ad copy. Since your ad copy informed the searcher about what they would find, the landing page should continue the conversation by assisting them to find their answer (see Figure 1.4).

Figure 1.4 The Bose landing page showcases the product and allows a searcher to either buy or get more information.

If your landing page does not meet the searcher's expectation, they will use the most common navigational element on the entire Web—the dreaded Back button. You paid for the click; this is something you definitely want to avoid.

The landing page should show someone the answer to their question or instructions on how to get the answer to their question. For an e-commerce site, the answer is contained in the product someone will receive once they've checked out through your shopping cart. When they're looking for a plumber, the answer comes after they make a phone call. At other sites, the answer will come after the searcher fills out a form for more information. For most businesses, when the consumer receives the answer to their question, the business has a new customer.

The landing page is critical to your AdWords success. A bad landing page leads to wasted advertising dollars due to the searcher leaving your site without conducting any business with your company. A good landing page will turn shoppers into buyers.

The process of someone searching and buying on the Web is much different from other forms of advertising. While many advertising campaigns are structured to create emotional need within a consumer, the search process is driven by giving someone the correct information at the correct time. This concept extends from choosing the correct keyword to creating your ad copy, and ultimately answering the searcher's question on your website.

Advertising Is Not Advertising When It Is Information

Once upon a time I was riding on the top of a First Avenue bus, when I heard a mythical housewife say to another, "Molly, my dear, I would have bought that new brand of toilet soap if only they hadn't set the body copy in ten point Garamond." Don't you believe it. What really decides consumers to buy or not to buy is the content of your advertising, not its form.

DAVID OGILVY

Often people are resistant to advertising. Ads are something you are bombarded with on a daily basis. You hear ads on the radio when you are driving to work. You see ads on TV when you are trying to relax in the evening. You see ads in the daily paper as you are trying to read the local weather forecast. You see ads in search results as you are trying to find information.

But ads do not have to be annoying or intrusive. Ads can be very helpful if they are created properly, because advertising is not actually advertising when it is information.

By aligning your ad copywriting, landing pages, and Google AdWords account with this concept, you are much more likely to see success in your search marketing efforts. This is a concept much better visualized than explained.

Ads Should Lead Searchers to Answers

If you performed the search, "plasma TV features," do you think clicking on this ad would help you find the information you are looking for?

Plasma TV. Massive new TV offerings. Visit us today to buy your new TV!

Unfortunately, ads that are not directly related to the search query and do not mirror the search process are quite common.

Now consider this ad for the same search, "plasma TV features":

Compare plasma TV features. Find a new plasma TV that fits your lifestyle and budget.

Someone searching for features is most likely looking to compare products and is not ready to buy yet. They are still in the comparison shopping stage of the buying cycle. An ad focused on buying does not fit into their decision making process.

Ad copy needs to both reflect the search query and recognize where a searcher is within the buying cycle; we will examine both of these elements in future chapters.

Imagine this weekend will be nice and sunny and you would like to spend it with your family at the beach. The drive will take several hours, but you manage to pack the kids and the spouse into the car and begin your journey.

You start driving down the interstate while the kids are glued to a DVD player in the backseat. Billboards whiz past on the side of the road, which you do not have to try to ignore; you have had the skill to tune out advertising for many years.

After a few hours, you start to get hungry and the kids start to get restless. It is time to find a restaurant for lunch. You have made the decision that you do not want to eat in the car as it is too messy with the kids, and you would like to get out of the car to stretch your legs.

Where do you start looking? Those ignored billboards. They are no longer advertisements cluttering up the roadside; they are now valuable pieces of information that will show you available lunch options.

You stop ignoring them and start reading them.

Why?

Because the advertisements are your source of information for finding the answer to your question. Your question is along the lines of "What are my lunch options?" Your answer will be found in the billboards alongside the interstate.

When ads become part of the information gathering process, they cease to be ads. At this point in time, they are pieces of information that consumers are seeking. Wouldn't you like your ads to be sought after, not ignored? By aligning yourself with the search process, the quest for answers, your ads will not only help consumers find the answer to their questions, they will help your business make sales.

Stop thinking of ads as advertisements.

Start thinking of ads as pieces of information.

Goal Alignment: Google vs. You vs. the Searcher

Every search result has three different entities trying to reach their goals. Sometimes, these goals get in each other's way, leading to poor search results. Other times, they work in conjunction, leading everyone toward success. It is important to examine Google's goal, the advertiser's goal, and the searcher's goal for each search result.

All search results start with the same element, a searcher looking for the answer to a question. The searcher inputs a query, and search engine results pages (SERPs) appear.

Google's goal is to have that same searcher use Google for their next query. The more search queries that occur on Google properties, the more chances Google has to make money by people clicking on ads. Therefore, Google wants searchers to always find the answer to their question quickly, easily, and on a Google-owned property.

This is why Google also spends so much time and money on the natural results (also known as organic or free listings). Not all searchers can be monetized, but if someone always finds their answer on Google, regardless of whether it's a monetized or nonmonetized query, that person is more likely to use Google for their next search. In addition, if someone finds their information on Google quicker and easier than on other properties, they will always return to Google to find information, which leads to more total queries per month for Google, which leads to more chances of Google making money.

Note: Several studies have found that a user spends only 10 to 12 seconds on a search results page.

The advertiser's goal is to show an ad that is related to both their products and the searcher's query. The advertiser wants to control when their ad is shown, wants to choose which ad is shown, and then wants to take the searcher to the landing page of their choice.

The advertiser wants to make money with their Google AdWords budget. That's the endgame—profitable advertising. Advertisers want control over how their money is being spent. They also want insight into the ad display process so they can expand their profitable advertising and stop their unprofitable ads.

Google's goal and the advertiser's goal are not the same. Since Google's goal is first and foremost to satisfy the searcher, not the advertiser, a conflict often arises between the two parties.

The advertiser will scream that it's their money and they should be able to display whatever they want in an ad and take someone to any page on their site they deem desirable. AdWords customer service reps will remind the advertiser about relevancy and attempt to help the advertiser make their keywords and ad copy more relevant. These relevancy rules are defined by Google.

Since Google is ruled internally by a quality control team—a team where relevancy trumps dollars—advertisers often feel like they are constantly trying to play catch-up in learning all the rules. Having an internal team that is more concerned about relevance than making money is beneficial to all parties, if everyone can align their goals.

It is critical to remember that the only person who makes Google or the advertiser any money is the actual searcher. Google does not make you money. You do not make Google money. Google is an intermediary between you and the searcher. You make money on AdWords because a searcher decided to do business with your company. You define a budget that you are willing to give to Google; however, if the searcher does not click your ads, you do not owe Google a penny.

Both you and Google make money from each other only if a searcher is involved. If there is no searcher, there is no search query, your ad is not displayed, and Google is not paid. Therefore, the person to actually align your goals with is the searcher. If you align yourself with the searcher, you help the searcher find information on your site. If they are finding information on your site, they are conducting business with your company, which helps you reach your end goal—a profitable business.

 Note: Google made nearly $22 billion in 2008. Approximately 97 percent of all Google's revenue comes from showing ads.

Because Google's goal is to assist the searcher in finding information, you will end up aligning yourself with Google as well. You will find that if you think of the searcher first, AdWords is much easier, and much more likely to be a successful advertising medium for your business.

After all, the searcher's only goal is to find the answer to their question.

Best Practices for Applying Search Theory

The basics of search are not difficult to understand; the principles have been the same ever since people started looking for information. By referring back to the fundamentals of search throughout your marketing, you keep your efforts aligned with the searcher, which can bring long-term success to your company.

- PPC marketing was created and revolutionized in less than a decade. As the industry is ever-changing, those who can continuously evolve their marketing can find great success.

- Search engines have transformed how people find their information. As more consumers use search engines as their starting point for finding information, more advertisers will find success with search marketing.

- The search process starts with a question. That question is translated into words by the searcher. Therefore, keywords are individual thought processes.

- Every time someone does an action, there is an expectation of results. Meeting these expectations with both ad copy and landing pages helps increase your PPC marketing returns.

- Advertising is not advertising when it is information. When your ads help a searcher find the answer to their question, your CTR and conversion rates often increase.

- On any search page there are three goals: the search engine's goal, the searcher's goal, and the advertiser's goal. Align your goal with your potential customer—the searcher—and success usually follows.

In future chapters, we will examine keyword research, ad copy writing, and multiple ways to target consumers. At each step, we are trying to enhance these fundamentals. If you can help the searcher find what they are looking for, you will continue to gain new customers.

Keyword Research

Keywords are the foundation of a successful AdWords campaign. If you have a keyword that matches a searcher's query, your ad could show. If you do not have a keyword that matches a searcher's query, your ad is not shown. It is pretty simple: If you decide not to use a certain keyword, your company will not be visible to those searchers.

Keywords are so paramount to an AdWords campaign that PPC advertising is frequently called keyword advertising or keyword-driven advertising.

Not all keywords are created equal. Some keywords will have high search volume, others small search volume. Some have high conversion rates, and others will provide low quality traffic.

Choosing the correct keywords is the first step to advertising with Google AdWords.

Chapter Contents

Understanding the Buying Funnel

Before diving into all the different ways to research, group, and choose keywords, you must first take a step back and examine how people buy products or services.

There are five stages to the buying funnel (Figure 2.1):

- Awareness
- Interest
- Learning
- Shopping
- Buying

Understanding where a keyword falls in the buying cycle can help signal where a consumer is within the buying process so you can ensure that your ad and landing page match the consumer's shopping phase.

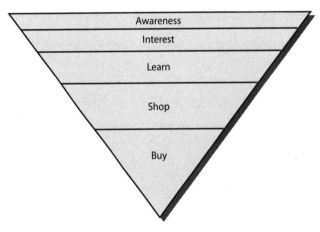

Figure 2.1 The buying funnel

While the buying funnel often refers to actual physical product sales, the same principles apply to B2B (business to business), service, retail, and other industries.

Note: The buying funnel is a subset of the broader known buying cycle. The entire buying cycle has two additional phases known as retention and advocacy. While customer loyalty and lifetime visitor values are important considerations for your entire marketing program, they can be distracting when we initially discuss keywords. Hence, we will only work with the initial aspect of the buying cycle, the sales funnel, during keywords and revisit the full buying cycle in later chapters.

The shopping cycle is illustrated as a funnel because many searchers will enter the beginning of your product's buying funnel. However, as consumers learn more information about your product as compared to others, fewer consumers will transition from one section to the next. As a marketer, one of your jobs is to move as many prospects as possible through the funnel so they become customers.

Examining the Buying Funnel Phases

Awareness leads off the top of the funnel. If a consumer does not know about your products, they can never buy from you. A marketer's first job is to make sure that consumers know that your products exist. If a consumer does not know about your product, they may not realize that your product can fix their problem, let alone understand that you offer a way to help them. At this stage of the buying funnel, your job is to shout from the rooftops that your product exists.

When we correlate this part of the buying funnel to keywords, the keywords are very general. Consumers do not yet know enough to do a search for the product's benefits, features, or part types. These keywords are often high volume, low converting words such as TV, plumber, laptop memory, and real estate.

Once a consumer understands that your product exists, your next function is to generate *interest* for your product or service. At this stage, you want consumers to think about your product and how it will make their lives better. We will discuss features and benefits more in Chapter 4 during ad copy writing. At this stage of the buying funnel, you want to focus on benefits. Essentially, a benefit is what your product will do for consumers so they desire your product.

After consumers have become aware of and interested in your products, they need to *learn* more about the product so they have enough information to make informed purchasing decisions. This is known as the learning or information gathering phase of the buying funnel.

This is where consumers start to delve into product specifications and features and begin to compare products. If a searcher were looking to buy a new HD TV, this is where they would start to examine the features and differences associated with plasma versus LCD vs. DLP televisions. Consumers want to know about pixel burnout rates, what the magic mirrors are in DLPs, and what size TV they actually need for optimal viewing.

If you were an accounting firm, this is where you would showcase that you offer payroll services, are integrated with Intuit QuickBooks, and have a lawyer on staff for incorporation services.

It is in the learning stage where searchers first learn your industry jargon. The searcher's query is often more specific and commonly includes brand names and service specialties. Showcasing both benefits and features is useful for consumers during this phase.

Using these examples, you could easily put keywords such as "Chicago QuickBooks accounting firm," "Samsung DLP TV," and "plasma TV pixel burnout rate" into your keyword list.

Once consumers understand enough about the industry or product that they can start looking at product specifications to make informed decisions, they will begin to compare similar products to each other. This is known as the *shopping* phase.

At this phase, a consumer might have decided they would like a plasma TV because it's light enough to hang on the wall, and based upon how far their couch is from the wall, they want a 52-inch set. However, the consumer might not know if a Sony TV has certain features that a Samsung TV does not have. Therefore, while the consumer has decided on a 52-inch plasma TV, the brand and actual model are still in question. Or the consumer might have determined that they want a Sony, but there are multiple types of Sony plasma TV, and therefore the consumer needs to compare the different model types to each other.

Keywords at this phase are often quite specific and indicate a certain level of knowledge about the product. "Sony Vaio Z series laptop," "Sony plasma 52-inch TV," and "Chicago accounting services with lawyer on staff" are keyword searches that describe consumers in this aspect of the buying funnel.

Finally, a consumer has made up their mind on the actual product they are willing to purchase. At this point, the only question left to answer is where to *buy* the plasma TV or which accounting service can offer both a lawyer on staff and quick phone support.

These keywords are often product part numbers or company names: "Jim's accounting service" or "Samsung hl-61ssw DLP TV." A consumer will examine prices, warranties, shipping costs, service contracts, return policies, and similar items before finally making a decision on where to buy the specific product.

How Do Consumers Flow Through Your Buying Funnel?

The buying funnel is different for every business. It is important to consider your company to determine how people find their information, make their decisions, and finally engage companies within your industry.

There is no time limit to the buying funnel. A used book sale might consist of five minutes from initial query to buying. A B2B $100,000 software integration package may take six months or more.

Some consumers will jump directly into the learn or buy phase of the buying funnel. If you are shopping for a new book, and you already know an author you like because of a previous book you have read, you do not need to learn more about the author, you just want to see what other books they have written and maybe take a quick look at customer reviews.

> **Note:** Jargon terms can be useful both as keywords and in ad copy. However, always keep in mind whether someone knows enough about your product to use jargon or understand the jargon you are using. If searchers are early in the buying funnel, jargon terms will confuse them, as they are still learning about your product. Later in the buying funnel, jargon can be useful as keywords. When someone uses a jargon keyword, you know that they know something about your products or services.

If you are tasked with finding both a software package and an integration vendor to move your company's email to a lower total cost of ownership system, the search may take many twists and turns through many months of discussions and searches.

Always keep in mind that every single keyword you choose for your AdWords campaign will fall into at least one phase of the buying funnel. Some keywords may be somewhat ambiguous as to which exact phase of the buying funnel they fall into. In those cases, you may wish to test different landing pages for these keywords to see if the informational page or a product page has a higher return for your company.

It can be a useful exercise to examine your keywords and see at what aspect of the buying funnel you are reaching prospects. If all of your keywords fall into the awareness and learn phases, but you do not have any in the buy phase, you might help a consumer decide which product to buy but then not capitalize on their search when they are finally buying.

Conversely, if all of your keywords fall into the buy phase, you might be generating very few sales, and by using keywords further up in the buying funnel, you can generate more awareness and sales for your company.

Of course, having the keyword in your account just means your ad might show for the search result. Both your ad and landing page need to continue engaging the consumer so you receive both the click and the conversion associated with that keyword. The first step is making sure you have the proper visibility.

Understanding Keywords

Keywords are thoughts put into words. We search to find the answer to a question. Always remember that when you choose a keyword, you are telling a consumer that you can help them find the answer to their question.

When doing keyword research, you should always keep the searcher in mind. It's their thoughts put into words that you want as keywords so your ad can be shown on a search results page.

Before we delve into the four main types of keywords, let us take a closer look at the scenario from Chapter 1 to see how any scenario can utilize these types of words.

Our searcher is sitting in his Chicago suburban house in January watching TV on a Saturday afternoon. Suddenly, his spouse calls up from the basement that there is water everywhere. Upon investigation, our searcher determines that a pipe froze, causing the pipe to break and flood their basement. This happens every year in Chicago. What are the possible keywords?

First, keywords or thoughts are often segmented into four key areas:

- Explicit
- Problems
- Symptoms
- Product names or part numbers

We will examine each individually.

Types of Keywords

Explicit keywords are the easiest to research. These keywords often have the highest search volume of all the keyword types. They directly describe the product or service, and very little creativity is necessary to research these keywords. Some examples are:

- Dermatologist
- Computer memory
- Plasma TV

In our above example, if we were to list out keywords for a plumber, we might have:

- Plumber
- North Chicago plumber
- Chicago plumbing services
- Emergency plumber
- Plumber phone number
- Saturday plumbing

The second type of keywords are problem-based words. These keywords describe the conditions or problems that your product solves. These are also known as curing searches. Some examples are:

- Acne
- How do I get rid of acne
- Can't run Excel
- Toothache
- What toothpaste will help cure a toothache?

If you examine your products and services and think of what you solve for a consumer, or how you make their life better, these are often problem-based keywords. In our plumber example, a "flooded basement" search would describe the root problem.

Symptoms make up the third type of keyword search. These keywords describe the symptoms of the actual problem. Some examples are:

- Oily skin

- Slow computer

In our earlier example, symptom searches may include:

- Frozen pipes

- Burst pipe

- Broken pipes

The fourth type of keyword is *product names or part numbers*. These are common keywords late in the buying funnel. Some examples are:

- P-10113/4 (a printer cartridge)

- Mint Soufflé Cleanser

- 512 MD DDR2-533 SODIMM (computer memory)

If we look closely at the keyword examples above, we can devise our own story from them.

We need a dermatologist because we have acne, which is caused by oily skin, but we could use the Mint Soufflé Cleanser to help care for our skin.

Our slow Sony Vaio is causing large Excel files to not load because we don't have enough computer memory. After researching the problem, our choice for the best computer memory is two 512 MD DDR2-533 SODIMMs.

By not just looking at keywords, but by also examining the scenarios that cause someone to need your product, you can quickly expand your keyword research into new, untapped areas.

There are other keyword types that might be more applicable for your industry. The next most common keyword search is an informational query. These are often harder keywords to monetize for those selling products or services; however, with a bit of creative thought to both answering the question and engaging the searcher, you can find new keyword search volume.

Some examples of informational queries are:

- How to turn off the water in the basement

- How to install memory in a computer

- Computer memory installation

- Candle burning times

- Differences between plasma and LDC TVs

These keyword searches may not have any commercial intent. However, they are excellent top-of-the-funnel keywords to create more awareness for your business and to engage a searcher to start them down the buying funnel.

Finding Keyword Ideas

When conducting keyword research, you should first consider your themes instead of actual keywords.

A theme is a collection of closely related keywords. In AdWords accounts, these are also known as ad groups. By first concentrating on your themes, you will build a high level list of how your products or services coordinate with the keyword types.

Often the navigation on a website is already broken down into themes, and much of your initial work is already conducted. However, these are only the direct keywords, and you will still need to do research on the other types of keywords for those direct keywords.

If your website does not have a good navigational structure, then as we walk through the following keyword research ideas, instead of thinking in individual keywords, first take a look at the high level themes and once those are established, come back to each theme and fill in the keywords.

For example, if you were a plumber, here's a list of some of the more popular themes:

- Plumber
- Broken pipes
- Fix shower
- Kitchen remodeling
- Bathroom remodeling
- Overflowing toilet
- Emergency plumbing
- Weekend plumbing
- Flooded basement

And the list goes on. You should be able to come up with more than 50 different themes for a plumber. With some work, you might even come up with a few hundred themes. While you know your business well, your potential customers—the searchers—do not; your business is actually quite complex when you start researching every problem you can fix.

Starting Your Keyword Research

You should start by analyzing your website: your website's navigation and the words used on your site. We will showcase the AdWords keyword research tool in Chapter 3, which will help you take a deep look into your own website.

If you have offline marketing material, examine your print collateral. Often direct mail pieces are carefully optimized over years of time. Are there hot-button words in your materials?

Analyze your top competitor's sites. Do they have navigational elements that are different from yours? Why? Is it that they offer different services than you or that they have broken down their site differently? If their site is just broken down in different ways, make note of those themes and see how their organization might jumpstart new ways for you to consider additional themes.

Examine the natural search results. Search engines try to diversify their results by including both authority and hub sites. The authority sites are worth taking a deeper look into as they are displayed on page one of the search results for some of your major keywords. Wikipedia.org or JustAnswer.com are common authority sites.

Hub sites are places where consumers can find a variety of information and links to other similar sites. Follow what the search engines consider hubs to see what other keywords and navigational elements these sites use. Since a hub site is trying to link to the most relevant sites for a category, they often have refined navigation that can help you organize themes. Do not forget to take a look at whom they link to, as a good hub will showcase a large variety of information. DMOZ.org and DexKnows.com are good examples of hub sites.

Hopefully, you have an analytic system in place. If not, Google offers a nice free system to get you started called Google Analytics. Your analytic system will show you what keywords someone searched on various search engines to find your website. If you have goals or conversion tracking configured, you can even see which keywords led to higher conversion rates.

One of the best places to mine for new keywords and themes is your internal search engine. If your site has internal search, you should be tracking what keywords visitors are searching for within your site. This information will tell you exactly what someone was trying to find. It is also a good place to examine your landing page's effectiveness. If you have a page with a high search percentage, essentially, the searcher did not find what they wanted on your landing page and had to do another search to find their information.

> **Note:** Google has a product called Custom Search Engine which is a free search engine for your site. This product is easy to integrate into both your site and your Google Analytics system so you can track what users are searching for on your website.

My absolute favorite tool will be the subject of Chapter 3: the AdWords Keyword tool.

When doing research for both your keywords and themes, there are two points to remember.

First, always keep the searcher in mind. The searcher is who you are trying to reach. You are advertising on a keyword you think they will type into a search engine and click on a result afterward. The searcher is the one who will ultimately make you profitable.

Second, always keep your products in mind. Your products or services are the lifeblood of your company. It's by selling those items that you can satisfy a searcher. When choosing keywords, make sure they are an accurate reflection of your products and services.

Do You Know Your Keywords?

Who searches for the word "bleach"?

If you thought the most common searcher was a 20- to 50-year-old female, then you have joined a large group of people who do not watch Japanese anime.

The most common searcher for the word "bleach" is a male under 24 years of age.

A few years ago a new Japanese anime program launched entitled *Bleach*. That show has completely changed the dynamic of that word.

There are words whose meanings have changed, and there are other words that describe multiple items.

A search for the word "ceramic" could be for a $0.99 figurine or a $10,000 factory part.

A search for "buy pipe" could mean a nice meerschaum tobacco-smoking pipe or a replacement for the busted pipe in your basement.

Sometimes relatively few people searching on a particular keyword will actually fit your ideal customer profile, and you may want to just avoid using that keyword altogether. For instance, if you sold Clorox and realized that the majority of people searching for the word "bleach" do not meet your website goals, you may wish to not advertise on that specific keyword. There are other times when the word is essential to your advertising campaign.

There are ways to write ad copy so you can showcase whether you are selling Clorox bleach or *Bleach* DVDs. This will help the searcher understand what products you offer. However, the first step is that you have to know it's a commonly confused word.

The best way to start understanding your words is to look at the natural search results. If you see sites or ads for seemingly unrelated industries, you should investigate further.

Another place to find these differences is in your keyword reporting, which we will discuss in later chapters. If you see words that seem highly targeted yet do not convert, it is worth your time to take a quick look and see if that word has multiple meanings.

Another fantastic tool is Microsoft adCenter Labs. One of the various tools available attempts to predict the demographic characteristics (age and sex) of a keyword (Figure 2.2).

Query: bleach

Gender: Male-oriented, with the following confidence:

:0.62

:0.38

Age: 18~24 Oriented with following distribution:

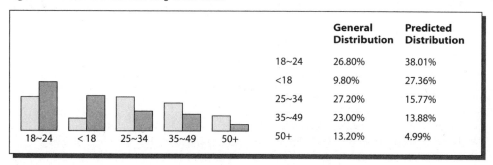

	General Distribution	Predicted Distribution
18~24	26.80%	38.01%
<18	9.80%	27.36%
25~34	27.20%	15.77%
35~49	23.00%	13.88%
50+	13.20%	4.99%

Figure 2.2 Microsoft adCenter Labs demographic targeting

Understanding when your keywords might be confused with other products or services can help you to be more specific with the words and themes you choose to keep you from spending money on keywords that do not lead to sales.

How Many Keywords Should You Have in Your Account?

You have probably heard someone mention an AdWords account that has over a million keywords. Yet, by most estimations the English language only contains roughly one-quarter of a million words. How can an AdWords account have more than four times the number of words in the entire English language?

The answer is simple: by creating keyword lists.

Before creating keyword lists and generating millions of keywords, it is important to first consider what you are going to do with those keywords.

Most companies do not need millions of keywords. There is not a magic number for how many keywords you should have in your account. The answer to "How many keywords should I have in my account?" comes back to relevancy.

You should only have relevant keywords in your account. If the keywords you create help a searcher find the answer to their question, then these are good keywords. If your keywords start to become ambiguous and could have multiple meanings, you need to make a financial decision about whether it is worth it to your company to advertise on a word with marginal (or worse, negative) results.

For example, if you were to search for "TV," what would you expect to find?

- TV reviews
- TV guide
- TV repair
- TV celebrities
- Plasma TVs

These highly unrelated terms could all be shown for a keyword such as "TV." The keyword is not specific enough to have any definitive user intent. Here are some issues to consider:

Examining Your Keywords If you cannot determine the user intent of a keyword, it is probably not specific enough for your account. This is a rule of thumb, and there are definitely exceptions. It is useful to first test out the more specific keywords, and then once you have an idea of cost per conversion and conversion rates on the more specific keywords, try out some of the more general keywords to see if they are profitable for your advertising dollars.

Determining the Right Number of Keywords The next consideration in determining how many keywords you should use comes back to management time. If you have a 100,000 keywords, you will need to find a scalable way to manage that many. Excel files and database reports are highly time consuming for organizing that much data and determining your profit on each keyword so that you can decide how much you would like to bid for each word. You may need a bid management system to handle that many words.

Understanding Google AdWords Account Limits The last consideration is Google AdWords account limits. A standard Google AdWords account can only have 50,000 active keywords. If you need more than 50,000 keywords, you have two options.

> **Option 1: Larger Spenders** Google has an enhanced account that can hold up to 50 active campaigns and a much larger keyword list. You will have to have your AdWords rep enable this for you. If you do not spend well into five figures a month with Google, you will most likely not be able to have this feature turned on.

> **Option 2: Linking Accounts** Google can link accounts together on the back end so they share some data and only serve one ad per search result. If you need multiple accounts, then talk to an AdWords rep.

If you are wondering why Google has caps on keywords, you can examine it from their perspective. Every keyword entered into their system has to be stored in multiple databases. Every local database is examined for keyword matches every time someone conducts a search on Google. Google is trying to filter through millions of keywords to serve ads to a searcher in less than one second. The less total database space being used to house keywords, the easier it is to sort through the keywords to quickly serve results to the searcher.

Therefore, while you will learn techniques for creating millions of keywords, it is best to initially keep your list to fewer than 50,000 keywords unless you are spending tens of thousands of dollars each month with Google.

Creating Keyword Lists

Most words in the English language can be categorized as a noun, adverb, adjective, preposition, pronoun, or verb. The same can be said for products. Most products can be described by product types, product attributes, adjectives, and so on. By breaking down your products or services into their base elements and then recombining these words, you can easily create huge keyword lists.

For example, Table 2.1 is a chart for maternity clothing that is by no means exhaustive, but can be used to illustrate this point.

▶ **Table 2.1** Maternity shirt example keywords

Category Adjectives	Product Types	Product Attributes 1	Product Attributes 2	Example Keywords
Pregnant	Shirt	Long sleeve	Cotton	Pregnancy shirt
Pregnancy	T-shirt	Short sleeve	Rayon	Pregnancy shirt long sleeve
Maternity	Dress blouse	Sleeveless	Silk	Pregnancy shirt cotton
	Tops		Stretchable	Pregnancy shirt long sleeve cotton
	Polo shirt		Natural fibers	
	Sweatshirt		Wool	

In the table, if we always used a word from both the Category Adjectives and Product Types column and then mixed and matched the rest of the words, the words in Table 2.1 would become 504 keywords.

If you were to make five lists of five keywords and mix and match them all, that would create 7,775 keywords. As you can see, keyword listing is powerful but can easily grow out of control. Therefore, it is important to keep in mind your account structure when creating keyword lists. You should first diagram your final ad groups before creating the lists. If you create keyword lists first, then you have to try and categorize them all into ad groups.

In Table 2.1, the minimum number of ad groups should be seven, one for each product type. You could easily have a few hundred ad groups from this information.

For example, at the most granular level, each keyword generated this could instead be an ad group. To fill in the keywords within the ad group, you could use plurals, misspellings, and similar words such as "t-shirt," "tshirt," and "tee shirt."

Creating keyword lists to generate thousands of keywords is useful. However, if done improperly, you could quickly end up with more keywords than you know how to organize, let alone manage. You can use the exact same techniques of creating lists to first diagram your ad groups, and then you can create lists within each ad group to generate the final keywords used within your account.

By first creating your ad groups and then filling in your keywords, it is much easier to organize your account and keep your keyword lists from spiraling out of control.

Using Long Tail Keywords

The *long tail* is a term first coined by Chris Anderson in an article in *Wired* magazine (October 2004) to describe how niche markets can sell a large number of infrequently sold items that together create more total sales than the top-selling product lists.

For example, before the days of the Internet, bookstores had to keep physical inventory in their stores. There is a finite number of books that can be housed and displayed upon shelves within a store. The top-selling books in each category were most prominently featured. A book had to constantly sell to continue to maintain space on the shelves; otherwise, it was regulated to the discount bin to make space for a book that was selling. While some of these books might have sold a few copies each month, it was not worth the shelf space to try and keep them in stock.

Then came Amazon.com, which had no physical storage limit for its products. Suddenly, a book that only sold one copy a month, or only a hundred copies a year, could still be profitable for Amazon. When you combine the millions of books that only sell a few copies, those total sales can be equal to or even exceed the top best-selling books.

You can repeat the same logic for any niche-based business, such as Netflix. Netflix carries thousands of copies of the most rented titles. However, the power of Netflix comes from their ability to carry even a few copies of each low-demand title. It is a powerful value proposition to the Netflix customer that even these niche movies can be rented. The total rentals for the low-demand movies in aggregate numbers may be equal to the total rentals of the top hundred movies.

This same logic can be applied to keywords. Single word keyword searches make up roughly 20 percent of the search volume in the United States. However, search queries that are five or more words in length make up nearly 20 percent of the search volume as well.

There are two main ways that marketers use the phrase "long tail keyword" when discussing keywords:

- The first refers to keyword searches that are three or more words in length. Essentially, someone typing in three or more words in a search box is being specific in defining the information they are wishing to discover.
- The second refers to low search volume. Instead of focusing on how many words are in the search query, these marketers consider long tail keywords to have low search volume. In this instance, even a one-word keyword with low search volume would be a long tail word.

Each year, the number of words used in search queries grows (see Table 2.2). As the general search population starts to search with more words, the popularity of two- and three-keyword phrases will grow as well.

Therefore, when considering the long tail, I favor applying it toward search volume. The principle of the long tail is to aggregate infrequent data points. In searches, this would be keywords with low search volume.

▶ **Table 2.2** U.S. clicks by number of keywords

Subject	January 2008	December 2008	January 2009	Year-over-Year Percent Change
1 word	20.96%	20.70%	20.29%	–3%
2 words	24.91%	24.13%	23.65%	–5%
3 words	22.03%	21.94%	21.92%	0%
4 words	14.54%	14.67%	14.89%	2%
5 words	8.20%	8.37%	8.68%	6%
6 words	4.32%	4.47%	4.65%	8%
7 words	2.23%	2.40%	2.49%	12%
8+ words	2.81%	3.31%	3.43%	22%

Note: Data is based on four-week rolling periods (ending Jan. 26, 2008; Dec. 27, 2008; and Jan. 31, 2009) from the Hitwise sample of 10 million U.S. Internet users.

Source: Hitwise, an Experian company: http://press.experian.com/documents/showdoc.cfm?doc=3430

There are several advantages to using long tail keywords and incorporating them into your keyword lists:

- There is often less competition on these words. It takes more keyword research and keyword creation discipline to have an encompassing keyword list. By expanding your reach to these less frequently used words, you can often find gems that cost very little.

- The much more important reason is that many long tail words are more specific, and it is easier to match the user intent with both the proper ad copy and the proper landing page.

Regarding the second reason, if someone searched for "long sleeve silk maternity shirts" and one ad copy talks about generic maternity shirts and another one talks about silk maternity shirts that have long sleeves, which do you think a consumer is more likely to click on?

Keyword advertising is about choosing keywords and ad copy that can answer a user's initial question. The closer you can associate the ad copy to the user intent, the higher the click-through rate. If you pair that ad copy with a landing page that also includes that same product or service, conversion rates are usually higher as well.

Utilizing the long tail for both ad group organization and keyword research will let you associate your marketing more closely with the user intent, which has benefits for both the searcher and the advertiser. The searcher finds the answer to their question, and the advertiser receives more conversions on their website.

Wide vs. Deep Keywords

When enacting keyword lists or using the long tail approach, it is crucial to consider wide versus deep keywords. They are very different, and the wrong approach can send you spiraling down a path of tens of thousands of closely related keywords that do not accurately encompass the best keywords for your account.

Instead, consider the different ways someone looks for information about your product and services. Earlier in this chapter, we discussed explicit, problem, and symptom keywords. Each of those types of keywords represents different ways of finding the exact same product. You first need to aggregate the different keywords used before drilling down into the specific keywords.

For example, if you were advertising a spyware removal product, it would be easy to expand this list to create thousands of keywords from the simple list in Table 2.3.

However, what you would end up with is a list of keywords that all include the root keyword "spyware." That does not represent the way people search for spyware removal.

Adjectives	Brands or Adjectives	Product	Program Types
Free	Microsoft	Spyware	Removal
Cheap	Download		Scan
Discount	McAfee		Remover
Low cost	Norton		Programs
			Protection
			Detector

The above list would be considered a deep keyword list. It only encompasses the way people search when they are using the root keyword "spyware." Before you start to go deep, you will first want to go wide with your keyword list.

A more encompassing keyword list would look like Table 2.4.

► **Table** 2.4   Wide spyware keywords

Action Words	Wide Keywords	Software Type
Delete	Spyware	Software
Destroy	Adware	Program
Remove	W32	Download
Find	Virus	Freeware
Scan	Keylogger	Trial

Instead of relying on the word "spyware" to be included throughout your keyword list and in the search query, this keyword list examines the different root keywords used in searching for spyware removal. If your product converted much higher for "adware" keywords, and you started with all "spyware" keywords, you would be missing your most profitable keywords.

This also makes it easier to concentrate on the correct keywords. Start with a very wide list. First, you should think of all the different ways that someone can search for your product or services. From those different thinking patterns, create a root keyword list. These are the major words used to describe your offerings.

Run these keywords (with their appropriate modifiers) for a while in your AdWords account. Once you start to see which wide keywords are receiving more clicks and conversions, you can focus on going deep within those root keywords.

By taking this two-step approach to both keyword and ad group creation, you will be spending your time more wisely building out profitable keyword lists. It is easy to create massive amounts of keywords, but it makes more business sense to create profitable—and manageable—keyword lists.

Discerning Keyword Match Types

AdWords gives an advertiser a significant amount of control in determining when an ad will be shown. We will continue to discuss many of these additional options in later chapters. However, if you do not match your keywords appropriately, these additional controls will only have marginal increases in producing high quality traffic.

There are three different match types that AdWords uses to determine if your ad should be displayed based upon the user's search query: broad, phrase, and exact match.

Broad Match

A word is considered *broad matched* when you enter a keyword into an ad group with no formatting around the word (Figure 2.3).

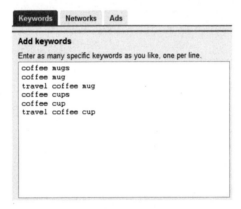

Figure 2.3 Broad matched keywords in an ad group

Broad matched keywords can trigger your ad to show if the searcher uses a query that is related to your keywords. Broad matched keywords match to misspellings, plurals, and even similar words.

For example, if you had the broad matched keyword "coffee cups," you could match to "coffee cup" (singular), "cofee cup" (misspelling), or "coffee mug" (similar word).

In addition, the order of the words does not matter. To continue our example, if you used the broad match "coffee cups," you could match to "cups coffee" or "mug coffee."

Lastly, you can be matched if the search query contains similar words to your keyword with additional parameters. For example, if your keyword was "coffee cups," you could match to "coffee red mug," "blue mugs coffee," or "coffee cup holder."

If you only sold coffee mugs, being matched to a keyword such as "coffee cup holder" is probably not a good match. In these cases, we will show you how to keep your ad from showing when we visit negative keywords later in this chapter.

You will hear many marketers disparage broad match. This is because broad match provides the least amount of control of any of the match types. In general, the higher your quality score and the better your click-through rate, the more your keywords can be matched to similar keywords.

This becomes an issue if you sell coffee mugs and suddenly start being matched to tea cups, as tea and coffee are related and mugs and cups are related. This is why it is important to understand all of the match types to best control when your ad is shown.

There is one huge advantage to broad match. In a November 2008 article, Google announced:

> *Did you know that 20% of the queries Google receives each day are ones we haven't seen in at least 90 days, if at all?*

HTTP://ADWORDS.BLOGSPOT.COM/2008/11/REACH-MORE-CUSTOMERS-WITH-BROAD-MATCH.HTML

When one-fifth of all searches on Google have not been seen by Google in the last 90 days, and that engine receives millions of searches every single day, it is easy to see that it is impossible to have every single keyword related to your products or services within your account.

Broad match has its uses. It will let your account reach individuals who are typing in very specific queries. However, it must be measured carefully and optimized over time.

There is a way to see exactly what search queries your keywords are being matched to—with the Search Query Report. In this report, you can see exactly what is triggering your ads and refine that ad exposure as necessary. We will cover this report, and how to make keyword refinements based upon this data, in Chapters 16 and 17.

If you want the maximum exposure possible for all of your keywords, broad match will help you get there.

Phrase Match

A keyword is considered *phrase matched* when you enter the word in an ad group within quotation marks as seen in Figure 2.4.

In order for your phrase matched keyword to display your ad, the search query must contain your keyword in the same order you typed it into your ad group.

Figure 2.4 Phrase matched keywords in an ad group

For example, if your keyword was "coffee cups," your keyword would match to phrases such as:

- Coffee cups
- Blue coffee cups
- Coffee cups blue
- Red coffee cups for traveling

In each of the above instances, there could be words before, after, or before and after your keyword phrase. It could also be the keyword phrase itself. However, your keyword phrase was always included in the search query.

Phrase matched words do not match to misspellings or plurals. Therefore, if you had the keyword "coffee cups," the following searches would not trigger your ad:

- Coffee cup (singular)
- Cofee cups (misspelling)
- Cups coffee (different word order)

Your ad would not trigger if someone entered a word between your keywords. In the "coffee cups" example, if someone searched for "coffee blue cups," your ad would not show as the search query did not contain your phrase exactly.

Just to clarify, the user is not typing in quotes or adding formatting when entering their query into Google. The user is searching as usual; the quotes are only used to signal to Google that you would like your keyword to be triggered if it matched the search pattern. For example, in Figure 2.5, if you had the phrase matched keyword "coffee cup," your ad would be displayed.

Figure 2.5 Google search query that will display an ad for coffee cup phrase matched keyword

Phrase match is one of the best match types to use for a new account. In new accounts, you do not yet know all the keyword variations. You can use phrase match to find some of the additional variations with the search query report while ensuring that your ad is not being matched to broader items that might not bring you a positive ROI (return on investment).

Exact Match

Exact match is the most specific matching option that AdWords offers. First, you must enter the keywords into your ad group within brackets, as shown in Figure 2.6.

Figure 2.6 Exact matched keywords in an ad group

Exact match works just how it sounds: a user must type into the search box a query that is identical to a keyword in your ad group for your ad to be displayed.

Exact match keywords do not match to misspellings, similar keywords, plurals, or singular forms of the words.

If you have the exact match keyword "[coffee cups]," your ad would not be shown if someone types in "coffee cup" (singular), "cofee cups" (misspelling), "blue coffee cups" (additional word), "coffee mugs" (similar word), or any other possible variation.

The biggest advantage of exact match is that you know exactly what someone is typing into the search box. You can examine your ad copy, landing page, and keyword to ensure that a perfectly formed synergistic chain has been established that will maximize your conversion rate.

In longer queries, exact match will also show user intent. A keyword such as "buy plasma TV" shows commercial intent. A keyword search such as "LCD vs. plasma TV" or "advantages of accountants over tax prep software" signals a comparison shopping intent. In this case, the user needs more information before they are ready to buy a product. A search such as "congressional term lengths" has an informational intent.

While we all use a search engine to find answers to questions, our intent upon finding those answers can vary quite significantly. The main intents online are commercial, informational, and navigational. However, just because you have a shopping site does not mean you should not use informational terms in your keyword list. It means you need to make sure you are engaging those users first with information and then have that information lead them to your products.

Which Match Type Is Best?

Now that you know the three match types, how should you use them within your AdWords account?

First, you should know you can use all three match types for the same keyword within the same AdWords account. You could have the same keyword exact, phrase, and broad matched within the same ad group.

Second, when determining which match types to use, there are two major considerations: budget and reach.

If you are starting with a small budget and only want to increase your budget as you find profitable keywords, you will want to start with mostly exact match keywords. Once you find keywords that are meeting your business goals, then you can add the phrase matched and eventually broad matched versions of those keywords.

If you are starting with a large budget and are willing to throw everything at the wall to see what converts, you will want to start with all three match types.

If you have multiple match types, you want to make sure that you have exact match bid the highest, phrase match a little lower, and finally broad match at the lowest bid.

The reason why you want to set bids will become very apparent in Chapter 7 when we discuss quality score. Essentially, if all three keywords can be triggered in a search result, Google will show the one with the highest ad rank. Ad rank is a number derived from multiplying your quality score by your maximum CPC (cost per click). By bidding the most on exact match, you are essentially forcing a higher ad rank for the exact match than the phrase or broad matched keyword.

Another reason you would want to bid exact match the highest is that you know exactly the keywords used in the search query. It is much easier to determine user intent with exact match words than with the other match types. With phrase or broad match, the search query should be related to your keywords but will not be exactly related.

You should find that exact match has the highest conversion rate, then phrase match, then broad match. If you find that broad match has a higher conversion rate than phrase or exact match, it is generally because you are being matched to some search queries where you do not have that corresponding keyword in your account. This is another reason to use the search query report: to find those converting keywords you do not currently have in your AdWords account.

Lastly, if you use this bid technique, every time your phrase or broad match keyword is shown, it signals that you do not have that exact match keyword in your account.

Due to how many unique queries are seen on Google within a day, you will never have every exact match keyword in your account. It is just not possible to find every single variation. This brings us to the second point to consider when using multiple match types: reach.

Broad and phrase match will help you reach a larger user base. If you only have exact match keywords, you are considerably lowering the possible search queries that your keywords could be matched to, and thus, will not reach nearly as many users.

By examining both your budget and desired reach, you can determine how many different match types you wish to use when creating a new ad group (Figure 2.7).

Once an ad group starts to collect statistics, then you can use the search query report to determine what keywords you wish to add to your ad group, and what keywords you do not wish to trigger your ad.

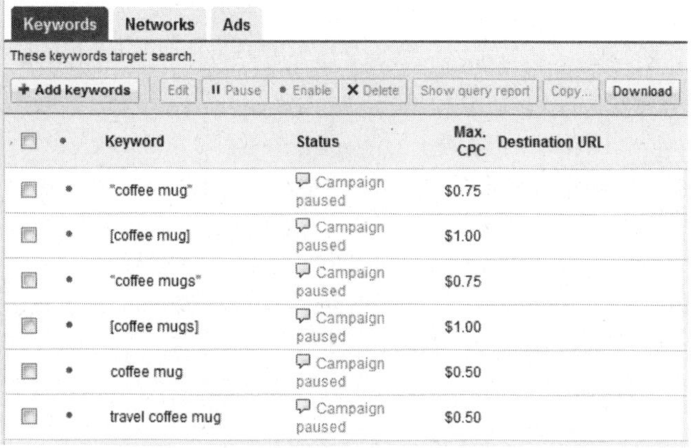

Figure 2.7 Ad group using all three match types

As a starting point rule of thumb, bid phrase match 25 percent less than your exact match bid. Then, for your broad match bid, choose another 25 to 50 percent less. If you are looking for a significant amount of broad match exposure, 25 percent less is a good number. If you want some exposure on broad match, but you are not ready to pay a lot of unknown search queries, a 50 percent less bid is a good starting place.

Using Negative Keywords

Negative keywords are filtering words. This type of keyword stops your ad from being displayed on a search result. If you have phrase and broad matched keywords in your account and some of the variations do not have good conversion rates, you could use a negative keyword to stop your ad from showing on a search result.

Before implementing negative keywords, you should have a way to measure your conversion rates and cost per conversion. In Chapter 15, we will discuss a free conversion tool that Google offers to measure your results.

The reason why you need conversion tracking implemented into your account is that when you add negative keywords to your account, some very specific things should happen:

- Your click-through rate should increase. Since you are now choosing to stop your ad from showing on irrelevant search queries, the times your ad is shown should be more relevant and thus gain a higher click-through rate.
- Your conversion rate should increase. Since you are now only showing your ad for queries relevant to your product or services and are not being matched to more obscure words that are not directly reflective of your offerings, you should see your conversion rate go up.
- Your cost per conversion should decrease. As negative keywords keep your ad from displaying on less relevant results, when you do receive clicks, those clicks should be of higher quality and lower your overall cost per conversion.

If you do not see these three items happening, you need to revisit your negative keyword list to see if you added negative keywords that stopped your ads from showing on keyword searches that were driving sales. It is common for someone to know about negative keywords and automatically add the word "free." However, a search for "plasma TVs with free shipping" would not trigger your ad if you used the negative keyword "-free." If you happened to sell plasma TVs and offer free shipping, that is a wonderful query for you to show your ad. Therefore, you need to be careful when adding negative keywords.

Implementing Negative Keywords

There are two places within your account to add negative keywords. The first is within an ad group.

Navigate to an ad group, and when you enter a keyword, add the minus (-) sign in front of any words that you do not wish to trigger your ad.

For example, if you were using the broad matched keyword "coffee cups," and you wanted to make sure you would never show for "tea cups," you would add the negative keyword "-tea" to your ad group, as shown in Figure 2.8.

Figure 2.8 Negative keyword "-tea" in an ad group

When you add a negative keyword within an ad group, it only affects the keywords in that group. Therefore, in this example, you could have one ad group selling coffee mugs with the negative keyword "-tea," and another ad group selling tea cups with the negative keyword "-coffee." In this instance, you could now use some broad matched words and ensure that the correct ad was displayed.

Please note that in this example, if you only had the just described two ad groups, a search for "tea and coffee mug set" would not display any ads. This is because both "tea" and "coffee" are within the query, and each ad group has a negative keyword that would keep your ad from showing on that query.

The second use for negative keywords is at the campaign level. If you navigate to the Tools menu and click on Edit Negative Campaign Keywords, you can input negative keywords. In this instance, these negative keywords will affect every ad group within that specific campaign.

There is also a tool within the campaign negative interface that allows you to find other negative keywords in your account in case you wish to add them as campaign negatives. Be careful when using this tool as you may have negative keywords in specific ad groups that you do not wish to have affecting every single ad group. It is useful when used properly, just use with caution.

Negative campaign keywords are easy to forget about since they are not displayed within your ad group. If you are troubleshooting why an ad is not displaying, you might want to check your campaign negative keyword list to see if that is the cause.

Just as with regular keywords, AdWords offers three different match types for negative keywords. These three match types are called broad, phrase, and exact negative keyword match. However, while the names are the same, the rules for how the match types work are different for negatives.

Negative Broad Match

When you navigate to your ad group and just type in a minus (-) sign and a keyword, you've created a *negative broad match*. Negative broad keywords stop your ad from showing if that word is anywhere within the search query. Negative broad keywords do not match to misspellings or plurals.

For example, if you had the negative keyword "cups" ("-cups"), a search for "coffee cups" or "tea cups" would not display your ad as the search query contains the word "cups." However, a search for "coffee cup" (singular) or "coffee cps" (misspelled) would display your ad as the word "cups" was not explicitly stated within the search query.

You can also use multiple words in a negative broad keyword. In this instance, the order of the words does not matter, as long as all of the negative words are in the query. Once again, these do not match to plurals or misspellings.

If you added the negative keyword "coffee cups" ("-coffee cups") in your ad group, your ad would be displayed on a query such as "blue coffee cup" (singular) or "cofee cups" (misspelled).

However, your ad would not be displayed for:

- Coffee cups
- Blue coffee cups
- Coffee blue cups
- Cups coffee blue
- Cups of coffee

This occurs because every example above contains both the word "coffee" and the word "cups."

Negative Phrase Match

Negative phrase matched keywords must be contained within the user query in the exact order you entered them. Additional words can be contained before or after the search query; however, if the search query contains your negative phrase in the same order, then your ad will not be displayed.

As with broad match negative keywords and regular phrase matched keywords, this match type does not match to singular or misspellings.

For example, if you had the negative phrase match -"coffee cups", your ad would not be shown for queries such as:

- Coffee cups
- Blue coffee cups
- Coffee cups and mugs

This is because every one of those examples contains the keyword "coffee cups" in the same order.

However, if you have the negative phrase match word -"coffee cups", your ad would be displayed for queries such as:

- Cups coffee (different order)
- Coffee cup (singular)
- Blue coffee cup (singular)
- Coffe cups (misspelling)
- Coffe cups and tea (misspelling)

When adding negative phrase matched words, the formatting is straightforward. Add a minus (-) sign and then the keyword in quotes: -"negative phrase match" (Figure 2.9).

Figure 2.9 Negative phrase matched keywords used in an ad group

You can use negative phrase matched words at either the ad group or campaign level.

Negative Exact Match

In the *negative exact match*, your ad is not displayed when the search query matches your negative keyword exactly.

For instance, if you had the negative exact match keyword -[coffee cups], your ad would only not be displayed if someone typed "coffee cups" into the search box.

If the search query was "coffee cup" (singular), "cup coffee" (different order), or "coffe cup" (misspelling), the negative exact match keyword would not stop your ad from displaying.

As with the regular exact match, the negative exact match does not match to plurals and misspellings.

The formatting is also the same as the exact match keyword, except you add a negative sign in front of the formatting brackets. The formatting is -[keyword].

▶ **Table 2.5** Will the ad show?

Negative Keyword	Search Query
-mug (broad match single word)	~~coffee mug~~
	coffee mugs
	mugs blue coffee
	blue coffee mugs
- coffee mugs (broad match, multiple words)	coffee mug
	~~coffee mugs~~
	~~mugs blue coffee~~
	~~blue coffee mugs~~
-"coffee mugs"	coffee mug
	~~coffee mugs~~
	mugs blue coffee
	~~blue coffee mugs~~
-[coffee mugs]	coffee mug
	~~coffee mugs~~
	mugs blue coffee
	blue coffee mugs

Putting Negative and Positive Keywords Together

When discussing negative keywords, it can be useful to call regular keywords *positive keywords* to signify the difference between keywords that trigger your ad and their negative counterparts that keep your ad from showing.

When using both negative and positive keywords together, you should first determine when you want your ad to show, and if there are specific variations when you do not want your ad to be displayed. Once you have determined those conditions, it becomes easy to choose the proper negative and positive keywords and respective match types.

For example, let us create a fictional company that sells Disney videos. After running their ads for a while, they realize that when a searcher just types in "Disney video" their conversion rates are low and they are not profitable on those keywords.

However, upon further investigation, the company realizes that if the searcher types in anything *with* the keyword "Disney video," they convert quite well.

Therefore, they would not want their ad to show on the actual search "Disney video," however, they do want it to show for variations such as "Little Mermaid Disney video," "Disney video for sale," and "newest Disney video."

This can be accomplished quite easily. The company would have an ad group with the negative exact match keyword -[Disney video] and the positive keyword "Disney video" as seen in Figure 2.10.

Figure 2.10 Disney video negative exact match used with positive keywords

In this instance, the ad would only be displayed if someone searched for "Disney video" and any accompanying word. If someone just searched for "Disney video," the ad would not be triggered.

Often, you will want to use broad or phrase matched words to capture a wide variety of search queries. However, this often results in your ad displaying on queries that do not accurately reflect your company's products. Using negative keywords to filter your ad from showing on these queries can allow you to maintain control over when your ad is shown and maximize your ad's reach.

Researching Negative Keywords

It is just as important to keep your ad from showing on irrelevant queries as to show your ad on the correct queries. That also means it's just as important to conduct negative keyword research as it is to research positive keywords.

The easiest place to find negative keywords is the search query report. If you navigate to the reporting section of your AdWords account, one of the reports is called a search query report. Run this report, and you will have an Excel file that looks like Figure 2.11.

	A	B	C	D
			Search Query Match	Cost/
		Search		
1	Ad Group	Query	Type	Conversion
2	Coffee Cups	Blue coffee cup	phrase	$2.34
3	Coffee Cups	Red coffee cup	broad	$1.76
4	Coffee Cups	Starbucks coffee cup	broad	$4.55
5	Coffee Cups	coffee cups	exact	$2.34
6	Coffee Cups	coffee mugs for RVs	broad	$19.56

Figure 2.11 Search query report in Excel

If your business is selling coffee mugs, but you must have a cost per conversion of fewer than $5 to be profitable, you can see that the actual search query that contains "RV" is not profitable.

Assuming that you had enough data to prove this was a trend, or you did not sell RV coffee mugs, you would want to stop your ad from showing when "RV" was used in the search query. By adding the negative keyword "-RV" to that particular ad group, you can stop your ad from showing when the word "RV" is used in the search query.

If you happen to sell RV coffee mugs and do not want to lose that traffic, you could create a new ad group with keywords and ad copy that specifically spoke to those searchers looking for RV coffee mugs.

The search query report will give you a significant amount of insight into which actual queries are triggering your ads.

The other way of finding negative keywords is during your regular keyword research phase. In the next chapter, you will learn about Google's powerful keyword research tool. As you use the tool, if you see words that are unrelated to your business or words where you just do not want your ad to be displayed, make note of those potential negative keywords so you can add them to your account.

Taking Control of Your Ad Display

Positive keywords are the lifeblood of Google AdWords. If you do not have a keyword that will match to a searcher's query, your ad will not show. It's quite simple.

It is crucial that you not only conduct keyword research, but when you use these keywords in your account, you understand what search queries someone can search for that will trigger your ad to show on a search result.

Conversely, when you find search queries that you do not want your ad to show for, block your ad from showing by using negative keywords. Negative keywords should raise your CTR (click-through rate), lower your CPA (cost per action), and increase your conversion rate.

As you add negative keywords, always keep an eye on total conversions. Even if the negative keywords are doing their job, if your total conversions drop significantly, you may need to trim some of your negative keywords.

If keywords lead to conversions, but at a higher cost per conversion than you are comfortable paying, you should lower the bids to a profitable level instead of just keeping your ad from showing by using negative keywords:

- Positive keywords trigger your ads.
- Negative keywords stop your ad from showing.

By using these two keyword types together, you can take control of your account to ensure you receive the maximum exposure and profit from your AdWords campaigns.

Best Practices for Conducting Keyword Research

Keywords are the foundation of your AdWords account. If you do not have a keyword that matches to the search query, your ad will not be shown. Comprehensive keyword research is essential to maximizing your account's exposure to potential customers.

- Every keyword falls into a section of the buying funnel. Understanding where your keyword falls in the funnel is important to ensure you are reaching consumers at different stages of their buying behavior.

- Keywords can be broken down into four major aspects: explicit, symptoms, problems, and product names or part numbers. Utilize each type of keyword to reach the maximum number of searchers.

- Start keyword research with your site, your competitor's site, the natural search results, internal site search, and the dictionary.

- Make sure you know your own keywords. If your keywords describe one or more different products or ideas, then use ad copy to tell the consumer which keyword variation is related to your company.

- A good way to start expanding your keywords is to create keyword lists. By creating lists for both ad group and keyword organization, you can create larger, yet more focused, lists.

- When starting long tail keyword research, do not use deep keywords. Deep keywords only describe a single aspect of how someone searches. Instead, start with wide keywords, and when you find keywords that are converting, do deep keyword research on those particular keywords.

- There are three different match types: broad, phrase, and exact. Use a combination of these various match types based upon your budget and marketing objectives.

- Negative keywords stop your ads from showing. It is just as important to conduct negative keyword research as it is to find new positive keywords.

- The search query report will show you what someone actually searched for that triggered your ad to show. Use this report to find new positive and negative keywords.

Keyword research can be time consuming. However, it is necessary for maximum exposure. There are many tools that will help you along in your keyword research efforts to help save you time and give you ideas you may have overlooked. In the next chapter, we will examine one of these tools: the AdWords Keyword tool.

Keyword Tools: Extracting Valuable Data from Google

Understanding where keywords fall into the buying funnel is critical. Choosing your keywords wisely and then measuring results will ensure the best chance of success for your campaigns. By starting with wide keywords and then moving to deep keywords, make sure you are directing your keyword research time into the proper areas.

After examining your site, competitors' sites, search results, and internal site search, where do you go next to look for keywords?

There are a variety of tools available online that will help you discover new keywords.

Chapter Contents

AdWords Keyword Tool

Google's Search-Based Keyword Tool

Google Sets

Google Trends

Google Insights for Search

Google Labs and Microsoft adCenter Labs

Best Practices for Using Keyword Tools

AdWords Keyword Tool

Google has a tremendous amount of search data. Between its organic and paid search listings across its web properties such as news, Google.com, Google sites in various countries, images, and even products, Google has compiled a massive amount of data about search queries.

One of the most powerful tools you can use to start your keyword research process is Google's own Adwords Keyword Tool that can examine the information collected across all of these various properties.

The AdWords Keyword Tool can be accessed from a few different places:

- Access the tool directly: `https://adwords.google.com/select/` KeywordToolExternal
- From the Tools menu in your AdWords account
- From an individual ad group

Internal vs. External Tool Access

If you access the AdWords Keyword Tool from the URL (or any other way that is not clicking into the tool from within your AdWords account), there are a few features you will not see. This is because Google does not know which AdWords account to associate this data with and therefore cannot show you data items from within your AdWords account.

The two major features you will not see (which will be discussed more) are a way to find information from an existing keyword within your account, and the ability to view and add negative keyword information.

However, if you access the tool from within your account, the results are tailored to your campaign's geographic and language settings. Therefore, you cannot easily see data from different countries or languages (Figure 3.1).

Keyword Tool

Use the Keyword Tool to get new keyword ideas. Select an option below to enter a few descriptive words or phrases, or type in your website's URL. Keyword Tool Tips

Important note: We cannot guarantee that these keywords will improve your campaign performance. We reserve the right to disapprove any keywords you add. You are responsible for the keywords you select and for ensuring that your use of the keywords does not violate any applicable laws.

new Want more keyword ideas? Try the Search-based Keyword Tool, a new tool that will generate ideas matched to your website.

Results are tailored to the languages and countries you choose below:

English		All Countries and Territories	
Chinese (simplified)		------	
Chinese (traditional)		United States	
Danish		Australia	
Dutch		Austria	
Finnish		Belgium	

Figure 3.1 Changing geographic and language settings within the AdWords Keyword Tool

There are three ways you can use the tool to find new keywords (see Figure 3.2).

- Phrases—similar to a Thesaurus tool
- Content—find keywords from a webpage
- Keyword—expand your current keywords

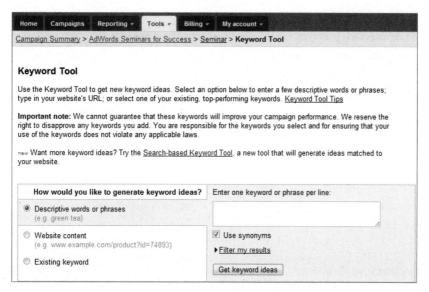

Figure 3.2 AdWords Keyword Tool main screen

You can also choose to filter the data you are seeing when you are using the above types of research (Figure 3.3):

- Do not show keywords already in an ad group (only available if the tool is accessed via the AdWords interface).
- Include adult content.
- Do not show new keyword suggestions, only show data for entered keywords (not available for website content).

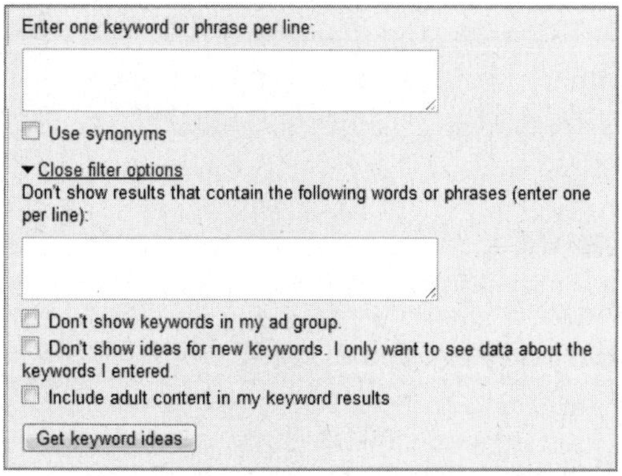

Figure 3.3 Filtering keyword information

Although the AdWords Keyword Tool has only a few options for finding and filtering data, when used correctly, it will be your main resource for keyword research. There are a couple of ways to use this tool to generate keyword ideas, which we will examine in depth.

Generating Keyword Ideas

When using tools to generate ideas, it is important to note that they are just tools that are run by computers. These tools do not know your business, they do not think, they do not understand your customers. While there is tremendous data available from these tools, you are the one responsible for choosing your keywords.

Ensure that the keywords you choose accurately describe your products or services, what problems they solve, and the conditions someone may be in when they need your business. Remember, keywords are thought processes.

You should start by finding wide keywords—those keywords that describe the vast ways people search for words that are not closely related (for example, spyware, adware, virus, keylogger)—before diving deep into one specific keyword (for instance, spyware, spyware remover, spyware program).

We will first look at the three main ways of conducting keyword research.

Descriptive Words and Phrases

The first way to use the AdWords Keyword Tool is to input words or phrases and ask Google to show you related keywords. If you click the synonym box, you will also see synonyms of the keywords entered (Figure 3.4).

Use this tool when first starting your keyword research to look for the synonyms of your major keywords. When you find different wide keywords, note them in a separate list from your keyword research. This will help you keep tabs on the wide keywords and sort them from the thousands of keywords you might normally add to your ad groups.

However, when you use the synonym tool, these keywords are closely related; therefore, the descriptive words and phrases section of the tool is better for finding deep keywords than wide ones. After advertising for a period of time so that you have enough data to examine your conversion rates and cost per conversions, you may realize that a few sets of wide keywords are driving most of your sales. This tool is then very valuable for you to dive into all the variations of those keywords.

Website Content: Jumpstarting Your Keyword List

Since you already have a website, and most likely you spent quality time writing your content, would it not be useful if you could just receive suggestions based on each of your website's pages?

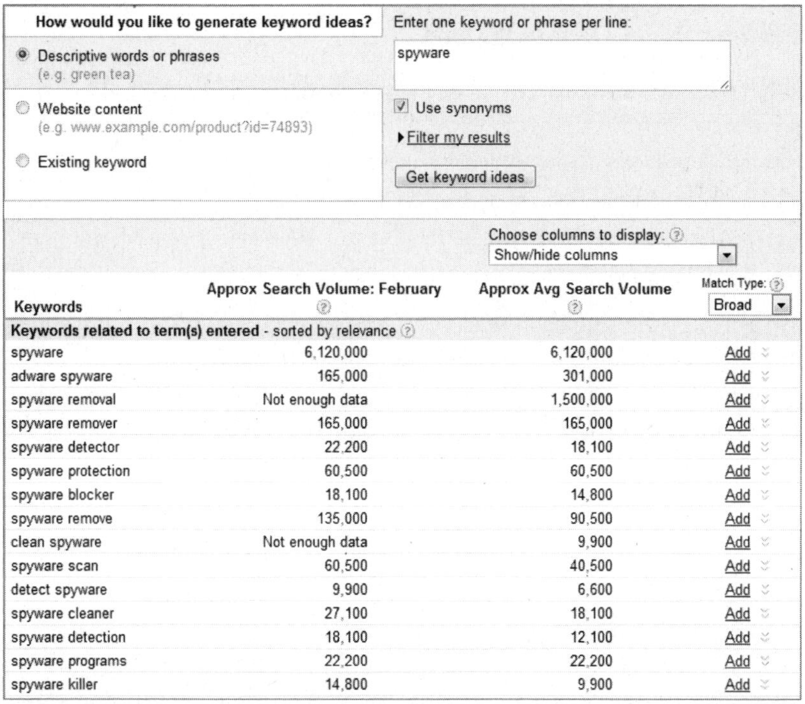

Figure 3.4 Viewing related phrases in the AdWords Keyword Tool

That is exactly what the AdWords Website Content Explorer accomplishes. You can either enter a landing page URL or copy and paste text into the text field, and then the Keyword Tool will suggest keywords based on what it finds on those landing pages (Figure 3.5).

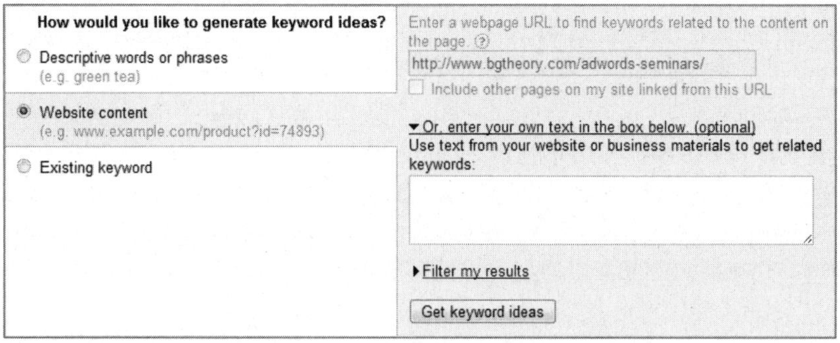

Figure 3.5 AdWords Website Content Explorer

This is an excellent way to start finding your wide keywords. Take a look at your landing page, and then enter the URL into the search box. AdWords will crawl your page attempting to decipher what keywords that page describes.

Understanding a Spider's Role in the Web

When a search engine wants to index the Web, it uses a program called a spider or robot. The search engine sends out its spider to crawl the Web to find new pages to index so it can build a database from the information it discovers. The spider indexes content such as HTML, images, PDF files, or any other file found on the Web. The terms *spider*, *spidering*, *crawl*, or *crawling* are commonly used to describe the process of the spider discovering and indexing the content it finds.

There is a checkbox option that lets you crawl one page deeper into your site if you desire. You can try and spider multiple pages at once or you can repeat this process for each of your landing pages. If your pages link to unrelated products or services, it is more useful to spider each page individually. If you are looking to gather many keywords at once and then organize them later, it can be useful to check the option to spider another page deeper into your site. Having Google spider your site is a fantastic way of finding wide keywords.

Note: We will discuss quality score in Chapter 7; however, inputting your landing page into this tool also helps you see if Google thinks your page is about what you think it is about. If the two of you disagree, you may see much lower quality scores.

Most Adobe Flash pages have problems being crawled and understood by search engines. However, Google and others have made great strides in attempting to crawl sites designed in Adobe Flash. You can input an Adobe Flash website into the tool to see if AdWords has any understanding of the website. Often, Adobe Flash sites have a difficult time achieving relevancy in AdWords because Google's crawlers cannot understand their pages. Just because the Keyword Tool brings back information about your page does not always mean it can be crawled well; however, it is good directional information if Google has some understanding of your website.

There is no restriction on what sites you can input into this tool. You can attempt to crawl any page on the Web. If someone has amended their robots.txt file to not allow crawlers to access the page, the tool should respect the robots.txt file.

Note: A robots.txt file is an instruction manual for your website that tells a spider what pages they can crawl and index. It is found at yoursite.com/robots.txt. If you do not have a robots.txt file, then a spider assumes it can index any page of your website. To learn more about robots.txt files, see `http://robotstxt.org`.

This means you can spider competitor pages, industry pages, search results, and so on to help build out your wide keyword list. Here is a list of sites to spider when you are first starting your wide keyword research: (Please note that you may want to do a search on some of these sites for your keyword first. For example, spidering the homepage of thesaurus.com is not useful while spidering the search result page for your keywords at http://thesaurus.reference.com/browse/YourKeyword will be more relevant to your company).

- Your website
- Your competitors' websites
- DMOZ.org category for your site
- Thesaurus.reference.com
- Dictionary.reference.com
- Wikipedia.org
- Ask.com (related results are very useful)
- Google or Yahoo! news
- The top authority magazine or journal for your industry
- Sites where you receive your industry news
- Any sites or blogs where you regularly receive your industry information
- Any directory related to your industry

Every time you see a page on the Web that is highly related to your business, make note of the page so you can spider it when you do keyword research. This simple exercise will help you expand your keyword list over time.

If you have offline marketing materials, or internal materials that are not published, you can also elect to copy and paste those materials into the website content tool. This is useful when you have information you do not wish to publish on the Web but that does contain good content about your products.

The Keyword Tool can also help with your search engine optimization (SEO) efforts. With SEO, you do not get to pick keyword match types—you have to choose exact keywords. Please note, there are more advanced versions of SEO that examine traffic more than individual keyword rankings, but you have to start somewhere. When using this tool for SEO research, make sure you only look at the exact match of a keyword when trying to predict keyword volume.

Even beyond SEO and pay-per-click advertising, if you are looking for related keywords, or for thesaurus, competitor, trend, and other data, this is a useful tool. It has uses within social media as well as competitor research.

The website content tool is a powerful resource for conducting keyword research about your specific website and almost every other website on the entire Internet. Always keep this tool in mind when you are trying to find new wide keywords or when you come across an authority site related to your industry.

Existing Keywords

The third way that the AdWords Keyword Tool finds keywords is based on existing keywords within an ad group. To use this feature, you must access the tool from within the ad group. If you access the tool from the external link or from the Tools menu in your AdWords account, this option will not be displayed.

When you access the tool from within an ad group, you will see a bread-crumb trail at the top of the page that shows you which campaign and ad group you are currently researching (Figure 3.6). The keywords displayed on the page are the ones currently in that particular ad group.

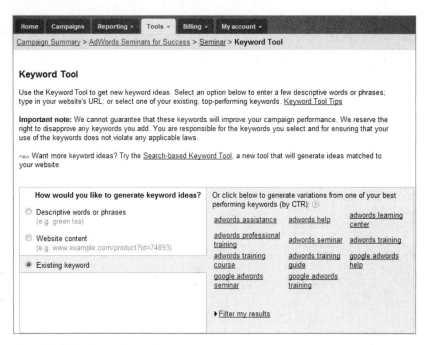

Figure 3.6 Existing keyword research

To view additional data about a particular keyword and to receive new keyword ideas, all you have to do is click on the keyword. This is a useful exercise if you find keywords that are performing well, and you want to find closely related keywords.

As with the descriptive words and phrases tool, the more specific the keyword the better the additional suggestions will be. If you want to find very broadly searched keywords, then start with one- or two-word phrases. If you are looking for very specific long tail keyword expansion, then start with two- to four-word phrases.

Now that you've seen how to generate keyword data, let's examine the data you can view for each of those words.

Interpreting the Keyword Data

Once you use one of the above methods to find keywords, you can also see a variety of data about each of the possible keywords. Not all of the data is displayed by default. If you examine the customize columns drop-down selections (Figure 3.7), you can choose which data you wish to examine.

Figure 3.7 Customizing columns in the AdWords Keyword Tool

When examining the information, there are three pieces of data that are very important to note, as they will change all of the other statistics on the page depending on their inputs.

The first is the bid you are using to calculate the estimated ad position and estimated average CPC, seen in the top left of Figure 3.8. If you access the tool from within an ad group, the maximum cost per click (CPC) used will be your maximum CPC from your ad group. If you are not logged in, you should set a maximum CPC if you wish to see the estimated ad position and average CPC for each keyword.

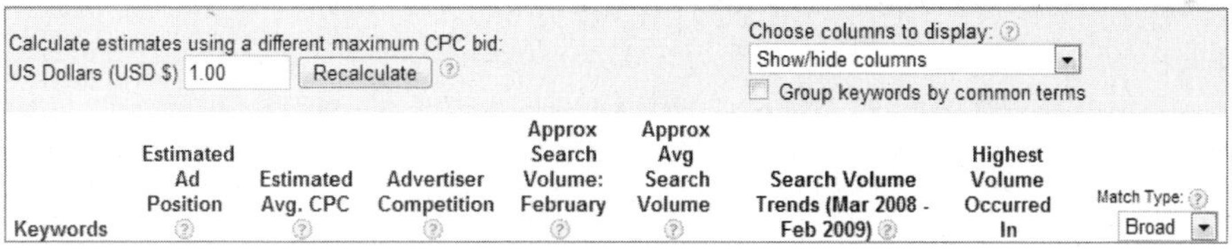

Figure 3.8 Data inputs for maximum CPC and match type

Please note that this tool is not hooked up to the quality score within your account, and if you have never used that keyword before, your account does not even have that information available for the tool. Therefore, the average CPC and average position data are very rough estimates. Since there are so many factors that go into average CPC, such as other advertisers changing their bids, advertisers within a specific geography, and a plethora of other variables, the suggested CPC should be used as a guide and not as a definite number. You should use your common sense and the historical information you have learned about your industry to determine how useful those two numbers are to your specific account.

The second important piece of information is the match type (as seen in the bottom right of Figure 3.8). The displayed information is based on the match type of the keyword. If you change the match type, the data will change based on the match type chosen (Figure 3.9).

Keywords	Estimated Ad Position ⓘ	Estimated Avg. CPC ⓘ	Advertiser Competition ⓘ	Approx Search Volume: February ⓘ	Approx Avg Search Volume ⓘ	Search Volume Trends (Mar 2008 - Feb 2009) ⓘ	Highest Volume Occurred In	Match Type: ⓘ Broad ▾
- sorted by relevance ⓘ								
google adwords	4 - 6	$0.75	▭	673,000	550,000	▮▮▮▮▮	Feb	Add ⌄
adwords	4 - 6	$0.78	▭	1,830,000	1,500,000	▮▮▮▮▮	Feb	Add ⌄
adwords keyword tool	1 - 3	$0.71	▭	33,100	22,200	▮▮▮▮▮	Feb	Add ⌄
Keywords	Estimated Ad Position ⓘ	Estimated Avg. CPC ⓘ	Advertiser Competition ⓘ	Approx Search Volume: February ⓘ	Approx Avg Search Volume ⓘ	Search Volume Trends (Mar 2008 - Feb 2009) ⓘ	Highest Volume Occurred In	Match Type: ⓘ Exact ▾
- sorted by relevance ⓘ								
[google adwords]	4 - 6	$0.18	▭	246,000	201,000	▮▮▮▮▮	Feb	Add Exact ⌄
[adwords]	4 - 6	$0.19	▭	550,000	550,000	▮▮▮▮▮	Feb	Add Exact ⌄
[adwords keyword tool]	4 - 6	$0.21	▭	18,100	9,900	▮▮▮▮▮	Feb	Add Exact ⌄

Figure 3.9 The data changes based on match type.

The third piece of data is advertiser competition. This is a bar that goes from empty for no competition to full (as seen in Figure 3.9) for a highly competitive word. It is always nice to find a highly relevant word with high search volume with little competition. They are very difficult words to find. Just because a word has many competitors does not automatically make it more expensive. While the bar is useful to get an idea on a keyword, this data point alone should not be one you use to make decisions if you choose to add a keyword to your account.

Viewing Competition, Trends, and Adding Keywords

The next two data points show approximate search volume. The first is the approximate search volume from the previous month. This is one of the few times you will see an actual month volume from Google, so it can be useful to save this data point. This information is followed by approximate average search volume, which is the average search volume of that keyword for the past 12 months.

The graph that follows shows the search volume trends—how the keyword has changed in search volume over the past year. Right next to that information is the month with the highest search volume over the past 12 months. This information is so useful that we will feature Google Trends information later in this chapter and dive into how to use trending data.

Finally, the last column is the Add link. When you click on this link that keyword is added to a column on the left. As you find keywords you would like to use in your account, click the Add link to grow your list. Remember that the match type chosen earlier will determine which match type is added to your list.

If you use the website content option, be very careful with the Add All button, as you most likely will have keywords in the list that are not related to your products. For instance, if you spider "Google news," you will get keywords related to breaking news in your keyword list.

Lastly, you can add negative keywords to your list if you are accessing the tool from within your AdWords account. When adding negative keywords from this tool, be sure you are adding the correct negative keyword. This tool often shows very broad keywords in this list, which could preclude your ad from showing in a significant amount of searches. In addition, you can only add a broad negative keyword. If you wish to add an exact or phrase match negative keyword, you will have to add those negative keywords by hand.

Luckily, this tool makes it easy to add your own keywords (or negative keywords) by hand to your keyword list (Figure 3.10). Just click Add Your Own Keywords and a text box will open up where you can add anything you want.

Figure 3.10 Add your own keywords and additional options for handling your keyword list.

Where to Save Your Keyword Data

Once you have added several keywords and built a list you have a few more options.

The first is adding those keywords to an ad group. If you accessed the Keyword Tool from within an ad group, they will be saved to that specific ad group. If you accessed the tool from the AdWords Tool menu, you have the option of saving them to any ad group.

Another option is to estimate traffic. With this option, Google will attempt to determine not just the search volume, but how many possible clicks you will receive for those keywords (Figure 3.11). This is another tool that does not know your quality score or your click-through-rate (CTR). If you write fantastic ads that have very high CTRs, you could receive significantly more clicks than what is estimated. Conversely, if your ads have low CTRs, or you have a daily budget that is lower than what is required to capture all of the clicks, you may receive fewer clicks than what is estimated.

Traffic Estimates

View the ad performance estimates for your selected keywords on the Google Search Network below. Estimates are provided only as a guideline: your actual costs and ad positions for your keywords may vary. Learn more

Your keyword and CPC changes have not been saved.
You may continue making changes and re-calculating estimates below.
When satisfied, please save your changes.

Without budget limitations:
At an average CPC of $0.06 - $0.15 these keywords could potentially generate 8 - 16 clicks per day (which would cost you $1 - $3).
▼ Hide total potential clicks in the table below

Keywords ▼	Max CPC	Search Volume ⑦	Estimated Avg. CPC ⑦	Estimated Ad Positions ⑦	Potential Clicks / Day ⑦	Potential Cost / Day ⑦
Search Network Total			$0.06 - $0.15 was $0.00	4 - 6	8 - 16 was 0	$1 - $3 was $0
google adwords (to be added)	$0.15		$0.06 - $0.15	4 - 6 delete	2 - 5	$1
"google adwords" (to be added)	$0.15		$0.06 - $0.15	4 - 6 delete	4 - 9	$1 - $2
[google adwords] (to be added)	$0.15		$0.05 - $0.14	4 - 6 delete	1 - 2	$1

Figure 3.11 Traffic estimates by keyword

Lastly, you can export the data. If you conduct a significant amount of keyword research and have hundreds or thousands of keywords in your list, you may opt to export those keywords into Excel instead of saving them directly to an ad group. In Chapter 12, we will cover the AdWords Editor, which has a feature for adding thousands of keywords to your account. This import feature will save you time compared to adding your keywords to individual ad groups via the AdWords interface.

AdWords Keyword Tool versus Wordtracker

There are several keyword tools on the market that can help you learn more about your keywords. The most popular, and one of the original keyword tools, is Wordtracker.

Wordtracker draws its data from a few meta search engines, such as Dogpile.com. These meta engines did have decent search volume years ago when pay-per-click (PPC) was new. However, they make up a miniscule amount of the search volume. Wordtracker takes the data it receives from these engines and extrapolates the numbers to determine search volume. Estimating search volume from such a small data set often creates a large difference in the suggested search volume versus the impression you actually receive when you advertise on those same keywords.

Another tool is Keyword Discovery. This tool draws data from a large variety of search engines and once again extrapolates the data to show search volume

Since Google accounts for roughly 70 percent of all search volume in the United States (and higher in many European countries), it is often best to rely on Google's numbers to estimate traffic. If you are doing some advanced calculations, you can use all three data sets together to attempt to determine search numbers.

However, that does not mean that Wordtracker and Keyword Discovery are useless. Quite the contrary, when you are doing specific research into wide and deep keywords, they both have some nice features to dig into your keyword lists. They are useful for keyword research and both are tools I use regularly—just be careful of the search volume numbers.

In addition, they both have free trials. This makes it easy to test out their keyword research capabilities to see if they work for you before committing any money to other keyword research tools.

Using Google's Search-Based Keyword Tool

In November 2008, Google quietly launched a new keyword tool where the information was not based on their keyword database, but on your website's content. The Search-based Keyword Tool, often referred to as the SKTool, is yet another Google product you should add to your keyword research arsenal.

Google crawls a large part of the Web on a regular basis. It also tracks massive amounts of keywords on a regular basis. When it sees that you have pages on your site with relevant content to their actual searched keywords, it will suggest both keywords and landing pages for your website.

> **Note:** The suggested search volume information is only based on the last month or two of search data. Therefore, it does not contain a significant amount of seasonal information. If you have seasonal keywords, use the AdWords Keyword Tool or Google Trends to track the changes in search volume.

This is also another tool where if you are logged into a Google account that is associated with your AdWords account you can see some additional data about the website. If you are logged into your account, on the home page of the SKTool (Figure 3.12), you should see a prepopulated Website drop-down box, with websites that are associated with that AdWords login. If you are using a My Client Center (MCC, discussed in Chapter 14) login, you should see all of the websites associated with that login.

There are two main ways of finding keywords with this tool: keyword ideas based on your site and category browsing. To see all keywords related to your website, just click the Find Keywords button on the home page after you have selected a particular website. You can also input a root keyword to only see keywords related to a specific word.

Below the text box is a link to see all keywords across categories, which we will visit later in this chapter in the section "Keyword Suggestions by Category."

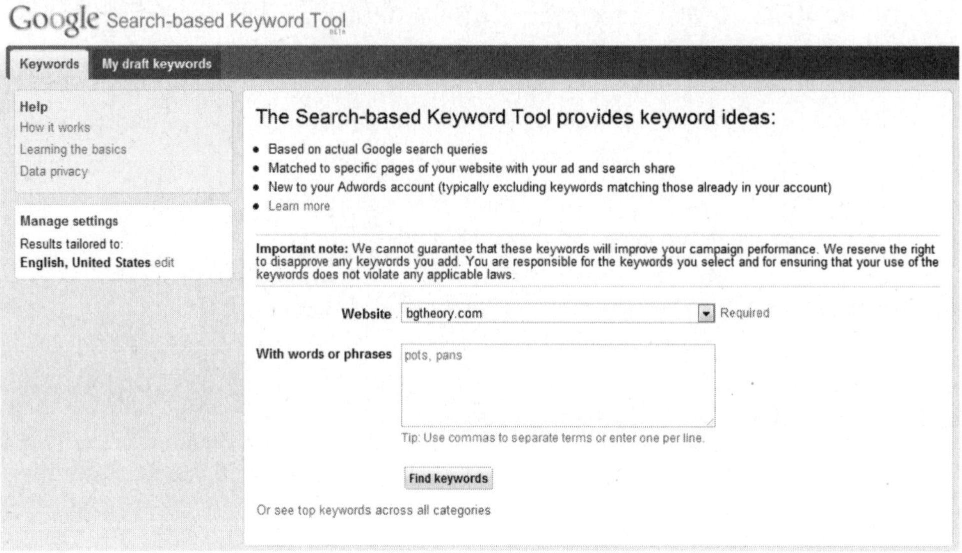

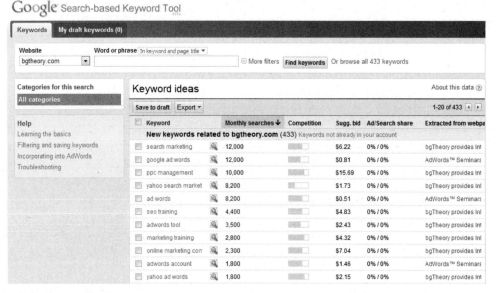

Figure 3.12 Search-based Keyword Tool home page

Finding Keywords Based on Crawl Information

Once you have clicked the Find Keywords button, you will be presented with a screen of information about those keywords (Figure 3.13). Usually, these are new keywords for your AdWords account. Since you are logged into your AdWords account, the SKTool attempts to filter out your current keyword list to only show you new keyword ideas.

Figure 3.13 SKTool keyword ideas

The first few columns are similar to the AdWords Keyword Tool discussed earlier: keyword, monthly searches, competition, and suggested bid.

There are a few differences between the first few columns in the SKTool and the AdWords Keyword Tool. First, the monthly search volume draws on different data sources; therefore, the search volume information may differ for the same keywords across the two tools. Secondly, clicking on the keyword will open a window to a Google search result for that keyword. Lastly, if you click on the magnifying glass icon next to the keyword, it will open a new window showing Google Trend information for that keyword. Google Trends will be examined later in this chapter.

Learning Your Ad/Search Share

The ad/search share information is only displayed if the URL you are examining is associated with your AdWords account for the Google account login you are using to access the SKTool.

The ad/search share is composed of two different pieces of data. The ad share is the percentage of time your ad shows for that search. The search share is how often your website appears on page 1 for that particular search query in the organic results.

This information has become more accurate over time, but it is by no means completely accurate. In Figure 3.13, the website bgtheory.com has appeared almost 100 percent of the time in the organic results for several of the keywords shown in the last screenshot. In addition, if you do not filter the data, these keywords are new keywords for your account, so it would make sense that your ad share is 0 percent since you have not added them to your account yet. Therefore, if you do SEO (search engine optimization) and you see that your website does not seem to have a large search share percentage for words you see traffic from, do not panic. It could be that there is an error with the data.

The data is also based on the entire country. Therefore, if you are geo-targeting (advertising to just one particular area, discussed in Chapter 11), your search share could be a very low number as you are not trying to reach an entire country.

Where Did Google Find These Keywords?

The last column is one to pay attention to: Extracted from webpage. This is the page on the examined domain that Google thinks is most relevant for that keyword. Instead of having to hunt through your site for which keywords belong to which pages, this tool can help you quickly associate keywords to a particular landing page.

If you see keywords you would like to add to your account, all you have to do is click the box next to the keyword and they will be added as draft keywords. The My Draft Keywords tab will show you the keywords you have added in such a manner (Figure 3.14).

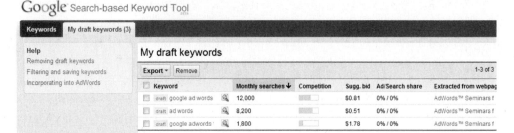

Figure 3.14 SKTool draft keywords

Note: At present, you cannot save these keywords directly to your AdWords account. If you would like to add them, the easiest way is to export the keyword data to an Excel file, and then use the AdWords Editor or copy/paste via the AdWords interface to add those new keywords to your account. You can also export all the keywords from the main page and save them in a CSV file.

While doing your keyword research, there are several ways you can filter the data (Figure 3.15). The first way is based on where Google is finding the keyword information on your website:

• In keyword and page title

• In keyword only

• In page title only

Figure 3.15 Filtering the SKTool data

In addition, you can filter based on

• Competition

• Monthly search volume

• Suggested bids

• URL contains

• Partial matches to keywords in my account

The first three are self-explanatory. The URL Contains filter allows you to only see keywords based on a particular webpage or section of your site. For instance, if you only wanted to see keywords related to the page bgtheory.com/adwords-seminars/, you could input "adwords-seminars" into the URL filter.

The last filtering item, Partial Matches To Keywords In My Account, is an important filter to understand. By having this box checked, you are informing the tool that you would like to see additional words that partially match your broad match or expanded match keywords. This can be a good place to find more wide keywords, but you may see unrelated keywords from this list as well.

As explained in Chapter 2, taking control of your broad match keywords is extremely important for controlling your ad serving. This tool can not only help you find new ideas, it can also help understand some of the other matches for your key-words. If you are doing research within this tool and see keywords you do not want your ad to show, then add them as negative keywords in your AdWords account.

It is important to note that Google has several disclaimers in their help files that the suggested keywords might not be the best words for your account, but they are suggestions based on your website. As with all keywords added to your account, make sure they are relevant to helping a searcher find their answer. You are responsible for choosing to spend money on any given word.

Keyword Suggestions by Category

The other way to use this tool is by browsing through the categories. On the home page of the SKTool, you can click the link to view keywords by categories.

On the left side of the page, you can drill down into various categories to see suggested keywords for each of these categories (Figure 3.16).

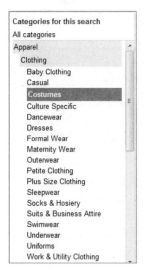

Figure 3.16 SKTool keyword drill-down by category

With the category keywords, since they are not based on a particular website, there is no correlating ad/search share or associated landing page information.

Most of the keyword suggestions will be wide keywords. In many cases, the keywords will be so general you might not even want to use them in your AdWords account.

One of the best uses of the categories is to find other keyword themes you may have missed. This is good information for not only your AdWords keywords, but also for your natural search rankings. You may see better ways to structure your site navigation based on some of the category information. In addition, this can be useful for how you might want to structure your ad groups.

For instance, if you sold all types of greeting cards, the suggested keywords under the Congratulations Cards category (Figure 3.17) could be keywords in one ad group. For better ad copy to keyword relationship organization, each of the suggestions could even be its own ad group.

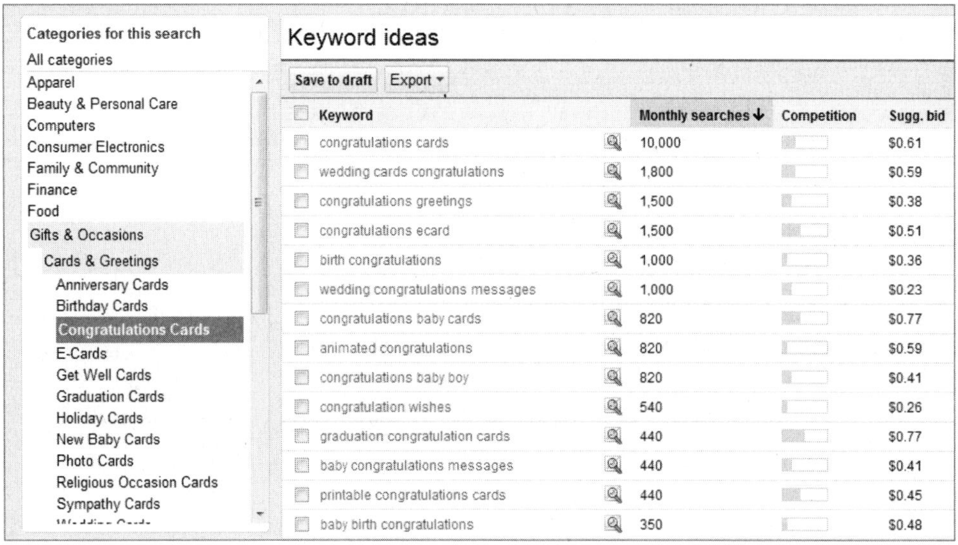

Figure 3.17 Congratulations Cards keywords from SKTool

The SKTool is useful for finding new keywords and associated landing pages for your AdWords account. Since its data is based on Google's crawling of your site, often you may see landing pages you missed or new opportunities for keywords.

This tool is also very useful when you are first launching a new AdWords account. If you are slowly building an account over time, the tool can help direct you to landing pages and keywords you have not yet utilized. Look through the tool for appropriate keywords and then export the data, which will contain both keywords and landing pages. The keyword and landing page data can be reformatted as an upload to import these suggestions into your account via the AdWords Editor. When building new accounts, this can save you a significant amount of time.

However, always remember that the Search-based Keyword Tool's suggestions are an automated process. Any tool can make mistakes. Just because Google is suggesting a landing page or keyword, do not assume that you should blindly accept that suggestion. You will always know your account and business better than a tool. Use the information that makes sense, discard the rest, and then check back with the tool at a later date to see new suggestions.

Google Sets

After you have spidered your website with the AdWords Keyword Tool and then examined the results for the Search-based Keyword Tool, if you are still stuck for new keyword ideas, it is time to turn to Google Sets.

Google Sets can be accessed from http://labs.google.com/sets. It is a simple tool that takes a few ideas and expands them into a larger set of ideas.

To use this tool, simply enter a few keywords into the text boxes on the home page of Google Sets (Figure 3.18).

Google™
Sets

Automatically create sets of items from a few examples.

Enter a few items from a set of things. (example)
Next, press *Large Set* or *Small Set* and we'll try to predict other items in the set.

- [mortgage]
- [refinance]
- [ ]
- [ ]
- [ ]

(clear all)

[Large Set] [Small Set (15 items or fewer)]

Figure 3.18 Google Sets home page

Choose a small or large set, press a button, and you will quickly be presented with words related to your original inputs.

Note: Because the tool attempts to match words related to your inputs, it is useful to only try two or three words at first and play with how many words help define your set.

With Google Sets, you will see more appropriate data if you use broad phrase matching instead of specific words. Using one or two words usually results in better information. The more specific the word you use, the less likely Google Sets can present you with meaningful ideas.

If you are stuck on finding new themes, add a few of your current themes, try them in different combinations, and examine the results for ideas you may have missed.

The other use of Google Sets is when you are looking for new modifiers for existing keywords. For instance, if you sold clothing you would want to make sure you listed all the different sizes for all your apparel based on how people search. Inputting "small," "medium," and "large" into Google Sets brings back approximately 44 additional possibilities with roughly 20 being different ways people search for clothing sizes (Figure 3.19).

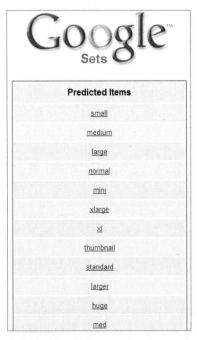

Figure 3.19 Viewing Google Sets data

Google Sets is a simple tool. It does one thing well: it attempts to find sets of words based on a set of inputs. However, if you are stuck for keyword themes, or even keyword modifier ideas, Google Sets can help you jumpstart your thought process.

Google Trends

In an online world, it is easy to forget the lessons taught through hundreds of years of data from the offline world.

A brick and mortar store has a limited amount of inventory. Each month they have to consider the goods that will need to be stocked in the upcoming months based on what will sell in the store. If a store stocks goods that are not sold, it is wasted space that can lead to loss of profits. The inventory specialist examines what goods were sold in the previous years in order to predict the inventory they need in the store in any given month.

Almost every business has some seasonality. Seasonality in the flower industry is one of the most obvious. Valentine's Day, Mother's Day, Easter, etc., have correlations with spikes in searches, sales, and even conversion rates. However, even an office supply store will see trends in their sales. During various holidays, spikes will occur in the number of searches for holiday stationery and printable cards. At Father's Day, it is common to see a spike for Cross pens, a popular Father's Day gift. During Christmas, high-end pens such as Waterman or Mont Blanc see search spikes (Figure 3.20).

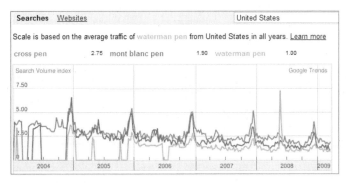

Figure 3.20 Trend data for Cross, Waterman, and Mont Blanc pens

Not all seasonality is driven by holidays. An office supply store will want to stock low cost laptops and computer desks in the fall when the college semester starts. It is always important to keep in mind the daily factors of life that drive search and buying behavior.

When you examine AdWords reports, which we will cover throughout this book, you are always looking backward in time at data. If you are making bid or budget decisions by only utilizing the past month or two of data, you are missing possible changes in conversion rates and search behavior that are driven by trends that may only occur a few times a year. If you sell computer desks, it can be useful to make changes to your inventory and ad copy based on fall back-to-school season versus the spring when both people and businesses move and need new furniture. Instead of making changes based on your account's past history, examine the history to project changes to conversion rates, sales, bids, and budgets.

This is where Google Trends shines. It is a free tool that will display changes in keyword search volume or even in visitors to a website. You can segment this data by various time frames and by regions. Once you have the data, you can click into a region to drill down into states and cities.

The most important thing to note when examining the region, city, and language data is that it is normalized by population (Figure 3.21). The data shows the likelihood of that search term being used in that language or region. In the chart shown in Figure 3.21, the data does not mean that Singapore and the United Kingdom conduct more searches for Waterman pens than the United States. It means there is a higher chance of a user in one of those countries searching for a Waterman pen than in the United States.

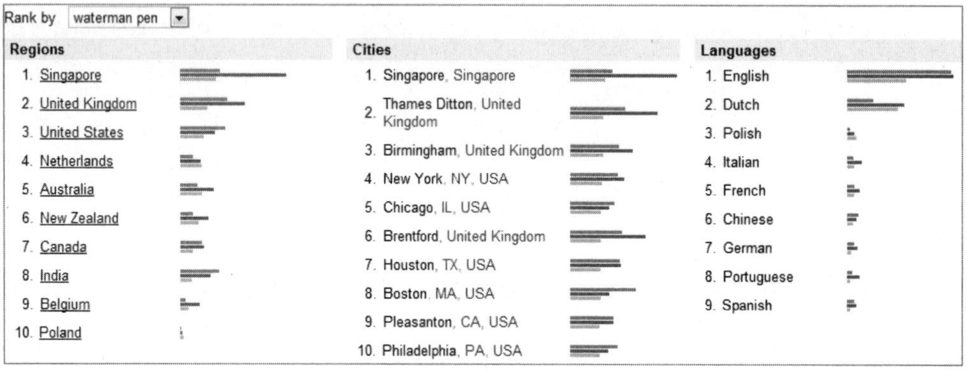

Figure 3.21 Search trend information normalized by population

You can also view trending data by individual websites. If you are using placement targeting campaigns (discussed in later chapters), it is useful to see changes to website traffic.

With trending data for websites, you can see which geographies are more likely to visit a website, other websites visited, and even other websites also searched for (Figure 3.22). These sets of data can give you ideas about placing ads on various sites, keyword ideas, or just some competitive research information.

Google Trends is an easy tool to use to gain insight into changes in search behavior for either specific words or websites. You can export the data to easily see changes in the search behavior on a weekly basis. This makes it easier to visualize what weeks lead to higher or lower search volume.

One exercise that can be useful for visualizing all of your keywords and trend information is to export the data into Excel and then cross-reference the Excel file with a calendar. This can help you build a reference source for your business so you can quickly look at a week or month to help anticipate the changes to search volume.

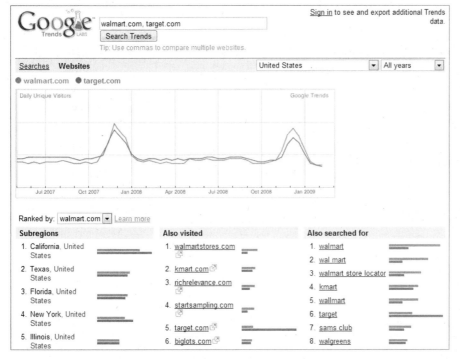

Figure 3.22 Trend data for Walmart.com and Target.com

Google Insights for Search

One of the more complex tools that Google offers is Google Insights for Search. This tool will let you compare groups of search terms, view terms by locations or time frames, and then segment the entire data set by industry.

There is a tremendous amount of insight you can gain from Google Insights for Search. It can be useful to first consider your goals when using this tool to stay focused on the information that will help you make actionable decisions.

There are three major ways by which you can search for information:

- *Search term*: You can compare up to five different groups of up to 25 keywords (Figure 3.23).

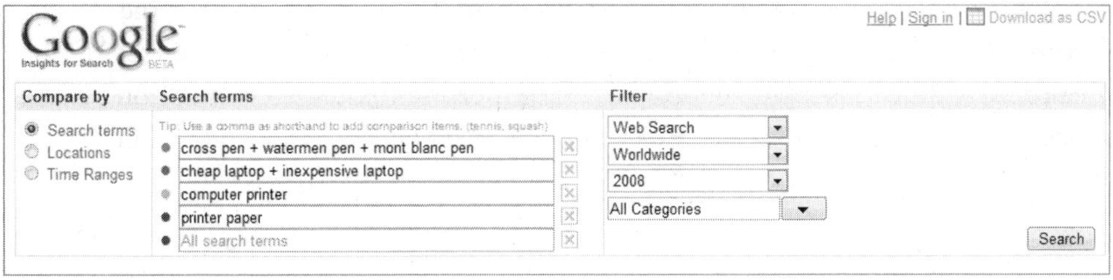

Figure 3.23 Multiple items compared to view search volume

- *Location*: See which locations have higher search volume.
- *Time frame*: Compare search volume by different time frames.

You can filter the data by several items depending on how you are searching for information. The most common filters (seen in Figure 3.23) are

Search Type You can see just image, product, news, or general web search information. This is very useful if you specialize in a specific type of search.

Location For search terms and time frames, you can either view a specific country or worldwide. If you are comparing by location, you can specify particular metros or states. In addition, you can drill down into more granular locations, which we will show in the What Services Should You Offer section.

Time Frame There are several options to view different time frames.

Category Category drill-down is very useful. If you have a word, such as bleach, that falls into many categories, understanding the search volume for that keyword in a specific category can give you a better understanding of the search volume available.

There are more possible uses for Google Insights for Search than we could possibly cover in a chapter; therefore, we will take a look through some of the more useful comparisons.

What Service Should You Offer?

If you have several different services, it would be useful to know which ones have higher search volumes and how those volumes change so you know where to put your online marketing efforts.

With Google Insights for Search, it is easy to compare several items to see which has a higher search volume and if there are definitive trends. If you are a plumber who specializes in kitchen and bathroom remodeling, where should you spend more search time (Figure 3.24)?

In this chart, we can clearly see that the trends for kitchen remodeling and bathroom remodeling are very similar. However, there is consistently a higher search volume for kitchen remodeling. Therefore, while it is useful to bid on both of these terms, there is a higher possible payoff when you focus more attention on kitchen remodeling as the search volume is higher.

However, there are more drill-downs available on the page. Below the search volume chart is a chart that shows regions and a heat map based on the search volume in various regions. You can see this at a country, region (state), or city level.

If you tailor your search campaigns for geographic regions (which will be covered in depth in Chapter 11) you can gain more insight by drilling down into various regions.

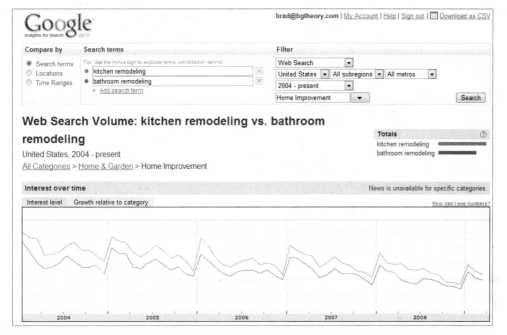

Figure 3.24 Kitchen remodeling vs. bathroom remodeling search information

For instance, if you were a Miami plumber, it would be useful to know that Miami is one of the few regions where there is more search volume for bathroom remodeling that kitchen remodeling (Figure 3.25). Therefore, a Miami plumber might focus his campaign differently than a Tampa Bay plumber who sees the exact opposite in terms of top searches.

Figure 3.25 Kitchen and bathroom remodeling search volume in Florida

Lastly, at the bottom of the page, you can find information about top searches and raising searches.

The top searches are just what they sound like—the top searched keywords related to the keywords you chose and the geographic region. If you choose different regions, you may see the top related searches change as well.

The top gaining searches are words that have gained in popularity based on the time frame you chose. It is useful to select the past year, or even the past 90 days in a quick-changing industry, to see what additional words are gaining in search volume. This can be useful to see if there are new products you should offer (Figure 3.26). Occasionally you may see a word labeled "breakout." This means the search volume has changed by more than 5000 percent. If it is related to your business, that is a trend you want to make sure your company is aware of and possibly testing.

Search terms related to kitchen remodeling	United States, 2008		
Top searches		**Rising searches**	
1. home remodeling	100	1. green kitchen remodeling	+130%
2. kitchen remodeling ideas	95	2. budget kitchen remodeling	+60%
3. remodeling ideas	90	3. kitchen remodeling contractors	+50%
4. kitchen ideas	90	4. kitchen remodeling contractor	+50%
5. remodeling kitchen cabinets	80	5. remodeling my kitchen	+40%
6. kitchen cabinets	80	6. cheap kitchen remodeling	+40%
7. remodeling a kitchen	70	New! Google	
8. kitchen remodeling design	70		
9. kitchen design	65		
10. bathroom remodeling	65		

Figure 3.26 Top searches and raising searches for kitchen remodeling

In this case, we see that the top raising search for kitchen remodeling is "green kitchen remodeling." If you do not offer an environmentally conscious kitchen remodeling product, it might be worth your time to investigate if that is a product your company should offer.

Determining Your Messaging

If you were selling cars, should you promote a family car or a luxury car? What about car safety versus fuel efficiency versus financing? If you could compare the search volume for these different aspects of a product, it could help you decide how to position your product (Figure 3.27).

In Figure 3.27, we can see that the search volume changes slightly for family versus luxury cars, with family cars having a slight edge. This might not be enough of a difference for you to change your product positioning.

However, it becomes easy to see that car safety is much more important than either fuel efficiency or auto financing. While fuel efficiency had a large spike in the middle of 2008 with the drastic changes in fuel pricing, even then, car safety always remained a larger consideration. So, although in 2008 you might have added more information about fuel efficiency, if you had a message around car safety you would never have abandoned that message.

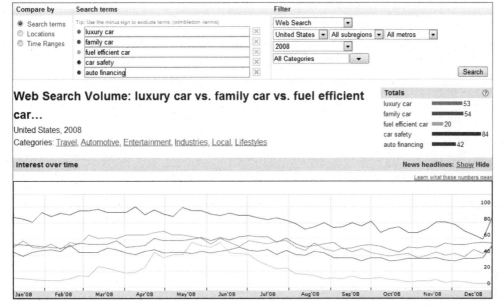

Figure 3.27 Comparing car positioning

By comparing features of your products, you can see which features have higher search volume and are often a larger consumer concern. This can help shape your ad copy and landing pages to address the consumer's greatest questions.

Determining Consumer Interest

If you are expanding your market, knowing which areas have a greater interest in your product can help you create test markets and determine where your expansions will have the best chance for success.

For example, if you created an add-on for the popular Nintendo Wii game console, where should you market your product? You could attempt to look at market interest by individual city or by country. How much do you want to expand your marketplace?

By comparing searches for Wii across different geographies (Figure 3.28), it is easier to determine a list of regions where the interest for Wii is high. As Google Insights for Search shows interest, and not total search volume, you will need to reference this information with the actual population size, but Google Insights for Search creates a much easier starting place for your additional research.

There are many other creative ways you can use Google Insights for Search. Whenever you are conducting research that involves keywords, locations, or trends, keep it in mind to see how you can use the tool to help with your research.

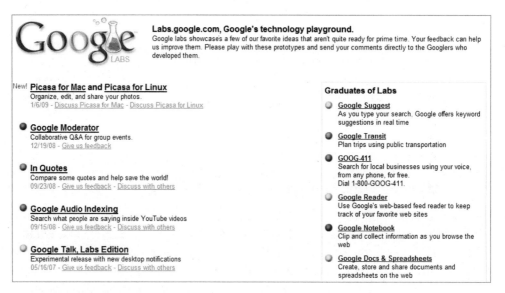

Web Search Volume: United Kingdom vs. United States vs. France...

for wii, 2008

All Categories > Games > Video Games
Subcategories: Cheats & Hints, Online Games

Totals	⑦
United Kingdom	43
United States	36
France	30
Germany	20
Australia	29

Interest over time   News is unavailable for specific categories.

Learn what these numbers mean

Figure 3.28 Search interest for Wii

Google Labs and Microsoft adCenter Labs

Google is constantly adding and tweaking their tool sets. You can find a list of and links to all the Google tools at labs.google.com (Figure 3.29). In addition, there are beta items that Google eventually graduates from labs to become full products. You can see a list of those products on the Google Labs page.

Labs.google.com, Google's technology playground.
Google labs showcases a few of our favorite ideas that aren't quite ready for prime time. Your feedback can help us improve them. Please play with these prototypes and send your comments directly to the Googlers who developed them.

New! **Picasa for Mac and Picasa for Linux**
Organize, edit, and share your photos.
1/6/09 - Discuss Picasa for Mac - Discuss Picasa for Linux

● **Google Moderator**
Collaborative Q&A for group events.
12/19/08 - Give us feedback

● **In Quotes**
Compare some quotes and help save the world!
09/23/08 - Give us feedback - Discuss with others

● **Google Audio Indexing**
Search what people are saying inside YouTube videos
09/15/08 - Give us feedback - Discuss with others

○ **Google Talk, Labs Edition**
Experimental release with new desktop notifications
05/16/07 - Give us feedback - Discuss with others

Graduates of Labs

○ **Google Suggest**
As you type your search, Google offers keyword suggestions in real time

○ **Google Transit**
Plan trips using public transportation

○ **GOOG-411**
Search for local businesses using your voice, from any phone, for free.
Dial 1-800-GOOG-411.

○ **Google Reader**
Use Google's web-based feed reader to keep track of your favorite web sites

● **Google Notebook**
Clip and collect information as you browse the web

○ **Google Docs & Spreadsheets**
Create, store and share documents and spreadsheets on the web

Figure 3.29 Available software in Google Labs

Not to be outdone, Microsoft has one of the most interesting sets of tools that you should spend some time learning. At Microsoft adCenter Labs (Figure 3.30) you can see tools that help to predict and understand

- Audience intelligence
- Keyword research
- Content analysis
- Video and interactive media
- Social network tools

There are more than 20 tools at Microsoft adCenter Labs. You can find Microsoft adCenter Labs at http://adlab.microsoft.com.

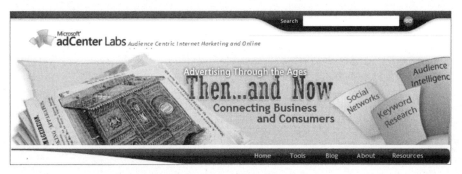

Figure 3.30 Microsoft adCenter Labs has many tools worth exploring.

The most important point to remember about tools is that they are only as good as their inputs and interpretations. If you put bad data into a tool, you will see bad data come out. If you do not understand the information being presented, or the business rules behind how the data is calculated, then you may not be able to interpret the data to come to the correct conclusions.

Understanding what the tool does and how it calculates and presents the data is crucial in extracting valuable, actionable data from any toolset.

Best Practices for Using Keyword Tools

Keyword tools do not tell you what keywords you should use; they give you keywords suggestions that you can choose to either use or bypass. However, using keyword tools is essential to researching the full breadth of keyword possibilities for your account. Keywords are thought processes, and everyone thinks differently.

- The AdWords Keyword Tool should be one of the first tools you utilize when you are conducting keyword research.

- Use the descriptive words and phrases section of the AdWords Keyword Tool when you have a list of words and would like suggestions based on that list.

- Use the website content section of the AdWords tool when you wish to extract data from a website. Try inputting your website, your competitor's website, search results, or the dictionary to find new keywords. Whenever you see a page on the Web and think that page is highly related to your products, input the page into the tool to see if there are new keywords that are relevant to your account.

- Once you find keywords with the AdWords Keyword Tool, you can either save those keywords to an ad group or export them for organization and later use.

- The SKTool (Search-based Keyword Tool) can help you find not only new keywords, but the corresponding landing pages on your website.

- The SKTool has category keyword lists that can help you think of new keywords or ad groups that you wish to add to your account.

- When you are stuck and need a tool to help jumpstart your thinking, turn to Google Sets. It's an easy tool to use and can help you find new keyword themes very quickly.

- Google Trends is useful for looking backward in time to help you project changes in keywords search volume.

- Always remember with Google Trends that the data is not absolute but is relative to the geographies population size and the propensity of its inhabitants to search for a keyword or visit a particular site.

- Google Insights for Search is a powerful tool that can help you in many unique ways, such as by crafting marketing messages or seeing the differences between multiple locations.

Finding keywords is not difficult, although it can be time consuming. What is important with keyword research is that you understand the search intent behind the keyword so you can show the searcher a compelling ad copy so they will visit your website. In the next chapter, we will discuss how to write effective ads based on the keywords you have found.

Writing Compelling Ads

Ad copy is the only part of your AdWords account a consumer will ever see. When a searcher sees your ad, the ad needs to stand up, wave its arms, jump up and down, and shout, "I have the answer to your question!"

However, there are many subtleties to writing ad copy. The messaging, value proposition, editorial requirements, and information need to be tightly wrapped into just a few characters. Accomplishing this type of writing can be quite tricky.

Chapter Contents

Do Your Ads Reflect the Search Query?

Ads serve as a bridge between the search query and your landing page. Your goal is to have enticing ad copy that causes a user to "cross the bridge" from a search result and arrive at your website.

AdWords ads do not need to be gimmicky. The ads need to quickly convey to the consumer that the answer to their search can be found on your website. If your ad has enticed someone to cross the bridge, the ad copy has done its job.

Of course, it's not quite that simple. There are many types of bridges. Some ads emphasize conversions, and others focus on clicks. Your job is to build an ad that produces results for your company, based on your company's goals, by bringing the correct prospects to your website.

The ad should reflect both the keywords in your account and the user's search query. If the ad is not highly relevant to both of those items, it will be less effective (Figure 4.1). Ad copy that does not cover both the search query and your keywords is like a bridge that leads to nowhere. Either your ad leads someone to the answer to their question, or it leads off in an irrelevant direction. Make sure you are always bringing the consumer closer to the answer to their question, assuming the answer is a conversion on your website.

The VIERA from Panasonic
Gather Your Friends and Family.
It's Time for Some VIERA® Time.
Panasonic.com/VIERA

Panasonic **tv** sale
Low Prices on LCD & **Plasma** HDTVs.
Fast Shipping And Secure Checkout!
www.BuyDig.com/PanasonicHDTVs

Samsung **Tv** Sale
Enhance Your HD Experience
Shop Dell For HD TVs By Samsung!
www.Dell.com

LCD Monitors
Save on LCD Monitors at Staples.
Guaranteed Low Prices & In Stock.
www.Staples.com

Figure 4.1 For the highly commercial search "buy plasma TV," these ads do not speak to the user's query.

Therefore, it is imperative that you go through the exercise of ensuring that your ad copy will be reflective of your keywords and the search query. As you know your keywords, and what type of related queries should trigger them (refer to the search query report in Chapter 16), one of the most important exercises to undertake before writing ads is to ensure you have *granular account organization*. I will mention this concept several times throughout this book because this organization can determine the minimum effectiveness of your account.

Granular account organization means that the keywords in an ad group are highly related and you do not see additional ways to separate out the keywords. In addition, your ad copy should reflect every single keyword in your ad group. For example, let's say your ad group is about HDTVs and contains these keywords:

- LCD TV
- Plasma TV
- HDTV
- Hi-def TV

With these keywords, your ad group is not granular enough. The keywords could be in several different ad groups: one for plasma TVs, one for LCD TVs, and so on.

First, write an ad copy with one explicit meaning. Imagine that if someone saw this ad copy, they could only assume you do this one particular thing, such as you only offer weekend plumbing services, small business accounting solutions, or used books under $5. Now, look at your keywords. Does the ad copy reflect the keywords? If yes, the keywords are in the correct place. If no, move the keywords to a new ad group.

Consider someone who searches for "buy plasma tv" and sees the two pieces of ad copy shown in Figure 4.2.

Buy a Plasma TV
Compare features of all Plasma TV:
TVs for your budget & lifestyle
example.com

Hi-Def TV
Compare features of all Hi-Def TVs
TVs for your budget & lifestyle
example.com

Figure 4.2 "Buy plasma TV" ad copy

Which one would you click? While a plasma TV is a hi-def TV, there are other types of hi-def TVs, such as LCD or DLPs. The use of the word "buy" in the query informs us that this is a commercial query with a high purchase intent. This searcher is not likely to change their TV choice from a plasma TV. Therefore, you would want to show this searcher a plasma TV ad.

The exercise of breaking down your ad groups into very specific keyword and ad copy combinations will take a while, but it will assist greatly in ad copy writing. Because you now only have to reflect one specific theme in your ad copy, you only need to write ads for one explicit meaning.

Note: It is much better to have 100 ad groups of 10 keywords than to have one ad group of 1,000 keywords. When it comes to searching, there is not a magical number of keywords that belong in an ad group. When you go to organize your ad groups, it is vital that you make sure the keywords and ad copy are closely related.

Writing Effective Ads

Once your granular ad group organization is completed, it is time to think about the content of the ad copy. There are many ways of writing ad copy, some of which we will revisit in Chapter 15 when we discuss ways of testing different ad copy messages to see which are more effective.

Note: If you have a dozen ideas for ad copy, which one is best? There is no way to know without running a test to find out which ad has a higher conversion rate or click-through rate (CTR). Split testing is essentially testing multiple elements (such as ad copy or landing pages) to find out which one is the best for your business.

Ad copy must promote your goals for success. Before you begin advertising, it is important to determine the goals for your campaigns (which will be discussed in depth in Chapter 13). Once you have established the goals, your ads should reflect those goals.

Your ad should display your products' features and benefits. This is so important that an upcoming section focuses on features and benefits.

You want to make sure that the consumer identifies with your ad copy. Marketing is about identifying and connecting with consumers. Using your consumers' language is important. If you use terms that your consumers do not understand or terms they do not often see, it can cause them to not identify with your ad copy and click on a competitor's ad instead of yours (Figure 4.3).

Deep Vein Thrombosis
Do You Suffer From **DVT**? Learn About
Diagnosis, Treatment Options & More
www.vdf.org

Deep Vein Thrombosis
Info for HCPs about **DVT**, the most
common form of VTE. View Videos
www.VTEConsultant.com

Defective BARD IVC Filter
G2 and Recovery IVC Filters
Aggressive Representation
www.filterlaw.com

PPT Vision
Compact Intelligent Cameras for
Machine Vision & Vision Inspection
www.ONExia.com
1220 American Blvd, West Chester

Deep Vein Thrombosis- DVT
Symptoms, Diagnosis and Current
Treatment Options for **DVT**.
www.**dvt**answers.com

Figure 4.3 How many ads do you understand?

Using Words Consumers Understand

It is useful to read writers and columnists who write about your local area and industry. If you are advertising in a specific location, the local newspaper columnists usually try to make interesting points about that particular area within their column. If you see words that are not typically used in your location, these could be words that are common to another area (which could be state, city, or country). By reading the local columnists, you can find words your audience understands and finds familiar. This is a fantastic place to find some unusual adjectives to test in ad copy.

Each industry can get lost in its own jargon, but consumers often do not know these industry words. Read magazine reviews of your products and services that are written for the general populace and not just your industry. When you find places where you feel words or concepts are not quite accurate, the wrong word is being used, or a common word is used instead of a specific one (denoting jargon), note that these words might be used because the general populace does not understand the jargon. If you are using this jargon, do you think consumers can understand your ad?

Calls to Action

Direct a consumer to take action. What do you want someone to do once they arrive at your site? When you tell someone what to do within the ad copy, it is going to predispose them to look for that action on the landing page. Some generic examples of calls to action are

- Call us today

- Subscribe to our newsletter

- Download our whitepaper

Those who do not wish to take such action may not even click on your ad. If you are looking to increase CTR and views to a new product page (regardless of who buys the product), you may not want to add a purchasing or prequalifying call to action within the ad copy as it could lower CTR. This will be discussed in more depth in Chapter 6 when we examine optimizing your account for conversions.

Often in search advertising, a straightforward marketing message connects cerebrally with visitors. By using logic and informational ad copy, you are trusting that the consumers can make decisions if they are presented with all of the facts. This is very useful in ad copy writing—the purpose is to answer a searcher's question, and an answer is made up of facts. This is also useful when you are trying to reach consumers who do intensive research before making a decision, which is common in B2B and technical fields. However, you will see higher CTRs and conversion rates if you also connect emotionally with a visitor.

Touching the Emotional Core

It is possible to connect both informationally and emotionally with a searcher. There are some common assumptions about what any person wants and what one would most likely try to avoid:

What people want:

- More control
- Independence
- Freedom
- More time
- More money
- Better health
- Better appearance
- Promotions at work
- To feel included
- Social advancement
- To be appreciated
- Security
- Confidence
- Enjoyment

And what people try to avoid:

- More work
- Unacceptable risk
- Doubt
- Criticism
- Guilt
- Embarrassment
- Pain
- Feeling stupid
- Being ignored

By combining emotional and informational factors (Figure 4.4), you can create ads that elicit emotional responses in your visitors while still directing them to find their necessary information on your website.

Gaming Laptop Computer
4 Gigs Memory. 512 MB Graphics.
Own your enemies like never before
example.com

Be the Hero - MS Exchange
Save your company Thousand$
Download hosted exchange whitepape
example.com

Secure Travel Laptops
Keep your information secure with
Fingerprint and Biometric Security
example.com

Buy a Dell Computer
Be productive on European flights
with our 8 hour extended battery
example.com

Figure 4.4 Ads that combine emotion and information

Following Google's Editorial Guidelines

Before we continue examining different aspects of ad copy writing and creating effective ads, let us examine the editorial policies. If an ad will not be approved by Google to show on a search result, there is no need to waste your time writing that type of ad.

Google has gone to great lengths to ensure that ads meet a certain standard before being shown to their visitors. As one of Google's major success metrics is a returning visitor, they want to ensure that the ads are just as relevant as the natural search results.

Character Lengths

The first consideration is character length. There are stringent requirements for how many characters can appear in an ad:

Ad Copy Section	Character Length
Headline	25
Description line 1	35
Description line 2	35
Display URL	35
Destination URL	1,024

It is commonly said that the best headline is 26 characters. Attempting to write creative marketing messages in a matter of 95 characters is very difficult and takes some time to master. This is why it is important to test out different messages.

Even though description lines 1 and 2 appear as different lines when ads are created, it can also be useful to test out writing one 70-character sentence to see if the ad reads better as a single sentence than as two distinctive messages on separate lines. This is especially true if your ad regularly appears at the top of the page, where the two description lines are run together.

Editorial Requirements

The most ambiguous of the editorial rules is "accurate ad text." While Google explains this requirement as ensuring that your ad reflects what the consumer will find on your landing page, it is also a rule they can fall back on if they want to disapprove ad copy for various reasons.

Following this rule is important for conversion rates. If your ad copy claims someone will find something on your landing page and that item is not there, the user will hit the Back button and you have just wasted the price of the click. Following this rule can also help your quality score (discussed in depth in future chapters) as "relevancy" is a word Google uses repeatedly to describe their AdWords program.

The second rule is accurate capitalization. While you can capitalize the first letter of each individual word, you cannot have a word in all caps: exceptions include acronyms or words that naturally always appear in all caps. For instance, if you wrote the ad copy "FREE Software," the ad would be disapproved because "FREE" is not a word that should appear in all caps. However, if your ad copy was "Learn PPC Marketing," this would be approved, as the acronym PPC should be in all caps.

You must back up all competitor claims on the landing page. If you claim that your product is better than another product, you need supporting evidence on that page. This could be an accurate comparison chart or a third party who has verified that information.

All ads must use proper grammar and spelling. You cannot use misspellings in ad copy, with the exception of some common misspellings or words that have alternate spellings. For instance, the words "optimize" and "optimise" are both acceptable as they are alternate spellings of the same word (optimise is the U.K. spelling, optimize is the U.S. spelling).

Ads cannot have offensive or inappropriate language. This is another ambiguous rule that helps to keep hate-based ads, some adult ads, and other offensive items out of search results.

If you make a claim of a price, discount, or special offer, you must show the consumer that offer within a couple of clicks from your landing page. If you make the claim that DVDs are 60 percent off, and that offer is not on your site, the ad should be disapproved. Following this rule will also help conversion rates. If you make a claim of free shipping, and a searcher navigates throughout your site and is about to check out but has yet to determine if they will receive free shipping, odds are they will not enter their credit card.

You must use proper punctuation marks and symbols. This means you cannot bullet point each line of your ads to make them look different on a search result. In addition, an ad copy can only have one exclamation point, and that exclamation point cannot be in the headline. We will discuss trademarks and copyrights later in this chapter; however, since there are so few symbols used in ad copy, adding a ®, ©, or ™ symbol (assuming you have the right to use it) can help make your ad copy stand out from the other ads.

You can not repeat the same word multiple times in a row in ad copy. For instance, "Free Free Free ads" would be disapproved for gimmicky repetition.

In general, superlatives such as "best" are disapproved in ad copy. The exception is if you can prove it. If you claim to be the best at something, you will need third-party verification. If you do have third-party verification, it can be very useful to use a word such as "best" in your ad copy, as very few other ads will make superlative claims.

You also cannot imply a Google affiliation or relationship that does not exist. Making the claim of "Recommended by Google" will be disapproved in almost all cases.

While some of the editorial restrictions can be annoying, in general they foster an environment of fair play between advertisers and help consumers find their information.

Following the relevancy aspects of the editorial guidelines often leads to higher conversion rates and more profit for your company. Knowing the editorial restrictions will help you create ads that will be approved by editorial so you do not have to keep trying new ads in hopes of them becoming approved. Too many companies spend time trying to work around the restrictions, which just creates short-term work that does not give long-term results. The goal of writing ads within the editorial guidelines is to find unique ways to differentiate your ads regardless of any restrictions.

Developing Unique Selling Propositions

Why should someone buy from you instead of your competitor? That is one of the fundamental questions you need to answer about your business, as it should permutate your marketing efforts.

To visualize different unique selling propositions, it is easy to turn to the car industry. What is the first thought that pops into your mind as you read this list of cars?

- Porsche
- BMW
- Ferrari
- Lexus
- Subaru
- Volvo

Lexus, BMW, Porsche, and Ferrari are all luxury cars that will make a serious dent in your wallet. However, even among these cars there are differences in their unique selling propositions (USP). A Porsche can be driven off a lot and raced that same day. A Ferrari is a status symbol that stands out wherever it is seen. A BMW is a German-engineered luxury driving machine. Lexus is the pursuit of driving perfection.

Volvos often tout their safety record, while a Subaru is great for all-weather driving. That does not mean a Subaru is not a safe car or that a Volvo cannot drive well in the snow. These are marketing statements that are top-of-mind to consumers when they consider which cars to purchase.

While these are extreme scenarios dealing with companies who have many years and millions of dollars behind their marketing efforts, any business can come up with something unique about their particular company. You can find anything at eBay. You can compare insurance quotes from competitors at Progressive. Customize your new computer at Dell. Zappos is powered by service.

If you are unsure of what your USP should be, you can test this through AdWords ads. Create several different ads with different USPs and see which ones gather the highest CTR and conversion rates on your website (For full details on testing ad copy, please refer to Chapter 15).

If you are a local company that advertises against national companies, your USP may include the fact that your business is local and someone can walk into your office or easily call and talk to a human.

By choosing a USP that is core to your business, it is easier to make decisions about how to position yourself in the marketplace. The USP also makes for a good line of ad copy as it showcases why someone wants to do business with your company. Do not blend into the crowd. Stand apart by showcasing your company's uniqueness.

Distinguishing Features and Benefits

Features and benefits are often misunderstood. They are very different, and each has its own place within the buying funnel.

A *feature* is a component or function of your products and services. This is often the big list of details found on the outside of a product's box or included in the PDF description of a product. Features are facts about the product or services. Features are easy to list—just create a bullet point list about the product.

For instance, this book is being written on a Sony Z laptop with these features:

* 13.1-inch wide screen display
* 4 GB of memory
* 128-GB solid-state drive
* 128-MB hybrid graphics card
* 9-hour battery life
* Carbon fiber casing

- Built-in webcam
- Less than 4 pounds is good

This list could go on for hundreds of bullet points. Look at any product or service, and start writing down its components. Features are easy to determine.

A *benefit* is something the product or service will do for you. How will the service make your life better? Why should you spend your hard-earned money on a particular product? Essentially, if you can answer "What's in it for me?" you've come up with the product's benefits. Benefits are based on evoking emotional responses.

It is easy to turn a feature into a benefit by adding a "so," "to," or "will" to the end of the feature and completing the sentence.

- The laptop has a 9-hour battery life so you can be productive on an international flight.
- The Sony Z weighs less than four pounds to save your back from excessive strain.
- Having 4 GB of memory will easily let you analyze a million rows of Excel files to find the most profitable keywords.
- Use the built-in webcam to see your family when you are traveling.
- The carbon fiber casing will protect your investment if you accidently drop your laptop.

Always keep your customer in mind when creating your benefits. If your customer does not travel, a 9-hour battery life might not be a benefit. However, if your customer is constantly examining large Excel files to optimize keyword lists, being able to manipulate a million rows in Excel could save them both time and money.

You can take the extra step of segmenting your customers into different demographics and then examining what features and benefits are most important to each segment. For instance, if you sold the Sony Z laptop I just described, which features and benefits would be most beneficial to these groups?

- Frequent travelers
- Gamers
- PPC marketers

By segmenting your audience into groups, you can send custom messages to those users. This can sometimes be difficult with keywords on the search network; however, across the content network (discussed in Chapter 9), you can examine the demographics of individual websites and then write appropriate ads based on the website's visitor demographics.

What do your customers want? Your benefit list can be paired with the lists earlier in the chapter about what people want and what they avoid. By creating emotionally beneficial statements about your product, you can move past the features of a product to showcase how buying your product will improve someone's life in a particular way.

Benefits, Features, and the Buying Funnel

When writing ad copy, you need to keep the buying funnel in mind (we covered the buying funnel in Chapter 2). Users have different concerns and questions throughout the buying funnel, and adjusting your ads appropriately can help engage users to click on your ads and eventually do business with your company.

The buying funnel starts with the awareness and interest phases. At this point in time, searchers do not know much about your products or services. Using jargon confuses consumers as they do not yet know enough about the products to understand what the jargon terms mean.

At this phase of the buying funnel, you need to emphasize why your products will make someone's life better. Why should they want the product or want to learn more about your services? Using benefit-driven ad copy that tells a story of how you will improve their life will help to engage users.

The next step of the buying funnel is the learn phase. It is in this phase that a consumer's research transitions from just understanding the benefits to also learning about the features. Mixing both benefit and features within your ad copy is useful. This will help transition the user to understanding why they need the product, and then start down the next path of the buying funnel into feature comparison.

If you do not know where a keyword lives in the buying funnel, it can be useful to first treat the keyword as being part of the learn phase as your ad copy showcases both benefits and features. Once you write your initial ad copy, you should test these keywords with different ad messages to see which resonates better with the consumer to determine where the keyword lives within the buying funnel. These are excellent keywords to start some of your testing (discussed later).

In addition, often the search buying funnel starts at the learn phase. As a consumer cannot search for something they have no knowledge of, the content network is more useful in reaching users at the top of the buying funnel (more on the content network in Chapter 9).

Once a consumer has learned more about a product and has decided they want to buy a product, or engage a company's services, the consumer moves into the shopping comparison phase.

When someone is comparing products, they already understand why a product will enhance their life (which is a benefit of your product). At this stage of the buying funnel, it is important to showcase features. However, while you want to start emphasizing features during this phase, never forget benefits. Consumers eventually buy because of benefits; don't lose sight of this fact.

It is very easy for a customer to compare products side by side to see which product has which feature. It is usually more beneficial for you to make a comparison chart for the customer so you can highlight your best features.

You may test some ad copy (more on testing in Chapter 15) that shows features, and then list the benefits of those features on the landing page. Other ideas for ad copy are all features that tell a story about why your product is superior to the other products in the marketplace. You can always fall back on the standard ad copy to test one feature and the major benefit of that feature.

In the shopping comparison phase, you can also make an assumption that the consumer has a basic understanding of the jargon associated with the products. It is now okay to use some jargon in your ads. Price-conscious shoppers will compare both features and prices. When the economy is in a downturn, often you will see consumers buy "good enough" products that are less expensive as opposed to the "best" product in the market.

Finally, it is time for the shopper to make a purchase. While we comparison shop on features, we buy because of benefits. When your keywords fall into the buying stage of the buying funnel, you should include benefits in your ad copy. These are also excellent ads to test. In some cases, you may find an all-benefit ad copy works best. In other cases, a benefit-and-feature ad copy may work best. In many industries, the feature may not be about the product, but instead about the final cost of the product. Therefore, items like shipping, prices, and discounts can serve to enhance your ads.

While ads should be written that reflect the keywords that trigger the ad to be shown, the content of the ads should change based on searcher behavior and knowledge. Do not just write all-benefit or all-feature ads regardless of where someone is in the buying funnel. Determine where someone is in their decision-making process and then write ads appropriate to their current mindset.

Ad Copy Format to Start Utilizing Features and Benefits

There will be times when a keyword does not fit neatly into one aspect of the buying funnel. In this instance, since you might be unsure of what type of ad to write, start with one of the standard ad formats:

- Captivating headline
- Product or service feature
- Product or service benefit
- Display URL

This is an excellent starting ad. It might not be the best ad in the long run, but you have to start somewhere. Once you have created this standard ad type, you can test it against other ads that focus more on user benefits and product features to see which ad type consumers respond to for those particular keywords.

If you are certain where the searcher is within the buying funnel, emphasize the benefits or features of your products; doing so can serve to increase your CTR, conversion rates, and ultimately, your company's profits.

Employing Themes That Get Clicks

An ad copy has three lines where you can be very creative: the headline and the two description lines. (You can be creative with display URLs, but there's a limited amount of creativity possible.)

The Headline This is generally used to captivate the audience. The headline should draw the consumer's eye so they read your two description lines. You can use the headline as a benefit or feature line as well; it does not always have to be a line to draw the eye.

The Two Description Lines These are your chances to show off two different aspects of your products or services. These description lines could be benefits, features, prices, USPs, etc.

No matter how you choose to use these three lines, there is a maximum number of themes or different thoughts you can include in an ad copy.

Themes are the high level classifications of different types of ad writing styles, such as:

- Ads that include prices or discounts
- Ads focused on testimonials
- Ads that convey information
- Ads that include negative information

We will focus on themes with concrete examples in the next section.

Due to character restrictions, you must pick and choose which messages you are going to use to create these haiku-like ads to bring a searcher from viewing your ad to your website. If you decide to showcase two product-specific benefits, you probably do not have room to also talk about pricing and shipping and customer service within the same ad copy. There just is not enough room in these brief lines to add every marketing message you desire.

There are various themes that you can utilize in your ad copy. Each theme emphasizes a different message. None of the themes are better or worse than any other. Your goal is to test different themes to see which one performs best for your marketing goals.

Every time you include a theme in an ad, you are also excluding another theme. This goes for your competition as well. Your goal is to make your ad stand out, show the searchers you can answer their questions, and make them desire to view your website. If all of your competition is using just one theme, you may decide to test some completely different themes to see if that can make your ad stand apart from the other text on a page.

Utilizing Numbers in Ads

You can use psychology to help determine how searchers view different types of ads. There are two prevalent themes you will see when you utilize numbers in your ads: number ranges and exact numbers.

People often focus on the number that is most beneficial to their current situation. In ad copy writing, you can use this type of psychology to test out single numbers versus ranges for numbers in your ad copy (Figure 4.5).

Bluetooth Headset Sale
Great selection from $89-$199
Free Shipping on All Orders
bgTheory.com/BluetoothHeadsets

Bluetooth Headset Sale
Great Selection from $99
Free Shipping on All Orders
bgTheory.com/BluetoothHeadsets

Bluetooth Headset Sale
Great Selection from $89 and up
Free Shipping on All Orders
bgTheory.com/BluetoothHeadsets

Figure 4.5 Prices in ad copy

There will be times when the competition's prices are similar or you do not want to include the actual price in the ad—you may want to showcase a discount offer instead of an actual price point. You can apply the same principles of using numerals in ad copy to discount ranges (Figure 4.6).

Bluetooth Headset Sale
25% Off all Headsets.
Free Shipping on All Orders
bgTheory.com/BluetoothHeadsets

Bluetooth Headset Sale
Great selection. 25%-60% Off.
Free Shipping on All Orders
bgTheory.com/BluetoothHeadsets

Figure 4.6 Discounts in ad copy

The last number to try in ad copy is a very exact number: "I saved $241.56 last year by using Tax Software." These exact numbers draw consumers' eyes as they do not look like standard pricing and discount numbers. Using exact numbers in ad copy is best when

- Your ad shows how much of something you can save someone
  - Learn how I saved 37 hours using the Getting Things Done methodology for managing my email
  - Our IT department cut costs by $238,021 by instituting Google Apps for domains
  - Our customers can lose 26.5 lbs in just 3 months
  - Reduce your calorie intake by 354 calories a day

- Your ad shows how much money you made
  - Learn how I made $328,282 selling real estate
  - Our staffing agency increased salaries by $23,055

Using prices and discounts in ad copy is useful to test when
- Consumers are very price conscious
- You are advertising highly competitive product industries
- There are large price ranges for the same type of products
- You are using shopping comparison keywords

There are times when you might have an opportunity to change the pricing rules. If a customer sees two ads with the prices $10 and $50, usually they will assume these two products are quite different even if they are the same. If you were to create an ad with a $40 price point, then the $10 ad looks cheap, and the $50 and $40 ads look similar. In this case, the $40 price point might win out. However, in that same scenario, if you were to create an ad that listed a $15 price point (so the ads would be $10, $15, and $50), the $50 looks quite expensive and the $10 ad might turn out to be the winner.

Two price points do not give consumers a good comparison if there is a significant difference in prices. Three prices on a page are enough data points that consumers can start to compare products from just the ad copy.

You should always take into consideration your competitors' ads. If all of your competitors are using prices in their ads, you may want to test an ad that showcases features and benefits of the product instead of pricing. This is especially true in industries where everyone is trying to showcase the lowest price. If you lower your price to a point where you no longer make money on the sale, then why buy that keyword? In those cases, you may want to forego showing a price at all and instead focus on the other customer benefits.

How Strong Is Your Call to Action?

A *call to action* is a statement in your ad copy that informs the customer what you want them to do once they arrive at your website. Some calls to action are very straightforward:
- Subscribe to our newsletter
- Call for an appointment
- Buy a new TV today!

You can mix and match ad types and lines. You could have a call to action that is also a benefit. You can use a USP that is also a company feature.

Consider the ads shown in Figure 4.7. Which would one would you click?

| Secret AdWords Tips |
| Discover new AdWords Methods |
| Signup for our newsletter today! |
| bgTheory.com/AdWords |
| Secret AdWords Tips |
| Discover new AdWords Methods |
| Receive Your Secrets Today! |
| bgTheory.com/AdWords |
| Secret AdWords Tips |
| Discover new AdWords Methods |
| Signup for Powerful Marketing Tips |
| bgTheory.com/AdWords |

Figure 4.7 Different calls to action

"Sign up for our newsletter today!" is a very generic call to action. It does not add any additional benefit for the searcher.

"Receive Your Secrets Today!" is not necessarily a call to action. It is showcasing a benefit to the customer. When these three ads were run in a test, this one did receive the highest CTR of the three ad types. That often has to do with the words "free" and "secret." Secret is an interesting word to use in ad copy as it makes people feel included in a little-known club. However, this ad did not have the highest conversion rate of the three ads.

"Sign Up for Powerful Marketing Tips" had the second highest CTR but the highest conversion rate, and when you combine the actual numbers, this ad was the most profitable of the three. This line still includes a call to action but also tells a consumer they are going to receive "powerful tips." Who does not want powerful information?

In this example, there are many other calls to action you could test:

- Using the word "inbox" reminds consumers it will go to their email.

- The word "inbox" could also be associated with spam, so showcasing multiple delivery options, such as RSS feeds, could be tested.

- Using the word "daily" or "weekly" would let someone know how often they would see this information.

- Is "powerful" overused? Try different adjectives such as "effective" or "persuasive." A thesaurus is one book that should always be at your fingertips.

Once you find an effective message, it does not mean your job is complete. It means you have a nice starting place from which you can continue to refine your ads and increase your profits.

Writing Informational Ad Copy

The reason someone uses a search engine is to find the answer to a question. That answer is a piece of information. Showcasing informational statements in ad copy (Figure 4.8) can be a useful way to connect with the searcher.

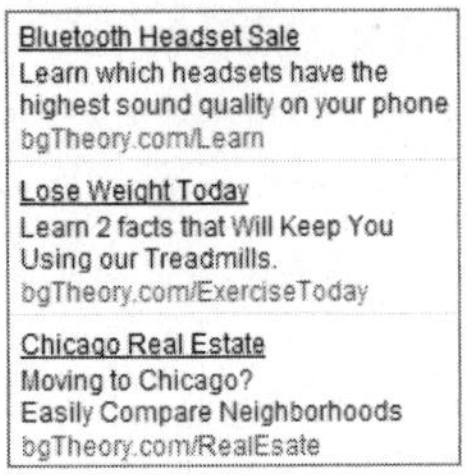

Figure 4.8 Informational ad copy

These informational ads can also showcase pieces of information that might not be part of the product, but when included with the product help increase its usefulness.

How much exercise equipment is bought, used for a month, relegated to the garage for the next six months, and up for sale on eBay the following year? Since this is a common aspect of buying exercise equipment, including bonus information that showcases ways to help someone continue to use a treadmill could be a highly effective.

When they are buying headsets, some of the biggest consumer questions revolve around clarity, background noise, and volume. By addressing one of the important issues about a product within the ad copy, you show that you do not just sell the product, but that a searcher can also learn about the products on your site.

Examine the top questions, issues, complaints, and user behaviors that exist with your services. What additional information could you include in the ad copy that helps a consumer make a decision on which product to buy?

Reflecting the Consumer's Question

You have a question for which you would like to know the answer. Therefore, you go to a search engine to find that answer. If you see an ad that reflects your original question, it is easy to assume that website has relevant information to help you find the information you seek.

It is worthwhile testing questions in ad copy. Since your ad will be reflecting the reason why someone originally went to a search engine and the question that user is currently trying to answer, you may see some nice increases in CTR by utilizing questions in your ad copy (Figure 4.9).

Figure 4.9 Questions in ad copy

When writing questions in ads, it is more important to have the question mark (?) in the ad copy than to write a properly structured sentence. By just adding the question mark to your current headline, you may see a difference in click-through rate.

Including Testimonials or Reviews in Ad Copy

Often we sit isolated behind a computer when making online purchasing decisions, without another person to ask what they think about a product. We understand that we are not experts in every field. Therefore, reading testimonials others have left, or expert reviews about a product, can help us feel more confident in making a decision (Figure 4.10)

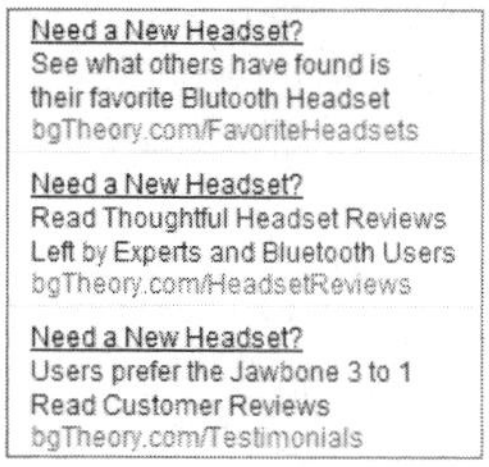

Need a New Headset?
See what others have found is
their favorite Blutooth Headset
bgTheory.com/FavoriteHeadsets

Need a New Headset?
Read Thoughtful Headset Reviews
Left by Experts and Bluetooth Users
bgTheory.com/HeadsetReviews

Need a New Headset?
Users prefer the Jawbone 3 to 1
Read Customer Reviews
bgTheory.com/Testimonials

Figure 4.10 Ad copy testimonials and reviews

The actual testimonial or review does not have to be included in the ad copy, although a short review can be useful. Your ad copy just needs to let the consumer know that upon visiting your site, they can read the opinions of others.

The actual testimonial information can even change based on the buying funnel. If someone is in the comparison shopping phase, they are most likely looking for product reviews. However, if someone has decided on the actual product and they are now looking for which site they are going to buy the product from, testimonials about your company could be more useful.

Expert reviews about different types of products (LCD versus plasma TVs) are more aligned with the buying funnel if the consumer is in the learning phase.

Even with different ad themes, these various types of ads should consider which phase of the buying funnel the consumer is in to ensure your ad is resonating with the searcher.

Utilizing Negative Ad Copy

When you read the newspaper, view TV headlines, or watch political campaigns, a common theme emerges: negative information.

Negative information stops many people from looking elsewhere and immediately draws their attention. If you consider what people want and don't want (the lists earlier in this chapter), often negative information reflects those types of conditions. Many people are drawn to negative information. This includes search ads (Figure 4.11).

Be Careful of Bluetooth
Think Bluetooth Headsets are Safe?
Get the Real Information Here!
bgTheory.com/Caution

Do Not Buy A Headset
Without Reading the Secret Shoppers
Guide to Bluetooth Headset Reviews
bgTheory.com/SecretShoppers

Headsets Waste Money
Don't buy non-compatible headsets
Free Bluetooth Compatibility Info
bgTheory.com/SaveMoney

Figure 4.11 Negative information advertisements

While negative ads often stand out in a search result, especially if none of the other ads is negative, it is important to consider your company positioning before utilizing negative ads.

Negative ads are read by consumers. Your ad copy not only contains your website's URL, it directs consumers to your website. The information contained within an ad is a reflection of your company. Therefore, before running a negative ad, please make sure that it is in line with your company positioning:

- If your company wants to be known as a friendly company, you may not want to run negative ads.
- If your company is about consumer warnings and recalled product information, for example, then negative ads may be in line with your company's image.

If you are an agency or part of a marketing department within a larger company, before creating and testing negative ads, you should first check with the CEO or the department that runs brand management and company positioning to make sure that negative ads are okay to run and test.

Do Not Forget the Display URL

The display URL tells the consumer where they are going after they click. However, the display URL can also help signal a user where on the site they will be directed.

Google has more than 5 million pages indexed from IBM.com. Knowing you are going to IBM.com is not necessarily useful. If the display URL is IBM.com/BladeServer, suddenly you know that you are not just going to one of the 5 million pages on IBM.com, but that you will end up on a page about blade servers. If you are in the market for a new server, that is a much more useful page than the home page of IBM.com.

Google does have two editorial rules that you must follow in regard to display and destination URLs:

- The display URL must be the site where the user ends up. In other words, if you were Dell, you could not have IBM.com as your display URL and then direct someone to Dell.com.

- All of the destination URLs within an ad group must go to the same website. In other words, you could not have one ad that goes to IBM.com and a second ad within the same ad group that goes to Dell.com.

The other thing you need to consider when using display URLs is that you make sure how your consumer will read it. For instance, these are two commonly used display URLs that showcase information about ad copy writing:

- adwordsexample.com
- AdWordsExample.com

In the first example, there will be many consumers who do not see the entire display URL but instead focus on the word "sex" that is in the middle. By capitalizing the first letter of each word, most consumers no longer see the word "sex" in the URL, but instead see "AdWords Example."

This concept extends to not just single words within a display URL, but to other ways of interpreting your URL. Always take a look at your URL to see how many different ways it can be interpreted.

With the display URL, that exact URL does not have to exist within your website. It also does not have to be the same as the destination URL. The root domain must be the same for your destination and display URL, but the URLs themselves do not have to be the same. For instance, you could have the following display and destination URLs:

- Display URL: bgTheory.com/AdWordsSeminars
- Destination URL: http://www.bgtheory.com/adwords-seminar-for-success-philadelphia

In this case, the root domain, bgtheory.com, is the same for both URLs and therefore the ad would be approved.

The two most common display URLs are either the root domain of the website or a folder containing the product name. However, there are other ways to write display URLs (Figure 4.12).

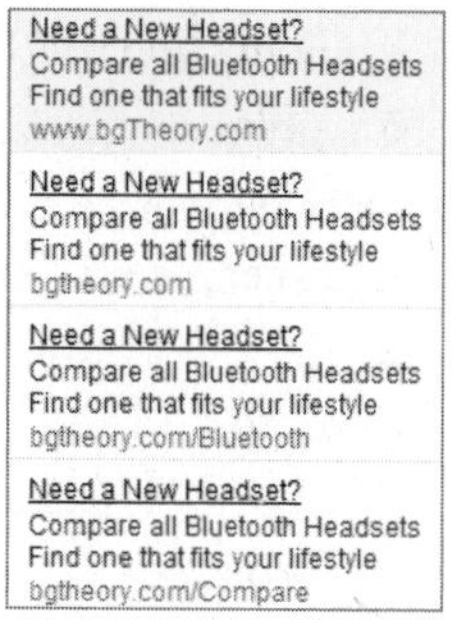

Figure 4.12 Display URLs

If you have a narrow theme site, just including the domain name, and no additional information can be useful. If a searcher sees AdWords.com and is familiar with AdWords, this domain name signals they will arrive at the AdWords program's website. No additional information is necessary in that case.

Adding a folder, such as /ProductInfo, can help you show a user where on the website they will arrive. Folders are useful to test on larger websites.

However, when you add a folder, it does not just have to be about the product or service. You can also create synergies with the ad copy that reinforce the ad's message. In the examples in Figure 4.12, the ads speak to comparing headsets. Therefore, using /Compare in the display URL reinforces to the user that they will arrive at a site that is comparing products. If someone is comparison shopping products, this synergy of reinforcing the ad copy can help your company attract the searcher's click.

The display URL is a line of ad copy. Since you only have four lines that you can control, do not forget to test this particular line of ad copy. The display URL CTR is also a quality score factor (more about quality score in later chapters). Testing out display URLs is useful not just to examine click-through and conversion rates, but to test for ways to improve your overall quality score.

Following the Law: Trademarks

Google's editorial policies regarding trademarks vary by country. In most countries, an advertiser can choose any keyword they desire. According to Google's trademark policy, it does not matter if the word is trademarked, you can use it as a keyword to trigger your ad copy. However, in those countries, if the trademark holder has filed an exception request with Google, then the keyword can still be used to trigger an ad, but that trademark cannot be used in ad copy. In general, in the other countries, a trademarked word cannot be used as either a keyword or in ad copy.

To view a list of the editorial policies regarding trademarks, please visit:
`www.google.com/tm_complaint_adwords/complaint.html`.

If you are a trademark holder and want to protect your trademark from being used, you can visit the above URL to view the exception process, which is straightforward:

1. Fill out and fax paperwork to Google.

2. Google will investigate if you own the trademark.

3. If you do, Google will then disapprove other ads within the same industry that are using your trademark.

"Within the same industry" is an important caveat when it comes to trademarks. For example, there are over 2,600 records at the U.S. Patent and Trademark Office (uspto.gov) for the search word "apple" in their database. While the word "apple" is trademarked in many industries, an orchard farmer can use the word "apple" in his ad copy. If you submit an ad and a form pops up that tells you a word is trademarked, but it is not trademarked for your industry, then just put that information on the exception request form ("not trademarked for my industry").

Note: Since trademarks are held at the country level, it is also important to consider in which countries your campaign will be displayed. If you choose to have your campaign shown to two different countries that each have different trademark laws, your ads and keywords will then have to follow the laws of both countries. There are many reasons to limit your campaigns to only show in one country, and one of them is based on trademark laws.

There are a few different ways that brands can think about their trademark utilization within ad copy. Let us walk through a few scenarios that show why a company may have various feelings about the enforcement of their trademarks. I will use Nike in this example since they sell both directly and through other outlet channels. However, please note that this may not be Nike's current policy.

Many stores sell Nike shoes. Regardless of whether a consumer buys shoes from Nike.com, Zappos.com, or yet another store that sells Nike shoes, Nike will sell a pair of shoes. Therefore, they might not file an exception request with Google and may allow other companies to use the Nike trademark in ad copy, as Nike can gain additional sales through their distribution partners.

Nike could take another approach and decide to selectively give accounts permission to use their trademark. They may decide there are certain retailers they have a special relationship with and only allow those retailers to use the Nike trademarks in ad copy. Therefore, Nike would first file an exception request with Google. Once it was granted, then Nike would file some more paperwork that gives permission for specific accounts to use the Nike trademark.

This is very common in franchise companies. If the corporate office holds the trademark, they may want their actual franchises to be allowed to use the trademark. This means the corporate office would need the AdWords account ID numbers for each franchisee account. However, you cannot selectively give permission until Google has completed their initial trademark investigation.

The most restrictive approach Nike could take is to not allow anyone but Nike.com to use their trademarks. Nike could decide that since they sell shoes online, they do not want additional competition for their trademarked words. In this instance, in the United States, consumers could see a wide variety of ads on a search for the word "Nike," but only the Nike.com ad would actually display the word "Nike."

Currently, Nike has not taken a restrictive approach. I'm not attempting to call out Nike specifically but to walk you through the conversations that should occur within your organization about the usage of trademarks.

In addition, just because Google may allow you to use a trademark in your ad copy does not mean the trademark holder could not sue you anyway. While Google's editorial policies may be introduced into the court case, a company can sue another company regardless of Google's policies.

This is especially true of company names. In the above case, there is a good reason for other companies to use Nike's trademarks in ad copy. However, if you use a competitor's name in your ad copy, regardless of the word being trademarked, you could end up in a lawsuit. A competitor could also sue you for using their name as a keyword even if it does not appear in the ad copy. While your competitor may or may not win, you will still have to pay to defend your keyword usage.

It is a worthwhile exercise to sit down with your marketing and legal departments to create rules around your usage of trademarks and competitor's names. If you use a third party to manage your AdWords account, make sure that party understands your policies surrounding these items.

The Quest for the Holy Grail of Advertising

Wouldn't it be nice to be given a magical formula where an ad always received a click and a conversion? Unfortunately, there is no magic formula for writing ads. Writing the perfect ad copy is like the search for the Holy Grail. It is a never-ending search of examining where you have been, ascertaining where others have gone, and plotting new paths to see where they lead.

Ad copy not only changes depending upon your industry, but upon your company's specific customer base as well. Consider two different accounting companies, one specializing in Quicken and the other in Peachtree. Quicken is generally used for personal finance. Peachtree is generally used for business bookkeeping. While these are technically both accounting firms, their customers are different. Therefore, their ad copy should also be different to showcase why they are distinct from each other.

Just because an ad works for your competition does not mean it will work for your company. Sometimes a company will start advertising, choose an ad that has been running for a competitor, and just duplicate that ad copy in their account. Ignoring the ethics of such tactics for a moment, you should know that this tactic will often fail. Each business has a different website, different sales pitches, and various benefits and features. These differences often cause an ad for one company not to work for another.

Each ad will have different CTR and conversion rates when paired with different keywords. Let's say you wrote ad copy about high definition televisions and used these keywords to trigger that ad copy:

- Plasma TV

- Buy a plasma TV

- LCD TV

- Compare LCD to plasma TVs

- HDTV

Each of those keywords will have vastly different conversion rates and click-through rates. The user intent, commercial intent, keyword specificity, landing page, and ad copy all come together to form different metrics for keyword and ad copy pairs.

These are important points to keep in mind when looking at ads used by other companies. Just because a company has used an ad for several years does not mean it's effective. You do not know how much another company is testing ads, what their success metrics are, or how well those ads blend with your landing pages.

You do need to examine your competitors' ads to make sure your ads stand out on a search page. If all the ads showcase pricing, try a different message. If all the ads only speak of benefits, try using a question in your ad copy.

PPC success is measured with hard numbers. You should know statistics such as CTR, conversion rate, average sale amount, lifetime visitor values, and profit per sale. These numbers will show you which ad copy and keyword combination is most successful based on your metrics.

When you are ad copy writing, it is one of the few times you can escape from numbers and use the right side of your brain for a while. Ad copy writing can be a fun exercise in utilizing different adjectives, marketing messages, unique selling propositions, features, and benefits. Let your creative juices flow. The numbers will eventually tell you which ad is the most successful for your company. However, until that time, be creative, test, and find new messages that resonate with searchers.

If you do not test various messages, you will never know what messages actually resonate best with your customers. Knowing which ads drive the most profit will not only make you more successful but will shift you from chasing your competitors to being a market leader.

Best Practices for Writing Compelling Ads

Writing, refining, and testing ad copy is an ongoing process that can lead to higher CTRs, higher conversion rates, and ultimately higher profits for your company. Below is a checklist of items to continuously keep in mind as you strive to find that perfect ad copy.

- Ensure that your ads reflect the search query. When a consumer conducts a search, they are seeking out specific pieces of information. Make sure that your ads can speak to the consumer's search query and show them how you can assist in helping them find their answers.

- Create granular ad groups to create a scenario where your ads are appropriate to both your keywords and the search query.

- Ensure that your ads are understandable. Jargon is only acceptable if the consumer knows the jargon. Do not use jargon for keywords that fall into the beginning stages of the buying funnel, as the searcher may not know the lexicon in their early research phases.

- Create a unique selling proposition for your business. This will differentiate your business from the other ads on the page.

- Features are facts about your product or service. Showcase features when someone is comparing products or services.

- Utilize benefits to connect emotionally with the searcher. Benefits inform someone why your product will make their life better.

- Direct a consumer to take action. By informing the searcher what you want them to do after the click, they are more predisposed to seek and conduct that action.

- Test informational, negative, and testimonial ad copy.

- Use the display URL to clarify to a searcher where they will arrive after they click.

- Never be satisfied with your ad copy. Journey down the never-ending quest to find the perfect ad copy.

These best practices should help guide you in creating effective ads that will connect with the searcher and lead them to your website where you can continue to engage them and show them how your company can fulfill their needs.

Landing Pages That Convert Searchers into Buyers

Where should you send a searcher after they click your ad? The home page is rarely the best place. You have several options, and choosing the correct one will ensure that the visitor does not just view your website, but becomes engaged with it.

First impressions last a lifetime, and that fact is just as true for websites as it is for people. If your website is trustworthy, friendly, and easy to use, it can help set a good first impression so the visitor does not just look at your website, but eventually becomes a customer.

Chapter Contents
Does Your Landing Page Answer the Searcher's Question?
Everything about Destination URLs
Choosing Landing Pages That Increase Conversion Rates
Employing Usability, Trust, and Web Technology to Increase Your Conversion Rates
Best Practices for Landing Pages

Does Your Landing Page Answer the Searcher's Question?

You advertised on a keyword. Your ad copy was compelling enough for someone to click on it. You paid for a click, you received a visitor. Now it's time for your website to convert that visitor into a customer.

The term *landing page* is industry jargon for the first page of your site someone visits after clicking on an ad. It might not be the home page of your website. It could be any page within your site or a page built specifically for your ad campaign.

Often, the only information the searcher has about your website is what was contained in your ad copy. A searcher only has a maximum of 130 characters of knowledge about what they are about to find after the click. Most searchers will only spend a few seconds looking at your landing page before deciding to continue interacting with your website to click the Back button. Therefore, the first thing your landing page must do is answer several questions that are going through the searcher's mind. These questions are not all related to their initial search query; they are related to the quality of your website and a searcher's ability to extract information from the webpage:

Am I in the Correct Place? This is the very first question your website must quickly answer. Someone did a search attempting to find an answer to a question. If you look at your landing page for three to five seconds, does the page appear to lead someone down the path to finding their answer?

Is This What I Expected? Is your landing page an extension of your ad copy? Is the information contained in your ad showcased on the landing page? If your ad mentioned product comparisons and your landing page only shows a single product review, you are not setting the expectations properly in the ad copy, and a visitor is likely to leave your website. Ensure your ads are not just the same theme as the keyword, but that they are setting the proper expectations for what someone will see after the click.

Do I Trust This Site? Trust is a major concern for many searchers. It is common for demographics that are not overly familiar with the Web to need additional reassurance that their credit card or personal information will be safe. Conversely, those who are more familiar with the Web know how to quickly look for SSL certificates, whether a site has HTTPS (secure pages) components, and if there's a privacy policy. We will cover more on trust elements later in this book.

How Long Will This Take? People value their time. Before committing to any action, many people unconsciously calculate how long it will take to accomplish that action. If the landing page consists of a long, intimidating form, the perception will be that there will be a high time commitment to complete the action on the site. Make sure that process seems quick. If your landing page is a form, just tell how long it will take (i.e., this is a three-page form that will take five minutes of your time).

What Should I Do Next? Does your landing page have a clear call to action? Once someone sees your landing page and has been satisfied that the preceding questions have been answered, what do you want them to do? Though people can be resistant to being told what to do, when they are unsure of the next action, they are more open to being informed about what their next action should be. Tell your visitors what the next step is for them to obtain their answer.

Where Should I Go Next? This aspect is closely related to "What should I do next?" If someone knows what to do next, do they know how to do it? Does your site have a clear path to action? The human mind can hold five to seven thoughts in short-term memory. If your website has 20 links on the landing page all going to different places, you can confuse the visitor. Your main button or image on the landing page should be where you want the visitor to go next. The button could be a subscription, add-to-cart button, or "contact us" form. Make sure that your primary action for a landing page stands out from the rest of the page's content.

Should I Click the Back Button? One of the most common navigational elements on the Web, and the one that loses websites the most visitors, is the dreaded Back button.

Regardless of how you code your site, choose your design, and lay out information, there will be visitors who click the Back button. You cannot be all things to all people. You can try to minimize how often the Back button is clicked by making sure all of the these questions are quickly and easily answered. If any of these questions are not quickly answered, you risk losing a visitor.

You're a Bad Judge of Your Website

Unfortunately, this is a true statement for almost all marketers and designers. You know that the big red button is a link that takes someone to the subscription page. You know that the images are not linked and that clicking on them will not let you see a larger image or take you to that product page. You know that your phone number is buried in your banner-like header.

Ask a colleague, spouse, customer, or someone else not familiar with your website to complete an action on your site. Give them a specific direction such as "contact us," "buy this product," or "subscribe to our newsletter." Now watch how they navigate through your website.

Even better, take five to seven people and ask them to do the same action. If you ask ten people to complete an action, you may see five to seven different ways that the exact same action was completed. Do not just watch how they completed the action; look for signs when they are lost, such as clicking on a non-hyperlinked image.

Many analytics programs have a reverse goal path report. This report shows you the different pages that someone visited before completing an action. By examining the reverse goal path report, you can get an insight into how visitors are navigating through your website.

The first question echoing through someone's mind when they visit your landing page is, "Am I in the correct place?" Does your landing page reflect the ad copy? Choosing which page you send the traffic to is an important decision since it is the first step in engaging visitors. You have several options about where to send the traffic depending on if you use keyword level, placement level, or ad copy level destination URLs. First we will focus on how and where to create destination URLs, then we will look at where to send the traffic.

Everything about Destination URLs

There are three ways within AdWords to choose where you send traffic for a particular click.

The first is at the ad copy level. In this instance, every click from that ad goes to the same landing page. An ad group can have several different ads (or even different ad types, as discussed in Chapter 8). Each ad can have a different destination URL (Figure 5.1). You must assign each ad a destination URL.

Figure 5.1 The destination URL is the last entry in your ad copy.

You can also set a destination URL at the individual keyword level. This is an optional, not required. If you create keyword level URLs, this URL is used instead of the ad copy destination URL (Figure 5.2).

Figure 5.2 Editing a destination URL for a keyword

For the keyword content network (detailed explanation in Chapter 9), if you set keyword level destination URLs, Google will attempt to determine which keyword best matches the content of that page and use the keyword's URL. If the keyword that best matches the landing page does not have a URL, then the ad copy destination URL will be used for the content network.

If you use placement targeting (see Chapter 9 for more details), you can set a destination URL for each placement (this is optional). If you have a destination URL at the placement level, that URL is used when someone clicks on your ad. If you do not have one, and you have keywords in the ad group, then Google looks to see what the best matching keyword is for the content. If that keyword has a destination URL, it is used; if it does not, the ad copy destination URL is used to determine where to send the visitor.

The search hierarchy for destination URLs is:

- Keyword destination URL

- Ad copy destination URL

The content network hierarchy for destination URLs is:

- Placement destination URL

- Keyword destination URL

- Ad copy destination URL

Building destination URLs for accurate tracking can be tricky, as you need to consider the wildcard variables that Google will fill in for you (such as the keyword) and what your analytics system can understand. In the next sections, we will walk through examples of how to build destination URLs so you can gain insight into visitors' behavior once they have reached your website.

Using Destination URLs for Tracking

For tracking purposes, you might want to add additional parameters to your destination URLs. Some may be dictated by your tracking system, and there are some variables that Google supports. This is why a destination URL can be 1,024 characters—when you start adding tracking parameters to a URL, they can grow quite long.

These additional parameters are not for visitors. They should not affect where a visitor goes on your site. These additional variables are for your tracking purposes, whether you are parsing them out in log files or in a separate analytics system.

URL Parameters: Understanding the Basics

In a URL, the question mark (?) and ampersand (&) are used to denote a new parameter (or variable). Most content systems only support one instance of a question mark, while they will support many instances of an ampersand. The question mark should be the first parameter used in a URL, and the remaining variables separated by ampersands. In addition, do not leave spaces in destination URLs. Some systems interpret spaces as %20 or %2B, some leave them as spaces, and some add a plus (+) sign. By using a space, you could break the URL for some visitors, causing them to see a 404 (error) page on your website.

For instance, if you wanted to send a visitor to http://www.bgtheory.com for the search term "AdWords seminars," and you wanted to add a source (src) and keyword parameter to the destination URL for tracking purposes, your final destination URL would be:

http://www.bgtheory.com?src=AdWords&keyword=adwords+seminars

The most common tracking parameters to add to an AdWords URL are:

- Src (meaning traffic source such as AdWords)
- Medium (what type of traffic, in this instance PPC)
- Campaign
- Ad group
- Ad copy ID
- Keyword
- Keyword match type
- Network (search or content source)
- Placement

Some of these inputs are supported by Google with variable replacements, meaning you can input a variable into your URL and Google will fill in that variable with the actual information. This is very useful if you want to track at the ad copy level.

Adding Custom Parameters to Destination URLs

Some of the earlier information (such as match type) is not supported by Google. If you wanted to track that set of information, you would need to build keyword level destination URLs.

The variables that Google supports are shown in Table 5.1.

▶ Table 5.1 Destination URL variables

Inserted Data	URL Formatting
Keyword	{keyword}
Ad copy ID	{creative}
If click came from search	{ifSearch:YourName}
If click came from content	{ifContent:YouName}
Placement of click	{placement}

The keyword input is based on the keyword that caused your ad to be triggered. The ad copy ID is unique to every ad in your AdWords account. The easiest way to associate an ad copy with the ad copy ID is to either use the API (a back-end program that lets your database communicate with the AdWords database) or run an ad text report and include the ad ID data point in the report.

The two interesting variables are ifSearch and ifContent. All clicks come from either search or content. AdWords will automatically include which network sent you traffic. If your click originated from a placement, the placement's information will be included in the URL.

Step-by-Step Guide to Building Destination URLs

We will illustrate how to build destination URLs at the ad copy level. As one of the variables is placement, you can use this same URL at the placement level as well.

While we are not going to dive deep into Google Analytics, it is important to incorporate your tracking system's variables into your destination URLs. Therefore, in these examples we will use the main variables of Google Analytics.

Google Analytics does have a URL builder tool (Figure 5.3), which can be found at www.google.com/support/googleanalytics/bin/answer.py?hl=en&answer=55578 (or you can search for "Google Analytics URL builder").

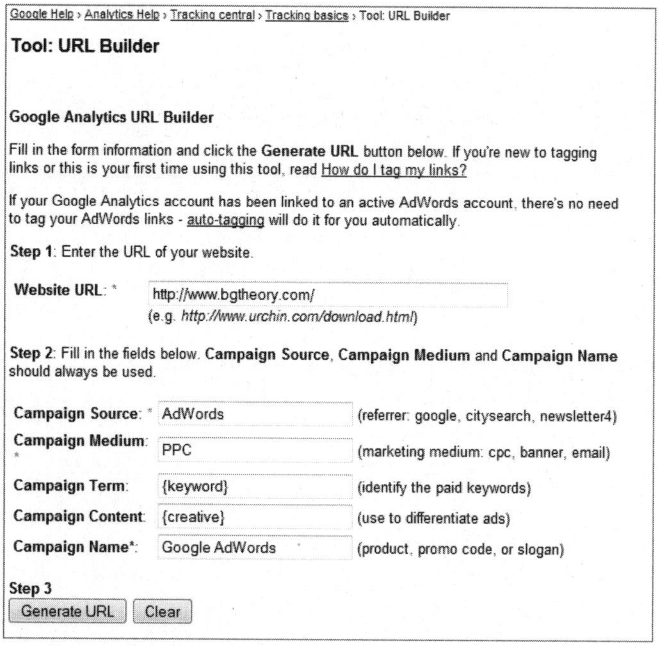

Figure 5.3 Google Analytics URL builder

Google Analytics uses the main variables shown in Table 5.2. When you see "YourName," this means you can input anything you desire to help you understand what data point is being referenced.

Google Analytics Name	Google Analytics Formatting
Campaign Source (traffic source)	utm_source=YourName
Campaign Medium (marketing type)	utm_medium=YourName
Campaign Term (keyword, optional input)	utm_term= YourName
Campaign Content (ad types, optional input)	utm_content= YourName
Campaign Name	utm_campaign= YourName

It is important to note that you can link your AdWords account with your Google Analytics account and see much of this data without having to code all of these URLs in AdWords. In some cases, you can combine both the analytics and the AdWords inputs together, which will pass large amounts of information to your analytics program.

If you were building ad copy level URLs, the one piece of data that is missing from the Table 5.2 variables is ad group. Therefore, you will have to code that information directly into the URL.

The following URL contains information for Google Analytics data, Google AdWords variable replacements, and the manual coding of the source ad group. This would be your final ad copy URL:

```
http://www.bgtheory.com/?utm_source=AdWords&utm_medium=PPC&utm_term=
{keyword}&utm_content={creative}&utm_campaign=AdWordsSeminars&Network=
{ifContent:Content}{ifSearch:Search}&SiteTarget={placement}&AdGroup=
ChicagoSeminar
```

While this would be your ad copy destination URL, it is not what the URL will look like when someone makes it to your website. To illustrate the final URL, let's assume that these are the variables that triggered your ad:

- Keyword: AdWords
- Ad Group Name: Chicago Seminars
- Campaign Name: AdWords Seminars
- User clicked on a search click

Here is the final destination URL once the variables are replaced by actual values:

```
http://www.bgtheory.com/?utm_source=AdWords&utm_medium=PPC&utm_term=
AdWords&utm_content=123456&utm_campaign=AdWordsSeminars&Network=
Search&SiteTarget=&AdGroup=ChicagoSeminar
```

You will rarely look at these URLs after you build them. What is important is to know how to build the URLs so that your tracking system can parse the information from the URL and store it appropriately in a system where the data is easily understandable.

This same URL can also be used at the keyword level. Since match type is not one of the variables, you may wish to add a match type parameter, such as &match=MatchType (i.e., &match=exact), to the destination URL.

There are a few reasons to have destination URLs at the keyword level. One is if your keywords are going to different pages. If this is your reason, be careful that the keywords in your ad groups are tightly themed. Rarely will you send different keywords to different pages. It's most common in very large accounts that are supporting hundreds of thousands of keywords.

If you want to track additional variables such as match type with the URL, you will need keyword level URLs. This data cannot be automatically added to a URL since the variables do not exist that support this data point. Another reason is that some tracking systems need keyword level destination URLs as they use different variables for tracking keywords, or they may add additional parameters to the URL for other purposes. This is a system by system consideration, and your vendor should be able to help you format these URLs (or they may do it automatically for you).

Some systems grab the keyword from the URL and do a site search or add keyword specific information into the landing page. In these cases, the systems will want to ensure they know the exact keyword being clicked by coding it into the URL.

Note: If you are using Google Analytics, and this seems like a huge amount of work, do not despair. There is an easy way to pass most of this data from AdWords to Google Analytics. The data that is not passed can easily be accessed from AdWords reports, which will be covered in depth in Chapter 16.

When you first set up your Google Analytics account, do so from within your AdWords account. During the setup process, Google Analytics will recommend that you auto-tag your links so that information can be passed from AdWords to Analytics. Just answer yes to this question.

If you have already set up a Google Analytics account and you are unsure if the data is being passed, there are two things to check.

1. Navigate to Google Analytics from within your AdWords account (Tools > Google Analytics). You will either see the Google Analytics interface (in which case move to step 2) or you will see a setup wizard. In the setup wizard, there is an option to link an existing Analytics account to AdWords. Just follow those instructions to link them together.

2. Navigate to My Account > Account preferences. Under Tracking (see Figure 5.4), make sure Auto-tagging is marked Yes.

Destination URLs only occur at the ad copy, keyword, or placement level within your AdWords account. You can add additional parameters however you want to the URL, as long as the final URL renders to an actual page in the browser.

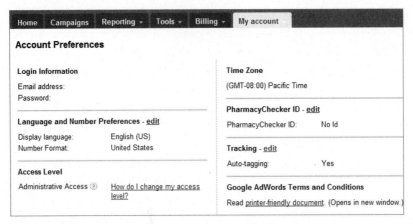

Figure 5.4 Auto-tag AdWords data for Google Analytics

By using custom destination URLs, you can pass certain pieces of information to your tracking, lead generation, e-commerce, or custom database that will help you understand what keywords, ad copy, placements, etc., are sending you high quality traffic.

There are a few editorial policies that your destination URL must meet before it will be approved by Google. First we will cover these policies, and then move on to where on your website you should send the traffic.

Complying with Destination URL Editorial Policies

There are a few editorial policies that your destination URLs must follow. The first is quite simple: the URL must be 1,024 or fewer characters. Secondly, every destination URL must go to the same root domain as the display URL of the same ad copy. Table 5.3 shows examples of display and destination URLs and how they comply with the editorial guidelines.

▶ **Table 5.3** Display and destination URL editorial examples

Display URL	Destination URL	Editorial
bgTheory.com	`http://www.bgtheory.com/article name`	Approved: Both root domains are the same.
bgTheory.com/AdWords	`http://www.bgtheory.com/Google-AdWords`	Approved: Both root domains are the same.
bgTheory.com	`http://google.com`	Disapproved: Root domains (bgtheory.com and google.com) are different.
Google.bgTheory.com	`http://www.google.com`	Disapproved: Root domains (bgtheory.com and google.com) are different.

The one exception occurs if your domain name is over 35 characters in length. As the display URL can only be 35 characters, you cannot enter a 36-character domain into the display URL.

In this case, you can work with the AdWords team to use a shorter display URL for your ad copy, and then the destination URLs will still have to go to your full domain name. When working with the AdWords team to choose a shorter domain name, the main consideration is that the chosen display URL does not cause confusion with another website.

If you have to choose a shorter domain name for your display URL, it is best if you purchase the domain so that another site will not spring up using your shortened URL. You do not have to use the new domain, but redirecting the shorter domain to your primary site will ensure that you do not lose any branding traffic from using a different display URL and that another site will not purchase your display URL, causing confusion between the two sites.

The third editorial policy also influences your display URL: all ads within the same ad group must go to the same root domain. This means that you cannot send traffic from one ad (or keyword) to a different root domain from any other ad (or keyword) within the same ad group.

If you owned two domains, such as bgtheory.com and ewhisper.net, even if the content on both sites is the same, you could not send traffic within the same ad group to those two separate domains.

Since this editorial rule is for each individual ad group, you can send traffic from one ad group to one domain (such as bgtheory.com) and then have the traffic from a second ad group sent to a different domain (such as ewhisper.net). Therefore, if you want to test two different domains, you can accomplish this by using two different ad groups.

Many of the display URL and destination URL policies revolve around where to send the visitor and are intertwined with each other. Therefore, always keep the policies of both these ad copy aspects in mind when writing destination and display URLs.

Choosing Landing Pages That Increase Conversion Rates

You can send traffic to any page on your website (assuming it conforms to editorial policies), but you will see drastic differences in conversion rates depending on where on your site you are sending your paid search traffic.

The best page is the one that answers the advertiser's question. Where on your site can they receive the answer to their original search question? Another way of thinking about this concept is to send traffic to the page that is the furthest logical page in your website that starts the conversion process for each keyword.

Note: Please remember that the searcher might have to buy a product, fill out a lead generation or contact form, or place a phone call to receive their answer. On your website, you are answering the question or showing the consumer how to receive the answer.

In most cases, this page will be the same for all keywords in the same ad group. If you have done the hard part of organizing your keywords granularly, then the keywords will often share the same landing page. There are exceptions to this rule based upon account organization, but in most cases this rule should hold true.

Consider these three points:

- People enjoy being lazy.
- People do not want more work.
- You are the expert on your website.

Why would you not choose the exact page on your site the visitor should see first? If you do not send someone to the best page on your site for the query, visitors will start to wander around your website, which will take them off the conversion path, or they will just hit the Back button and visit the next site on the list.

Taking the extra time to link your keywords or ad groups with the most specific page on your website will help keep visitors focused and moving down the buying funnel toward becoming a customer.

Choosing Landing Pages Based upon the Type of Query

To best determine a landing page, you need to understand the three main types of keyword queries:

Transactional Query Transactional queries are those in which there is an intent to buy. These are often called commercial.

Informational Query Informational queries, or noncommercial queries, are those in which the searcher is looking for a specific piece of information, or is trying to learn more about a specific item or concept.

Navigational Query Navigational queries are those in which the searcher is just trying to navigate to a specific website or webpage. There is often only one satisfactory result for the user. This type of query might be "Amazon.com Prime shipping information." In this case, the user wants to find one specific page on Amazon.com, and the other results hold little interest for the searcher.

These query types are described in detail in the following sections.

Leveraging Transactional Queries

The easiest examples to use when deciding where to send traffic are commercial-based queries. Most shopping carts have a home page that provides navigation into categories and from the category to the product page. Category pages showcase all of a product type (for instance, all Samsung or all DLP TVs), and finally, a product page highlights a single product. While many shopping carts contain many more types of pages, almost all have these three types of pages (home, category, and product).

When examining where to send traffic, imagine, for example, someone is doing a search for Samsung HL61A650 (which is the part number for a Samsung DLP TV) and you send the searcher to the home page of your site. In this instance, the visitor has to search again (or attempt to browse through your website) using the same query they just preformed on Google. This additional action of searching again is redundant and akin to giving the searcher more work. The more tasks you assign your visitors, the more visitors are going to refuse your tasks and go back to Google and look at your competitors' ads.

If you send the searcher to the Samsung DLP category page, the searcher then needs to look through the available selections and try to find the same TV. If your category pages do not have part numbers listed, or if the searcher knows your product under a different name than is listed, the visitor has no idea where to go next, and will often click the Back button.

If you send the searcher directly to the Samsung HL61A650 product information page, you have done the hard work of finding the best page for them. The searcher will spend less time trying to find the information and more time engaged with the information on your website. This example of a good search experience should lead to higher conversion rates.

If you know where on your website you should send traffic, why make the searcher take the time to find the information? The more freedom you give someone to wander around your site and make decisions, the lower the conversion rates you will see.

There is a balance between giving someone enough information and options to make a decision and maximizing conversion rates. Always make sure you answer the searcher's question. That and any offer made within the ad copy (such as free shipping) is the minimum amount of information you should present on your landing page.

While product searches are common on the Web, and an easy first example, let us examine some different classifications of search queries to see where conventional wisdom would suggest sending the traffic.

Getting Conversions from Informational Queries

A Pennsylvania State University study, "Determining the Informational, Navigational, and Transactional Intent of Web Queries," by Bernard Jansen, Danielle Booth, and Amanda Spink (http://ist.psu.edu/faculty_pages/jjansen/academic/pubs/jansen_user_intent.pdf) concluded that over 80 percent of all queries are informational, while the remaining 20 percent are about half navigational and half transactional. Often this information is misinterpreted to assume that only 10 percent of queries can lead to a purchase.

If we keep the buying funnel in mind, we are reminded that purchase decisions are usually based upon research and learning before buying. While there are informational queries that cannot be monetized, often informational queries are under-monetized, and one of the most common reasons is choosing an incorrect landing page.

If a searcher does not have enough information to make a decision, even a perfectly designed sales page will not convert most visitors. In some cases, the information may be on the product page, and sending a user to the product page is the best course of action.

It is important to look at your keywords and think like the searcher. If a searcher input a particular keyword, what scenario going on in their life might have caused that search? It is that scenario that your landing page needs to address. By addressing those scenarios, you can include additional information on the landing page to help you monetize informational queries.

For instance, the query "candle burning times" is an informational query. Often the ads for this type of query end up sending the user to a specific candle type or maybe a candle product page. Those pages do not have an easy way for the user to see the burning times of all the candles.

Why would someone want to know how long different candles burn? Here are a few reasons:

- Romantic dinner
- Religious service
- Emergency lighting
- Meditation
- Halloween haunted house
- Relaxing bath
- Wedding

The list could continue with hundreds of examples. In each of those instances, you could imagine wanting to know how long a candle will burn. For example, a host would not want his candles to burn down halfway through a dinner party.

Instead of sending the search traffic to a candle product page or category page, send them to a page that lists the types of candles (votive, taper, etc.) and how long those different candle models will burn. Then you can link the candle type, a call to action, or a buy-now button to the product pages so the visitor can buy the candle that best meets their needs.

Any Business Can Leverage Informational Queries

Informational queries and shopping carts are easy examples. However, the concept of answering the question and then showing a way for a searcher to do business with your company can be accomplished regardless of your business model.

What about Publishers?

If you are a publisher, such as a newspaper, most of your traffic will come from informational queries. Publishers often make money by selling ads to their advertiser base. Usually publishers are paid on an impression basis (often called CPM, cost per thousand impressions). Then the publisher buys traffic from a search engine. The difference between what they make on a page view from the ads they sold and the cost of the click they paid to the search engine is their profit. (Profit = income from displayed ad − cost per click.) If a searcher visits several pages, the publisher makes money on each page view. One of the key success metrics, and often a conversion action, for publishers is page views per visit. If publishers can double their page views per visit, they've increased their profits significantly.

Publishers generally have secondary conversions, such as subscriptions. It is important that publishers do not just measure page views for informational queries, but also their secondary conversions to determine not only what the click is worth to their company in terms of ad revenue, but to continue to optimize their paid subscription offerings that should be built into the page.

Often, informational queries have fewer advertisers, are cheaper clicks, but are harder for product companies to monetize. For publishers, this can be a big opportunity, especially on review or breaking news queries, to buy traffic and give the searcher the information they are seeking, and also attempt to sell that same visitor a subscription.

In April 2008, at the height of the tax season, a search for "sales tax deduction" in Washington, D.C. yielded zero ads for accounting firms (and only four total ads, all going to search result pages of various search engines). Yet a search for "sales tax deduction" was conducted over 50,000 times in the United States that same month. During April, bids for tax-based keywords skyrocket. This is another example of an informational keyword being under-monetized.

If your accounting firm can create a page that explains what sales tax deduction is and how your firm can help someone decide to use sales tax or income tax as their deduction, this can help your company monetize an informational query.

In this case, even if the informational query has a lower conversion rate than more commercial queries, the lack of advertisers will most likely cause this keyword to be an inexpensive click. Lower converting, inexpensive clicks can often result in a lower cost per acquisition than a high converting, expensive click.

Informational queries make up a large percentage of the total web searches. If you treat these types of searches like transactional searches where you just send visitors to shopping cart pages or form fills, you will not find a lot of success with informational queries.

If you answer the searcher's question first and then try to monetize the searcher based upon the information you presented to them, you will have much more success advertising on information-based keywords. Never forget to answer the searcher's question. That's the searcher's primary objective for conducting a search.

Once you have answered the question and the searcher has engaged with your website, then you should introduce commercial actions. Selling is not just about the best sales pitch. You need to wait for the proper moment to introduce the pitch.

Getting the Most from Navigational Queries

Navigational queries are difficult to monetize as the user is often looking for a specific company or webpage and only that result will satisfy their search.

For most companies, monetizing navigational queries for other companies is difficult. For example, a search for "barnes and noble" usually means someone wants to go to the Barnes & Noble website and does not want to go to Amazon.

You can attempt to buy some navigational queries to see how they work for your company, but they are keywords you should put in separate ad groups and watch the traffic. If these keywords are not providing clicks or conversions, feel free to delete these keywords.

If your business is not easily found for your brand terms, website name, or business name, then you will want to make sure you are buying those terms so searchers can find your website. If your product page is listed number one in the organic results for a navigational query, then you should test sending AdWords traffic to a different page. As ranking organically takes time and effort, and changing a page could jeopardize your rankings, testing dedicated PPC landing pages that are built for conversions can lead to higher profits.

In addition, if you are considering a site redesign, buy the navigational keywords to the new design to see if the new design will have a positive effect on the page's profitability.

Differentiating Local Business Queries

The term "local business" is often misunderstood. A local business is one with a physical address or that only serves a specific geographic area. This means that while the plumber down the street is a local business, so are Best Buy and JCPenney.

With local businesses, you first need to ask a few basic questions:

- Who is your target audience?
  - Locals
  - Non-locals (i.e., travelers)
- Who travels to whom?
  - Customer travels to business (Best Buy, lawyer)
  - Business travels to customer (plumber, lawn care)

- Where are the products sold?
  - Online
  - In store

Until you answer these questions, it is impossible to determine where to send a user.

If you have both a physical store and sell online, the rules of sending traffic are very similar to the commercial query information just listed. Adding additional conversion options, such as in-store pickup or the benefits of viewing a product in person, to your landing page gives consumers more reasons to do business with your company. If you do not sell online, the very first question to answer about local business marketing is with your target audience. Are they locals or non-locals?

Locals know the area. They understand your specific use of geography. They want to know if you serve their area or they want directions to your business. Only after the user is satisfied with the geographic issues will they examine whether they should do business with your company. We will focus on some of these distinguishing factors of why someone should do business with you instead of your competitors later in this chapter.

Non-locals are often business or leisure travelers. They do not immediately need to know that a hotel is located at a specific address, for example. Travelers want to know how close the hotel is to the airport, shopping districts, or major attractions. Your landing page should show what is around your location and why your hotel should be chosen over the competition.

You should not market to local and non-locals in the same way. These two groups have different knowledge sets about the area and different questions that need to be answered by your website. A local wants to know specific information right away. A non-local first needs to be reassured that they are in the correct place before moving to the next stage of evaluating your business.

These differences extend to the ad copy as well. Consider these two description lines for our example hotel:
- Located in the Water Tower
- 5 blocks from shopping district

Both refer to major shopping areas in downtown Chicago. A local already knows where the shopping districts are located; therefore telling them your hotel is five blocks away does not give them additional information. Informing a local that you are in the Water Tower gives them precise information to make a decision about traveling to the business.

Conversely, telling a non-local about the Water Tower is a waste of ad copy characters. If someone does not know where the Water Tower is located, why tell them your business location? Informing a non-local that your hotel is walking distance from the shopping district gives them the general information they need to know in planning for their trip.

With local advertising, you need to break down the messages based upon the user's knowledge of your area and based upon who needs to travel. Once a searcher is confident that your business serves their area, or they can easily travel to your business, only then should you move the visitor into the conversion funnel.

Using Segmentation Pages

There will be many times when you do not know the consumer intent of a keyword. It could be that the keyword is ambiguous or that the word could describe multiple aspects of your business. In these instances, using segmentation pages can help the consumer pick the option that describes their question. A segmentation page is where a user can self-select which aspect of your business they are interested in learning more about.

Consider a search for hotels or plane travel; is the searcher a business traveler or a leisure traveler? They each have different concerns; yet they will use the same keywords when searching for information.

The keyword "accounting jobs" could either mean a company is looking to hire an employee or that a searcher is looking for a job. By using a segmentation page (Figure 5.5), you can help the user find the correct information when the query is ambiguous.

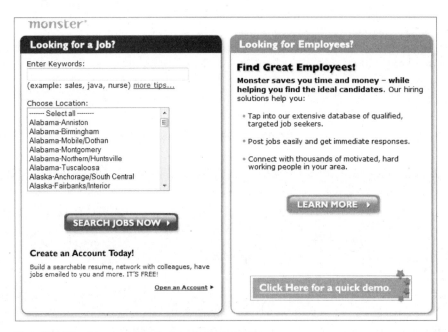

Figure 5.5   A Monster.com segmentation page for general queries

Segmentation pages are most commonly used with narrow theme sites, but they can also be useful even within a larger site to help narrow down choices. Consider the TV buying process. You ask the consumer to select an answer from each of these bullet points:

- TV Type (DLP, plasma, LCD)

- TV Size (63, 61, 55, 51, 43, or 28 inch)

- Price (Over $2,000, $1000–2000, under $1000)

Once you know those three answers, you will be able to narrow down which products are most relevant to the consumer. While the above is usually referred to as a category search or product refinement, the resulting page is a segmentation page, as it segments the products that are being presented to the user so the user can self-select which avenue to explore.

The downfall of a segmentation page is that it adds another page view and customer decision between the search query and the final conversion. The more pages in your conversion process and the more decisions you force someone to make, the higher your abandonment rate will be.

For most of your keywords, you will probably not need a segmentation page. If you have keywords that have multiple meanings or speak to different audiences, or if your website has multiple audience types, testing segmentation pages can allow you to successfully advertise on a larger set of keywords by presenting the consumer with an option for where to go next.

Using Forms as Landing Pages

The primary focus of your landing page can be a form. This is common if you are collecting contact information for lead generation or generating online quotes (such as insurance and mortgage).

While a form can be a good landing page, be sure you are also answering the searcher's question. It is common to see a scenario where a user searched for "merchant accounts," made it to the second page of the form, and then encountered a question such as, "What type of merchant account do you want?"

If the consumer has not learned about the different merchant accounts you offer, this question may cause them to abandon the form and start searching for different merchant account types. Make sure that product, company, or personal information you are asking for can be easily accessed from the form (Figure 5.6).

While the AdWords signup process is not perfect, it does contain some of the more important form elements:

- Easy-to-follow steps

- Short process that shows progression (top-left side)

- Ability to easily find additional information without abandoning the form

- Ability to contact company for more questions (although phone numbers are usually a good supplement to chat and contact-us links)

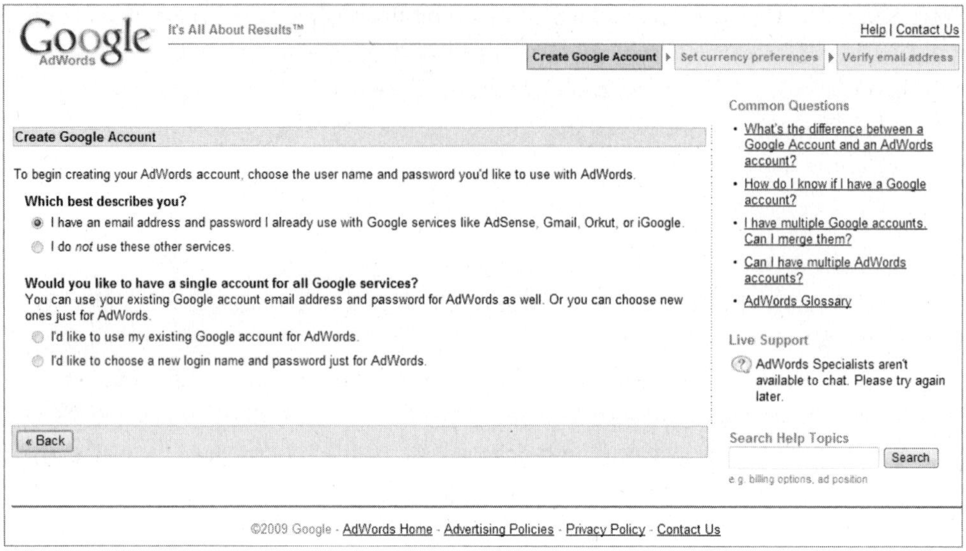

Figure 5.6 Google AdWords signup form contains FAQs on the right side

A good example of adding information to a form is the CVV (Card Verification Value) information from your credit card. Most credit cards have a three-digit code on the back of the card which is the security information for that card. It has become common practice to show a picture of where to find that information on the card. However, American Express is different from most cards. The security number on an American Express card is a four-digit number on the front. For some time, American Express card holders had a difficult time checking out on websites that either validated a three-digit CVV or did not show where to find the number on an American Express card.

An e-commerce checkout is also a form. While it will not be your landing page, ensuring the information a consumer needs can be accessed from your form is important regardless of where the form is on your website.

In addition, a page that is just a form is often not a good landing page as the consumer may not have enough information about your company or the products to make a decision. Your form landing pages should include benefits and calls to action within the text of the page.

In the English language, we read left to right, so it is usually best to put your text on the left and your form on the right so that searchers' eyes keep ending up at the form after reading your content.

As forms are such a common element of websites, we will cover forms more in the next chapter.

Thanking Your Customers

While thank-you pages are not landing pages, they are an essential part of your website that your converting traffic will see. If someone converts on your website, they trusted your company enough to give you a credit card number, email address, or phone number. This is the start of your relationship with a customer. A properly framed landing page can turn a simple inquiry into a relationship.

Some of the more common thank-you pages are:

- Thank you for shopping with us.

- Thank you for contacting us.

- Thank you for downloading our whitepaper.

While these thank-you pages are essential, they may be the least effectively utilized pages on the entire Web.

Thank-you pages are essential as they communicate to the customer that an action has been completed. But what does your thank-you page really say to the visitor?

- Thank you for shopping with us. You will receive an email with your shipping confirmation. Now go away.

- Thank you for contacting us. We will get back to you within 24 hours. We're done with you until we have time to call you back.

- Thank you for downloading our whitepaper. Enjoy reading our hard work. We hope you come back one day.

One of the hardest and most expensive goals to accomplish in marketing is to acquire a new customer. It is generally cheaper to maintain a customer than to gain a new customer. Thank-you pages can be the starting place of maintaining that relationship.

Instead of making your thank-you page a place where the visitor stops interacting with your website, give the visitor additional options:

- Thank you for shopping with us. Would you like to join our loyalty program and gain 10 percent off your next purchase?

- Thank you for contacting us. We will call you back within 24 hours. Here's a whitepaper about our company and products for you to read while we find the answer to your inquiry.

- Thank you for downloading our whitepaper. Would you like to subscribe to our newsletter to stay on top of industry trends?

You can have multiple conversion funnels on your website. If your first conversion funnel is an e-commerce checkout; your next conversion funnel should be for the user to either join your newsletter or join your loyalty program.

It is also useful to cross-sell or up-sell from within your website. Adding a subscription form to a "thank you for shopping" page, or driving a consumer into an e-commerce experience after downloading a whitepaper, is acceptable as long as the consumer is finding their information and trusting your website. You rarely want to surprise a user, but adding some twists here and there can be useful if the customer is having a good experience on your site. Of course, to find out if they are having a good experience, you need a solid analytics platform in place to make sure they are continuing on your website after seeing some of these options.

If you are a B2B company with a six-month sales cycle, do not waste the opportunity to keep communicating with a potential client. Do not just let them download a whitepaper and walk away. Let the customer download the whitepaper and then subscribe to your newsletter or request a product demonstration.

The thank-you page is a great place to test:

- Loyalty programs
- Customer satisfaction surveys
- Downloads such as whitepapers or catalogs
- Offers to tell a friend or other social media options such as "join our Facebook page"

Changing the messaging on your thank-you pages from being an ending point to a continuation point so you can keep moving visitors through your conversion funnels is essential to increasing the profitability of your company.

Crafting Perfect Landing Pages

The perfect landing page is one that answers the searcher's question and accomplishes your marketing goal. In this scenario, the searcher is satisfied with what they have learned (which could be a new accounting firm to handle their taxes, a purchase, or a new subscription) and you have accomplished your marketing goal, which is usually what keeps your company open and in business.

There will be many times when you are not sure where to send the traffic. In these cases, you can test different landing pages and different layouts for those pages. Testing your landing pages is essential to refining your marketing efforts and receiving the highest return for your marketing investment dollars. We will cover how to test ad copy, landing pages, and traffic extensively in Chapter 15.

Choosing a landing page is the first step in sending visitors to your website. The next step is making sure the visitor can easily find the information on your landing page. This does not just mean that the webpage contains the answer, but that the webpage is coded in such a way that the user can both find and read your information so they can continue to interact with your website.

Employing Usability, Trust, and Web Technology to Increase Your Conversion Rates

Usability is a catchall word used to describe how well users can navigate, find information, and accomplish their goals on your website. Usability is often associated with users. However, usability should also be associated with conversion rates. If a user cannot find information on your website, they cannot complete an action.

If a user does not trust your website, they will click the Back button. With the increasing number of phishing attacks, security concerns, and worms and viruses, users are becoming more concerned with protecting their computer and personal information. If your site does not appear trustworthy, you will see visitors quickly leave.

Providing a good experience on your website is not just so users have a better experience and will return, it also ensures they can convert and your business can make money with your online marketing efforts.

As usability is so important, there are entire books devoted to the subject. In this section, we will highlight some of the more important and essential usability elements to ensure your website has embraced the basics.

There are two main aspects to usability and conversion analysis: technical and psychological.

Technical aspects stem from the technology being used by both the visitor and the website to render the information. Different browsers, operating systems, servers, plug-ins, and your website's code can completely change how a visitor sees and interacts with your information.

The second major factor that affects your usability is psychological: how a visitor sees, understands, trusts, and is persuaded by your website. There are subtle ways of using images, color, and testimonials that can help increase your website's profit.

Using Web Technology to Implement Usability and User Security

The foundation of any website is the actual code. There are different ways you can code your website so it has the exact same look and feel. However, while your website might appear the same on the surface, there are other technical issues (such as browsers or operating systems) that might render your website differently.

The browser market is diverse, offering Internet Explorer, Firefox, Safari, Opera, Chrome, and several others. Some are aimed at special market segments, such as social network users. There are three different browsers with over 15 percent of the market share each. Four operating systems (Windows XP, Windows Vista, Windows 7, and Mac OS), combined with various browsers and dozens of ways to code your website, create almost infinite variations of ways your website could be viewed.

Luckily, there are only a few major factors that you need to be concerned with when examining the technical aspects of usability on your website, as explained in the following sections.

Accessible Information

The text on a website can be coded in a few different ways. There are usually two outcomes to the coding:
- Font size is absolute (i.e., is not rendered smaller or larger in a browser).
- Font size is relative (can be rendered smaller or larger in a browser).

If your website that sells eyeglasses is coded in absolute font, and a searcher has their browser set to show larger text (Figure 5.7), the searcher will still see your small text. If someone cannot read your website, they cannot convert on your website.

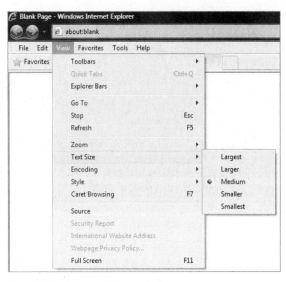

Figure 5.7 Resizing text in Internet Explorer

It is important to take a look at your demographics. If your website caters to groups that use screen readers or surf your website while viewing a larger font size, ensure they can view your information in their preferred font size. Do not take away someone's ability to read your site.

Browser Compatibility

Different browsers render sites in different ways. Your site could look one way in Firefox and another way in Internet Explorer. You should surf your website, checkout, test your contact forms, and so forth in the browsers used by your visitors to ensure they can actually convert on your website regardless of their browser choice.

w3schools.com maintains global statistics on browser, JavaScript, screen resolution, and many other web stats. As of November 2009, this is what w3schools.com report is the browser market share:

2009	IE7	IE6	IE8	Firefox	Chrome	Safari	Opera
November	13.3%	11.1%	13.3%	47%	8.5%	3.8%	2.3%

You can always view the updated information at this URL: `www.w3schools.com/browsers/browsers_stats.asp`.

Between Firefox (47 percent), and all versions of IE (37.7 percent) if your website worked in both browsers, could you assume that 84.7 percent of all traffic could view your website?

The answer is an absolute no. These numbers are global statistics and may not apply to your site at all.

For instance, my blog's (bgtheory.com/blog) statistics (Figure 5.8) show a very different picture of Chrome usage.

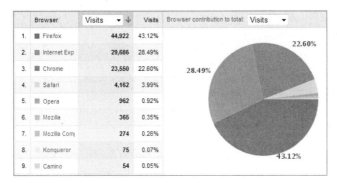

Figure 5.8 Google Chrome is 22.6 percent of Theory blog traffic.

If you examined the global browser usage statistics, you might not even test your site in Chrome. This is why you should look at your analytics system to determine what browsers your actual visitors are using. In this case, Chrome is more than 22 percent of the traffic and is an essential browser to test to ensure that visitors can convert on your website.

Note: Never rely on global statistics to show you the entire picture of your site. Use actual data to determine how your site needs to be coded for your visitors.

When testing your website in different browsers, install just the default version of the browser, as many people do not change the default settings. Here's how to do this in Internet Explorer: Go to Tools > Internet Options > Advanced Options. There you can reset the browser to its default conditions (Figure 5.9).

There are many errors that you can tell your browser not to display to you again. If you choose not to see these errors, then you cannot find them when surfing your website.

In general, look to see which browsers contribute more than 5 percent of your traffic (if you see a browser with a small percentage of traffic, but a high conversion rate, you should also include it) and keep a default installation of those browsers on your computer. For Firefox, you can add a new profile that contains the default settings.

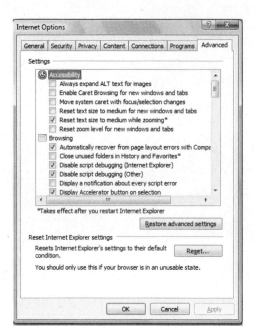

Figure 5.9 Advanced Internet Explorer options

When you make changes to your site, load up each browser and surf through your site. Are there navigational elements that are not loading? Checkout on your site (or complete all conversion activities); are there some actions you cannot accomplish?

There are also services, such as AnyBrowser.com (`http://anybrowser.com/siteviewer.html`) that help you see your site in different browsers. There is no substitute to having someone check your site in an actual browser, but sometimes these services are useful if you do not have multiple operating systems or computer types (such as a Mac) in your office.

In addition, often a developer browser version is launched before the final public version. Your design team can test your website in new versions—before your customers think your site is broken.

Enhancing Browser Functionality: Flash, Java, and Plug-Ins

Most plug-ins are optional. Installing Firefox does not mean your computer suddenly has Flash support. Microsoft Silverlight, for example, is essential for seeing graphics on particular websites (Figure 5.9). But ask yourself: do your visitors want to see the graphics enough to install something unknown on their computer?

Most users will not install additional software to view a page. In some cases, it could be that their browser does not support particular plug-ins (especially on a mobile device). Other users do not trust plug-ins as they don't know what side effects they might cause with their computer or browser. Rather than extend the functionality of their browsers, these users are cautious and no amount of cajoling will ever get them to install a plug-in. It is just as easy for these users to find similar products or services on a different site. This is where your analytics system can let you know how many of your visitors do not have Flash, Java, or other plug-ins installed.

Figure 5.10 MSN toolbar page without Silverlight installed

If your website uses plug-ins, and even 10 percent of your users do not have support for those plug-ins, you are immediately lowering the number of possible conversions on your website.

It is also important to note that robots (those programs search engines use to index the Web) have very rudimentary understanding of Flash and other scripts. If your navigation is in all Flash or all JavaScript, a robot might not be able to index your entire website.

Note: There are two plug-ins for Firefox that make it easy to view your website without certain features (such as Java or CSS) enabled. The first is a very powerful plug-in called the Web Developer toolbar. The second is Flashblock, which simply turns Flash on or off.

This does not mean you should not use Flash or other plug-ins across your website. It means you should be aware of your users' browser capabilities to ensure they can navigate and convert on your website based on how your website is coded.

Is Your Website Fast for Everyone?

The numbers for U.S. broadband penetration rates vary significantly. Some studies say that more than 60 percent of users have broadband at home. Others claim that more than 75 percent of the country still does not have broadband. The issues that come into play that create such a wide span of statistics are broadband type (DSL, FiOS, cable), ISP traffic throttling, and how fast a connection has to be before it's considered high-speed.

Regardless of the numbers involved, the United States and Canada have a large number of users who are on slow networks. Typically, rural areas have slower connections than urban areas, but even in urban centers, there are plenty of users on slow connections.

Impatience is a common human trait. People with slow connections are not granted more patience than those on a broadband connection. Therefore, you should consider how long it takes your site to load on all connections. Are you losing visitors because all your images are high resolution? They may only take a few seconds to load on your connection, but five minutes to load on a dial-up connection.

Examine your analytics to see if you have a large percentage of visitors on slow connections. If 99 percent of your visitors are using broadband, it might not make financial sense to add another version of your website.

Securing the User's Data: SSL Certificates

Users are becoming increasingly aware of and concerned about the security of their data online. If you accept personal information, especially credit cards, having an SSL certificate is a necessity.

Secure Sockets Layer (SSL) and the newer Transport Layer Security (TLS) encrypt data sent from a browser to a website so the data is harder to intercept and provide greater security for the users' information. Most host providers can help you set up a security layer for your website. VeriSign and GeoTrust are two of the leaders in providing security for websites.

It is useful to not just have a security layer for your website, but to also let users know their data is secure. This can increase users' trust of your website and help increase conversion rates.

When adding secure layers, it is important to look through your website for one of the more common errors on the Web: the browser message that some content on the page is not secure (Figure 5.11).

Figure 5.11 Security error warning

The error shown in Figure 5.11 is for Internet Explorer; each browser displays security error messages differently.

Usually, but by no means always, this is not a nefarious error. It commonly occurs when a logo or script is being rendered on a secure page from a nonsecure server. To fix this error, view the source of your webpage (either by right-clicking and choosing View Page Source or navigating to the View menu and choosing Page Source), and look for images, scripts, and other files where the source is http instead of https.

The worst error is when the browser interrupts the process of loading a website, informs the searcher that there is an issue with the website's security certificate, and asks if they really want to continue (Figure 5.12). This keeps any part of the page from loading until the user has made a choice. If a user sees this screen instead of your website after clicking on an AdWords ad, their most likely action will be to leave the website immediately.

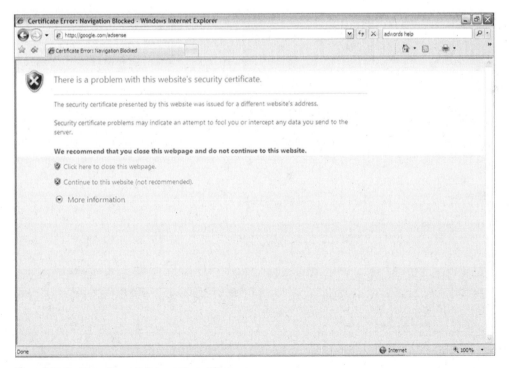

Figure 5.12 Problem with a website's security certificate

Data security is going to continue to be a growing concern. Do not let this easy-to-fix technical issue lower your conversion rates. Keep your customers' data safe and let them know that the information they send you is secure.

Is Your Information Above the Fold?

What a consumer first sees in their browser when your website loads is known as *above the fold*. This is information the visitor sees without having to either scroll down or to the right. It is your website's first impression.

The most complex issue with the above the fold concept is that monitors come in all shapes and sizes. Some laptops have only nine-inch monitors, while some wide-screen monitors are more than two feet wide. This creates a scenario where there is no definite above the fold that you can code into your website.

This is another place where your analytics system can tell you about your visitors (Figure 5.13). While w3schools.com does publish statistics about the most common browser resolutions, those stats do not necessarily apply to you. If your target audience is business travelers, you may see some very small browser resolutions with the advancement of ultraportable laptops. If your audience is web developers, you may see some extremely large browser resolution sizes.

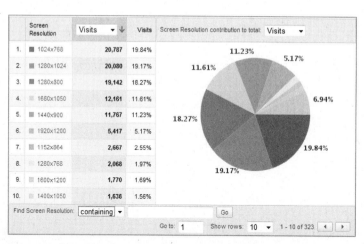

Figure 5.13 Google Analytics showing visitor browser resolutions

Harald Weinreich, Hartmut Obendorf, Eelco Herder, and Matthias Mayer published a paper titled *Off the Beaten Tracks: Exploring Three Aspects of Web Navigation* in which they examined where people clicked after arriving at a website. Table 5.4 highlights why showcasing your most important information—especially the actions you want someone to take—at the top of your website can dramatically increase conversion rates.

► **Table 5.4** Where Users Click

TableHeadCol1	Visible area	Right of visible area
Visible area	76.5 percent	0.3%
Below visible area	23.1%	0.1%

As more than three-fourths of all clicks occur in the area that loads above the fold, you always want your call to action, major benefits, and conversion actions above the fold. Users do not scroll right. If you have a website where a user has to scroll horizontally to see more of your website, most visitors will never see that information.

Note: The Firefox add-on Firesizer allows you to see your website in different resolutions. This is a useful plug-in to quickly view how your website looks in different browser sizes.

The concept of above the fold is both a technical concept as it concerns your website's coding and a psychological concept as it showcases human behavior and where consumers look for information.

The proper coding and security of your website can increase your website's usability and trust. These concepts can be enhanced by examining additional psychological factors that help your website convert browsers into buyers.

Psychological Factors That Increase Conversion Rates

It is easy to get caught up in a world of statistics that make you blind to the actual person sitting behind the computer. Stats do not pull out their credit card and buy from your website. You need to convince the human who is referenced in those statistics to pick up the phone and call your business.

Next we will examine several ways your website can convey trust and usefulness to the user.

Testimonials and Reviews Lead to Sociability

There are two truths about humans that have been proven over and over again in studies:

- People act differently when they are alone than in a group.
- People conform to those around them.

Often the word "conform" is taken harshly, but try these two experiments and see what happens:

- During a face-to-face conversation, keep looking over someone's shoulder at something in the distance.
- Stand in the middle of your office (or on a street corner) and stare up.

How long did it take for someone to stop and try to determine where you were looking? Humans are social creatures, and we want to feel included within the group around us.

Browsing the Web is an isolated activity. Rarely do searchers sit on the couch with a group of friends and search for information. Rarely do searchers have someone sitting next to them telling them where to click next or to scroll down the page. Therefore, you need to find ways to make the solitary activity of browsing the Web more social and instill a sense of being included in a group; doing so can change the way people feel about your site. The two most common examples of this are the use of testimonials and reviews. These two items are very closely related as they are the words of actual people who have used a product or a company's services.

When reading reviews or testimonials, people are no longer alone. They no longer have to form an opinion about a website by themselves. Now a searcher can incorporate the opinions of others in forming their decision about a product or service that your company offers.

Featuring testimonials or reviews on your landing pages or the page where someone is making a decision about using your service (or buying your product) often leads to higher conversion rates.

Note: Be careful about using fake reviews or testimonials. The old axiom about "if something looks too good to be true, it usually is" also applies. Often reviews contain some positive and some negative information. People have different writing styles, and the adjectives and phrases used in reviews should vary accordingly. It is generally easy to spot fake reviews. This can hurt your credibility more than not having reviews in the first place.

Testimonials are usually positive, but allowing some testimonials that contain both positive and negative information shows that you are human like everyone else. This is something to test, not just blindly incorporate. For example, a testimonial might say, "Phil's Accounting Service did our taxes quickly and saved us a couple thousand dollars, but they are slow to respond on the phone and prefer communicating via email or in person." There will be some people who do not care that Phil is slow on the phone, as they prefer email communication. In this case, the negative information that made the review seem honest is actually positive for some people. Other searchers will just like the fact that Phil saved people some money and will want to see how Phil can help them.

Just remember, your primary goal is to ensure that your visitor feels part of a group and to raise your conversion rates. If your reviews and testimonials are not changing conversion rates, you need to examine why that is happening. We all like to feel included. Utilizing testimonials, reviews, or other social aspects in your website can help turn a solitary decision into an easier one as the searcher joins a group that has already enjoyed using your company.

Associations: What Company Do You Keep?

Many industries have governing bodies, associations, and networks that are well recognized within that particular industry. Showing which associations you are a member of is another way to instill trust in your visitors. You may be able to go beyond just showing your associations to why you are a market leader. Include any awards received within your field, speaking engagements, press clippings, and other demonstrations of authority to your visitors.

For example, at this point you have read almost five entire chapters of this book, yet you know little about the author. If I were to show just a small sample of associations and statements that I have been able to use over the past few years for myself or companies I have worked for, the list would look something like this:

- Google AdWords Seminar Leader
- Google AdWords Professional
- Google AdWords Qualified Company
- Google AdWords reseller
- Microsoft adExcellence member
- Yahoo! Search Ambassador
- SEO class speaker
- 2008 SEMMY runner-up
- 2009 SEMMY nominee
- Certified Yahoo! Affiliate
- Member of the American Marketing Association
- Member of the eMarketing Association
- Member of Search Marketing Association of North America
- Member of Search Engine Marketing Professional Organization (SEMPO)
- Speaker at SES Latino
- Speaker at ad:tech Latino
- Speaker at Search Engine Strategies Chicago
- Speaker at Search Engine Strategies New York
- Speaker at Search Engine Strategies San Jose
- Speaker at Search Engine Strategies Local
- Speaker at Search Marketing Expo (SMX) Local
- Speaker at Search Marketing Expo Advanced
- Speaker at Pubcon Boston
- Speaker at Pubcon Vegas
- Local Search Ranking Factors contributor

- Search Engine Land columnist
- Over 100 hours of public speaking in each of the last three years

By now, most readers will have a different opinion of the material they are reading based upon the author's authority. This is due to our ever-changing expectations based upon the information we have with which to make decisions. While I listed many associations, there is no mention of any business I've worked with or worked for; it is only a list that helps to gain trust.

It can be useful to also show your partnerships and featured clients. Most people will assume that if a company chose to work with you, that company did their due diligence in researching your company before engaging your services. This statement is even truer if the featured client is a well-known business. Most people assume that Amazon does more research than Joe's Used Books in choosing a partner. Essentially, there is a transference of trust from the featured client or partner to your business.

People are also visual, and images can quickly show your authority instead of just bullet points (Figure 5.14). If you can use association seals or images, they can help break up the text on the page with subtle reminders of your authority.

Figure 5.14 Brad Geddes's associations

The goal is for visitors to be able to examine your company and quickly find reasons why you are a better company to engage with than your competitors. If you have symbols of authority, or memberships in organizations such as the Better Business Bureau or Chamber of Commerce, test using them on your website.

Using Coupons or Discounts

A common marketing tactic is to offer coupons or discounts. If you use either of these items in the ad copy, make sure you also show the same offers on your landing page.

It is common to see a discount code listed in an ad. The user clicks to the landing page and does not see the discount code. They navigate through the site, add items to the shopping cart, and go to checkout. If they cannot remember the code, they often go back to the search engine to try and find the code. If the searcher cannot find the same ad again, they can become frustrated and abandon the cart completely.

Reinforcing the discount code on the landing page, or even adding the code to a navigational frame so that it stays with the user throughout that visit can help increase conversion rates, as the visitor will not have to abandon the shopping cart to find the coupon.

Using coupons is also a way to track in-store shopping. If you have both a physical store and an online store, it can be difficult to see your marketing effectiveness. By tracking in-store coupon redemption from your AdWords visitors, you can start to see if your AdWords campaigns are driving visitors into your store.

The end of 2008 saw a higher increase in searches for coupons and discount codes than previous months. In a down economy, consumers become more price conscious. By not only advertising discounts, but buying those keywords on your products ("discount TV," "TV coupon"), you can bring additional visitors to your website.

Using coupons is also a way to increase customer loyalty. If you have an email marketing list, make sure you showcase your coupons in your newsletters.

A 2008 survey by Prospectiv (`www.prospectiv.com/press172.jsp`) found that consumers find 15 percent of their coupons on websites and 6 percent in newsletters. However, when asked where they would like to receive coupons, 16 percent said on websites and 26 percent said in email. There is currently a large gap between where coupons are found and where consumers would like to receive their coupons. Use that gap to your advantage by giving your customers what they would like.

Using Images to Direct a Consumer's Focus

People are drawn to images of other people. That is a well-known fact. We are compelled to not just look at images of people, but to look closely at their faces. Earlier in this chapter, we saw how if you look behind someone while talking to them, the person will turn and look at where you are looking. The same thing happens on the Web with images of people. If you have a face on your website, searchers will follow the eyes in the picture to see where they are looking.

If your image is at the bottom-right corner of the page, often consumers will skip your text content to look at the image. If the image is then looking down and to the right—where if you drew a line from the eyes they would be looking off the monitor onto the desk—the searchers' eyes will no longer be on your website, but distracted by elements on their desk.

Make sure that if you use faces on your website that the image is looking back into your content at either your major benefits or the Submit button where you want them to take action. Images are excellent to use on websites as they break up the monotony of text. However, you must make sure that the image is enhancing your conversion rates and not distracting your visitors.

What Color Is Your Website?

The subtle use of color is another way to subconsciously influence your visitors. Some common color associations are:

- Green conveys trust or money.
- Red conveys aggressiveness.
- Blue is calming.
- Black and white are neutral colors.

However, even within colors there are variations of meaning. Deep purple is associated with royalty and riches while light purple is romantic. Experimenting with color on your website can lead to combinations that are highly effective; just be careful with your meanings.

Red might seem like a good color for a DUI attorney as they need to go in and fight. Red is probably not a good color for a family planning attorney. Green conveys both trust and money, which is a good color if you are a nonprofit trying to attract donations, but it might make you seem expensive if you are selling stocks.

You must also be careful with overuse of a color. Looking at blue for too long can cause one to go from a calm state to almost a depressed state (that's why it's called "the blues").

White works well with any other color, and it is easy to read black text on a white background. In general, you do not want to overdo background colors where someone must spend a lot of time reading. A poorly chosen color scheme can doom your website to failure. In the United States, Canada, and western Europe, most users prefer light background colors, with other colors used to denote different aspects of a website (such as sidebars, navigation bars, and headers). Most websites should not be bold and sparkly, but that is not always true if you are trying to reach a younger demographic, for example. This is why it's important to test different color schemes (more about testing in Chapter 15).

Beyond just your website's navigation bar and sidebars, experiment with the color of your Submit button. A red Submit button on a white and blue page stands out from all other elements. If your page only has one or two conversion activities, using a different color for those actions can help those items draw visitors' eyes.

Buttons vs. Text Links for Conversion Activities

Most websites have several links on any one page. If your call to action is also a link, it can get lost in the myriad of other links and text on the page. A button stands out from the rest of a page, making it more effective than a text link, and it invites the visitor to take action.

Consider the three possible links shown in Figure 5.15. Which stands out the most to you?

Figure 5.15 Button and text links

If you use buttons, only use one or two on a page. You do not want to overuse them so they no longer stand out. Changing your main actions (such as add to cart, checkout, subscribe, download, etc.) from a link to a button should have an effect on conversion rates.

Privacy Policies

Privacy policies are at a crossroads in several countries. In the United States, a privacy policy is not required, but if you have a privacy policy it becomes a legal document that you must follow. This is a general statement, and not necessarily true for all industries and company types, such as public, private, and governmental, within the United States.

Adding a privacy policy can be a difficult choice for a company to make. There will be users who look for a privacy policy before submitting their information. If you wish to maximize your conversion rates, adding a privacy policy should help. In addition, one of Google's mantras for websites is transparency to the user. Google suggests that websites have privacy policies. They require them for AdSense publishers, but not for advertisers. Falling in line with Google's guidelines often leads to higher quality scores.

Your privacy policy could state, "We will sell your data to anyone who is willing to buy it." Now, that might not increase conversion rates for those who read it, but if you are trying to be transparent to the user, at least they know what will happen if they give you their email address.

Everyone is concerned about spam these days. Most searchers want empathy and reassurance more than they want to read through an entire privacy policy. Just by adding a small message to your Submit button (Figure 5.16) you can help reassure your visitors that they will not end up with spam from your company.

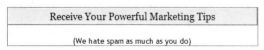

Figure 5.16 Add empathy and a benefit to your Submit button.

Your Website's Usability Goals

There are many books devoted to website usability. There is no way to cover all of the possible tricks and elements in just one chapter. We have also examined conversion elements such as associations (and we will examine more about increasing conversions in the next chapter). What you should take away is that your website should accomplish these tasks:

- Allow the customer to find the answer to their question
- Allow the searcher to easily find information about your products and services
- Allow the customer to be able to access that information regardless of their browser, operating system, or eyesight
- Instill a sense of trust
- Showcase your authority
- Protect the privacy and data of your customers
- Make the conversion process easy

If your website can accomplish these goals, you can engage the customer and hold their attention. This is the first step to increasing conversion rates: making sure your website is accessible, readable, and trustworthy. If you cannot accomplish these three actions, the quality of your services and products do not matter, as searchers will not stay on your website long enough to learn more about your offerings.

Your landing page is the first impression a visitor has about your website. Therefore, you should examine the usability and conversion paths of your landing page very closely. Most websites are not a single page, so incorporating these elements over your entire website is also a must for increasing your website's effectiveness.

Best Practices for Landing Pages

Devising the right landing pages is a crucial technique for converting searchers into buyers. A misstep here can send potential customers back to square one or to rival sites. The following are some crucial issues that you must address to enhance your potential for success:

- Make sure that your landing page answers the searcher's questions—not the search query itself, but the searcher's need to know whether your site can fulfill their needs.

- Craft the destination URL to comply with Google's editorial policy and to add additional tracking information that you can utilize to see how AdWords visitors navigate and convert on your website.

- Send the user to a page on your site that is the furthest logical page within the buying funnel for your website or a page dedicated to the search query.

- Correctly directing AdWords traffic is crucial. To do so, you need to understand the different types of user queries: transactional, informational, and navigational.

- Your site must be user friendly and trustworthy in the mind of your potential customer. You can accomplish these goals by understanding web technologies and using those technologies to your advantage.

- Use testimonials, reviews, and certifications to show that not only can your website be trusted, but your business can be trusted.

By utilizing the techniques in this chapter, you should be able to accomplish a good conversion rate. In the next chapter, we will examine techniques for bringing more visitors to your site and ways of increasing the conversions of those who view your landing pages and interact with your website.

Advanced Optimization Techniques

Once you have done the difficult part of choosing keywords and writing ad copy, you will start to see some results from your campaigns. Based on these, you can optimize your account in a few ways.

The first optimization technique increases traffic to your website. We will address how to gain more impressions and more clicks from them. Once you have visitors, learn how to gain more page views from them.

The second technique increases conversion rates. Learn techniques that increase these rates and address additional conversion types to help move visitors through the buying funnel.

6

Chapter Contents
Optimizing for Traffic
Optimizing for Conversions
Best Practices for Advanced Optimization Techniques

Optimizing for Traffic

The most common analytics metrics to examine for any website are total page views and unique visitors. How many different people visited your website? How many page views did those visitors generate? The reasons these metrics are useful is they give a high-level picture of your website's exposure.

While these are common metrics for website measurement, they can also be applied to any AdWords advertising campaign. How often were your ads shown (keyword impressions), how often were they clicked, and how engaged were those visitors with your website (page views or conversion rates)?

These numbers are important because they will direct you toward what type of traffic optimization you need. If you have a good click-through rate (CTR is clicks divided by impressions), then you need more impressions. If you have plenty of impressions, but very few clicks, then you need to raise your CTR.

Often publishers are paid per page view by selling cost per thousand impressions (CPM) ads. In that case, a conversion can be counted for each page view, and increasing page views per visitor has a direct influence on the site's profitability.

You might find increasing page views useful if you have an e-commerce or a local business website, especially if you have one customer recruit another person to visit your website, or if you want more total visitors to see your offerings. These viral characteristics help you receive multiple customers from a single click.

First, we will look at techniques for increasing traffic to the website. Then we will examine various methods to receive multiple visitors from a single click.

Exploring Strategies That Display Your Ads More Often

Before you can determine how to receive more impressions for your ad, you need to know why your ad is not being shown in the first place.

The first setting to examine is your daily budget. If you are spending your daily budget every single day, then odds are you are capping your impressions due to budget limitations. In this case you have two options:

Raise Your Daily Budget If you raise your daily budget, your ads should be shown more often. Your CPCs (cost per click) and cost per conversion should remain stable.

Lower Your Bids If you lower your bids, your ads may receive more impressions and clicks for the same budget. This is not a guarantee, as some of your keywords may not have a high enough CPC to be displayed on page 1, which will end up lowering your total impressions.

If your average position is 5 or higher, it is usually best to lower CPCs. If your average position is below 5, lowering your CPCs may or may not gather more impressions. This average position is a rough rule of thumb as sometimes there are 12 ads on a page, and other times there may be a maximum of 8 depending on how many ads are shown above the organic results (more about the premium ad slots when we discuss quality score in Chapter 7).

> **Note:** It is not uncommon to see different conversion rates by position. We will examine this phenomenon in Chapter 13. The two other major items that can limit your ad exposure are ad scheduling (Chapter 13) and geography (Chapter 11). If you have chosen to only show your ads between 1:00 a.m. and 2:00 a.m. in Fargo, North Dakota, for example, then you will not see many impressions.

When you lower bids, there is no guarantee that your conversion rate or cost per conversion will stay the same. If you do not want to spend more but want to receive more clicks, then lowering bids is useful. However, daily budget is the most common reason your ad is not being shown. If you are not reaching your daily budget, or would like more information about why your ads are not being shown even if you are reaching your daily budget, the first step is to run the impression share report.

Creating and Reading an Impression Share Report

Impression share report is the name the industry has adopted for one of the AdWords reports. This report will tell you the percentage of times your ad was shown when it was eligible to be shown and the reasons it was not displayed. For instance, if you set your ad to be shown only between 1:00 p.m. to 2:00 p.m., and the user searched at 4:00 p.m., your ad was not eligible to be shown.

To create this report, select the Campaign Performance report option from within the AdWords interface. Under the optional advanced settings section, check the boxes that contain "IS" (Figure 6.1), which stands for impression share.

Campaign	Ad Distribution	Impressions	Clicks	CTR	Impression Share (IS)	Lost IS (Budget)	Exact Match IS

Level of Detail : These columns reflect this report's coverage and level of detail

☑ Campaign

Attributes : These columns report on your current ad settings and status

☑ Ad Distribution ☐ Ad Distribution: with search partners ☐ Daily Budget
☐ Campaign Status

Performance Statistics : These columns feature data about how your ads are performing

☑ Impressions ☑ Clicks ☐ Invalid Clicks ⑦
☐ Invalid Clicks Rate ⑦ ☑ CTR ☐ Avg CPC
☐ Avg CPM ☑ Impression Share (IS) ⑦ ☐ Lost IS (Rank)
☑ Lost IS (Budget) ☑ Exact Match IS ⑦ ☐ Cost
☐ Avg Position

Figure 6.1 Creating an impression share report

You can run this report with additional data fields if you wish, but the impression metrics are the minimum amount of data you need to examine. Once the report has been created, you will have a high level snapshot of your current impressions and why your ads are not showing, causing you to lose impressions (Figure 6.2).

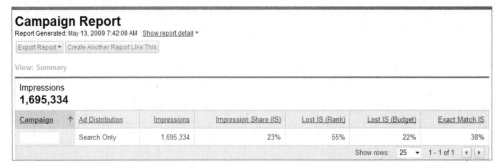

Figure 6.2 Reading impression share report results

The first three columns give you general information, such as the campaign name, the ad distribution, and the number of impressions the campaign has received during the time frame you chose for the report.

The fourth column, Impression Share (IS), is the percentage of time your ads were shown. In this instance, the ads were only shown 23 percent of the time when they were eligible to be shown. Eligible to be shown means the number of times the searcher could have seen your ad, based on your campaign's ad scheduling choices, network options, keyword choices, and geography.

When your impression share is 85 to 95 percent or above, depending on how many advertisers are in your industry, it is very difficult—sometimes impossible—to raise your impression share. This is due to the sheer number of ads and advertisers Google is trying to serve.

The fifth column, Lost IS (Rank), shows the percentage of times your ads were not shown because of your rank—your ad's position. If your ad position was too low to be shown on page 1 and the user did not go to page 2, then your ad lost its impression due to its rank being too low. In this case, raising your quality score (see Chapter 7) or your bids is one of the few ways to receive these impressions. There are situations where you might always lose some impressions due to rank.

To illustrate a situation in which you might lose impression share even if your average position is number one, consider this scenario:

- Search partner only shows two ads.

- Keyword is ultra-competitive only in Miami.

- Companies in Miami bid 500 percent normal cost price for this keyword.

Micro-situations like this exist, and trying to track down areas where you are only losing a few percentage points of rank might not be worth your time—even if you found it, you still might not raise your bid to a profitable level.

The sixth column is Lost IS (Budget). This column shows the percentage of time that your ads were not shown because your daily budget was too low. Once your daily budget is exhausted, your ad no longer shows for that day. If you are consistently reaching your daily budget, you will want to consider raising it to receive more impressions. If you have a high daily budget that is rarely reached, and you see that you are losing impressions due to budget, there are a couple other common possibilities:

- The keyword was in the news and created an unusually high search activity for that keyword.

- Your keyword's search volume changes based upon day of the week or month, and that's the only time you are losing impressions.

In these scenarios, try running the impression share report over different time periods and then comparing the reports. You may see some days or months where your ad is shown much more often than other periods of time.

The Lost IS (Budget), Lost IS (Rank), and Impression Share (IS) columns should equal 100 percent.

The last column, Exact Match IS, is a bit tricky to work with. Exact match impression share is how often your ads would show if all your keywords were set to exact match. If all your keywords are exact match, this column should be 100 percent. The higher this number, the more impressions you would receive if you added phrase or broad match variations of your keywords.

When examining your share of voice, or online visibility, the first place to start is learning how often your ads are not being shown due to the limitations you have put on your account. If your ads are not being shown due to rank or budget, those are easy fixes. If your impression share report shows that your ads are being shown most of the time, then the only way to increase your impressions is to add new keywords.

The impression share report only measures impressions for search. There are often new impressions available from the content network, which we will discuss in Chapter 9 and Chapter 10.

But what if your ad is being shown and you want more of those clicks? The second way to optimize for more clicks is not to get more impressions, but to make better use of the impressions you are receiving by increasing your click-through rate.

Taking Advantage of Dynamic Keyword Insertion

When someone does a search on Google, their search query is bolded in both ad copy and organic results on the search results page. In general, if the keyword is in the ad copy (and therefore bolded), the ad copy receives a higher click-through rate. Wouldn't it be fantastic to be able to automatically insert the searcher's keyword into your ad copy? This is almost what dynamic keyword insertion accomplishes.

What's in a Name?

Google did not publicly acknowledge dynamic keyword insertion when the feature was first released, as it was meant for internal use. Since it was not recognized by Google, the community ended up choosing the name dynamic keyword insertion (which was influenced by some Googlers who privately talked about the feature).

Both Yahoo! and Microsoft released public information about this feature on their systems before Google finally acknowledged the feature existed. Google chose to name the feature *keyword insertion*; however, by that time the term *dynamic keyword insertion* (commonly referred to as DKI) was so ingrained that the official label is rarely used. Suffice it to say, DKI is keyword insertion, which is also called dynamic keyword insertion, and whenever you hear someone mention any of the above names, they all refer to the same feature.

When your ad is shown, it's because a keyword in your account triggered that ad to be shown. With dynamic insertion, you can automatically insert the keyword that caused your ad to be displayed in the ad copy. For example:

1. Your account has the broad matched keyword "computer memory."
2. Your account does not have the keyword "laptop computer memory."
3. Someone searches for "laptop computer memory."
4. This search triggers your keyword "computer memory" to display an ad.
5. Since the keyword "computer memory" was what triggered the ad, that keyword would be inserted into your ad copy.
6. If your account had had the keyword "laptop computer memory" in it, the searcher would have seen their keyword query inserted into the ad copy.

If all of your keywords are exact match, you are inserting the searcher's keyword into every single ad. Since you will most likely be using different match types, you are inserting the closest match in your account.

There are a few restrictions to using dynamic keyword insertion. The first is that the ad copy must still follow editorial rules. If the keyword is trademarked and cannot be shown in an ad copy for legal reasons, dynamic keyword insertion will fail. This is also true for capitalization and misspellings.

There are several options for how to display your ad, and understanding the capitalization is essential to creating effective keyword insertion ads.

How to Create Keyword Insertion Ads

To create a keyword insertion ad, you replace part of the ad copy with a special syntax that denotes that the keyword should be inserted into to a specific section of the ad copy. Along with denoting where the keyword will be inserted, you need to define what will show if the keyword cannot be inserted (such as trademarks, misspellings, or exceptionally long keywords).

For instance, if you allocate the entire headline to keyword insertion, but the keyword is 30 characters long, the keyword cannot be inserted into the ad copy as the headline is limited to 25 characters. Therefore, you also specify text that shows if the keyword cannot be inserted into the ad copy.

The syntax is very straightforward: insert {**keyword:*Backup Text***} into any part of your ad copy, replacing *Backup Text* with what you would like to see in your ad copy if the keyword could not be inserted. Figure 6.3 shows several examples of keyword insertion in ad copy. With keyword insertion you can:

- Allocate an entire line to keyword insertion
- Allocate only part of a line to keyword insertion
- Add keyword insertion into any line of ad copy
- Use keyword insertion in multiple lines

When a keyword is inserted into the ad copy, the words *Backup Text* will not appear, having been replaced by the inserted keyword.

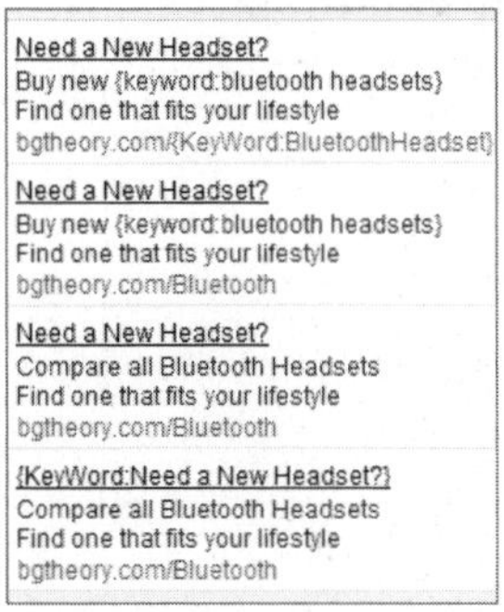

Figure 6.3 Examples of dynamic keyword insertion

The secret to keyword insertion is the way the word "keyword" in the ad copy is capitalized (see Table 6.1). This only applies for the way you write "keyword" in the ad copy—the way you format your actual keywords in each ad group does not matter for keyword insertion.

Your Ad Copy	What a Searcher Sees	Notes
{keyword:marketing seminar}	chicago adwords seminar	All lowercase
{Keyword:marketing seminar}	Chicago adwords seminar	Sentence case
{KeyWord:marketing seminar}	Chicago Adwords Seminar	Title case
{KEYword marketing seminar}	CHICAGO adwords seminar	KEY determines capitalization of first word
{KEYWord:marketing seminar}	CHICAGO Adwords Seminar	First word all caps, rest is title case
{KeyWORD:marketing seminar}	Chicago Adwords SEMINAR	WORD determines capitalization of last word
{KEYWORD:marketing seminar}	CHICAGO ADWORDS SEMINAR	All uppercase
{keyWord:marketing seminar}	chicago adwords Seminar	If k and w are different capitalizations, then w only affects last word

Note: Be careful when using keyword insertion: often companies become lazy and either forget the rules of successful organization, or write some very poor ads. If you ever seen ads where the capitalization seems incorrect (acronyms such as TV spelled Tv or ROI spelled Roi) or the word order seems wrong (such as TV Sony), this is often due to lazy use of keyword insertion.

Keyword insertion is one of the few times when the order of the words in your account matters (excluding match type, where it is very important). If you are creating keyword lists and have the keyword "TV Sony" in your ad group, "TV Sony" will appear in your keyword insertion ad and not the more commonly stated "Sony TV." Poorly formed keyword insertion ads can lower your click-through rate.

When using dynamic keyword insertion, you should keep a second ad in the same ad group that does not use the feature to see which one receives the higher click-through rate. It is very useful to test keyword insertion versus non–keyword insertion ads, as it is common to see search results where all the ads start to look the same (Figure 6.4).

The use of keyword insertion in this search result is not the issue. The larger problem is that the ads blend together as the headlines are so similar. In this case, writing a different ad that stands out can dramatically increase the click-through rate.

If your ad was among those in Figure 6.4 and you wanted to use keyword insertion, you could move the feature to the second or third line of ad copy. This way the word is still bolded in the ad copy, but you could write a headline that stands out from the crowd and increases your CTR.

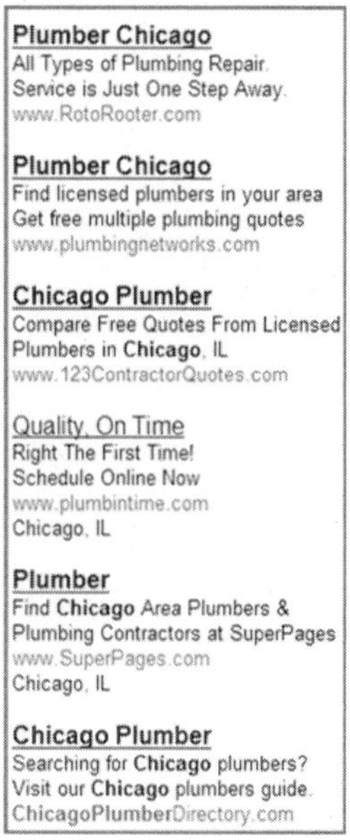

Plumber Chicago
All Types of Plumbing Repair.
Service is Just One Step Away.
www.RotoRooter.com

Plumber Chicago
Find licensed plumbers in your area
Get free multiple plumbing quotes
www.plumbingnetworks.com

Chicago Plumber
Compare Free Quotes From Licensed
Plumbers in **Chicago**, IL
www.123ContractorQuotes.com

Quality, On Time
Right The First Time!
Schedule Online Now
www.plumbintime.com
Chicago, IL

Plumber
Find **Chicago** Area Plumbers &
Plumbing Contractors at SuperPages
www.SuperPages.com
Chicago, IL

Chicago Plumber
Searching for **Chicago** plumbers?
Visit our **Chicago** plumbers guide.
ChicagoPlumberDirectory.com

Figure 6.4 Does your ad stand out from the crowd?

Keyword insertion is fantastic if you have thousands of part numbers and do not want to create thousands of ad copy versions to show the actual part number. However, keyword insertion is not always the best ad feature for your account. While keyword insertion might increase the click-through rate, do not forget the conversion rate. If you are a publisher being paid per page view, dynamic keyword insertion will probably work well. If you are selling a product, you need to measure if your keyword insertion ads have different conversion rates than your other ads. More visitors are not useful if it leads to fewer conversions.

Please note that the use of keyword insertion does not automatically increase your quality score. (We will discuss quality score in the next chapter.) The ad (after keyword insertion) is used in determining a keyword's quality score so it might have a slight effect on increasing your quality score, but the larger effect on quality score is usually from an increase in click-through rate. CTR is the largest component of quality score, and if your keyword insertion ad receives a higher CTR, this will help your quality score.

Keyword insertion works on both the search and content networks. For the search network, the keyword inserted is very straightforward; it's the one that triggered your ad to show.

On the content network, keyword insertion is more ambiguous. On the content network, the keyword that is inserted into your ad is the one that Google determines is the most likely to trigger your ad for that particular page. For example, say your ad group contained these keywords:

- Plumber
- Kitchen remodeling
- Fixing showers

If a user were reading a news article about the increase in home owners remodeling their kitchens and bathrooms for resale, the most likely match for that article would be the keyword "kitchen remodeling." Therefore, your keyword insertion ad would use the keyword "kitchen remodeling" in your ad copy for that particular page. If your keyword list contained both the keywords "kitchen remodeling" and "bathroom remodeling," either of those could be inserted into the ad copy.

On a content page, your keyword may or may not be contained within the article. Therefore, it is common to see very different response rates for the keyword insertion feature across content and search. We will cover the content network in Chapter 9, but this is another example of why you should always separate out search and content reporting.

Keyword insertion can be a powerful tool when used correctly. The ability to automatically add keywords into the ad copy can help increase your ad's relevance to the consumer. However, when used poorly, a keyword insertion ad can lower your CTR.

Keyword insertion can help make better use of your current impressions. Instead of finding new keywords, if you increase your click-through rate on your existing keywords, you will receive more visitors to your website. Once someone has clicked on your ad and visited your site, how do you increase the number of pages each searcher visits?

Increasing Page Views

With Google AdWords, you pay every time someone visits your website. While this can be a very profitable endeavor, finding ways of increasing the page views from each visitor or even having a visitor bring someone else to your site for free can increase your profits and site visibility.

E-commerce companies are often focused on return on investment (ROI) and not page views. This focus can lead to creating landing pages dedicated to a single product where the page does not offer any navigation except to add an item to a shopping cart. If you only have one product on the landing page and the searcher does not want that product, their only option is to click the Back button and leave your site. When optimizing for page views, always consider the options—or lack of options—that you present to searchers.

The other consideration is that when surfing the Web, searchers often do not know what to do next. They have read a page of content, or looked at a product and decided they do not want it, so what is the next thing they should do on your website?

There are two main ways to increase page views:

- Give the reader additional or related information
- Have the reader send information to a friend that there is content they will enjoy on the website

These two ways can be broken down into several different techniques.

Related Articles If someone reads an entire article on your website, they are generally interested in that topic. Give the reader related articles where they can continue learning more. If your site is a news site, usually you want your related articles based on the same overall story. If it is an informational article, the timeliness of the articles generally does not matter as long as the information is related.

Related and Supporting Products In the grocery store, as you are waiting to check out, there are many last minute impulse items you can add to your shopping cart. On the Web, there is no last minute aisle that features candy, gum, and magazines. Each page of your website can be customized with impulse items and last minute related products.

Showcase your related and ancillary products across your product pages. You can also use this tactic to engage a user who is in the learning phase of the buying funnel. If someone is interested in purchasing an iPod, they may not know if they want an iPod Touch, 80GB iPod, or a Nano. Help the user easily navigate between the related products or show a comparison of all the products on a single page.

This is also true for supporting products. If the iPod is being purchased as a gift, many users will also want to give an iTunes gift card along with the iPod. By showing additional products, you can increase not only your page views, but often your average order amount.

Recommended Articles Have you created an authoritative set of informational articles? Do you have some articles that readers absolutely love? Put these articles in a recommended article section. This not only helps increase the page views on your website, but it also showcases your best writing so that users will have a higher level of trust for your content.

Recommended Products You are the authority on your website. Searchers look to a website to guide them. If they are unsure about what to buy, a recommended product section can help put them on track toward a checkout. Often gift buyers have no idea what to purchase for another person. By organizing your products by age, price, gender, and so on, you can create a recommended buying section to help a user narrow down their gift options.

Buying Guides Have you ever bought a camcorder, laptop, or high definition TV? The different types of technologies, displays, recording devices, and acronyms associated with buying these products are staggering. Creating a how-to buying guide, or recommendation wizard, can not only increase page views, but it can also help your site become an authority in a specific area. If you have the best resources for determining how to buy a particular product, showcase these resources so others will find them and tell their friends.

Top-Read Articles and Top-Selling Products It is commonly noted that we live in a world of fads. From choosing a watch because a celebrity is wearing it to reading a news article that everyone is discussing in the break room, people want to be included. One way you can incorporate these desires on your website is to show the top-read articles and top-selling products.

Highest Reviewed Articles and Products Do you let users rate your articles or products? Do you allow users to write reviews that you show on your pages? If so, take advantage of that content by showcasing the highest reviewed pages or products of your site.

Breaking Long Articles into Multiple Pages If your goal is page views and you write very long articles, break the content into multiple pages. This is especially useful if you sell CPM ads on your site and are looking to maximize page views.

Search Box If you have been online for more than six years, you remember the days when the best navigation was drilling down through the Yahoo! directory to find the proper category and then finally a website. Today, there is an entire generation that does not even look for navigation, but starts the browsing behavior within the search box.

Regardless of how your site is designed, incorporating a search box into your website will increase not only page views, but functionality and user satisfaction. When you incorporate your search box, remember to track the words being used to search. These are not only good keywords for your search campaign, but if you see frequent searches from particular pages, it can be a sign that the page is lacking some critical information.

Bookmark or Save This on Social Media Sites Just about every user knows that you can bookmark a web page, but it is often forgotten. Adding subtle reminders, such as "bookmark this" or "save to Delicous.com" can help get more page views from return visitors.

Social media sites (such as Digg, Facebook, MySpace, and Twitter) can drive a massive amount of traffic to your website. Incorporating social media tactics so that your content is easy to share on these sites can help you find new avenues of traffic.

Send to a Friend The oldest of the sharing tactics is send to a friend. If someone likes your site's content, is there an easy way for them to email it to someone they think will also like it?

Print This Page One thing that has amazed me over the years is how often people print pages and either call a business at a later date, read the story on the train, or pass the pages on to someone else they think would enjoy the information. As much as we live in a digital world, paper is still greatly used. Creating printer-friendly pages is useful as you can customize your site's logo and URL on those pages so the searcher can always remember how to get in touch with your business or where the information originated.

None of the above examples are exclusive. On a site like NYTimes.com, for example, you will see "print," "email," "search," and "save" functionalities. On a site like Amazon.com, you will see "recommended," "top rated," and "top reviewed" products. Incorporating social and related information can help increase page views across your site.

Too Many Options Lead to Confusion

The more information you give to someone at a single time, the more mental processing it takes to absorb all the information. In psychology circles, this is known as *cognitive load*. Giving your visitor too many options can lead to *cognitive overload*, in which your visitor no longer has enough mental processing left to make a decision.

This phenomenon is often coupled with short-term memory capacity. Most people can only hold five to nine concepts in short-term memory. If you give someone too many options, they could forget the original reason for coming to your website, or decide to wait until later to make a decision, as your site requires too much mental processing and memory capacity for the user.

Most users already have part of their short-term memory occupied with other tasks, such as why they visited your website or the fact that they have a meeting in 15 minutes. They only have a percentage of their cognitive load and short-term memory to dedicate to your website. Therefore, provide the user with options that are most beneficial for your company. If you are an e-commerce site, your primary option would be a sale. Your secondary option might be to create an account or subscribe to a newsletter. Your tertiary option might be social network sharing. You can test adding additional options, but your test should not just examine if users are taking advantage of secondary or tertiary options, but if the percentage of users engaging in your primary options is decreasing.

Increasing the number of page views per visitor on your website is not just about selling more CPM ads. It also ensures that your visitors are finding the information they seek so they have a positive experience with your site and either return, recommend it to another person, or buy from your company.

The information could be a product or an article. Incorporating some of the above ideas on your website should not just increase page views, it should also increase conversion rates as consumers find exactly what they are seeking and maybe a bit more (in the case of related products).

There are also techniques specifically geared toward increasing the conversion rate. These techniques do not rely on making sure the consumer can wander around your site to find the specific information. Instead, they try to sell one product per keyword and do everything possible to have the consumer take one specific action.

Optimizing for Conversions

Instead of focusing on traffic, you could put your efforts into increasing conversion rates. These two optimization techniques are generally at odds with each other. With traffic, you are looking to entice someone to come to your website regardless of their intent. When trying to increase conversion rates, you are only trying to bring people to your website who may perform some action.

A 100 percent conversion rate is not useful with one visitor a month. Conversely, a million visitors a day with zero conversions is a quick way to go out of business. Therefore, you generally want to use a combination of both conversion and traffic optimization when fully optimizing your AdWords campaign.

There are two aspects of increasing conversions: the ad copy and the landing page. We will start with techniques for writing high-converting ad copy, and then move to additional landing page options you can implement to increase conversion rates.

Writing Ad Copy That Sells

Ad copy is the bridge between the search query and your website. If the bridge is inviting to all, then all the cars will cross if the bridge leads in the generally correct direction. Conversely, if you hang a warning sign that says the bridge can only support up to certain weight and height limits, then those who do not fit will not cross the bridge.

The sign serves as a filter to keep those who do not fit into your criteria away from your website, saving you money on those potential clicks. When trying to increase conversion rates, your ad copy should only be inviting to those whom you determine wish to perform an action on your website.

Usually, the ad copy's job is to stand up and shout, "You can find the answer to your question here." For increased conversion rates, the ad copy should instead be saying, "We have the answer to your question if you want to perform this one action. If you do not want to perform that action, then do not cross the bridge." That action could be:

- Call us to schedule a visit
- Buy an HD TV
- Subscribe to our newsletter
- Fill out a form to receive free quotes

The second line of your ad copy should be a very specific item you want the user to complete on your website (Figure 6.5).

Figure 6.5 Use calls to action in your ad copy.

By letting visitors know exactly what you want them to do, you are accomplishing two goals:

- Those who do not wish to complete that action are less likely to click on the ad.
- Those who do click are more predisposed to both perform the action and to seek ways to conduct that action on your website.

As discussed in Chapter 4, a call to action can still contain a benefit. Testing benefit-laden calls to action ads is one of the most important tests you should run to keep unqualified searchers from clicking, it is natural to see your click-through rates.

Your CTR will decrease when you use ad copy that discourages unqualified searchers from clicking your ads. Since CTR is one of the most important quality score factors, you could see a drop in quality score. This is why it is crucial to test your ads. You have to balance your AdWords account between quality score, traffic, and conversions. This is a difficult balance to find, and only through trial and error will you find the correct combination for you.

When your ad does receive a click, it should be from a prequalified searcher who is ready to continue down the conversion path. The next step is making sure that your landing page can keep the searcher on the path toward reaching your goal of conversion.

Creating Landing Pages That Increase Conversions

When designing landing pages to increase conversions, there is one decision to make before you move to the next step, whether to use:

- A dedicated landing page designed only for conversions and single actions
- A page of your existing website

If you use a page in your existing website, you most likely have additional navigational and other elements on the page. You can still use some techniques to increase conversions, but some users will wander off your primary conversion path. Most e-commerce sites send traffic to pages in their existing website. You may choose a few of your top-selling products or late sales cycle keywords to send to dedicated landing pages with a different layout than your usual site. However, it is rarely cost effective to design a dedicated landing page for every product.

If you use a dedicated landing page for the search query, you can control every option a user has, which can help increase conversion rates. However, be careful of limiting someone's options too much if the keyword falls into the early buying cycle phases. Someone who is researching a product is not yet ready to purchase and will want some additional options to learn more about the product or service.

Using Dedicated Landing Pages

Dedicated landing pages are excellent for form actions, such as receiving quotes, filling out a contact form, or subscribing to a newsletter. With dedicated landing pages, you need to choose only one or two actions you want someone to complete. If you don't overwhelm the user with choices, you have made the conversion choice for them. Now your page needs to move them from viewing the page to taking action.

When limiting a user's options, it is also important to keep in mind Google's landing page criteria:

- Relevance
- Navigation
- Transparency about the business and personal information collection

"One-page wonders"—single-page websites that often contained 100 paragraphs of scrolling sales copy with only one option on the page, usually an email signup— were saddled with very low quality scores a few years ago. This was due to the fact that the user had no options, rarely was there a privacy policy, and there was little business transparency.

You can be very creative with dedicated landing pages as long as you keep the major AdWords landing page criteria in mind.

Keep Your Dedicated Landing Pages from Hurting Your SEO Efforts

If you spend time on search engine optimization (SEO), you want to make sure that your dedicated landing pages are not hurting your SEO efforts. If Google finds the same content on multiple pages, they will choose which one to rank; this is called the duplicate content penalty. Usually dedicated landing pages are not built for ranking; they are only built for conversions. Therefore, you do not want them included in the regular Google index.

The easiest way to keep these pages from being spidered by Google is to put them in their own folder (such as yoursite.com/landingpages). Then in your robots.txt file, exclude Googlebot from indexing that folder. You can also exclude all bots from indexing the folder. If adsbot-Google, the bot that spiders your page for AdWords, sees a global disallow in your robots.txt folder, it will ignore the instructions, as Google assumes that if you are buying traffic to a page you want that page spidered for quality score purposes. If you accidentally block adsbot-Google, then Google cannot spider your page and you will see very poor quality scores.

When designing dedicated landing pages, make sure that your primary action is above the fold and the page centers around that one particular action. The action could be a form fill, add-to-cart button, or any other action you desire. The most important aspect is to make sure that there is a very clear call to action that is the first thing your visitors notice.

Increasing E-commerce Conversion Rates

Add-to-cart buttons are essential for e-commerce websites and should appear anyplace the product appears. This means users should be able to add a product to the shopping cart from the product page, category page, specials page, and even search results pages.

Detailed product information should be available within one click of the landing page. Even if you have a dedicated landing page for a product, detailed information should be easily accessible. While people ready to purchase may ignore it, you will engage those who are still learning about a product before they are ready to buy.

Bose has an excellent example of an e-commerce landing page (Figure 6.6). The major actions on the page are "Buy Now" or "Learn More." The information above the fold for most monitors ends at the "Learn More" link. In addition, you can mouse over aspects of the headset to see the headset's benefits.

Figure 6.6 Bose headset landing page

Keeping with Google's policies, there is also navigation at the bottom of the page for those who wish to view other Bose products or headsets.

While Bose went with limited navigation, Amazon did something quite different. Once you enter the shopping cart, all your options change. You still have navigational options, but those options are items like change shipping address, add a credit card, etc.—all options that only keep you moving toward finishing your purchase.

Shipping prices should be easily accessible. Consumers are very conscious about shipping prices. If you offer free shipping, make sure your landing page reinforces that message. If you ship to multiple countries, also make that obvious.

Make sure the shopping cart is easy to find. On some sites, you cannot view the cart unless you have just added a new product, which means that if someone adds a product, then starts shopping around, they cannot checkout until they add another product. On other sites, the shopping cart is difficult to find. Use a highly visible shopping cart icon.

Do not put a registration barrier between the shopping cart and the final checkout. Registration requirements only serve to increase the number of abandoned carts on your site. If you would like users to register, give them the option to do so, and a reason why it will benefit them, after you have processed their credit card.

The shopping process should be no more than three pages. The longer the checkout process takes, the higher the chance of shopping cart abandonment.

Increasing Form Fill Conversion Rates

Web-based forms are used to collect email addresses and other contact information, check out at an e-commerce site, or register for a download. They are heavily used, but may be the least optimized pages across the entire Web. How intimidating do your forms look?

Even if you only want to collect name, email address, physical address, phone number, and credit card information, it still is common to see a form with at these fields.

- First name
- Last name
- Email address
- Confirm email address
- Address line 1
- Street type
- Address line 2
- City
- State

- Zip code
- Area code
- 3-digit phone exchange
- Last 4 phone digits

For our purposes, we are going to keep the form simpler to illustrate a point and assume that your billing address is same as the shipping address. If the above fields are just tossed on a web page, it looks like it will take a while to fill out (Figure 6.7).

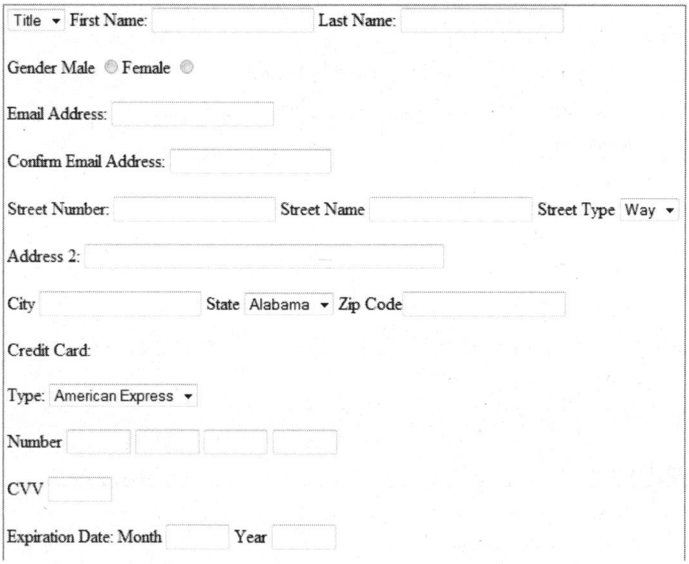

Figure 6.7 Poor form collection layout

While this form is not that long in comparison to many forms on the Web, compare the form in Figure 6.7 to another form that collects the exact same data (Figure 6.8).

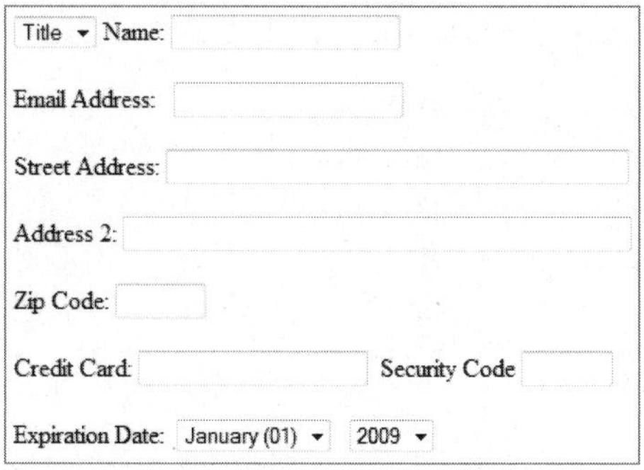

Figure 6.8 A simple form that collects a lot of data

In the second form, Figure 6.8, the title field (Mr., Mrs., etc.) is used to determine the gender. The zip code field will let the merchant know the user's city and state. The credit card number denotes the card type. Consumers type first name and then last name. There is little need to make someone fill out separate fields. Your development team can parse out this information.

These simple form design principles work very well in most areas outside of e-commerce. If you have shipped to rural areas, or dealt with individuals who have hyphenated last names, then you have come across exceptions where you might need the first name field or where someone's zip code does not match their city shipping address.

In cases where you need to ensure the information is exactly correct, you have three options:

- Ask more explicit questions, but try to keep to as few fields as possible.
- Collect basic information with simple fields on the first form page. Save that information (especially basic contact information), and then present them with specific fields on page 2 of the form.
- Show a final review page before submitting the order, which is common with shipping carts, where you present your full information to the user and then let them edit any mistakes.

In most cases, the user will not need to edit their information. However, there will be some exceptions, and using a final review page will allow those few users to edit their information, while the majority of users who have standard addresses and names will quickly go through the entire form process.

Note: Did you know that all American Express cards start with a 3? All Visa credit cards start with a 4, MasterCards start with a 5, and Discover with a 6. Asking for both the credit card type and the credit card number is redundant.

The following are a few crucial considerations when designing forms:

Sales versus Marketing Many companies have a fight between marketing and sales. Marketing tells sales that if they only ask for a name, phone number, and email address, then sales can contact the prospective customer. Sales wants to know the contact's cell phone, best time to call, industry, how much money they make, the total income of the company, and the person's title. This is enough to make many customers abandon a form.

There is a compromise that can occur between marketing and sales. On the first page of a form, ask for basic information that sales needs to contact the customer. On page 2, inform the customer that you would like to personalize their phone call, but to do so you need to collect some additional information about their company. This second page is where you can ask some of the more instructive questions such as cell phone and gross sales numbers. Sales will not receive everyone's full information, but they can still put their calls in a queue based on the information they do receive.

Making Buying Easy Have you ever filled out a credit card form where your information was rejected because you did not use spaces? Or received the error that the form will not accept spaces or dashes in the credit card field? If someone is trying to give you a credit card number, take it. Your developers can parse out spaces and dashes on the back-end and accept the customer's data regardless of their personal preference for typing out their card information.

Respecting the Customer's Time Setting proper expectations is important for any business, especially when it comes to respecting someone's time. If you have a very long form, just tell the customer how long it will take to complete. If someone fills out page 1 and then sees page 2, then page 3, that prospective customer will start worrying about their time investment and may abandon the form. Tell the customer, "This is a three-page form and will take five minutes of your time. If you need assistance, do not hesitate to call us and we will walk you through the form." That small message sets the expectation of how long it will take, respects the customer's time, and gives them additional conversion options.

Many customers feel reassured of their progress by seeing a graphical navigation bar at the top of the page showing their progress. Let's say your checkout process is:

1. Review cart
2. Choose shipping method and address
3. Enter credit card billing
4. Review everything one last time
5. Check out

Showing those steps at the top of the page—and which page the customer is currently on—can help people understand the process, see if they have a chance to review their information, and know when they will be finished.

An Informed Searcher Is a Happy Searcher Make sure the searcher has the necessary information to complete a form before they start filling in the form's fields. There are many landing pages that are simply forms with limited information. Many of these forms contain detailed questions that require some knowledge about the industry. If your form contains a field for which a searcher does not know the answer, they will have to abandon your form to do some research. Whenever you ask a specific question that the consumer might not know the answer to, make sure that information can be easily found on your website.

For example, say someone searched for "merchant accounts" and came to a form page on your site. They happily fill out the first page of the application. Then, the second page of the application asks a required question, "What type of merchant account do you want?" If the searcher does not know that there are different types of merchant accounts, they have to abandon your form to do this additional research.

 Note: One of the best ways to optimize forms is to track where the forms are being abandoned and then investigate for potential causes. If you find there are two or three fields where abandonment consistently happens, then add information to the page or change those particular fields.

A poorly designed form can drastically lower conversion rates. A well-optimized form can significantly raise conversion rates. Take a look at your forms, see how intimidating they seem, and find ways of making them friendly and easy to complete.

What If the Consumer Is Not Yet Ready to Buy?

Not everyone is ready to conduct an action when they visit your website. It is important to consider what is happening in the searcher's life that would cause that person not to convert so that you can engage these potential customers.

- Many office workers hide in their cubicles and shop online. However, while they may surf at work, they might not be ready to pull out the credit card while still in the office.

- Administrative assistants are often asked to conduct research on a topic and compile a list of resources and papers. This information is then handed to a second person to evaluate and make a decision.

- A shopper spends the afternoon on a site configuring options for the next computer they wish to purchase. Before they buy, they need to wait for the next payday and get the spouse's opinion.

In all three of these scenarios, someone may give your company money, but it will not be today. What options do you give those who are not ready to purchase immediately?

Empowering the customer to be able to print pages, download whitepapers, save items in a cart, send a configuration in email, and so forth can help entice the user to come back to your site when they are ready to purchase.

This is especially important in industries with long sales cycles. It is common for business-to-business companies to have six months pass between initial contact and final purchase.

One of the reasons to ask for an email address in upfront fields is to send reminders when forms are abandoned on your website. If a consumer adds products to their shopping cart, makes it through two steps of the cart and suddenly abandons your site, you can increase conversions by sending them a reminder email that their shopping cart is about to expire. You can do the same for whitepapers or any form that captures an email address. There are times when the phone rings or someone walks into the office and disrupts the conversion process. Please note, when sending emails such as this, make sure you are following any applicable laws, such as the CAN-SPAM act.

In many of these cases, you might need to add additional conversion types so you can track the initial conversion and keep in touch with your prospective customer as you move them through the analysis of your products to finally purchasing.

Allowing Consumers to Contact You Their Way

Do you force searchers to email you? Do you only list a phone number? Do you offer live chat? Different types of consumers have their favorite ways of contacting a business. If that choice is not available, they may not contact you at all.

You might want to offer more conversions than necessary for a while, see which ones are being used, and then remove the rest. If your customers do not use live chat, there is no reason to support it.

If you only offer phone support, and you only answer the phone during business hours during the week, what do you expect customers to do when they click on your ads during the weekend or at night? You should offer them a different course of action, and maybe even a different landing page, to make sure you are not alienating those searchers.

Many businesses find that by offering both email and phone support their conversion rate increases due to additional consumer choice.

Making Additional Conversions to Increase Your Profits

In Chapter 2, we discussed the consumer decision-making process, known as the buying funnel. Many companies can benefit by adding conversion actions to different segments of this process to keep in touch with the consumer, and to keep moving the consumer through the buying funnel toward a final purchase.

If you have a long sales cycle, what does your conversion funnel look like?

Too many conversion funnels look like this:

1. Offer a free whitepaper download.
2. Hope the customer calls you (or add the customer to your email list).
3. If the customer calls you, try to sell them something.

This type of conversion funnel relies on the customer to read your whitepaper, do their research, understand your business, and then decide to contact you.

Consider a conversion funnel such as this:

1. Searcher downloads a whitepaper to learn more about the product.

2. Searcher is sent an email to attend a free webinar to learn more about your company and how the product will benefit them.

3. Searcher attends free webinar and becomes more confident about your company.

4. Salesperson calls customer to offer free demo.

5. Salesperson conducts personalized demonstration with customer.

6. Customer makes a decision.

The second conversion funnel allows for more customer contact, more hand-holding, more interaction, a better customer relationship, and usually more sales.

Even if the customer's decision is to not buy from you, often the effort you put into the second conversion funnel is the same or less than the first one, as you do not have salespeople constantly calling or emailing to reach a bad prospect—the prospect has made up his or her mind. In addition, in this second conversion funnel, the prospect knows more about your company and may feel confident in recommending you to someone else as an option, or they might call you back when their situation changes.

When sales teams call customers after they have only attended a webinar or read a whitepaper, customers are usually resistant as they do not have enough information to make a decision. When there are multiple touch points, the customers naturally move though the conversion cycle into having enough information to make a decision.

By adding additional conversion options and tracking them all, you can see what patterns lead to higher conversion rates. In the previous scenario, you might find that the free demo does not increase conversion rates, so you could remove it. Or you could find that when someone attends your webinar, your contact ratio increases significantly, so you push that conversion option to more consumers.

Understanding Your Conversion Options

A conversion is anything you want to define on your website. Often conversions lead toward your company becoming profitable, such as contacts, purchases, or subscriptions. You do not necessarily have to be paid on each conversion for it to be useful. A conversion can be someone entering your conversion funnel or viewing a key page of your website.

Some of the more common conversion types that are worthy of tracking are:

Contact Us Use this conversion action to track how often someone is contacting your business.

Any Form Fill Every time a form is filled out on your site, you gain some information or a searcher has taken an action.

vCard Download A vCard or "save to contacts" option allows you to be part of someone's Outlook or other email program.

Whitepaper Download Whitepapers are often PDF files that cover details about a product or idea. Offering whitepapers is critical in business-to-business selling where the person doing the research is not the decision maker.

Webinar A webinar is an online presentation.

Subscription When someone subscribes to your newsletter, RSS feed, or protected section of your website, you have a chance to continue the conversation.

Save to Cart and Add to Wish List These are various ways to let someone save a product to buy at a later date. Allowing people to publish their wish lists can also help your website's visibility and conversion rate.

E-commerce Checkout Someone gave you money—track it!

Send to Friend (or Self) via Email Allow someone to send product or article information to another person, or even to themselves to investigate at a later date.

Send to SMS or Mobile Phone This is useful to allow customers to send your contact information or driving directions to their phone.

Driving Directions If you have a physical store, track how often people are getting directions to visit you in-store.

Phone Call Phone call tracking takes some work, but it allows you to understand how many calls and sales your marketing is generating. With more sophisticated systems, you can even correlate phone calls to keywords, ad groups, landing pages, and ad copy.

Bookmark or Save to a Social Network Site While this does not lead to direct revenue, it shows some interaction with your site.

Print Page Offering a printer-friendly page and Print button can allow you to see how often your information is being printed. It is not uncommon for searchers to print a website and call a business at a later date.

Coupon Print If you have a physical store, track both how often coupons are printed and how often they are redeemed in the store. With proper coding, coupon redemption can be traced back to a keyword, landing page, and ad copy.

While offering too many conversion options can cause consumers to be overwhelmed and unsure which is correct for them, offering too few can cause you to lose consumers either on the initial visit or by not being able to move them through the shopping and conversion funnels.

Best Practices for Advanced Optimization Techniques

The first step to any pay-per-click campaign is to send traffic to your website by bidding on relevant keywords. There will be many times when you want to increase the traffic your website receives. In those cases, these practices can help bring more visitors from the search engine to your site.

- The impression share report will help you identify why your ad is not being shown, and then you can take action to improve the situation:
    - If you are already hitting your daily budget, then either raising your budget or lowering your maximum CPCs can increase the number of clicks you receive without adding new keywords.
    - If you are not reaching your daily budget, and you have a high impression share, the next step is to either increase your ad's CTR or add more general keywords.
- One technique for raising click-through rates is using dynamic keyword insertion to automatically insert keywords into your ad copy.
    - The trick to proper use of dynamic keyword insertion is to correctly use your ad copy capitalization syntax, as this will determine how your keywords are displayed in the ads.
    - When using dynamic keyword insertion, make sure your ad stands out from the other ads on the page.

It does not matter whether you send traffic to a dedicated landing page or an existing page of your website. There are some best practices you should follow to increase conversion rates:

- The visitor should feel that the landing page is what the ad was describing—that is, it should be an extension of the ad copy.
    - The call to action that appears in the ad copy should be on the landing page.
    - Any claims, pricing, or special discounts should be echoed on the landing page.
- Create a synergy between the ads and the landing page so that visitors feel they have arrived at the correct site.
    - When using media-rich ads, echo the same images in the ads on the landing page to avoid confusing the visitors by a landing page that has a very different look and feel. The graphics can be different sizes and shapes, but the same basic images.
    - Make sure visitors see the same offer so they can continue converting on your website without wondering whether they have arrived at the correct place.

- Leverage the few simple principles of increasing conversion rates:
  - Have a clear call to action.
  - Have a clear path to action.
  - Offer a compelling benefit and message.
  - Ensure your information is accessible to all.
  - Ensure the user has the correct information to make a decision.
  - Make the conversion process painless.

The principles are easy to grasp. The execution of those principles is difficult.

Furthermore, testing ad copy and landing page layouts is essential to maximizing both traffic and conversions. Once you test, you need to let both the results of those tests and your analytics systems tell you the story of what combination provides the best response rates to turn searchers into customers.

Demystifying Quality Score

Quality score is the most important number in your AdWords account, as it has far-reaching effects on your Google AdWords success. This number can decide the fate of your account. Low quality scores can doom your account to failure. High quality scores can place your ad above your competitors while you pay less per click than they do. It is also the hardest number to quantify and try to improve across your entire account.

We will examine what quality score affects within your account and the factors that influence your quality scores. Finally, you will learn how to improve your quality score to gain a strategic advantage over your competitors.

7

Chapter Contents

What Is Quality Score?

Quality score is the single most confusing number in your entire AdWords account. It is often considered an ambiguous number that is almost impossible to consciously change. This number has more impact on your account's performance than any other number, and that includes your bid.

The reason this number is so important is that quality score determines:

Your First Page Bid First page bid is an estimate given to you by Google for each of your keywords that is an approximation of what you need to bid for your ad to show up on page 1 of the search results.

Ad Rank for the Search Network Ad rank is a number that is derived from multiplying your quality score with your maximum CPC. Ad rank is calculated for all advertisers who are shown on any given page. The highest ad rank is shown in the first position on Google, the second highest ad rank is shown in the second position, and so on.

Eligibility to Appear on Specific Content Sites Content network ads appear on non-search pages. In search, Google looks to see if the search query is related to your keywords. On the content network, Google looks to see if the article's contents are related to your keywords. For example, if someone is reading an article about airline travel on the *New York Times* site, the content ads will also be related to airline travel. Your quality score, along with several other factors, is used to determine if your ad can appear on one of these sites.

Whether a Placement Targeted Ad Will Appear Placement targeting allows you to select individual websites across the content network where you would like your ad to appear. Your quality score will help determine if your ad can appear on the sites you select.

Essentially, if you can increase your quality score, you can pay less for clicks and increase your ad's visibility by having it shown higher in the search results.

Google displays the quality score number that is shown within your account at the keyword level. Therefore, every keyword in your account will have a quality score.

Quality score is a number that can be understood, quantified, and optimized in your AdWords account if you examine all of its parts and associate those different aspects to your account, ad copy, keywords, and landing page. By breaking down quality score into its associated factors, this number can be influenced and you can optimize your account to increase your quality score.

Some Essential Terminology

Here are the definitions of the various types of networks covered in this and other chapters:

Search Partners Sites where you conduct a search, but which are not owned by Google, such as AOL.com and Ask.com.

Continues

How Quality Score Affects Ad Rank

Every time your ad is shown, the keyword is given an ad rank number. The higher your ad rank, the higher the position in which your ad will appear. Google then determines the ad rank for all the other ads that could be shown. The highest ad rank is shown in the first position, the second ad rank is shown in the second position, and so on.

Ad rank is calculated by a very simple formula:

(maximum bid) × (quality score)

To increase your ad rank, you can either increase your quality score or increase your bid. You will encounter many instances when working with your AdWords account when you should not raise bids, but instead attempt to increase your quality score.

It is also possible to pay less than a competitor for a higher position. Consider the scenario shown in Table 7.1.

▶ **Table 7.1** How quality score calculates ad position

	Advertiser A	Advertiser B
Max CPC	$0.75	$2
Quality Score	8.5	3
Ad Rank	6.375	6

In this scenario, advertiser A's ad will show higher in the search results than advertiser B because advertiser A's ad rank is higher. Advertiser B is already bidding 266 percent higher than advertiser A. Just because you are willing to pay more than your competitors does not mean your ad will be displayed higher in the results.

If advertiser B wanted to leapfrog advertiser A and have their ad appear higher, they could continue to increase their bids. However, paying a significantly larger amount for each click than your competitor is not a good long-term strategy. It makes more sense to raise your quality score so you save on advertising costs, or put that money to good use in gaining more clicks by increasing your budget or developing new creatives and adding new marketing channels. In this scenario, Advertiser B should not focus on increasing their bid. Instead, they should attempt to raise their quality score.

Determining Actual CPC from Quality Score

There is usually a difference between your maximum CPC and your actual CPC. In many cases, you may bid $2, but actually pay $1.57. This is because Google uses a discount ad system so that you only pay $0.01 more than is required for your ad to appear just above your competitor.

The formula that determines actual CPC is:

$$\text{actual CPC} = \frac{\text{(ad rank to beat)}}{\text{(your quality score)}} + \$0.01$$

If we plugged in the numbers from Table 7.1, we would arrive at this formula:

$$\$0.71 = \frac{6}{8.5} + \$0.01$$

Therefore, even though advertiser A is bidding $0.75, they are actually only paying $0.71 per click. If there were more than two advertisers, the above ad ranks and actual CPCs would be calculated for every single advertiser.

Because AdWords is a blind auction system, it is impossible to know what your competitors are bidding. The AdWords system is built around setting bids based on your advertising profits. To profitability increase bids, you may need to increase your website's conversion rates, change match types, or try different ad copy. If you increase conversion rates, you are increasing the searcher's satisfaction with your website, which again aligns your advertising with Google's goals: make the best search experience possible for the searcher.

Quality Score Factors for Search

There are a few quality score factors that are used in your AdWords account. The most transparent of all these scores is the one used for search, as you can see this number in both your account and your AdWords reports.

One of the confusing aspects of quality score is that you have one number displayed in your account that is determined by a set of factors, and a different set is used to calculate first page bid and ad rank. First let us examine all of the factors used to determine the quality score that is shown in your AdWords account, and then we will look at some of the exceptions. The quality score factors are as follows:

Click-Through Rate on Google.com The single most important factor in determining your quality score is your click-through rate (CTR). The higher your click-through rate, the higher your quality score can be for each keyword.

The click-through rate is normalized by position. This means that your ad is not penalized for being shown in a lower position. Google does directly compare the CTR of an ad in position 5 with the ad in position 1. Google understands that position 5 generally receives a lower CTR than position 1. Therefore, Google normalizes the CTR across positions to determine how effective your ad is at gathering clicks.

When ads are shown on the Google search network, only the CTR of the Google search network is used. Your content CTR and search partner CTR do not matter whatsoever for determining your quality score for search when your ad is shown on a Google search network site.

When your ad is shown on a search partner, such as Ask.com or AOL.com, the CTR of your ad on that partner site is used along with your CTR on Google.

Click-Through Rate of Display URLs within an Ad Group Google tracks the display URLs used within your ad group separately from your text ads. The higher your display URL CTR, the higher your quality score can become. This is another reason to vary your display URLs and test to see which ones lead to higher CTRs.

Relevance of the Keywords to the Ad Copy within an Ad Group Relevance is one of Google's mantra words, and one of the places where this word takes on a special significance is in your ad copy. How closely does your ad copy describe and reflect your keyword? You do not have to use the actual keyword in the ad copy, but they should be closely related.

For example, the words "flowers" and "roses" are closely related. If the keyword is "flowers" and it triggers an ad copy about buying rose bouquets, these are closely related terms, as roses are a type of flower. A searcher may search for the word "flowers," but really want to buy roses.

However, the keywords "real estate" and "mortgage" are very different. When looking for real estate, the location, price, and number of bedrooms are pieces of the same puzzle. While most people who are looking to buy a house will need a mortgage, the search process is very different. A user looking for a mortgage is more interested in financial information than the number of bedrooms a house contains. In this instance, the ad copy will have a low relevance score as it is not helping someone arrive at the answers to their search query.

Note: The term *relevance* is similar to *latent semantic indexing* (LSI). The layman's explanation of LSI is that all words are related by degrees of separation. The more you use words that are closely related in your ad copy, the higher the relevance of your copy. In a later section we will examine a few ways to gain insight into keyword, ad copy, and landing page relevance.

Relevance of the Keyword and Ad Copy to the Search Query Google made a change in October 2008 when they moved to a real-time quality score analysis. In real time, Google examines the relevance of your keyword and the ad copy that will be shown in the search result and then compares your keyword and ad copy to the actual search query. Therefore, if you are using dynamic keyword insertion, it can help improve this one factor.

Since this factor is in real time, it does not influence the quality score shown in your account, but it does affect the quality score used when determining your ad's position in a search result.

Development of Quality Score

When Google AdWords PPC program first launched in 2002, your ad rank was calculated as bid times click-through rate. To increase your position, you could either increase your CTR or increase your bid (all other factors being the same). However, if your CTR was low, your ad was simply not shown and was placed into a disabled state where it was very difficult to ever have that keyword active in your account again.

In July 2005, Google revamped the rules by introducing quality score and minimum bids. At first, quality score was simple and mostly determined by predicted click-through rate. Over the years, Google has tried to align quality score with searcher satisfaction. Usually the closer your ads and landing page are aligned with giving the consumer the answer to their question, the higher your quality score becomes.

Landing Page Quality This is very similar to the relevance of ad copy to the keyword. How relevant are your landing pages to the keyword? You do not have to have the actual keyword on the landing page; the landing page must be thematically related to the keyword.

Landing pages are considered relevant or non-relevant. Once your landing page is considered relevant, there is nothing more you can do to optimize the page for a higher quality score.

I will show how to determine if your page is deemed relevant later in this chapter in the section "Landing Page Quality: Making Your Pages Relevant." In addition, as there are several factors that make up landing page relevance, we will also examine those factors in depth in a later section.

Landing Page Load Time The speed at which your landing page loads for the user is also a factor in determining quality score. This is another factor where if you pass the threshold, there is nothing more to optimize. In the following section, "Viewing Your Quality Score," you can see how to determine if your landing page load time is acceptable or not.

The AdWords system follows all keyword level destination URLs (or ad copy level if you do not use keyword level URLs) to determine the final page to analyze.

When Google determines if your page loads fast enough to be considered acceptable to the user, it is just looking to see if the HTML of your page loads as fast as the other pages hosted in that same geography. Since Google only looks at the HTML—not image sizes, scripts, etc.—this should never be an issue for most accounts.

If you are having landing page load time issues and are not using redirects, you have a larger problem than your AdWords account. You need to evaluate your host and website to find out why your site is loading so slowly.

If you are using redirects, make sure your redirects are not slowing down the searcher before they reach the final landing page. In the case of redirects, your site could load quickly, but if the redirects are slow, then you may see issues with landing page load time.

Account Performance in Geographic Region Where Your Ad Will Be Shown This is another factor that has more influence on your ad's actual position than the displayed number in your account. Google examines the different geographies where your keyword and ad are being shown. If a pattern emerges where your ad receives a higher CTR in one geography over another, your ad will be shown more in the geography with the higher CTR and usually have a higher position in that geography (assuming the completion and other bids are relatively similar).

This quality score factor could be at odds with your conversion rates. You may find that you have a higher conversion rate in one geography, but in a completely different area you have a higher CTR. In this instance, Google will show your ad more in the area with the higher CTR and you could lose out on conversions.

There is a geographic performance report that will give you insight into different statistics by geography, which we will cover in depth in Chapter 11.

Account History Google examines the entire account, both the keywords and the ad copy, to determine how the account has done overall. Your overall account history is used when determining quality score.

With most AdWords statistics, such as account history and keyword CTR, the most recent history matters more than the overall history. Think of it as "What have you done for me lately?" Since most recent matters more than overall, accounts and keywords can almost always be saved when the proper techniques are applied.

Quality Score Is Only Calculated by Precise Matches

When examining the quality score factors, do not worry about the click-through rate or related queries for your phrase and broad match keywords. If you add the same keyword as an exact match, phrase match, and broad match keyword, all three versions will have the same quality score. That quality score will be derived from the exact match version. If you have a broad match keyword that does not have the exact match equivalent in your ad group, then Google will calculate the quality score for that keyword based upon the times when the search query matched your keyword precisely.

Therefore, it is useful to either use an exact match version of all your keywords or run the search query report to see the actual CTR of your phrase and broad match words when attempting to optimize for quality score.

Other Relevancy Factors Google has many other relevancy factors that only sometimes apply. Most of these factors are fairly minor, are extremely difficult to optimize, and do not always come into play. Therefore, they are not disclosed by Google. However, they are usually so minor, they are also not worth worrying about and you can instead focus on the other factors described earlier.

For example, let us assume there are two advertisers using the broad match keyword "teeth whitening." One of the advertisers is a dentist located in Chicago. The other advertiser is an e-commerce site that sells a teeth whitening product. Now consider a searcher sitting in Chicago doing a search for teeth whitening. Most dental queries are inherently local and the Chicago dentist is geo-targeting the Chicago area. In this instance, odds are that the Chicago dentist is a bit more relevant. Now let's say the searcher changes their query to "online teeth whitening." While the user is still sitting in Chicago, their search query has turned more product oriented than local oriented, and in this case the online e-commerce store might see a slight bump.

The above scenario may not be used by Google, but it is intended to give insight into one of many reasons why Google might have these other relevancy factors that only sometimes come into play.

Most of the these factors are used when you are determining the displayed quality score in your account (with the exception of the factors that vary by user, such as the relevance of the keyword and ad copy to the actual search query). However, for the actual quality score used to determine your ad rank for search, Google does not use the landing page quality score.

While it is useful to know the factors involved in determining quality score, it is equally useful to be able to see the actual quality score by keyword to understand how your keywords are doing.

Viewing Your Quality Score

Quality score is listed as a number from 1 to 10. The higher the number, the better your quality score. Technically, Google keeps a different number strung out to many decimal places that is used in their calculations; however, they only display whole numbers to advertisers.

There are three places where you can view a keyword's quality score. The first is within the AdWords interface. At the ad group or campaign level, when you view keywords, you can also view the quality score (Figure 7.1).

		Keyword	Status ⑦	Max. CPC	Quality score ↓
☐	●		Total - all keywords		--
☐	●	internet marketing seminars	🗩 Eligible First page bid estimate: $0.20	$0.13	10/10
☐	●	web marketing seminars	🗩 Eligible First page bid estimate: $0.35	$0.13	10/10
☐	●	online marketing seminars	🗩 Eligible First page bid estimate: $0.15	$0.13	10/10
☐	●	business seminars	🗩 Eligible First page bid estimate: $0.35	$0.13	10/10
☐	●	seminar marketing	🗩 Eligible	$0.13	10/10
☐	●	marketing seminars	🗩 Eligible First page bid estimate: $0.20	$0.13	10/10

Figure 7.1 Viewing your quality score

The quality score column is hidden by default. If you do not see your quality score listed at the ad group or campaign level when viewing keyword, then you will have to customize the columns.

Click on the Filters and Views button on the far-right side of any page that displays your keywords and you will be presented with options for which statistics you would like to view (Figure 7.2).

Edit columns

Select columns
- ☐ Performance
- ☐ Destination URL
- ☑ Quality score
- ☑ Clicks
- ☑ Impr.
- ☑ CTR
- ☑ Avg. CPC
- ☐ Avg. CPM
- ☑ Cost
- ☑ Avg. Pos.

- ☑ Conv.
- ☑ Conv. (many-per-click)
- ☑ Cost / Conv. (many-per-click)
- ☑ Conv. Rate (many-per-click)
- ☑ Conv. (1-per-click)
- ☑ Cost / Conv. (1-per-click)
- ☑ Conv. Rate (1-per-click)

Preview
drag and drop to reorder

- Keyword
- Status
- Max. CPC
- Avg. Pos.
- Quality score
- Clicks
- Impr.
- CTR
- Avg. CPC
- Cost
- Conv. (many-per-click)
- Cost / Conv. (many-per-click)
- Conv. Rate (many-per-click)
- Conv. (1-per-click)
- Cost / Conv. (1-per-click)

Figure 7.2 Customizing ad group columns

Once this quality score is shown for your account, you can click on the conversation box next to Eligible to view more specific information about that keyword (Figure 7.3).

Figure 7.3 Detailed quality score information

When you see a low quality score in your account, this is the very first step you should undertake to diagnose problems. Often if there is a reason why your ads are not showing, it will also be shown within this dialog box. Please note that "landing page performance" is the exact same factor as "landing page load time."

The second place to view your quality score is in the AdWords Editor (Figure 7.4). The AdWords Editor is free software that Google maintains so you can manage your account on your desktop (or when you are offline). We will discuss it in detail in Chapter 12; for now, please note that this is another place where you can view your quality score.

		Max. CPC (USD)	First Page Bid Est. (USD)	Quality Score
		0.75	0.40	9
		0.75	0.25	9
		0.75	0.35	9
		0.75	0.03	9
		0.35	0.40	9
		0.75	0.03	9
		0.75	0.20	8
		0.75	0.25	8
		0.75	0.80	8
		0.75	1.25	8
		0.75	0.70	8

Figure 7.4 Viewing quality score in the AdWords Editor

The final place to view your quality score is within keyword reports. When creating a keyword report, in the Attributes section under Advanced Settings, be sure that the Quality Score box is checked (Figure 7.5).

This will give you an AdWords report, which can be exported into Excel, a list of your keywords, and quality score by keyword. We will revisit some ways to utilize this report in the section "Increasing Your Quality Scores."

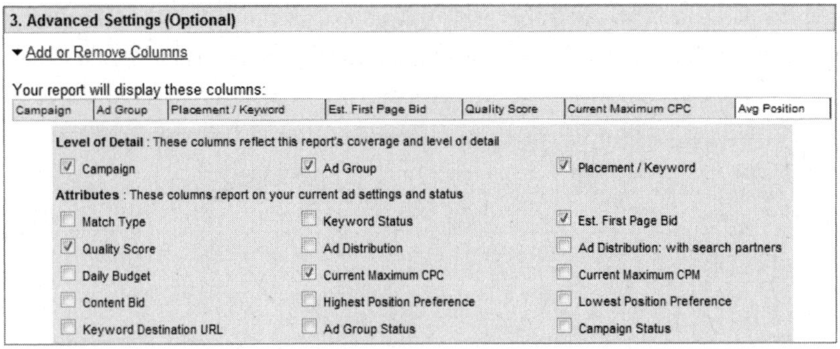

Figure 7.5 Adding quality score to a keyword report

Your choice of landing pages is not only important for increasing conversions, it is also essential to maintaining high quality scores. Later in this chapter, we will discuss ad group organization that will make it easy to choose the appropriate landing page. However, you also need to ensure that your landing page meets Google's guidelines.

Landing Page Quality: Making Your Pages Relevant

Google has developed landing page guidelines for AdWords based on giving the searcher the best possible experience after the click when they leave Google's property and enter your website.

Luckily, most of these guidelines actually help with conversions and your website's usability. By following these guidelines, you can make your page relevant for the consumer and for Google's quality score formula.

Spiderability

The first step to creating a relevant landing page is making sure that Google can read the page with their spiders (programs that index websites). If Google does not understand your landing page, it cannot ascertain if your landing page is relevant or not.

Google uses two different robots to spider your site for AdWords:

- Adsbot-Google
- Googlebot

A robots.txt file is an instruction manual that tells a robot what it can or cannot crawl on your website. If you use disallow all robots from crawling a page, then Adsbot-Google will ignore your robots.txt instructions. Adsbot-Google ignores these global disallows because it assumes since you are buying traffic to that page, you want the page to be indexed so a quality score can be created.

There are times when Googlebot may index your site instead of Adsbot-Google. If Googlebot has recently visited your site, Adsbot-Google may ignore your website as AdWords will use the information from the Googlebot crawl to determine your quality scores. However, if you block Googlebot in your robots.txt file, then Adsbot-Google will crawl your site so your account can be assigned quality scores.

If you are unsure how Adsbot-Google is treating your site, you can create a free Google Webmaster Central account (google.com/webmasters/) and use their tools to analyze your robots.txt file and make sure the site can be crawled.

Once you know that your site can be crawled, the next step is creating relevant pages.

Relevance

The destination URL should lead the searcher to a page on your website that answers the searcher's question or shows them how to receive their answer. This relevance is very similar to the ad copy relevance, as you do not have to have the actual keywords on the landing page. The page needs to be topically related.

If you are unsure what Google thinks your page is about, use the AdWords keyword tool discussed in Chapter 3. Input your landing page and let Google crawl your site. Now examine the keywords. If the keywords are similar to the keywords in your ad group and what *you* think the page is about, then your page should be relevant to the search query.

If the keyword tool thinks your page is about something completely different, you need to revisit the content on your page and possible rewrite some paragraphs. If you have a page that is mostly images and Flash, you may just wish to add some HTML content.

The content should also be unique to your site. You can have the content on multiple pages of your site, but you do not want the content to appear on other pages across the Web.

Note: For paid search, it is acceptable to have the same content on multiple pages of your website. However, for organic search engine optimization, having the same content across your website can lead to either a duplicate content penalty or Google ranking one page of your website when you would rather have a different page rank for that term. Use the robots.txt file to make sure only one version of your content is crawled and indexed by Googlebot. To learn about robots.txt files, visit www.robotstxt.org.

Sites that utilize manufacturer descriptions in their content can run into problems with this guideline. If there are a hundred sites with the same content, why should the searcher read it on your website? Mixing in some additional content, or writing some original content for your top-selling products can help increase the originality of your website.

This same concept holds true for *affiliates*. Affiliates are companies that refer consumers to another company to buy a product and in return receive some sort of compensation. An easy example is travel agents who are affiliates for airlines and cruise ships. Often affiliates feel that Google dislikes them. This is not true. There are many affiliate sites that have fantastic user experiences within them. The question affiliates should ask themselves is:

- Should the user have gone directly to the merchant instead of to my site first?
- What did I include on my site to enhance the search experience?

Your landing page should contain unique and relevant content that can be read by Google's bots. However, that is not quite enough to satisfy all of Google's landing page requirements. Transparency to the user about your business and website is also considered.

Transparency

Consumers are increasingly becoming aware of scams, phishing attempts, and privacy issues online. Being transparent with your offers and business information goes a long way toward meeting Google's editorial guidelines, landing page quality, and often increasing conversion rates as searchers have a better understanding of your company. For example, if you make a claim in your ad copy, such as free shipping, discounts, or a third-party authorization, put that information on your landing page.

Respect the searcher's computer. Do not alter their browser settings, disable the Back button, or attempt to auto-install software. Violating any of these three rules usually results in your ads quickly becoming disapproved. In addition, auto-installing software may result in your website being marked as untrusted in some privacy software.

In the United States, privacy policies can be tricky. In unregulated industries, privacy policies are not legally required. However, if you have one, it becomes a legal document. Please note that the European Union and other countries have different laws regarding privacy policies and whether they are required.

If you collect personal information, such as email addresses, credit cards, or phone numbers, then adding a privacy policy can increase your landing page quality, as you are giving consumers the ability to learn what you will do with their information. You do not need that information on the page; a simple link called "Privacy policy" is all that is required. Do not automatically sign up users for your newsletters if you collect their email address for other purposes, such as sending an ecommerce receipt. Allow a user to choose to receive your newsletter.

If you require registration to view the content on your site, allow someone to see a preview of the information before they are required to register on your website.

Navigation

If the searcher does not find the information they are looking for on the landing page, do they have additional options? In Chapter 6, we covered best practices for dedicated landing pages and reasons to include some additional navigation to your site from your landing page.

Another reason to add some navigational elements is that navigation is a factor in determining landing page quality. Your landing page does not have to have your typical full navigation; however, if the consumer does not find what they are looking for on your landing page, or if they want to learn more about your company, offers, etc., can they easily find that information on your website?

Generally, if you have the following links on your landing page, you will meet Google's navigational requirements:

- Home page
- About us page
- Contact us page
- More about the product or service
- Privacy policy

You should avoid pop-ups on the landing page. Hover items that do not open new windows are currently acceptable. However, adding pop-ups on load or exit often results in disapproved ads or low landing page quality scores.

Landing page quality is generally considered to have less weighting in the quality score formula compared to some of the other factors such a CTR. However, a low landing page quality score can hurt your quality score more than any other factor. A low landing page quality score may result in your ad not even showing.

Once your landing page has been deemed relevant by Google (which you can see earlier in Figure 7.3), your work is done. There is no need to keep changing your landing page for quality score reasons. You should test your landing pages and layouts to increase your conversion rates, but there is no need to test landing pages in attempts to increase your quality score.

Estimating Your First Page Bid

The first page bid is an approximation of what you need to bid for your ad to be shown on page 1. If your bid is below this number, your ad will rarely be shown on page 1. If your bid is above this number, your ad will usually be shown on page 1.

This approximation is based on the exact match version of the keyword. You may find that phrase match and especially broad match may be shown in much higher or lower positions than the exact match version. The search query report, discussed in Chapter 16, will give you insight into these broad and phrase match keywords. The first page bid is more accurate when your campaign is set to only show in one country.

Due to each region having different advertisers, each with their own daily budgets that affect how often their ads are shown, even if you bid above the first page bid, there may be times when your ad is not displayed on page 1. However, it is a decent number to work from when you are looking to ensure that your ads are receiving exposure.

When you view keywords at the campaign or ad group (Figure 7.6), one of the columns is labeled Status. If your current bid is above the first page bid, you will not see the first page bid estimate. If your current bid is below the first page bid, Google will display the estimated first page bid.

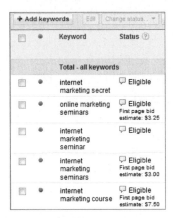

Figure 7.6 Viewing first page bids

It can be time consuming to look for instances of first page bids within each ad group. The easiest way to determine if your bids are below the first page bid is to create a keyword report where you include the current bid and first page bid attributes (Figure 7.7).

Placement / Keyword Report

Report Generated: May 28, 2009 5:36:56 AM Show report detail ▼

Export Report ▼   Create Another Report Like This
View: Summary

Avg Position
3.67

Placement / Keyword ↑	Est. First Page Bid	Current Maximum CPC	Avg Position
adwords class	$0.55	$2.50	3.0
adwords classes	$1.25	$2.50	3.0
adwords conference	$0.05	$2.50	2.0
adwords course	$0.85	$2.50	4.2
adwords courses	$0.65	$2.50	4.5
adwords faq	$0.05	$2.50	6.5
adwords forum	$0.05	$2.50	3.0
adwords help	$6.00	$2.50	15.5

Figure 7.7 Viewing first page bids in AdWords reports

Note: Microsoft Excel has a feature called *conditional formatting*, which lets you change the formatting of a cell or column based on particular criteria in that Excel file. One use of conditional formatting is to highlight the current bid column in red if the current bid number is below the first page bid number. This will allow you to quickly find which keyword bids are below the first page bids.

By viewing current bid and first page bids side by side in either Excel or the AdWords reports, it is easy to determine where your ad is not receiving page 1 placement.

Just because your current bid is below page 1 does not mean you should raise your bid to the page 1 bid amount. You may have keywords that are not profitable on page 1 and thus may be willing to have them not appear on page 1.

When Google determines page 1 bids, they use most of the quality score factors listed in the earlier section, "Quality Score Factors for Search." The factors that are not used are the ones that require real-time analysis, such as relevance of actual search query to the ad copy and keyword.

Understanding the Content Network Quality Score

The content network will be analyzed in Chapter 9, but there is one detail about the content network that you must understand when you are examining quality score. For the content network, Google examines all the keywords within an ad group to determine the ad group's theme. Google then tries to show your ad based upon that particular theme.

For instance, if you are reading an article on the *New York Times* website about airline travel, you will see a list of travel-based ads that are marked "Ads by Google." These ads are served based on the article's content and are not triggered by a user conducting a search.

This means there are two considerations when you are thinking about your content quality score:

- The ad group's theme matters more than individual keywords.
- Your content performance statistics are displayed at the ad group level (and ad copy level), not at the keyword level.

Your content network quality score is not a displayed number within your account. There is generally a correlation between a good search quality score and strong network placement. However, this is not always true because content advertising is quite different from search advertising.

Your content quality score determines:

- If an ad will be shown on a particular content site
- The ad's position on that content site

The factors that determine your content network's quality score are described here.

The Ad's CTR on that Exact Site and Similar Types of Sites Google examines how an ad performs on a specific site and sites with similar themes to determine if they will show an ad on a specific site. There are many thousands of sites in the content network, and often your ad has not been shown on a site previously. Therefore, Google uses a combination of how an ad has performed on similar-themed sites and the site where your ad will be displayed to determine if your ad should be shown on any specific site.

The CTR utilized for the content network will not affect your search CTR or search quality score. Often, content network CTRs are much lower than search CTRs. Therefore, the CTRs from these two different networks do not affect each other.

The Relevance of the Ads and Keywords within Each Ad Group to a Particular Website Google examines the keywords within an ad group to determine the ad group's theme. Google also examines the relevance of the ad copy to the website where your ad might be shown. The closer these two items are to the website's theme, the more likely your ad will be shown on that site.

Landing Page Quality The landing page quality used for the content network is the exact same as for the search network described earlier. We examined what makes a quality landing page in the section "Landing Page Quality: Making Your Pages Relevant" earlier in this chapter.

The above three factors are all that is used to determine your content network quality score. As this quality score can be thought of as being kept at the ad group level, when you want to optimize this quality score, you will either need to reorganize the keywords or write some new ad copy.

These factors are used to determine if an ad is shown across the content network when you have not chosen specific sites to place your ad, known as *placement targeting*. However, when you have chosen specific sites where you want your ad displayed, there are different factors used to determine if your ad will be shown, and where it will be shown, on those sites.

Placement Targeting Quality Score

With placement targeting, you choose exactly the sites where you want your ad to be displayed. Since you have chosen these sites, Google does not have to spend as much computing power determining the ad group's theme and whether an ad is appropriate to be shown on a particular site. Therefore, the factors used in quality score are different.

If you are bidding CPC (cost per click) on a placement, the two factors used in determining if your ad is shown are:

- The ad's CTR on that exact site and similar types of sites
- Landing page quality

The description of these two factors is the exact same as for the content quality score factors described earlier.

When placement targeting across the content network, you have an option to pay by CPM (cost per thousand impressions) instead of the usual cost per click. With CPM bidding, Google knows exactly how much they will make when your ad is shown because you are paying for each impression; therefore, they do not need to determine how likely your ad is to be clicked so they can get paid. This means that most of the relevancy factors do not come into play.

For CPM bidding on the content network, the only factor that is used to determine the quality score is landing page quality.

Since there are so many different places where Google stores and utilizes data to determine if, when, and where your ad should be shown, the first step to optimizing quality score is to determine where you want to increase your exposure (and decrease click prices). Once you have determined where you want to increase exposure, examine the factors that make up the quality score for that specific exposure type and work within those variables. (See Chapter 9 for more on placement targeting.)

Now that we have looked at how quality score is determined for different aspects of your account, let us dig deeper into Google's mantra—relevance.

Creating Highly Relevant Ad Groups

Relevance is a subjective word, and yet being relevant determines much about your account's success. There are four main places where Google attempts to ascertain relevance:

- Keyword to ad copy
- Ad copy to landing page
- Keyword to landing page
- Ad copy and keyword to content network sites

In these four instances, you might not be able to quantify relevance; however, there are exercises and research you can conduct to help ensure you are coming close to meeting Google's relevance guidelines.

The most time-consuming exercise, and the one that will give your account the best chance of long-term success, is successful account organization. Make no mistake, this organization will take time, but the rewards are worth the effort. Creating tightly themed ad groups where the ad copy is closely related to the keywords will not only lead to a higher quality score due to Google's relevancy algorithms, but it will also lead to higher click-through rates, which is the major component in your quality score.

To begin, write one highly targeted ad copy—an ad copy that does not have to be used within your account, but if a searcher reads it, that searcher could only assume that it describes exactly one service or product. After you write this ad copy, examine the keywords within that ad group. If the ad copy describes those keywords, then the keyword is in the correct ad group. If the ad copy does not describe the keyword, then the keyword needs to be in a new ad group.

The best organization possible would be to write one ad copy for one keyword. This way, the keyword and the ad copy are always closely related. However, that is not usually possible due to the restrictions on how many ad groups can be in a campaign and the fact that it would take significantly more time than the vast majority of people have. Therefore, it is much better to have 10 ad groups of 10 keywords that are closely related than one ad group of 100 keywords that are only marginally related.

It is common to see an ad such as:

John's Plumbing Service

Servicing the Chicago area

Call for an appointment today!

be shown for an ad group with these keywords within it:

- Chicago plumbing
- Plumbing service
- Broken pipes
- Emergency plumbing
- 24-hour plumbing
- Fix shower
- Overflowing toilet
- Saturday plumbing
- Weekend plumbing
- Flooded basement

The common argument is that plumbers offer all of these services, therefore, I only need to write one ad to describe all of these keywords. The truth is that while you might have some keywords that are fairly generic (such as plumbing) where this ad copy would serve, an account would be much better served to break this copy into more targeted ad groups.

An emergency plumber is one who is willing to come to a house at 3:00 a.m. on Tuesday. You might want to hire a weekend plumber who will not charge double time for the visit to your house. Instead of using a single ad copy, consider the ads and keywords shown in Table 7.2.

Ad Group	Ad Copy	Keywords
Emergency plumbing	Emergency Plumbing Service	Emergency plumbing
Emergency plumbing	Call 24/7 for immediate service	24-hour plumbing
Emergency plumbing	We will be there in an hour or less	Midnight plumber
Weekend plumbing	Weekend plumbing service	Saturday plumbing
Weekend plumbing	Don't pay high weekend rates	Weekend plumbing
Weekend plumbing	We work all day, every day	Sunday Chicago plumber

This granular grouping of keywords and ad copy will allow you to write ads that truly reflect your keywords. In addition, because your ad groups now contain only a single theme, it is easier to pick (or create) the landing page on your website that best reflects your keywords. Almost every ad group will use a different landing page.

While not a factor in quality score, you may often see higher conversion rates when you use ad copy and landing pages that are closely related to the original search query.

By organizing your account in this manner, it is common to see:

• Higher click-through rates

• Higher relevancy

• Higher quality scores

• Higher conversion rates

• Lower cost per lead

• Lower cost per click

Compared to accounts that are organized in the original manner described that contain one ad copy and a handful of semi-related keywords, this might take some time, but it is some of the best time investment you can make with your account.

Using the Tilde Search Command to Find Relevant Keywords

There are several advanced search operators that you can string together to find related keywords on a Google search result.

• When you do a search on Google, your keyword is bolded in both ad copy and the natural results.

• When the tilde (~) character prefixes a search on Google, it signals that you want information related to that search query.

• When you use a negative sign in a search query, it signals to Google that you do not want to see that word in the search results.

Continues

Therefore, the search query "~roses -roses" tells Google that you want information related to roses, but that you do not want to see the word "roses" in your search results. The search results will then bold the next most related keywords, as shown in the following illustration, which in this case are "flower," "flowers," and "rose."

You can continue this search string and continue to add negative search queries to the search to find all of the related keywords. In this example, your next search would be "~roses -roses -flowers -flower -rose."

What to Do if Your Quality Score Drops

There will be times when your quality score may suddenly drop. In these cases, there are some steps to follow to find the problem and try to fix it.

The very first step is to look at the quality score pop-up (refer back to Figure 7.3) to see if Google will let you know what the problem is. However, the problem will not always be listed.

A good corporate practice is to make sure your company has a communication system between your IT and marketing departments. It's possible that IT has launched a new version of the website and has broken your URLs. In this case, you are sending traffic to error pages. If you also have an SEO (search engine optimization) department, then make sure there is communication with this department as they might institute mod rewrites, modify a robots.txt file, or make other changes to your website that could affect your quality score. Having a record of website changes, and preparing for website changes, can save many headaches at a later date.

Keep track of and archive your quality score data. When you run a report in Google, the quality score listed is the number at that exact moment in time. You cannot see previous quality scores. You can schedule a report to be automatically run and emailed to you (Figure 7.8). Set up a keyword report that includes your quality score to be emailed to you on a regular basis (daily or weekly) so that you have an archive of your keywords and quality scores.

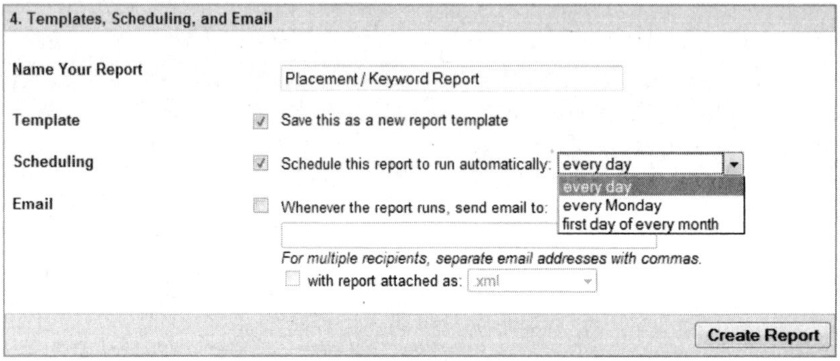

Figure 7.8 Schedule reports to be sent to you automatically.

When you find that a quality score has dropped, look through your reports to find the time frame where the drop occurred. Once you have isolated the time frame, use the My Change History tool (Figure 7.9) to see what changes were made in your account during that time. You will find times when new destination URLs, ad copy changes, or campaign changes affected your quality score.

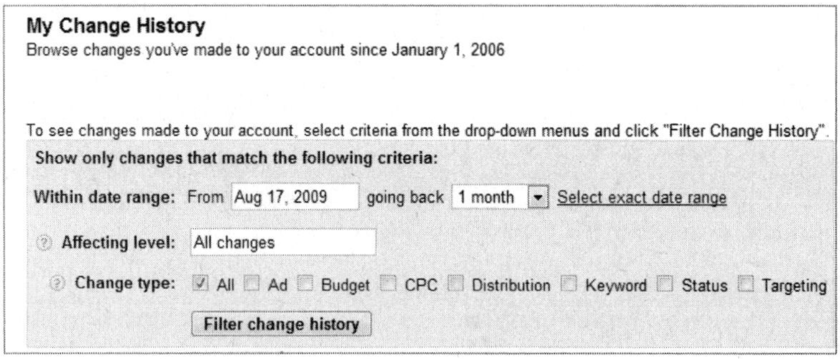

Figure 7.9 My Change History tool

If you have yet to turn up a reason for the lower quality score, then examine the natural search results. Has the keyword changed in search intent? In Chapter 2, there was an example of the word "bleach" having a higher search volume for the anime show than for the cleaning product. There are many examples of news stories, new products, and new services changing the meaning of a word, which could result in changes to that keyword's quality score.

The AdWords Editor (featured in Chapter 12) allows you to keep notes associated with data points in your account. Using the AdWords Editor notes helps you keep track of your changes, reasons, and investigations into quality score changes.

There will be times when none of these investigations turns up a reason for that change. If the quality score box does not list a reason for the low quality score, then your landing page, keyword, and ad copy should be relevant. In these situations, the best steps to take are the ones you take to improve quality score in the first place:

- Check your ad group organization. Can it be more granularly organized?

- Does your CTR vary widely by geography? You can determine this by looking at geographic performance reports (covered in Chapter 11). If so, use geo-targeted campaigns to write more effective ad copy.

- Does your CTR vary widely by time of day, day of week, or even days of the month? If so, try utilizing ad scheduling (see Chapter 13).

- Test new ad copies. Determine if a different ad copy has either a higher CTR or higher relevancy, which will raise quality score.

If Google does not give you a reason for the lower quality score, then almost always you need to increase relevancy or CTR. Focus on those two items to see what combinations of ad delivery, ad copy, and keyword usage increase your quality score. However, never forget your profit. There may be times when a campaign is highly profitable and you make a business decision that working with lower quality scores is acceptable for your account.

Increasing Your Quality Scores

Spending all day looking for low quality scores, clicking on the text box to see the detailed quality score information, and then trying to reorganize your ad groups or write new ad copy can be a daunting task. There is a more efficient way to spend your time by isolating the problem areas:

1. Run a keyword report that includes at least these six columns:
    - Campaign
    - Ad group
    - Keyword
    - Cost
    - Quality score
    - Impressions

2. Once you become familiar with this method, you may wish to add conversion data to the process.

3. After you have run the report, export the data into Microsoft Excel.

4. Create a pivot table using your keyword report as the data source.

Creating Pivot Tables

A pivot table summarizes data sets. Using pivot tables is an easy way to combine many data points into a higher level data set that makes it easier to analyze the data.

Creating pivot tables in Excel 2007 takes less than 10 seconds. Follow these steps:

1. Import the data into Excel.

2. Delete all rows above the title row (the row that contains the label keyword, ad group, quality score, etc.).

3. Go to the Insert tab, and push the PivotTable button (on the far left of the Ribbon).

4. Make sure that the entire sheet is selected, and then click OK.

A new worksheet will be created that contains the pivot table information.

Microsoft help files for creating pivot tables can be found at `http://office.microsoft.com/en-us/excel/HP101773841033.aspx`.

With pivot tables, you can choose to see the average quality score of an ad group, which we will show in a moment. However, when you look at the average quality score by ad group, each keyword is given the same weight regardless of clicks and impressions. For instance, if your ad group contained these statistics:

Keyword	Impressions	Quality Score
Keyword 1	1000	4
Keyword 2	10	7
Keyword 3	1	10

the average quality score of this ad group would be 7—that is, $(4+7+10) \div 3$.

However, if you weighted the quality score of this ad group by impressions, you would have a much different picture. If you take a keyword's impressions multiplied by its quality score and add these numbers together for all keywords within the ad group, then divide by the ad group's total impressions:

$$\frac{(1000 \times 4) + (10 \times 7) + (1 \times 10)}{1011}$$

you would see that this ad group really has a quality score of 4.03, not 7.

The reason to work with the weighted average is that you are going to create a pivot table that will let you find places where you have low quality scores and high spends. Therefore, once you have your keyword report imported into Excel, add one more column labeled QS * Impressions. To populate this column, just create a formula that multiples the keyword's quality score by its impressions.

Now create the pivot table. Once the pivot table is created, use ad groups as the rows, and Sum of Impressions, Sum of QS * Impressions, and Sum of Cost as the columns.

Finally, create a column for real quality score where you look at the weighted average. All you need to do is divide the Sum of QS * Impressions by Sum of Impressions. This will create a column that shows you your real quality score. When you are done, you should have a pivot table that looks like Figure 7.10. In some Excel configurations, you cannot create a formula that utilizes pivot table data. Therefore, copy and paste the pivot table columns you want to work with (such as Sum of QS * Impressions and Sum of Impressions) and paste them as values only, then use these values-only columns when you write the real quality score column's formula.

Row Labels	Sum of Impressions	Sum of QS * Impressions	Sum of Cost	Actual QS
Ad Group #1	24446	122230	25.79	5.00
Ad Group #2	20934	104670	46.18	5.00
Ad Group #3	10608	53040	43.31	5.00
Ad Group #4	37975	189875	89.03	5.00
Ad Group #5	11222	56110	18.8	5.00
Ad Group #6	2542	12710	1.56	5.00
Ad Group #7	12062	60310	20.48	5.00
Ad Group #8	703392	5498936	7823.28	7.82
Ad Group #9	1491940	4188542	7862.72	2.81
Ad Group #10	383472	2684303	1737.79	7.00
Ad Group 11	25130	125650	155.41	5.00
Ad Group 12	334848	2343936	2145.51	7.00
Ad Group 13	120801	845084	1595.61	7.00
Ad Group 14	103553	724871	2488.97	7.00
Ad Group 15	7564994	37824970	20874.08	5.00
Ad Group 16	12556	62780	351.45	5.00

Figure 7.10 Pivot table with real quality score and cost data

What you want to look for is ad groups with both high spends and low quality scores. In Figure 7.10, Ad Group 9 has the highest spend and the lowest quality score. That is the best ad group for you to spend your time optimizing. As you become more familiar with pivot tables, you can add additional data points such as conversions or ROI (return on investment) to the table. This table will not tell you what to do. It will present summary information that should be easy to analyze to find a starting place for your optimization. Looking at ad group data is easier than looking at tens of thousands of keyword quality scores.

Once you have found ad groups with high spends and low quality scores, then navigate to these ad groups in your AdWords account and click on the dialog boxes (Figure 7.3) to see what the problems are with those keywords.

Pivot tables are so useful that we will use them in other chapters when there are too many data points to find meaning. Instead, you can summarize the data, find the weaknesses, and then investigate and optimize the ad groups.

Quality Score FAQs

There are a handful of questions that always present themselves when quality score is being discussed.

What Happens if a Keyword or Ad Is Paused or Deleted? When a keyword or ad copy is paused or deleted, it does not accrue impressions. If no data is being collected, this ad copy or keyword does not currently affect your quality score.

Can I Save this Keyword? If you have a keyword that has not done well for you, but you believe in it and want to run it, then, yes, you can save it. Most recent history matters more than all-time history. If you have a problem keyword, do this:

1. Delete it everywhere in your account. This will help you isolate its appearance.
2. Create a new ad group with just that keyword.
3. Write a few highly targeted ads for just that keyword, and send the traffic to a relevant landing page.

It will take some work, but if the keyword is relevant to your business, then you should be able to make it work.

When Reorganizing My Account, What Keywords Should I Move? If a keyword is performing in your account, do not move it. When you move a keyword, it needs to build up a new history within the new ad group. Instead, always move low performing keywords to new ad groups.

Can't I Just Buy My Way Out of Trouble? Relevancy trumps money at Google. There are times when you can buy your way to the top with enough money if your landing page and ad copy are somewhat relevant. If they are completely irrelevant, your dollars will not help you. Spend your money on creating a more relevant experience on your website and writing appropriate ads. You will find much better success in this manner.

I Resumed a Paused Keyword and It Dropped in Position and Quality Score Pausing and resuming keywords or ad copy does not affect your quality score. Pausing campaigns will not affect your quality score. It is not uncommon to see new competitors enter the market, changes in keyword intent, and changes in quality score formulas occur over time.

When you resume a keyword, it may drop in position due to the new competitors driving up the keyword price or a new quality score formula being released.

How Do I Get My Ad Above the Natural Search Results? Sometimes you will see no ads above the search results, and other times you may see several ads (Figure 7.11) in that same spot. There are two things that need to happen for your ads to show in the top spot:

1. Google examines a keyword for commercial intent and how often that keyword results in clicks (and some other secret sauces), and determines how many ads they might show in these premium positions.

2. Assuming Google has decided to show at least one ad in the premium position, they look at your CPC and quality score.

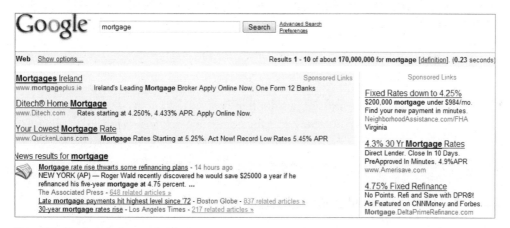

Figure 7.11 Premium ads shown on Google

Your quality score is held to a higher standard than normal and must meet certain minimum guidelines for your ad to be shown in these top positions. If your keyword meets the minimum quality score guidelines, then Google examines your CPC. If the combination of your CPC and quality score are high enough, then your ad can be shown in the top spot.

If your quality score and CPC do not meet their minimum requirements to be shown in the top position, and your competitor's ad in a lower position does meet those requirements, Google may leapfrog your competitor's ad over yours and display it in the premium position.

How Often Is Quality Score Updated? Google currently updates quality score approximately 10 times per quarter. While this is roughly once a week, sometimes quality score can be updated twice in one week and then not updated for two weeks.

However, this does not mean that if you change your landing page the landing page quality score will be reflected in each update. Google crawls landing pages on occasion; the more traffic you receive, the more often your site is crawled. When your landing page changes have been processed, the changes should be reflected within your account the next time quality score is updated.

Google updates the quality score algorithm about once per month. These are slight tweaks to the algorithm that may or may not affect your account.

Quality score was created to ensure that Google shows searchers relevant ads and sends those searchers to websites that help them find the answers to their search queries. While there are some factors and rules that can be quantified to help you optimize your keywords for higher quality scores, always keep the searcher in mind when making changes to your ad copy and landing pages.

Google tries to show the most appropriate ads to each searcher, but the searchers also vote by clicking on your ads. As click-through rate is the highest weighted factor in determining quality score, those clicks ultimately decide if your keywords will receive high quality scores.

Best Practices for Optimizing Quality Scores

Quality score is one of the most important numbers you can understand and optimize in your account. While the number can seem ambiguous to work with, once you understand these principles, it is a number that can be quantified and improved.

- To increase your ad rank, you either need to raise your bid or increase your quality score.
  - If you have a low quality score, you should optimize your quality score instead of raising bids.
  - If your quality score is high, you need to raise your maximum CPC. When raising your maximum CPC, always make sure the new bid does not make your keyword unprofitable.
- It is essential that you create granular ad groups with very closely related keywords and ad copy.
- To make your landing page relevant, make sure it possesses the following four attributes:
  - *Spiderability*: Ensure that Google's bots can find and read your landing pages.
  - *Relevance*: Your landing page must reflect the keyword or its general theme.
  - *Transparency*: Tell the searcher what you will do with their private information.
  - *Navigation*: Enable the searcher to navigate to other sections of your website if they do not find what they are looking for on the landing page.

- It is useful to always have your quality score displayed in your account and the AdWords Editor so you can easily notice quality score changes.

- Look for areas where your first page bid is higher than your maximum CPC. These words receive little exposure, and raising the maximum CPC or optimizing their quality score will help raise their ad rank so they appear on page 1.

- Your quality score will change over time. This is due to your keywords and ad copy accruing more data from clicks or from Google updating their quality score algorithm. Use the My Change History tool, AdWords Editor notes, and report scheduling to keep historical data about your account.

- When trying to increase quality scores for search, there are three main steps:

  1. Examine the detailed quality score information inside your AdWords account. If there is a problem, fix that problem first.

  2. If there are no problems listed, examine your ad group's ad copy and keyword organization. Move any unrelated words to a new ad group.

  3. If the ad group is already closely related, then write new ad copy to examine its relevance and click-through rate.

- Your content quality score is not shown by Google. However, you can still optimize your content quality score by keeping these two points in mind:

  - The theme of your keywords should match the theme of your landing page and ad copy. Individual keywords on the content network do not matter as much as keywords on the search network. The theme of your keywords is the most important factor to consider for content placement.

  - The click-through rate of your ads on a single site or similar types of sites is used in determining if your ad will show on a site. Do not focus on overall content CTR, focus on the CTR of sites bringing you valuable traffic (discussed in Chapter 9).

- Use pivot tables to save time in identifying quality score problem areas.

By following these principles, you should be able to track your quality score and its change over time. Then, when you find areas that can be improved, you should be able to improve your quality score, which will lead to higher ad position or a decrease in cost per click.

Up to this point in the book, we have primarily covered text ads and the search network. In the next chapter, we will cover some of the additional ad types found in Google AdWords, such as video and image ads, which are shown not on search, but across the content network.

Beyond Text: Image, Video, and Mobile Ads

Mobile usage has been on the rise for several years and is a significant challenge for all web developers. You can use available techniques to reach and engage this mobile audience. Google AdWords also supports several types of ads that enable you to reach desktop users in new ways. You can use rich media (such as video, interactive, or image) to boost your campaign and increase clicks to your site and brand recall.

Building image or video ads can be costly and time consuming. We will examine Google's tool that allows you to build rich media ads within the AdWords interface, saving you time and money.

This chapter focuses on building additional ad types, and then in the following two chapters we will discuss places to utilize these ads in your AdWords content campaigns.

Chapter Contents

Beyond the Desktop: Creating Mobile Ads

Mobile users have different needs than people on a desktop computer. They often want different information when they are out in the community than when they are at home or in the office. For example, if someone searches for the brand Best Buy while on the computer, they may be looking for an actual location, to purchase an item, or for some price comparison. If that same user is looking up Best Buy on a mobile phone, the searcher is most likely not looking to buy an item over the phone (e-commerce activity on mobile devices is still quite low compared to desktops). It is more likely that the user is either comparing prices or trying to find the nearest location. In this case, the landing pages could be completely different for the mobile search versus the desktop search.

The desktop search will take someone into Best Buy's main website, where the user can decide where to go on the site. For a mobile phone user, waiting for a site to load and then trying to search throughout a website can be a frustrating experience. Sending the mobile user to a landing page that has driving directions or location lookups for the nearest locations as a primary action, and then viewing products as a secondary action, could lead to a higher user engagement for that mobile site.

As another example, someone searching for a locksmith on a desktop computer might want to know more about locks, pricing options, redoing the locks on their front door, or maybe adding an alarm system to their house. You do not know the intent of such a general search. However, if someone is on the phone searching for locksmiths, that user is probably locked out of their car or house. Those two experiences should be met with two different landing pages.

For many businesses, mobile advertising is highly effective. Before starting mobile advertising, first think about the reasons someone might search for your products or services from a mobile phone. Once you have those pieces of information, some of the later decisions we will walk through in setting up mobile campaigns will be easier to make.

There are a few different ways to reach mobile users with Google AdWords, depending on the user's mobile technology. The sophistication of the user's phone will determine what type of ads they can see and what type of ad you need to create to reach them.

Reaching iPhone Users

There are two types of browsers that come installed on mobile phones:

- A full Internet browser, also called a full HTML browser
- A basic browser that does not display entire websites

The full HTML browser is the type that an iPhone or BlackBerry Storm user has. These browsers can support scripts and render most websites very similarly to what you would see in a desktop browser.

However, cell phone speeds are slower than broadband speeds. Therefore, web elements such as large images, scripts, and so on can take a long time to load. When designing landing pages for iPhone or Storm users, keep in mind the total time it will take for your page to load on a mobile device. Most users understand that it takes a few more seconds, but if the page takes too long, these users will navigate back to the search results and visit someone else's website instead of yours.

In addition, not all full HTML browsers support Flash or all web elements. Be careful not to add too many design parameters to mobile landing pages even if the user has a full HTML browser.

Reaching a user on a full Internet browser can be done quite easily. Navigate to your campaign settings screen, where you can choose on what networks you wish to display your ads. One of the options is Devices (Figure 8.1) where you can choose to display your ad on:

- Desktop and laptop computers
- iPhones and other devices with full Internet browsers

Networks, devices, and extensions

Networks ⑦   **Content**   Edit

Devices ⑦

○ All available devices (Recommended for new advertisers)
◉ Let me choose...
  ☑ Desktop and laptop computers
  ☑ iPhones and other mobile devices with full Internet browsers
    ⊟ Advanced device and carrier options
    Devices
    ◉ All mobile devices
    ○ Target only selected mobile devices
      ☐ Android ☐ iPhone/iPod Touch ☐ Palm webOS
    Carriers
    ◉ All mobile carriers ⑦
    ○ Target only selected mobile carriers
      Canada: ☐ Bell Canada ☐ Rogers ☐ Telus
    United States: ☐ AT&T ☐ Cricket Communications
        ☐ Metro PCS ☐ Nextel ☐ Sprint ☐ T-Mobile
        ☐ Verizon

  Save   Cancel

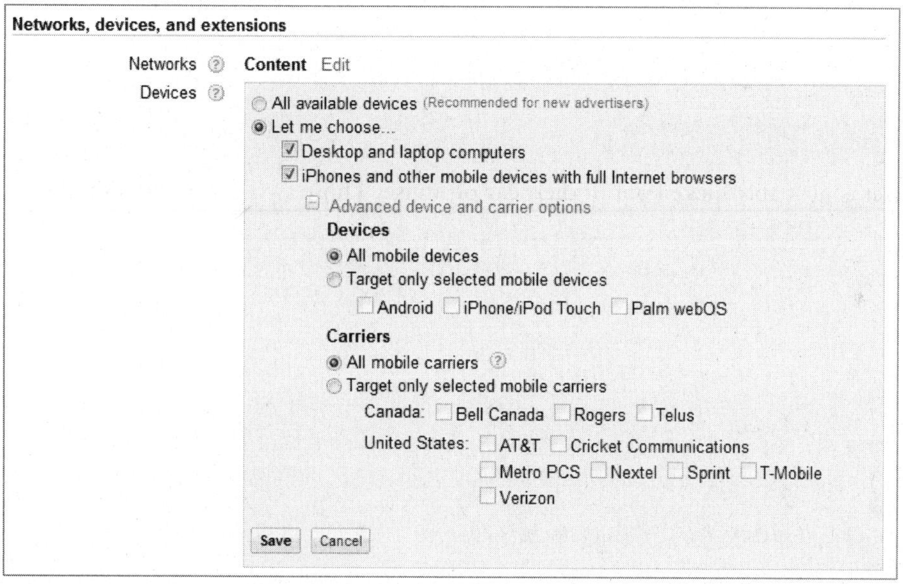

Figure 8.1 AdWords campaign device settings

You can choose one or both options. If you choose both computers and mobile devices with full Internet browsers, then your search text ads will be shown to users of either of these devices. Be careful about using that method. If you want to show a different landing page to mobile versus computer users, you will want two campaigns.

The first campaign will be your existing campaign that reaches computer users. Duplicate that campaign (when you use the AdWords Editor discussed in Chapter 12, duplicating a campaign will take only a few seconds), and then set the new campaign to only be shown on mobile devices. The last step will be to change the landing pages of your ads and keywords in the new mobile campaign to send the users to your mobile landing pages.

You can target mobile users based upon the phone's operating system or the carrier. If you are selling iPhone applications in the United States, then you would only want your ad shown to iPhones that are AT&T's network. If you had created an Android application, then you will want to show your ad on all carriers, but choose to only show your ad on Android devices. A local store using mobile ads to send searchers to driving direction pages should not filter ads by device or carrier and choose all carriers and all devices.

Viewing Your Site's iPhone Usage

You can view your site's current mobile usage in some analytics systems. If you use Google Analytics, navigate to the Advanced Segments option in the right corner of your Google Analytics account. There you can choose to only view iPhone visitors, as shown in the following illustration. Please note, this will not include visits from other full Internet browsers, such as the BlackBerry Storm.

Not all users have sophisticated phones with full Internet browsers. To reach these users, you need to utilize Google's mobile ads.

Reaching Other Mobile Users: Google Mobile Ads

Most phones do not have full Internet browsers. Cell phones such as the BlackBerry Curve or Motorola Razr have basic web browsing capabilities. These phones can access the Internet, but they can only view pages that are designed to be rendered on a mobile device.

Because these phones need specifically created pages, their users do not see the typical text ads on a Google search page. These users only see Google mobile ads on their search pages.

Google mobile ads are created at the ad group level. They are only shown if your keywords within that ad group are triggered. These ads follow all of your typical campaign settings such as location or time of day targeting. To create a Google mobile ad, follow these steps:

1. Navigate to the ad group where you wish to create the ad.

2. Click on the Ads tab.

3. Click New Ad.

4. Choose Mobile Ad (Figure 8.2).

Figure 8.2 Choose Mobile Ad to create a new mobile ad.

You should be presented with an ad creation screen (Figure 8.3). Your new ad can be either text or an image. Since mobile screens are smaller than computer monitors, so are the mobile ads.

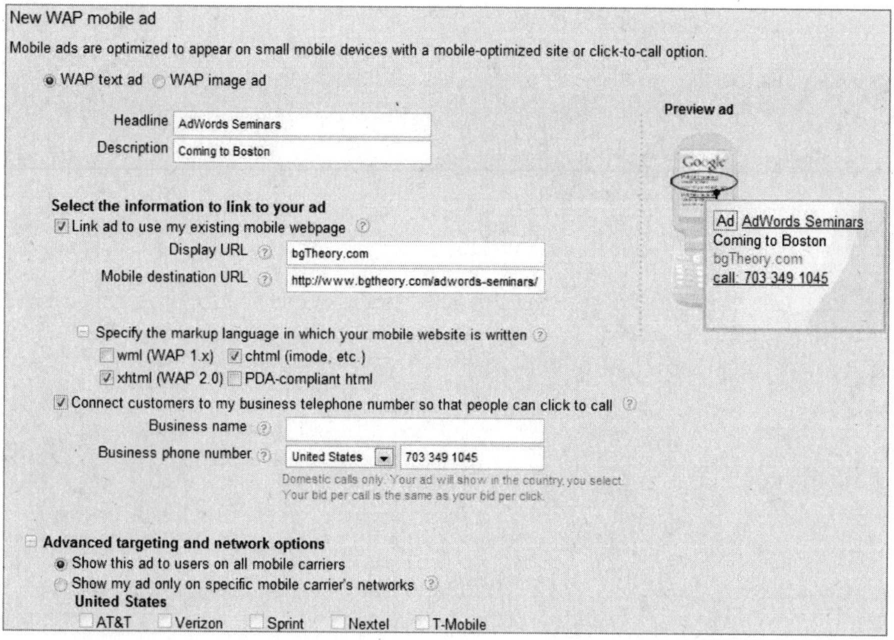

Figure 8.3 Mobile ad creation wizard

If you choose to create a text ad, your new ad will only contain two 18-character lines along with a display URL. Mobile text ads must still meet all of the editorial requirements of typical ads as discussed in Chapter 4.

Mobile image ads are smaller in size than normal image ads. If you click the WAP Image Ad button (as seen in Figure 8.3) you will be presented with an upload button and the image size requirements. Mobile image ads must meet image ad editorial requirements (discussed later in the chapter in the section "Technical and Editorial Requirements for Image Ads").

Once you have created the ad, the next step is deciding what options you will present to a user who clicks on your ad. There are three options:

- Send the user to your website
- Initiate a call to your phone number
- Give the user both choices

If you want to send users to your website, your website must be mobile compatible. You cannot send users who click on a mobile ad to a typical HTML-coded website.

An Easy Way to Create Mobile Compatible Sites

If you want to test out mobile advertising but do not want to pay to have a full website developed, there is an easy way to create a small mobile site to test the traffic.

First, install WordPress, an open source content management system that takes only a few minutes to set up on a server that supports PHP and MySQL.

WordPress supports a large variety of plug-ins that expand the functionality of the CMS (content management system). One of these is WordPress Mobile Edition. Information for the plug-in can be found at bgtheory/go/mobile/. Install the plug-in.

Lastly, create your landing pages based on what you want a visitor to see, such as phone number, driving directions, etc.

If you are technically minded, you can set up WordPress, install the plug-in, and create some new pages within an hour. And best of all, as it is open source, the entire system is free outside of your hosting fees.

If you do not have a mobile compatible site, or you want users to call you instead of visiting the site, then you can only choose to allow visitors to call your business. This is often the best choice for locksmiths, towing companies, and other service-based businesses.

You can give the user a choice of calling or clicking. In this case, the ad will be clickable and there will be a call feature next to the ad for someone to initiate a call to your company.

The last option is to have your ad show across all carriers or only specific carriers. For most companies, you will want to choose all carriers. However, if you are offering services that only certain types of phones can install, then you might want to limit your ads to the carriers that support that phone.

Tracking Mobile Conversions

AdWords conversion tracking (covered in Chapter 13) works with mobile ads; put your conversion tracking script on your mobile site's thank-you pages. However, not all phones support all scripts, so while conversion tracking is supported, the numbers will not be 100 percent accurate.

If you allow users to call you from your mobile ads, it is beneficial to use a separate phone number from your website so you can track how often you receive calls and the quality of those phone calls.

Viewing Google Mobile Ads

If your customers search for your services, products, or business while away from their computers, it can be worth your time to test mobile ads. Seeing what your ads look like if you do not own a phone on each carrier can be difficult, however. The easiest way to view mobile ads is to use Google's mobile ad preview tool (Figure 8.4), which you can access at `www.google.com/m/adpreview/`.

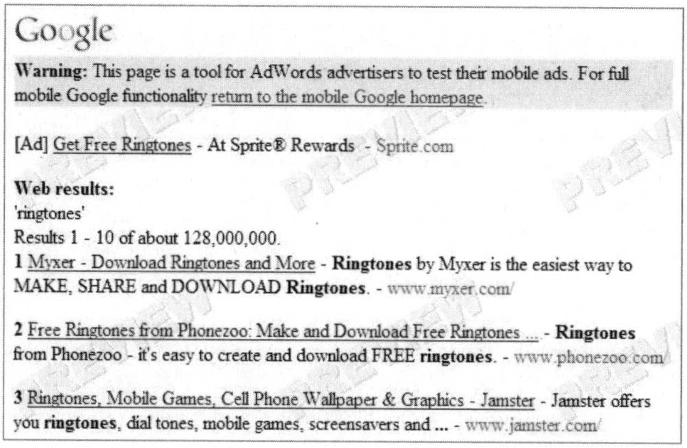

Figure 8.4 Previewing Google mobile ads

While you can do a search on Google mobile (`www.google.com/m`) in an attempt to see mobile ads, Google rarely shows mobile ads to desktop users, and odds are you will not see your ad at that property.

The other option is to use Firefox plug-ins such as WMLbrowser (`https://addons.mozilla.org/en-US/firefox/addon/62/`), which make your browser appear to be a mobile device. This is useful for previewing both ads and mobile web pages.

The total inventory for mobile ads is still low. The number of searches on phones is only a fraction of what occurs on the desktop. However, often the buy intent is higher on a mobile device. You might comparison shop different locksmiths from a desktop computer, but if you are searching for a locksmith on a mobile device, you probably need a locksmith pretty quickly.

While mobile ads allow you to reach those not on a desktop, Google offers many ad types besides text ads to reach users who are still on their computers. In the next section, we will examine additional ad types that will increase your company's visibility across the Internet.

Beyond Static Text: Creating Rich Media Ads

AdWords support different ad formats beyond text ads. The most simple of these are *image ads*. Image ads look like your standard banner ads. The second ad format is known as *rich media ads*. Rich media ads are ad formats with which a user can interact, such as video ads.

These additional ad formats only show up on the content network (which will be discussed in depth in the following two chapters). Image and rich media ads are not shown on Google.com or search partners.

Image and rich media ads are typically paid for the same way you pay for text ads, cost per click. There is an additional feature of AdWords where you can bid cost per thousand impressions (CPM) for the image types, which will be discussed in Chapter 9. While the bidding methodology and setting bids are the exact same for these additional ad formats, it is not uncommon to see slightly higher prices for image ads due to the fact that you need to win the entire ad block for your ad to be shown.

Some of the benefits of using image and rich media ads are:

- Creating product awareness
- Establishing higher brand recall value
- Associating your brand with a product line
- Introducing new products or services
- Educating consumers on the product
- Creating higher content network CTR
- Seeing an increase in search CTR due to brand recognition
- Increasing product's awareness
- Moving consumers into the buying funnel

Creating Effective Image Ads

Image ads serve two main purposes. The first use of image ads is to direct traffic to your website. These ads are measured in total clicks, conversions from those clicks, and cost per click.

The second reason to use image ads is to increase awareness of your products or services. These images should match other advertising efforts you are conducting, such as TV, print, or banner ads. Matching online and offline images can help increase your brand's awareness by connecting the consumer's awareness of your brand across channels.

Often the success of image ads is measured in brand lift, increased searches for your branded keywords, or increased click-through rate of your search ads. It is not uncommon to see your search CTR rise while your image or banner ads are being displayed across the Web. As images should lead to a higher awareness of your brand, you may see a higher search CTR as your brand becomes more recognizable and your site increases in authority.

There is a reason the old adage "A picture is worth a thousand words" has stood the test of time—it is true and can be applied to search. Text ads have very little recall. After a consumer sees your text ad, there is little chance they will remember the benefits the product promised. Image ads have much higher recall values. Often a consumer can recall the benefit of an ad that included images. If one of your advertising goals is not just to click, but to increase your brand presence or align your company with a product, image ads are much more effective at accomplishing these goals.

The Tenants of Effective Image Ads

There are a few commandments you should follow when creating image ads:

Image Ads Should Command Attention Most banner-type ads can be camouflaged in the page. If your ad blends in with the rest of the page, it will be easy for users to ignore the image. Use visuals that stand out from the page and illustrate your point (Figure 8.5).

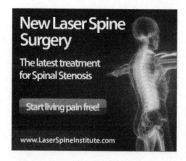

Figure 8.5 While this ad does many things correctly, the highlighted spine enhances this ad's point of living pain free.

Image Ads Should Be Easy to Comprehend While image ads should contain some text that lets the reader know what you offer, if you have too much text in a small ad, your main points will be lost. You should be able to glance at your image ad and know exactly what is being advertised without having to study it.

The first ad's offer (Figure 8.6) is less expensive than the second ad (Figure 8.7). However, the text in Figure 8.6 makes it difficult to quickly comprehend all the information in the ad. Most users will not study your ads before clicking. The information should be clear and concise.

Figure 8.6 Ads that contain too much text are difficult to comprehend

Figure 8.7 An ad that lacks a call to action

Image Ads Should Clearly Offer Consumers a Benefit Search ads are shown to individuals who are researching your market and are learning the features and benefits of different products and services. Image or banner ads are shown to an individual regardless of their purchase intent. Therefore, showing a clear benefit is essential. In addition, as these individuals may not even be in the buying funnel yet, offering free information or a compelling reason to click is also essential (Figure 8.8). This can help you move someone who is unaware of your product into the buying funnel.

Figure 8.8 Offering free information can entice someone into the buying funnel.

Image Ads Should Contain a Call to Action There is a difference between someone reading your ad and someone clicking on your ad. Without a clear call to action, a user will often read the ad, understand the information, but without further instructions will wander back to the content on the page. Make sure there is a clear call to action, such as a button that stands out from the rest of the ad.

Figure 8.9 "Get Yours Now" is a red button that stands out from the rest of the ad.

If you know the website where your ad will be displayed, you can also direct your message differently to the consumer. For instance, an image ad that displays across various networks needs to have a general offer, such as a free download, free trial, or compelling benefit for the user to visit your website. The biggest reason for these offers is that the user may not be in the buying funnel for your products, and you need to use the image ad to enter them into the buying funnel so you can eventually do business with them.

If the user is on a website that indicates they have entered the buying funnel, then you could show them an ad that does not offer a free or low cost entry point to your services, but instead directs them further into the buying funnel (Figure 8.10).

Figure 8.10 If someone is on a site that contains LCD TV reviews, this is a perfect ad to show them so they enter the buying funnel on your website.

If you know additional information about a user, utilize that information within your ads as well. This ad from Ford (Figure 8.11) shows the user's location and how far a single gallon of gas will take them by incorporating a map program into the ad. This type of ad helps the user visualize exactly the benefit of buying this car.

Figure 8.11 A Ford ad that incorporates a map to illustrate a vehicle's gas mileage

These same tenets of effective ads apply to both static and dynamic (such as Flash) image ads. With dynamic ads, the user may not watch the entire ad, therefore the opening and ending images should follow the exact same rules as static ads. However, while any additional animations are being displayed within the ad, feel free to be creative as long as you can keep the user's attention. Do not let an image animate for too long (more than a few seconds) without showing a benefit to the user. Long-running animations might be fun for the graphics department to create, but a user's attention will start to wane after a few seconds.

Technical and Editorial Requirements for Image Ads

While the above guidelines will help you make more effective image ads, there are certain standards your ad must meet before Google will approve your images:

- Image ads must meet all of the standard editorial guidelines for text ads that were covered in Chapter 4.
- Image ads can be in any of these formats:
  - JPG
  - GIF
  - SWF (Flash)
  - PNG
- Image ads must be one of the standard Internet Advertising Bureau (IAB) sizes:
  - Banner: 468 × 60
  - Square: 250 × 250
  - Small square: 200 × 200
  - Leaderboard: 728 × 90
  - Medium rectangle: 300 × 250
  - Large rectangle: 336 × 280
  - Skyscraper: 120 × 600
  - Wide skyscraper: 160 × 600

- Animated ads can be submitted only in the following size formats:
  - Banner: 468 × 49
  - Square: 250 × 239
  - Small square: 200 × 189
  - Leaderboard: 728 × 79
  - Medium rectangle: 300 × 239
  - Large rectangle: 336 × 269
  - Skyscraper: 120 × 578
  - Wide skyscraper: 160 × 578
- All ads can be no larger than 50k in size regardless of the file format.

Note: Google will add a small footer to your image ad. This footer will contain a line stating "ads by Google," your destination URL, and possibly other information. You can submit an ad that is already resized so that Google does not cover part of your ad. Please note, you can only submit these additional sizes for static ads.

While your ad must meet all of the editorial requirements for standard ads, there are some additional requirements for image ads. Most of these requirements follow the four tenets of landing pages:

- *Respect the user's privacy.* For instance, you cannot use click tracking in Flash ads.
- *Do not be obnoxious.* An animated ad cannot expand beyond its frame. You cannot use strobing or Flash effects.
- *Do not trick the user.* You cannot mimic computer functions, computer error warnings, etc.
- *All image ads must be family friendly.* Google does not allow adult image ads.

If you would like to see the full details and editorial policies for image ads, please visit Google's editorial policy page at `http://adwords.google.com/support/aw/bin/static.py?page=guidelines.cs`.

Image ads can effectively increase the recall rate of your brand, drive traffic to your website, and increase the search volume for your business. However, image ads contain a limited amount of information. If you wish to convey more information to Internet users or tell them a story about your products, video ads are a more effective communication tool.

Developing Profitable Video Ads

The massive increase in broadband penetration and Internet bandwidth around the world has given rise to an increase of video usage, from sites that contain user-generated videos such as YouTube to entire TV programs on Hulu.com.

The rise of video usage has not escaped marketers. Video allows you to both visually and audibly communicate a message to consumers. This increased interaction allows markets to show how their products are used, utilize video testimonials, or create a more traditional message similar to a TV commercial. (An actual TV commercial is rarely useful for video ads unless it is complementary to the TV commercial and you are creating a cross-medium message.)

There are three major ways to measure the effectiveness of your video ads:

- The first is by examining how many people clicked on your video ad and then visited your website and conducted business with your company.

- The second is similar to image ads, where you examine the increased searches and CTR of your search campaign on branded terms.

- The third is a combination of the two, where you examine your play rates (the number of people who saw the video ad compared to the number who watched the video) and optimize your account to increase your play rate. Play rate is a useful metric if you are launching a new product or service that currently does not have search volume. The use of video can increase the awareness and benefits of a service.

When you create video ads, you will have access to additional reports that include:

- *Play rate.* The percentage of people who play your video.

- *Average percent played.* The percentage of your video that is being watched.

- *Cost per view.* How much it costs you each time your video is watched.

- *Frequency.* How often users are being exposed to your ads.

- *Reach.* Estimated number of different individuals who have seen your ad.

- *Click-through rate.* The percentage of people who clicked on your ad.

- *Cost per click.* The average cost you pay when someone clicks on your ad.

You can choose to pay either CPC or CPM with video ads. You are not charged when someone watches the video, you are only charged for the impression or the actual click. We will discuss these two options in Chapter 9.

Video ads look very similar to image ads (Figure 8.12) with the exception that they each contain a play button and video bar at the bottom.

Figure 8.12 A perfect pairing of medium and subject

How to Create Videos that Are Actually Watched

There are a few guidelines that will help you get the most out of your video ads.

Utilize a Compelling Opening Image AdWords video ads do not autoplay. A user has to click the Play button to start playing the video. Therefore, the opening image (an image that you choose and upload along with your video ad) must be compelling so that someone will want to watch the video. Using a combination of testing opening images (testing will be discussed in Chapter 15) with the guidelines for creating image ads can help increase your play rates.

With image ads, you want a commercial feel to them. With opening images for video ads, noncommercial images tend to increase play rates. Use an image that has a compelling visual, is easy to comprehend, and contains a user benefit or call to action. Keep commercial items such as prices or shipping out of the image.

Keep Videos to the Point A video ad can be up to 2 minutes in length. However, after roughly 30 seconds, a user's attention starts to decrease and you may see a lower percentage of your video being viewed. Try to keep your videos on the shorter side.

Utilize a Strong Call to Action As a user can stop watching your video at any time, make sure you have a strong call to action at multiple points within your video so that the viewer will want to click on the ad to visit your website. Do not have your only call to action at the end of the video. If you do, and no one finishes watching the video, your call to action will never be seen.

The Video Is a Story, Not an Ad Videos that do well usually do not look like advertisements. These videos tell a story, educate the consumer, entertain the watcher, and give them a reason why they need to learn more about your business. Remember, the user can stop watching the video at any time. If your storyline is boring or appears to be a commercial, you will see fewer visitors continuing to interact with your ads. Educate, inform, and entertain your viewers.

Technical and Editorial Requirements for Video Ads

The editorial requirements for video ads are quite simple: Follow the editorial requirements for both text and image ads. To view the latest information about video ad requirements, please see the AdWords page at: `http://adwords.google.com/support/aw/bin/answer.py?hl=en&answer=66788`.

The technical requirements for video ads are also straightforward.

- The audio cannot be louder than 12 dB.
- The maximum length of the video is 2 minutes.
- The size requirements are the same as for animated image ads described earlier.
- The supported formats are:

- AVI, ASF
- QuickTime
- Windows Media
- MP4
- MPEG

- The suggested frames per second is around 30, however, the minimum is 14.
- A 4:3 aspect ratio is preferred for best viewing. Other aspects may be accepted, but the video may be shown in letterbox format.
- The maximum file size is 75 MB.

Video ads allow you to tell your company's story to its viewers. They can take a viewer who is not in your buying funnel and show them how your business can help them fill a need in their lives. As soon as a viewer thinks you can assist them with a need, they have now entered the first steps of the buying funnel: awareness and interest.

The keys to effective AdWords video ads are the opening image that induces someone to watch the video, and then the story itself.

Video ads are a challenge to create. They take time, money, and technical resources. If you want to create video or image ads, but do not have the resources to start yet, there is another tool Google offers that can help you get started. The Display Ad Builder is a free tool that lets you create image and interactive ads within Google's interface.

Using Google's Display Ad Builder

Display Ad Builder is a tool that allows you to quickly create image, rich media, and interactive ads. Google has designed a significant number of ad templates. All you need to do is fill in the template's blanks to customize those ads for your own business.

To access Display Ad Builder, navigate to an ad group where you would like to create the ad. Click on the Ads tab, then New Ad. In the drop-down list, choose Display Ad Builder (Figure 8.13).

Figure 8.13 How to access the Display Ad Builder

Once you've chosen to create a new Display Ad Builder ad, you can examine the various templates to find one that fits your needs (Figure 8.14).

One useful feature of the Display Ad Builder is that you can build multiple ad sizes at once. Below the ad template image you will see the available sizes. You do not have to build a different ad for each size. If you build one ad, the same ad can then be saved as all the different image sizes. This is a huge timesaver when you are testing out various formats and sizes.

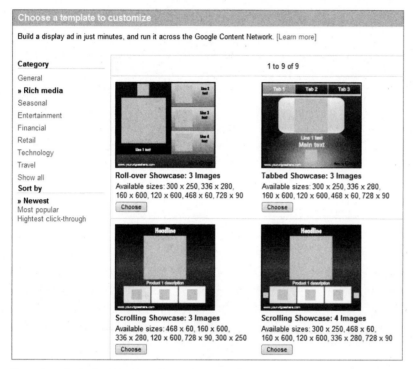

Figure 8.14 The Display Ad Builder screen to select an ad design

After you have chosen an ad size, it is time to build the ad. Building the ad is a straightforward process (see Figure 8.15). All you need to do is:

- Fill in the text boxes
- Choose the colors of that text
- Choose the font for the text
- Upload images or logos where applicable
- Choose your background colors (if you wish to change them from the defaults)
- Choose the display and destination URLs

Note: AdWords launches new templates on a regular basis, and often there are seasonal templates (such as Valentine's Day or Halloween) released before each new holiday. Utilizing the holiday templates can keep your ads fresh and relevant to the current seasons.

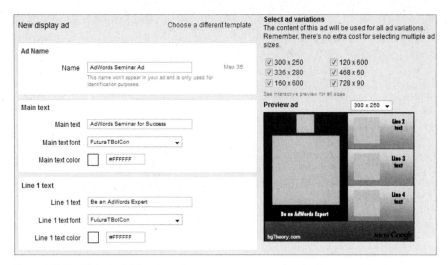

Figure 8.15 The Display Ad Builder ad creation screen

Depending on the amount of customization you add to an ad, it can take as little as 5 minutes to build an ad from scratch using this tool. It can be useful to first test out different types of images, layouts, color schemes, and sizes before hiring a more expensive designer to perfect your images. First find out what works for your company, then move to a more polished design step. Of course, you do not have to hire a designer; you can exclusively use the Display Ad Builder templates and still find advertising success.

Best Practices for Employing Image, Video, and Mobile Ads

Image and rich media ads allow you to target the content network in new and interesting ways. These ads usually have response rates higher than you can receive from text ads. However, mobile users and the content network can be tricky to effectively target and reach your goals.

- When utilizing mobile ads, always consider if the searcher has different needs than when they are on a desktop so that you send the searcher to the proper place on your website.

- Watch your iPhone usage statistics in Google Analytics to determine if you need to create a mobile website for your current users.

- If you want to reach all mobile users regardless of their mobile browser type, you need to utilize mobile ads and ensure your campaigns are set to be shown on "iPhone and other mobile devices with full Internet browsers."

- Use image ads to increase the recall of your brands and to increase the CTR of your content campaigns.

- When using video ads, always test opening images to see which image increases play rate, CTR, and conversion rates.

- Measure the changes to your branded search volume, search CTR, and conversion rates when using rich media ads. Image and video ads can not only increase branded search volume, but also increase your search metrics.

- Use the Display Ad Builder seasonal templates to take advantage of the changes in search behaviors during holidays.

Image and video ads are only shown on the content network. The content network is significantly different from search. In the next two chapters, we will dive into exactly what the content network is and how to effectively use the network to increase your advertising reach with text, image, and/or video ads.

Understanding the Content Network

The content network is an often misunderstood aspect of Google AdWords. The content network will show your ads on non-search pages, such as news articles. As search page views are a small percentage of the Web, utilizing the content network can increase your advertising reach tremendously.

However, the content network uses different rules to display your ads than search. Users are in a different mindset when reading articles compared to when they are searching. Therefore, understanding how the content network works and how to reach your prospects is essential to creating successful content campaigns.

Chapter Contents

What Is the Content Network?

When we think of Google, we naturally think of search. After all, it's the premiere search engine on the Web. If someone has to conduct a search before they can view your ad, then your ad is being displayed on Google search or Google search partners.

However, there are many times when someone does not have to conduct a search to see your ads. In these circumstances, your ads are displayed based on the content of the page.

If someone is reading an article on a newspaper site, would it not make sense to show ads based on what the article is about? Unrelated ads are easy to ignore, but when the ad is related to the article, it can help a consumer understand their choices or products and services related to that article.

For instance, if you are on the *New York Times* website reading an article entitled "T-Mobile to Unveil 2nd 'Google Phone'" (Figure 9.1), and the article talks about smart phones and cell networks, would it not make sense to also show ads related to cell phones?

Figure 9.1 *New York Times* article about cell phones

Below this *New York Times* article is a list of ads based on the article (Figure 9.2). You will notice that all of the ads are similar to the article's content.

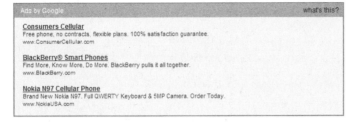

Figure 9.2 Cell phone related ads

If you have ever seen "Ads by Google" around the Web, you have seen Google's content ads.

Advantages of the Content Network

There are a finite number of searches conducted every month. That number continues to grow, but search page views are still a small percentage of the Web. According to numerous studies, search page views make up approximately 5 percent of all page views on the Web. Some other studies have stated that search page views make up approximately 5 percent of consumers' time online.

If a page view is not a search result, it is a content page view. For instance, do you go directly to a news site every morning to read the news? If so, you could be making 20 or 30 content page views and no search page views. Those who go directly to Amazon.com to read product reviews often make 10 or 20 content page views and no searches. Of course, there are those who combine searches and page views. However, when you want to expand your advertising efforts, there is no larger network than *contextual advertising*.

Individuals who search for a product already have a need in mind. They are conducting a search to find the answer to their need. These individuals are a small percentage of everyone online who could benefit by your product. Generally, these searchers are in the learning or later stages of the buying funnel (Figure 9.3), which is described in detail in Chapter 2.

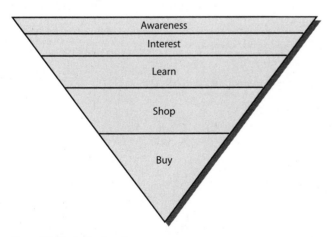

Figure 9.3 The buying funnel

The buying funnel starts with awareness and interest. If no one is aware of your products or services, then they do not know enough to search for them. As the content network reaches those who do not yet have a need for or awareness of your product, it can introduce many new prospects into the buying funnel.

Another advantage of utilizing Google's content network is that you can use the dynamic ads covered in Chapter 8. Image and video ads are very visual; combining rich media ads with the content network is a good technique for introducing your company to new prospects who otherwise wouldn't have become aware of what you offer.

Creating a Successful Content Network Campaign

The way Google displays content ads is a three-step process:

1. Google scans a page within their content network (such as the NYTimes.com page displayed earlier) and they assign a theme to that page. There are times when they might only scan a section of a page, as items such as links or other advertisements do not always help determine the theme of a page.

2. Google scans your ad groups, and based on the keywords in each ad group, they assign a theme to that ad group.

3. When the content page and your ad group contain the same theme, your ad can be displayed.

This is a very simplistic look at how Google displays content ads; for organization and optimization purposes, there is no need to dive further into the nuances of this ad serving. Instead, we will show some tools and tips to help refine your organization.

It is important to note that the content obeys all of your campaign settings, such as location, time of day, or daily budget. Therefore, you can have your content ads only shown to a specific city, or only shown at certain times of the day.

Another important note is that Google does not look at any individual keyword within your ad group to determine if your ad should be shown. In fact, Google does not even look at the match types (other than negative) of your keywords. Google looks at all of the keywords combined to create a theme for that ad group. You can only set a content bid at the ad group level.

Content placement is much different from search. With search, each individual keyword and its associated match type is used to determine if your ad should be shown. In addition, you can set a different bid for each keyword and match type intersection.

Since these two networks (search and content) are so different in how the ads are displayed and bid, it is best to have different search and content campaigns.

Creating Search- and Content-Only Campaigns

To set a campaign to only show on search or on content, navigate to the Settings tab for a campaign. Under Networks and Devices, click the Edit button and you will be presented with your network and device options (Figure 9.4).

Figure 9.4 Network settings to change so your ads only show on search or the content network

Choose to have your ads shown only on search or only on content and then click the Save button. Now you have a campaign running only on search or content. This will make creating ad groups and setting bids and budgets much easier.

Once you make these changes, it can be useful to include the network type in your campaign description so you know which campaigns are shown on different networks (Figure 9.5).

Figure 9.5 Campaign names can help with organization.

> **Note:** You can also make these changes within the AdWords Editor, which will be addressed in Chapter 12. In addition, if you already have existing campaigns and want to change your account structure so that you have both search and content campaigns, there is an easy way to accomplish this with the AdWords Editor.

Ground Rules for Creating Effective Content Network Ad Groups

Content campaigns examine the keywords within an ad group to try to establish the theme of that ad group in order to show it on appropriate pages. There are a few rules when creating content ad groups:

Only 50 Keywords Are Examined Google only looks at 50 keywords within an ad group when determining the theme of that ad group. Never use more than 50 keywords in any content ad group. If you use more than 50 words, you may not know which 50 Google is using in determining your theme.

Match Types Do Not Matter Google does not give more weight to exact match keywords over broad match keywords in determining your ad group's theme. Match types are ignored. Therefore, if you have a keyword with all three match types in a content campaign, you are just wasting your time in adding these additional match types. Ignore match types.

Google *Does* Take into Account Negative Keywords While Google ignores whether a keyword is a broad, phrase, or exact match, they do take into account negative keywords when trying to determine your theme. If there are words that when used in an article signal to you that the article is not being read by your desired audience, then you should add them as negative keywords.

For example, let us assume you are marketing an iPhone application. You regularly check the pages that are sending you traffic but are not converting. Over time, you find a pattern that when the words "jailbreak" or "jailbreaking" appear on the page, the traffic does not convert. As jailbreaking an iPhone is a method of unlocking the iPhone that makes the phone incompatible with other features, it turns out these jailbroken iPhones can't take advantage of your app; therefore, these clicks do not convert. In this case, you would then add "jailbreak" and "jailbreaking" as negative keywords in the ad group so your ads no longer show up on those pages.

The Use of Very General Keywords Is Acceptable There are many keywords that are so general you would never want to use them for search. For example, the word "wi-fi" has no standalone meaning. That search could refer to wi-fi hotspots, routers, phones, cards, etc. However, if general words are paired with other words to define a theme, they are okay to use for content campaigns.

Choosing the Correct Words for Your Content Network Ad Group

A successful content network ad group should contain words that together create a theme. These words should appear often on the page where you want the ad to show.

If you are trying to sell TVs, this first example will usually give poor results. Consider an ad group with these keywords:

- TV
- Plasma TV

- Hi-def TV
- Samsung TV
- DLP TV
- Television

The preceding ad group could be displayed on a wide variety of sites, such as:

- TV reviews
- TV repair
- TV listings

Those three types of content are quite different, and running the same ad across that variety of sites will usually yield poor results.

Consider an ad group with these keywords:

- Cell phone
- Mobile phone
- App store
- Wi-fi
- Bluetooth
- Apple
- iPhone

When examining any page about the iPhone, the above words usually appear on the page. One way to organize your content campaigns is to play the game Taboo with your products. In this game, the "giver" is given a card with a primary word on it. The object of the game is to have the giver describe the word on the card so that the other players can guess the word. In addition, there are taboo words on the card that the giver cannot use in trying to describe the product, as they will easily give away the primary word.

Content organization is very similar to the game Taboo. You will have words that if someone sees them they will automatically guess the product (the taboo words). You will have other words that help to describe the product, but are not taboo (the words the giver chooses to say).

In the earlier ad group about the iPhone, if you read the words one by one, how long does it take you to guess that an iPhone is being described?

Since the content network works on themes, and there is automated technology involved that does not make qualitative decisions, it can be useful to create several variations of ad groups to see which ones give you the better placement. If we return to the TV example, we might have several ad groups to describe the products being sold.

If you specialize in DLP TVs, then you would know there are two major types of DLP TVs. One is a projector, and the other is a more typical thin TV set. Projector brightness is measured in lumens. A typical TV review would not use the word "lumens." Therefore, you might start with these ad groups to determine which works best for you.

- DLP TV Ad Group:
  - -Projector (negative keyword)
  - DLP TV
  - Digital light processing
  - HDTV
  - 1080p
  - Rear projection
- DLP TV Ad Group 2:
  - DLP TV
  - Digital light processing
  - HDTV
  - HDMI
  - 1080p
  - Rear projection
  - Rear projector
  - -Lumens (negative keyword)
- DLP TV Projector Ad Group:
  - DLP projector
  - Digital light processing
  - HDTV
  - Lumens
  - -Rear (negative keyword)
- DLP TV Projector Ad Group 2:
  - DLP projector
  - HDTV
  - Lumens
  - Distance

The reasons for duplicating the same themes in multiple ad groups is to see which one Google places better based on the keywords being used. It can be useful to try several different word combinations. In the second DLP projector example, the word "distance" is used. That is because many reviews look at the distance a projector can be from a wall and still receive an accurate picture. However, some review sites use the term "lens and throw distance" as one of their standard terms for reviewing all projection devices. Therefore, you could even have another ad group that uses the more specific set of words on that review than just the single word "distance."

The ad groups just listed might receive nice placement on product review pages, which are viewed by someone further along in the buying funnel. Many new hi-def TV buyers research the different types of TVs before deciding which to buy. Therefore, if you wanted your ad to show on a page dedicated to comparing rear projection DLP TVs to DLP projector TVs, you might want a third ad group with these keywords:

- DLP TV

- Projector DLP TV

- Rear projection DLP TV

- Lumens

- Digital light processing

- Distance

- 1080p

Other consumers have decided they want to buy a projector and compare LCD and DLP projectors to see which one they prefer. If you wanted to be on such a page, utilizing a different set of keywords could gather placement on those pages. The LCD vs. DLP Projector ad group might contain

- DLP projector

- LCD projector

- Rainbow effect

- Contrast

- Home theater projectors

all types of TVs, all of these ad groups would be useful to try so you combinations of keywords lead to the best placements and ultimately OI for the content network. As different type of sites use their own termi- useful to test out multiple combinations of words and even leave all of the unning at once, as they may be shown on different types of pages. other way to try to find the correct words to use in an ad group is to use a keyword density analyzer (Figure 9.6).

Note: A *keyword density analyzer* is a program that examines a page, or set of pages, and tells you the frequency at which words and phrases appear on the pages.

phrase		frequency ▽	words	dispersion	▲
DLP	🔍	76	1	6383.5	
LCD		55	1	4394.1	
TV		44	1	5436.7	
color		29	1	6073.8	
will		24	1	3247.6	
TVS		23	1	6480.1	
have		22	1	5364.1	
you		21	1	5076.6	
DLP TV		21	2	5050.4	
can		18	1	6939.1	
light		18	1	7579.8	
image		17	1	7055.7	
than		17	1	6274.2	
projection		17	1	5323.6	

Figure 9.6 Textanz keyword density analyzer

When using a keyword density analyzer, there are a few rules to keep in mind:

Choose the Types of Pages Where You Want Your Ad to Be Shown If you want your ads to be shown on review sites, examine the density of the review page. Different words are used in describing a product review versus an editorial page versus a news article. By using words in your ad group that show up on these pages, your ad is more likely to be placed correctly.

Analyze Several Pages and Combine the Data Before Choosing Your Keywords Authors vary in writing styles. Different types of sites have different editorial guidelines. If you were to analyze only a single page, your results would be skewed and your placements could suffer. Choose several different pages across multiple websites when you are analyzing the top keywords.

Always Use Common Sense When you use a density analyzer, you will find instances of common words (you, submit, can, have, etc.) that do not describe your services or goods. Just because a word has a high frequency of occurrences does not mean it is a good word to use in your ad group. Always use common sense in choosing words that create a cohesive theme.

Go through the exercises just described to choose keywords for each theme. As each ad group should be a complete theme, no single keyword matters as much as the overall theme. Therefore, while you rarely want to use the same word in different ad groups for search, it is okay for different ad groups to contain some of the same keywords for the content network. For instance, if you sell iPods and iPhones, these two products will not only be two different ad groups, but you may have the same keywords (such as Apple, MP3, video, etc.) in different ad groups.

Once you have created a content campaign with tightly themed ad groups, the next step is refining your ad exposure to make sure your ads are only shown on sites where you feel comfortable about it showing.

Before we jump into reporting, let us first examine success metrics for the content network. The content network is priced differently than search, which means there are different metrics to focus on when optimizing for content campaigns.

Smart Pricing: Why Cost per Conversion Is the Best Metric to Measure Success

In search, Google uses a feature called the AdWords Discounter so that you only pay a penny more than necessary to appear just above the ad below yours. Google uses a different set of pricing rules for the content network, called *smart pricing*.

With smart pricing, Google looks to see if a page is more or less likely to end in a conversion action. If a page is less likely to end with a conversion, Google may discount the price of that click. If a click is more likely to turn into a conversion, they may charge more for that click (up to your maximum CPC).

Note: While Google may discount your click prices for the content network, you should set different bids for the content network based on the return of ad spend or what it will cost to reach your marketing goals. You may have ad groups where you are willing to bid more per click than on search. Conversely, you will have ad groups where you are willing to bid less than on search. Do not use the same bid for both networks. If in doubt, using a content bid of 75 percent of your search bid will get you started. For example, if you were willing to pay $1 for a click on search, set your content bid at $0.75.

The smart pricing feature creates a scenario where your conversion rates are not nearly as important as your cost per conversion.

Let's assume for a moment that you sell digital cameras, and that your maximum CPC is set to $1. The first site where your ad is shown is an authoritative review site where your ad was shown alongside an article that reviewed the digital camera you are selling. This type of site is far along in the shopping cycle and the traffic is more likely to convert on your website, therefore you are also going to pay a higher CPC than a less authoritative website. Let us also say that your ad was shown on Johnny's blog alongside a story where he talks about how he used his new digital camera on a trip to Aruba. This site is less commercial in nature, and therefore, less likely to convert for your products. However, that does not mean you do not want your ad to show on Johnny's blog. The numbers should tell you the story of your ad's effectiveness on each of these two sites (see Table 9.1).

▶ **Table 9.1** Comparison of two sites

Metrics	Authoritative Review Site	Johnny's Blog
Clicks	100	100
CPC	$1	$0.25
Total Cost	$100	$25
Conversions	10	5
Conversion Rate	10%	5%
Cost per Conversion	$10	$5

In this scenario, Johnny's blog has half the conversion rate of the review site (5% vs. 10%). However, because you are paying significantly less per click ($0.25 vs. $1), Johnny's blog has a better cost per conversion ($5 vs. $10) and you make more profit from a visitor to Johnny's blog instead of the review site.

Each site has different types of users and will therefore send different types of traffic. You may see large differences in CPC and conversion rate for each website where your ad is shown. However, conversion rates and CPC are not nearly as important as cost per conversion when examining success for the content network.

Once your ads have some exposure across the content network, you should examine the websites where your ad is being shown to determine where you are receiving both good and bad returns.

After your ads have run for a while and accrued enough data for you to make sound decisions, it is time to run AdWords reports and fine tune your content campaigns based on success metrics.

Learning How the Content Network Is Performing for You

Once you have created a content campaign, Google will start to show your ads across the content network. As the AdWords content network reaches approximately three-fourths of all Internet users, your ads can be placed on a multitude of different sites.

While the first step in successful content campaigns is account organization, the second step is measuring what types of sites and categories are sending you traffic so you can refine where your ads are shown.

In this section, we are going to assume that you are using the Google AdWords conversion tracker (a system of tracking conversions in your AdWords account that will be discussed in depth in Chapter 13).

Understanding the Placement Report

Several years ago, it was very difficult to optimize for the content network as Google did not show advertisers a list of sites, or metrics, about where their ads were placed. This led to many companies abandoning the content network because the network was so opaque. However, Google has made great strides in the past couple of years to provide marketers with enough metrics to extract value from the content network.

The most useful of the new reports is the placement report. This report shows you the domains (or individual URLs) where your ad was displayed (Figure 9.7) along with the corresponding metrics for those domains or URLs.

The placement report can be configured to show a variety of metrics; we are only going to concentrate on a few metrics at present. The two most important pieces of data you can extract from this report are the domain (or URL) where your ad was shown and that site's cost per conversion.

Export Report   Create Another Report Like This

Jan 1, 2009 - Jun 28, 2009

View: Summary

Impressions	Clicks	Avg CPC	Cost	Conversions (1-per-click)	Conv. Rate (1-per-click)	Cost/Conv. (1-per-click)
12,268,785	31,709	$0.41	$13,109.94	627	1.98%	$20.88

Ad Group	Domain	Special Category	Impressions	Clicks	Avg CPC	Cost	Conversions (1-per-click)	Conv. Rate (1-per-click)	Cost/Conv. (1-per-click)
	about.com		991,381	1,169	$0.39	$456.01	30	2.57%	$15.20
	annecollins.com		75,171	1,261	$0.34	$426.43	28	2.22%	$15.23
	ezinearticles.com		90,689	720	$0.45	$320.54	28	3.89%	$11.45
	thecaloriecounter.com		267,064	1,187	$0.43	$510.77	23	1.94%	$22.21
	about.com		374,361	354	$0.41	$146.15	14	3.95%	$10.44
	thedailyplate.com		392,180	613	$0.34	$206.71	10	1.63%	$20.67
	about.com		361,506	348	$0.44	$152.56	10	2.87%	$15.26
	everydayhealth.com		214,829	400	$0.41	$164.93	10	2.50%	$16.49
	everydayhealth.com		55,822	237	$0.39	$92.13	10	4.22%	$9.21
	about.com		418,409	239	$0.42	$99.81	9	3.77%	$11.09
	ezinearticles.com		20,087	182	$0.46	$83.22	8	4.40%	$10.40

Figure 9.7 AdWords placement report showing which sites are sending you traffic

Once you see each site's cost per conversion, then you can control your ad's exposure based on actual metrics. The next step to optimize your content campaigns is to either change the CPC per content website or block traffic from sites that are not meeting your performance goals.

To bid differently per website where your ad is being shown, you will have to use placements, which will be discussed later in the section "Placement Targeting: Choosing Which Content Sites Display Your Ads."

Stopping Google from Showing Your Ads on Sites That Do Not Convert

Once you run a placement performance report, you will have data about what sites are not performing for your campaigns. If you want to block your ad from being shown on certain sites, it is a straightforward process.

First, navigate to the Tools menu in your AdWords account. One of the tools is called Site and Category Exclusion. This tool has several different ways to block traffic from seeing your ad.

When using this tool, you will first choose the campaign where these settings will apply. If you want to block traffic in several different campaigns, you will need to enter the information into the tool for each campaign.

Being able to block traffic at the campaign level creates a scenario where you might have one campaign where you are not filtering traffic and another one where you are, so that you can have even greater control in displaying your ads. We will explore this concept further in Chapter 10.

Blocking Domains from Showing Your Ads

The first way to control your ad display is by blocking domains from seeing your ads (Figure 9.8). Enter the domains you want to block, and your ad will no longer be shown on those domains.

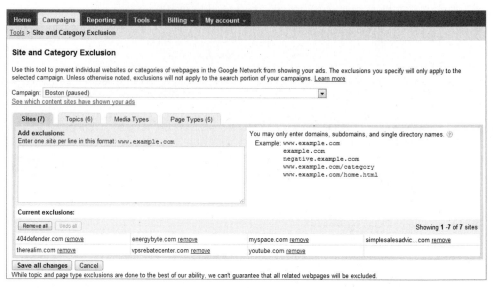

Figure 9.8 Blocking domains from showing your ads

You can block traffic at three different levels within a domain:

- Top level domain name: example.com
- First level subdomain: widget.example.com
- Single directory name: example.com/widget/

If you block a top level domain name, your ad could still be shown on a subdomain. Google does not currently support wildcards for blocking subdomains; therefore, if you want to keep your ad from showing on a site and all of its subdomains, you need to enter all of the subdomains into the tool.

If you choose to block a single directory, such as example.com/widget/, then your ad could be shown on example.com or example.com/redwidgets/, as those pages do not fall into that exact directory.

Blocking Your Ad from Being Shown Next to Undesirable Content

The second use of this tool is to inform AdWords that you do not want your ad to appear on certain types of content pages. AdWords will attempt to discern the type of content on a page and, if you choose not to have your ads shown on that content, will keep your ad from appearing on those pages.

You can block six different types of content (Figure 9.9):

- Crime, policy, and emergency
- Death and tragedy
- Military and international conflict
- Juvenile, gross, and bizarre content
- Profanity and rough language
- Sexually suggestive content

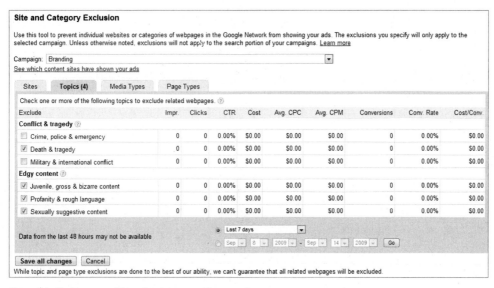

Figure 9.9 Blocking your ad from showing on specific types of content

This is a useful tool for brand protection. If you sell vacation packages, for example, you might not want your ad to be displayed on a news article describing an airline crash. While Google does a good job of classifying these pages and keeping your ad from showing, it is not 100 percent accurate. You might find pages that are misclassified where your ad is not showing or is showing improperly.

Google will display your performance statistics for each of these content sites for the currently selected campaign to help you decide what returns you are receiving on each of the different content types that you can block.

Keeping Your Ad Off Video Sites

A publisher can design video ads that show content ads within that video. In addition, users can embed those videos on their own websites (such as you might embed a YouTube video on a blog). You can control whether you want to keep your ads from being displayed within this type of content (Figure 9.10):

- If you exclude video, your ad will not be shown within any video.

- If you exclude embedded video, your ad can be shown within the video on a publisher's site, but if users embed the video on their own site, the ad will not be displayed.

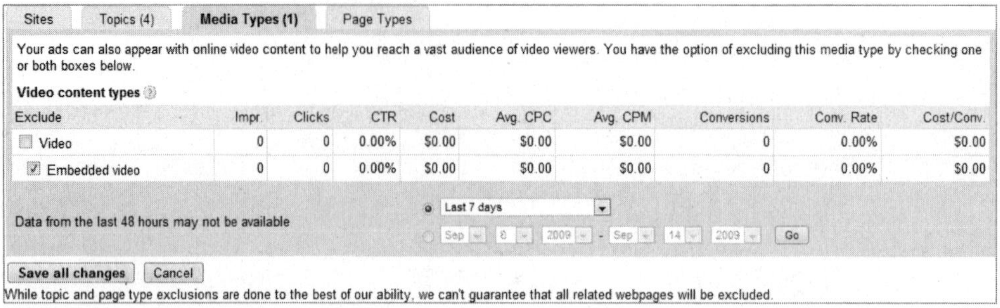

Sites	Topics (4)	**Media Types (1)**	Page Types								

Your ads can also appear with online video content to help you reach a vast audience of video viewers. You have the option of excluding this media type by checking one or both boxes below.

Video content types ⓘ

Exclude	Impr.	Clicks	CTR	Cost	Avg. CPC	Avg. CPM	Conversions	Conv. Rate	Cost/Conv.
☐ Video	0	0	0.00%	$0.00	$0.00	$0.00	0	0.00%	$0.00
☑ Embedded video	0	0	0.00%	$0.00	$0.00	$0.00	0	0.00%	$0.00

Data from the last 48 hours may not be available

◉ Last 7 days ▾

○ Sep ▾ 8 ▾ 2009 ▾ - Sep ▾ 14 ▾ 2009 ▾ [Go]

[Save all changes] [Cancel]

While topic and page type exclusions are done to the best of our ability, we can't guarantee that all related webpages will be excluded.

Figure 9.10 Keeping your ad from being displayed within video

Blocking Various Types of Pages from Displaying Your Ad

Lastly, you can block certain types of pages from showing your ad:

- Error pages
- Parked domains
- User-generated content sites

An *error page* is a page that is displayed when a page does not exist. This is a common tactic for ISPs (Internet service providers) to employ. If you attempt to navigate to a domain that does not exist or do a search from your address bar that leads to an error page, the ISP will show a page of ads based on the mistyped URL or search query instead of a 404 (not found) error page.

Parked domains are domains that have been purchased, but the content is never developed; instead all you see is ads when you navigate to these pages. Most of the traffic from parked pages comes from user's mistyping URLs into their browser or typing a domain name into their browser's address bar that does not exist.

With both error pages and parked domains, you can see their effectiveness in placement reports (Figure 9.11) or within the blocking tool. In the placement report, you can see the actual domain where your ad was shown if the page was a parked domain. However, Google does not show who displayed your ads on an error page.

Domain	Special Category
stacysweightlossstory.com	Parked domains
wholegraindiet.com	Parked domains
wrpdiet.com	Parked domains
betterlivinghypnosis.com	Parked domains
myally.com	Parked domains
Error pages	Error pages
Error pages	Error pages
Error pages	Error pages
Error pages	Error pages
Error pages	Error pages
Error pages	Error pages
Error pages	Error pages
Error pages	Error pages
Error pages	Error pages

Figure 9.11 Placement report showing statistics for parked domains and error pages

Lastly, you can block your ads from being shown on certain types of *user-generated content sites*. You can keep your ad from being shown on pages such as:

Forums Sites where users discuss topics, such as webmasterworld.com.

Image-Sharing Pages Pages where users can submit, browse, or download images, such as zooomr.com or Google's Picasa.

Social Networks Sites where users can interact with friends, such as Orkut or MySpace.

Video-Sharing Pages Pages where users can upload, watch, or download video, such as YouTube.

To block page types, check the box next to the type of page where you do not want your ad to be displayed (Figure 9.12) and then save your settings.

Sites (7)	Topics (6)	Media Types (1)	**Page Types (5)**							

There are several page types that can show your ads. You can choose to opt out by checking one or more of the following options. ⓘ

Network types

Exclude	Impr.	Clicks	CTR	Cost	Avg. CPC	Avg. CPM	Conversions	Conv. Rate	Cost/Conv.
☐ Error pages ⓘ	0	0	0.00%	$0.00	$0.00	$0.00	0	0.00%	$0.00
☑ Parked domains ⓘ	0	0	0.00%	$0.00	$0.00	$0.00	0	0.00%	$0.00

User-generated content ⓘ

Exclude	Impr.	Clicks	CTR	Cost	Avg. CPC	Avg. CPM	Conversions	Conv. Rate	Cost/Conv.
☑ Forums	0	0	0.00%	$0.00	$0.00	$0.00	0	0.00%	$0.00
☑ Image-sharing pages	0	0	0.00%	$0.00	$0.00	$0.00	0	0.00%	$0.00
☑ Social networks	0	0	0.00%	$0.00	$0.00	$0.00	0	0.00%	$0.00
☑ Video-sharing pages	0	0	0.00%	$0.00	$0.00	$0.00	0	0.00%	$0.00

Data from the last 48 hours may not be available

Last 7 days ▾ Jun ▾ 22 ▾ 2009 ▾ - Jun ▾ 28 ▾ 2009 ▾ Go

Save all changes   Cancel
While topic and page type exclusions are done to the best of our ability, we can't guarantee that all related webpages will be excluded.

Figure 9.12 Blocking your ad from being shown on user-generated content, error pages, or parked domains

Managing Automatic Placements

Google has two types of content targeting techniques:

Automatic Placements These are places where your ad is displayed based on matching your keywords and the website.

Managed Placements These are places you choose for displaying your ad, which is the topic of the next section, "Placement Targeting: Choosing Which Content Sites Display Your Ads."

By navigating to the Networks tab and clicking Show Details next to the Automatic Placements text, you can view information similar to the placement report within the AdWords interface (Figure 9.13).

	Clicks	Impr.	CTR ⓘ	Avg. CPC ⓘ	Cost	Avg. Pos.	Conv. (1-per-click) ⓘ	Cost / conv. (1-per-click) ⓘ	Conv. rate (1-per-click) ⓘ
Search	193	33,098	0.58%	$1.58	$305.40	3.7	6	$50.90	3.11%
Google search	161	17,106	0.94%	$1.60	$257.33	4.4	6	$42.89	3.73%
Search partners ⓘ	32	15,992	0.20%	$1.50	$48.07	3	0	$0.00	0.00%
Content	327	833,270	0.04%	$0.54	$177.15	3.5	0	$0.00	0.00%
▦ Managed placements ⓘ show details	3	32,680	0.01%	$2.21	$6.62	2	0	$0.00	0.00%
▦ Automatic placements ⓘ hide details	324	800,590	0.04%	$0.53	$170.53	3.6	0	$0.00	0.00%
Total - All networks	**520**	**866,368**	**0.06%**	**$0.93**	**$482.55**	**3.5**	**6**	**$80.42**	**1.15%**

Tabs: Campaigns | Ad groups | Settings | Ads | Keywords | **Networks**   Filter and views ▾

Figure 9.13 Viewing automatic placements in your account

Once you show these details, you can now view the websites where Google has placed your content ad at the account, campaign, or ad group level (Figure 9.14).

Content: automatic placements

Buttons: Manage placement and bid | Exclude placements | See URL list | Download

	Domain	Campaign	Ad group	Clicks	Impr.	CTR	Avg. CPC	Cost
	Total - all automatic placements			324	800,590	0.04%	$0.53	$170.53
☑	gmail.com	Washington DC	Seminars	0	346	0.00%	$0.00	$0.00
☐	gmail.com	Washington DC	PPC	1	324	0.31%	$0.42	$0.42
☑	gmodules.com	Washington DC	AdWords	0	2,430	0.00%	$0.00	$0.00
☐	motorloa.com	Cell Phone Example	Motorola	4	5	80.00%	$0.15	$0.59
☐	pakpoll.com	Cell Phone Example	Motorola	1	1	100.00%	$0.08	$0.08
☐	wikihow.com	Cell Phone Example	Motorola	1	1	100.00%	$0.25	$0.25

Figure 9.14 Automatic placement details

From the details screen, you can add these sites as managed placements (discussed in the next section) or block an ad group or campaign from showing your ads.

When managing your account on a day-to-day basis, it is easy to manage placements from within the Networks tab. When you are doing a significant amount of organization and analysis of the content network, it is easier to run the placement report and work from data that is easy to import into Excel to conduct additional analysis.

Follow these steps to create a profitable content network campaign:

1. Create tightly themed ad groups. If you are not happy with the pages where your ads are being placed, the first step is to choose different sets of keywords within an ad group.

2. Once your ads are being placed on the appropriate pages, become familiar with the placement performance report. This report shows exactly where your ads are being shown and how each of those sites is performing for your account.

3. To ensure the continued success of your content campaigns, understand how to keep your ad from being shown on sites that do not meet your cost per conversion goals or are on types of pages and websites where you do not want your ad to be displayed.

The content network is vast. There is no way to know in advance all of the pages where your ads can be shown. If you want to just have your ads placed on websites that you choose, or if you want to set a separate bid for various websites, Google has another feature that allows you absolute control, where you can pick and choose exactly which sites can display your ad. This is known as placement targeting.

Placement Targeting: Choosing Which Content Sites Display Your Ads

The content network contains a vast number of websites where your ad can be shown. Automatic placements are useful for finding websites that are sending you excellent traffic and maximizing your ad's exposure. With managed placements (often called *placement targeting*), you can choose which websites you want to display your ads. If you only use placement targeting, your ads will only be shown on sites that you approve.

There are ways of using a combination of both automatic and managed placements to maximize your exposure that will be discussed in Chapter 10.

With placement targeting, you do not need to choose any keywords. Since you are explicitly informing Google where you want your ads to be displayed, Google does not need to match the themes of your keywords to the content of the webpage to find matches where your ads will be displayed.

Placement Tool

The first step in placement targeting is to find websites where you want your ads to be displayed. The easiest way to find these websites is with Google's placement tool. To access the tool, follow these steps:

1.   Navigate to the Placements tab.

2.   Click on Show Automatic Placements.

3.   Click Add Placements.

4.   If you are viewing information for your account or a campaign, walk through the wizard to choose to which ad group you want to add placements. If you are viewing information at the ad group level, there is no need to drill down to find an ad group.

5.   Once you have chosen an ad group, the placement tool icon (Figure 9.15) will be displayed. Click on the icon.

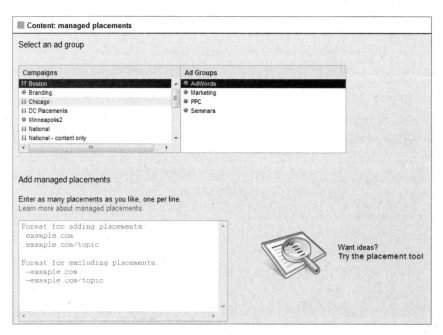

Figure 9.15 Clicking on the placement tool icon will show you the placement tool

The goal of the placement tool is to help you find websites where you want your ad to be displayed. There are four ways of using this tool to find information (Figure 9.16):

Browse Categories   Drill down through categories to find your industry.

Describe Topics   List your topics and search for sites that match your topics.

List URLs If you have websites in mind, you can input their URLs to see if those sites accept Google's placement targeting.

Select Demographics You can choose your demographics and find sites that house those demographics. Please note that this tool shows sites where the propensity of users for a particular website fits into the selected demographics, but any demographic can see your ad.

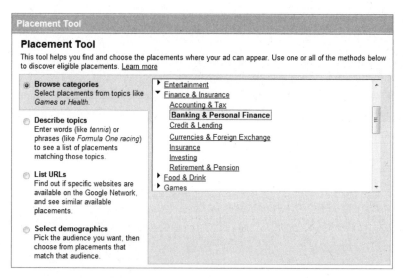

Figure 9.16 Browsing categories via the placement tool

Each time you search for placements, a list of sites that match your criteria will be displayed at the bottom of the tool's page (Figure 9.17), along with the accepted ad formats and how many impressions a day that site receives.

If you want to advertise on a particular site, click the Add link and you can create a list of websites where your ad can be displayed.

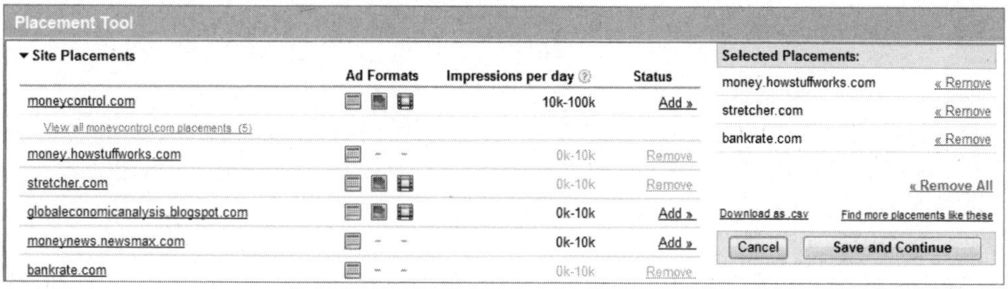

Figure 9.17 Websites available for placement targeting

Note: Some websites publish *Really Simple Syndication* (RSS) feeds. RSS feeds are a standard content format that can be displayed within a feed reader (such as reader.google.com). Feed readers provide an easy way to keep up with news content, and many use them to read articles instead of having the articles delivered via email or visiting websites to read them. Publishers can place ads within feeds. When browsing through websites to show your ads, you may occasionally see *feed placements*. If you choose a feed placement for your ad, your ad will be placed in that publisher's RSS feed.

All publishers display text ads. However, not all publishers display video or image ads. In addition, since a publisher has to allocate space on their website for the ads, the publisher only shows a set number of ad sizes. Not all publishers display all ad sizes.

You can filter by the type of ad and the ad size that the publisher displays. Click on Choose Formats and you will be shown a screen where you can choose certain ad types and sizes (Figure 9.18). Once you save these formats, you will only be shown websites that accept the ad types you have chosen.

Only show placements that offer these ad formats:

☐ Text ads

☐ All image ad sizes
- ☐ Banner (468x60)
- ☐ Leaderboard (728x90)
- ☑ Square (250x250)
- ☐ Small Square (200x200)
- ☐ Large Rectangle (336x280)
- ☐ Medium Rectangle (300x250)
- ☐ Skyscraper (120x600)
- ☐ Wide Skyscraper (160x600)
- ☐ Mobile Leaderboard (300x50)
- ☐ Flash Overlay (480x70)
- ☐ Flash Overlay (IAB) (450x50)

☐ All video ad sizes
- ☐ Leaderboard (728x90)
- ☑ Square (250x250)
- ☐ Small Square (200x200)
- ☐ Large Rectangle (336x280)
- ☐ Medium Rectangle (300x250)
- ☐ Skyscraper (120x600)
- ☐ Wide Skyscraper (160x600)
- ☐ Flash Overlay (480x70)
- ☐ Flash Overlay (IAB) (450x50)

[OK] [Cancel]

Figure 9.18 Filter websites by ad type and size.

There are some websites that are easily broken down into categories, such as a newspaper sites. With some of these sites, you can choose to have your ad displayed only within a section of those websites. If you see instances of "View all website placements," you can click on that listing to see all of the available placements for that website (Figure 9.19).

Note: If you find a significant number of websites and do not want to add them all to the same ad group, you can export your list to a .csv file. You can then organize the placements in Excel, and use the AdWords Editor (discussed in Chapter 12) to import all of those placements back into your account.

	Ad Formats	Impressions per day ⓘ	Status
nytimes.com	▤ ▦ ▥	500k+	Add »
– U.S. & World News Pages.Bottom right	▤ – –	10k-100k	Add »
– Business Pages.Bottom right	▤ – –	10k-100k	Add »
– Art, Dance, TV & Music.Bottom right	▤ – –	10k-100k	Add »
– Fashion & Style Pages.Bottom right	▤ – –	10k-100k	Add »
– Travel Pages.Bottom right	▤ – –	10k-100k	Add »
– Health Pages.Bottom right	▤ – –	0k-10k	Add »
– Movies Pages.Bottom right	▤ – –	0k-10k	Add »
– Sunday Magazine Pages.Bottom right	▤ – –	0k-10k	Add »
– NY Region .Bottom right	▤ – –	0k-10k	Add »
– Books Pages.Bottom right	▤ – –	0k-10k	Add »
– Science Pages, Top center	▤ ▦ ▥	0k-10k	Add »
– Home & Garden Pages.Bottom right	▤ – –	0k-10k	Add »
– Home & Garden Pages, Top center	▤ ▦ ▥	0k-10k	Add »
View all nytimes.com placements (21)			

Figure 9.19 The *New York Times* offers 21 different placement opportunities.

The first step in placement targeting is to find websites where you want your ads to be displayed. After you have conducted research to find those websites, then you will want to save them to your ad group.

You may not want to save all your placements to a single ad group. There are ways of organizing placements and ad groups to achieve better results with your placement efforts.

Organizing Placements

When creating search keyword ad groups, the ads should be closely related to the keywords. Granular ad groups usually lead to higher click-through and conversion rates.

The same organization can be applied to placement ad groups. Examine the placements where your ads will be shown to create themes for these placements. Then group these different themes into different ad groups.

This organization will make your ads more relevant when they appear on placement targeted sites, which should increase both click-through and conversion rates. For instance, if you sold wedding supplies you could start with ad groups such as:

- Wedding dresses
- Wedding cakes
- Wedding favors
- Wedding flowers
- Wedding pictures

With this organization, you no longer have to write generic ad copy about how your company handles everything related to weddings. You can now tailor your ads to each type of website where your ads will be shown. This will create higher relevancy between your ad, placement, and landing page, which will in turn make your marketing more effective.

By taking this extra step in organizing your placement campaigns, it becomes easier to see not only what sites are converting for you, but which ad groups (or themes) are bringing in revenue.

Choosing CPM or CPC Bidding

With the content network, placements, or keywords, there are two ways you can choose to pay for your ads. The typical method is cost per click. However, if your ad is only shown on the content network, then you can chose to pay per impression instead of by click.

Cost per thousand impressions (CPM) is the way most banner ads are purchased on the Web. With CPM bidding, you are informing Google how much you want to pay for a thousand impressions. As with CPC bidding, you could pay less than your bid amount, but you will not pay more.

With CPM bidding, your goal is not just traffic to your website. Your goal is also to increase the recognition of your brand, products, and services. It is not uncommon to see a company buy banner ads and then see an increase in search volume for their company's name or products.

Since you are paying for an impression, you need to make sure each impression is worth your marketing dollars. Therefore, you should always use a visual ad when bidding CPM. Text ads have little recall value, and bidding CPM on a text ad is a waste of money. If you decide to bid CPM, make sure that you are using image or video ads.

Every time your ad shows, you pay for an impression. It does not matter if a user actually sees your ad or not—if the ad appears, you pay. So be careful about buying CPM ads on sites where users are highly engaged in the content, or where the site generates many page views but very little time on each page. Some examples are:

- Forum sites
- Image-sharing sites
- Social networks
- Ads below the fold

This does not mean you should not buy CPM ads below the fold or on a social network site. What you should take away is that those impressions may be worth less to you, and therefore, you may want to bid lower on those individual websites. CPM bids start at $0.25 for 1,000 impressions.

Before you can bid CPM, the campaign must be set to only appear on the content network (Figure 9.20).

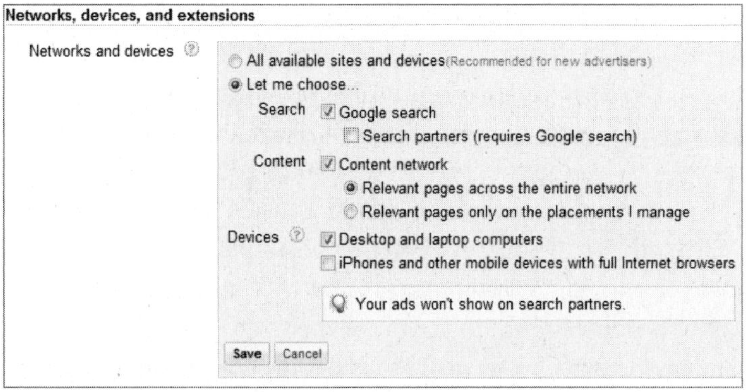

Networks, devices, and extensions

Networks and devices ⑦

○ All available sites and devices (Recommended for new advertisers)
◉ Let me choose...

Search ☑ Google search
☐ Search partners (requires Google search)

Content ☑ Content network
◉ Relevant pages across the entire network
○ Relevant pages only on the placements I manage

Devices ⑦ ☑ Desktop and laptop computers
☐ iPhones and other mobile devices with full Internet browsers

💡 Your ads won't show on search partners.

[Save] Cancel

Figure 9.20 Campaign that only appears on the content network

Once you have enabled a campaign to be only shown on content, when you examine your bidding options in your campaign settings, you will now have an additional option to bid CPM (Figure 9.21).

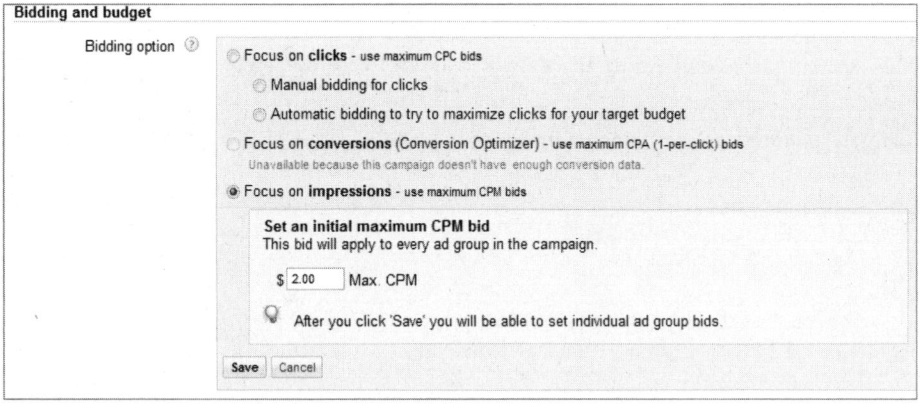

Bidding and budget

Bidding option ⑦

○ Focus on **clicks** - use maximum CPC bids
○ Manual bidding for clicks
○ Automatic bidding to try to maximize clicks for your target budget

○ Focus on **conversions** (Conversion Optimizer) - use maximum CPA (1-per-click) bids
Unavailable because this campaign doesn't have enough conversion data.

◉ Focus on **impressions** - use maximum CPM bids

Set an initial maximum CPM bid
This bid will apply to every ad group in the campaign.

$ 2.00   Max. CPM

💡 After you click 'Save' you will be able to set individual ad group bids.

[Save] Cancel

Figure 9.21 Enabling CPM bidding in the campaign settings

Note: A campaign can have only one bidding type associated with it. You cannot have one ad group in a campaign that bids based on impressions and another ad group within the same campaign that uses cost per click bidding.

With CPM bids, you will first set a bid at the campaign level. This is the default bid that all new placements will receive. You can adjust this bid either higher or lower for each placement.

When utilizing CPM ads, you are generally trying to raise the awareness of your products, services, or brand. Therefore, your ads should not contain specifics, such as prices. They should be memorable and easy to recall. If you want to add a call to action, do not make it commercial in nature. Instead, use a call to action that lets the consumer know that you will teach them valuable information.

CPC bidding gives you more control of your spending each time someone visits your website. If you want to examine the cost per conversion for an ad group or placement and then set a bid based on those metrics, you should use CPC bidding. If you are using text ads, then use CPC bidding. If you are unsure of which bidding type to use, start with CPC bidding, as you should have more experience with it since that is the primary method that AdWords utilizes.

In general, if you want to control costs, use CPC bidding. If you want to maximize your exposure, then CPM bidding is more effective. Once you have created a placement ad group and chosen the bidding type for the campaign where that ad group resides, then it is time to manage the bids for each of those placements.

Ongoing Management of Placement Targeted Ad Groups

Once you have created a placement ad group, you can manage bids, pause, resume, or delete each individual placement. Your ad group will show the same statistics you can view in keyword ad groups, only the data will be for each placement (Figure 9.22). Within the ad group or campaign, navigate to the Networks tab, and click Show Details next to the managed placements.

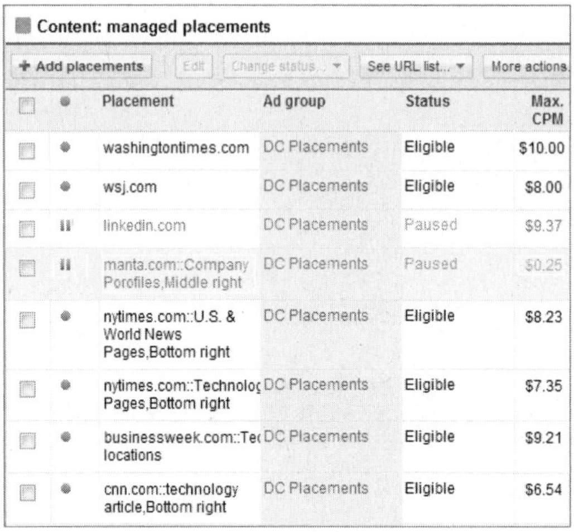
Content: managed placements
+ Add placements
Edit
Change status...
See URL list...
More actions
Placement
Ad group
Status
Max. CPM
washingtontimes.com DC Placements Eligible $10.00
wsj.com DC Placements Eligible $8.00
linkedin.com DC Placements Paused $9.37
manta.com::Company Porofiles,Middle right DC Placements Paused $0.25
nytimes.com::U.S. & World News Pages,Bottom right DC Placements Eligible $8.23
nytimes.com::Technolo(Pages,Bottom right DC Placements Eligible $7.35
businessweek.com::Te(locations DC Placements Eligible $9.21
cnn.com::technology article,Bottom right DC Placements Eligible $6.54

Figure 9.22 Managing CPM placement bids

Begin by viewing the conversion statistics next to the placement within the interface, or run a placement report. Once you have the data, then set bids based on your goals (we will discuss bidding in Chapter 13) for each individual placement.

If your goal is to bid by ROI for each placement, which is a similar goal to keyword bidding, use the exact same techniques for determining and setting these bids. Your goal might be to maximize video plays. In that case, you can run a report to examine the play rate for various placements and adjust your bids appropriately.

If your goal is to maximize the total number of people who are seeing your ads, then it can be useful to limit the number of times any single user can see your ad. This is done by frequency capping.

Using Frequency Capping to Limit the Number of Times a User Sees Your Ads

There are times you might want to limit the number of times a unique user views your ads. If you are trying to reach the most users possible, especially if you are bidding by CPM, you might only want to pay for a single person to see your ad a few times. This is called *frequency capping*. If you limit the number of times a single user sees your CPM ads, you will not use your budget on only a handful of users, but instead spread out your budget among many users.

Frequency capping only works to control the exposure of your content ads. However, it applies to both keyword and placement content exposure.

You cap impressions by both a time frame (day, week, or month) and at an ad group or ad copy level. To enable frequency capping, navigate to the Campaign Settings tab and click Edit next to the frequency capping text. You will be presented with a screen where you can select the maximum number of impressions, a time frame, and the data (ad group or ad copy) where you want to cap impressions (Figure 9.23).

Figure 9.23 Frequency capping interface in your campaign settings

For CPC bidding, frequency capping is usually not necessary, as you are only paying on a per click basis. You might want to enable it to reach more users and test out if that helps your campaign reach its goals. Frequency capping is most commonly utilized in CPM campaigns. Why pay for one person to see your ad a thousand times? Instead, pay for someone to see it a few times and then use the rest of your budget to reach more total users.

Best Practices for the Content Network

Running your ads across the content network can help increase exposure for your business by increasing your reach, reaching nonsearchers, and introducing your product and services to start someone down the buying funnel. In other words, the reach of the content network is so vast that you can find many new customers on websites who will never search for your products. By utilizing content campaigns, you can introduce your products to a significant number of web surfers who have never heard of your business. The following is a recap of critical points to remember when utilizing the content network:

- You should always run a campaign that is either based on content or search. Never combine search and content in a single campaign.

- Choose groups of keywords that create a theme. Do not use more than 50 keywords in an ad group; otherwise, you may not be able to determine which 50 words Google is using in determining your theme. While match types are ignored, negative keywords are used by Google in determining your theme.

- It is okay to use general keywords on the content network. It is also okay to have the same keyword in multiple ad groups in a content-only campaign.

- Focus on cost per conversion. With smart pricing, the click price and conversion rates are not nearly as important as cost per conversion.

- Become familiar with the placement performance report. This report will give you insight into your metrics for every site where your ad is displayed.

- When you find sites that do not meet your performance goals, block those sites with the category and site exclusion tool. Alternatively, you could add that site as a placement targeted site and then write ad copy specific to that site or set a bid for that site.

- Use placement targeting to reach users on specific websites.

- Use CPM bidding only with rich media or image ads. Usually, you want to use CPM bidding when you are trying to increase awareness of your products and you want someone to see your ad.

- Use CPC pricing when you want to focus on bidding by cost per conversion or you are only utilizing text ads.

- Break down placement ad groups by themes so you can write targeted ads for each site where your ad is displayed.

In this chapter, we have only outlined the basics of creating content and placement campaigns. There are ways of structuring your account that can help you take greater advantage of the content network. You can even change bids based on the demographics of users viewing your ads. In the next chapter, we will dive even further into additional features, placement research, and structure that will help make your content campaigns a success.

Advanced Content
Network Techniques

The content network reaches across the United States and worldwide. However, you may want to refine your ads to a smaller, more targeted audience.

In this chapter, you learn to refine your ads by adding keywords to your existing placements or by setting different bids by using placements versus the general content network. You can also adjust your bid based on demographic characteristics. You learn how to organize the content network by using a discovery campaign to reach the entire content network and a placement campaign to reach only sites that meet your marketing goals.

We wrap up this chapter by examining the Google Ad Planner, a free research tool that gives you valuable insight into the users of individual websites.

Chapter Contents

Enhancing Your Content Campaigns

In the previous chapter, we showed how you can use placement targeting to put your ad on just a single website. You can also be more specific with larger sites, such as the *New York Times*, and have your placement ad only show in the business section, for example. However, the specific sections of the *New York Times* can still result in hundreds of thousands of page views per day (Figure 10.1) according to the AdWords placement tool.

Placement Tool	Ad Formats	Impressions per day ⓘ
nytimes.com	▦ ▨ ▤	500k+
– U.S. & World News Pages.Bottom right	▦ – –	500k+
– Business Pages.Bottom right	▦ – –	500k+
– Sports Pages.Bottom right	▦ – –	100k-500k
– Health Pages.Bottom right	▦ – –	100k-500k
– NY Region .Bottom right	▦ – –	100k-500k
– Movies Pages.Bottom right	▦ – –	100k-500k
– Travel Pages.Bottom right	▦ – –	100k-500k
– Art, Dance, TV & Music.Bottom right	▦ – –	100k-500k
– Technology Pages.Bottom right	▦ – –	100k-500k
– Fashion & Style Pages.Bottom right	▦ – –	100k-500k
– Sunday Magazine Pages.Bottom right	▦ – –	100k-500k
– Dining & Wine Pages.Bottom right	▦ – –	100k-500k
– Science Pages.Bottom right	▦ – –	100k-500k
– Books Pages.Bottom right	▦ – –	100k-500k
– Science Pages, Top center	▦ ▨ ▤	10k-100k

Figure 10.1 *New York Times* estimate daily page views

While placement targeting is fantastic for sites with a small number of page views, when reaching a large site that has millions of daily page views, your ad could be seen by those outside of your target audience. Enhanced content campaigns allow you to further refine your ad exposure by using both keywords and placements to signal to Google where you would like your ad placed.

Refining Your Content Exposure with Keywords

Each ad group has the ability to house automatic placements, managed placements, and keywords. You control exactly what level of targeting you would like for each ad group.

When you combine both placements and keywords within an ad group, then your ad will only be shown to users on the website (or website section) you specify and when the article is related to the keywords you have chosen.

For example, let's assume your company sells a product that helps stockbrokers track breaking news related to their portfolio. In this instance, showing a placement ad in the *New York Times* business section seems like a good idea as many stockbrokers visit those pages each day. However, the business section of the *New York Times* is estimated to have over half a million page views every day (refer back to Figure 10.1). Instead of showing your ad to anyone in the business section, you could add keywords to your ad group that are related to stockbrokers. Now someone would have to be in the *New York Times* business section, and the article would have to match your stockbroker keywords, and only then would your ad be displayed.

You can start with either placements or keywords in your ad group. When targeting large numbers of smaller sites, it does not matter which you add first. If you are targeting larger sites, however, first add the placements, and then examine the articles of the placement websites to see what keywords their writers utilize in creating your keywords.

For example, let us assume you sell cell phones. Some review sites will use "mobile phone" to describe the product, while others may use "cell phone," and yet others will use "cellular phone." By examining a larger site's lexicon, you can use more targeted keywords to make sure your ads are placed correctly.

Note: When choosing keywords so your ad will be displayed correctly on a single site, use a keyword density analyzer as discussed in Chapter 9. However, instead of examining many different pages across the Web, find a handful of articles on the site where you want to see your ad displayed, and only look through the keyword density of those articles when selecting your content keywords.

For our purposes, we will first create an ad group that contains managed placements (Figure 10.2) in the Networks tab of an ad group.

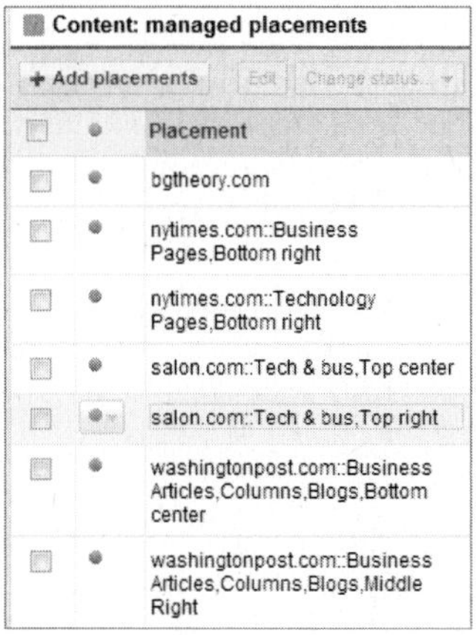

Content: managed placements

		Placement
☐	●	bgtheory.com
☐	●	nytimes.com::Business Pages,Bottom right
☐	●	nytimes.com::Technology Pages,Bottom right
☐	●	salon.com::Tech & bus,Top center
☐	●	salon.com::Tech & bus,Top right
☐	●	washingtonpost.com::Business Articles,Columns,Blogs,Bottom center
☐	●	washingtonpost.com::Business Articles,Columns,Blogs,Middle Right

Figure 10.2 Managed placements in an ad group

Next, in the exact same ad group, click on the Keywords tab and create a keyword list (Figure 10.3) using the information from Chapter 9 in the section "Choosing the Correct Words for Your Content Network Ad Group."

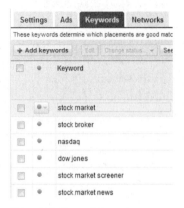

Figure 10.3 Keywords in an ad group

Using both keywords and placements in conjunction with each other can help refine your exposure across the content network so that your ad is only shown to visitors who are on the website you targeted and reading an article related to your keywords.

While it is simple to use a combination of keywords and placements, an additional campaign setting is crucial to understand when you are using placement targeting so that your ad is only displayed on the websites you have selected.

Controlling Your Placement Ad's Display

In your campaign settings, you can define if you want your ads to only be displayed on sites you choose or the entire content network (Figure 10.4).

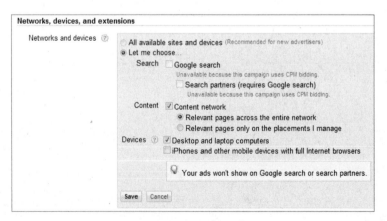

Figure 10.4 Defining where you placement ads are shown

Relevant Pages across the Entire Network

If you choose the first option, Relevant Pages Across The Entire Network, your ad can be shown on any site in the content network, but you can set separate bids for each placement you have chosen (Figure 10.5).

		Placement	Status	Max. CPM
☐	●	bgtheory.com	Eligible	$1.00
☐	●	nytimes.com::Business Pages,Bottom right	Eligible	$0.57
☐	●	nytimes.com::Technology Pages,Bottom right	Eligible	$0.25
☐	●	salon.com::Tech & bus,Top center	Eligible	$0.31
☐	●	salon.com::Tech & bus,Top right	Eligible	$0.65

Figure 10.5 Different bids by placement site

When using the option Relevant Pages Across The Entire Network, you can set a content network bid for each ad group and a default bid for placements you choose (Figure 10.6). Within each ad group, you can choose to have placements where you set separate bids.

Figure 10.6 Setting the ad group bids

This creates a bid hierarchy system. Google goes through this list, and as soon as it finds a bid it stops:

- Individual placement bid
- Ad group placement bid
- Ad group content network bid
- Campaign content network bid
- Ad group default keyword bid

For instance, if your ad was shown on a site where you chose a placement, and you did not set either a placement level bid (Figure 10.5) or an ad group placement bid (Figure 10.6), but you did have an ad group content network bid, then Google would use the ad group content network bid for the maximum CPC calculations.

If you do not want to manage an entire placement campaign where you might have anywhere from one to thousands of placements, then using this content bidding technique can be useful as it will allow you both content exposure and the ability to set different bids by sites based on their returns.

If you want to have one campaign that is only shown across the content network, and then another campaign where you choose exactly where your ad is shown, then the second campaign setting can help you control your ad's exposure.

Relevant Pages Only on the Placements I Manage

The second option in your campaign settings is Relevant Pages Only On The Placements I Manage (refer back to Figure 10.4).

When you select this option, your ad is only shown on pages where you have specifically chosen that placement. If you are looking to control your ad exposure to only certain sites, this is a better option. In addition, if you have a content campaign where you are trying to find new sites, but once you find them, you want to write specific ads for those sites, then this option gives you more control. You can read more on this in the section "Organizing Your Content Campaigns."

With Relevant Pages Only On The Placements I Manage, the same bid hierarchy system as discussed will be utilized in determining your maximum CPC.

Knowing the difference between the two options and selecting the correct one based on your content organization are crucial to understanding the breadth of your content advertising. Since these options are set at the campaign level, you could have one campaign that uses option 1, and another campaign that uses option 2. We will discuss using both of these options in different campaigns to maximize your content exposure and control later in this chapter.

Optimizing Your Content Campaigns

In the previous chapter, we showed how to block a site from showing your ads. While this is a crucial step in content optimization, it is best to first know if your offer is converting, and if your ad is being placed appropriately, before blocking traffic.

The first step to content optimization is ensuring that your ad is being placed on the proper sites. Run a placement performance report, and include individual URLs where your ad was shown (Figure 10.7).

Ad Group	Domain	URL
AdWords	650rider.com	650rider.com
AdWords	about.com	desktoppub.about.com/od/word/Microsoft_Word_Tips_and_Tutorials.htm
AdWords	about.com	google.about.com/od/googleblogging/ss/embedyoutubesbs_2.htm
AdWords	affhelper.com	www.affhelper.com/blog/2007/05/23/google-cash-detective-automator
AdWords	best-top-tips.com	www.best-top-tips.com/BB/bbimager.html...
AdWords	blogspot.com	c12hriscg.blogspot.com
AdWords	cssreflex.com	www.cssreflex.com/2009/07/5-essential-google-cheat-sheets-which-surely-will-come-in-handy.html

Figure 10.7 Placement performance report with actual URLs

Then click on some of the URLs to look at the actual pages where your ad has been shown. If these pages are related to your ad group's theme, then there is nothing else to do at this step. If the pages do not look relevant to your ad group's theme, you need to change the keywords in the ad group so that your ad is shown on more appropriate pages. Once you change the keywords in an ad group, let the content network accrue some more impressions, and then repeat this step until you are seeing your ads on relevant sites.

Once your ad is being shown on the proper pages, the second step is to find high quality sites where your ad has been shown. Look for newspaper sites or sites you recognize by name without having to look them up. These types of sites should be sending you high quality traffic. If the traffic from these sites is converting, then again, you are done and can move to the next section about content campaign organization.

Understanding Site Quality

Personally, I like to place websites into one of three categories: low-traffic, medium quality, and high quality sites. I define them as follows:

Low-Traffic Sites Usually these are small sites that do not have much traffic and therefore do not send enough traffic to make it worth your time to create specific offers for them.

Medium Quality Sites These could be local newspapers, for example, or sites in your niche that you are familiar with, but they are not the authority sites in your industry.

High Quality Sites These sites are either the authority in your niche or sites that everyone knows. These sites have the potential to send large amounts of high-converting traffic.

If the traffic is not converting, then your ad copy and landing pages may not be in proper alignment with your keywords. Especially if you find that it's not only high quality sites that are not converting, but that most sites are not converting as well, then you need to improve your ad copy, landing pages, or both before it is worthwhile to spend money on the content network or refine your exposure by blocking these sites.

In the case of low-converting traffic, instead of having your ad shown all over the content network and trying to find where you are receiving high quality traffic, only use placement targeting until you perfect your offer.

 Note: A publisher can choose to block an individual advertiser or to not allow placement targeting on their website. If you find sites where you cannot seem to have your ad displayed, it might not be your marketing efforts. There is no way to know if a publisher has blocked your ad from showing.

Choose a handful of high quality sites in your niche, and only have your ads shown on those sites. You can also run some ad copy and landing pages tests (discussed in Chapter 15) to find what combination of ad copy and landing page converts. Once you have found a combination that works well, it is time to turn on the entire content network again and use the following organizational techniques to refine your exposure over time.

There will also be times when you find that a category of websites is not working for you. For instance, if you are doing well on high quality sites, but local newspapers are not converting, instead of just blocking these sites, you could use an enhanced campaign (the keywords in your ad group and the placements in the local papers) to test out different ad copy and landing pages to find if some different combination works well on just those types of sites.

You may often see that social networking sites (such as MySpace or Facebook) perform quite differently than local newspaper sites or forum sites. Therefore, even testing different types of websites together can help you determine if you are more or less likely to convert the traffic on those sites. The exact same user is in a different mindset when on MySpace as opposed to a newspaper site, and that difference in mindset can make a difference in conversion rates.

Whenever you find good traffic from an individual website or a combination of similar websites that is not converting, your first thought should not be to block these websites from sending you traffic. Your first thought should instead be to try to optimize the ad copy and landing page for that traffic. The more traffic you block, the fewer potential customers your company can have. By trying to convert the traffic with different offers first, and then blocking second, you will constantly be improving your campaigns and finding more total customers.

Organizing Your Content Campaigns

There are two main ways to use the content network to reach your audience:

- List keywords in an ad group and let Google place your ads across sites in the content network that have similar themes to your keywords.

- Target individual websites where you want your ad to be placed with placement targeting (placement also includes keywords plus placements in enhanced campaigns).

The easiest way to block your ad from being shown on a specific website is at the campaign level. Hence, you can have one campaign where your ad is shown on a website and another campaign where your ad is not shown on that same website. Please note you can block an individual website at the ad group level as well.

By utilizing each of these targeting options, placements and general content network, in conjunction with each other, you can start to control the content network so that your ads will meet your company's goals.

Before using this technique, make sure that your offer is converting using the criteria from the previous section, "Optimizing Your Content Campaigns."

The first step is to create two campaigns:

Discovery Campaign The first campaign will contain targeted keywords in each ad group. In your campaign settings, select only the content network for placement. Do not have this campaign shown on search. Google will then place your ads across the content network when the theme of your ad group matches the theme of the webpage. For our purposes, we will call this a *discovery campaign*. The goal of this campaign is to discover sites that are meeting your performance goals.

You will set a daily budget for this account lower than your search campaigns or the next campaign type, the placement campaign. You may see limited returns from this campaign (and you might see nice returns); however, as the goal is discovery, your ads will be shown on both sites that do well for you and sites that do not.

Placement Campaign Next, create a second campaign, which we will call a *placement campaign*. This campaign is for websites that are meeting your campaign goals. When you find a site that does well, move it into the placement campaign. As these websites are performing, you always want your ad to be shown on these placements.

When you move the site to your placement campaign, examine your placement report and set a bid for that specific placement based on the ROI it is bringing your company. Then block this placement from being shown in your discovery campaign. Since you have targeted this site explicitly in your placement campaign, you want to utilize your discovery campaign to find new sites that are performing.

This campaign will have a higher budget than the discovery campaign as it only contains websites that have proven they will send your company traffic that meets your goals. You always want your ads to be shown on these websites, and setting a higher daily budget than the discovery campaign can help you sustain this converting traffic.

The second step is to run a placement performance report. When you first start using this organization technique, you will not have any websites listed in your placement campaign; therefore, start by examining data from your discovery campaign. Use the data in this report to segment sites into three categories:

- Sites that are not performing
- Sites where you do not have enough data to make a decision
- Sites that are meeting your goals

When you find sites that are not performing for you, block them in your campaign settings. If you are not receiving the proper returns from a website, you no longer want your ad to be shown on that website.

How Much Data Should I Have Before Blocking Websites?

In Chapter 15, we will discuss statistical significance in performing tests. However, many companies do not wait to achieve significant data when deciding to block websites, and with good reason. There are more websites across the content network than most companies could ever find to place their ads. Thus, it can be easier to quickly block low-performing websites, because your ad will just be shown on another site.

Make sure that you are receiving conversions from high quality sites. If you are not, you will not be blocking sites appropriately. In addition, if you find categories of websites that are not performing, use the enhanced campaign techniques described earlier to help convert traffic before you block it.

Low-Traffic Sites If I receive 50 to 100 clicks and no conversions, I usually block these sites. There are enough sites floating around the content network to fill the traffic from these sites. If you look at a site and it does not seem highly related to your offer, feel free to block it with much less data.

Medium Quality Sites If you have received 200 or more clicks and no conversions, then feel free to block this traffic, assuming you do not see a nonconverting theme, such as newspapers you should test before blocking.

High Quality Sites If one of these sites is not converting after a few hundred clicks, then I like to create an enhanced ad group (keyword plus placement) first to test out a different offer. If the site just cannot convert even with offers, then feel free to block it. Just remember, blocking high quality sites can remove many potential customers, so you are better off trying to convert this traffic before blocking it.

If you do not have enough data to make a decision for some sites, do nothing. Let these sites accumulate more data before you decide what to do with them.

When you find sites that are doing well for you, you will want to add them as placements in your placement campaign. Since these sites are doing well, ensure that your ad will continue to be shown on these websites.

Before you add this site to your placement campaign, first use the placement tool (Figure 10.8, also discussed in Chapter 9) and type in the URL of the website to see if there is more than one placement available on that website. Smaller websites, or websites that are not easily broken down into categories, may only have single placement options. In the case of single placement options, choose that placement. However, if it's a larger site that can be broken down into sections (for instance, the *New York Times* has 22 different placement options), you may want to only choose a few of the available placements.

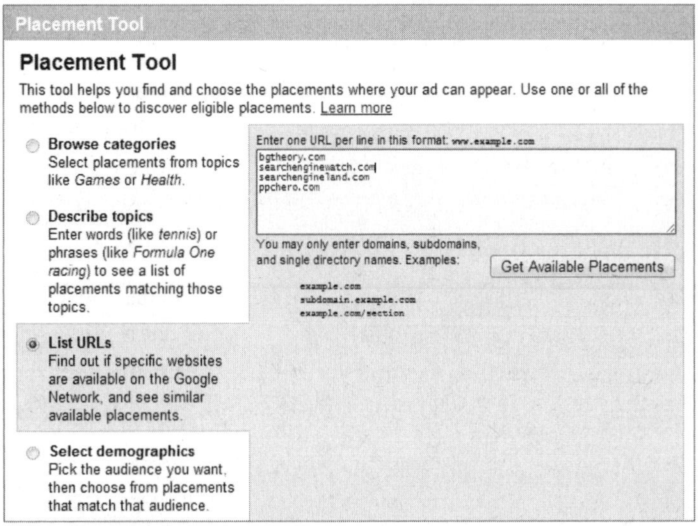

Figure 10.8 Listing URLs in the placement tool

If you want to be shown on every placement of a site that has multiple placement opportunities, instead of selecting the entire site, choose each individual placement. The reason to add all of the smaller placements is that you can set a different bid for each placement even within a website. For instance you could set a bid of $0.50 for the *New York Times* travel section, a $0.75 bid for the *New York Times* business section, and $1 for the *New York Times* technology section (Figure 10.9).

In addition, you will want to block these sites from being shown in your discovery campaign. The discovery campaign's purpose is to find new sites to place your ads. If you do not block a site from being shown in the discovery campaign, then your ad could still be shown on a site that is also listed in the placement campaign and it will slow down the process of finding new sites that are performing for you.

☐ Content: managed placements				Hide details

☐	●	Placement	Ad group	Status	Max. CPC
☐	●	nytimes.com::Business Pages,Bottom right	bg Theory	Eligible	$0.75
☐	●	nytimes.com::Technology Pages,Bottom right	bg Theory	Eligible	$1.00
☐	●	nytimes.com::Travel Pages,Bottom right	bg Theory	Eligible	$0.50

Figure 10.9 Different bids for different sections of the *New York Times*

Since each placement in the placement campaign can have its own bid, calculate the bid based on the returns that site is sending you (more about calculating bids in Chapter 13), and set that as the starting bid. Next, run a placement performance report for the placement campaign and continue to refine bids based on each placement's performance.

Repeat this process to find sites doing well and sites not performing, and then block and add them as necessary. You can use the flow chart diagram in Figure 10.10 to follow the steps just outlined.

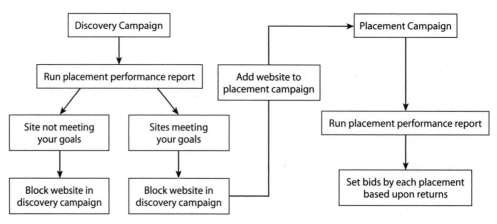

Figure 10.10 Content network organization flowchart

By using the process of first making sure your offer converts, then placing your ad around the content network, then refining your exposure based on individual websites, you can achieve excellent results from the content network.

Our bidding process so far has only encompassed setting a bid at the ad group level with respect to keywords or at the placement level. These bids are static regardless of who is seeing the ad. There is one more level of complexity you can add to the content campaigns: automatically changing your bid based on the gender or age group of the person viewing your ad. This is known as demographic bidding.

Setting Different Bids By Demographics

When a user creates a MySpace profile, they enter additional information about themselves such as their gender and age. There are a number of social networking sites, such as MySpace, that partner with Google to send anonymous demographic data about people who are viewing your ads. You can then use this data to set different bids by both gender and age.

> **Note:** Demographic targeting and bidding apply only to the content network. Each of these partners is a content network partner.

As users don't log in on every site they access, and not all sites know their users' demographics, demographic bidding only applies to certain sites in Google's content network. To see the entire list of websites where demographic bidding is available, go to http://adwords.google.com/support/bin/answer.py?answer=88168&topic=13665.

Viewing Your Demographic Performance Stats

The first step in creating demographic bids is to run a demographic report (Figure 10.11), which is available in the Reporting Options screen.

Demographic Report

Report Generated: Jul 21, 2009 9:25:13 AM   Show report detail

Export Report   Create Another Report Like This

View: Summary

Ad Group	Domain	Age	Gender	Impressions	Clicks
Red Sonja	myspace.com	55-64	Male	1	1
Dark Tower	friendster.com	25-34	Male	5	1
Spider-Man	myspace.com	65+	Female	25	1
Captain America	myspace.com	45-54	Female	52	1
Hulk	youtube.com	25-34	Male	52	1
Spider-Man	friendster.com	Unspecified	Male	519	3
Buffy	myspace.com	35-44	Male	666	1
Iron Man	myspace.com	18-24	Male	1,059	1
Dark Tower	myspace.com	35-44	Male	1,240	1
Spider-Man	myspace.com	0-17	Female	3,648	2

Figure 10.11 Demographic performance statistics

While the reports allow you to drill down into the performance stats of every single domain, age, and gender combination, when first getting started it can seem like a huge amount of data. As with most AdWords reports, there is a plethora of data available. One data point that can cause the demographic report to be unwieldy is Domain. If you deselect Domain from Level Of Detail (Figure 10.12), you will see combined demographic data by ad group in the information being filtered by domain.

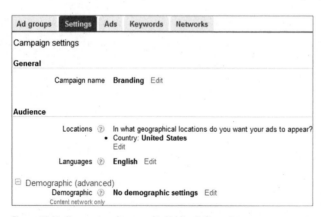

Figure 10.12 Removing domain information from reports

This non–domain filtered report will give you more information about the performance stats by demographics. In addition, you can see demographic information where you set the demographic bids, shown in the next section.

Setting Demographic Bids

In your campaign settings, click on Edit in the Demographic section (Figure 10.13).

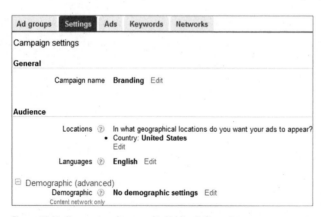

Figure 10.13 How to view demographic bidding information

This will bring up a page where you can see the last seven days of performance statistics by demographic as well as set different bids by demographic (Figure 10.14).

Demographic bidding ⊠

This summary shows how your ads have performed on sites that offer demographic data. Click any row to adjust your bid for that demographic group. You can also use the exclude checkboxes to hide your ad from that group.

0.00% of total impressions are from sites with demographic data. ⓘ

Traffic Reports by Gender and Age (for last 7 days)

Gender	Exclude	Modify bid	Impr.	Clicks	CTR	Cost	Conv. rate (1-per-click)	Cost / conv. (1-per-click)
Male	☐	Bid + 25%	0	0	0.00%	$0.00	0.00%	$0.00
Female	☑	Bid + 0%	0	0	0.00%	$0.00	0.00%	$0.00
Unspecified			0	0	0.00%	$0.00	0.00%	$0.00
Total			**0**	**0**	**0.00%**	**$0.00**	**0.00%**	**$0.00**

Age	Exclude	Modify bid	Impr.	Clicks	CTR	Cost	Conv. rate (1-per-click)	Cost / conv. (1-per-click)
0-17	☑		0	0	0.00%	$0.00	0.00%	$0.00
18-24	☐	Bid + 35%	0	0	0.00%	$0.00	0.00%	$0.00
25-34	☐	Bid + 22%	0	0	0.00%	$0.00	0.00%	$0.00
35-44	☐	Bid + 12%	0	0	0.00%	$0.00	0.00%	$0.00
45-54	☐	Bid + 0%	0	0	0.00%	$0.00	0.00%	$0.00
55-64	☑	Bid + 0%	0	0	0.00%	$0.00	0.00%	$0.00
65+	☑	Bid + 0%	0	0	0.00%	$0.00	0.00%	$0.00
Unspecified			0	0	0.00%	$0.00	0.00%	$0.00
Total			**0**	**0**	**0.00%**	**$0.00**	**0.00%**	**$0.00**

Figure 10.14 Setting demographic bids for a campaign

In this screen, you can exclude demographics from viewing your ads by clicking the Exclude box next to the age or gender information. You can also set different bid boosts by age or gender. This is the percentage you want your maximum CPC to be multiplied by in determining your bid for that gender or age range.

It is important to note these percentages are additive. For instance, if this is your bid information:

- Ad group maximum CPC $1

- +25% if the viewer is male

- +35% if the viewer is 18–24

  then your maximum CPC used by Google would be:

- $1 if gender and age is unknown

- $1.25 if the viewer was male, but between the ages of 45–54

- $1.60 if the viewer is a 18–24 year old male

Since these numbers are additive, it can be useful to set low maximum CPCs at the ad group or placement level and then use demographic bid boosts to increase your bids when your target market is viewing your ads. This lower maximum CPC will be the maximum CPC of your ad groups for non-demographics seeing them. Therefore, it can be useful to create demographic-only campaigns.

Organizing Your Demographic Campaign

There are two major ways to organize your demographic campaigns based on your objectives. If you find that you receive enough returns from the sites that allow demographic targeting that you are willing to set a different budget for demographic targeting, and you are willing to write ads for each site, or category of sites, then creating a demographic campaign with site placements can be worth your time.

If you do not want to set a different budget for a demographic campaign, or you are still experimenting with demographic targeting, then setting demographic bids in current content campaigns is probably your better option.

Creating a Demographic Campaign with Site Placements

If you want to set a different budget for demographic targeting versus your regular content network reach, or you find that demographic optimization is leading to good returns, you can create a demographic-only campaign.

The first step is to create a content-only campaign as normal (in your campaign settings, set this campaign to only be shown on the content network). Next, choose to only allow this campaign to be shown on placements you have chosen. Then you can add each of the demographic targeted sites as placements. This will ensure that your ad is only shown on sites that allow demographic bidding.

In this organization, you have the option to write specific ads for each demographic site by adding just one placement per ad group and then creating corresponding ads in that same ad group.

If writing a different ad per website is more work than you are willing to undertake, you can add all of the placements into a single ad group, or break the placements into like-minded sites and write ads for only the ad groups you create.

In this method, since you have set a different budget for the demographic sites and are writing custom ads for these sites, you need to block these sites from being shown on your discovery content campaign. If you do not block these sites from that campaign, Google could use your content bids and budget from the discovery campaign instead of your demographic bid and budget when showing your ads on those sites.

Setting Demographic Bids in Your Current Content Campaigns

Demographic bidding only applies if someone is on one of the websites that passes demographic information to Google. The bid changes do not apply to any other content network sites. Therefore, you could add the list of demographic sites as placements in your current content campaigns.

As with the previous method, you can add all of the demographics to a single ad group or break up the list of demographic sites into different ad groups. It all depends on how you want to organize the ad copy.

If you add these sites to your discovery campaign, or any campaign that is shown across the content network, Google can use your keyword-based ad groups and their associated bids when your ad is shown on these sites. Therefore, this method can cause a conflict if you only have a single content campaign, unless you block all of the demographic placements in all the other ad groups in this content campaign.

If you add these sites to a placements-only campaign, like the one discussed earlier in content organization, then add the demographic targeted sites to your blocked sites list in your discovery campaign settings.

In either method, if you do not like the returns of a single site, you can remove that site from your list of placements, and then ensure that site is also blocked in any general content campaigns.

Why You Should Add the Demographic Sites as Placements

In both methods, placement targeting was used instead of just setting demographic bids for that content campaign and letting Google adjust your bids based on where the searcher is viewing your ad. The reason for this is that demographic bids can only increase your CPC, they cannot lower it.

If you set low bids for an individual placement, and then use demographic bidding where you are increasing your bids based on the demographics of someone seeing your ad, you can be highly accurate in determining what you are willing to pay based on both the site where your ad is being displayed and the demographics of the visitor.

If you just set demographic bids and do not use placements, you lose some ad serving control. Since you should set bids at the ad group level based on returns (although in some discovery campaigns, you might bid higher because you want the exposure on various websites so you can find good placements), you might only have the option of bidding even higher than your returns when specific demographics see your ads.

If there are only a couple of age ranges or a single gender where you see higher conversion rates, this is acceptable. If you see widely different conversion rates, or cost per conversion by demographics, especially on the demographic targeted sites, then you will run into scenarios where you cannot set your desired bid without using placements.

For example, say you have this scenario:

- Want to bid $0.50 if someone is between 18–24

- Want to bid $0.30 if someone is 55–64

- Want to bid $0.40 if someone sees your ad from a random content network site

In this scenario, because you wish to pay less for the 55-64 age group than your standard bid, there is no way to set appropriate content bids without the use of placements.

With demographic bidding, since you can only raise your bid, you should set the bid for that placement at the minimum you are willing to pay when someone clicks on your ad from that placement, which would be $0.30 in this scenario. Then use the bid boost to bring your bid price up to the point you are willing to pay when someone from a specific demographic clicks on your ad.

Creating Scenarios to Understand and Reach Your Targeted Audience

Using discovery, placement, and potentially demographic campaigns will lead to a scenario where you can start to control and refine your targeting based on returns. However, if you have a smaller budget, or you only want to reach a very specific user, having a general content campaign might not be cost effective or possible for you.

If you have a smaller budget, starting with placements, determining what type of placements are doing well for you (news, social, forums, etc.) and then finding additional placements that meet that criteria can help you grow your content advertising in a more returns-oriented environment.

As we start to layer on more targeting options, it can start to become confusing to determine how to reach your target market. Instead of focusing on all of the options, let us focus on creating real-life scenarios and then see what options apply to your audience.

Here's a list of the ways you can target a content ad:

- Time of day (discussed in Chapter 13)

- Day of the week (discussed in Chapter 13)

- Location (discussed in Chapter 11)

- Individual website or section of a website (placement targeting)

- Keywords (standard content targeting) or keywords plus placements (enhanced campaigns)

While you have to use either keywords or placements as a starting point, you can use all or none of the additional targeting options. Instead of trying to think through all the options, first let's create a scenario for reaching your target market.

Even though someone is viewing your ad online, they still have a physical presence in the world where their life is dictated by offline factors and daily routine. Examine the life of your customer, and the targeting options can become apparent.

For instance, let us expand on the earlier scenario that your company has just developed a product that allows stockbrokers to get real-time U.S. news results based on their portfolio. And let us also assume that you are doing a limited test to view the response rate and have chosen Minneapolis as your target market. In addition, you do not have a limitless budget, so you want to refine your targeting as much as possible.

Therefore, the question is how do you reach stockbrokers who live in Minneapolis? Let's begin by building a profile of how they receive their current news, as that is what your product addresses.

Since your company only wants to reach users in Minneapolis, the first setting is quite easy: only show the ad in Minneapolis.

Next, a stockbroker has to be ready for the New York Stock Exchange to open at 9:30 a.m. EST. However, Minneapolis is on Central time, therefore, the stockbroker has to be ready for work at 8:30 a.m. Some will read the news at home, others at work. Therefore, let us run the ad from only 5:00 a.m. until 10:30 a.m.

Most people behave differently on weekends than on weekdays. The weekends are for relaxing, the weekdays are about work. Therefore, let us only run the ad from Monday to Friday.

Where do stockbrokers read their morning financial news? Use the placement tool (and the Google Ad Planner, discussed later in this chapter) to research financial news sites. For our purposes, we will choose a starting place of:

- Bloomberg.com, only one placement available
- *New York Times*, business pages placement
- *Business Week*, all placements except Asia and Europe

These three websites have a tremendous amount of daily page views, even when only that handful of sections is chosen. Therefore, also choose some keywords such as "stock market," "NASDAQ," "Dow Jones," "NYSE," and so on.

Now, when we add all those components together, the ad will only be shown to those who meet all these criteria at once:

- Located in Minneapolis
- Viewing the *New York Times*, Bloomberg.com, or *Business Week* in one of the chosen placement sections
- During a weekday
- In the morning from 5:00 a.m. until 10:30 a.m.
- The article matches your keyword list

It is important to note that the more you segment your audience, the smaller the potential audience is, as they have to meet all of the criteria.

If you have ads that are already running, when you start to refine your ad's exposure, always track total conversions and conversion rate to make sure you did not remove your ads from being seen by converting customers.

If you feel overwhelmed by the possibilities of the content network and all the options, step away from Google's options and start thinking about the user:

- Who is your ideal customer?

- How do they live their life?
- When during their daily routine are they more open to reading your ad and viewing your offer?

By examining those three simple questions, you can learn how to reach your customers.

How to Write Effective Content Ads

Writing ads for the content network is different from writing search ads. With search ads, someone has conducted an actual search, which shows they are aware of the product and service. The fact that a searcher has conducted a search means they are somewhere in the buying funnel.

When reaching individuals with the content network, many users may not be in the buying funnel at all. Your ads are shown based on the article's contents, not the user's intent of actively seeking information. Therefore, you should be writing content ads to reach users who are not in the buying funnel so that they will enter your buying funnel.

While some people who are in the buying funnel will see your content ads, they are often not your primary audience for such ads. Those individuals you will reach when they are searching for your products. Your content ads will help reinforce your message for those who are in the buying funnel, and you may see conversions from these individuals. However, as those already in the buying funnel usually make up a small percentage of those who see your content ads, they should rarely be your primary audience (with placement targeting being the common exception).

When examining these ad copy writing rules, we are making the assumption that you are using the content network to introduce your existing product or service to consumers to start them down the buying funnel. There are many other reasons to use the content network, such as CPM image ad buys to create awareness for a new product. If you are using the content network for some of these specific reasons, then borrow what makes sense from the ad writing sections (here and in Chapter 8) to create your own ads that meet your company's goals.

Showcase Relevancy The more relevant an ad is to the consumer, the more interest it will attract. Relevancy is attained by your keyword or placement selection. Make sure your ad is relevant to the website it is being shown on. This point is as much about choosing the proper placements and keywords as it is about the ad's design or chosen text. Ads that seem to underperform might not be underperforming; it could be they are being seen by the wrong audience. Always check to make sure your ads are being placed on the proper pages.

Showcase Benefits The reason people move further into the buying funnel is that the product or service has made some promise about how it will make their life better.

We become interested in products because of benefits. As consumers who are reading related articles might be aware of similar products or services—and in someone else's buying funnel—if your product or similar products are well known, you should test adding a feature or two in the ad along with your primary benefit.

What Will They Learn After the Click? This is not necessary in every ad copy, but it is worthwhile testing. Tell consumers what they will receive if they click on your ad. By letting them know what they will learn, you might give those who have entered the incentive they need to click on the ad to view your landing page.

Call to Action All ads should have a call to action. Tell a customer why they should click on your ad and what they should do on the landing page. Phrases like "begin your free trial" are a call to action that lets them know the next page will be a free trial sign-up.

Use General Offers Too specific an offer can confuse a visitor who is not yet in the buying funnel and does not know about your products. General offers, such as "download a whitepaper," "free trial," and "calculate your savings," create a compelling message for a general audience.

While these rules generally apply to all content network ads, you can be more specific with placement targeted ads. For instance, if you sell server monitoring software, and your ad is being placed on a site that caters to advanced IT individuals, then you are reaching an audience that understands the benefits of server monitoring. In this case, your general consumer benefit may not be that compelling to an audience who already understands the entire monitoring process and knows they need it. They are interested in new features that will make their lives easier that are not typical in other software. Therefore, you might need more specific benefits in your ad copy such as why this monitoring software is easier to use, that it is less resource intensive, or that it can SMS you when servers go down when most software just sends email notifications.

As a general rule, the more you know about your audience and the more specific the audience, the more your ads can be tailored to meet their needs. Conversely, the more general the audience, the more general the ads should be written.

Google Ad Planner: Free Access to Expensive Data

Data is expensive. The more data you desire, the more it will cost your company. While many large companies use comScore or Hitwise for market intelligence, their price points often exclude small and medium enterprise businesses who do not have the data research budgets to pay for such information.

Luckily, Google has introduced Google Ad Planner, which gives some information about websites for free. While this data is by no means as complete as comScore or Hitwise, it is excellent data to use when researching information about various websites.

As there is more data available in Google Ad Planner than we could cover in an entire chapter, we are going to concentrate on how to use it to find effective placement targeted websites.

To start using Google Ad Planner, visit `www.google.com/adplanner/` and sign in with your Google account (Figure 10.15).

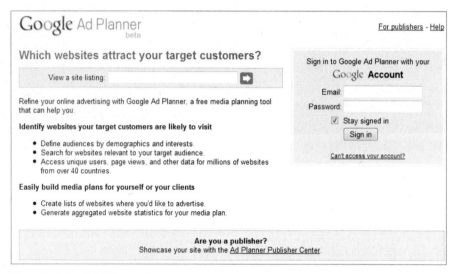

Figure 10.15 Google Ad Planner main page

The first step in using Ad Planner is to create a media plan (Figure 10.16). This is a collection of websites you have added to your plan from research you have conducted. You can have as many plans as you wish; therefore, name it something descriptive so you can easily find your research at a later date.

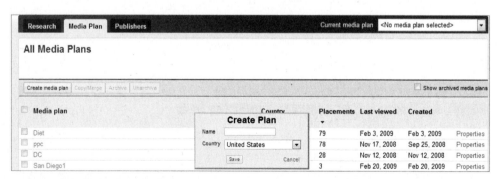

Figure 10.16 Create and access your media plans.

Once you have created a media plan, select the plan and then it is time to start researching websites.

Conducting Google Ad Planner Research

Upon accessing the research page, a list of the more common websites visited will be shown. You can segment the websites based on both audience and website characteristics to narrow down the selection of websites you are viewing. Once you have found specific websites that you want to know more about, you can receive detailed information about those websites' visitors.

As our goal for this chapter is to find new websites to use in your placements, we are going to walk through a few different methods of using your AdWords data to find these sites. Please note, while we are going to walk through some of these options individually, in most cases you can combine these methods together. The more you segment the data, the fewer websites will meet your criteria.

Google Ad Planner shows details for:

- Sites that accept advertising

- Sites that are in Google's content network

- All sites regardless of the above two criteria (if you uncheck both boxes, you can see information from almost any website regardless of what ads are shown on a site)

For our research purposes, the first step will be to only view details of sites that are in the Google content network (Figure 10.17).

Figure 10.17 View information for sites only in the Google content network.

Along the top of the Ad Planner research page is a filtering bar (Figure 10.18). In the next few sections, you will see this bar several times but with only one item selected. Each of the filtering options is available somewhere along this main filter bar.

Figure 10.18 Ad Planner filtering bar

To help explain the filtering options, let us first examine what data is available for any website.

Detailed Website Information

As you filter your audience, the bottom of the screen will refine the websites listed based on those filters. You can click on any of the websites to find detailed information (Figure 10.19) that contains some of these data points:

- Categories
- Traffic statistics
- Daily unique visitors
- Gender
- Education
- Age
- Household income
- Children in household
- Sites also visited
- Keywords search for
- Ad specifications

(Please note that Figure 10.19 only contains a third of the available data points that are shown when you actually use the Ad Planner tool.)

Figure 10.19 Detailed stats for Yahoo.com

Demographic Research

One of the options for Google Ad Planner is to segment the audience by demographic characteristics. If you run a demographic performance report in your AdWords account, and have data that shows what gender and age range are converting on your site, you can only view sites that have a high composite of that specific audience.

However, Google Ad Planner allows more demographic inputs (Figure 10.20) than you can achieve from your AdWords reports. You can filter by:

- Gender
- Age
- Education
- Household income
- Children in household

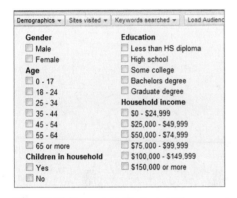

Figure 10.20 Demographic filtering in Ad Planner

Therefore, it can be useful to build an ideal customer profile. Determining additional statistics such as income and education can help you find more specific placements.

If your AdWords reports do not give you demographic data as your ads have not been placed on those sites, then examine the demographic statistics discussed in the next section to see if you find a pattern.

Finding Related Websites

When you run a placement performance report, you can see which sites are sending you traffic that meets your advertising goals. Take those sites and input them into Google Ad Planner. This will give you detailed statistics about each of those websites.

The goal is not to examine each website individually. With composite data (high-level data mixed together) there are always anomalies because the data comes from multiple sources and is mixed together. Therefore, instead of looking at all the stats of each website that has performed well for you, look for patterns among the data.

For example, if you do not have a clear demographic picture yet, look for commonalties of gender, age, income, and education levels among all the sites that are performing for you across the content network. Make note of any patterns and see if you can start to build a demographic profile.

When examining the data items, look for:

- Sites also visited (Figure 10.21)

- Categories

- Keywords searched for

Sites also visited

Site	Affinity ⑦
ppchero.com	950.0x
roirevolution.com	590.0x
seroundtable.com	190.0x
seomoz.org	160.0x
shoemoney.com	160.0x
searchengineland.com	140.0x
marketingpilgrim.com	140.0x
clickz.com	130.0x
searchenginewatch.com	130.0x
hubspot.com	110.0x

Figure 10.21 Sites also visited for bgTheory.com (the author's blog)

You can copy and paste them into an Excel sheet. Repeat that process for your top-performing content network websites. As you copy and paste, you will start to form a list that contains some sites listed multiple times as they are related to other high-performing websites. Once you have compiled a list of websites, use a pivot table in your spreadsheet program to create a single list of websites where column 1 is the website name and column 2 is the number of times it appeared in the sheet. Repeat this step for keywords searched for, related websites, and categories. We will use this data in the next few research techniques.

Sites Also Visited

Another way you can filter websites in the Ad Planner tool is by other sites your audience has visited (Figure 10.22). Either use the top-performing sites from your placement performance report, or use the most common sites also visited from the previous research step that you created in a spreadsheet.

Figure 10.22 Filtering based on related websites

If you have a defined demographic, you can leave those items selected so that the related sites will be included if they also reach your demographic.

In this filtering list, click on a website and view its detailed information. If there is a website where you want to place your ads, click the box next to the website from the research screen (Figure 10.23) and it will be added to your media plan.

	Placement	Category	Comp Index	Audience Reach	UV (users)	Country UV (users)	PV
☑	bgtheory.com	Search Engine Optimization & Marketing	950000	89.9%	20K	22K	100K
☑	seomoz.org	Search Engine Optimization & Marketing	15000	32.4%	7.2K	520K	16M
☑	searchengineland.com	Search Engine Optimization & Marketing	13000	26.4%	5.8K	470K	4.6M
☑	searchenginewatch.com	Search Engine Optimization & Marketing	12000	23.9%	5.3K	480K	3.1M

Figure 10.23 Adding sites to your media plan

Each time you add a site to your media plan, the top of the research pane will be updated with the number of placements in that media plan and its overall reach (Figure 10.24).

Summary	Placements	Unique visitors	Country reach	Page views
Media plan	4	1.3 M	0.6%	28 M
Selected	4	1.3 M	0.6%	28 M
Combined	4	1.3 M	0.6%	28 M

Figure 10.24 Media plan summary

Keywords Searched For

You can also view sites based on what keywords people search for that lead to that website. You can run a keyword performance report and see what keywords are your highest-converting keywords. Then you can input those keywords into Google Ad Planner (Figure 10.25) to see what other sites these searchers are visiting. If they accept advertising, you can place your ads on those websites.

Figure 10.25 Input keywords into Google Ad Planner to find related websites

By placing your ads on related sites, you get a second chance with the user who conducted a search for one of your keywords yet chose to go to another site instead of yours. You can visit the detailed profiles of several related websites and copy the list of keywords for each site into Excel. Then, you can create a pivot table from the keyword list to see the most common words used to navigate to those sites. Examine the most commonly used words to see if they should be added to your content network keywords.

You can also use demographic filtering, related site filtering, and the other filtering options along with the keyword filter. However, if you filter by too many data points, you will eventually end up with a message that no websites can be found.

Pre-defined Audiences

If you are unsure of your audience, and you are lucky enough to be in an industry where Google has created a pre-defined audience, it can be useful to take a look through their suggestions. Navigate to the Load Audience button and you will be presented with many options for audience choice (Figure 10.26).

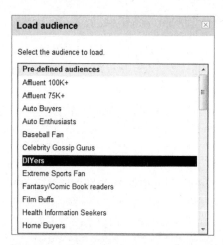

Figure 10.26 Choosing among pre-defined audiences

You can always see your current filters listed below the audience and filters information (Figure 10.27).

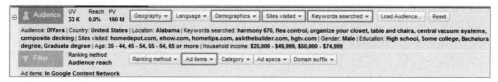

Figure 10.27 Current audience and filters selected

Filtering the Information by Category

If you only want to see what sites fall into pre-defined categories, you can use the category filtering option (Figure 10.28) to either view all the websites within a category or use some other filtering items (such as demographics) to only see sites within a category that match your audience characteristics.

Figure 10.28 Filtering Ad Planner data by categories

If you saved all of the previous research in Excel with the categories listed per website, you can utilize a pivot table to see which categories are already performing for your ads.

Filtering the Information by Ad Size and Type

Not all websites, even in the Google content network, accept all ad formats. You can view websites based on the ad types and sizes that they accept. For example, if you are beginning to analyze video ads to see if they are performing for your company, but you have only created a 250×250 video for testing purposes, you could choose to only see sites that show video ads of that size format (Figure 10.29).

After you have conducted your research, added sites to your plan, and saved your plan, it is time to move those sites into your AdWords account.

Figure 10.29 Viewing websites that only accept specific ad formats and sizes

Adding Ad Planner Sites to AdWords

Unfortunately, Google AdWords and Google Ad Planner are not linked products. Therefore, you need to follow a few simple steps to add the sites you have found for placement targeting into your AdWords account:

1. On a media plan's detailed information page, or on the research page, there is an Export button. Click this button to export the files to a .csv (comma separated value) file, which can be opened in most spreadsheet programs.

2. Open this file in Excel (or your chosen spreadsheet program) and copy the list of websites.

3. In AdWords, navigate to the ad group where you want to add these sites.

4. In the placement tool (as described in Chapter 9) click on List URLs.

5. In the text box, paste the URLs you copied from your spreadsheet (refer back to Figure 10.8) and let the tool find the sites for you.

6. Click the Get Available Placements button; Google will add any placements it finds from the URLs you listed directly into the Selected Placements box for you to save to your ad group.

It is common for the tool to not find all the placements you have listed, even if they are available for placement targeting. Therefore, there are two steps you should undertake before saving these placements to the ad group:

- If the website has additional placement options, such as the *New York Times* with its 22 available placements, the tool will add only the root domain into the placement box. If you want to only add specific placements within larger sites,

  1. Delete the placement from the Selected Placements box.

  2. Scroll down to that website's placement opportunities and only select the ones where you want your ad to appear.

- Some sites will be listed as not available for placement targeting. This happens on occasion even if the site is available. In this case,

    1. Go to the keyword search box and search for the website's name, or a keyword that would bring up that website.

    2. If you find the website through the search process, add it for placement targeting.

    If you do a few searches and cannot find the website, it might not be available for placement targeting after all.

Once you have added all of the placements where you want your ad to appear, save those placements to an ad group. Navigate to the ad group and write your text ads, or upload any image or rich media ads that you would like to appear on those websites.

Google Ad Planner gives you access to a tremendous amount of data. However, you need to combine it with an advertising outlet, such as Google AdWords, before you can find the full value in the research for advertising purposes.

Best Practices for Advanced Content Network Usage

The content network has multiple layers of complexity you can utilize to display your ads, from using keywords to placements to keywords plus placements to demographic targeting. In addition, all of your typical campaign settings such as geography, time of day, and budget also apply to content campaigns. With so many options available, it is often simpler to create scenarios for reaching your target audience and then examine the list of possible targeting options to best reach that audience.

- If you are placing your ads on either very large sites or a large number of small sites, refine your ad exposure by adding keywords in the same ad group as your placements. This way your ad will only show on the sites you want when the article also matches your keywords.

- When using placement targeting, set the campaign's reach to either be on any site in the content network or only on the placements you have chosen.

- You need to be familiar with the placement performance report to accomplish any content campaign optimization.

- Run the placement performance report. If a site is not performing for you, then block your ad from being shown on that site. If a website is performing for you, then block it from the discovery campaign and add it to a placements-only campaign.

- Become familiar with the demographics that convert on your website so you can set demographic bids and use that information to find new sites to place your ads.

- When writing ads for the general content network, create general offers that are laden with benefits.
- Google Ad Planner can give you free insight into many statistics about most websites on the Internet. Use the Ad Planner to find new sites where you want to place your ads.
- Once you have found new websites with the Ad Planner tool, export the data and add those websites to your AdWords account.

The content network is about reach. There are more possible impressions and clicks on the content network than on search. Therefore, understanding your audience and writing ads to reach that audience will help you not just get clicks from the content network, but conversions as well.

In the next chapter, we will discuss another way of reaching your target audience based on their location. With location targeting, you can make sure that only users in specific locations can view your search or content ads.

Advanced Geographic Targeting

Location targeting allows you to show your ads to consumers in specific geographic regions, whether it is multiple countries or five miles around a single zip code. The first part of this chapter focuses on how to show your ads to specific locations and some pitfalls that you should understand.

The second half of the chapter focuses on writing ads for different geographies and on using methods to engage users based on their knowledge of your target area and what they consider credible.

Finally, we will close with a geographic report where you can find opportunities to optimize your account based on your performance in specific geographies.

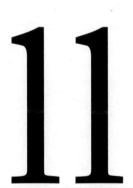

Chapter Contents

What Is Geographic Targeting?

AdWords allows you to choose where your ads will be displayed. This is useful if you want to show a different message in different locations, set different budgets by location, or optimize your spending based on returns from different geographies.

The benefit for location-based companies, such as a New York dentist or the Best Buy in Fargo, is fairly obvious: you reach only consumers who will travel to your business location. Therefore, a plumber in San Francisco or a pizza delivery company in Dallas only needs to show their ads to those who are in their business area.

However, e-commerce or national companies often overlook the advantages of using location-based ads. If you examine the marketing of a company like Coca-Cola, you will notice different billboards and commercials in San Francisco as opposed to those that appear in New York or London. This is because consumers react differently to various messages based on their location norms.

Please note, all campaigns must choose in which geographies the ads in each campaign will appear. The default option is usually a country or bundle of countries. However, regardless of the reach you want your ads to have, it is a setting you should be aware of so that you know exactly where Google is displaying your ads.

Before discussing the location targeting options and how local, national, and multinational companies can take advantage of them, you must understand how the technology that is used to identify a user's location works.

The Technology Behind Location Targeting

There are four main ways that Google identifies a user's location:
- By looking at the Google property used for the query
- By examining the explicit geographic keywords used in a search query
- By inspecting the previous geographic keywords used in searches
- By determining the searcher's location based on their IP address

For our purposes, I will simplify these as much as possible and leave out some of the technology so these concepts are easy to understand in the framework of a single chapter.

The first factor used to determine a user's location is based on the extension of the Google search engine being used. For instance, users in France go to Google.fr while users in Canada go to Google.ca. The country extension tells Google from which country a searcher wishes to see information.

The second is when a searcher uses an explicit geographic qualifier in their search query, such as "Austin plumber." When a geographic qualifier is used, Google must feel confident that they understand the area in which the searcher is seeking information.

In the Austin plumber example, there are a few locations in the United States that use the word "Austin." However, the vast majority of them are looking for Austin, Texas, information; therefore, Google is fairly confident that the user is looking for that information and will therefore serve ads for Austin, Texas.

If you consider a query such as "Washington plumber," the query could refer to Washington, D.C., Washington State, Washington, Utah, or any of the other Washington-named cities or counties. In another example, there are two large cities named Kansas City. In both of these cases, Google will show fewer (or no) ads because they are not highly confident that they understand the user's location.

The third method that Google uses to show ads is based on previous search history. If you use explicit geographic qualifiers in the search query, which is the second method, Google has an idea of the location where you want to find information and may use that information to target ads for other queries. If you do a search for "Washington DC plumber," and then follow that query with "Washington kitchen remodeling," you may see geographic ads, as Google now has some idea that you have defined Washington, D.C., as your target location. In addition, if you search for "Washington DC plumber" and follow that query with "kitchen remodeling," you might also see location-based ads even without a geographic qualifier in the search query, as Google remembers previous searches.

The fourth way they show location-based ads is based on your IP address. When a computer logs on to the Web, it is assigned an IP address. This could be considered your computer's location on the Web. Many IP addresses are mapped to physical locations so that Google understands where you are actually located.

However, the IP address for your computer is not always your computer's actual location: it's your ISP's (Internet service provider) location, otherwise known as your host provider. Therefore, the third method looks at ISP locations and attempts to discern your location with the assumption that most people live close to their ISP provider.

This leads to the following scenario: When you do any form of location targeting, whether it's for a country to a city, three things are going to happen:

- A searcher inside your target location will see your ad.

- A searcher outside your target location will see your ad.

- A searcher inside your target location will not see your ad.

If you only want to show your ads in Chicago, these are the three scenarios (Figure 11.1) that will occur:

- Searcher 1 is inside your target area. The host provider is in your target area. This is a perfect match.

- Searcher 2 is outside your target area. The host provider is in your target area. Though this searcher is outside your target location, they will still see your geographic ad.

- Searcher 3 is inside your target area. The host provider is outside your target area. Though this searcher is in your target area, they will still not see your geographic ad.

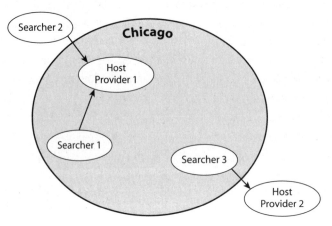

Figure 11.1 Location targeting examines host provider locations.

Location targeting will help you reach an audience with a unique message, give you the ability to raise your CTR and conversion rates in different locations, and make better use of your budget. Understanding the basics of how location targeting works will help you troubleshoot why certain groups of people are or are not seeing your ads.

How Accurate Is Location Targeting?

The first step in location targeting is to choose a location. This is a required setting for every campaign. Even if you used a geographic keyword, such as "Chicago dentist," you must still set the United States as the location targeting option in that same campaign.

Since you are often not targeting a consumer's location but their host provider location, how accurate is location targeting? Before we get into the numbers, let us look at a few exceptions that adversely affect location targeting.

The AOL Conundrum AOL dial-up users all appear to come from Reston, Virginia. This means that Google cannot always show ads to AOL users based on their IP addresses; they must use other forms of technology or dissect geographic search queries to understand AOL dial-up user's locations. AOL dial-up has more than 26 million subscribers in the United States and more than 6 million in Europe. To reach AOL dial-up users, it is best to use geographic keywords in a campaign targeted at the country level, which will be fully explained in the section "How to Reach Users in an Area Smaller than a Country."

Corporate VPNs When a user logs into their corporate VPN (virtual private network) and then accesses the Web, their location is often shown as their VPN's location, which is commonly the corporate headquarters, not their actual location.

Data Cards These are often called air cards or cell cards. They are connection devices you can attach to your computer so that your computer can access the Web via a cell connection. Often these cards show completely different locations than your cell phone on the same network. While cell phones can use cell tower triangulation to determine location (and a few other methods, such as GPS), these additional data points are not always used in determining a computer's location when accessing the Web from a data card. The search engine may not realize you are using a data card to access the Web. Therefore, a data card user may be assigned an IP address from the cell company, which might be in the exact same location or in a completely different state.

Cities That Cross State Lines The Chicago metro area is primarily in Illinois, but it also encompasses areas in Indiana and Wisconsin. The Washington, D.C., metro area crosses into Maryland and Virginia. In these cases, you may see IP addresses assigned from an incorrect state. It is not a common occurrence, but it does happen.

The following unofficial numbers were calculated by talking with the search engines and by my own testing. The accuracy of these numbers is thrown off by the above factors, as well as some other technological idiosyncrasies. Therefore, this is a rough compilation of all geographic areas; some areas will have higher degrees of accuracy and others lower. Here are the unofficial numbers for the United States.

99.9999 Percent for Determining a Country The country of origin is very easy for a search engine to determine. More than just IP data is used to determine country of origin, and the search engines are highly accurate at determining country information. The most common issue that throws off country-level targeting is corporate VPNs.

90 to 95 Percent at the State or Region Level That is a global U.S. average. There are some states, such as California, where most of the population does not border another state. Therefore, most of the ISP providers are in that state and the accuracy of state-based targeting is exceptionally high. Illinois has cities that border and spill over into other states: There's Chicago in the North, which flows into both Indiana and Wisconsin, and in the southern tip of the state, there's the St. Louis, Missouri metro area. These two areas cause some users in both the north and the south to potentially see ads from other states. However, the users in the middle of Illinois will mostly see Illinois-based ads. Each country has widely different accuracy levels at the state or regional level. Canada's numbers are fairly similar to the United States'. However, the accuracy of regional targeting in the United Kingdom is quite poor.

80 to 90 Percent at the Metropolitan Level A metropolis is a city that influences adjacent neighborhoods or cities. For instance, San Francisco is a city with a population around 800,000 people. San Francisco influences San Jose and Oakland. Therefore, the San Francisco metropolitan (often called metro) area is considered the entire region around San Francisco, Oakland, and San Jose with a population nearing 8 million people.

This is another global U.S. average. There are some cities where user location is pretty easy to determine due to lack of ISP competition and rural areas outside of the city. Fargo, North Dakota, borders Morehead, Minnesota. The same metro area has two different names based on which state you live in. The areas outside Fargo are very rural. If you want to reach users in the Fargo metro area (users in Fargo and Morehead), your accuracy will be fairly high. However, if you only want to reach users in Fargo and not Morehead, then your accuracy will be lower as some of the same ISP providers service both areas.

75 to 80 Percent at the City Level Since a city is a predefined geographic area, and yet most ISP providers create their infrastructure based on the metro area, reaching only users in a city can be challenging at times.

If you are targeting a city that is not in a metro area and is surrounded by more rural areas, the accuracy increases. If you are trying to target a city in a metro area, the accuracy decreases.

For instance, if you are attempting to reach only users in Chicago city proper, your accuracy is high for the middle of the city, as the middle of the city does not border any other cities. Many users on the north side of the city of Chicago see ads from Evanston, a city just north of Chicago. Therefore, your accuracy when targeting the city of Chicago is high in the middle of the city and will decline for users in the north. Since Evanston is still in the Chicago metro area, if you are targeting the entire metro of Chicago, the north side residents would see your ads. This is why metro targeting is often more accurate than city targeting.

These numbers are very rough guidelines, as there are many exceptions where the numbers could be higher or lower. None of these numbers should scare you away from trying geographic targeting. Targeting a specific location with ads written for that location is one of the more powerful combinations you will find in AdWords, regardless of whether you are a national company or a local company that only serves a single region.

Marketing is about connecting with users. People love and defend their local areas. Reaching consumers based on their geography allows you to connect with searcher not just by their search query, but by their location as well.

Reaching Users in Specific Locations

The region where you want your ads to show is a setting at the campaign level. You can choose to have different campaigns show in different regions. In AdWords, there are several location targeting options:

- Country
  - Single country
  - Multiple countries

- Region or multiple regions in a county
  - State
  - Metro area
  - City
- Customized

To access these settings, navigate to the campaign Settings tab. In the Audience section you will see your current settings (Figure 11.2). To change your location settings, click the Edit link near your current location list to choose where you want your ad to be displayed.

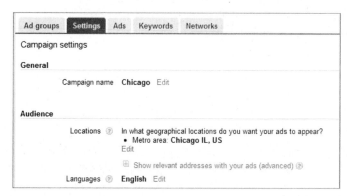

Figure 11.2 Viewing and changing your location settings

Reaching Users in Multiple Countries

Once you choose to edit your location settings, you will be presented with a screen that contains maps and a text listing of geographic areas. From this screen, you can choose all of your location options.

If you want your ad to show in multiple countries, there are two ways of accomplishing this goal.

First, be aware that Google has prebuilt country bundles from which you can easily choose multiple countries to display your ads, as shown in Figure 11.3. Click on a bundle and your ad will be shown in all of the countries you have chosen.

Every time you add a region, the map will highlight your selected region. If you want to remove selected countries from the bundle, in the Selected Locations box in the corner, click the X next to the location name and your ad will no longer be shown in that area.

The second option is to click on the Browse tab at the top of the location editing wizard and click the check box next to the individual countries (Figure 11.4). As you choose countries, they will be highlighted in the map. To remove a country, either unselect the check box next to the country or click the X next to the country name in the Selected Locations box.

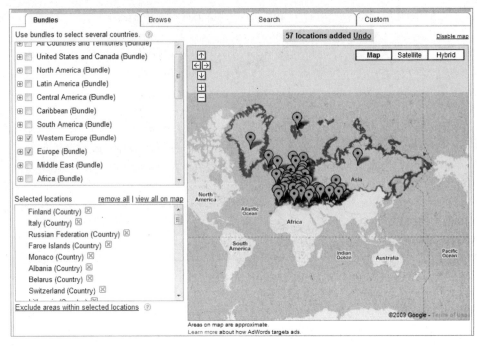

Figure 11.3 Choosing the Europe country bundle

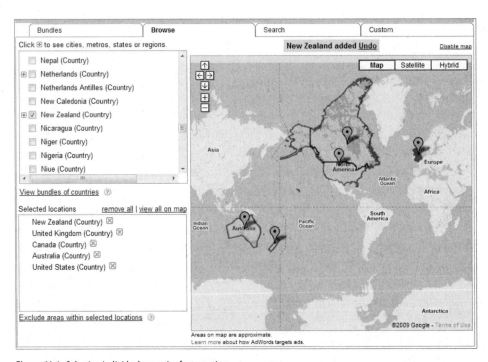

Figure 11.4 Selecting individual countries for targeting

Choosing to show your ad in multiple countries is easy and straightforward, yet it is rarely best practice. It is common to see advertisers choose United Kingdom, New Zealand, Australia, Canada, and United States in a single campaign because all of these countries speak English. However, that can lead to problems down the road.

For example, if you choose these five countries, how do you spell a word such as *color*? It is spelled *colour* in some countries and *color* in others. While the basics of English are the same in most English speaking countries, there are many colloquialisms, slang, and local customs that can cause a breakdown in communication even though the "correct" words are being used.

There are many words that not only have different spellings by country, but have different meanings as well. For instance, the word *currar* is a Spanish word that means "to work" when used in Spain. However, in Argentina that same word means "defraud."

Country-Based Optimization

If you group all of your countries into a single campaign, what is the next step to optimization? If you learn that the stats for your countries look like those in Table 11.1, what would you do next?

► **Table 11.1** Statistics for multiple countries

Country	Click-Through Rate	Conversion Rate
United States	10%	1%
United Kingdom	1%	10%
Australia	3%	5%

In this case, you are receiving traffic in the United States, but the ad and landing page are not converting, therefore you would want to choose a different combination to show to your visitors. However, in the United Kingdom, you are converting quite well, but your ad is not being clicked on very often, and you might want to test different ad copy to increase the click-through rate.

Since you have chosen all of your ads to be shown it in these different countries in the same campaign, you would not be able to accomplish these changes in the same campaign. Therefore, the first step would be to duplicate the entire campaign and change the location targeting options for each campaign to show to the appropriate countries. If you only advertise in a handful of countries, it is useful to limit yourself to one country per campaign.

When to Ignore the One Country per Campaign Rule

Multinational companies may want to disregard this rule of thumb due to the 25 active campaign limit on most accounts. Please note, if you are a larger advertiser you can have more active campaigns.

Even if you are a multinational company that serves more than 25 different countries, if you do not have a large budget to effectively penetrate every single country you serve, it can be better to concentrate your budget in a small list of countries.

If your multinational company's goal is to advertise to searchers who have a high chance of converting, then choose a handful of countries you do well in and limit your ads to only show in those few countries. Once you have effectively penetrated the marketplace and are seeing returns on your ad spend, expand your list of countries.

If your multinational company's goal is to penetrate new markets, then selectively choose those new markets, reach your goals in those markets, and then move on to the next set of countries you want to learn more about your products.

For multinational companies, if you have a small budget and try to reach every single country, you will often fail at your objectives—you cannot be everything to everybody. Therefore, choose your country list wisely based on your marketing goals. Once you reach those goals, you should have higher revenues and can increase your budget as you expand your reach to new countries.

For most accounts, limiting yourself to one country per campaign will help you write better ad copy and allow you to send your visitors to country-specific pages in your website. This combination will lead to a better user experience, and higher conversion rates usually follow good user experiences.

How to Reach Users in a Single Country

If you are following the best practice suggestions, then you only want the ads in each campaign to be shown to a single country. In the location targeting interface, you will often see a plus sign next to the locations (Figure 11.5). When you click on this plus sign, the system will display a list of subregions.

In the bundles screen, expand the box to see the list of countries in the bundle. Then click on the single country where you want your ads to be displayed.

You can also view the Browse tab, which lists all of the countries, and select a single country from that screen, or you can do a search for your country name from the Search tab.

Reaching users in a single country is easy to accomplish in the interface. When attempting to reach users below the country level, such as at the city or state level, the process becomes more complex.

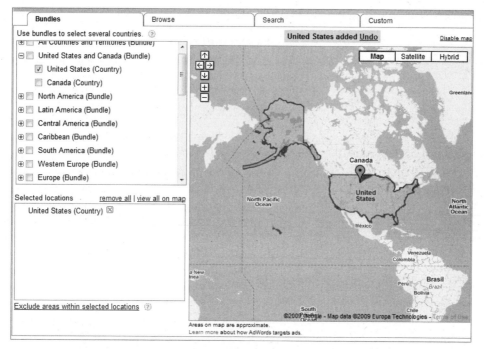

Figure 11.5 Viewing the countries in the North America bundle

Your Geographic Ads Will Purposely Be Served to Searchers Outside Your Region

While you can choose to show ads only to users in a region, Google tries to show ads to users based on the area where they want to find information. Therefore, when selecting regions you want to target, you are not telling Google you only want to show ads in a region, you are actually informing them that you want to display ads to individuals who are searching for information in your target locations.

When a searcher uses an explicit geographic keyword in their search query that falls into the region where you want your ads to serve, that searcher can still see your ad.

For instance, if you use the keyword "plumber" in a campaign that is targeted to only Chicago and a searcher in California searches for "Chicago plumber," your ad can be displayed.

There are times when a geographic query is ambiguous, such as the Washington example in the earlier section, "The Technology Behind Location Targeting," where Google is not confident enough to show geographic ads based on the user's query. However, if Google is confident that the user is looking for information in your geographic targeted areas, then your ad can be seen by searchers outside your target region who are explicitly searching for information about your keywords and target region.

How to Reach Users in an Area Smaller than a Country

If you only want to reach all searchers in a city, metro area, or state, follow this two-step process:

1. Visit the Browse tab and drill down into the country, state, or metro area by clicking on the plus box until the location where you wish your ads to display appears. For instance, if you want your ads to show in Alameda, CA, you will click: United States, California, San Francisco, Oakland, San Jose, and then check the box next to Alameda, CA.

2. Once you see the expanded list, select the location where you want your ads to appear.

For instance, if you only wanted your ads to appear in Chicago, you would expand the United States list to see all of the states, and then expand the Illinois list to see all of the metros, and then select the Chicago metro area (Figure 11.6).

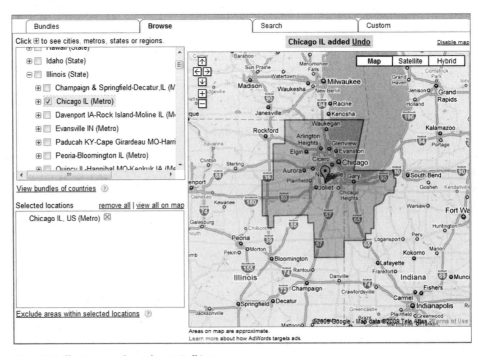

Figure 11.6 Showing your ads to only users in Chicago

You can also choose multiple city and state combinations by selecting multiple regions. The metros you select do not have to be in the same state or even country. You could choose to show your ads from a single campaign to all users in California, Chicago, and Long Island (Figure 11.7). You can have ads displayed to New York City and London. If you ever want to see which region is selected in the map, click on the map icons to see what locations you have selected.

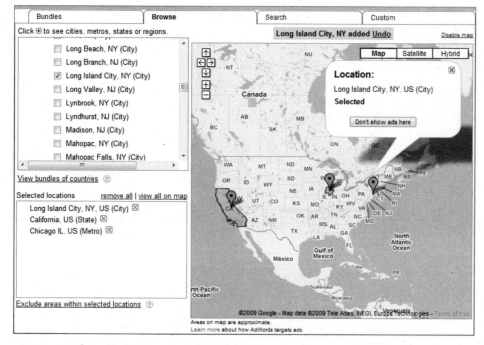

Figure 11.7 Reaching multiple locations in a country

When you target ads to a region smaller than a country, your ads will sometimes display a fifth line of ad text denoting a geographic area. Just below the display URL, you will see a region in the ad copy (Figure 11.8). This additional line of ad text can help the user understand your target area, and it often increases CTR as you are identifying locally with the consumer.

Figure 11.8 Geographic locations shown below the ad copy

Do Not Use Geographic Keywords in a Campaign Targeted to an Area Smaller than a Country

When you choose to show your ads to users in a specific location, such as Chicago, you should not use non-geographic qualified keywords. For instance, if you are a plumber, your campaign is targeted to Chicago, and you use the keyword "Chicago plumber," your ad will only be shown to those identified as being in Chicago or explicitly looking for plumbers in Chicago, and those who search for "Chicago plumber." This double qualification of both keyword and location targeting is unnecessary. Since the campaign is already targeted to Chicago, you can use the keyword "plumber" and those users who search for "plumber" and are identified as looking for Chicago information will see your ad. Therefore, you can use non-geographic keywords such as plumber, kitchen remodeling, and so on, in location targeted campaigns.

If you were to use the keyword "Chicago plumber" in a campaign targeted to only Chicago, someone would have to be identified as being in Chicago and using "Chicago plumber" as their search query for your ad to be displayed.

As many users do not search with geographic queries, using a geographic qualified keyword in a campaign targeted only to Chicago would result in far fewer impressions than using a non-geographic keyword in the same campaign.

Utilizing Multiple Campaigns to Reach All Searchers

Google is excellent at detecting the country of origin. However, there are many times when a user's location cannot be discerned, such as those listed in the earlier section "How Accurate Is Location Targeting?" In these cases, your geographic ads will not be displayed to these users. Therefore, if you want to make sure every searcher looking for your services sees your ad, you will need to use two campaigns.

IP Campaign This campaign is named after the IP detection technology used to detect a user's location. In this campaign, choose the location targeting of the area where you want to show your ads and do not use geographic keywords.

GEO Campaign This campaign will contain all geographically qualified keywords. In this campaign, choose your ads to be shown to the entire country, and then every keyword you use will have a geographic qualifier attached to it.

For instance, if you were an accounting service that was trying to reach searchers in Dallas, you would use the campaign structure shown in Table 11.2 to make sure the maximum number of searchers could find your ad.

Campaign Name	IP Campaign	GEO Campaign
Target Geography	Dallas	United States
Example Keywords	Accounting services	Dallas accounting services
	Tax preparation	Dallas tax preparation
	Bookkeeping services	Dallas bookkeeping services

If you are constrained by the total number of active campaigns you can have in your account, keep in mind that most accounts will have more total impressions from an IP campaign than from a GEO campaign. However, many accounts find that their conversion rates are higher in their GEO campaign. Therefore, if you can only have one campaign to reach geography, choose based on your goals: more total searches or a higher conversion rate. When you want to reach all the searchers possible, using a combination of both GEO and IP campaigns will maximize your exposure.

Are Your Visitors Traveling Long Distances to Reach Your Business?

If your customers search with geographic qualified queries to find your business, do not rely on IP campaigns to reach your customers. For instance, searchers looking for hotels are rarely in the local area. Most searchers looking for hotels are searching for a city name and a hotel-based keyword, such as "San Francisco hotel." While Google attempts to discern if there is a local intent in the search query to show IP targeted ads, you should take greater control of your ad serving by using geographic qualified queries as keywords in your account.

You can still run two different campaigns to reach all the users searching for your hotel; however, in this case if you only wanted to run a single campaign, you would reach more qualified users by utilizing a GEO campaign instead of an IP campaign.

The Most Popular Geographic Keywords

In GEO campaigns, you will want to utilize geographic qualified keywords. Most accounts will not use every possible geographic keyword. Based on the area you want to reach, choose the ones most applicable to your campaign's geo-targeting goals.

State Names When reaching all users in a state, use the state name as a keyword qualifier. Some common examples would be "California car insurance" and "Alabama BMW dealership."

State Abbreviations The longer the state name, the more common it is to see searchers use the state abbreviation instead of the full state name. Keywords such as "NJ car insurance quote" or "AZ golf courses" are common searches. However, be careful when automating these abbreviations. Oregon's abbreviation is OR, which is such a common word that Google often ignores it and often does not consider it a state-based search. It is common to see ads for "plumber MD." While plumber doctors are not common businesses, MD is the abbreviation for Maryland. Maine is such a short state name that the residents rarely search for "plumber ME," which is a good thing, as their abbreviation ME could be mistaken as the common use of the word and not as a state abbreviation.

County Names Some states, such as Ohio, identify greatly with their local counties. Other states see very little search volume for county names. If you are licensed in a county or see a decent search volume for your local county, then use it as a keyword, such as "Orange County contractor."

There are times when a geographic name is used in many locations. For instance, Orange County, California, is near Los Angeles and home to Disneyland. Visitors to Disney World have passed through Orange County, Florida. There are several Orange Counties in the United States. When your geographic area's name, whether it be a county, city, or other area, is the same in multiple locations, then use your ad copy to identify which location you serve.

While the electrician in Orange County, California, and the electrician in Orange County, Texas, are competing for impressions on the keyword "Orange Country electrician," they are not competing for the clicks. The electrician in California does not want the users from Texas clicking on his ad. By adding the state abbreviation or some other geographic qualified keyword, such as the city name, the ad will inform the users of the actual area you serve. Santa Ana is the country seat of Orange Country, California. In this example, the ad copy "Orange County TX plumber," or "Santa Ana plumber" will help differentiate your ad from the other ads targeting Orange Counties in other states.

City or Metro Names Some of the most common geographic keywords are city and metro names. "Los Angeles museums," "Orlando resorts," and "Seattle travel agents" are good examples of using a city name as a keyword. There are also a handful of cities where the city abbreviations are worth considering; NYC for New York City and LA for Los Angeles are the most common U.S. examples.

Zip Codes and Area Codes "72113 plumber" is searched for by those looking for a plumber in Maumelle, Arkansas. Zip codes are hyper-local queries that generally have low search volume, but highly targeted consumers. Area codes can also be used to designate a very specific local search.

When using area codes or zip codes as keyword qualifiers, do not utilize broad match. Google does not always realize that 60606 is different than 60406, yet anyone who lives in Chicago will tell you that one is in south Chicago and the other in north

Chicago. Plumbers rarely serve both of those areas as it can take well over an hour, depending on traffic, to go from one zip code to another.

Neighborhoods Some larger cities, such as Chicago, have many residents who identify with their neighborhood and use their neighborhood names as geographic qualifiers in their search results. The search "Rogers Park apartments" was conducted an average of 1,300 times a month throughout 2009. While that is not a high search volume, the search query has a very explicit geographic intent. If you rent apartments in Rogers Park, it is a keyword you should use. Searching by neighborhood names is not common in smaller cities; however, it is always worth examining the areas you are reaching to see if the consumers in your target market search with their neighborhood terms.

Airport Codes Many frequent travelers have been stuck in a city overnight due to the weather. Their first search is usually for the airport code and the word hotel followed by the airport code or restaurant. For instance, LAX is the abbreviation for the Los Angeles Airport. The search query "LAX hotel" is often searched more than 60,000 times a month.

There are instances where searchers have used airport code iPod headphones and gone shopping during a long layover. If you are near an airport, test out using the airport codes as qualifiers. For example, if you were at the Hilton hotel located in the Chicago O'Hare airport, "ORD Hilton" and "ORD hotel" would be excellent keywords. In the LAX example, the query "LAX sushi" is searched a few hundred times each month. While the search volume is small, that is a very explicit query. The more explicit the query, the higher the likelihood that conversion rates will be high.

If you serve the airport in some unique fashion, such as a taxi or limousine company, for instance, you should use airport codes as geo-qualifiers to your usual keywords.

Regional Lingo Every area has ways they describe themselves that are not official designations. Some of these words have high search volume, as that is how the locals think about their geographic area.

For instance, downtown Chicago is called the Loop. The query "loop restaurant" frequently breaks 15,000 searches a month, while "loop hotel" often breaks 27,000 monthly searches on Google. Since the word "loop" could describe multiple places, such as the Loop Restaurant in Minneapolis, adding additional ad copy such as "Serving Chicago's West Loop" can help weed out searchers looking for a different service.

While regional lingo can provide good geographic keywords, it is also excellent to use in ad copy. Using the local lexicon in your ad copy helps identify your company as understanding the local area and can often increase your click-through rate. Ad copy such as "Sushi Delivery in the Loop" or "Located in the Water Tower" instantly tells the searcher your location or delivery area, and it can help prequalify searchers who click on your ads.

However, always be careful when using regional lingo. Chicago is known as the Windy City. That term refers to Chicago politics, not the wind blowing off Lake Michigan.

When a local hears someone refer to Chicago as the Windy City, they usually assume the person is not from Chicago.

Custom Targeting

The last location targeting option is *custom targeting*. With custom targeting, there are three options for choosing locations:

- Radius targeting
- ISP targeting
- Bulk import

In *radius targeting*, you will first choose a map point, such as a zip code or city (Figure 11.9), and then inform Google how far from this location you want your ads to be displayed.

If you read the text closely, you can see that Google recommends a 10-mile minimum radius around your map point. There are two things to keep in mind as you choose a radius:

- How far will people travel to visit your business?
- How far are you willing to travel?

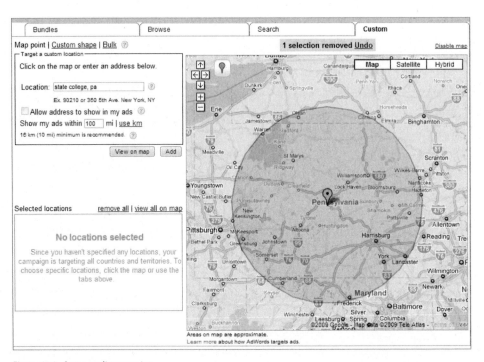

Figure 11.9 Custom radius targeting

In State College, Pennsylvania, for example, it is not uncommon for searchers to drive over an hour to one of the major cities from the rural center of Pennsylvania. Choosing a large radius could be a good choice for your business if you were targeting a rural area. However, even a five-mile radius could be over an hour drive during rush hour in Washington, D.C. Therefore, examine how far you travel to your customers, or how far your customers travel to you when selecting your target radius.

The second item to keep in mind is that you are often targeting *ISP providers* and not always someone's physical location. For instance, Rogers Park is a neighborhood in Chicago consisting of over 60,000 residents. Yet, almost everyone in Rogers Park sees ads from either Evanston or downtown Chicago. If you were to target your ads to only Rogers Park, your ad impressions would be much smaller than actual searches for your company from people who live in Rogers Park.

Another way to use custom location targeting is to draw shapes on a map. You can click on the map and play connect-the-dots to form custom shapes of where you want your ads to show (Figure 11.10). As with the preceding advice, as you draw custom shapes remember that if you draw an area that is too small, you might not receive any impressions.

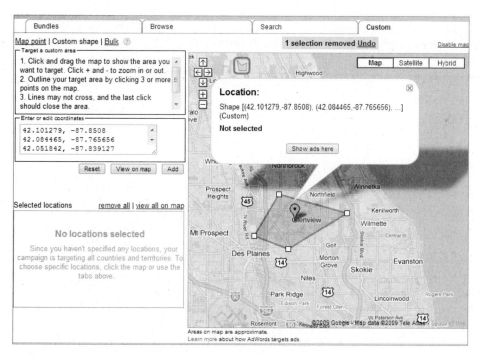

Figure 11.10 Create custom location targeting shapes

The final way of using custom targeting is actually a time saver. If you have a list of locations that you would like to target, but you do not want to spend time in the interface trying to find all of the regions, you can copy and paste your list into the *bulk import* feature (Figure 11.11).

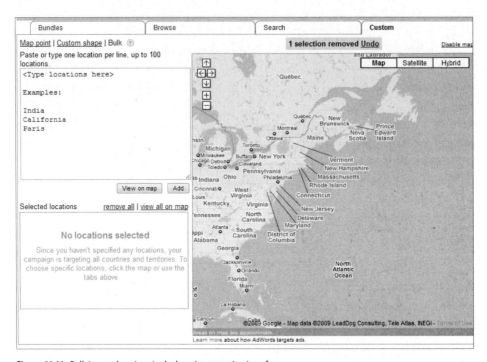

Figure 11.11 Bulk import locations in the location targeting interface

So far, we have examined many ways to target your ads to reach consumers. However, there are times when you want to make sure that consumers in specific areas do not see your ads. To keep your ads from showing in a region, you can use the excluded regions feature.

Excluding Your Ads from Showing in a Location

AdWords also gives you the ability to exclude your ad from being shown in regions. You can only exclude regions in the area you have chosen. For instance, if you are only showing your ads to the United States, you cannot exclude Russia, as your ads are not being shown there anyway. However, say you are an e-commerce site and want to reach everyone in the United States, but you do not ship to Alaska and Hawaii. You could include the entire United States and exclude Alaska and Hawaii (Figure 11.12).

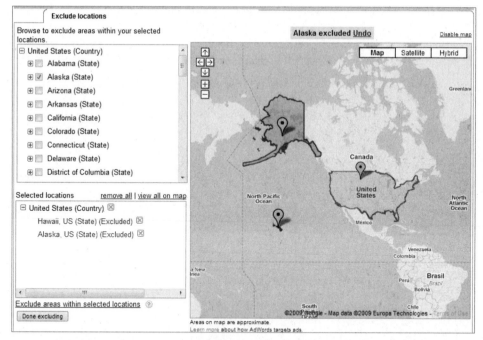

Figure 11.12 Exclude Hawaii and Alaska from seeing your U.S. targeted ads.

To access the excluded regions feature, click on the Exclude Areas Within Selected Locations link at the bottom of the location targeting screen. Then you will choose the regions where you do not want your ads to show using the same interface as you use to include regions. The regions you are excluding will be highlighted in a different color than your selected regions and will be shown in the Selected Locations box in the bottom corner of the interface.

There are times you may want to use this feature for organizational purposes so you can showcase different ads based on a user location. For instance, if you sell renter's insurance, you might want to have three different campaigns based on the benefits in the ad copy and the landing page you want to send visitors to on your website. Let us assume these are the goals of your benefit messages in ad copy:

- Showcase fire insurance benefits in San Diego

- Showcase earthquake benefits in San Francisco and Los Angeles

- Showcase a general benefit to the rest of California

In this instance, you would have one campaign that was targeted to California and excluded San Diego, Los Angeles, and San Francisco (Figure 11.13). Then you would create a campaign that was shown to just users in San Diego, and another one that targeted San Francisco and Los Angeles.

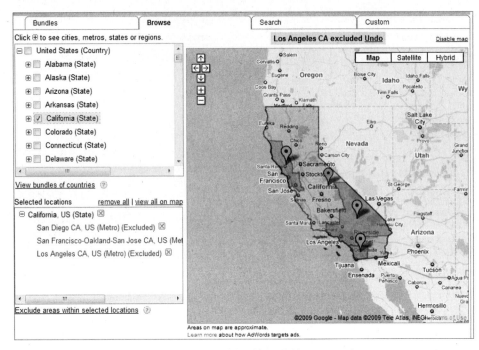

Figure 11.13 Excluding San Diego, San Francisco, and Los Angeles in a California targeted campaign

By utilizing a combination of location targeting and excluded regions, you can narrow down exactly who will see your ad copy. This is also useful for showing different offers, messages, and benefits in different sections of the same country.

However, one of the most important aspects of writing ads for specific locations is to determine if the user is a local or non-local. Each of those groups has different concerns and knowledge about your area, and therefore you need to engage them in different manners.

Treating Locals and Non-locals Differently in Your Ad Copy

A *local* is someone familiar with the location you are targeting. They have an understanding of the region, landmarks, and culture. A non-local is someone who has limited knowledge about your location, and therefore needs a different set of information than a local. Let's examine a few different ways to treat these two audiences differently.

Geographic Descriptions A local searcher knows the area you serve. They want to know if you serve their actual location. Therefore, when a local searches for "Chicago plumber" they want to know if the plumber will come to their house. Using descriptors such as "Serving North Chicago" or "Located in the heart of the Triangle" tells a local exactly where you are or where you service.

A non-local may not have enough information about the area to understand the locations in the preceding ad copy. They are looking for very blunt descriptors such as "New York City hotel" or "Downtown Pittsburgh hotel." When using geographic descriptors in ad copy for non-locals, rarely should you use regional lingo. Reassure the searcher that you serve the location where they are searching for information.

Where Are You Located? A local will look for precise information. What building is your office located in? How long does it take to drive to your store? Using ad copy such as "Near Rush Street," "Located in the Water Tower," or "Rogers Park Real Estate Specialists" gives a local exact information.

However, a non-local will be confused by much of that language. A non-local wants to know if you can even serve their needs. A traveler wants to know general information such as how far you are from shopping, if you are near the airport, or if you are close to downtown.

Rush Street and Michigan Avenue are both in the heart of the Chicago shopping district. A local knows that fact. Therefore, "On Rush Street" tells a local more precise information than "In the Shopping District." However, a non-local may not know that fact about Rush Street; therefore, the more general ad copy "Located in the Shopping District," is better non-local ad copy.

Engaging the Searcher Once someone has clicked on your ad, your landing page needs to continue to engage the searcher based on their knowledge of the local area. A local will look for driving directions, phone numbers, maps, and detailed business information on your website. If you are a delivery company, show a map that highlights the areas you deliver to so the person can quickly see if you serve their area.

Conversely, if you are a hotel catering to non-locals, showing a map of the area with your location, the airport, the shopping district, or the nearest amusement park will let them understand how far you are from those various items that maybe related to the purpose of their trip.

Conversion Activities Since locals know precise information about your area, they often jump to items such as driving directions, online delivery ordering, or in-store pickup once they realize you can serve their needs.

However, non-locals rarely have enough information to make that quick of a decision. It is common for a non-local to make a phone call or send an email looking for a specific piece of information before finishing any conversion processes you have. Take note of the most common questions you receive as you can put those as pieces of information on your landing page to help a non-local make a quicker decision.

Rarely are locals and non-locals looking for the same information. Think through what someone who knows your local area would want to find. If you are an actual store, it's most likely driving directions or a phone number. If you are a pizza delivery company, it is most likely delivery area and online ordering, or a phone number to order over the phone.

For non-locals, you may need to give out as much information about the local area, such as shopping opportunities or the local amusement park, as you do about your actual business. By thinking through the differences between these two groups of individuals, you can write better ads and send the searcher to appropriate landing pages that can answer their questions so they can take the next step of doing business with your company.

If you use regional targeting, your ad could show a fifth line of ad text denoting the region your ads are targeted to. This is good for locals and excellent for non-locals. However, there is a way to put an actual address below your ad copy using location extensions.

Automatically Inserting Your Address into the Ad Copy

Google retired Local Business Ads in the fall of 2009 with the introduction of location ad extensions. If you still have Local Business Ads in your account, they are grandfathered into the system and will exist for a while.

Local Business Ads were replaced with location ad extensions. Location ad extensions allow you to store data in your campaign settings, such as your physical address, and the extra data will be displayed alongside your ads under particular conditions.

To access the location extension options, navigate to your campaign settings. Under the Audience and Location settings you can add custom location information (Figure 11.14).

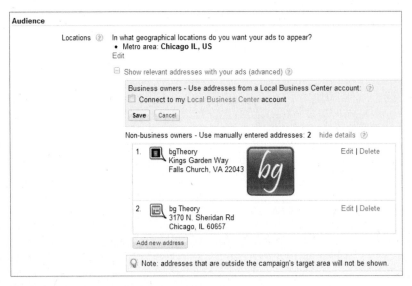

Figure 11.14 Location extensions in your campaign settings

The easiest way to accomplish this is to link your AdWords account with your Local Business Center account.

If you do not want to link your Google Local Business Center account, you can enter addresses manually (Figure 11.15).

Figure 11.15 Adding a location extension

When entering your information, you can choose from Google's icons or upload your own icon. In addition, you can upload an image that will show next to your ad in certain conditions, such as when the image is displayed on maps.google.com (Figure 11.16).

The default icons on Google Maps are red. Therefore, it can help your listing stand out on the map by utilizing yellow or blue in your icons. At a minimum, use your website's favicon (the icon that shows up in most browsers next to the site's URL in the location box) so that you can extend your branding to multiple properties.

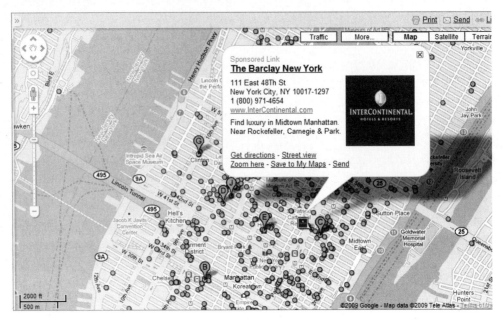

Figure 11.16 Location extensions in action on Google Maps

Once you have saved addresses in your campaign settings, Google will display your address in the text ads on Google.com (Figure 11.17) when Google determines that your address will help the searcher find the information they are seeking. Your address will almost always show on Google Local properties (Figure 11.16) like maps. google.com.

Figure 11.17 Address shown in text ads on Google.com

If you have multiple addresses in the same campaign, then each ad could be shown with any of your addresses. Generally, Google will display the address that is nearest the searcher. If you want to limit an ad to only display one address with an ad, then navigate to the ad group's Ad tab, and edit the ad. In the edit box, you will be informed of how many addresses are connected with that ad, and then you can choose to only have an ad show with one particular address (Figure 11.18).

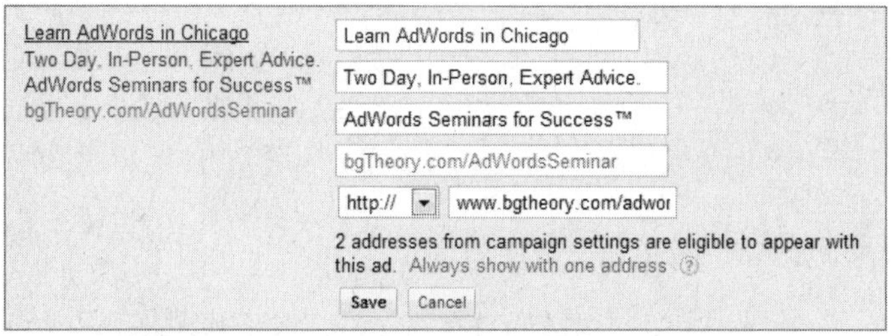

Figure 11.18 Edit an ad to choose a single address to show with each ad.

Using location extensions will help your business connect with searchers on Google.com by showing the additional address and giving the consumer more information about your business. However, location extensions really shine when your ads are shown on Google Local properties. Utilizing custom icons and images that stand out from the typical text ads can dramatically increase your presence on local properties.

A Case Study into Local Belief Systems

Local residents usually respect and defend their cities. One does not walk on stage in Boston and disparage the legacy of the Boston Celtics. Each area also has different beliefs and uses different criteria to determine whether information is credible.

These beliefs carry over into response rates for advertising. It is not uncommon to show the same ad in two different geographies and find two very different click-through rates or conversion rates. I'm going to walk through a study I did with a company that serves ads in the northeast United States.

This company has several locations throughout multiple states. As they were trying to drive awareness of their new locations and attempting to drive foot traffic into their buildings, the main goal was to bring qualified visitors to their website so they could showcase how easy it was for anyone in the northeast to find one of their locations. They wanted to show that same ease in the ad copy as well as create a synergy between the ad copy and the landing page.

The headline, description line 1, and display URL of these ads were identical. The only difference was description line 2. The two lines were:

- Locations throughout the state
- Convenient locations near you

Both of those lines of ad copy talk about multiple locations, but the difference in response rates between Pennsylvania and New Jersey (two states that border each other) was stunning (Table 11.3).

	Convenient locations near you	Locations throughout the state
New Jersey	13.6%	2.1%
Pennsylvania (All)	5.6%	11.3%
? Philadelphia	8%	5.5%
? Rest of state	2.3%	16.4%

New Jersey is a state where most people, except for commuters, do not drive from the north side to the south side of the state on a regular basis, even though it takes less than three hours to do so. Therefore, the ad copy "Locations throughout the state" did not do well. New Jersey is a state of convenience. The adage "if it's more than 15 minutes away, it doesn't exist" can be used to explain much of the state's behavior. Hence, the ad copy that used the word "convenient" did well in the state.

The middle of Pennsylvania is rural. Consumers often drive an hour or more to shop at the outlet malls. It is not uncommon to see someone from State College, which is in the middle of the state, drive to Philadelphia, Pittsburgh, or the Poconos to do their shopping. All of those options take more than an hour of driving time. Overall, people in the middle of the state do not believe the word "convenient" applies to them. Therefore, outside of Philadelphia, the ad copy using the word "convenient" did poorly. However, telling people in Pennsylvania the truth—we're not close, but we are all over the state—increased response rates.

Philadelphia, one of the largest cities in the United States, was the exception in Pennsylvania. It is common to see residents of large cities behave differently from people who live in rural areas. The CTR difference between Philadelphia and the rest of Pennsylvania highlights these differences.

If this were your account, you would want to divide your targeting into four campaigns:

- The first campaign would target only New Jersey with the "convenient" ad copy.

- The second campaign would target Pennsylvania and use the excluded regions feature so consumers in Philadelphia do not see the ad. This campaign would use the "Locations throughout the state" ad copy.

- The third campaign would only target Philadelphia with the "convenient" ad copy, and test a few other variations of ads to see what else resonated in this city.

- The fourth campaign would utilize geographic keywords. This campaign would have a large number of ad groups that all use the geographic modifiers, such as New Jersey, Pittsburgh, Pennsylvania, Allentown, Trenton, and Philadelphia.

The difference in belief systems by geography is one of the reasons you see different billboards and TV commercials from national companies in different locations. Each area has different cultural norms. If no one believes your ads, the ads will not get clicked and you will not receive conversions from those searchers.

Viewing Geographic Results

When you start adding multiple addresses or showing your ads in a variety of geographies, it can be difficult to see your ads and the local competition as you might not live in all of your target markets. Google provides a nice tool that allows you to see ads in various locations.

Navigate to http:\\adwords.google.com/select/AdTargetingPreviewTool. At the top of the page you can enter specific criteria to preview ads (as shown in Figure 11.19):

- Searcher information:
    - Keyword
    - Google domain (Google.com, Google.co.uk)
    - Language
- Location information:
    - Country
    - State or city in a country

        If you choose a metro area, you may see another list of cities in that metro area.

    - Specific coordinates

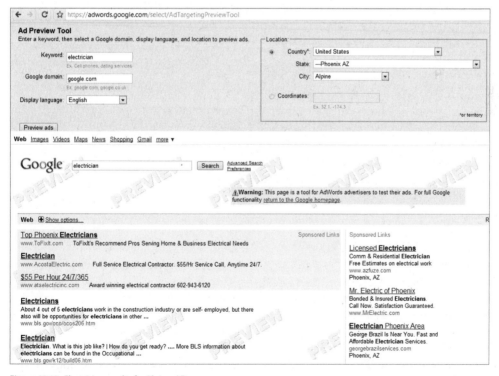

Figure 11.19 Electrician results for Alpine, AZ

Once you fill out the information, you can preview what a user who is conducting a search at that moment in time would see in that target geography. This is an important caveat: at that moment in time. If your daily budget is exhausted for the day, your ad will not show up on Google.com, and therefore, it will also not show up in the ad preview tool.

If you want to see what someone who lives in Alpine, Arizona, would see when conducting a search for "electrician" on Google.com in English, enter the information into the tool. The bottom of the preview page will reload with your search results (Figure 11.19).

If you conduct searches for your ad and then never click on them, it appears to Google that your ads are not relevant to you as a searcher. When this happens, Google may stop showing your ads to you when you conduct searches. When your ad is displayed on the ad preview page, it does not count as an impression or affect the statistics in your account in any manner. You should always use this tool when searching for your own ads.

Geographic Performance Reports

AdWords offers the Geographic Performance Report, which will give you performance statistics broken down by geographic region. For instance, you can see the cost per click, click-through rate, conversion rate, and cost per conversion by geographic region (Figure 11.20).

Country/ Territory	Region	Metro Area	City	Impressions	Clicks	Avg CPC	Avg CPM	Daily CTR	Cost	Conversions ▼	Conversion Rate	Cost/ Conversion
Netherlands	Noord-Holland	(all other Metros)	Amsterdam	4	1	$0.04	$10.00	25.00%	$0.04	1	100.00%	$0.04
India	Delhi	(all other Metros)	Delhi	82	4	$0.30	$14.51	4.88%	$1.19	1	25.00%	$1.19
Israel	HaMerKaz	(all other Metros)	Petah Tiqwa	6	0	$0.00	$0.00	0.00%	$0.00	1	0.00%	$0.00
United Kingdom	England	(all other Metros)	West Bromwich	0	0	$0.00	$0.00	0.00%	$0.00	1	0.00%	$0.00
United States	Nebraska	Omaha NE	Omaha	2	1	$1.08	$540.00	50.00%	$1.08	1	100.00%	$1.08
India	Tamil Nadu	(all other Metros)	Chennai	21	1	$0.26	$12.38	4.76%	$0.26	1	100.00%	$0.26
United States	(all other Regions)	(all other Metros)	(all other cities)	1,126	3	$0.22	$0.58	0.27%	$0.65	1	33.33%	$0.65

Figure 11.20 Geographic Performance Report

One good use of this report is to find areas where you are not performing well. If you are targeting the entire United States and find that only 1 percent of your conversions are coming from New York City, yet that metro area is almost 15 percent of the entire U.S. population, then you are not fully taking advantage of the region.

You may find there is more competition in New York City for your services and that your ads are on page 2 or 3, and to receive more exposure you need to raise your bids in just that area. Or you may find that you are receiving the visitors, but your conversion rate there is much lower than in other areas.

In this case, you might want to create a new campaign that is targeted to just New York City where you can showcase a different offer, and bid separately from the rest of the United States. You should also exclude New York City from showing ads in your original campaign that is targeted to the entire country.

An easy way of working with this report is to use Excel pivot tables, as discussed in Chapter 7. If you examine your data by geographic region, you can see conversions, conversion rate, and other data points by individual region (Figure 11.21).

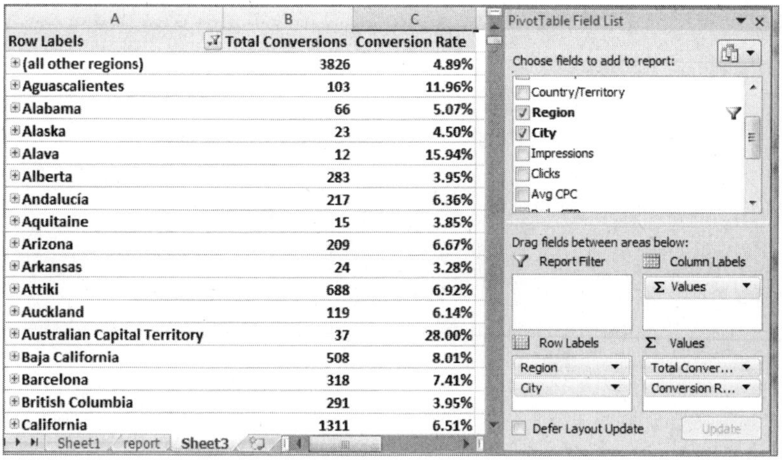

Row Labels	Total Conversions	Conversion Rate
(all other regions)	3826	4.89%
Aguascalientes	103	11.96%
Alabama	66	5.07%
Alaska	23	4.50%
Alava	12	15.94%
Alberta	283	3.95%
Andalucía	217	6.36%
Aquitaine	15	3.85%
Arizona	209	6.67%
Arkansas	24	3.28%
Attiki	688	6.92%
Auckland	119	6.14%
Australian Capital Territory	37	28.00%
Baja California	508	8.01%
Barcelona	318	7.41%
British Columbia	291	3.95%
California	1311	6.51%

Figure 11.21 Geographic Performance report in a pivot table

One of the quality score factors for search is your click-through rate in a geographic region. If your ads have a high CTR in Seattle and a low CTR in Phoenix, then your ads will be shown more in Seattle due to a higher CTR in that region. The geographic performance report will allow you to see CTR by geographic area (Figure 11.22).

It is useful to layer other statistics with CTR to see where you want to spend your time optimizing an account. For instance, this account has only spent $0.60 in Arta. Regardless of CTR, this probably is not a place to spend your time, especially when combined with the knowledge that Arta is a city in Greece with a population of 23,000. This account's overall CTR is 14.62 percent. However, in Baja, California, the CTR is 3.11 percent. In Attiki, Greece, the CTR is only 1.54 percent. As both of those locations have more than 3 million residents, and have higher spends than many other locations, optimizing the ads for those locations would be a more appropriate place to spend your time.

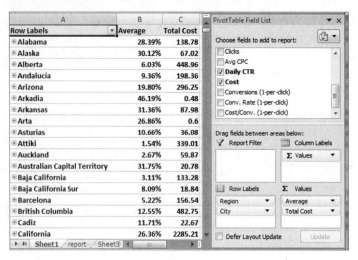

	A	B	C
Row Labels		Average	Total Cost
⊞ Alabama		28.39%	138.78
⊞ Alaska		30.12%	67.02
⊞ Alberta		6.03%	448.96
⊞ Andalucía		9.36%	198.36
⊞ Arizona		19.80%	296.25
⊞ Arkadia		46.19%	0.48
⊞ Arkansas		31.36%	87.98
⊞ Arta		26.86%	0.6
⊞ Asturias		10.66%	36.08
⊞ Attiki		1.54%	339.01
⊞ Auckland		2.67%	59.87
⊞ Australian Capital Territory		31.75%	20.78
⊞ Baja California		3.11%	133.28
⊞ Baja California Sur		8.09%	18.84
⊞ Barcelona		5.22%	156.54
⊞ British Columbia		12.55%	482.75
⊞ Cadiz		11.71%	22.67
⊞ California		26.36%	2285.21

Figure 11.22 Examining CTR and spend by region

When optimizing local ads, the first step is to use the ad preview tool and see if the ad is blending into the others in that region. If the ad does stand out, it could be that the locals just do not respond to your current ad copy. If you wanted to reach Attiki differently than the other regions where the ad is shown, then you could create a different campaign for just Attiki.

The geographic performance report allows you to examine your statistics for each region where your ad has been shown. When combined with location targeting, you can optimize your account by geographies to make sure searchers are responding to your ads in every area where you want to reach consumers.

Best Practices for Geographic Targeting

The first step in location targeting is to understand where your target market lives and then make sure you are targeting those users appropriately. The second step is to ensure that your ads are being received properly in the various geographic regions and to then adjust your ads and location targeting properly. By following the best practices in this chapter, you should be able to accomplish those two concepts in an effective manner.

- Define where your users are located. Then ensure that your ads are only being shown to the appropriate users.

- You should try to limit your exposure to a maximum of one country per campaign. This will allow you to create more targeted ads and send users to more specific landing pages.

- Use a combination of location targeting and excluded regions to organize your campaigns and to make sure you are reaching your target locations.

- As much of the technology behind geo-targeting is based on a user's host provider's address, the smaller the area you target, the more people you will miss. It can be useful to target a larger area than you serve to reach more potential prospects and then use ad copy descriptors to let searchers know exactly the areas you serve.

- Geo-qualifiers are useful as both keywords and in ad copy. Here are a few guidelines:

    - Be careful when using state abbreviations as keywords. Some state's abbreviations, such as Maine (ME), Oregon (OR), and Maryland (MD), have alternate meanings.

    - When two areas share the same name, use a metro, state, or regional qualifier in the ad copy to let the searchers know which area you serve.

    - When using zip codes, do not use broad match; always use phrase or exact match.

    - Using regional lingo both as keywords and in ad copy will help you connect with local searchers.

- Define if your target market is comprised of locals or non-locals so you can write ads and use landing pages based on their knowledge of your area.

    - Non-locals need to be reassured that you can serve their needs and that you are in the area where they are searching for information.

    - Locals want precise information such as address and driving directions.

    - Examine the local belief systems to make sure consumers consider your offers credible.

- Always use the ad preview tool when searching for your own ads as it will not count in your account's statistics. The ad preview tool should be your first step when researching local competition for your ads.

- The Geographic Performance report will give you insight into your metrics in the various locations where your ads were shown. Use these metrics to optimize your account.

By following these best practices, you should be able to target your ads to the locations that house your target market. Then write ad copy that engages users based on their knowledge of the area. Finally, run reports that will show you if you are being successful and show you areas where you can improve.

These past few chapters have been about reaching your audience through location targeting and the content network. Many of these best practices can be time consuming when you use the AdWords online interface. In the next chapter, we will introduce the AdWords Editor which will speed up how quickly you can make account changes. We will also walk through methods to scale your account in a quick, yet efficient manner.

Save Time and Scale Accounts with the AdWords Editor

The AdWords Editor is a free downloadable desktop program offered by Google that allows you to manage your AdWords account on your computer instead of using Google's online interface. Learning how to use the AdWords Editor can save you tremendous amounts of time in day-to-day account management.

The AdWords Editor also supports the bulk importing of ad copy and keywords. Combining the editor with Excel can help you scale your account to house thousands of pieces of ad copy with tens of thousands of keywords.

In this chapter you will learn how to define and organize your ad groups offline so that you can still use best practice management even with extremely large accounts.

12

Chapter Contents

AdWords Editor Overview

Google's AdWords Editor makes it easy to manage your account. You can add, remove, or pause keywords, ad copy, ad groups, or campaigns from a single interface. You can see your statistics, quality score, first page bids, and other metrics within this program. You can make the vast majority of changes to your account within this editor. This should be the program you use to optimize your account. Since the editor sits on your computer, and not on the Web, you can work on your account quickly instead of waiting for the AdWords interface to load.

Once you download your account into the editor, the changes do not go live within the Google interface immediately. You can make any number of changes and upload them when you are satisfied with the adjustments. Once you post the changes, they will go live within your AdWords account.

While most of the options available through the AdWords interface are also in the editor, there are a handful of more advanced options, such as ad scheduling and custom location targeting, that are not available in the AdWords Editor.

However, the AdWords Editor does have capabilities, such as import and export, that are not available in the online interface. Whenever you need to make bulk changes to your account, you can save yourself a significant amount of time by using the editor instead of the online interface.

We will walk through the interface and basic functionalities of the editor and then look at some tricks to save you time and headaches.

To download the editor, you can go to www.google.com/intl/en/adwordseditor/ or go to the Tools menu in your AdWords account and click on the AdWords Editor link, which will take you to the this webpage.

When new features are added to the interface that can easily be added to the editor, they usually appear in the next release of the editor. When you open the AdWords Editor, it will automatically check for new versions and prompt you to download a newer version if there is one. The editor is available for both Windows and Mac computers.

Choosing Your Viewpoint

The layout of the AdWords Editor is similar to the interface that Google launched in the summer of 2009. You can choose how much data you want to view and the type of data you want to view and have access to several tools. Figure 12.1 shows what the editor looks like in its entirety.

In the left column (Figure 12.2), you select how much data you want to view. You can see all data points in your account, a campaign, or an individual ad group.

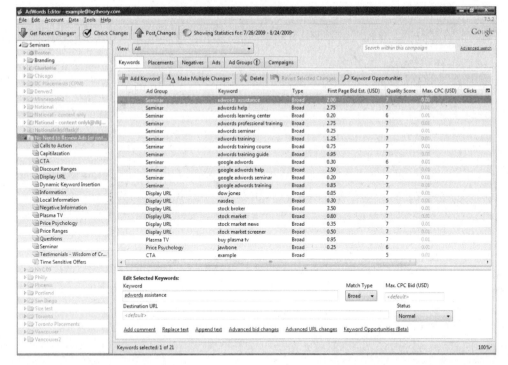

Figure 12.1 The AdWords Editor Interface

Figure 12.2 Account
navigation column

Along the middle horizontal bar, you can choose what data points you want to see: keywords, placements, negative keywords, ads, ad groups, or campaigns (Figure 12.3). In addition, you can filter the data by unposted changes, errors, warnings, or all the data available.

Figure 12.3 Choosing the data you want to view

In the top navigation column, you can right-click to choose exactly what types of data you want to view (Figure 12.4). Depending on the data you are viewing, you will see different customization options. For instance, on the Ads tab you will see items such as Headline, Description Line 1, and so on, whereas on the Keywords tab you would see items such as Match Type and Bids.

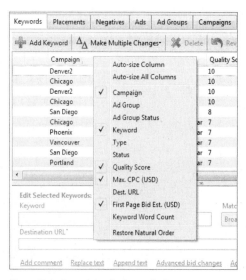

Figure 12.4 Customizing the keyword column

The combination of the navigation and data columns allows you to work with any type and amount of data you wish to view. You can see all ads in your account or just negative keywords in a single ad group. How you want to view the data is entirely up to you.

AdWords Editor Shortcuts

Since this is a desktop application, your standard desktop shortcuts also work. For instance, Ctrl+C lets you copy the data point you are working on, and Ctrl+V lets you paste that same data point into another area. Becoming familiar with the available shortcuts will allow you to quickly navigate though the interface and make bulk changes. Table 12.1 lists the shortcuts you've probably been using for years in various Windows and Mac applications. Table 12.2 deserves special attention, as it provides the special AdWords Editor shortcuts.

▶ **Table 12.1** Common keyboard shortcuts

Command	Shortcut
Open account	Ctrl+O
Search	Ctrl+F
Search and replace text in selected items	Ctrl+H
Copy selected items	Ctrl+C
Cut selected items	Ctrl+X
Paste items	Ctrl+V
Delete selected items	Delete key
Post changes (the standard Save command)	Ctrl+S
Exit AdWords Editor	Ctrl+W

▶ **Table 12.2** AdWords Editor keyboard shortcuts

Command	Shortcut
Get recent account changes	Ctrl+R
Get recent account changes with first page bid estimates	Ctrl+Alt+R
Check changes	Ctrl+P
Check changes in selected campaigns	Ctrl+Alt+P
Post changes in selected campaigns	Ctrl+Alt+S
Open advanced search	Ctrl+Shift+F
Select all items in data view	Ctrl+A
Revert selected changes	Ctrl+Z
Copy just keyword text or placement URLs	Ctrl+Shift+C
Paste items into selected ad groups	Ctrl+Shift+V
Paste negatives into selected campaigns	Ctrl+Alt+V
Append text to selected items	Ctrl+Shift+H
Sort rows in the data view	Ctrl+Shift+S
Add keyword	Ctrl+K
Add or update multiple keywords	Ctrl+Shift+K
Delete multiple keywords	Ctrl+Alt+K
Add placement	Ctrl+B
Add or update multiple placements	Ctrl+Shift+B
Delete multiple placements	Ctrl+Alt+B
Add negative keyword	Ctrl+L

Command	Shortcut	
Add multiple negative keywords	Ctrl+Shift+L	
Add campaign negative keyword	Ctrl+M	
Add multiple campaign negative keywords	Ctrl+Shift+M	*Continues*
Delete multiple campaign negative keywords	Ctrl+Alt+M	
Add negative site	Ctrl+Y	
Add multiple negative sites	Ctrl+Shift+Y	
Add campaign negative site	Ctrl+E	
Add multiple campaign negative sites	Ctrl+Shift+E	
Delete multiple campaign negative sites	Ctrl+Alt+E	
Add text ad	Ctrl+T	
Add multiple text ads	Ctrl+Shift+T	
Delete multiple text ads	Ctrl+Alt+T	
Add image ad	Ctrl+I	
Add multiple image ads	Ctrl+Shift+I	
Add local business ad	Ctrl+U	
Add multiple local business ads	Ctrl+Shift+U	
Delete multiple local business ads	Ctrl+Alt+U	
Add mobile ad	Ctrl+J	
Add multiple mobile ads	Ctrl+Shift+J	
Delete multiple mobile ads	Ctrl+Alt+J	
Add ad group	Ctrl+G	
Add or update multiple ad groups	Ctrl+Shift+G	
Add CPC campaign	Ctrl+N	
Add CPM campaign	Ctrl+Shift+N	
Add draft CPC campaign	Ctrl+D	
Add draft CPM campaign	Ctrl+Shift+D	

Credit for these tables and an online reference guide to see additional shortcuts as they are added are available on Google's AdWords Editor website at www.google.com/support/adwordseditor/bin/answer.py?answer=54654.

Using Visual Cues

As you add and remove data from the editor, there are visual symbols that will appear:

- Plus (+): Added item
- Delta (Δ): Edited item
- Minus (−): Deleted item
- Red colored circle: Item may violate AdWords policies, and an exception request will need to be filed before you can make the change.

- Yellow colored circle: Item may violate AdWords policies, but you can still upload the changes.
- Red push pin: A comment is associated with that data point (Figure 12.5).

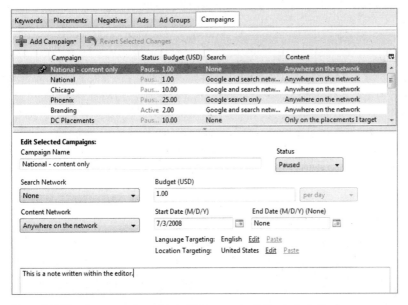

Figure 12.5 There is a comment associated with the campaign National - Content only

The comments feature in the AdWords Editor is extremely useful for keeping notes on why you made a change or why you added or removed a data item, or just for keeping track of something you need to check on in the future.

These are the basics of how the editor functions. There are many more options you will discover when using the editor. As it's an intuitive interface, it is easy to learn its functionality once you understand the basics.

Viewing Your Account in the AdWords Editor

When you first install the editor, it will not be associated with any AdWords accounts. The first step is to open your AdWords account in the editor. Use either the shortcut Ctrl+O , or navigate to the File menu item and click Open Account (Figure 12.6).

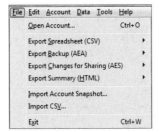

Figure 12.6 Opening your AdWords account in the editor

This will present you with a dialog box where you can enter your AdWords login email address and the password. Once you enter the information, your account will be downloaded into the editor.

You can enter the credentials of several different accounts in the AdWords Editor for quick access to all of those accounts. If you enter a My Client Center (MCC) email address, you will be able to see every account that is linked to that MCC.

In the editor, you can perform typical account management items such as:

- Change bids
- Add or remove keywords
- Add or remove text ads
- Create or delete ad groups
- Create or delete campaigns
- Change campaign settings

When you first start, your AdWords Editor file and your AdWords interface will contain the same data. As you make changes within the AdWords Editor, those changes are not automatically added to your account. To post the changes, click the Post Change button, and you will be presented with a box listing your changes (Figure 12.7). If your current view is not the entire account, but either an ad group or a campaign, then you will have the option to either post changes for the entire account or for just a single campaign.

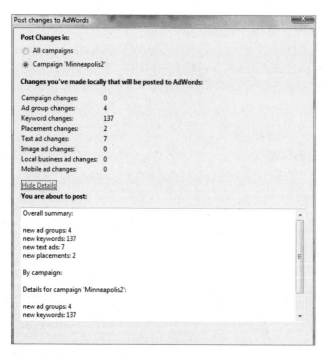

Figure 12.7 Reviewing and then posting your changes

If you are posting a handful of changes, you can post them for your entire account at once. If you are posting more than 10,000 keywords, or more than 1,000 pieces of ad copy, it is not uncommon for the AdWords Editor to appear to be working but actually to have timed out on the back-end. Therefore, if you are making large bulk changes, only upload the changes to a single campaign at once. If you are making a few keyword changes or adding a dozen text ads, it will take the editor seconds to make the changes. It could take a few hours to do large bulk changes.

While the AdWords Editor is posting changes, do not change the setting to those same campaigns in the interface. The AdWords system could become confused as to which changes should be in effect.

If you have gone into the interface and made changes, your AdWords Editor file will not be synced with your AdWords account. To sync your AdWords Editor file with your Google AdWords account, you can use the Get Recent Account Changes button to download your account. If you want to download your entire account and over-write any local changes you made in the editor, then use the Get Full Account feature (Figure 12.8).

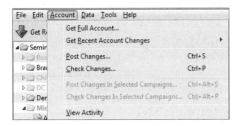

Figure 12.8 Downloading new changes to your AdWords Editor file

Giving Multiple People Access to Your AdWords Account

In either your AdWords account or your MCC, you can create a user login for each person who has access to your account (Figure 12.9).

This is useful from both security and tracking standpoints. If someone leaves your company, you can disable a single login and not worry about having to change all of your access passwords. When someone makes changes in your account, that change shows up in the My Change History tool with the associated login that made each change.

When someone first opens your account in the AdWords Editor, they can download your account with their login credentials. When that person posts changes to your account from the AdWords Editor, the account used to post those changes will show up in the My Change History tool as well, so you can track which login is making changes to your account.

Figure 12.9 Giving account access to additional people

However, if you would like even more control over who can make changes to your account, the AdWords Editor has an additional feature called Export Changes for Sharing (AES) (Figure 12.10). An .aes file is the AdWords Editor file extension.

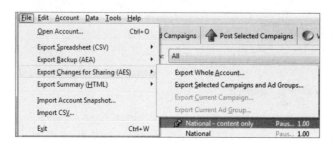

Figure 12.10 Exporting your editor account for sharing

You can export your editor file and send it to another person who can open your account in their AdWords Editor program. That person can then make changes to your account, and instead of uploading the changes, they can send the file back to you. Then you can see what their proposed changes are and have the capability to accept or reject changes (Figure 12.11).

Once you have saved the changes you would like to go live in your account, you can post those changes. If you have several people who work on your account, having a central gatekeeper who understands all of the changes and their implications can be useful in maintaining control over what is happening inside your AdWords account.

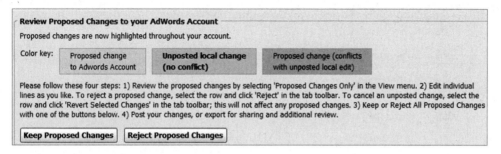

Figure 12.11 Accepting or rejecting changes

How to Scale Your Account

Most of the best practices examine how to create small ad groups of tightly themed keywords and hand-write ad copy that can be tested for those keywords.

While this is best practice, it is not always practical when you are managing thousands of ad groups, tens of thousands of keywords, and thousands of pieces of ad copy. However, there are ways of mass-creating keywords and ad copy inside a spreadsheet program and then using the AdWords Editor to import that information into your account.

First we will examine how to import anywhere from a single keyword to thousands of keywords into your account. Then we will examine how to import ad copy for those keywords.

Importing Keywords

One of the AdWords Editor functions allows you to copy and paste data from a spreadsheet into the AdWords Editor. This allows you to use a spreadsheet program, such as Excel, to create and organize your keywords, and then you can copy that data and paste it into the AdWords Editor. Just follow these steps:

1. To access this function, navigate to the Keywords tab, and then click on Add/Update Multiple Keywords (Figure 12.12).

Figure 12.12 Mass importing keywords into the AdWords Editor

This will bring you to a screen where you can paste large amounts of data. There are a couple of different ways that you can import the data; for now, we are going to focus on importing everything so that you can automatically create new campaigns, ad groups, and keywords at once.

2. Create an Excel file where each column, in this order, contains these data points (Figure 12.13):

- Campaign name
- Ad group name
- Keyword
- Keyword type (same as match type; this is optional, but strongly recommended)
- Max CPC (optional)
- Bid (optional)
- Destination URL (optional)
- Keyword status (optional)

	A	B	C	D	E	F	G
1			Required (or Strongly Suggested)			Optional	
2	Campaign	Ad Group	Keyword	Keyword Type	Max CPC	Destination URL	Keyword Status
3	Austin	Seminars	advanced marketing seminar	Exact			
4	Charlotte	Seminars	advanced marketing seminar	Exact			
5	Austin	Seminars	advanced marketing seminars	Exact			
6	Charlotte	Seminars	advanced marketing seminars	Exact			
7	Austin	AdWords	adwords class	Exact			
8	Charlotte	AdWords	adwords class	Exact			
9	Austin	AdWords	adwords classes	Exact			

Figure 12.13 Excel file with the proper headers

3. In Excel, you can then create all of the data you want to add to your AdWords account. If you conducted research with the AdWords Keyword Tool (from Chapter 3) and have hundreds or thousands of keywords, you would not want to go through the AdWords interface to add all of those keywords to various ad groups. Instead, put your keywords in column 3, and then add the campaign name, ad group name, and so on for the data you want to import.

When you import the data, if there is not a campaign or ad group name within a campaign that you are adding, the AdWords Editor will automatically create those campaigns and ad groups for you.

4. Once you have organized the data, copy all of it, except for the header row, and paste it into the AdWords Editor (Figure 12.14).

5. Click the Next button, and the editor will inform you of how many ad groups, campaign, and keywords will be added to your account.

If you created new ad groups or campaigns, you will need to navigate to those items in the editor to set your bids, daily budget, and other campaign or ad group settings (refer back to Figure 12.6).

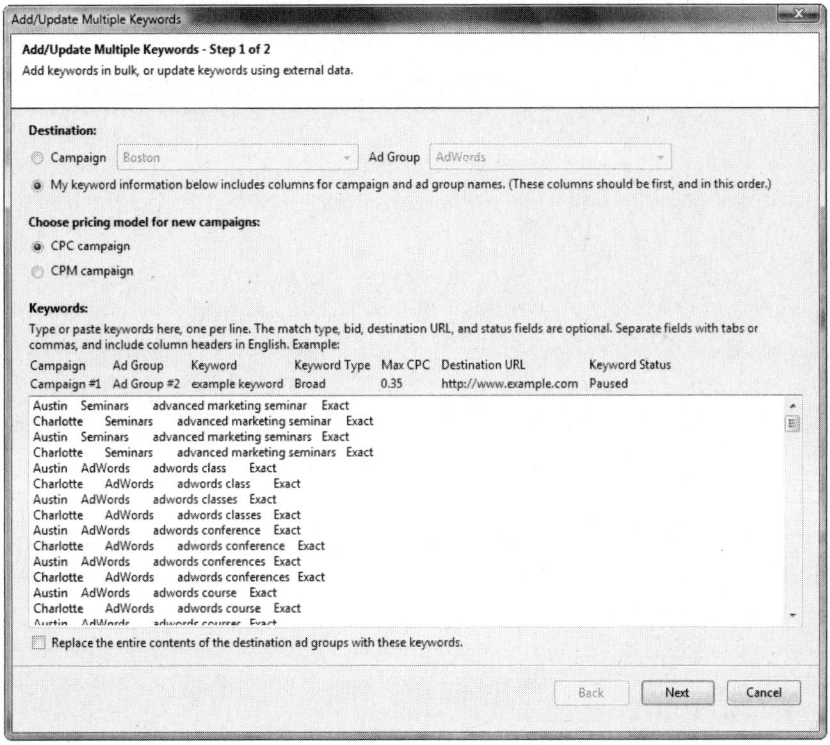

Figure 12.14 Importing keywords into the AdWords Editor

Creating Thousands of Keywords and Ad Groups

You can also use Excel to create hundreds of thousands of keywords, although when doing so, it is suggested that you just create one campaign at a time.

Let us re-examine the keyword methodology chart from Chapter 2. In the keyword listing methodology, you will create several lists of several keywords. Table 12.3 is the maternity shirt example from Chapter 2.

▶ **Table 12.3** Maternity shirt example keywords

Category Adjectives	Product Types	Product Attributes 1	Product Attributes	Example Keywords
Pregnant	Shirt	Long sleeve	Cotton	Pregnancy shirt Pregnancy shirt long sleeve
Pregnancy	T-shirt	Short sleeve	Rayon	Pregnancy shirt cotton
Maternity	Dress blouse Tops Polo shirt Sweatshirt	Sleeveless	Silk Stretchable Natural fibers Wool	Pregnancy shirt long sleeve cotton

The first thing to do when scaling your accounts is to determine your campaigns and ad groups. For ease of explanation, in this example, we are going to assume it is a national retailer who is just getting started, and therefore they only need national search campaigns.

In addition, make the assumption that the lists in Table 12.3 are much longer. For instance, there are many more product types, attributes, brands, and so forth that could be listed in the lists in Table 12.3.

Since we are using a single campaign, the next step is to decide upon the ad groups. In the earlier list, the words are not yet defined as ad groups or keywords. For instance, you could have the ad group Maternity Cotton Shirts with keywords such as "xl maternity cotton shirts." Or you could have the ad group Maternity Shirts with the keyword "cotton maternity shirts." There are many possibilities. Therefore, determine how many ad groups you want to devote to your current list.

If this company sold men's, women's, children's, and other clothing, then we might not want to use thousands of ad groups for just maternity clothing. As we would also have hundreds or thousands of ad groups for each of men's, women's, and children's clothing categories, it would not make sense to start with thousands of ad groups for a specific clothing type, such as maternity, shoes, or outerwear. An account might get there after learning what is converting and optimizing the account, but we are going to start more simply.

If the company only sold maternity clothing, and therefore all your ad groups were going to be related to maternity, then you could be more liberal in your ad group selection and have thousands of maternity ad groups.

Organizing Your Account

Account organization is so important to long-term success that it can be useful to create a document that covers how you are going to reach your audience, how that audience searches, and how you are going to break down your ad groups and campaigns into a manageable account structure before even opening your AdWords account. In Chapter 14, we will take an in-depth look at successful account organization.

Let us assume that after doing research we found out these points (and these are made up, so please do not use them for your organization):

- The words "maternity" and "pregnancy" are used interchangeably, and user intent did not vary based on the word being searched.
- "Cotton" and "stretchable" are the most common attributes searched, and the search volume for the other materials is much smaller.
- There is a large search volume for branded terms, and the branded terms can be used in the ad copy as they will be compliant with the trademark policies and laws.
- It is summertime, and while the search volume for "swimsuits" and "sun dresses" is high, those words do not combine well with our list in Table 12.3, and we will need a second list for sun dresses and swimsuits.

This is a short list of points for illustration purposes only. Your research should uncover more information about the searchers.

Armed with this information, it is now time to create the ad groups. The information leads us to making these assumptions about our organization:

- The words "maternity" and "pregnancy" are used interchangeably, and user intent did not vary based on the word being searched.

  We are going to use the words "maternity" and "pregnancy" as keyword modifiers and not as different ad groups. Therefore, whenever a keyword is added, it will be added twice, once with the "pregnancy" modifier and once with the "maternity" modifier. For instance, your keywords would be "maternity cotton shirt" and "pregnancy cotton shirt."

- "Cotton" and "stretchable" are the most common attributes searched; the search volume for the other materials is much smaller.

  For each product type, there will be three ad groups: Cotton, Stretchable, and Other. Therefore, we will have Cotton Suits, Stretchable Suits, and Other Suits as ad groups.

  In the Other Suits ad group, we will use all of the additional product attribute modifiers as keyword modifiers. For instance, "pregnancy wool suit," "maternity wool suit," "pregnancy rayon suit," and "maternity rayon suit" would be some of the keywords in that ad group.

- There is a large search volume for branded terms, and the branded terms can be used in the ad copy as they will be compliant with the trademark policies and laws.

  Since there is such high brand search volume, and we want to use the branded terms in the ad copy, we need to create brand-specific ad groups.

  Therefore, we will make a list of all the brands and what ad groups contain keywords that each brand sells. For instance, if Chiarakruza only sold shirts, pants, and sun dresses, then we would take the nonbranded ad groups that contain those items and make them again, adding Chiarakruza as another product attribute to those ad groups.

  However, if we have one ad group that is Chiarakruza Maternity Shirts and another one that is Maternity Shirts with some broad match keywords, then Google could choose which keyword to trigger and which ad to serve. Therefore, in the nonbranded ad group, Maternity Shirts, we would add the negative keyword "Chiarakruza."

- It is summertime, and while the search volume for "swimsuits" and "sun dresses" is high, those words do not combine well with our list from Table 12.3, and we will need a second list for sun dresses and swimsuits.

  This information will start our next action list. We will need to do more research on sundresses and bathing suits and create new lists before adding these ad groups.

With this information, we would then re-create our lists to first create ad groups, as shown in Table 12.4.

▶ **Table 12.4** Maternity clothing ad groups

Brand	Attributes	Product Type	Ad Groups
Chiarakruza	Cotton	Shirts	Cotton shirts
Belabumbum	Stretchable	Pants	Stretchable shirts
	Other	Suits	Other shirts
			Belabumbum shirts
			Chiarakruza shirts

Once you have listed all of your ad groups, you can use your keyword list information to create the keywords that fit into each of these ad groups. By going through this exercise in a spreadsheet, you can use formulas to create thousands of ad groups and tens of thousands of keywords fairly easily. The hard part is the initial research into the keyword lists and laying out your account structure. For larger accounts, the actual keyword creation can be easier than the planning stages.

Importing Keywords and Ad Groups into the AdWords Editor

Once you have this organized, it is a simple copy and paste from your spreadsheet into the bulk import function of the AdWords Editor to get them into your editor file. If you have created new ad group or campaigns, make sure you set the appropriate bids, budget, and other settings.

If you are creating a campaign that will have more than 10,000 keywords or 1,000 pieces of ad copy, before creating text ads, upload the data to your AdWords account. These ad groups will show a warning because there is no associated ad copy. However, when selectively uploading from an AdWords Editor file, the smallest amount of data you can upload is a single campaign. The AdWords Editor can time out when uploading huge amounts of data; therefore, by selectively uploading the keywords first, you are uploading less total data at once and mitigating the chances of the data not being uploaded into your account. After you have created the ads from the next section, upload just the ads as the second step to create whole ad groups.

Now that we have created potentially hundreds of ad groups with tens of thousands of keywords, it is time to create ad copy for those ad groups.

Easily Creating Thousands of Ads

An ad group is not complete until it contains both keywords and ad copy. After determining your ad groups and populating those ad groups with keywords, the next step is to write associated ad copy.

The AdWords Editor also supports the bulk importing of ad copy. In the editor:

1. Navigate to the Ads tab and click on Make Multiple Changes.

2. Select Add/Update Multiple Text Ads (Figure 12.15).

Figure 12.15 Finding the ad copy import tool

This will bring you to a similar screen as when you were importing text ads (Figure 12.16).

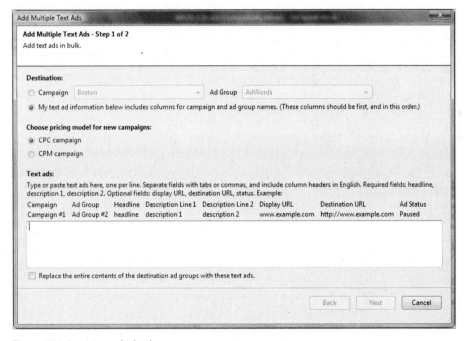

Figure 12.16 Importing multiple ads

3. In your spreadsheet program, create a sheet with these column headers (Figure 12.17)

- Campaign
- Ad Group
- Headline
- Description line 1
- Description line 2
- Display URL
- Destination URL
- Status (optional)

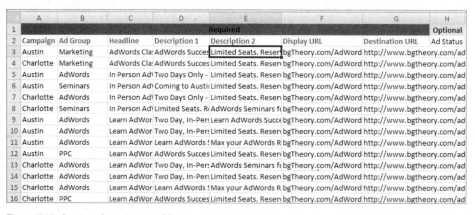

	A	B	C	D	E	F	G	H
1					Required			Optional
2	Campaign	Ad Group	Headline	Description 1	Description 2	Display URL	Destination URL	Ad Status
3	Austin	Marketing	AdWords Cla:	AdWords Succe:	Limited Seats. Resen	bgTheory.com/AdWord	http://www.bgtheory.com/ad	
4	Charlotte	Marketing	AdWords Cla:	AdWords Succe:	Limited Seats. Resen	bgTheory.com/AdWord	http://www.bgtheory.com/ad	
5	Austin	AdWords	In Person Ad'	Two Days Only -	Limited Seats. Resen	bgTheory.com/AdWord	http://www.bgtheory.com/ad	
6	Austin	Seminars	In Person Ad'	Coming to Austi	Limited Seats. Resen	bgTheory.com/AdWord	http://www.bgtheory.com/ad	
7	Charlotte	AdWords	In Person Ad'	Two Days Only -	Limited Seats. Resen	bgTheory.com/AdWord	http://www.bgtheory.com/ad	
8	Charlotte	Seminars	In Person Ad'	Limited Seats. R	AdWords Seminars f	bgTheory.com/AdWord	http://www.bgtheory.com/ad	
9	Austin	AdWords	Learn AdWor	Two Day, In-Pers	Learn AdWords Succe	bgTheory.com/AdWord	http://www.bgtheory.com/ad	
10	Austin	AdWords	Learn AdWor	Two Day, In-Pers	Limited Seats. Resen	bgTheory.com/AdWord	http://www.bgtheory.com/ad	
11	Austin	AdWords	Learn AdWor	Learn AdWords :	Max your AdWords R	bgTheory.com/AdWord	http://www.bgtheory.com/ad	
12	Austin	PPC	Learn AdWor	AdWords Succe:	Limited Seats. Resen	bgTheory.com/AdWord	http://www.bgtheory.com/ad	
13	Charlotte	AdWords	Learn AdWor	Two Day, In-Pers	AdWords Seminars f	bgTheory.com/AdWord	http://www.bgtheory.com/ad	
14	Charlotte	AdWords	Learn AdWor	Two Day, In-Pers	Limited Seats. Resen	bgTheory.com/AdWord	http://www.bgtheory.com/ad	
15	Charlotte	AdWords	Learn AdWor	Learn AdWords :	Max your AdWords R	bgTheory.com/AdWord	http://www.bgtheory.com/ad	
16	Charlotte	PPC	Learn AdWor	AdWords Succe:	Limited Seats. Resen	bgTheory.com/AdWord	http://www.bgtheory.com/ad	

Figure 12.17 Creating ad copy in a spreadsheet

Note: The ad group name is for your purposes only. It does not affect items like quality score; however, it can be useful to name ad groups with names that reflect the keywords so you understand what the ad group is about and also so you can use Excel formulas to help to help create ads.

When creating the ad groups and campaign names for your ad copy, please make sure that you use the exact same names from your keyword import sheet. If you use different campaign names, you will have one campaign with ad copy and a different campaign with only keywords. There are simple tricks you can use that will help you write multiple ads at once to save you precious time.

Writing Multiple Ads

If you are only writing a handful of ads, please write them customized by hand with the best practices from Chapter 4. However, if you are creating thousands of ads for hundreds or thousands of ad groups, you will need to write formulas to create this many ads.

The first step in writing multiple ads with formulas is to break down your ad groups into similar product lines where formulaic ads will still be relevant to the searcher. For instance, if you sell maternity and men's clothing, a tagline such as "Maternity Wear for Fashionable Moms" would not resonate with the men searching for clothes.

Once these are broken down into various ad groups, then write some calls to action, some headlines, and some taglines for those ad groups.

For instance, let us say these are some of the initial ad copy lines we want to try:

- Headlines:
  - Ad Group Name (in this case, we are assuming the ad group name is closely associated to the keywords in the ad group and that it would make a good headline)
  - Fashionable Maternity Clothing
  - Shop at Company Name
- Taglines:
  - Shop today, wear it tomorrow.
  - Free shipping on all orders!
- Destination URL:
  - Company URL
  - Company URL/AdGroupName
  - Company URL/Shop

Next, we will write a set of formulas where we will insert this information (see Table 12.5). The more traffic you are going to buy, the more ads you can write. Because we are writing formulas that will be used across multiple ad groups, we can also run reports where we are looking at which formulaic writing is leading to clicks and conversions, so we do not have to rely on testing at the ad group level.

▶ **Table 12.5** Example ad copy formulas

Headline	Description Line 1	Description Line 2	Display URL
Ad Group Name	Headline1	Tagline1	Display URL 1
{Keyword:Ad Group name}	Shop at Company Name	Tagline2	Display URL 2
Headline1	Buy {Keyword: Ad Group Name}	Tagline1	Display URL 3
Headline2	Tagline1	Tagline2	Display URL 2

Once you have the formulas written, then plug in the ad copy variables. You can easily do this in Excel by calling information from different cells within the spreadsheet. For instance, if your headline was Ad Group Name, and the ad group is located in column B of your spreadsheet, you could write "=B3" and the cell would be replaced by the content of cell B3. Since Excel automatically adjusts formulas as you copy, paste, and drag them, it is simple to write the formulas for one ad group, and then copy and paste the selection multiple times or drag the cells down across multiple ad groups. If our ad group was Chiarakruza Maternity Shirts, then our final ad copy would look like Table 12.6.

▶ **Table 12.6** Maternity clothing ads

Headline	Description Line 1	Description Line 2	Display URL
Chiarakruza Maternity Shirts	Fashionable Maternity Clothing	Shop today, wear it tomorrow.	CompanyName.com
{Keyword: Chiarakruza Maternity Shirts }	Shop at Company Name	Free shipping on all orders!	CompanyName.com/ ChiarakruzaMaternityShirts
Fashionable Maternity Clothing	Buy {Keyword: Chiarakruza Maternity Shirts }	Shop today, wear it tomorrow.	CompanyName.com/Shop
Shop at Company Name	Shop today, wear it tomorrow.	Free shipping on all orders!	CompanyName.com/ ChiarakruzaMaternityShirts
Chiarakruza Maternity Shirts	Our friendly return policy means	Guilt Free Shopping	CompanyName.com/Chiarakruza

The last ad copy is just one we added to test out what a multiple line ad copy would do. Feel free to add additional ad copy as it makes sense to your goals. In this example, you would replace Company Name with your actual company, and the same with the display URL.

In addition, you will have a destination URL based on where you are sending traffic to on your website; however, you would not use a formula to create the destination URL. You want to make sure the destination URL resolves to the correct page on your website.

Character Limits and Naming Conventions

When you write formula-based ads, some of them will be outside of character limit policies. If you are writing these ads in Excel, use the conditional formatting to highlight instances where you have gone over character limits. Then you will need to adjust the ads appropriately.

For instance, in the previous example, the word "Chiarakruza" contains so many characters that a few of the ad copy lines have exceeded their character limits, such as the display URL CompanyName.com/ChiarakruzaMaternityShirts. In this instance, we would remove the MaternityShirts aspect, leaving the CompanyName .com/Chiarakruza, which might be within the 35 allocated display URL characters depending on how long the company's URL is.

When you create the ad copy to match your existing keyword ad groups, make sure the naming conventions for your campaigns and ad groups are identical. If they are not the same, you will have one ad group with keywords and another ad group with just ad copy.

Once you have finished writing your ad copy, then copy the new ads and paste them into the AdWords Editor. The AdWords Editor will inform you of how many ads you are adding and if any new ad groups or campaigns will be created. If you have already imported the keywords, you should not be creating new ad groups or campaigns. Hence, if the editor informs you that new campaigns or ad groups will be created, check your naming conventions.

Advantages of Using Excel with AdWords Editor

Using a spreadsheet and the AdWords Editor together allows you to easily import large amounts of information into your AdWords account in a quick and scalable manner. The hard work of scaling your accounts should no longer be the AdWords front-end interface. The hard work should be in mapping your ad groups, keywords, and ad copy together so that you can still use many of the best practices from those who create ad groups by hand, yet in a scalable manner.

Once you have larger accounts, especially ones written through formulas, you can use the best practice optimization techniques discussed in Chapter 17 to find your strengths and weaknesses, and be able to find ad groups that need to be further broken down based on returns. Even if you have smaller accounts, the exact same optimization techniques apply, only you will have a smaller number of ad groups to analyze.

Optimizing Content with the AdWords Editor

In the last two chapters, we went through examples of why it is best to have your campaigns only set to search or to content. If your campaigns are currently set to both, do not fret—with the AdWords Editor, it will take you only a minute to duplicate your campaigns and change the appropriate settings.

First, navigate to the campaign that you want to duplicate. Then use the copy (Ctrl+C) and paste (Ctrl+V) functions to duplicate that campaign. With those two simple keystrokes, you now have two identical campaigns.

The campaign you just created will have an error associated with it because it has the same name as another campaign (Figure 12.18). Rename the first campaign to Current Campaign Name - Search. Then rename the second campaign as Current

Campaign Name - Content. This will not only fix the error but let you quickly tell if you are working on a content or search campaign.

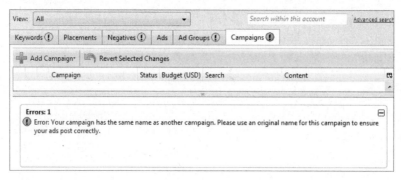

Figure 12.18 Campaign name error in the AdWords Editor

Once the campaigns are renamed, it is time to change the settings so that the first campaign is only displayed on search and the second campaign is only displayed on the content network (Figure 12.19).

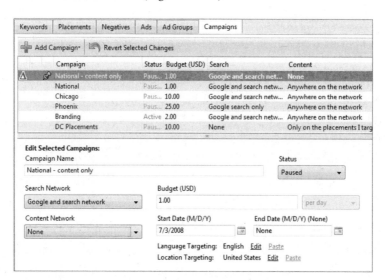

Figure 12.19 Choosing either search only or content only for your campaigns

Next, you will want to go through the typical content organization techniques discussed to choose your content keywords and placements. However, because your new campaign is only targeted to the content network, you can use more general keywords to help create a theme for your ad group and not have to worry about those keywords triggering your search ads.

Best Practices for Using the AdWords Editor

Whenever you are hesitant to start working on your AdWords account because of the front-end interface, it is time to use the AdWords Editor.

While there are a few features that are available within the AdWords interface that are not in the editor, they are generally settings that are not commonly used, such as demographic bidding or custom radius targeting. In addition, they are usually features that are not changed often; hence, they are not always necessary to have in the editor.

- Your view in the editor is determined by settings. To get started, use the left navigation column to select the amount of data you want to view (account, campaign, or specific ad group), and the middle horizontal bar to select the data points (ad copy, keywords, ad groups, or campaigns).

- Look for visual cues in the editor. The red or yellow warning labels let you find problems. The plus sign or minus sign shows what is being added or deleted.

- Use the notes feature in the AdWords Editor, designated by a red push pin. This will allow you to keep track of why you made certain changes for future analysis.

- At a minimum, you should give everyone who has access to your account their own login. If you have a large team, you can also export your account for sharing and then review any changes proposed to your account before they go live.

- The AdWords Editor allows the bulk creation of keywords, ad copy, campaigns, or ad groups. When you bulk create items, always adjust any bids, geographic targets, or other ad group and campaign settings before you push the changes live.

- When creating large numbers of keywords, follow these steps:

  1. Determine your ad groups.

  2. Populate those ad groups with the proper keywords.

- When creating large amounts of ad copy, use formula writing, but ensure that the ads are still relevant to the user and fall within the editorial requirements before posting the ads.

- Learn the keyboard shortcuts. While it is easy to duplicate a campaign for content and search targeting purposes, you can also use shortcut keys to select all ad copy that requires an exception request and fill out a single exception request at a time.

The AdWords Editor is a powerful tool to help you quickly add data, remove data, or change existing data, such as bids. Using the AdWords Editor import functions along with Excel can not only save you time, but it also allow you to use best practice account management in both small and large accounts.

However, it is not enough to create thousands of ads or tens of thousands of keywords if they do not fit within the goals of your business. In the next chapter, we will examine different bid strategies so you can set bids that increase your company's profits.

Profitable Bid Strategies

Is your AdWords account making money or costing money? The only way to know is to first understand the goals that your marketing initiatives must accomplish for your company to be profitable. Once you have determined your goals, you then need to find a way to measure them. Only after these two steps have been accomplished can you start to decide how much you should bid.

There are different bidding techniques you can use to set bids, control costs, choose ad positions, and reach searchers by time of day and day of the week. Learn how to extract the proper data from AdWords so you can take the necessary actions to develop a successful AdWords account.

13

Chapter Contents

Setting Your Marketing Goals
Measuring Results with Google's Conversion Tracking Code
Exploring AdWords Bidding Options
Bidding Strategies that Increase Profits
Calculating Your Max CPC
Position Preference: Controlling Where Your Ad Is Displayed
Ad Scheduling: Automatically Changing Bids by Time Periods
Understanding Attribution Management
Examining AdWords Reports to Make ROI Bid Decisions
Best Practices for Utilizing Profitable Bid Strategies

Setting Your Marketing Goals

The first thing you should do in any advertising campaign, before you spend a single penny, is to set the goals your advertising campaign needs to accomplish. It does not matter if your advertising outlet is Google AdWords, yellow pages ads, newspaper ads, radio, TV, or any other medium. If you do not have goals set for the campaign, you cannot define success and optimize the campaigns to increase performance.

Many companies will have multiple goals. You may also need to refine your goals over time. Let us examine the steps a plumber may take in setting and refining goals.

Before the advertising campaign starts, the plumber examines his phone records and realizes that he receives 50 calls per month. Of those calls, he closes five jobs a month. Therefore, his conversion rate is 10 percent. His average job is worth $1,000, and it takes about 20 hours to accomplish each job. Since he only works 160 hours per month, he realizes that he needs to close eight jobs per month. Since he has a 10 percent conversion rate, he needs to receive 80 calls per month. However, since each job is worth $1,000, he can do some math and realize that his breakeven point is paying $100 per phone call. He wants a 200 percent ROI (return on investment), and therefore, he is willing to pay $50 per phone call.

In the first month of advertising, he manages to receive 50 calls. However, all of the calls come from keywords for fixing pipes and broken showers. His conversion rate is much higher, 20 percent, but these smaller pipe repair jobs only take 3 hours each. Even though he hit his goal of 50 phone calls, he only ended up working 30 hours that month. Therefore, he needs to refine his goals.

After further examination of the phone call records, he realizes that he closes 1 in 5 calls for small jobs, such as pipe fixing and broken showers. However, his close rate for large jobs such as kitchen remodeling is only 1 in 20, or 5 percent. After doing some math, he realizes that he wants to do two kitchen remodeling jobs each month, and then fill in the rest of his time with small jobs. Therefore, his final goals are 40 phone calls for kitchen remodeling each month and 130 calls for small jobs. In addition, he is willing to pay $100 for the kitchen remodeling calls, but only $25 for the smaller job phone calls.

An e-commerce company might take a different approach. The company might look at their finances and realize that based on their margins, they need a 200 percent ROI for all products sold. However, they also have a newsletter and they find that if someone subscribes to their newsletter, they make at least two sales a year to those subscribers. The average sale from the newsletter is $50. Therefore, after doing some calculations on the returns they want from their email marketing, they are willing to pay $10 per newsletter subscriber. However, since they need to pay overhead and monthly bills each month, and the newsletters are long-term investments, they must have at least 1,000 e-commerce sales per month.

Many times a company will need to dig back into its business model to understand how the business makes money and what is required to not just hit payroll each week, but to also grow as a company. This is often harder than setting bids for ad groups or keywords. Consider a drop-shipper who realized that if they could sell 7 percent more goods, they could switch suppliers and receive a 10 percent discount on the wholesale price of the goods they purchase. If this is the case, that drop-shipper could run an additional campaign at a breakeven number just to hit the new sales numbers so they could save on the total cost of goods they buy, which would put more dollars back into their bank account without changing a single bid price.

Many companies do not know their internal numbers well enough to set goals that improve their supply chain. However, setting goals is essential.

Some of the more common goals are:

- Set percentage ROI on goods sold
- Minimum number of sales per month
- Minimum revenue per month
- Number of phone calls per month per product
- Cost per phone call per product
- Cost per acquisition of a new customer, newsletter subscription, or RSS feed subscription
- Number of new visitors per day
- Number of visitors per day (this is a common goal for publishers who make money by selling CPM ads on their website)
- Number of leads per month
- Cost per lead

Once the company examines itself and understands how it makes money, set the goals for what the marketing campaigns need to accomplish. Once these goals are set, they need to be measured.

Measuring Results with Google's Conversion Tracking Code

Optimizing Google AdWords campaigns can only be done with proper metrics. If you do not have the numbers to examine, there is no way to know if you are hitting your goals, or even what keywords and ad copy are helping you reach those goals.

Therefore, for every goal you set, you need to find a way to measure it. This may lead you to institute phone call tracking, FeedBurner for RSS tracking, Google Analytics for page views per visits, or other software as necessary.

Google offers a conversion tracking script you can institute that will add conversion metrics to your AdWords account. Once you install the conversion tracking code, you will be able to see cost per conversion (CPC), total conversions, and ROI numbers by keyword, ad copy, and landing page in both the AdWords interface and your AdWords reports.

AdWords Conversion Tracking Code

The AdWords conversion tracking code is powerful and easy to install. The first step is to navigate to the conversion tracking page within your account (Figure 13.1). This screen will show you all the previous conversion actions you have defined.

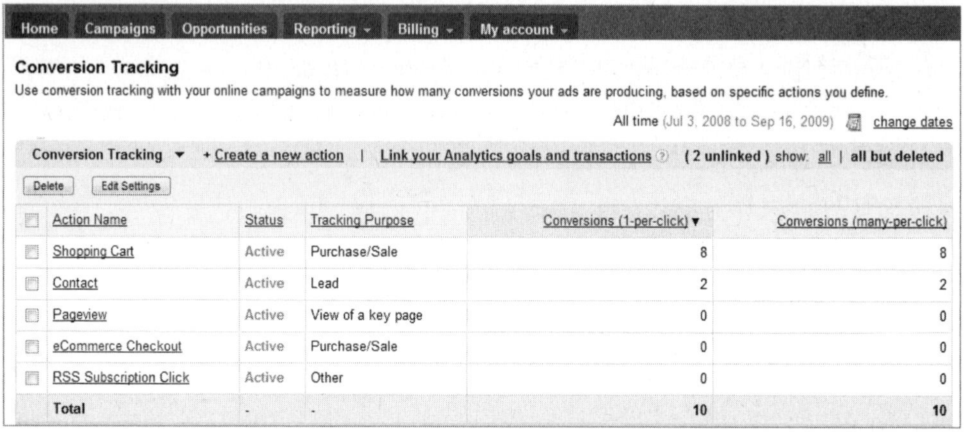

Action Name	Status	Tracking Purpose	Conversions (1-per-click)	Conversions (many-per-click)
Shopping Cart	Active	Purchase/Sale	8	8
Contact	Active	Lead	2	2
Pageview	Active	View of a key page	0	0
eCommerce Checkout	Active	Purchase/Sale	0	0
RSS Subscription Click	Active	Other	0	0
Total	-	-	10	10

Figure 13.1 AdWords conversion tracking overview

Click on Create A New Action and you will be presented with a screen where you can define your conversion information (Figure 13.2). The items are as follows:

Name Your Action Fill out the open text field with a name that describes the action. You use this naming field to help you remember which conversion is taking place on your website.

The second field, This Action Is Used For Tracking, will show up in your AdWords reports. Therefore, choose the action that describes what you are tracking. If you are tracking multiple items, choose a different field each time. That way you will be able to see that each keyword led to $10 leads and four signups.

Revenue for Your Action This field will populate your AdWords reports with the actual revenue you gained from an action. In your AdWords reports, you will be able to see that keyword 1 led to $15 in revenue, and keyword 2 led to $25 in revenue. There are three ways of defining this field.

The first is to leave it blank or use the number 1 as the field number. In this case, you will not see revenue in your AdWords reports; you will only see the total number of conversions.

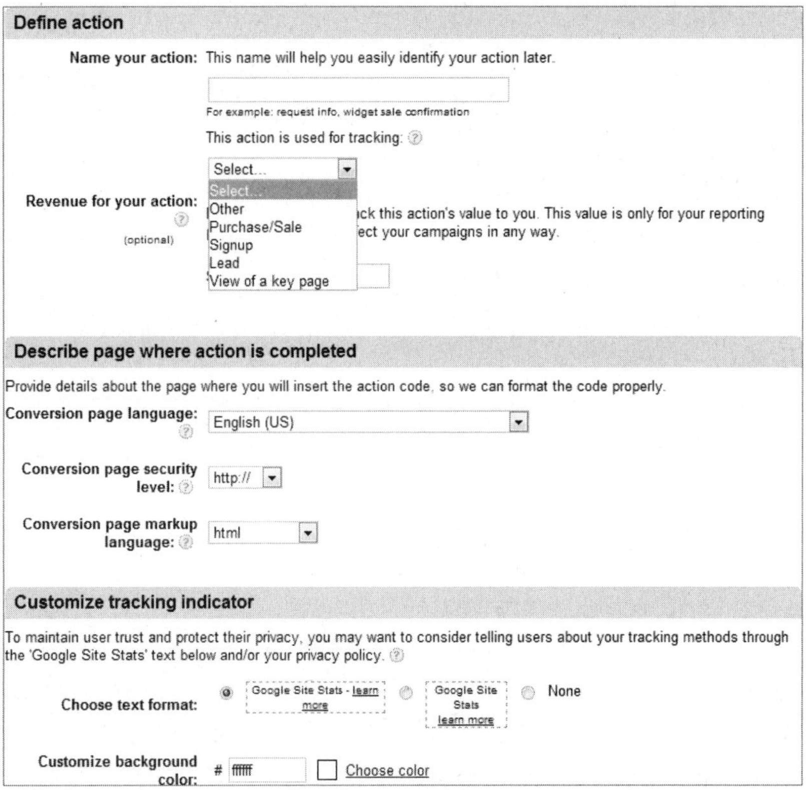

Figure 13.2 Conversion tracking script wizard

The second is to do some math and then put in the estimated revenue for that action. For instance, if the e-commerce company from the previous example were using this method to track their newsletter subscriptions, they would enter 50, as that is what they calculated a newsletter subscription was worth to their company.

The third way to use this field is to enter a variable from your shopping cart. Most shopping carts have three variables on the checkout page: total cost of goods, cost of shipping, and total cost to consumer. Most companies do not make money on shipping, so by entering the variable for total cost of goods, you will be able to see the actual revenue that each keyword or ad copy led to on your website. To find the variable, ask your shopping cart provider or web developer. They should be able to assist you.

Conversion Page Language   Choose the language in which your conversion page is written.

Conversion Page Security Level   This is an important setting to note so you do not cause trust errors with your customers. Choose whether your conversion page is a secure (HTTPS) or non-secure (HTTP) page. If you put a secure script on a non-secure page, most browsers show an error, "This page contains secure and non-secure items. Do you want to view the non-secure information?" You do not want users to see this message, as it can lower the trust they have in your company. It is OK to call a secure script from a non-secure page. Therefore, if you are in doubt about the security level of your website, choose the secure (HTTPS) script.

Conversion Page Markup Language Choose the coding language of your website. Please note that extensions such as .php or .aspx are still HTML pages. The other options are for mobile extensions such as .xhtml. If this is your standard website, choose HTML. If you are placing the code on a mobile site, examine the options to make sure you are calling the appropriate language code.

Customize Tracking Indicator When a user clicks on your AdWords ad, a cookie is placed on their browser. If that cookie is on a user's browser when they get to a page where you are using this conversion code, Google will display a piece of text to the user. You can customize this text to fit the look and feel of your website, or you can update your privacy policy to inform users that you are using a tracking script and not display any text to the user.

Once you have filled out all of the options, save the page. You will then be brought to a page that displays the code you need to install on your website (Figure 13.3).

Figure 13.3 AdWords conversion tracking code

Copy this code and paste it in the thank-you pages of your website. This code only goes on the page that the user sees after they have completed an action, such as the "Thank you for shopping" or "Thank you for contacting us" pages. If you install this code in a global footer, you will be tracking page views.

> **Note:** A browser loads a webpage in the order in which it receives. If after the open body tag <body> your website has several scripts, then the browser must load all of the scripts before the text of your website can be loaded. If a script is slow to load—or worse, it times out—the user will stare at a blank page for a while until the scripts finish loading or time out. Therefore, it is best to add all scripts at the bottom of your web pages before the close body tag </body>. When you add scripts to the bottom of a page, the user may still leave the page before the script loads, which will cause you to lose some tracking data; however, all users will be able to see the text of your site first and not think there is a problem if the page loads slowly. It is better to lose some tracking and keep the user's trust than to track everything and lose consumer confidence.

If you have multiple conversion actions, such as a newsletter and e-commerce conversion, use a different code for each action. If you use the same code for all actions, you will not be able to see which keywords, ad copy, or landing pages lead to the different types of actions on your website. Utilize the conversion tracking wizard once per action you want to track, and then install the code on the various thank-you pages associated with those actions.

Accessing Valuable Conversion Data in AdWords Reports

Once you have conversion tracking installed when you run AdWords reports, you will have access to valuable conversion data. In the reporting menu, scroll down to Add Or Remove Columns and open the tab. Under Conversion Type Columns and Conversion Columns you can select the conversion information you want to see (Figure 13.4).

Conversion Type Columns : These columns enable you to view conversion statistics broken down by type		
☑ Action Name	☑ Action Category	
Conversion Columns : These columns provide statistics on ad conversions and conversion rates		
☑ Conversions (1-per-click)	☑ Conv. Rate (1-per-click)	☐ Cost/Conv. (1-per-click)
☐ Conversions (many-per-click)	☑ Cost/Conv. (many-per-click)	☑ Total Conv. Value
☑ Value/Conv. (1-per-click)	☐ Conv. Value/Cost	☑ Conv. Value/Click
☐ Sales Conv. (many-per-click)	☐ Sales Conv. Value (many-per-click)	☐ Leads Conv. (many-per-click)
☐ Leads Conv. Value (many-per-click)	☐ Sign-up Conv. (many-per-click)	☐ Sign-up Conv. Value (many-per-click)
☐ Page View Conv. (many-per-click)	☐ Page View Conv. Value (many-per-click)	☐ Other Conv. (many-per-click)
☐ Other Conv. Value (many-per-click)		

Figure 13.4 Adding conversion information to AdWords reports

You can view these conversion columns in almost all of the AdWords reports (see Figure 13.5). Now you can see conversions, revenue, cost per conversion, and conversion rate by many data points, including:

- Keyword
- Ad copy
- Landing page
- Ad group

- Campaign
- Placement
- Geography

Placement / Keyword Report

Report Generated: Sep 16, 2009 7:44:50 AM Show report detail

Export Report | Create Another Report Like This

View: Summary

Impressions 19,531,484	Clicks 204,641	CTR 1.05%	Avg CPC $0.47	Avg CPM $4.94	Cost $96,403.88	Avg Position 2.93	Conversions (1-per-click) 2,979	Conv. Rate (1-per-click) 1.46%	Cost/Conv. (1-per-click) $32.24

Ad Group	Placement / Keyword	Impressions	Clicks	CTR	Avg CPC	Avg CPM	Cost	Avg Position	Conversions (1 per-click)	Conv. Rate (1-per-click)	Cost/Conv. (1-per-click)
		898,710	16,697	1.86%	$0.71	$13.20	$11,861.80	4.1	427	2.56%	$27.75
		1,499,317	19,886	1.33%	$0.31	$4.17	$6,250.87	3.3	417	2.10%	$14.99
		291,129	5,589	1.92%	$1.07	$20.46	$5,957.14	4.5	157	2.81%	$37.93
		624,680	13,692	2.19%	$0.16	$3.48	$2,173.61	2.8	134	0.98%	$16.21
		171,570	3,794	2.21%	$1.17	$25.93	$4,449.09	3.9	121	3.19%	$36.75
		253,505	3,959	1.56%	$1.03	$16.10	$4,081.53	4.0	105	2.66%	$38.83
		1,822,350	4,911	0.27%	$0.21	$0.56	$1,018.30	1.8	88	1.79%	$11.57
		363,667	9,491	2.61%	$0.21	$5.49	$1,998.23	3.4	85	0.90%	$23.50
		2,782,959	6,969	0.25%	$0.16	$0.40	$1,099.40	2.6	83	1.19%	$13.23
		318,282	3,687	1.16%	$0.58	$6.70	$2,133.35	3.5	66	1.79%	$32.32

Figure 13.5 AdWords report with conversion information

As we look at bidding techniques in this chapter and examine reports in future chapters, we will assume you have installed the AdWords conversion tracking script. If you are using another tool to track revenue, you can still use all of these techniques we will examine, but you will have to combine the AdWords reports with your own metrics system.

How to Track Phone Calls

There are several different ways to track phone calls, including using AdWord's conversion tracking code. Many vendors exist that will let you buy one or more tracking phone numbers. Some vendors will help you track phone calls by keyword, ad copy, or landing page. The more phone numbers you want, the more expensive the solutions become.

Unique Phone Number per Data Point This solution tracks search engine, ad group, keyword, and so on. It's the most accurate, but the most expensive.

Unique Extension per Data Point This solution can be cheaper to institute with a sophisticated in-house call system. However, you will need to correlate extensions with data points.

Code Identifiers You can generate a code underneath the phone number on your site that is associated with AdWords data points. Then have the sales reps collect the identifiers from callers and correlate sales to data points. This is not a hard method to institute, but it does require retraining sales reps, which can be difficult.

Utilize Confidence Factors If you have a high call volume, instead of having unique phone numbers or extensions by data points, you can create confidence factors so that when a certain keyword is clicked, on average the phone rings 2 percent of the time.

AdWords Conversion Tracking Code If you can get someone back to your website after the call, then you can use the AdWords conversion tracking code. You may have to be creative, such as by generating online receipts, to consistently get people back to your website to trigger the code. This method is the cheapest to institute and will allow you to see phone call conversion data inside your AdWords account.

AdWords Bidding Options

AdWords supports several different methods of setting bids. Setting max CPCs, also known as Manual bidding for clicks, is the default method; however, depending on your goals, the other methods may work better for you.

These options are at the campaign level in your account. Hence, you can have one campaign that uses one method and another campaign that uses a different method. However, all ad groups in the same campaign will utilize the same bidding methodology.

Navigate to the campaign Settings tab. Under the Bidding And Budget options (Figure 13.6), there are up to four methods listed that you can use to determine your bids.

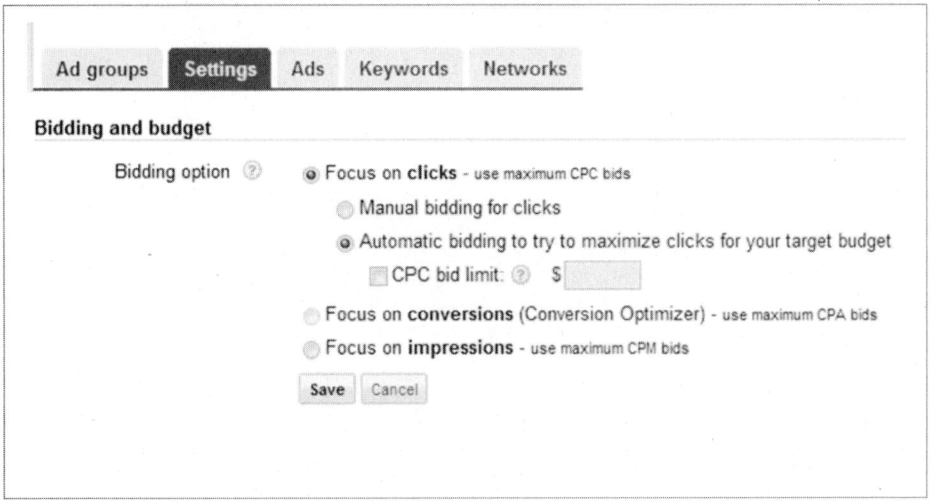

Figure 13.6 Campaign bidding methods

Focus on Clicks: Manual Bidding for Clicks The first option under Focus on clicks is Manual bidding for clicks. This is the default method of bidding. You will set a max CPC, and you will pay up to that max CPC. The advantage of this option is that it is compatible with all the advanced options in AdWords. For instance, if you want to use advanced ad scheduling where you change your max bid by time of day, you must use this bidding methodology.

Focus on Clicks: Budget Optimizer The second option under Focus on Clicks is "Automatic bidding to try to maximize clicks for your target budget," also known as the Budget Optimizer. With the Budget Optimizer, Google will attempt to maximize the number of clicks your campaign receives. You can choose to set a max bid cap or let AdWords take full control of the bidding. It is recommended that you set a bid cap, otherwise you could end up paying a significant amount per click, as Google will attempt to spend your budget.

If you consider your keywords to have different values for your company, then you should not use the Budget Optimizer. For instance, if you are willing to pay $4 per click for the keyword "Samsung 63 DLP TV," but only $2 for the keyword "DLP TV," then you should not use the Budget Optimizer. If you are looking to maximize traffic, however, then it can be useful.

The other reason to use the Budget Optimizer is if you have keywords that are good words for your industry, and you want to have some exposure on searches that use them, but those words are so early in the buying funnel that you do not see returns on searches that use them. In this case, you can put the early buying funnel keywords in a Budget Optimizer campaign with a branding budget, and then let AdWords maximize your traffic. For the other keywords for which you are receiving conversions and want to control the bids, leave them in a max CPC or Conversion Optimizer campaign.

If you use both a Budget Optimizer and a max CPC campaign to separate out keywords based on where they are in the buying funnel, make sure that the max CPC set for the Budget Optimizer campaign is lower than the max CPCs you are setting in your max CPC–based campaign. If your Budget Optimizer campaign uses broad matched keywords and has higher bids than your ROI-based campaign, a Budget Optimizer ad could be shown instead of your ROI-based ad. Since the Budget Optimizer ad is meant to get someone to enter your funnel, its value is less for someone who is already in the buying funnel who searches for a keyword in your max CPC campaign. Hence, you should never want to pay more for a Budget Optimizer keyword to show instead of a max CPC keyword where you are bidding on an ROI or profit basis.

Conversion Optimizer The second option, Focus On Conversions, is known as the Conversion Optimizer. To enable the Conversion Optimizer, the campaign must be using the AdWords conversion tracking script and must have at least 15 conversions in the past 30 days.

If you meet the criteria and want to use the Conversion Optimizer, then you will enter a cost per action (CPA). AdWords will adjust the bids for your keywords in attempting to meet your cost per action. You will still be charged on a cost per click basis. You will not just pay for actions. However, AdWords has access to many data points that you do not, and they will use this information, along with other information gathered, to manipulate your bids to try to maximize the conversions you receive for your target CPA.

Unfortunately, you cannot enter different CPAs for different conversions you have defined. For instance, in the earlier plumber example, the plumber was willing to pay different prices for a phone call that led to a small job versus a kitchen remodeling job. However, with the Conversion Optimizer, you can only define a single CPA. Therefore, you might have to separate out keywords into different campaigns based on your goals. For instance, the plumber could put the kitchen remodeling keywords in one campaign with a CPA of $100 and the pipe repair keywords in another campaign with a CPA of $25.

While companies have found great success with the Conversion Optimizer, the biggest drawback many companies find is that while Conversion Optimizer hit their target CPA, their total conversions dropped. Therefore, if you want to test out the Conversion Optimizer but do not want to turn over your entire budget to it, follow these steps:

1. Use the AdWords Editor to duplicate the campaign you want to test.

2. Split your budget among the two campaigns. If you are an aggressive tester, give the new campaign half your budget. If you are a conservative tester, only give it a quarter or less of your budget.

3. In the new campaign, set max CPC bids and try to maximize your conversions.

4. In the old campaign, turn on Conversion Optimizer and let Google take over your bidding.

5. After a few weeks, see who has the better results.

If you have a campaign that is doing very well right now, then instead of turning on the Conversion Optimizer in your established campaign, wait for the new campaign to reach at least 15 conversions and then test the Conversion Optimizer in the new campaign. This will help mitigate the risk of putting your current profits in jeopardy if the Budget Optimizer does not perform well for your campaigns.

This is one of the few times when it is okay to compete with yourself. Rarely do you want to let Google choose which keyword they should show from your account. Much of optimizing AdWords is taking control from Google so you know that when someone does a search they will see the exact combination of a keyword, ad copy, and destination URL you choose. In this case, you are testing bidding methods that can only be set at the campaign level. Therefore, it is okay to compete with yourself for a few weeks until you can determine which bidding methodology will work best.

Focus On Impressions The first three bidding methodologies can be used on both the search and the content network. However, this option will only be displayed if your campaign is only shown on the content network. When you choose Focus On Impressions, you are setting cost per thousand impression (CPM) bids. Please refer to the "Choosing CPM or CPC Bidding" section in Chapter 9 to learn more about CPM bidding methods.

When using Budget Optimizer or Conversion Optimizer, you should always measure profit and examine if those methods are helping your reach your goals. If you are using max CPC bidding, by far the most common method, then you need a strategy to set your bids based on your goals.

Profitable Bidding Strategies

If you are using max CPC bidding, you need to set your own bids. We will walk through some strategies for setting bids. There are a few different places in your account where you should set bids:

- Ad group for search
- Ad group for content
- Keyword for search
- Placement for content

If you set both keyword and ad group bids, the keyword bid will be used for search. If you set placement and ad group content bids, then if the user is on that placement, the placement bid will be used. If the user clicks on a content ad that you have not placement targeted, the content ad group bid will be used.

To maximize your bidding control, use placement and keyword bids. If you have many ad groups, you can set ad group level bids, and not keyword level bids. However, please note that you might find that similar keywords in the same ad group lead to different returns for your ad spend. While you can take the shortcut of setting ad group bids instead of keyword bids, if you want to maximize your bidding strategies, you should use keyword level bids.

Regardless of where you decide to set bids, these strategies apply to any of the four places you want to set bids.

ROI vs. Profit

In several of our bidding strategies, we will use ROI calculations to set bids. However, it is always worth noting that maximizing your ROI does not always maximize your profits. Hence, we will look at a strategy to maximize profits as well.

ROI is easy to calculate. The formula is ROI = profit / spend.

A 100 percent ROI is breaking even. A 200 percent ROI means for every dollar you spend, you make two dollars. A 50 percent ROI means for every dollar you spend, you make 50 cents.

For example, let's examine a company that sells both chocolates and flowers. Chocolates are less competitive than flowers, and therefore the CPC is less. However, flowers have a higher average sale than chocolates, and therefore, there is a potential for more profits. More profits do not always mean higher ROI.

Campaign	Average CPC	Conversion Rate	Cost per Conversion (Conversion Rate × Average CPC)	Profit per Conversion	ROI (Profit / Spend)	Profit per Sale (Profit – Cost per Conversion)
Chocolate	$1	10%	$10	$20	200%	$10
Flowers	$3	10%	$30	$50	166%	$20

In this example, the chocolate campaign has a higher ROI than flowers. Many companies would consider this the more successful campaign. However, the flowers campaign brings in more total profits each time it makes a sale. Other companies would consider this to be the more successful campaign. The success metrics can be correlated with your original goals, which can be modified whenever you learn more about your business or change your business direction.

ROI is an easy number to work with, and we will use it in several of our calculations throughout the next few sections. However, never forget to calculate profit. We will also examine a bidding strategy that focuses purely on profit.

Revenue per Click

Each time you attain a final business goal, there is revenue associated with the goal. With AdWords, you also pay each time someone clicks on your ad. Each click usually does not lead to revenue. It is a bundle of clicks that finally results in a conversion that leads to company revenues. When thinking about how much you should bid on a click, you should first calculate your breakeven point. This is easily determined by the metric revenue per click.

Determining Revenue per Click

To calculate revenue per click, simply divide the revenue that a keyword, placement, or ad group brought to your company by the number of clicks that same ad group, keyword, or placement received.

If a keyword received 100 clicks that led to $1,000 of revenue, then the revenue per click is $10 ($1,000 / 100 = $10).

If you are using AdWords conversion tracking and have associated revenue numbers with conversions, then you can easily gather this data from your AdWords reports.

When you run a report that includes conversion columns, check the box next to Conv. Value/Click (Figure 13.7).

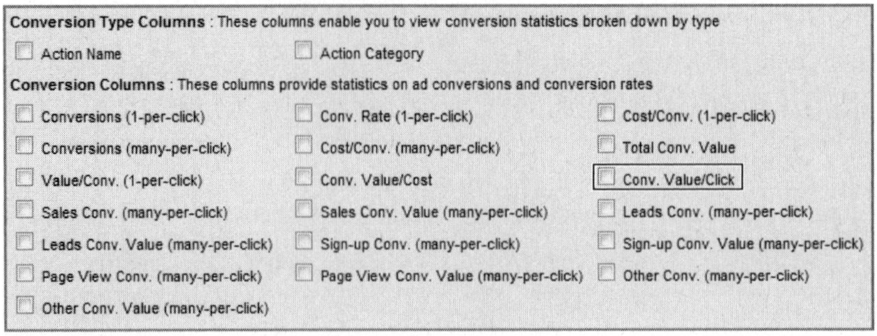

Figure 13.7 Include Conv. Value/Click when running AdWords reports.

Google will then divide how much revenue a data point received (for AdWords reports, this could be ad copy, ad group, keyword, campaign, placements, etc.) by the number of clicks that same data point received. Understanding your value per click will help you easily gain insight into your marketing effectiveness. It is one of the best metrics to work with inside your account.

To simplify the explanations, we are going to just look at keywords throughout the next several reports and mathematical calculations. However, please note that instead of keywords, these reports could be showing you data at the placement, ad group search, ad group content, keyword, or landing page level.

Once you run the keyword report including the value per click information, you should have an Excel file that shows your keywords, the number of clicks, conversions, total value, and value per click for those items (Figure 13.8).

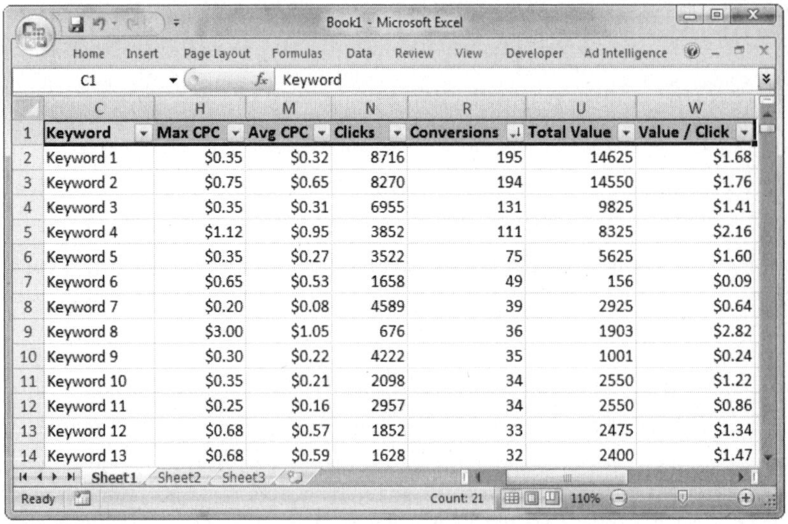

	C	H	M	N	R	U	W
1	Keyword	Max CPC	Avg CPC	Clicks	Conversions	Total Value	Value / Click
2	Keyword 1	$0.35	$0.32	8716	195	14625	$1.68
3	Keyword 2	$0.75	$0.65	8270	194	14550	$1.76
4	Keyword 3	$0.35	$0.31	6955	131	9825	$1.41
5	Keyword 4	$1.12	$0.95	3852	111	8325	$2.16
6	Keyword 5	$0.35	$0.27	3522	75	5625	$1.60
7	Keyword 6	$0.65	$0.53	1658	49	156	$0.09
8	Keyword 7	$0.20	$0.08	4589	39	2925	$0.64
9	Keyword 8	$3.00	$1.05	676	36	1903	$2.82
10	Keyword 9	$0.30	$0.22	4222	35	1001	$0.24
11	Keyword 10	$0.35	$0.21	2098	34	2550	$1.22
12	Keyword 11	$0.25	$0.16	2957	34	2550	$0.86
13	Keyword 12	$0.68	$0.57	1852	33	2475	$1.34
14	Keyword 13	$0.68	$0.59	1628	32	2400	$1.47

Figure 13.8 Excel report showing keyword value per click data

Clarifying Data with Conditional Formatting

If you have a large account, this is the point where you can easily become overwhelmed by data. There is another Excel function, called conditional formatting, which can turn large spreadsheets into visual references.

The basic use of conditional formatting allows you to highlight cells if they meet certain conditions. To use conditional formatting in Excel 2007, on the Home ribbon tab, click on Conditional Formatting and choose the type of rule you want to create (Figure 13.9). Then select the cells and the formatting you want to apply to those cells.

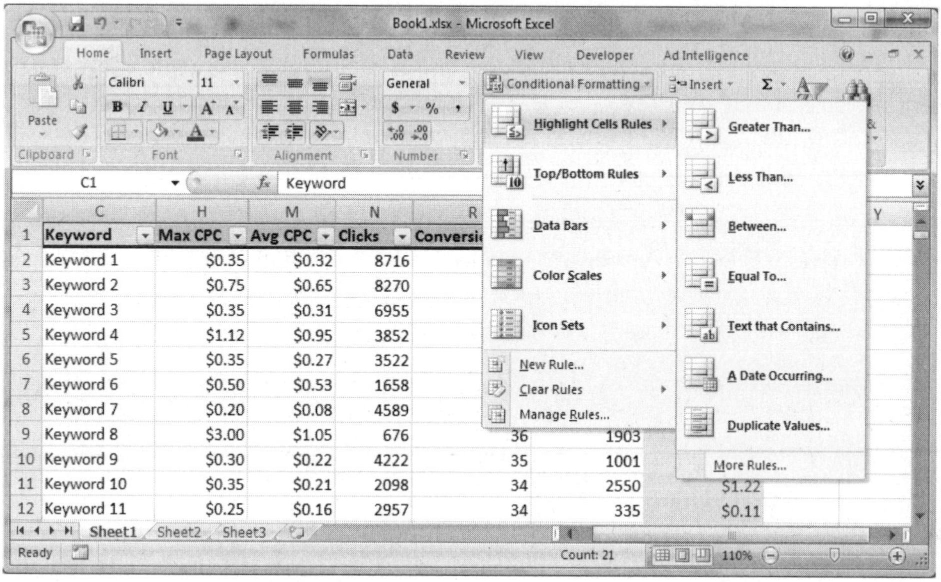

Figure 13.9 Creating conditional formatting rules

Use these conditional formatting rules to create a visual reference to see how various keywords, ad groups, and placements are performing:

Red *The value per click is lower than the average CPC.* The first rule you should create is to determine where you are losing money. Since value per click is your breakeven point, if your average cost per click is higher than your value per click, every time you receive a click, you lose money.

Orange *The estimated first page bid is higher than the value per click.* To receive first page exposure across all geographies where you are advertising, your maximum cost per click needs to be higher than the first page bid. When the value per click is lower than your first page bid estimate, these keywords can never be on page 1 profitably. This is a good place to do some testing to see if you can raise the value of those keywords.

Yellow *The value per click is higher than the average CPC, but lower than the max CPC.* When your value per click is higher than your average CPC, you make money on each click. However, if your value per click is also lower than your max CPC, then you could start to lose money on this keyword without changing the bid. These keywords need to be watched to see if they start losing you money. They are also good keywords to test to see if you can raise the value per click by testing different ad copy and landing pages.

Brown *The value per click is higher than the average CPC and first page bid estimate, but the max CPC is below the first page bid estimate.* These are words that are profitable as the value per click is higher than the average CPC. These words would also be profitable on page 1 as the value per click is higher than the first page bid. However, because the max CPC is below the first page bid, these words are not receiving first page exposure. These are good words on which to bid so that they receive page 1 exposure since they will be profitable at those positions.

Green *The value per click is higher than the max CPC, and the max CPC is higher than the first page bid.* These keywords are on page 1 and are making you money each time you receive a click. While you might adjust the bids so they receive more exposure or set bids based on ROI, they are not words that are currently losing you money.

By using these conditional formatting rules, you can transform large spreadsheets into visual reference charts that allow you to understand how your keywords, ad copy, landing pages, ad groups, or placements are performing.

Taking Margins into Account

Value per click only takes total revenue into account. This metric does not take margins into account. If you have hard costs, such as an e-commerce company that has to buy the products they are selling, then you need to move beyond value per click to look at profit per click.

If you are a lead generation company without hard costs of goods, then your value per click is usually your profit per click and you do not need to do any additional calculations.

There are a few ways to take margins into account so that you are setting bids based on actual profits. The most accurate method is to use Google's API or a third-party vendor to incorporate your backend system with AdWords so that you can see exactly which keywords are selling which products and then determine the margins automatically.

This is a costly solution, but the most accurate. We will examine a lower-tech approach that any company, regardless of budget, can incorporate.

First of all, your ad groups should consist of very closely related keywords. In this approach, you should create ad groups that only promote a specific product or closely related products with similar margins. For instance, let us assume these are the products you sell:

Keyword	Margin
iPod nano	25%
iPod touch	35%
Microsoft Zune	30%
Creative ZEN	20%
Sony Walkman	20%

Your best organization would be to group each of these keywords and their closely related variations (such as "pink iPod nano," "8GB iPod nano") together to form ad groups. However, if you have a tremendous amount of items, that organization is not always possible. In that case, the only two items you should combine into a single ad group would be the Creative Zen and the Sony Walkman because they have the same margins.

Note: From a conversion rate standpoint, this is not a good organization as you would want different ad copy and landing pages for these products. This is for illustration purposes only, so you can examine how to incorporate margins into your reports.

To create reports that include margin data, follow these steps:

1. Make a list of all your ad groups in Excel. The easiest way to get such a list is to run an ad group report or export your account from the AdWords editor.

2. In another column, list your margins for the product that the ad group should sell, just like in the earlier table.

3. When you run a report from AdWords, add a new column for margins. Then incorporate your margin data into the AdWords report using the VLookUp function.

4. Create an additional column called Profit per Click, and populate this column by multiplying your value per click times your margin (Figure 13.10).

5. Finally, use the above conditional formatting rules on the Profit per Click column instead of the Value /Click column. This will give you a visual reference of your actual profits.

Instead of applying margins at the ad group level, you could incorporate margins at the keyword level. However, determining your margins for each keyword could be so many man-hours of work that it might be cheaper to incorporate your backend system into a third-party vendor or utilize the AdWords API.

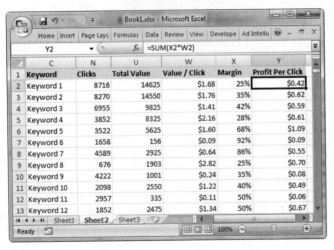

Figure 13.10 Taking margins into account when examining performance

This low-tech approach should be directionally accurate. However, what you will find is that some of your sales are for completely unrelated items. You will find that someone searches for an iPod and buys a plasma TV. Or someone searches for a plasma TV and buys a 10-cent pencil. Using this margin approach is better than not understanding how your profits are derived whatsoever, but it will be inaccurate at times.

How Can Publishers Determine Revenue per Click?

The metric that publishers, such as newspapers, should track is revenue per visitor (RPV). Sometimes RPV is calculated by individual user, and other times by 1,000 visitors, similar to CPM.

Most publishers have two main revenue opportunities. One is to sell ads on their site and the second is subscriptions. To calculate your revenue per visitor, you first need to find how much you make on any page view.

For instance, if a publisher sells $50 CPM ads (meaning an advertiser is willing to pay $50 for 1,000 page views), then each individual page view is worth $0.05 ($50 / 1,000). If a publisher has three ad display units on a page, then the page view is actually worth $0.15.

Once you understand how much you make on any single page view, the second step is to calculate average page views per visit. For our analysis, let us assume the average visitor sees three pages. By multiplying the average page views (3) times the RPV ($0.15), we can see that by getting a visitor to the site, the publisher makes $0.45. Average page views will vary by traffic source and by keyword.

The secondary metric to track is subscriptions. For ease of analysis, let us assume that one out of every 100 visitors buys a subscription for $10 per month. A subscription is not a one-time purchase. A publisher should then track how long someone is paying for a subscription. Our example newspaper finds that when someone buys a subscription, that user pays the newspaper for 10 months. Therefore, a one-time sale is actually a $100 lifetime value. At a 1 percent conversion rate, that means that the publisher makes $1 per visitor ($100 purchase × 1 percent conversion rate) when tracking subscription revenue.

Combining RPV and Subscription Revenue

You can take this even further and look at the number of page views per subscriber per month. For ease of calculation, let's say this newspaper finds that subscribers see 100 page views per month. When we calculate RPV ($0.15) times page views per month (100) times the number of months someone is a subscriber (10), we find that the actual subscriber is worth $150 over their lifetime. This is the lifetime RPV.

Adding the lifetime RPV ($150) to the lifetime subscription value ($100), we end up with a $250 product. Since only 1 percent of searchers is buying a subscription, the actual value per click for subscription conversions is $2.50: $250 (product value) × 1 percent (conversion rate) = $2.50.

When we add the original RPV ($0.45) and the lifetime subscription price value per click ($2.50) of each visitor together, we see that the newspaper on average makes $2.95 per visitor. Therefore, $2.95 is their actual lifetime value per click.

That value per click number is for all keywords and traffic sources combined. A publisher might find that one keyword leads to 10 page views per visit, but no subscriptions. Another keyword might lead to a 10 percent subscription rate, but only three page views. To set bids at the ad group, keyword, content, and placement level, you will want to be able to calculate those values for each data point.

Tracking Conversions in AdWords

The easiest way to view this data in AdWords so that you can see value per click by keyword, landing page, and ad copy is to use the AdWords conversion tracker. In the AdWords conversion tracker, set up one script that tracks page views. In the value column, you will enter $0.15 (the value per page view). Put this script on each page of your website. Then set up a second script that goes on the "Thank you for subscribing" page. In the subscription script, for the total value, enter $250, the lifetime value of a subscriber.

Technically, the most accurate number would come from tracking average subscription length and page views per subscriber by traffic source to adjust that $250 lifetime value appropriately based on actual data. To get to that level of tracking, you will need to incorporate your own tracking system, as that information cannot be gathered from AdWords alone. However, this is a good place to start to examine how profitable each keyword or placement is to your bottom line.

Once you have incorporated these tracking scripts, when you run an AdWords report, you can see the revenue associated with each keyword as a publisher. In the section "Calculating Your Max CPC," you will use this revenue per click number to set appropriate bids for each keyword, ad group, or placement based on actual revenue.

Tracking Long Sales Cycles with Conversion Funnels

Many companies do not make a final sale off their first conversion activity. If you are in a business-to-business environment, or selling high-end products, you may find that it takes several contacts with a user before you finally sell a product. In cases of multiple touch points, you need to build a conversion funnel to understand what each keyword and lead is worth to your company.

Let us look at a fictional company called RSI, which integrates BlackBerry mobile devices with Microsoft Exchange and a company's internal instant messaging desktop applications. This is a complex procedure, and their service is expensive; their average enterprise customer spends $100,000 per integration. RSI finds that they never make a sale from a single phone call. They need multiple touch points to move a corporation through the buying funnel before the customer finally signs a contract and writes them a check.

After some analysis, RSI builds a conversion funnel with five steps:

1. Buy clicks to their website from AdWords.

2. Offer those searchers a free whitepaper download. To receive the download, you must enter your contact information.

3. Invite everyone who downloads their whitepaper to a free webinar that showcases their product.

4. Call each person who attended their webinar to attempt to sell them a product.

5. Make a final sale for $100,000.

As RSI exists for illustration purposes only, you may find that you need to add more steps to your own conversion funnel, such as in-person demos.

RSI tracks the conversion rates from clicks to whitepaper downloads. As that action occurs on the Web, they can easily use the AdWords conversion tracking to see the percentage of downloads by keyword or placement to determine how much they are paying for a download. However, a download does not lead to revenues for the company; it just introduces a searcher to their buying funnel. Therefore, RSI needs to do some math and offline tracking to determine what an actual click is worth.

Buy Clicks to Their Website from AdWords RSI finds that they are currently paying an average $10 a click from AdWords. We can do this entire analysis at the keyword, landing page, or placement level. For now, we will keep it simple to illustrate how to analyze a conversion funnel. RSI buys 1,000 clicks at $10 a click, so their initial investment is $10,000.

Offer Those Searchers a Free Whitepaper Download Their whitepaper download conversion rate is a fantastic 25 percent. Of those 1,000 clicks, they have received 250 downloads. Therefore, they have paid $40 per download ($10,000 / 250 = $40).

Invite Everyone Who Downloads Their Whitepaper to a Free Webinar It seems those who like a free download also like free webinars. Forty percent of those who download the whitepaper attend their webinar. They receive 100 viewers of their webinar (250 downloads × 40% conversion rate). They have essentially paid $100 to have someone attend their webinar ($10,000 in clicks / 100 attendees).

Call Each Person Who Attended Their Webinar to Attempt to Sell Them a Product The sales team manages to get 10 percent of the webinar attendees on the phone. Doing some math, we can see that the cost per phone call contact is $1,000 ($10,000 in clicks / 10 phone calls = $1,000).

Make a Final Sale for $100,000 Of those 10 phone calls, the sales team makes one sale for $100,000. Now that we have a sale, we can finally calculate the ROI of that sale and the value per click. ROI is profit / spend. $100,000 profit / $10,000 spend = 1,000 percent ROI. While most e-commerce companies would love a 1,000 percent ROI, often in a B2B environment that ROI is necessary, as you have a large team making a single sale based on the customer touch points.

RSI is a savvy company, so they do not automatically assume that their ROI is actually 1,000 percent. They do some math and realize that, based on the time invested in paying sales reps, emailing customers, and conducting webinars, it cost them $50,000 in overhead to make that sale. Therefore, their actual profit is $40,000: $100,000 (total cost) – $10,000 (in clicks) – $50,000 (overhead) = $40,000.

By dividing the final profit ($40,000) by the number of clicks (1,000), they come to realize that their value per click is $40.

It can be useful to put these steps into a visual reference chart (Figure 13.11) so you can see the chain of events.

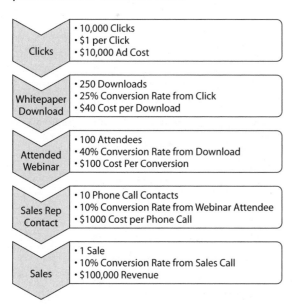

Figure 13.11 RSI conversion funnel

If RSI wanted to optimize their ability to sell their product, their first step should not actually be examining their AdWords account. Before a salesperson attempts to contact a business, the business has opted into two steps (whitepaper download, webinar attendance) with RSI. A 10 percent phone call contact rate to a company that has gone through only two steps of engagement is quite low.

RSI should examine how their sales reps are contacting companies and also examine the sales scripts. If their contact rate went to 20 percent, the company would have made another sale, leading to much higher profits than testing ad copy that led to another 5 percent of visitors. That does not mean RSI should not test ad copy, it just means if you have a full picture of your conversion funnel, you can spend your time making the biggest impact for your company. Once the phone call contact rate has been fixed, then RSI should work on optimizing their AdWords account.

Calculating Your Max CPC

There are two main ways to perform calculations to determine your bids. One is to bid based on your ROI. Setting ROI bids is preferred by many companies as it lets them build in a buffer of a higher ROI so they do not have to calculate such items as payroll, rent, and so forth.

The second method is to set bids by profits. When we examine this bid method, we are not going to take into account your lighting bill. We are going to try to maximize the profit that your account generates as if it operated in a vacuum from your typical operating costs.

Setting Bids Based on ROI

The difficult part of bidding is not setting bids. The difficult part in determining bids is understanding your revenue. Once you have determined the revenue for each keyword, ad group, or placement, setting a bid based on ROI is quite easy. There are a few different formulas you can use based on the information you have available to you.

In this section, we are going to use value per click, revenue per click, and profit per conversion, which is information you can ascertain from your AdWords reports (as we discussed in the section "Revenue per Click").

If you know your profit and conversion rates, you can use this method. For the keyword "chocolate," here are the metrics:

- Profit per conversion: $25

- Desired ROI: 200%

- Conversion rate: 10%

The basic formula for setting bids based on profits is:

- (Profit per conversion / desired ROI) × (conversion rate) = max CPC

- ($25 / 200%) × 10% = $1.25

- This can also be expressed by: ($25 / 2) × 0.1 = $1.25

If you know your value or revenue per click and do not have a margin, then you can use this information to set a bid:

- Value or revenue per click: $2.50
- Desired ROI: 200%

In this case, you can use the formula:

- Value per click / desired ROI = max CPC
- 2.50 / 200% = $1.25 is the max CPC

If you know your value or revenue per click, but you have a margin, then you need to go through two steps in calculating your max CPC. In this example, the metrics are:

- Value per click: $2
- Margin: 50%
- Desired ROI: 200%

The first step is to calculate the breakeven point:

- Value per click × margin = breakeven CPC
- $2 × 50% = $1

The second step is to calculate the bid from the breakeven CPC:

- Breakeven CPC / desired ROI = max CPC
- $1 / 200% = $0.50

Easily Make Multiple Bid Changes

Since setting bids by ROI is a simple calculation, you can build the formula in an Excel spreadsheet and calculate a bid by placement, keyword, or ad group. Once you have a spreadsheet that contains your bids, use the bulk import feature in the AdWords Editor to quickly make all your bid changes. After you import your existing keywords, ad groups, or placements with your new CPCs, post those changes to your AdWords account. Making bulk bid changes with Excel and the AdWords Editor will save you a tremendous amount of time.

The preceding formulas work for setting keyword bids, ad group bids, content ad groups bids, or placement bids. If you want to bid by ROI, regardless of where you want to set those bids, the same formulas apply. ROI is a very simple metric to use for setting bids. However, if you are more concerned with total profit, there is another way to set bids based on the profits you make from each keyword, ad group, or placement, based on bid simulator data.

Understanding the Bid Simulator

The bid simulator shows you a projection of the number of impressions, clicks, CPC, and costs you would see if you raised or lowered your bid for a particular keyword.

To access the bid simulator, navigate to the keywords in your account and look for the graph icon next to the max CPC (Figure 13.12).

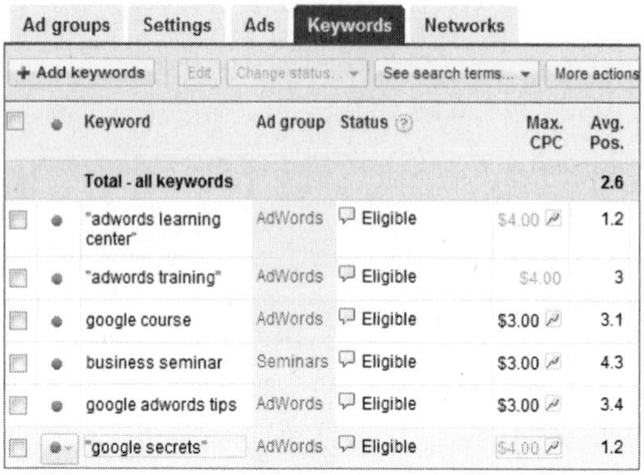

Figure 13.12 Accessing the bid simulator

Not all keywords will show the graph icon. If Google does not have enough data to project how many impressions and clicks you will receive at different CPCs, you will not see a graph. If you have a campaign that constantly hits its daily budget, you may not see the icon, as raising the CPC of one keyword might not get more impressions since other words are also using a percentage of your daily budget.

Once you find a keyword where the graph exists, click on the graph and you will be able to see projected clicks, cost, and impressions by different CPCs (Figure 13.13).

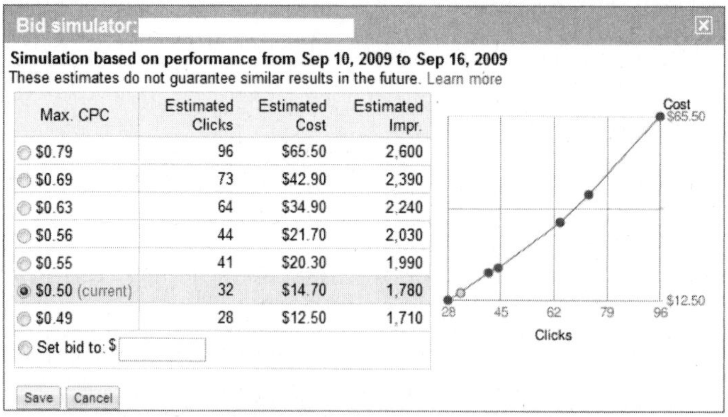

Figure 13.13 Projected changes by max CPC

Google refreshes this data daily, but changes in quality score, competitor's bids, or search behavior can cause these numbers to become inaccurate. You should use them for guidance purposes only and not rely on them as absolutes. However, these numbers can help you set bids based on profits and not just ROI.

Setting Bids Based on Profits

If you are trying to maximize your profits and not bid just on an ROI basis, you can use the bid simulator's information to walk through an exercise that determines what bid price is the most profitable.

The first step is to build a spreadsheet with these columns:

Column	Value
A	Max CPC from the bid simulator
B	Number of clicks from the bid simulator
C	Cost of the clicks from the bid simulator
D	Your conversion rate for the keyword from AdWords reports
E	The number of sales received: Conversion rate (Column D) times the number of clicks (Column B)
F	Revenue: The average revenue per sale associated with the keyword (from AdWords reports or your internal data)
G	Profit: Revenue (Column F) minus cost (Column C)

In the spreadsheet shown in Figure 13.14, I added some additional columns for illustration purposes:

Column	Value
H	Revenue per click: Revenue (Column F) divided by clicks (Column B)
I	Value per click: Profit (Column G) divided by clicks (Column B)
J	ROI: Profit (Column G) divided by cost (Column C)

When you have completed this exercise, you will have a spreadsheet that shows you the profit by max CPC (Figure 13.14) for a particular keyword.

Max CPC	Clicks	Cost	Conversion Rate	Number of Sales	Revenue ($25/Sale)	Profit	Revenue/ Click	Value/ Click	ROI
$1.75	1300	$1,690	10%	130	$3,250.00	$1,560.00	$2.50	$1.20	192%
$1.50	1250	$1,450	10%	125	$3,125.00	$1,675.00	$2.50	$1.34	216%
$1.25	1000	$1,150	10%	100	$2,500.00	$1,350.00	$2.50	$1.35	217%
$0.79	960	$651	10%	96	$2,400.00	$1,749.50	$2.50	$1.82	369%
$0.69	730	$421	10%	73	$1,825.00	$1,404.10	$2.50	$1.92	434%
$0.63	640	$341	10%	64	$1,600.00	$1,259.10	$2.50	$1.97	469%
$0.56	440	$217	10%	44	$1,100.00	$883.00	$2.50	$2.01	507%
$0.55	410	$200	10%	41	$1,025.00	$824.70	$2.50	$2.01	512%
$0.50	320	$147	10%	32	$800.00	$653.00	$2.50	$2.04	544%
$0.49	280	$125	10%	28	$700.00	$575.00	$2.50	$2.05	560%

Figure 13.14 Profit by max CPC

This example is for a $25 software download. Since there are no hard costs of goods for a download, the revenue per sale is the same as the profit per sale. If you have margins, take those into account when determining revenue per sale, and use your actual revenue per sale in Column F. In addition, this company has found that they have a 10 percent conversion rate on this keyword.

Upon examining this spreadsheet, we can see that our ROI is highest when the bid is low. However, low bids lead to fewer clicks and therefore fewer sales and less profit. When the bid is too high, our ROI is negative as our value per click is lower than our average CPC. As ROI is a percentage, a high versus low percentage gives you an indication as to your returns, but not to your actual profits.

Since value per click is dependent on both the number of clicks and the actual sales, the metric does not take into account volume of sales. It only takes into account what any one click is worth to your company's revenues.

Therefore, if you are trying to maximize your profits, often the highest ROI or highest value per click is not the best number to work from when setting your bids. In this spreadsheet, we can see that the $0.79 bid leads to more total profit than any other bids.

This calculation is also for a single sale. If you find that on average your visitor buys from you multiple times per year, you should use those metrics instead. For instance, if we found that this company sells three downloads per year to the customer at $25 per download, then the numbers completely change (Figure 13.15).

	A	B	C	D	E	F	G	H	I	J
1	Max CPC	Clicks	Cost	Conversion Rate	Number of Sales	Revenue ($75/Year)	Profit	Revenue/ Click	Value/ Click	ROI
2	$1.75	1300	$1,690	10%	130	$9,750.00	$8,060.00	$7.50	$6.20	477%
3	$1.50	1250	$1,450	10%	125	$9,375.00	$7,925.00	$7.50	$6.34	547%
4	$1.25	1000	$1,150	10%	100	$7,500.00	$6,350.00	$7.50	$6.35	552%
5	$0.79	960	$651	10%	96	$7,200.00	$6,549.50	$7.50	$6.82	1007%
6	$0.69	730	$421	10%	73	$5,475.00	$5,054.10	$7.50	$6.92	1201%
7	$0.63	640	$341	10%	64	$4,800.00	$4,459.10	$7.50	$6.97	1308%
8	$0.56	440	$217	10%	44	$3,300.00	$3,083.00	$7.50	$7.01	1421%
9	$0.55	410	$200	10%	41	$3,075.00	$2,874.70	$7.50	$7.01	1435%
10	$0.50	320	$147	10%	32	$2,400.00	$2,253.00	$7.50	$7.04	1533%

Figure 13.15 Lifetime revenue at $75 per sale

Suddenly, this company cannot buy enough clicks. They would be willing to pay more than any of the bid simulator's suggestions as their profits keep rising the more they pay and the more customers they can aggregate. However, once you are always in position 1, raising your bid does not give you a higher position on search.

If you find yourself in this scenario, then your next move should be to test ad copy to see if you can make better use of the inventory. For instance, if you could raise your average click-through rate by a few percentage points while still maintaining the same conversion rate, you would receive even more profit.

There are many times when position 1 might not bring in the most profits, and calculating profits by various bids can lead you to the most profitable bid for your company. There are other times when you cannot buy enough clicks, as a keyword is just working well for you; in those cases, start testing various ad copy to bring more visitors to your website from that same keyword, and then try to improve conversion rates.

However, if you find that certain positions bring in more profits, you can use the position preference feature to inform Google in which positions you would like your ad to show.

Position Preference: Controlling Where Your Ad Is Displayed

Position preference allows you to set a keyword to show in a desired ad position or range of ad positions in a search result. If you find that you have better conversion rates in certain ad positions, or you want to protect your trademark terms by only showing in the top positions, you can use the position preference feature to have your ad show in those desired positions.

Position preference is enabled at the campaign level. Navigate to your campaign settings and enable position preference (Figure 13.16).

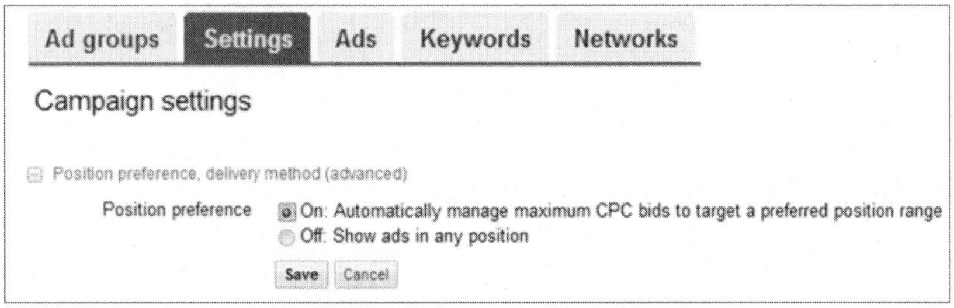

Figure 13.16 Enable position preference

Once position preference is enabled, you can navigate to your keywords and choose the positions in which you want your keywords to show (Figure 13.17).

If you do not set a position preference for a keyword, the keyword will be shown normally. You set both the top and bottom position where you want a keyword to be shown.

With position preference, you will never be shown below your desired position. That means that if you choose positions 1 to 1 (1 highest and 1 lowest), your ad will only be shown in position 1. However, that does not mean that your ad will appear in the top position. You must still have the highest ad rank (quality score times max CPC) of all the ads being shown for your ad to appear in that position. If your ad rank for a search would have shown your ad in position 2, yet you choose to only show your ad in position 1, then your ad would not show at all.

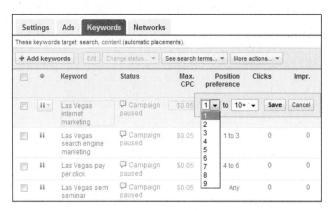

Figure 13.17 Setting position preference for a keyword

How Average Position Is Calculated

Average position is the average of all the positions your ad was shown in for a given time frame. If you have 10 impressions at position 1, and 10 impression at position 5, then your average position for that keyword would be 3.5. In the scenario where you only choose position 1, all the impressions you would have accrued in position 5 will be gone—your ad will not appear in that position at all. When you enable position preference, you should watch your metrics for how many impressions you lose.

While you will never be shown below your desired position, you could be shown above it. If there are three advertisers in an auction, and all three set their position preference at 3 or lower, then someone has to be shown in the first two positions before position 3 can exist.

With position preference, Google will charge you the CPC for the position where your ad was actually displayed. For instance, if you currently have the highest ad rank, then your ad would show in position 1. If you then set position preference so your ad will only be displayed in positions 3 to 5, and then your ad is shown in position 3, Google will only charge you the position 3 CPC, not the position 1 CPC. To review how actual CPC is calculated by position, please see Chapter 7, "Determining Actual CPC from Quality Score."

The most common usage of position preference is brand protection. Consider a company like Toyota: they may rather an ad not show on a page when someone searches for Toyota Prius if it means their Prius ad will show below a Ford Taurus ad. In cases like this, you can set your branded terms to highest position 1 and lowest position 1. Then the ad would either be shown in the top position or not shown at all on a search page.

Determining Conversion Rate by Position

If you find that you have different conversion rates by position, you may want to enable position preference so that your ad is shown in those positions. The easiest way to see conversion rates by position is to use Google Analytics.

In Google Analytics, navigate to Traffic Sources, then AdWords, then Keyword Positions. You can then look at all of your keywords and conversion rates by position (Figure 13.18).

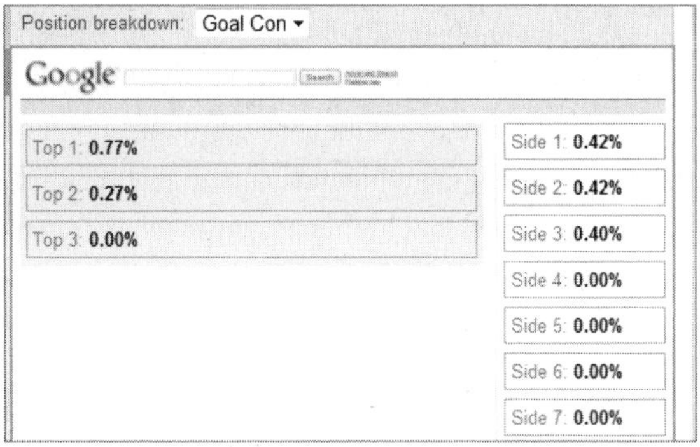

Figure 13.18   Google Analytics keyword conversion rate by position

Please do not see a trend where it does not exist. Many companies will not see any difference in conversion rate by position. You may only have a handful of keywords that have different conversion rates by position. When enabling position preference, make sure you have a clear trend of statistical significance before using position preference.

Conversion Rates Do Not Vary by Position

According to a Google blog post, Google does not see dramatic changes in conversion rates by position. When all of the factors are taken into account, there is less than a 5 percent difference in conversion rates by position. For instance, if your best position has a 1 percent conversion rate, your worst position should have a 0.95 percent conversion rate.

There are always exceptions to every rule. On an aggregate basis across transactional, navigational, informational, early buying funnel, and late buying funnel searches, Google's statement is easy to believe. However, you may find some exceptions among various keywords. It is important to understand how this feature works, especially for brand protection, but until you have all the basics of your account in working order, do not spend too much time on position preference.

To read more about Google's study, please visit http://adwords.blogspot.com/2009/08/conversion-rates-dont-vary-much-with-ad.html.

While conversion rates might not vary dramatically by position, you will often find different conversion rates by time of day or day of the week. Throughout the day, week, and month, search behavior changes and these changes lead to variations in conversion rates. To take advantage of these changes in search behavior, you can enable ad scheduling to automatically change your bid prices based on the changes in conversion rates.

Ad Scheduling: Automatically Changing Bids by Time Periods

Ad scheduling allows you to control what days of the week and times of the day your ads are shown. In addition, you can automatically change bids by a percentage higher or lower depending on the time of day or the day of the week. This feature is also called *day parting* in many circles.

Ad scheduling is enabled at the campaign level, and therefore it affects every ad group in your campaign. To enable ad scheduling, navigate to your campaign settings and click the Edit button next to Ad Scheduling (Figure 13.19).

Figure 13.19 Enable ad scheduling

Clicking the Edit button will bring up an interface where you can set exactly when you want your ads to show (Figure 13.20). The basic version of ad scheduling allows you to turn your ads on or off by time of day or day of the week.

The most important thing to note about ad scheduling is that the ads are shown based on your account's time zone. It is not based on the user's time zone. If you have an older account and have not adjusted the settings, your account is most likely in GMT −8 or Pacific Standard Time (PST). In the bottom-right corner of Figure 13.20 you can see your account's time zone.

If your account and target geography are not in the same time zone, then you need to manually adjust the times when your ad is displayed. There is a three hour time difference between PST and EST. If your account is in PST, and you want ads to be displayed from 8 a.m. to 5 p.m. in an EST location, such as New York City, then you would change your ad display by three hours. In this case, you would turn your ads on at 5 a.m. and turn them back off at 2 p.m.

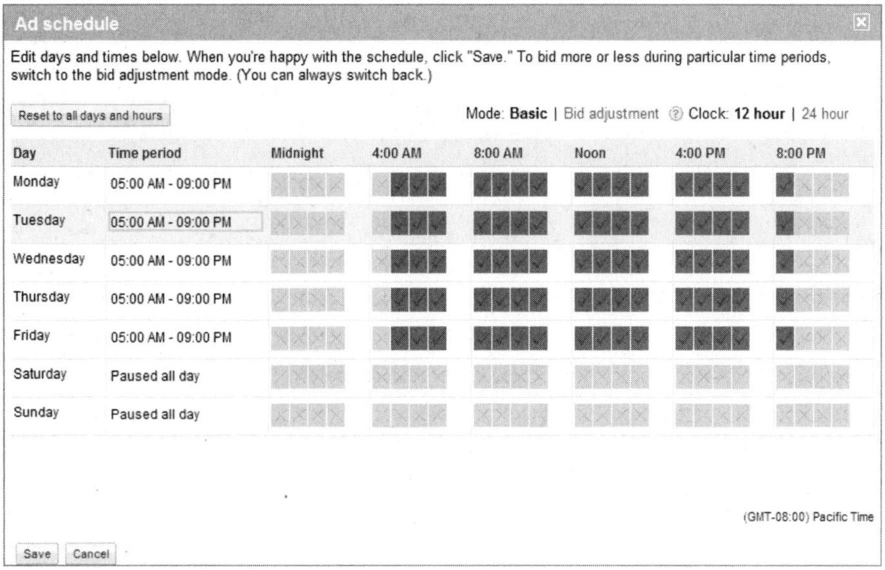

Figure 13.20 Turn ads on or off by day of the week or time of the day.

The advanced use of ad scheduling is to adjust your bids by a percentage by time of day or day of the week. If you were a catering company, you might find that:

- Between midnight and 6:15 a.m., you receive few phone calls, yet some people are looking for your service; therefore, set your bids to 60 percent of normal.

- Between 6:15 a.m. and 9:00 a.m., those who hire you for the day are starting to filter into the office, and therefore you want to run your bids at a normal rate.

- Between 9:00 a.m. and 11:00 a.m., your calls skyrocket for businesses who want their lunch catered. In this case, you set your bids to 120 percent of normal. This will cause all the bids in your campaign to be increased by 20 percent.

- Between 11:00 a.m. and 1:00 p.m., you are delivering orders and do not have time to answer the phone. Therefore, you turn off your account during these hours.

- Between 1:00 p.m. and 5:00 p.m., some companies order catering for the next day, and therefore you set your bids to 100 percent of normal. These are the standard bids you set for your account.

- Between 5:00 p.m. to 8:00 p.m., you receive some orders, but the call volume is lower, therefore you set your bids to 80 percent of normal.

- Between 8:00 p.m. and midnight, call volume drops significantly, and therefore you only want to pay 60 percent of your normal click price.

If this is your scenario, then in the ad scheduling interface, you would first create this scenario for a single day (Figure 13.21).

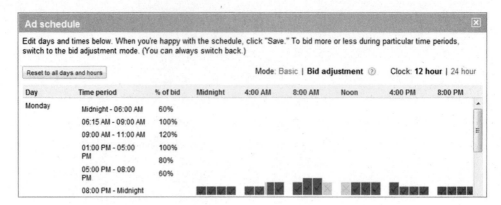

Figure 13.21 Catering company ad scheduling

After going through this exercise for a single day, you can use the interface to copy the schedule to the rest of the weekdays (Figure 13.22).

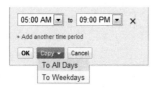

Figure 13.22 Copying ad scheduling data from one day to another

If you are trying to control costs, only run your ads when your conversion rates are highest. If you are trying to maximize returns, then examine when you receive conversions and change your bids based on that conversion activity.

How to Find Conversion Information by Time Frames

There are a few different methods you can use to extract conversion information by day or hour from Google products. You will need to use a combination of Google Analytics and AdWords reporting to see all the possible trend data.

Finding Day of the Week Conversion Information in AdWords Reports

Google AdWords allows you to see conversion information and most of your metrics by day of the week (Figure 13.23). In the Reporting menu, examine the unit of time under Settings.

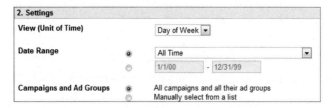

Figure 13.23 Viewing day of the week information in AdWords reports

In this example, I used an ad group report. However, you could see this information by keyword, placement, ad copy, and so on. The second step is to export the report to Excel and put the information into a pivot table (Figure 13.24). For ease of illustration, this information is not broken down into ad groups. However, you should examine this information on an ad group, keyword, or placement level.

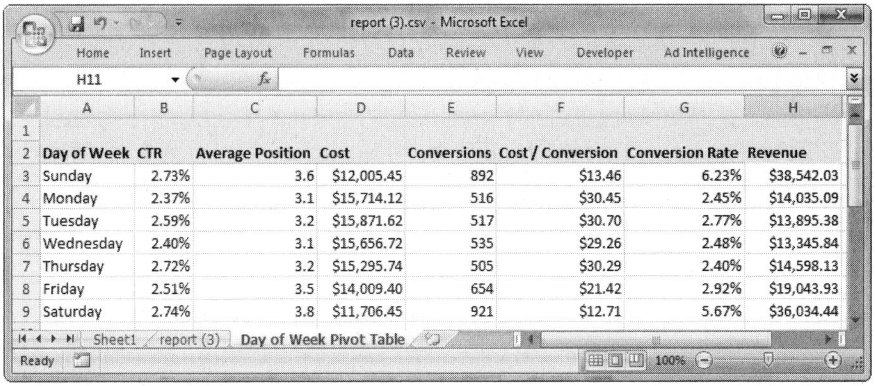

Day of Week	CTR	Average Position	Cost	Conversions	Cost / Conversion	Conversion Rate	Revenue
Sunday	2.73%	3.6	$12,005.45	892	$13.46	6.23%	$38,542.03
Monday	2.37%	3.1	$15,714.12	516	$30.45	2.45%	$14,035.09
Tuesday	2.59%	3.2	$15,871.62	517	$30.70	2.77%	$13,895.38
Wednesday	2.40%	3.1	$15,656.72	535	$29.26	2.48%	$13,345.84
Thursday	2.72%	3.2	$15,295.74	505	$30.29	2.40%	$14,598.13
Friday	2.51%	3.5	$14,009.40	654	$21.42	2.92%	$19,043.93
Saturday	2.74%	3.8	$11,706.45	921	$12.71	5.67%	$36,034.44

Figure 13.24 Day of the week pivot table

This account's conversion rate and cost per conversion are much better on the weekend than the weekdays. While their click-through rate is fairly static during the entire week, their average position drops slightly during the weekends. In addition, they are currently losing money during several weekdays (cost is higher than revenue), yet they are highly profitable on the weekends. In this case, during the week, they should lower their bids, and during the weekends, they should raise them.

Whenever you start changing bids by the time of day or the day of the week, or you turn off your account completely, track total conversion changes. You may find that someone is looking for you on a Sunday, but calling you on Monday morning.

You cannot see hourly information in the AdWords reports. However, you can view this information and more in Google Analytics.

Using Google Analytics to Find Time-Sensitive Conversion Data

Google Analytics allows you to graph conversion information by several time frames, including hourly, daily, or weekly. In your Google Analytics account, navigate to the Goals section. Then in both the Total Conversions and Conversion Rate sections, look for the graphing icons above the graph (Figure 13.25).

Once you have chosen the information you want to see, export it to Excel and create charts so you can view the information and see if there are clear trends. Some businesses will not see conversion rates change by time of day or by hour; others will see drastic changes.

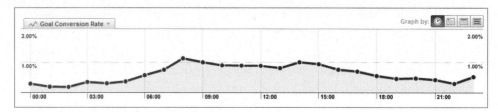

Figure 13.25 Graph conversion information by time frames

Often the differences can be explained by typical user behavior. Marketing is about reaching people. People's behaviors change based on the factors in their lives. Therefore, you need to ask the question, How do your customers go about their daily lives?

In-Depth Look at Two Companies That Found Ad Scheduling Success

Atlas One Point published an interesting paper on conversion rates by industry titled, "Search Conversion Rates by Day Part," by Esco Strong (available at `www.atlassolutions .com/institute_marketinginsights.aspx`). In this paper, they published several charts that showed conversion rates by time of day. Upon examining each of these charts, you can see conversion rates change based on what is going on in someone's life. The first chart (Figure 13.26) shows conversion rates for consumer finance.

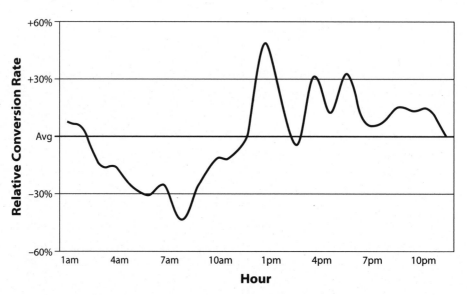

Figure 13.26 Atlas One Point conversion rates by hour for finance industry

Conversion rates are low in the morning as people are sleeping. Once consumers awaken, they are more concerned with getting to work and earning money than they are about their personal finances. However, lunch hour is their own time. The conversion rates over the lunch hour spike. After lunch, consumers go back to work, and then commute home. This is no longer their personal time, and conversion rates go down. Just before and after dinner time, the conversion rates again increase. As the evening wanes on, conversion rates steadily decline as consumers go to sleep. The chart looks interesting. When paired with a consumer's daily routine, it makes sense out of when to reach these consumers.

Examining your consumer's routine, and finding the times when the consumer is searching for you so you can adjust your targeting, applies to both consumer and business searchers.

Business-to-Business Case Study

When deciding to change bids by the day of the week or the time of day, it is essential that you have enough information to make solid decisions. This is a case study for a business-to-business company. Their goal was to offer an IT whitepaper download to bring consumers into their conversion funnel. The first step was to graph conversion rates by hour (Figure 13.27).

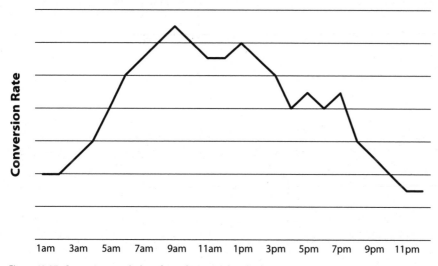

Figure 13.27 Conversion rates by hour for a whitepaper download

At first glance it appears that conversion rates are higher during work hours. The second step is to graph conversion rates by day of the week (Figure 13.28).

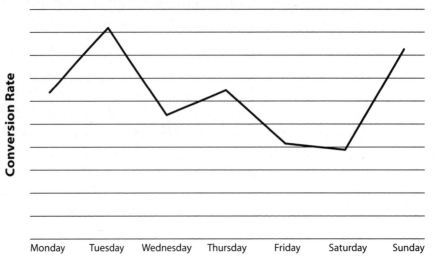

Figure 13.28 Conversion rates by day of the week for a whitepaper download

Now we have some interesting information. While the conversion rates seemed higher during working hours, it turns out that Sunday is their second highest converting day. If you stopped here and decided to make bid decisions, you would be making a mistake. As Tuesday and Sunday are their highest converting days, let us see the conversion rates by hour for those two days (Figure 13.29).

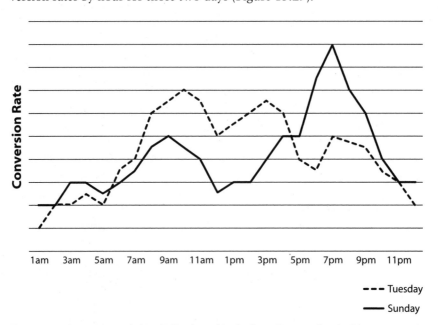

Figure 13.29 Conversion rates by hour for Tuesday and Sunday for a whitepaper download

While on Tuesday the thought holds true that conversion rates are higher during work hours, the opposite is true of Sunday. Sunday night is a common business-to-business search evening for people who left work early on Friday evening or did not finish all the work assigned to them the previous week. Only after this last chart is completed does this company have enough information to set bids by time of day and day of the week. Please note that these are the results for one company. You may not find the same results and should conduct your own research into your conversion rates by hour.

This company's goal was a whitepaper download. But what if you have multiple goals? Let us look at a company that needed to change their conversion actions based on user behavior throughout a month.

High-End Electronics Case Study

This study is for a company that sells expensive electronics. Their average order size is in excess of $2,000. Instead of graphing conversion rates by day and hour, they graph them by day of the month. Figure 13.30 shows a chart of their average conversion rates by day of the month for a three-month time frame.

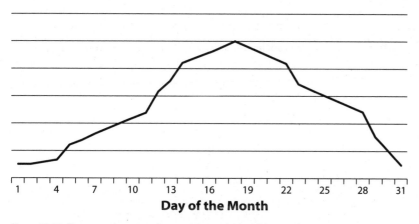

Figure 13.30 Three-month average of conversion rates by day of the month

It appears that conversion rates go up in the middle of the month, and at the beginning and end of the month their conversion rates are lower. However, if we graph their conversion rates by those three months individually, and not as an average, we see a much different picture (Figure 13.31).

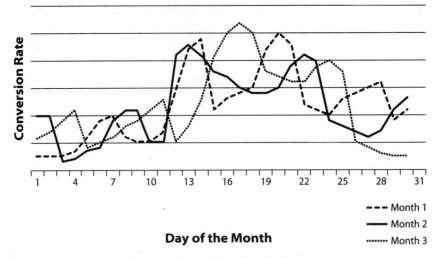

Figure 13.31 Three months of conversion data graphed against each other

This chart does not seem to make any sense. There does not initially appear to be any consistency to conversion rates. However, you must always take into consideration the lives of your consumers. When do they get paid? Most people in the United States get paid on the first and fifteenth of the month, or every two weeks. If we examine the data from the middle of the months, and then look at the weekends after the weekend paycheck, this data starts to make sense (Figure 13.32).

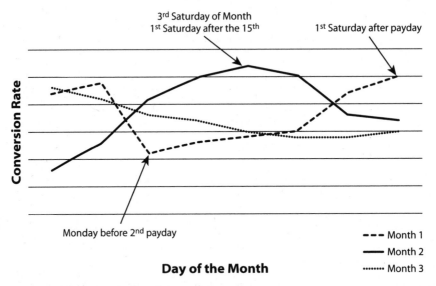

Figure 13.32 Graphing paychecks against conversion rates

The first paycheck of the month usually goes to mortgages, rent, gas, and utility bills. The second paycheck of the month is generally more disposable income. When consumers spend, their disposable income is directly reflected in this company's conversion rates.

After going through extensive analysis of their conversion rates, this company did something unique with their marketing. At the beginning and end of the month, their conversion goal was for consumers to sign up for their sales newsletter. Just before paychecks are distributed, the company sends out their sales newsletter and then sends their paid traffic to their e-commerce pages.

You do not need to be this sophisticated to take advantage of ad scheduling. There are simpler approaches that can help you engage customers.

Creating Time-Sensitive Offers

Marketing is about connecting with consumers. With AdWords, the first connection is based on keywords. The second connection is often location targeting. You could make the next connection to the content network by writing ads specific to a site or type of website where your ads appear. And finally, you can use day of the week or time of day in the ad copy.

Most restaurants have daily specials. You could create a campaign for every day of the week. In your ad copy, add the daily special (Figure 13.33). Your keywords will be the same for each campaign. The keywords will not compete with each other, as one campaign will only run on Monday, another only on Tuesday, and so on.

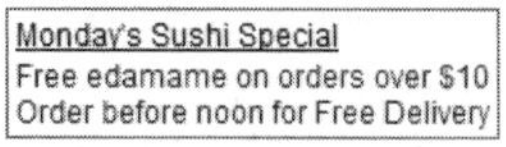

Monday's Sushi Special
Free edamame on orders over $10
Order before noon for Free Delivery

Figure 13.33 Time-sensitive offer for restaurant

Are there times when your business is slow? On Friday afternoons, most people in the office are more concerned with their evening plans than fixing a leaky pipe. However, you can write an ad that speaks to both the day of the week and the time of the day to help engage those who are searching (Figure 13.34).

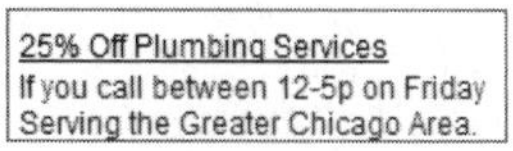

25% Off Plumbing Services
If you call between 12-5p on Friday
Serving the Greater Chicago Area.

Figure 13.34 Time-sensitive offer using day of the week and time of day in the ad copy

In this example, there would be two campaigns. One campaign would run from noon until 5:00 p.m. on a Friday. The other campaign would run from 5:00 p.m. on a Friday until noon the following Friday.

Once you understand all the possibilities of how ads are displayed, you can be highly creative in engaging your audience in unique methods beyond just changing bids and conversion actions.

So far, we have examined ways of bidding based on ROI or profit metrics, and then ways of engaging the audience or manipulating bids based on ROI or profit metrics. But should you always bid based on ROI? A look into attribution management may tell us there are times when we do not want to set bids based purely on ROI.

Understanding Attribution Management

Each of the bidding techniques we examined set bids based on the conversion rate of a keyword or ad group. AdWords conversion tracker only applies a conversion value to the last keyword, ad group, ad copy, and landing page clicked from your AdWords account.

For example, if someone clicked on your ad yesterday for the keyword "MP3 player," looked at your website, but did not convert, and then that same user saw your ad today for the keyword "16GB iPod touch," clicked it, and then converted on your website, what metrics would show in your AdWords account?

Both keywords would show that they received a click and incurred costs. However, only the last keyword clicked, "16GB iPod touch," would show a conversion in your AdWords account. Each time a user clicks on your ad, Google overwrites the conversion tracking code cookie. Therefore, Google AdWords conversion tracker is known as a last keyword clicked attribution management system.

To make matters more complicated, Google Analytics associates goals with the last entrance to the website. Therefore, if someone clicks on your ad today, then comes back to your site directly tomorrow and converts, Google Analytics will show that a direct traffic entrance received the conversion, and yet Google AdWords will show the last keyword clicked in your account received the conversion.

It is common for searchers to start out with general phrases to learn more about a product. As they learn more, their search becomes more specific in their keyword selection. The search behavior mirrors the buying funnel. Let's assume that you sell MP3 players and that a searcher did the searches shown in Figure 13.35; each time they clicked on your ad before finally purchasing from your company.

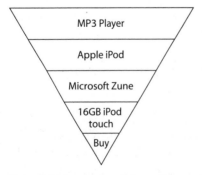

Figure 13.35 Search process before making a purchase

If you only bid by ROI or by profits, technically only the last keyword, "16GB iPod touch," would have a bid higher than zero. As the other keywords did not have a conversion associated with them, they did not bring ROI to your account and therefore are costing you money. However, are they *really* costing you money? Or is it that the searcher first became engaged with your company after searching for "MP3 Player" and the only reason they kept clicking on your ads before finally purchasing was that you helped them learn more about MP3 players after their very first click?

In this scenario, if you deleted all of the words except for "16GB iPod touch" you might find that your total conversions drop significantly. While your ROI would probably go up, as ROI is only a percentage, your total revenue and profits would most likely drop. In these cases, what do you do? You have two options.

The first is to use an attribution management system. There are third-party vendors that will track each of these clicks and tell you which keywords did not convert but originally brought a searcher to your site who converted at a later time. You could also build such a system in-house, but if you do, be prepared to invest some time and money. Even using a sophisticated third-party system is not cheap. If you do not have the money to invest right now, there is a second solution you can employ.

Take the keywords that are not receiving conversions, yet you feel really are good keywords for your company to bid on, and put them in a Budget Optimizer campaign as discussed earlier in the section "AdWords Bidding Options."

If you would like to use metrics to determine what keywords should be placed into a Budget Optimizer account, examine bounce rates, average page views, and goal conversions in Google Analytics for each keyword. If you see keywords that are leading to high interaction on your website, but those keywords are not converting and are early buying funnel keywords, then add the words to the Budget Optimizer campaign.

Attribution management is a buzz phrase that will receive more exposure in the future. If you buy banner ads and they seem to not lead to conversions, then your wallet will tell you that you should stop buying those ads. However, if you have data that shows you that when someone sees your banner ad your conversion rate for search increases for those individuals, you might have a different opinion on those banner ads. Multiple marketing channels do affect each other. Cross-channel attribution management will only continue to increase in sophistication over the coming years.

Examining AdWords Reports to Make ROI Bid Decisions

When you run AdWords reports, you are often buried in data. The first step to analyzing the information is to use conditional formatting to put the data into a visual reference, as discussed earlier in this chapter in the section "Revenue per Click." It can also be useful to put your ad groups into various buckets so that you can analyze similar ad groups together. Let's examine an ad group report (Figure 13.36) and sort the ad groups into a meaningful organization.

	A	B	C	D	E	F	G
	Ad Groups	Revenue	Spend	Average CPC	Value / Click	ROI	Profit (revenue - cost)
	Ad Group #1	$0.00	$1.49	$0.17	$0.00	0%	-$1.49
	Ad Group #2	$0.00	$31.47	$0.20	$0.00	0%	-$31.47
	Ad Group #3	$0.00	$3.87	$0.10	$0.00	0%	-$3.87
	Ad Group #4	$0.00	$20.84	$0.14	$0.00	0%	-$20.84
	Ad Group #6	$325.00	$495.92	$0.77	$0.66	66%	-$170.92
	Ad Group #7	$260.00	$354.64	$1.13	$0.73	73%	-$94.64
	Ad Group #8	$455.00	$159.71	$1.44	$2.85	285%	$295.29
	Ad Group #9	$8,775.00	$4,719.88	$1.11	$1.86	186%	$4,055.12
	Ad Group #10	$4,745.00	$3,596.16	$0.85	$1.32	132%	$1,148.84
	Ad Group #11	$5,980.00	$5,140.16	$0.20	$1.16	116%	$839.84
	Ad Group #12	$88,595.00	$26,869.74	$0.41	$3.30	330%	$61,725.26
	Ad Group #13	$22,165.00	$11,292.96	$0.25	$1.96	196%	$10,872.04
	Ad Group #14	$21,580.00	$19,046.49	$0.95	$1.13	113%	$2,533.51
	Ad Group #15	$5,005.00	$885.81	$0.45	$5.65	565%	$4,119.19
	Ad Group #16	$715.00	$127.29	$0.64	$5.62	562%	$587.71

Figure 13.36 Ad group report

You can do this analysis at the keyword, ad copy, landing page, or placement level. We will walk through it at an ad group level, but there are times you will want to go through this same exercise with different data points.

It is useful to add two columns to the AdWords reports. The first, Column F, is ROI. It is a percentage of how high the returns are for any ad group regardless of total dollars spent. The second data point is profit. Subtract cost from revenue to arrive at profit. In this case, we are assuming there are no margins involved. If there are, first calculate margins, then profit. Once we have those data points calculated, let us group these ad groups.

Low Cost, Low Return Ad Groups Ad groups 1 to 4 have zero conversions associated with them. They also have not spent much money. If you set a bid based on profits or ROI, these ad groups would have to be turned off, as the bids would be $0.00. First analyze if they are good keywords. Are they keywords that you tested and they failed? If so, delete them. Are they keywords that appear early in the buying cycle, and you like them, but they do not receive returns? If so, move them to a Budget Optimizer account.

Medium Cost, Solid Return Ad Groups Ad groups 6 to 11 have all spent some money and have decent revenue. A few of them have negative revenue numbers. For these ad groups, set bids based on profits or ROI. You should do some testing and tweaking of these ad groups over time, but they are not going to be top priority ad groups.

High Spend, High Return Ad Groups Ad groups 12 and 13 have high spends and excellent returns. While you might be tempted to significantly increase the bids on these ad groups based on profits, especially ad group 12, be careful about making dramatic changes in your profit centers. These two ad groups bring in more revenue than all of the other ad groups combined. It is not uncommon to find a handful of keywords or ad groups that are a large percentage of your overall revenue.

The AdWords system can be temperamental at times. In ad groups like these, change the bids by 10 percent or 20 percent and make sure your returns are the same at the higher bid prices. If the returns stay profitable, then raise the bids again by 10 or 20 percent. Do not make dramatic changes in these ad groups. In addition, on the home screen of your AdWords account you can set a watch list of items you want to keep a close eye on. Add these ad groups to the watch list. These are ad groups you should check on daily, as a slight change can cause a dramatic change in your profits.

High Spend, High Traffic, Medium or Low Return Ad Groups Sometimes the hardest part of AdWords is finding keywords with high search volume or keywords where you can drive a lot of traffic to your website. Ad group 14 has spent $19,046 and has only made $21,580. This ad group has a lot of traffic, but it barely makes money. However, it has potential to be a high revenue ad group. This is an ad group that you want to keep a close eye on because a slight change could cause you to start losing a lot of money instead of barely making money. Add this ad group to your watch list as well.

The best optimization you can take with an ad group like this is to start testing. In Chapter 15, we will examine how to test ad copy and landing pages to increase conversion rates. This ad group is a perfect candidate for testing.

High ROI Ad Groups The ROI of the first 14 ad groups does not break 330 percent. However, ad groups 15 and 16 both have over a 560 percent ROI. That is a significant difference from all the other ad groups. While these ad groups are not at the top in spend or profits, there is some combination that is leading to a fantastic customer experience. When you see ad groups like these, learn from them. Examine the keywords, ad copy, and landing pages to see if there are aspects of this search combination that you can utilize in other ad groups. With these ad groups, you can set bids based on profits or ROI; however, when you have outliers, examine and learn from the data.

Setting bids, controlling your marketing costs, and examining your profits are essential to making money with AdWords. However, it is equally important to understand how your customers buy from you so that you do not suddenly stop buying keywords that were indirectly leading to conversion or start making dramatic changes in your profit centers.

It is easy to end up in a paralysis-by-analysis scenario with AdWords as you have so much data available to you. Put your ad groups into meaningful groups so you can work on similar items together and continue to refine and improve your campaigns.

Best Practices for Utilizing Profitable Bid Strategies

Every single ad group must have a bid associated with it. You can set bids at the keyword, ad group search, ad group content, or placement level. However, a bid must exist for your ad to be shown. What is important is not just bidding to the top position, but bidding based on the profit your AdWords account is making your company. By following these best practices, you should be able to set bids based on conversion metrics:

- Do not spend a penny on marketing until you understand your company's goals.
- After you have written down your marketing goals, find a way to measure those goals. Use the AdWords conversion tracker to track goals that occur online. Use phone call tracking to track offline conversions.

- If you want to maximize conversions, test the Conversion Optimizer bid system.

- If you want to maximize traffic, put keywords into a Budget Optimizer campaign. If you have keywords you like that do not lead to conversions, put them in a Budget Optimizer campaign.

- If you want to change your bids by time of day or day of the week, utilize position preference, or maintain tight control of your marketing costs, then use the default bidding option, setting max CPCs.

- Calculate the profit for each keyword, ad group, placement, and the content network in your account.

- Once you have determined the profit by taking margins and other factors into account when necessary, set bids based on profit or ROI.

- When examining large spreadsheets, use conditional formatting to give yourself a visual reference of the data.

- If you want to protect your brand, use position preference. But do not use it if you do not see a clear pattern in conversion rates by position.

- Learn when your customers are most receptive to your marketing messages based on how they live their lives, then use ad scheduling to set bids based on your returns at those various times.

- Put ad groups into like-minded buckets so you can work on similar types of ad groups at once.

- Do not always set ROI or profit-based bids if they make dramatic changes in your most profitable ad groups. Be careful with your profit centers and make incremental changes.

- The more traffic an ad group receives, the higher the chance it has to bring profit to your company. If these ad groups are barely profitable, then test both their ad copy and landing pages.

- Be creative: the more you learn about AdWords possibilities, the more creative you can become in reaching users in unique ways.

Setting the proper bids will move your account from just spending money to making money. Knowing where your dollars are being spent, watching the returns, and making adjustments as necessary are paramount to finding profit with AdWords.

However, a bid just tells Google how much you are willing to pay for a click. The ad copy and keywords allow you to reach the consumer with the proper message. The ad copy and keywords are governed by the campaign's reach, be it by time of day, day of the week, geographic location, or content vs. network reach. The organization of your account will have as much to do with your success as the bid will.

In the next chapter, we will examine various ways of organizing your account based on the goals of your account and how you want to reach customers.

Successful Account Organization Strategies

Successful account organization is comprised of three levels of decisions. The first decision is determining how many accounts you need. The second requires you to look within an account at the number of campaigns you need based on your targeting and budgets and determine how to properly organize the campaign settings. Finally, you need to decide how to organize your campaign's ad groups so you have tightly themed ad copy and keywords. Account organization is not difficult if you understand your marketing goals and the AdWords settings we have discussed throughout the book so far. Proper account organization is essential if you want to gain the most benefit from your AdWords marketing dollars.

Chapter Contents
What Is an AdWords Account?
Developing a Successful Campaign Structure
Organizing an Ad Group to Increase CTR and Conversion Rates
Best Practices for Account Organization Strategies

What Is an AdWords Account?

An AdWords account represents a business. Each business should have only one AdWords account. Only one ad from an account will ever show in any given search result.

If you manage accounts on behalf of clients, such as a PPC (pay per click) agency, then each client should have its own account. If you are an internal marketer, even if you have multiple websites, you should have a single Google account.

There are times when a business might be very large, or the business has subsidiaries with multiple websites that you feel are so separated that the business should be allowed to show two ads on a given search result page or have multiple AdWords accounts. In these cases, talk to a Google representative before enabling multiple accounts for the same business to make sure you are not violating the AdWords terms of service.

 Note: In cases where you need multiple accounts because you are an agency managing accounts on behalf of third parties, no conversation is needed.

In the early days of AdWords, a search for many keywords might have lead to a page of ads for the same company. Often, these additional ads were affiliate ads that all lead to the same website. When multiple ads lead to the same page, searchers often become frustrated over lack of options. In January 2005, Google made a policy change: only one ad per website would be shown on a search results page. This expanded consumer choice on a search result and led to a much better search experience.

The policies around one account per company are also based on consumer choice. If you are creating multiple accounts to get around policies designed to enhance the search experience, then you could run into Terms of Service issues. This is why it is a good practice to talk to Google about why you need multiple accounts and let them help you.

What Are the Limits of an AdWords Account?

A basic Google account has maximum limits of

- 25 active campaigns
- 2,000 ad groups per campaign
- 50,000 active keywords per account

You can have more total campaigns that are deleted or paused; however, only 25 of them can be active.

When your account nears 50,000 active keywords, you will receive a message inside your AdWords account that your account is nearing an unmanageable size. This indicates that you need to either remove them from active status by pausing or deleting them or talk to your representative about transforming your account into an enhanced account.

If you are a large spender, your AdWords representative can change your account to an enhanced account. An enhanced account has maximum limits of:

- 50 active campaigns
- 2,000 ad groups per campaign
- 100, 000 active keywords

If you need more active campaigns or active keywords, your Google representative can link accounts together on the back-end. It is possible to have over a million keywords active in Google at one time; however, that would require several accounts being linked together. Just remember, you should always contact Google before creating a second account to make sure you will stay within their terms of service.

Unfortunately, there are no fixed guidelines defining a large spend or when an account qualifies for a representative. Google assigns reps on a "need-analysis" basis. If you spend more than $10,000 per month on AdWords, it can be worth your time to contact Google and ask them if you have a representative or any additional support options.

Not everyone will be allowed to have an enhanced account or link accounts together. Each keyword, campaign, ad group, and ad copy takes up space in Google's database. Each time someone searches for a keyword, Google must examine their entire database and perform an auction to see which keywords and ad copy should be shown to the searcher. If you are spending a low amount per month, then it is not cost effective for Google to store all of that data and use the processing power required to continually look through all of your keywords to see what should be shown. It can be useful to talk to your Google representative about your keyword and campaign needs to see if you can use an enhanced account or link multiple accounts together.

Managing Multiple Accounts the Easy Way

If you need multiple accounts, either because your account is so large that you need two linked accounts, or because you are an agency and manage accounts on behalf of multiple companies, the My Client Center (MCC) will be extremely useful to you.

A My Client Center account (Figure 14.1) allows you to link multiple accounts together in a single interface. From within the interface, you can easily navigate between the accounts, see account statistics in a single place, or run reports across all of the accounts in the MCC.

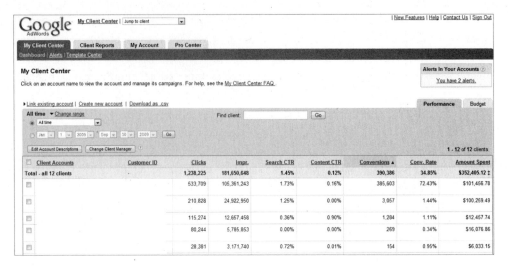

Figure 14.1 My Client Center overview screen

To navigate between the accounts, you can use the drop-down box at the top of the screen, click on a client name from the MCC screen, or use the search box. If you have thousands of clients, it is recommended that you name them appropriately so that you can easily use the search feature to find the account you want to view.

By default, one account in an MCC does not affect another. Therefore, items like quality score are not shared, and each account can show an ad on a search result (assuming they have different display and destination URLs).

If you are running a large account where Google linked the accounts together on the back-end, you can also add all of these accounts to the MCC so that you can enjoy the benefits of the MCC. In this case, the accounts can affect each other.

If you have a tremendous number of accounts, you can also nestle MCCs. For instance, if you manage clients, manage your own PPC spend, and have one large client that has five linked accounts, then you would want to organize your MCCs accordingly:

- Top-level MCC to see everything
- Sub-MCC for your large client with five accounts
- Sub-MCC for your own spend
- Sub-MCC for the rest of your clients

 Note: Although you can have multiple levels of sub-MCCs, unless you are managing more than 10,000 accounts, you will rarely need more than four or five levels of MCCs.

The two reasons to have multiple levels of MCCs are either for organizational purposes or if you are on consolidated invoicing with Google. *Consolidated invoicing* allows you to receive a single invoice for all clients either in all MCCs or for a specific MCC. Therefore, if you have one client paying their bill directly to Google, and other clients who are paying you for their spend, you may also want to organize the clients based on billing options to make it easier for the accounting department.

My Client Center Benefits

The My Client Center (MCC) comes with many benefits that will save you time and make it easier to manage multiple accounts.

Access Levels As with AdWords accounts, there are also different access levels you can give an individual. The first is administrative access. Someone with this access level can add and delete any user—and that can include you. Be careful with this access level. The second level is standard access. This user cannot add or remove users but can make changes to any account. The third level is report access. These users can run reports but cannot make changes in an account. When you give someone access through the MCC, they can see that MCC and any sub-MCCs. If you give someone access to a sub-MCC, they cannot see the MCCs above their level of access.

Linking Accounts If a user already has an existing AdWords account, then you will need to send them an invite to link their account to yours. Once you send them an invite, they will see a message in their AdWords account that they have to click on to give you permission to link to their account. Once the account is linked, then you can enjoy the benefits of having an account linked to from the MCC.

Creating Accounts Linking accounts can be time consuming if you have hundreds or thousands of accounts. Instead of creating accounts outside of the MCC and then having to link them at a later date, you can create new accounts in the MCC so that they are already linked.

Budget Controls The Budget tab of the MCC allows you to see the spend of each account. In addition, if the accounts are on invoicing or other payment methods instead of credit card billing, you can change the monthly spends, see the percentage of their budget spent, and other options from this tab (Figure 14.2).

Alerts If there are issues with your account, Google will show alerts at the account level. In the MCC, you can view the alerts for all the accounts in the MCC on a single screen, making it easier to troubleshoot issues.

Template Center You can create and store templates in the MCC. This makes it easier to create similar accounts at a later date. For instance, if your clients are all auto dealers, there are some keywords and placements that you might always use. Instead of creating accounts from scratch each time, you can save templates in the MCC and use them when you are creating new accounts.

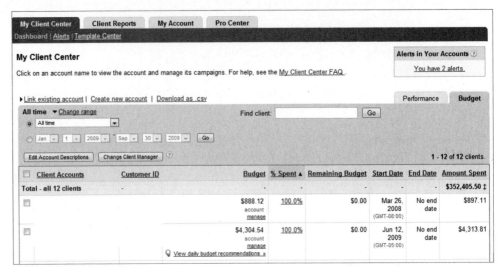

Figure 14.2 Viewing and managing budgets from the MCC

Cross-Account Reporting Finally, you can run reports across all accounts in an MCC at a single time. If you are a large advertiser and therefore need five different accounts, this will be a huge timesaver. Instead of having to log into each account to run a report, you can run reports that include data from all your accounts at once. You can select various reports to run and which accounts to include with these cross-account reports.

To create a My Client Center account, go to www.google.com/adwords/myclient-center and use the wizard to create a new MCC. Once you have access to the MCC, you can also join the Google Advertising Professionals Program.

Becoming a Google Advertising Professional

Google has a professional certification program called Google Advertising Professionals. To become a Google Advertising Professional, you must first have an MCC with at least one account linked to it. The accounts in that MCC need to spend at least $1,000 (for the United States) in a quarter. Next, you need to pass the Google Professional Exam. Once you have met these two requirements, you can be considered a Google Advertising Professional and gain use of a logo that you can use in various means with your marketing materials (Figure 14.3).

If a company has two such professionals, and has spent $100,000 in a quarter (for the United States; the spend requirements vary by country), then the company can be considered a Google Advertising Professional Company.

Figure 14.3 AdWords Qualified Individual Logo

Google Advertising Professionals Jargon

The AdWords Professionals program can be confusing to navigate at times due to all of the names involved.

- The entire program is called Google Advertising Professionals.

- As most people who advertiser with Google do so only through the AdWords program, it is common to hear this program referred to as AdWords Professionals or Google AdWords Professionals.

- You may also hear the term GAP used when referring to this program.

- When individuals join the program, they will be called Google Advertising Professionals. If you have been in the program for a while, your logo will say AdWords Qualified Professional Google.

- The newer logos for individuals are labeled AdWords Qualified Individual Google.

To sign up for the Google Advertising Professionals, go to `https://adwords` `.google.com/professionals/account/` and sign in with your Google account. You will walk through a wizard to create your professional account. Once you have an account, you will be able to invite new professionals, take the AdWords certification test, and gain access to helpful materials (Figure 14.4).

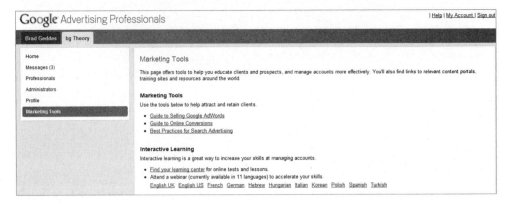

Figure 14.4 Google AdWords Professionals materials

You do not have to sign up for the Google Advertising Professionals program to gain access to an MCC account. It is an additional certification you can gain to help you sell your AdWords services to other companies or place as a nice bullet point on your résumé.

Since each AdWords account represents a business, items such as billing information, contact information, and access rights are stored at the account level. This is the basic information you need to open an AdWords account.

Developing A Successful Campaign Structure

A campaign is a collection of ad groups. Each ad group is comprised of keywords and ad copy. Google follows your campaign settings to determine where, when, and how you would like those ads displayed. If you would like keywords or ads displayed differently based on varying conditions, then you need a different campaign for each of those conditions.

As a basic account only has 25 active campaigns, you must first make a plan of how you want your ads displayed, and then map those campaigns appropriately before adding ad groups to them.

Therefore, the first question is: why should you create a second campaign? We will first examine the reasons to separate out campaigns, then we will use sample company objectives to see how that company should structure their campaigns based on their objectives.

Reasons to Create New Campaigns

The decision to create a new campaign is a big one. As most campaigns only have 25 active campaigns and must set a budget for each, they cannot effectively manage the overall budget with hundreds of campaigns. Here is a list of the most common reasons to create new campaigns.

Daily Budget Every campaign must have a daily budget. As you add more campaigns, you have to decide how much you want to spend on each. One way of organizing campaigns is by business objectives or conversion types, and then by deciding how much you want to spend to reach those objectives. If you have multiple products, and each product has its own marketing budget, then separating out the campaigns by products will help you reach those goals.

Network Reach This is the most common reason to separate campaigns. Have one campaign for content, another for placements, and a third one for search. This organization was discussed in depth in Chapter 10.

Location Targeting The second most common reason to have multiple campaigns is when you want to use different keywords, ad copy, or landing pages in different geographies, as covered in Chapter 11.

Bidding Type In Chapter 13, we examined the different bidding types: budget optimizer, conversion optimizer, and maximum CPC bidding. If you want an account to utilize multiple bidding strategies, each bidding type must have its own campaign.

Demographic Bidding If you find that you do well with certain demographics and receive a significant amount of volume on sites that support demographic bidding, as discussed in Chapter 10, then you should have a demographic campaign. Since you can only increase your bids based on demographic characteristics, and you cannot decrease them, create a campaign that only contains placements that support demographic bidding. Then, at the ad group or placement level, set low bids. Next, use demographic bids to increase your bids based on the cost per conversion of each demographic combination.

Device Platforms You can choose if your ads are shown to desktop users, mobile users, or both, as discussed in Chapter 8. If you want to show different ads, keywords, or landing pages to desktop versus mobile users, you will want both a mobile and a desktop campaign.

Ad Scheduling By default, a campaign is shown 24 hours a day, 7 days a week. Based on your daily budget, your ad might not show every time someone does a search; however, your ad is eligible to be shown all the time. If you want one ad to be shown on a Monday and a different ad to be shown on Tuesday, you will need a different campaign for each time frame that you want different ads, keywords, or landing pages to be displayed, as discussed in Chapter 13.

Whenever you want different keywords, ad copy, or landing pages to be governed by a different campaign setting, you need a new campaign. The items earlier in this list are the most common reasons to create new campaigns, but even items such as ad delivery method or ad serving methodology can be reasons to create new campaigns if you want different keywords or ad copy to follow different campaign rules.

Structuring Campaigns to Achieve Business Goals

There are thousands of ways to structure your campaign settings based on your business goals. If you do not know your business goals, you cannot set bids appropriately or understand the best way to structure your campaigns. This is why it is so important to know what you would like your marketing to accomplish.

Throughout this section, we will look at some common business goals and then examine how the campaigns in that account should be organized.

Basic Campaign Structure: Maximize Returns

When you want to maximize returns for all of your keywords, placements, and ads, there is a straightforward place to start that will utilize three campaigns.

Search Campaign Your first campaign will only be shown on search. In your campaign settings, choose only the search network. Then within your ad groups you will only choose keywords that you want to be triggered based on the searcher's query with appropriately written ad copy. This campaign will have a large percentage of your total budget, usually between 40 and 60 percent. For each keyword, you will use either ROI- or profit-based bids as discussed in Chapter 13.

Content Discovery Campaign Your second campaign will be a content-only campaign. The goal of this campaign is to find sites that are meeting your goals across the content network, as discussed in Chapter 10. When you find sites that meet your goals, you will exclude them from this campaign and add them to your placement campaign. As you find sites that do not meet your goals, you will block them from showing your ads in the future.

The keywords in these ad groups should form a theme. It is okay across the content network to use general keywords that you would not use for search but when combined with other keywords in the ad group create a theme so that Google can accurately place your ads on the proper types of content network pages.

As this campaign may or may not be profitable, you will set the lowest daily budget for it, usually 10 to 20 percent of your total daily budget. When you first open a new account, since you will not have placement data, this campaign may be 30 to 40 percent of your daily budget, and then as you add more sites to the placement campaign, your budget should be reallocated from this campaign to the placement campaign.

Placement Campaign When you find sites across the content network that are meeting your goals, you always want your ads to be shown on those sites. Therefore, add them to this placement campaign. Run the placement performance reports to see your cost per action for each placement, and then adjust the bids for each placement based on your goals. Follow the flow chart (Figure 10.10) in Chapter 10 to continuously refine your content discovery and placement campaigns. For larger placement sites, you can also copy the keywords from the original content network ad group to the placement campaign to create enhanced placements.

As this campaign should provide measurable returns for your AdWords account, this campaign's daily budget will be similar to your search campaign's budget. Eventually, this campaign should be spending 30 to 60 percent of your daily budget. As you add new placements, transition some of your budget from the content discovery campaign to the placement campaign.

This basic account organization (Figure 14.5) should get any account started. It combines the basic principles of using search, placements, and the content network appropriately. However, it does assume that you are only choosing one geographic reach for all your campaigns. If you want to show different ads to different users, you may want to restructure your campaigns.

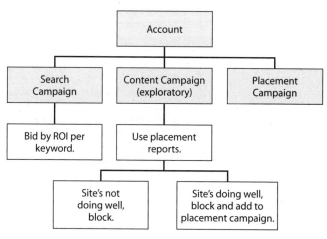

Figure 14.5 Basic account structure

Meeting Location-Based Goals

There are times when you will want to create campaigns that showcase different ads to users based on the user's location. A common reason for this is if you find different response rates by location from the geographic performance reports discussed in Chapter 11.

The geographic performance reports give you the data to refine your campaigns over time. In this example, we will look at a company that should start with multiple location-based campaigns.

Our fictional company, Illinois Insurance, is licensed in the state of Illinois to sell insurance; therefore, they only want users in Illinois to see their ads. After conducting some research, they find that people located in Chicago have different insurance concerns. Chicago is one of the largest cities in the world, and the residents want more information about car theft and home break-ins than the rest of the state. Illinois Insurance is headquartered in Rockford. They want to stress that customers in that city can come into their office and meet face to face with an insurance agent.

This company has three different goals for three different locations (Illinois, Chicago, and Rockford), therefore, they will need three search-based campaigns (Figure 14.6).

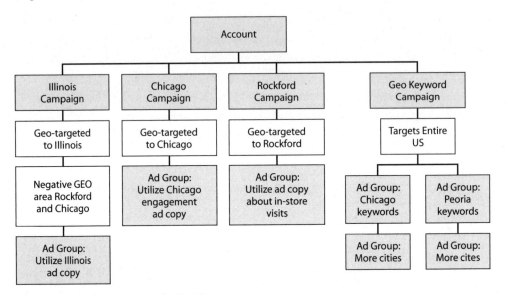

Figure 14.6 Search-based campaigns for Illinois Insurance

Illinois Campaign This campaign will be shown throughout the state of Illinois, so this campaign should use the location setting of Illinois only. However, as Illinois Insurance want different ads to show in Rockford and Chicago, the excluded regions feature (discussed in Chapter 11) should also be utilized to keep their ads from showing in those two cities. As this campaign is only shown to users in the state of Illinois, the keywords will not need geo-qualifiers such as "Peoria home insurance" or "Illinois home insurance." These ads will go to a landing page that corresponds to the keywords being searched.

Chicago Campaign This campaign is for searchers who live in the city of Chicago; therefore, in the location settings this campaign should only be displayed in Chicago. Since the company found that Chicago users had different insurance concerns, those findings should be echoed in the ad copy. As with the Illinois campaign, the keywords should not use geographic modifiers. Finally, the searcher should be sent to a page on the website that reinforces both the Chicago location and the keywords that were searched.

Rockford Campaign The Rockford campaign should also use the location feature so its ads are just shown in Rockford. The keywords should not use geographic modifiers. The ad copy and landing pages should be focused on the benefit of sitting down face to face with an agent.

Geo-Keyword Campaign If you want to reach everyone regardless of Google's ability to understand a searcher's location, then you will want to add a fourth campaign that utilizes geographic modified keywords.

In this campaign, your target area will be the entire country. Then, within each ad group, you will use geographic keywords, such as "Chicago home insurance" or "Peoria car insurance."

Each ad group should be a different city and insurance type combination. For the keywords that use the Chicago modifier, the searcher should be sent to the same landing page that is being used in the Chicago campaign. The same goes for Rockford-based keywords.

For other geographic keywords, such as "Peoria home insurance" or "Illinois home insurance," you would want to send someone to an appropriate landing page that reinforces the geography and insurance type.

> **Note:** If your budget is being stretched by the first three campaigns, you could skip the geo-keyword campaign.

Content and Discovery Placement Campaigns The big question this company needs to ask themselves is how do they want to treat the content network? There are a few options.

> **Option 1:** Showcase the same ads to all of Illinois. If your budget is being stretched, creating multiple campaigns for each location can be an accounting nightmare. Use display and text ads to showcase your general offer to anyone on insurance content pages and send them to a page that showcases the rest of your offers. You could test a general benefit page against a segmentation page (discussed in Chapter 15). In this case, turn on content only, use Illinois as your location target, and then refine your exposure by using a placement campaign for successful placements.

> **Option 2:** Create three content campaigns. Each content campaign will only be shown to a different location: Rockford, Chicago, Illinois (minus Rockford and Chicago). Then use placement campaigns as you refine your exposure. The benefit of this method is targeted content exposure that sends a user to the most appropriate geographic landing page on the company's website. However, it is a tremendous amount of work, and the results might not be worth the effort. In addition, you need to keep adding new daily budgets, which can start to thin how much any one campaign is allowed to spend, essentially handicapping your best keywords and placements.

> **Option 3:** Create a placement campaign only. Use the Ad Planner tool to find appropriate websites where your target audience spends time, and then put ads on

those pages. As you are guessing at placements, some of your ads will work, others will not. Use the placement performance report to remove websites or set appropriate bids. This method will not let you find random sites around the Web that would have been good placements for your ads, but it will let you test out sites you feel are appropriate and keep more budget control of the content network.

Reaching users with custom ad text and keywords based on their geography must be thought out carefully as you can quickly surpass the maximum number of active campaigns allowed (25). First create a strategy for search and content location campaigns. Then examine how many campaigns it will take to reach those goals. If you have exceeded the number, or spread your budget too thinly across multiple campaigns, refine your strategy and once again look to see how many campaigns that strategy will employ.

In this scenario, the company might show mobile and desktop users the same ads. However, there are times when you want to segment your campaigns based on the device one uses to access your website.

Showcasing Different Ads to Desktop versus Mobile Users

There are times when the user intent changes based on the device they use to access the Web. For instance, someone searching for a locksmith on a mobile phone is probably locked out of a house or car and needs immediate assistance. Someone searching for a locksmith on a desktop computer is more likely looking to duplicate keys or change the locks on their doors.

If someone searches for Best Buy on a desktop, they are probably looking for products and the main website. If someone searches for Best Buy on a phone, they are more likely looking for driving directions.

In these instances, you would want to show different ad copy to the searcher:

- Locked out of your car? We'll be there in less than 20 minutes
- Want to change the locks on your house? Call us for a free evaluation
- Find the nearest Best Buy
- Free delivery on orders over $50

In your campaign settings, you can choose on what types of devices you want your ads to be shown. This is known as the device platform setting. Your choices are:

- Desktop and laptop computers
- Mobile phones with full HTML browsers
- Both of the above

There are two ways that mobile users can see ads. If the user is on a device with a full HTML browser, such as a BlackBerry Storm or Apple iPhone, you must enable your campaigns to be shown on mobile devices. For devices without full HTML browsers, such as a BlackBerry Curve, you need to use mobile ads. It is worth noting that mobile ads ignore the device platform setting in your campaign. As a result, if we only examine how to reach the search network, we have two campaigns:

Desktop Campaign In the first campaign, set your ads only to be shown to desktop users. In this campaign, you will use text ads and keywords based on what you would normally use in a standard search campaign.

Mobile Campaign In the second campaign, choose to have your ads only shown to users on mobile devices with full HTML browsers. Most users on mobile devices use shorter search queries than on a desktop device. Therefore, you also might want to use more general keywords. For instance, on a desktop someone might search for "Coldplay ringtones for the iPhone." On a mobile phone, "Coldplay ringtones" is often specific enough. As usual, you should measure conversion rates and adjust keywords and bids based on returns.

Once you have created the keywords in your ad groups, write a standard text ad or two. These ads will be seen by those on iPhones and other HTML phone browsers. These ads can go to an HTML page on your website; however, send them to a page optimized for your mobile action, such as driving directions or a "call us for immediate assistance" webpage.

Next, create a mobile ad for each ad group. The mobile ads will be shown to mobile users without full HTML support. With mobile ads you can decide if someone should go to your website (which is what Best Buy should do by sending the user to a driving direction page), initiate a call (which is what the locksmith should do), or choose which action to take. You must send those who click on a mobile ad to a mobile-compliant site.

With this mobile strategy, you can engage users based on the device type they are using to access the Web and assist searchers based on their intent. As mobile campaigns also obey items such as location settings, you can choose to only have your ads shown in a specific city.

The campaign organizations just discussed have been focused around having the ability to set bids based on ROI or profit. However, there are times when you want to expand consumers' awareness of your website.

Creating Awareness or Branding Search Campaigns

There will be times when you like keywords, and those keywords accurately describe your products or services. If those keywords also lead to brand interaction, such as page views, low bounce rates, or video watches, yet by themselves do not convert for your primary conversion actions, you have three options.

The first option is to delete the keywords. If you are running a campaign strictly around profits and ROI, and these keywords are not performing, get rid of them.

 Note: Please note that just because a keyword does not lead directly to ROI does not mean it is not profitable. Keep in mind the keyword attribution funnel discussed in Chapter 13.

The first option is not fantastic if you have a long sales cycle or want to introduce new people to your buying funnel. When someone is in the early stages of the buying funnel, their conversion rates are naturally lower. Therefore, the second option is to create some monetary value for a page view or video view, and then bid by returns for those alternate conversions.

The last option is to create a branding campaign. This can also be called an awareness campaign as that is one of the first steps in the buying funnel. Your best option is to also track if these individuals do convert at a later date so you can see the full keyword attribution funnel. However, before you can see if they convert, you need the searchers to find your website. For these keywords, you should not care which ones get clicks. Your goal is to introduce people to your website.

To create this branding campaign:

1. Move all the keywords that you want to gain exposure into a separate campaign with the appropriate ad group organization.

2. Set a daily budget for how much you are willing to pay for people to find your website and learn more about your company.

3. Use the budget optimizer bidding strategy:

   • The budget optimizer attempts to maximize the number of clicks that a campaign receives. It does not care which keyword received the click, which is why you should not move keywords into this campaign if you know the returns for any of them.

   • In addition, the budget optimizer's maximum CPC should be set lower than any of the keywords in your search campaigns. If you know the returns for a keyword, then you want your search campaign's keywords to be triggered. Budget optimizer campaigns are for words that do not convert, but for which you want exposure, and they are usually less valuable than your search keywords.

When you are done creating the branding campaign, you will still have your typical search, content, and placement campaigns (Figure 14.7).

All of the organizations so far have been focused on showing the ads every day of the week and at all hours of the day. If you want your ads to show on different days of the week or at different times of the day, you need to utilize ad scheduling campaigns.

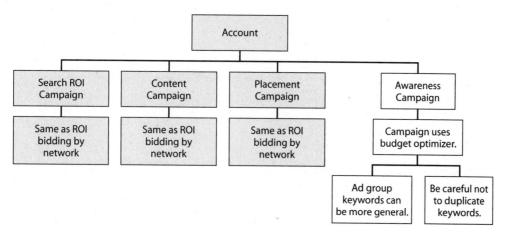

Figure 14.7 Campaign structure with a branding campaign

Showing Different Ads by Day of the Week

Marketing is about connecting with customers. With AdWords, the first connection point is with keywords. A second one can occur if you use the day of the week, or even the time of day, in an ad copy.

Most restaurants and bars have different specials each day of the week. If a restaurant wanted to put their daily special into their ad copy for the weekdays, and then highlight one weekend special, there is an easy way to accomplish this with ad scheduling (discussed in Chapter 13) by using a different campaign for each day of the week (Figure 14.8), as follows:

1. Build your ad groups within a single campaign. If you are a restaurant, also set the location targeting based on the city in which you are located.

2. Duplicate your campaign six times using the AdWords Editor (featured in Chapter 12). Name each campaign for a day of the week or weekend. The naming convention is for your organizational purposes; a campaign's name does not affect any of its data points.

3. Choose what day of the week you want that campaign to be active. When using ad scheduling, always look at the time zone for your account. You can view your account's time zone on the ad scheduling interface. Assuming that the time zone for the account is in the same time zone as your target area, then the first campaign would be set to only run on Mondays, the Tuesday campaign would only run on Tuesdays, and so on.

4. Go back into the AdWords Editor and download your account. In each campaign, change the ads so that they showcase both the day of the week that the campaign is active and the specials for that day. Upload the changes, check those changes in the interface, and then you will have custom ads for each day of the week.

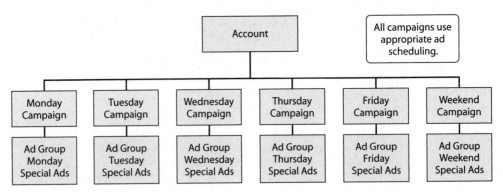

Figure 14.8 Ad scheduling campaign organization

You can also use advanced ad scheduling to change your bids automatically throughout the day. If you are a restaurant, and you find that most people are looking for driving directions and reserving tables in the late afternoon, you may want to raise your bids at those times, and then leave them the same or lower them at other times of the day. Using ad scheduling to reach consumers with time-sensitive ads, or changing bids by conversion rates, is a good method to help increase your profits.

Organizing Campaigns Based on Goals or Budgets

If you have different budgets for different goals on your website, then organizing your campaigns based on how much you want to spend for each goal is a good way of controlling costs. In addition, you can use campaign negative keywords to help segment traffic so the searcher sees the proper ad.

For this example, we are going to examine a timeshare company. TS Inc. is our fictional company, which has a website based on buying and selling timeshares.

TS Inc. only makes money when they sell an ad to someone who is looking to sell their timeshare. If you want to sell your timeshare, you can connect with one of their sales reps, and they will walk you through the advertising options so you can get your timeshare listed on their site and hopefully sell it.

However, TS Inc. has found that they need to drive traffic to the listings sections of their timeshares for those who are looking to buy. The sales reps like to tell prospective advertisers how much traffic each section of their site receives, as it helps increase conversion rates of their ad sales. However, when TS Inc. drives traffic to the timeshare listings, they do not make any money. While they need to drive traffic to their listings sections to help make their sales, it's a loss leader because they have to pay for traffic but they do not directly make any money on these clicks.

TS Inc. wants to spend a lot of money when someone is looking to sell a timeshare and is bidding based on their sales close rates. They have a lower budget when someone is looking to buy a timeshare. They also have a budget for those who are not decisive in their search query and just use a keyword such as "Aruba timeshare'; TS Inc." and TS Inc. does not know if that user wants to buy or sell a listing.

To accomplish their goals, and to send a user to the correct place on their website, they have devised three different campaigns based on their budgets (Figure 14.9).

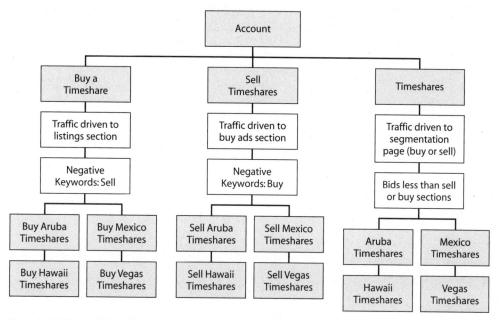

Figure 14.9 TS Inc. campaign strategy to separate out campaigns by marketing objectives

Buy a Timeshare The first campaign is reaching consumers who want to buy a timeshare. Since TS Inc. does not make money on these keywords, they have the lowest of their daily budgets in this campaign. Each ad group is a combination of a city name with the word "timeshare" and the word "buy" (Buy Aruba Timeshares). The keywords inside the ad group all have buying descriptors such as buy, buying, purchase, and so on.

TS Inc. has found that they need to use broad match to reach all their prospects. However, as they do not make money on the keywords in this campaign, they want to make sure that the consumer searching is using the word "buy" and does not use the word "sell" as they can monetize someone looking to sell a timeshare by selling them an ad. At the campaign level, they use all the variations of the word "sell" in their negative keyword list (discussed in Chapter 2). By using negative keywords, they segment traffic based on their marketing goals.

Sell a Timeshare This is the campaign that makes TS Inc. the most money. When someone wants to sell their timeshare, TS Inc. wants to sell that person an ad on their website. The ad groups in this campaign are very similar to the first campaign, except the "buy" based keyword qualifiers are changed to "sell" qualifiers. For instance, the keyword

"Buy Aruba Timeshare" from the buy campaign would be "Sell Aruba Timeshare" in this campaign.

As the goal for this campaign is conversions through selling ads, all of the traffic is sent to a page that shows how TS Inc. can help you sell your timeshare and provides a quick form for you to fill out to get in contact with a sales representative. For higher conversion rates, each landing page features the location in the headline, such as "Contact Us to Sell Your Aruba Timeshare" along with a picture of the location.

Finally, to help segment traffic into selling versus buying intent, TS Inc. uses negative keywords such as "buy" and "buying" at the campaign level. This helps keep their lead quality higher, and gives their listings sections more page views for those with a buying intent.

Timeshares The third campaign is for those searchers who do not use either buying or selling qualifiers. These searchers just type in "Aruba timeshare." Since TS Inc. does not know if these searchers are looking to buy or sell a timeshare, the users are sent to a segmentation page where they are presented with two options of where to go next. If someone clicks on the "sell your timeshare" link, they are sent to the contact form used in the Sell a Timeshare campaign. If someone clicks on the "buy a timeshare" link, they are sent to the listings page from the Buy a Timeshare campaign.

TS Inc. finds they receive quite a bit of traffic from these listings, and since some of the traffic is monetizable from selling these consumers ads, this campaign is the second highest daily budget, after the Sell a Timeshare campaign.

As the intent is ambiguous, and some users leave the segmentation page immediately, these searches are worth less to TS Inc. Therefore, all the keywords in this campaign have lower maximum CPCs than the keywords in either of the first two campaigns.

Lastly, as TS wants to make sure that users end up at the correct section of their website, they use all of the campaign negatives from the first two campaigns for this campaign. It is worth noting that, with this structure, they would not have any ads that would show for a keyword query such as "buy and sell timeshares" due to their negative campaign keyword usage.

In this example, we used a website that is both the seller and distributor of their own ads. There should be two takeaways from this section. The first is that if you have various objectives for your website, and you want the various objectives to have different marketing dollars, then you need to use your campaign organization to help you reach those goals. The second concerns user intent. Often you will find that you are willing to pay more if a user knows what they want or are more specific in their search query. If you can define the various intents of those who use your keywords, you can design campaigns and ad groups based around what the searcher is looking to find.

Defining Your Goals

A complex campaign structure is not difficult if you can define your goals. For the final example, we will examine the goals of a national e-commerce company that focuses on selling computers. As this is a larger company, their goals are diverse:

- Showcase offers to all of the United States and bid by ROI for both search and content
- Increase searchers finding their website for the first time
- Create demand for their goods on non-search sites

After examining their geographic performance reports (Chapter 11), they found they have low performance in Chicago. To increase performance in Chicago, they also want to test a B2B-focused ad on weekdays and a B2C-focused ad on weekends.

Showcase Offers to All of the United States and Bid by ROI for Both Search and Content This goal speaks to the basic campaign structure covered earlier in the section "Basic Campaign Structure: Maximize Returns." They start with search, content, and placement campaigns. Since the second goal is to showcase a different offer to Chicago users, they will use the excluded regions feature in their search campaign so this campaign is not shown in Chicago.

Increase Searchers Finding Their Website for the First Time This company has found that the buying cycle for new computers can be quite long. However, if they can reach a searcher early in the buying funnel, often that consumer will stay focused with their company as they move down through the funnel to a purchase. Therefore, they have a large list of keywords that are relevant to their products but are in the interest or learning phase of the buying cycle and the company has had a difficult time determining bids because the words do not directly lead to sales. These keywords will be placed in an awareness campaign.

This awareness campaign will use the budget optimizer feature to maximize the clicks that the company receives for these keywords. The company will still try to get these consumers to subscribe to newsletters and learn more about their products; however, they are also measuring interaction with their website and will remove keywords that don't contribute to them. They will also measure how many of these consumers buy at a later date. If any keyword starts to receive a significant number of conversions, the keyword will be moved to the search campaign that uses maximum CPC bidding.

Create Demand for Their Goods on Non-search Sites with Highly Targeted Ads This company would like to place ads on highly desirable review-based websites so that more people become aware of their brand. To accomplish this, they will use a placement targeted campaign with only image and video ads. In addition, as their goal is the ad view, the campaign will utilize CPM bidding (cost per thousand impressions) instead of CPC bidding.

The company will measure this campaign's success by examining the changes in branded queries, the number of people who watch a video, and changes to overall conversion rates on the website.

Test a B2B-Focused Ad on Weekdays and a B2C-Focused Ad on Weekends To reach this goal, they are going to use both location targeting and ad scheduling. The company should create two new campaigns that only target Chicago.

The first campaign will use ad scheduling to only show their ads on weekdays. As weekdays often contain more B2B-focused searches, they are going to write ads that use a B2B benefit message and send those searchers to a B2B-focused page on how the company helps other businesses who are buying multiple computers save time and money with their enterprise services.

The second campaign will use ad scheduling to only show their ads on weekends. As they are trying to reach more consumers who want to purchase new computers, these ads will focus on the consumer benefits of buying a new computer. These ads will lead to a consumer-focused landing page.

After the company has gone through the exercise of determining their goals and how to structure their campaigns to meet those goals, they create a chart (Figure 14.10) so they can visually understand their campaign's organization.

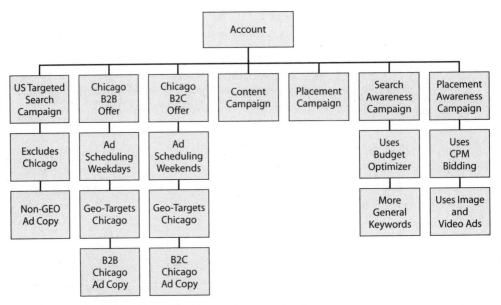

Figure 14.10 Complex campaign organization that meets the company's goals

Proper campaign organization can determine the success or failure of your marketing goals. List out the goals you want your marketing to achieve. Then examine all the options that AdWords gives you to help you reach those goals. Once you understand all the features in AdWords, you can create complex campaign structures that will help you reach your goals.

A campaign tells Google where, how, and when to show your ads. It does not inform Google which keyword, ad copy, and landing page should be used. The next step to a successful campaign is properly organizing your ad groups in a campaign.

Organizing an Ad Group to Increase CTR and Conversion Rates

An ad group is a collection of keywords and ad copy. Any ad copy can show for any keyword in an ad group. It is essential that all ad copy properly reflect each keyword. This is covered in depth in Chapter 7.

You should always ask yourself a few simple questions for each keyword you use in a search campaign:

- Does the searcher think the page reached after clicking on your ad will answer their question?

- Can you write an ad that is more related to this keyword?

- If you look at the other ads, is there one that is more closely related to the keyword than yours?

A simple exercise to go through is to write a highly targeted ad, an ad so specific that if a searcher sees it, they assume you only offer one item. Then ask yourself, does that ad describe the keyword? If yes, the keyword is in the correct ad group. If no, the keyword needs to go to a new ad group.

Going through this exercise and applying it to your keywords should lead to higher quality scores, higher click-through rates, and higher conversion rates. It is time consuming, but essential.

Once you have created relevant ad groups and have accumulated some data, run the search query report. This report is indispensable if you use broad and phrase match. It will let you find negative keywords, add new keywords, and even help organize your ad groups.

For instance, if a company sells various brands of MP3 players, they would want ad groups for Apple iPods, Microsoft Zune, and the Creative ZEN (among many other ad groups). Let us also assume that these ad groups are using broad matched keywords to capture as much search volume as possible. As both the Zune and iPod are MP3 players, it is easy to imagine a scenario where the search query is "Zune" and yet your "iPod" keyword is triggered and the iPod ad copy is shown to the searcher.

This is not an ideal scenario, as you have the keyword "Zune" in your account, accompanied by a Zune ad copy, and a Zune landing page. In this scenario, you would much rather your "Zune" keyword be triggered by that search query, and not the less specific MP3 ad or the competing product, iPod. When you have scenarios like this, use negative keywords to ensure the correct ad is being shown (Figure 14.11).

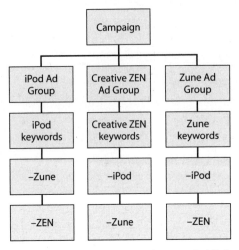

Figure 14.11 Using negative keywords to control ad display

For the Zune ad group, you would use the negatives "–iPod" and "–ZEN". For the iPod ad group, the negatives "–ZEN" and "–Zune" would be utilized. By using a combination of positive and negative keywords, you can make sure that the correct ad copy and keyword are triggered in your account when someone conducts a search that matches one of your keywords.

For organizing ad groups for content campaigns, please refer to the Chapter 9 section, "Choosing the Correct Words for Your Content Network Ad Group."

The ideal scenario is to create an ad copy and landing page for each search query where the ad copy and landing page are specific to every single keyword query conducted. While that might be ideal, there is no way to accomplish that organization with a medium sized account, let alone a large account.

To create effective ad groups, always think back to the search intent of any given query. If your keyword, ad copy, and landing page work together to answer the searcher's question, then your organization is on the correct path.

Best Practices for Account Organization Strategies

Google AdWords gives you a tremendous amount of control in determining the conditions in which your ad is eligible for the auction. You have control over:

- Keyword
- Negative keyword

- Match type
- Geography
- Time of day
- Day of the week
- Desired position
- Google search
- Search partners
- General content network
- Specific placement in content
- Specific placement if the article contains your keywords
- Bidding type (budget optimizer, maximum CPC, conversion optimizer, CPM)

There are so many options that it can become overwhelming when you are trying to figure out all the combinations, where you would like your ad to be displayed, and how much you want to pay for each of those clicks or impressions. To ensure your account is organized properly, follow these best practice techniques:

- First determine your business goals. You cannot be successful if you do not understand what your marketing needs to accomplish.
- Next, learn all of the targeting options available through AdWords.
- Once you have a grasp of the first two points, create a map of your campaigns, keeping in mind that each campaign must have a budget, and most accounts are limited to 25 active campaigns.
- For each campaign, create ad groups that meet the campaign's objective.
- For search campaigns, all keywords and ad copy need to be closely related.
- Run a search query report to learn when to break an ad group into multiple ad groups or add negative keywords and positive keywords.
- If you manage more than one account, create a My Client Center account to link all of your accounts together.
- If you want to sell AdWords or add a bullet point to your résumé, become a Google Advertising Professional.

Proper organization of your campaigns will help you reach the proper audience. Effective ad group organization will allow you to put the correct message in front of that audience.

However, creating ad copy and landing pages is just the first step in the process. You need to test different ad copy and landing pages to determine which message resonates best with searchers so you can continuously increase your account's profits.

In the next chapter, we will examine testing strategies for your ad copy and landing pages. First, we will look at different types of ad copy along with methodologies for testing those ads. Once you have obtained the click, you need the visitor to conduct an action on your website. We will then examine how to test where to send the traffic on your website along with how to test different landing pages so you can find ad copy and landing page combinations that lead to higher conversion rates.

Testing Techniques That Will Increase Profits

Testing is an essential component when optimizing any AdWords account. You should test both ad copy and landing pages to see what combinations improve the effectiveness of your account.

In this chapter, we will walk through not just how to test ad copy, but also different types of ads for you to test. We will examine how to test landing pages, offer ideas for where to send traffic, and lay out different types of landing pages that can increase conversion rates.

Finally, we will show how to test ad copy and landing pages in conjunction with each other. Profit per impression *is a metric that will let you find the most profitable combination of ad copy and landing pages that you should use in your AdWords account.*

15

Chapter Contents

Testing Is Essential to Increasing Profits

Throughout this book, we have discussed best practices for researching keywords, writing ads, and designing landing pages. But what if you have two or more ideas that seem like they could be successful? That is where testing comes into play. You can test out your ideas to see which ones lead to higher profits.

Testing is a crucial part of account optimization. Once you have created your AdWords account, it will start to accumulate metrics that will show you how successful your account currently is. These metrics can be improved over time by testing various ads and landing pages.

It is easy to impose your own will and designs when writing ads and creating landing pages. However, *you are not your target market*. Your target market will usually know less than you do about your products and your business. Therefore, whenever you say, "I think we should do it this way," when writing ads or designing your website, you need to test the ideas to see if consumers agree with you.

If marketing thinks a website should look one way, your IT department thinks it should look a different way, and the CEO wants to spatter the corporate logo all over the website, there is an easy solution. Create three landing pages and see which ones lead to higher profits. It is hard to argue with profits.

You should let consumers tell you what is best for them. The easiest way to do this is to test your ideas. The two major elements to test are ad copy and landing pages. We will start by examining different types of ads to test.

How to Test Ad Copy to Increase Conversions

There are two main ways to test ads: the unique approach and the methodical approach.

Unique Approach With the unique approach, you will write a few different ad types. For example, you may write one ad with prices, another that uses testimonials, and a third that answers a question. When you use this method, each ad will have completely different components than the other ads you are testing. This is a good place to start to determine which type of ad resonates best with your customers.

With this approach, it is also useful to look and see what types of ads your competitors are using, and then test out both their ad type and a completely different one. This will let you see how consumers in your industry are responding to different messages.

Methodical Approach In this scenario, you will write two or three headlines, description line 1s, description line 2s, and then mix and match them. If you have three headlines, description line 1s, and description line 2s, once you mix and match those ad components you will have 27 combinations. This is not the place to start. You need a significant amount of traffic to test 27 combinations. You may move to this approach at a later date once you have determined what type of ads and messages work best for your consumers, but do not start with this approach.

Before you can run a test, you need at least two different ads. We will examine different ad copy messages so you can find ones that resonate with your audience.

Ad Copy Messages You Should Test

There are various types of ads that will help you connect with your consumer base. Not all of these will resonate with your customers, which is why you need to test your ideas to see which ones increase profits. In chapter 4, these ad types were discussed:

- Numbers, prices, and discounts
- Call to actions
- Informational
- Question
- Testimonials and reviews
- Negative messages
- Display URLs

In this section we will introduce some more ads types to test as understanding message types is essential, not just for testing, but to understand what your competitors are doing as well.

Ad Copy Themes to Spark Your Creativity

There are ad copy themes you can test to see which resonate best for people looking at your ads. You may find that different types of ads perform differently depending on where someone is in the buying funnel.

> **Tip:** Ad copy is the only part of your account that a searcher ever sees. Your ad has only seconds to grab the searcher's attention, connect with them, and direct them to click on your ad to visit your website. If your ad fails to deliver visitors to your website, then designing exceptional landing pages is a waste of time since they will never be seen.

For instance, for those who are in the early stages of the buying funnel, information ads often do better than review-based ads. However, someone who is comparison shopping may like review-based ads more than informational ads.

You can also mix different themes within a single ad copy. For instance, you may use an informational description line 1 and a call to action for description line 2 in the same ad.

Test Discounts Instead of Prices

In Chapter 4, the psychology of numbers was discussed where a new ad can influence the consumers perception of prices. However, if you are not price competitive for some reason, instead of adding prices to your ads, you could instead test discounts (Figure 15.1).

Bluetooth Headset Sale
Great selection. 25%-60% Off.
Free Shipping on All Orders
example.com/BluetoothHeadsets

Bluetooth Headset Sale
Great selection. 25% Off
Free Shipping on All Orders
example.com/BluetoothHeadsets

Figure 15.1 Ad copy with discounts

If you are constantly changing the prices in your ads, you may want to use discounts instead of prices. Each time you modify an ad, you actually delete one ad copy and create a new one. As all new ads must go through editorial approval before they are shown on search partners or content sites, if you constantly change them you are lessening your potential exposure.

Note: While discounts will often increase conversion rates, they may not increase profits. You should examine the dollars lost from giving a discount compared to the additional revenue gained from selling more items to determine if you want to use discounts in your ads.

Geographic Ad Copy Are your customers locals or non-locals? You should always consider how much information someone has about an area when using that area in your ad copy (Figure 15.2). The more a user knows, the more precise the ad can be.

Chicago Bluetooth Headset
Touch the headsets before you buy.
Located in the Water Tower.
ChicagoElectronicsExample.com

Downtown Chicago Hotel
Located in the Shopping District
Easy access to All of Downtown
ChicagoHotelExample.com

Wicker Park Real Estate
Northern Chicago Specialists
Find Your Dream Condo Today!
RealEstateExample.com

Figure 15.2 Geographic ad copy

- When someone moves to Chicago, the very first decision they make is if they want to live in North or South Chicago. The third ad copy does not help someone reach that decision. Therefore, if someone has just decided to move to Chicago, it is a bad ad copy. However, if someone has decided they want to live in North Chicago, then the ad copy has meaning for the searcher. Therefore, this is a bad ad copy when someone is in the informational phase of the buying funnel, but a good ad copy if they are further down in the funnel.

- The second ad copy related to the hotel is a good ad copy for a non-local. A non-local wants to be reassured you are in the correct location. As most hotel bookings are for non-locals, you can make some assumptions about your audience.

- The first ad copy is a good ad copy if you are a physical business trying to get people to walk into your store. A precise location, the Water Tower, is used in the ad copy. However, this is a bad non-local ad copy as most people outside of Chicago do not know where the Water Tower is located.

Always consider the knowledge of your audience when writing any ads, especially location-based ads.

Dynamic Keyword Insertion   In Chapter 6, we discussed dynamic keyword insertion, which automatically changes your ad to include a keyword from your ad group based on the search query. Testing keyword insertion is simple. Write one or two ads. In the first group, do not use dynamic insertion. Duplicate the ads and use dynamic insertion in the second set (Figure 15.3).

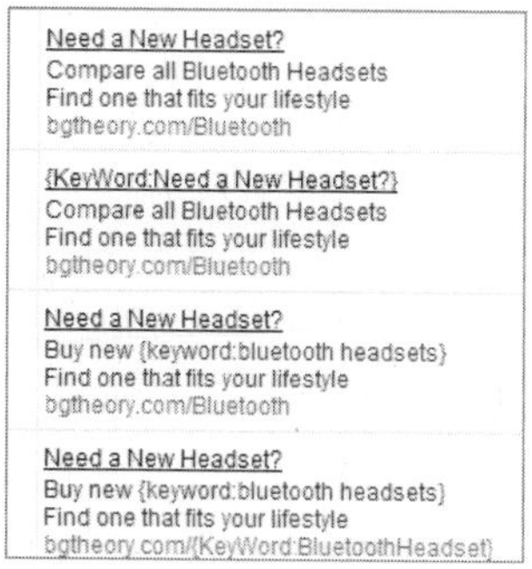

Need a New Headset?
Compare all Bluetooth Headsets
Find one that fits your lifestyle
bgtheory.com/Bluetooth

{KeyWord:Need a New Headset?}
Compare all Bluetooth Headsets
Find one that fits your lifestyle
bgtheory.com/Bluetooth

Need a New Headset?
Buy new {keyword:bluetooth headsets}
Find one that fits your lifestyle
bgtheory.com/Bluetooth

Need a New Headset?
Buy new {keyword:bluetooth headsets}
Find one that fits your lifestyle
bgtheory.com/{KeyWord:BluetoothHeadset}

Figure 15.3 Dynamic keyword insertion ads

The use of keyword insertion does not always increase both click-through rate and conversion rate. It commonly increases click-through rate, but not always; it may not affect conversion rates at all.

Be Creative in Writing Ad Copy

When choosing your ad copy type, you should always keep the landing page in mind as the ad copy sets the expectation for what will be found after the click. Creating synergies with the landing page is essential to any ad copy. For instance, if you used a testimonial in your ad copy, you should echo that call to action on the landing page. By using the same elements in the ad copy and the landing page, the ad copy and landing pages will work together to increase conversion rates. This same principle applies to testimonial or review ads (Figure 15.4).

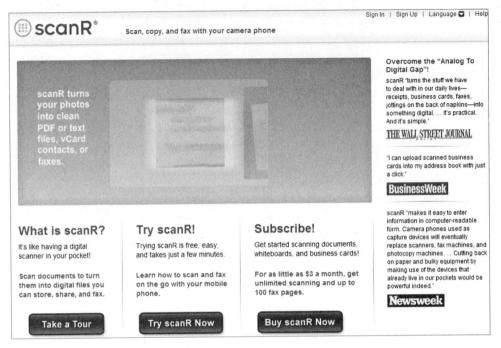

Figure 15.4 Reinforce testimonials on the landing page

As your ad copy initially connected with the searcher—it's why your ad was clicked—reinforcing that same message on the landing page will tell the consumer they are in the right place and the information presented is exactly what they were looking to find.

Although we've showcased a variety of ads, there are many additional items that you can test:

Shipping method

Customer benefits

Unique selling propositions

Product features

Service features

Title casing vs. sentence casing

Guarantees

Symbols: ©, TM, ®

One-line vs. two-line ad copy

When working with AdWords, most of your time is spent in spreadsheets crunching numbers. Writing ad copy is a good time to use the right side of your brain. The left side of the brain is focused on logic and facts. The right side of the brain is much more creative and emotional. As ad copy should connect emotionally with individuals, using the creative side of your brain to write ad copy can help you reach your target market.

Creating the Ad Copy Test

When starting with the unique ad approach, write a few different types of ads. For instance, write one informational ad, one with dynamic keyword insertion, and another ad that uses a discount. Do not forget to mix and match some of these concepts. For instance, you can use dynamic keyword insertion in an informational ad or a call to action in a geographic ad.

The next step in running a test examines how Google decides which ad from an ad group to display.

Ensure Your Ads Receive Equal Exposure

There are two different ways that Google will display the ads in the ad groups for your campaigns: optimize and rotate.

Optimize When optimize is enabled, Google will determine which of your ads has the highest click-through rate. Over time, they will start to show the ad with the higher CTR more often than the other ads in that ad group. Eventually, you may see one ad receiving 95 percent of all impressions for an ad group.

Rotate When you have this option enabled, Google will show your ads evenly. If you have three ads in an ad group, they will show ad 1, then ad 2, then ad 3, and finally ad 1 again. This option gives your ads equal distribution.

When you enable rotate, you will find that the ads do not receive exactly equal impressions. This is due to the complexity of Google's system and how they serve ads across many geographies and time zones. It is not uncommon to see that ad copy 1 has 450 impressions, ad copy 2 has 350 impressions, and ad copy 3 has 475 impressions. The ads should be directionally similar in impressions but will not be exact.

If your goal is to improve your conversion rate, increase your ROI, or find the ad with the highest profit, then you do not want to use the optimize feature, as that only maximizes CTR. In these cases, you want to enable the rotate feature. To enable the rotate feature, navigate to your campaign settings. Under the advanced settings, open the ad delivery section and choose Rotate (Figure 15.5).

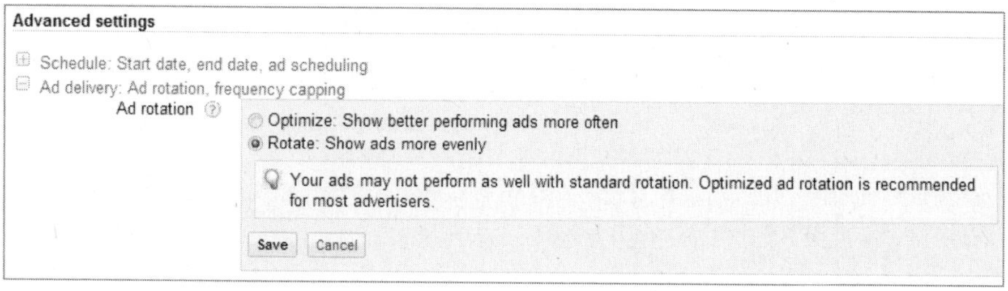

Figure 15.5 Choose Rotate in your campaign settings.

Please note that since this is a campaign setting, it will affect all the ad groups within that campaign. The next step of the testing process is entering the new ads in the test ad group.

Create the Test Ads

Navigate to the ad group where you would like to test your ads and enter them in the Ads tab of the ad group (Figure 15.6).

If you are testing ads across many ad groups at once, then you may want to use the AdWords Editor import function to add the new creatives to your account.

Now be patient as the ads run for a while so you can accumulate the necessary data to determine which of the test ads leads to the best results for your company.

Figure 15.6 Multiple ads running in one ad group

Rules of Thumb for Statistical Significance

When testing, the most important concern is that you believe in the data before you make a decision. If a single person converting vs. not converting makes a large difference in your conversion rate, then you do not yet have statistical significance.

For example, if 100 people click on your ad and 1 converts, you have a 1 percent conversion rate. If the very next person, click 101, leads to a conversion, then your conversion rate almost doubles. If your conversion rate doubles and you are using ROI-based bidding rules, then your bid doubles as well. In this case, you do not have statistical significance.

There are two ways that Excel will help you calculate when you have enough data. You can use either chi-square distribution or analysis of variance (ANOVA). Using either of these two methods will give you very accurate data of when you can end a test and make decisions on the data. However, both of them take some work to understand and implement in Excel. If you want to learn about these methods, Microsoft has online tutorials about using these two mathematical functions.

For our purposes, we will instead lay out some basic rules for how much data you need before you can end a test and measure the results.

> ### There Is No "Best" Ad Copy
>
> There is only a best ad copy as it relates to your marketing goals. If you are trying to bring more visitors to your website or raise your quality score, then you will focus on click-through rate. If you are bidding to maximize your profits, then you will examine how much profit you receive from each visitor. Testing ads without a goal in mind will leave you staring at a spreadsheet of data without any meaning.

How Long Should the Tests Run?

Search behavior is different on weekdays than on weekends. Often the search versus buy process changes over the course of a month, as with the high-end electronics sales example in Chapter 13. In these cases, you want to make sure that you capture search data over the lifespan of the entire buying funnel.

If your sales cycle is short, or searchers come to your site and either buy or do not return again, you should run a test for at least a week. This captures the differences between weekday and weekend buyers.

If your sales cycle is longer or you want more data (which is always useful), then let the test run for at least a month.

If you have a good idea of your sales cycle length, run the test over the course of three sales cycles. In the case of the high-end electronics company, three months would be good enough data. If you sell used books, then a week is long enough; however, waiting for a month is never a bad idea.

Even if you decide to use ANOVA or chi-square for your analysis, using these rules of thumb for making sure you capture searchers over the course of your entire sales cycle is a good idea. Neither of those systems will tell you that search behavior changes at different time periods. They will only examine the differences in the traffic and conversion numbers.

How Much Traffic Should Your Ads Receive?

The minimum amount of traffic each ad should receive is 300 clicks. That ensures that one person clicking versus not clicking will not change your CTR by a large amount.

Personally, I prefer 500 to 1,000 clicks for each ad copy before making decisions. This is where ANOVA and chi-square analysis can help significantly. If after the course of a month, one ad has 200 clicks and one has 500 clicks and they both have similar impressions, then you can make some assumptions about CTR, though you might not have enough data to make assumptions about conversion rate. In cases like this, utilizing higher level Excel functions will let you know that you have enough data to end a test.

If these numbers seem too high for you, which is often the case with accounts that only receive 1,000 clicks a month and any one ad group might not receive more than 100 clicks, there is another way to test ad copy.

In the cases of low-traffic accounts, you can write two tag lines. Put each tagline in two ads across multiple ad groups. When you are ready to examine the data, combine the metrics for those ads across all of the ad groups where you conducted the test. This method is not perfect, but it will let you test aspects of ads even with low traffic, which is better than not testing at all.

How Many Conversions Should You Have?

If you are testing for conversion rate, ROI, or profit metrics, you need conversions to tell you which ad is leading to higher metrics. A good rule of thumb is a minimum of 7 conversions per ad copy. A higher number, around 15, is better. If in doubt, let the test run longer.

Meeting All of the Requirements

Each test should meet a minimum number of days being run, clicks per ad, and conversions per ad. If you have enough data according to ANOVA, but the test has only run for a single day, then let the test run for a longer time frame. As each of the variables can affect your metrics, you want to make sure that your ads run under all of the conditions possible.

Lastly, you want to separate these metrics by search and content. Do not combine the data from the two different distribution methods. If on the search network you have accumulated enough data to finish running a test, then you can complete the test for search, but your content test must run longer.

Once your tests have met all of the conditions I have described, it is time to run an ad performance report to examine the test results.

Measuring the Results of Your Ad Copy Test

The ad performance report is one of many reports available in AdWords. This report will show you all your ad copy and associated metrics. For ease of showing metrics, we will assume that you are using the AdWords conversion tracker (discussed in Chapter 13) to show conversion information in your reports.

When you create the report, there are two important steps. First, choose the appropriate columns. Open the advanced settings (Figure 15.7) and choose these inputs:

Level of Detail

- Campaign
- Ad Group
- Ad Id

Attributes

- Headline
- Description Line 1
- Description Line 2
- Display URL
- Ad Variation
- Destination URL

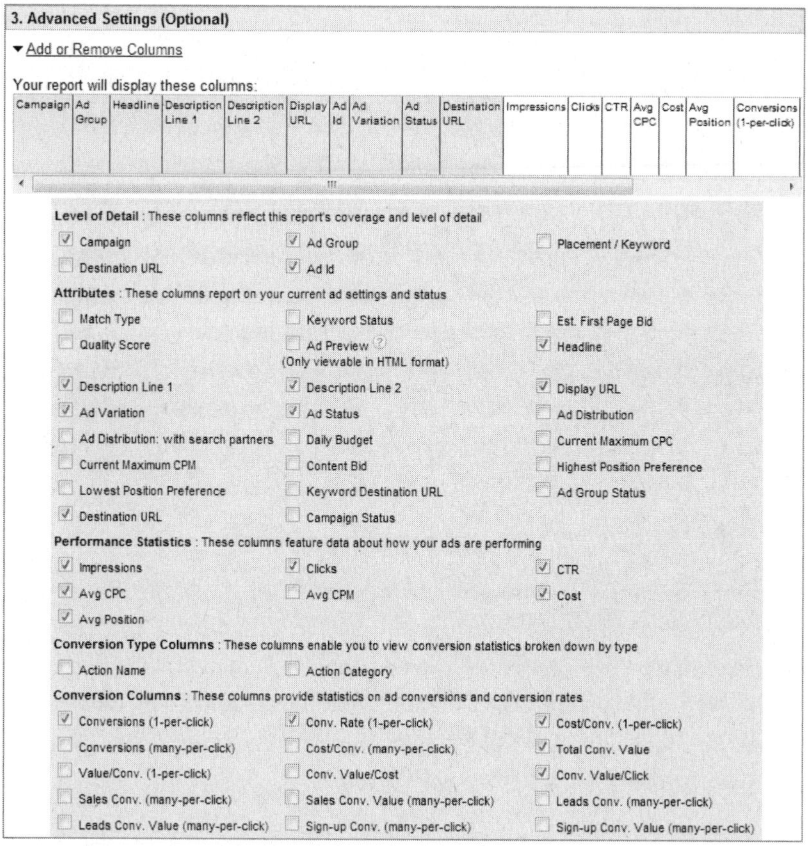

Figure 15.7 Advanced settings in ad performance reports

Performance Statistics

- Impressions
- Clicks
- CTR
- Cost
- Avg Position

Conversion Columns

- Conversions (1-per-click)
- Conversion Rate (1-per-click)
- Cost/Conv (1-per-click)
- Conv. Value/Click
- Total Conv. Value

You Can Test Any Ad Type

In the ad performance report, you can choose to see the metrics of your text, image, mobile, or display ads. The principles for testing ads are the same. If you want to test image ads across the content network, then create two to five images in an ad group. Wait for the images to collect enough data so you can make a decision. Finally, run the exact same ad performance report as discussed earlier and then make the decision on which ad to keep based on your website's goals.

You may find that certain images do better or worse on various types of sites. When examining the reports, if you see patterns that suggest certain types of images or videos are doing better on one site than another, you may want to create placement targeted ad groups using your best images for that particular website.

If you are testing multiple conversion types, you may want to choose additional conversion columns. Once you run the report, you will have a large Excel file that you can manipulate to view the data, which will help you make a decision.

Finally, below the conversion columns is a link called Filter. Click the link and choose Ad Distribution. Then choose to either see only search data or only content data in your ad performance report. Never mix these two distribution methods together.

For ease of illustration, we will show an Excel report with only a few data points selected (Figure 15.8).

	A	B	C	D	E	G	H	J	K
1		Impressions	Clicks	CTR	Cost	Conversion Rate	Cost / Conversion	Value Per Click	ROI
2	**Ad Copy 1**	30529	899	2.94%	$1,060.82	12.35%	$9.56	$6.17	523.18%
3	**Ad Copy 2**	30585	754	2.47%	$889.72	11.41%	$10.35	$5.70	483.30%
4	**Ad Copy 3**	23942	751	3.14%	$863.65	12.52%	$9.19	$6.26	544.20%
5	**Ad Copy 4**	31097	759	2.44%	$903.21	11.20%	$10.63	$5.60	470.54%
6	**Ad Copy 5**	31184	1546	4.96%	$1,793.36	5.69%	$20.38	$2.85	245.35%
7	**Ad Copy 6**	23953	696	2.91%	$953.52	13.22%	$10.36	$6.61	482.42%
8	**Ad Copy 7**	35326	1018	2.88%	$1,099.44	8.25%	$13.09	$4.13	382.01%

Figure 15.8 Ad performance report

Once you have this report, you need to make a decision about which is the best ad copy for your account:

- If you are looking to maximize customers, then Ad Copy 6 with the highest conversion rate is your best ad copy.

- If you are looking to lower lead costs, then Ad Copy 3 with the lowest cost per conversion is your best ad copy.

- If you are looking to get the most visitors to your website, or to increase your quality score, then Ad Copy 5 with the highest CTR is your best ad copy.

The first step is to save the ad that did the best for your company. Before you delete the losing ads, examine them to see what you can learn.

For instance, if your goal is to have the lowest cost per conversion, which is Ad Copy 3, but you want to increase total visitors to your website, then your next goal is to increase CTR for a similar ad copy. Ad Copy 5 is by far the highest CTR of all the ads that were tested. Therefore, see if there are elements that you can combine from Ad Copy 3 and Ad Copy 5 to write some new test ads in the ad group and continue testing.

At this point in time, you could use the methodological approach. If you want to go this route, mix and match the elements of each ad copy. For instance, if you wanted to use the existing elements from Ad Copy 3 and 6, then you would start to create new ads with these elements:

New Ad Copy 1

- Ad Copy 3 headline
- Ad Copy 5 description line 1
- Ad Copy 5 description line 2

New Ad Copy 2

- Ad Copy 5 headline
- Ad Copy 3 description line 1
- Ad Copy 5 description line 2

Keep repeating the process until you have created the new combinations. Then when you run an ad performance report, you will not just be examining each ad individually, but you can break down the metrics of each element within that ad copy. For instance, you would examine the CTR of ad copy 3's headline against the CTR of ad copy 5's headline. By looking at the metrics for the headline, description line 1, description line 2, and the display URL individually, you will see patterns that show which elements lead to higher conversion rates and higher CTRs.

Do not feel you need to use the methodical approach all of the time, as it does take significantly more traffic than a unique ad approach before each ad will have enough data for you to choose a winner. In the earlier case, you could keep the winner, then write a couple of new ads using variants from the two pieces of ad copy, and then test those new ads.

Once you have added the new ads to test, delete all of the losing ads from the initial test. By using this methodology, you can continuously test new ads to see which ones are helping you reach your marketing goals.

Along with testing ads, you should also test landing pages. The ad copy transfers a visitor from a search page to your website and sets the expectations for what the searcher will find post-click. Once the ad copy has completed its job, the landing page must continue to move the visitor through your website so that you receive conversions. The first step in landing page testing is deciding where to send the traffic.

How to Test Landing Pages to Increase Conversions

There are two aspects to landing page testing. The first is determining where you should send the traffic on your website. Once you have determined the best type of page to send your traffic, then you need to test out various layouts of the landing pages.

Testing Where to Send Traffic

In Chapter 5, we discussed where you should send traffic on your website. The conventional wisdom says traffic should be sent to:

- The furthest logical point in the buying cycle
- A page dedicated to the search query

While conventional wisdom is typically correct, there are definitely times when it is wrong. You should test your own traffic to make sure that you are sending the traffic to the correct pages before performing the more difficult work of testing different layouts on your website.

Let us examine some common queries to see where you should test sending traffic.

Informational Queries

Informational queries make up the majority of search queries on the Web. In Chapter 5, I illustrated a point that you must answer the searcher's question before attempting to monetize the query. In that example, we looked at the search query "candle burning times" and how that should not be sent to a shopping cart but instead to a comparison page that shows all of the candles and how long each burns.

However, each time you add a click to the final conversion process your conversion rates will decrease. Therefore, it is worthwhile testing what leads to higher profits, attempting to monetize an informational query, or answering the searcher's question with a comparison chart.

This is especially true for lead generation websites. If your goal is to gather a lead so you can call someone back with their information, it can be more profitable to send someone to the lead generation form, or shopping cart page, instead of the comparison page.

Ambiguous Queries

The search query "merchant accounts" is both an informational and ambiguous search query. You do not know if someone is looking to sign up for a merchant account or if they are looking for information on a merchant account.

Search queries such as "merchant account," "Chicago mortgage," or "auto insurance" often go to a landing page with a small amount of information and a form to be completed. This is not necessarily a bad search experience if someone knows enough to finish filling out the form.

A common search experience is that the searcher conducts a search for "Chicago mortgage," sees the landing page, and then starts to fill out the form. Halfway through the form, there is a required field that asks, "What type of mortgage account do you want?" If the searcher does not know the difference between an ARM, fixed, reverse, or interest-only mortgage, they cannot finish filling out the form.

What happens next? The searcher returns to Google, searches for the different mortgage types, and finds a page that explains what all the different mortgage options are. If that page also has a form on it, they are more likely to finish filling out the form on the page that helped them understand the options than return to the initial form page.

To see which is more profitable for you, create a chart that explains the different mortgage types, the advantages and disadvantages of each, and then has a section where there is a call to action to apply for each specific mortgage type.

Test out a form landing page against a comparison chart to see which one leads to higher total profits. Additionally, you could test out a combination page that has both the comparison chart and a form embedded into the page.

Local Business Queries

If the search query is "Pittsburgh kitchen remodeling," conventional wisdom says to send the user to a page that shows before and after pictures of a kitchen.

However, hiring a contractor is difficult. Everyone has heard horror stories about how they hired a contractor to remodel their house and three months later the job is over budget and still not completed.

Use the site overlay tool from Google Analytics to examine your website. This tool will show you where someone is clicking on your website and conversion information based on the searcher visiting specific pages.

In the case of a contracting business, their "about us" page might showcase how they have been in business for 25 years, say that they belong to the Better Business Bureau, and contain customer testimonials. If they use the site overlay tool, they may realize that when someone sees their "about us" page, their conversion rates go up. Therefore they have two options:

- Move some of the "about us" information to the kitchen remodeling page.
- Send traffic to the kitchen remodeling page and the "about us" page and see which leads to more business.

Narrow Theme Sites

If you conduct a search for "Washington DC nanny services," you expect to see a picture of the D.C. area, sample nanny résumés, and a form to sign up for access to their nanny résumés or schedule an appointment.

Hiring a nanny is a difficult decision. You are bringing a stranger into your house to care for your most prized possessions, your children. The question going through the searcher's mind is not just "Should I trust this site?" but "Where do these nannies come from?"

In cases like this, you want to increase the visitor's trust of your website. Using a segmentation page that shows a visitor two options might result in higher conversions. Option 1 is the "for families" link that goes into the family sign-up process. Option 2 is for nannies to apply for a job. Option 2 also shows that the nanny must pass a background check and meet minimum qualifications before they will be accepted.

What a page like this does is demonstrate to the families that nannies must meet certain qualifications before they are accepted, which can increase the level of trust. However, what is interesting about this example is that if you test the first example of the Washington, D.C., sample résumés and a second segmentation page, you may see completely different conversion rates in search versus content for those two examples.

At this point, searchers are in the buying funnel, and therefore they have thought about hiring a nanny, background checks, and the issues of trust. But consumers clicking content ads might not have thought about those items yet. Therefore, in this example, the segmentation page may mean higher conversions for search while the résumé page may mean higher conversions for the content network.

Testing segmentation pages is useful if your products have multiple uses (Figure 15.9) or if different types of searchers use the same keywords.

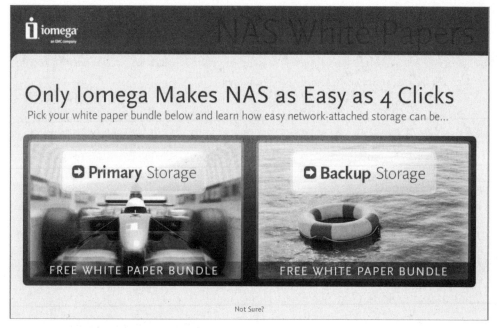

Figure 15.9 Iomega download segmentation page

In these cases, choose one product and send some traffic that way; often this will be the higher searched–for product or the higher margin product. Then send some traffic to a segmentation page. Measure results over time to see which leads to higher total profits.

Product Category Queries

If someone searches for "men's Seiko watches," the searcher expects to see a page full of Seiko watches for men. However, too many options can be just as detrimental to conversion rates as too few options. Most people can only hold five to seven items in short-term memory. One item is why you conducted a search in the first place. A second item might be that you have a meeting you need to attend in 15 minutes. That leaves only three to five open slots left for processing.

If you have a category page of 20 watches, searchers can become overwhelmed and confused over what to do next. In cases like these, the searcher may feel there is too much to process and decide to come back later when they have more time.

Instead of sending someone to a category page, choose three to five of your top-selling Seiko watches for men and feature them on a landing page. Many consumers will choose from these few items as they can easily process the difference between the designs and features of these watches. At the bottom of the page have a link such as "See all of our Seiko watches." You will have customers who want to look at every single watch, and this option allows them to see everything while keeping the total options limited.

Then test this limited product page against your typical category page. Does limiting options increase your conversion rates?

Brand Searches

Many companies use their own name as a keyword and then send the traffic to their home page. While this is an example of a navigational query, it is also a waste of money. The company should rank number one organically for their company name, and consumers can find the company via multiple means.

However, if competitors are also buying your name, it is a good idea to buy it yourself so you do not lose out on traffic. However, you may not want to send it to the home page of your website.

It is difficult to launch new products on the Web. There is often little search volume for brand new products, and you need to build awareness with your consumers that your new products exist. With branded terms, test by sending the traffic to a "what's new" page (Figure 15.10).

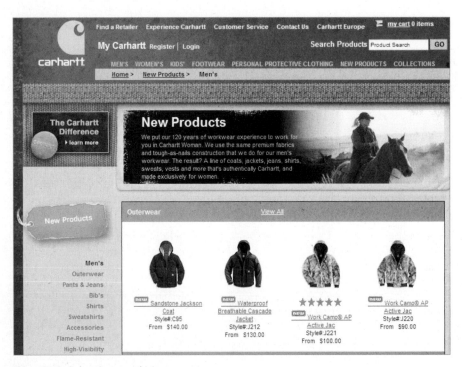

Figure 15.10 Carhartt's new products page

Then choose another action on your website, such as a newsletter subscription, and send some of the branded traffic in that direction. Measure if creating awareness for your new products leads to more revenue than trying to increase your newsletter subscriber list.

Thank-You Pages

Many thank-you pages say, "Thank you for your purchase. We will process your order within 2–3 business days," which says to the customer, "Thank you for giving us your money. We will get to your order when it is convenient for us." Most thank-you pages do not continue to engage the customer. The thank-you pages essentially tell the customer to close the browser because there is nothing left to do on your website.

If someone reached a thank-you page, they gave you a level of trust. Do not send these visitors away. Test different thank-you pages to see which one leads to a higher customer engagement.

Depending on your business model, there are different types of thank-you pages you can create. Here are some examples to get you started:

- Learn more about our company by downloading this whitepaper.

- Create an account to track your order.

- Subscribe to our newsletter.

- Suggested products.

- Send a 10% off coupon to a friend.

- Get 10% off your next purchase by referring a friend.

Once you have determined which page on your website is the best place to send traffic for each keyword or ad group, the next step is to test the layout of the individual pages.

Landing Page Testing Factors

Landing page testing is both a science and an art form. There are entire books dedicated to testing single pages that go into much more depth than we can allocate in a single section. We will examine the big factors you should test and items to be aware of while you are creating pages and marketing campaigns. This will get you started in the correct direction for creating landing pages and tests to help you improve your profits.

Start with Dramatic Changes

ArdenB.com uses very different pages for their top-level categories (Figure 15.11) compared to their sub-level categories (Figure 15.12).

Figure 15.11 Arden B. category page

Figure 15.12 Arden B. subcategory page

These pages are dramatically different. Although these pages do appear as different categories on their website, it would be worthwhile to test their current subcategory page with a similar layout to their main category page to see the differences in conversion rates.

You want to start your testing with dramatic changes. If you cannot see the difference within a few seconds, neither can your visitors. Once you have a handle on the larger items that affect conversion rates, then you can move to smaller changes.

Should You Add Navigation?

The more choices you give someone, the more likely they are to become confused over what to do next. Navigation options are additional choices. That does not mean you should always restrict navigation. There are different types of shoppers. Some shoppers want to make quick decisions, and limited choice is good. Other shoppers want to research the details and see all of the options; limited choice can isolate these shoppers.

In addition, one of the factors that makes a landing page relevant for quality score factors is navigation. Too little navigation can adversely affect whether your page is deemed relevant by Google.

There are often nice compromises you can use to engage both of these shoppers. Bose engages both with many of their PPC landing pages (Figure 15.13).

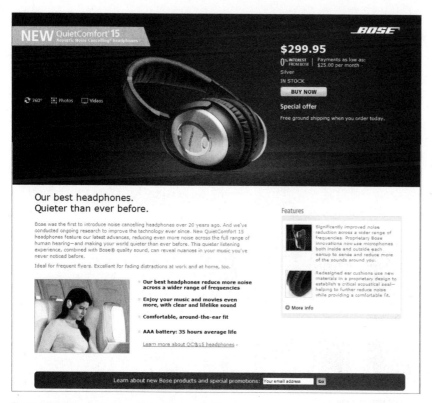

Figure 15.13 Bose landing page that restricts navigation

The main call to action above the fold is to "Buy Now." The secondary items on the page are product details and benefits for the research-oriented audience. At the bottom of the page is their secondary conversion, a newsletter signup.

Amazon takes a different approach to navigation. When you are in their main site, there are more navigational options than most people can comprehend. As soon as you enter the shopping cart, your choices become limited (Figure 15.14). You can change your shipping address, use a different payment method, and update quantities. What you cannot do is leave the shopping cart unless you click the Back button.

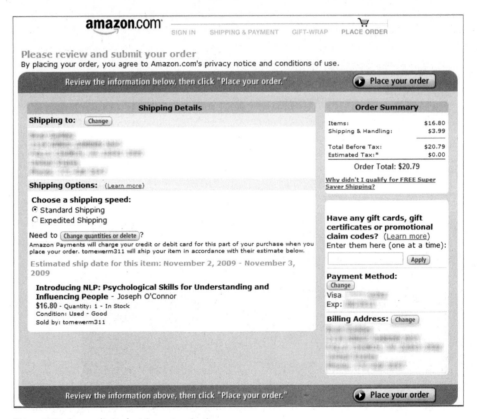

Figure 15.14 Amazon limits shopping cart navigation

You most likely have a product or service page you are sending traffic to now that includes navigation. Create a second page with limited navigation and clear calls to action. Then test to see which of those pages increases conversion rates.

Are You Using Faces?

We are drawn to human faces. When a face appears on a page, the first thing most searchers do is look at it. Next, they follow the eyes to see where they are looking. If the face on your page is looking away from your content, so will the searcher.

Make sure that any face you have on a page is looking toward the main items on your page you want the user to see. For some sites, this will be the service benefits. For others, it will be the Submit button or the Add To Cart button.

Create two pages, one where the eyes are looking into your product benefits and another where the eyes are looking toward your submit action. See which version raises your conversion rates the most.

English Speakers Read Left to Right

If there is not a face on the page, the next item that draws consumer's attention is an image. Once our eyes are drawn to an image, we then start reading left to right. If your images are on the far-right side of a page, then there is nothing left for the consumer to read and they can become distracted.

In Figure 15.15, the page on the right will perform worse in most cases. Since the page on the left also places the image on the left, as someone views the image their eyes will naturally be drawn back into the content of the page.

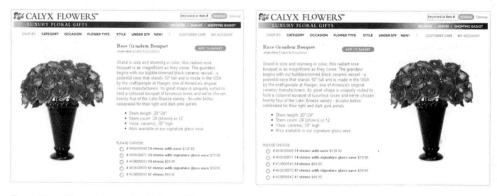

Figure 15.15 Identical pages with the image flipped

If you were advertising to a country where the population reads right to left, then the exact opposite information would be true. Ensure that your images are strategically placed so that the consumer's natural reading habit keeps bringing them back into your content.

Testing Video

Images and text allow you to show a product. However, video allows you to demonstrate a product or show real-life examples. When using video, you must first consider the searcher's environment to decide if you want the video to start playing or not. If someone is in a work cubicle and their computer starts to speak, they are likely to hit the Back button very quickly. If someone is at home or in an enclosed office, they are less likely to hit the Back button if their computer makes noise. There are four ways to test video:

- Autoplay with sound on

- Autoplay with sound off
- Do not autoplay
- No video

I work closely with Google to conduct the advanced sessions of the AdWords Seminars for Success program. The initial landing page that was used did not use video (Figure 15.16).

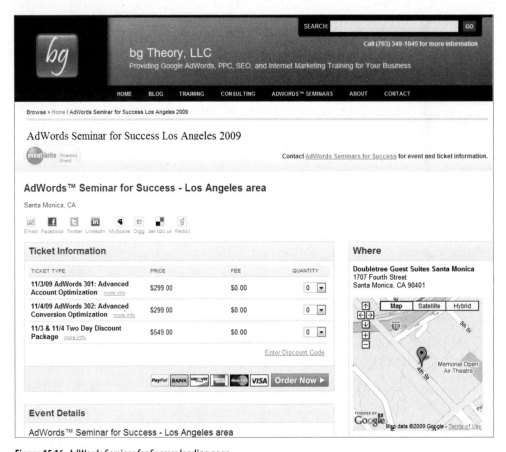

Figure 15.16 AdWords Seminar for Success landing page

These pages worked quite well for a couple of years. As video hosting and bandwidth significantly increased, I decided to test three versions of the page. One version did not use the video (Figure 15.16), the second version only used video testimonials, and the third version used even more video testimonials (Figure 15.17) followed by other videos on the Web where I have been interviewed. As most of the audience is in a business environment, I decided not to autoplay any videos.

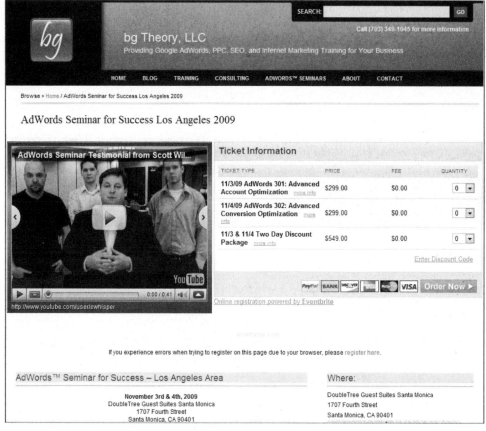

Figure 15.17 Video testimonials on the landing page

Table 1.1 shows a high-level set of metrics from the test pages. As the page without videos was the initial baseline page, there is no reason to include those statistics. Both versions of the page started with the same opening video, hence the same number of users who played a video.

▶ **Table 1.1** Conversion rate lift from using video

	Testimonial Video	Testimonial and Interview Video
Number of videos	3	9
Length of all videos	2 minutes	28 minutes
Percentage of users who started watching	32%	32%
Total time watched	1 minute 45 seconds	7 minutes 16 seconds
Conversion rate lift	31%	38%

What was fascinating is that once someone started playing the testimonial videos, they watched almost all of the them. Rarely did someone stop watching the video. Of course, if someone decided they were ready to buy and left the page to enter their credit card details before the videos finished playing, they would not have seen all of the videos in their entirety.

While this shows for my test that videos increased conversion rates, there are many more items to test, such as these:

- Opening video testimonial being a female
- Showcasing the seminar content in video before the testimonials
- Starting with a short interview before moving to testimonials

Any testing you do should evolve from what you have learned. This test first showed me that using video testimonial increased our company's conversion rates. The second thing it taught me was that consumers liked seeing who the speaker was by watching interviews. However, there is much more that can be learned by continuously evolving the video tests.

Making Ads and Landing Pages Work Together

Your landing page is only as good as the synergy it creates with your ad copy. If your ad copy is not compelling or does not set the proper expectations for the landing page, then the perfect page may still produce disappointing results. This synergy should extend not just to text ads, but to display ads as well.

Showcasing the Offer on the Landing Page

If your ad copy and landing page use different color layouts, themes, and calls to action, you can confuse visitors and they may think they have arrived at the wrong place. eTrade created a nice banner ad (Figure 15.18) with a simple call to action to open an account in minutes.

 Figure 15.18 eTrade banner ad

The ad itself is clean and easy to read. The effectiveness of this ad increased dramatically when the user clicked on the ad and then saw the majority of the ad as part of the landing page (Figure 15.19).

The color scheme of the ad and the landing page are the same. The numbers are the same. The benefit messages are the same. The user knows they have arrived at the correct page and can easily continue the action from clicking on the ad to applying for a new account.

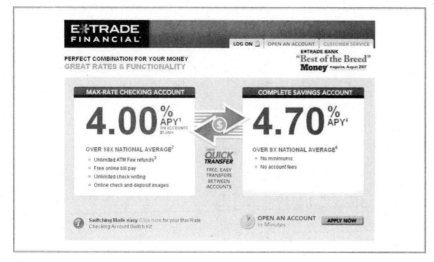

Figure 15.19 eTrade landing page

Ensure Relevance for Your Audience

Delivery.com delivers take-out food to your door so you do not have to leave the house. They came up with a fantastic marketing idea during the winter. Essentially, the offer is that the colder it is outside, the more bonus points you receive to your account (Figure 15.20) if you order from them.

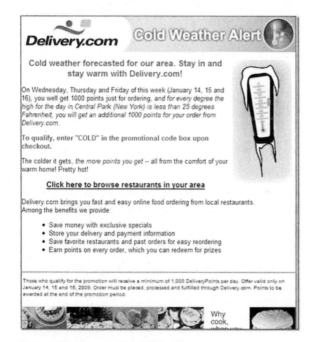

Figure 15.20 Delivery.com email promotion

While the idea was good, there were two areas where they could have increased the effectiveness of this campaign. This email was sent to many people in the northeastern United States. There are large weather differences between Pittsburgh, Washington, D.C., Boston, and New York. When deciding to stay in or go out, the weather outside your house is more important than the weather in a different city. However, the offer in the newsletter was based on the temperature of Central Park in New York City. If you lived in Boston, and it was cold in Boston but warm in New York, this promotion did not do you a lot of good.

Secondly, Delivery.com knows the zip code of everyone in their database, as they deliver to people's doors. The link in the email to "browse restaurants in your area" goes to the home page of Delivery.com. I hope by now you realize that the home page is rarely the best page to send traffic. In this case, they should have coded the links based on the zip code of the recipient so that when they visited Delivery.com's website they were directed to the restaurants that delivered to their address.

The overall idea for the marketing campaign was brilliant. The execution could have increased its effectiveness. Make sure you think through your campaigns as a consumer so that you are delivering effective messages.

Echo Special Offers on the Landing Page

Too often a consumer will see an ad that contains the text, "Use Discount Code EHCODE for 20% Off" and then they will visit the site and not see the code. They will navigate to the page where they enter their credit card information and not see the code. If the consumer looked around the site at all, odds are they have forgotten the code. Next, the consumer returns to the search results page and tries to find the ad again. If they cannot find the ad, they become frustrated and may not return to your site to complete the transaction.

If you add discount or special offer codes in either text or display ads, it is imperative that the exact same code and special can be found on the landing page (Figure 15.21).

Testing special offers and discounts is useful. The use of discounts will often increase conversion rates. However, your final profit on each sale is also less. Therefore, when testing discounts, what you should be testing to see is if the use of a special offer increases conversion rates enough that it is worth taking a lower profit on each sale, or if the lower conversion rate without a discount is more profitable.

Convey the Proper Experience

If you sell used books at a $5 price point, a searcher does not want to spend 20 minutes attempting to find their next used book. The searcher wants a quick Add To Cart button, an even faster checkout experience, and does not want to take time out of their day to deliberate over a $5 investment.

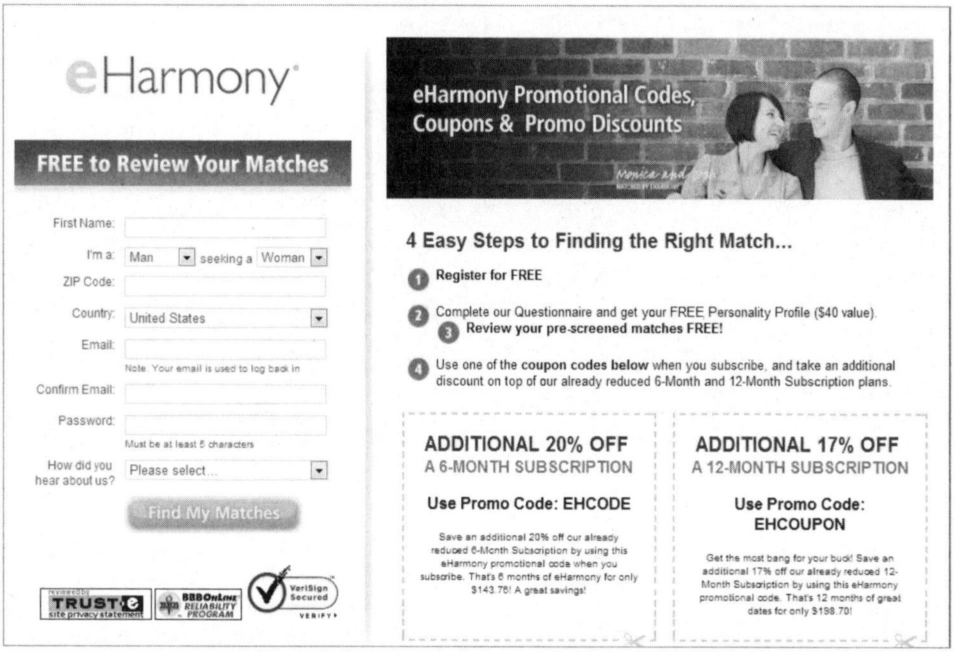

Figure 15.21 eHarmony's special offer landing page

When a consumer goes into a physical store to buy a diamond, they are treated to gorgeous showcases, helpful sales staff, and the ability to touch and examine not only the diamonds, but the rings and necklaces that make the diamonds sparkle.

If you sell diamond jewelry online, that same consumer does not want the same shopping experience as one buying a used book. The monetary investment is different, and the time between examining the products and buying a piece of jewelry is much longer. A diamond shopper wants to be treated to an exquisite sales experience (Figure 15.22).

ADiamondIsForever.com would not make for a good site to demonstrate how most e-commerce sites selling low-end products should be crafted. The site is mostly Flash, takes a long time to navigate, is full of high resolution images, yet one feels they are entering a website full of luxurious products.

While these are two extreme examples, when thinking of redesigning your website or changing the sales experience, do not assume your marketing and design teams know best. Create a few design variations to see which one helps you reach your marketing goals.

Ensuring Easy Information Retrieval, Not Perfection

Do not get caught up in creating landing pages that cost more to design than you can afford. You can spend thousands of dollars creating each landing page variation to test. For some companies, that price point fits into their marketing budget. For others, it does not.

Your pages do not have to be perfect Flash pages that mimic ADiamondIsForever.com. Your landing pages need to quickly and easily convey the information necessary for someone to get the answer to their question and make a conversion decision (Figure 15.23).

Figure 15.22 A Diamond Is Forever home page

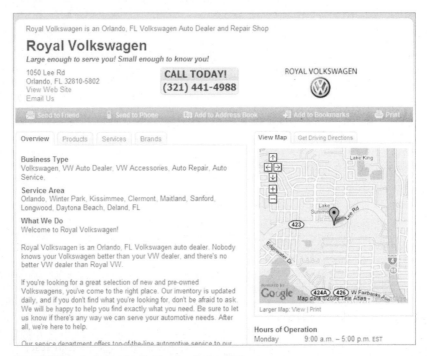

Figure 15.23 Logically organized landing page for Royal Volkswagen

This landing page, created by R.H. Donnelley for Royal Volkswagen, is not an expensive Flash driven landing page. It is a clean landing page that tells a consumer what the company does, shows their service area, and offers several conversion options. In the case of this site, the dark colored navigation bar is actually a conversion bar. The consumer's options are:

- Send to friend
- Send to phone
- Add to address book
- Add to bookmarks
- Print the page

One would not accuse this page of being an expensive-looking landing page or one that is hard to create. However, it is an effective page as it quickly conveys information to the consumer in a friendly, easy-to-digest manner.

Essential Items to Test First

When deciding which pages to test first, start with your landing pages that receive the most traffic. Even small gains in conversion rates for pages with high traffic will help increase your profits. The other pages you should start testing are ones that have the highest potential of profits. This might be a page of your top-selling products, your sales pages, or your high-margin products.

Once you have started testing the beginning part of the funnel, test the second step of the funnel. Do not start with the second or third steps. If someone does not make it from step 1 to step 2 of your funnel, then it does not matter how good your secondary pages are.

The main items to start testing are:

- Headline
- Hero shot (the picture on your page, either a person or a product image)
- Page layout
- Call to action
- Custom benefit
- Navigation

When thinking about your layout, additional items to test would be:

- Color scheme
- Logo
- Authority and trust icons
- Product or service descriptions

Once you have decided what you are going to test, it is time to set up your test.

Creating a Landing Page Test

There are two ways to test landing pages: an A/B test and multivariate testing.

A/B Test This is where you have two versions of a page and you send some traffic to page A and some traffic to page B. This method is good for testing websites with low traffic or testing where to send the traffic before testing different page layouts.

Multivariate Testing This testing methodology allows you to test several variables at once. For instance, you may have two headlines, two hero shots, two customer benefits, and two calls to action. Testing two variations of four variables is 16 different tests. Multivariate testing requires a significant amount of traffic.

Google offers a calculator, available at `www.google.com/analytics/siteopt/siteopt/ help/calculator.html`, to determine how long it will take to complete a multivariate test based on various inputs. In the multivariate example, if the page only received 100 visitors a day, has a 5 percent conversion rate, and we were expecting a 30 percent lift in conversions, it would take 651 days for the test to be completed (Figure 15.24).

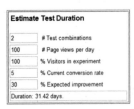

Estimate Test Duration

16	# Test combinations
100	# Page views per day
100	% Visitors in experiment
5	% Current conversion rate
30	% Expected improvement
Duration: 651.04 days.	

Figure 15.24 Website Optimizer duration calculator

Creating a test that will take almost two years before you can expect results is not the way to start testing. Instead, if that page had only two versions, such as found in A/B testing, it would only take 31 days (Figure 15.25) to see results from the experiment. Multivariate tests show confidence and lift factors by testing variable combinations. While this might sound complex, many systems, such as Google's Website Optimizer do the page serving and the math for you.

Estimate Test Duration

2	# Test combinations
100	# Page views per day
100	% Visitors in experiment
5	% Current conversion rate
30	% Expected improvement
Duration: 31.42 days.	

Figure 15.25 Duration calculator for 2 variables

An easy way to get started with multivariate testing is to use Google's free Website Optimizer. Google Website Optimizer is integrated into Google AdWords and allows for easy multivariate tests. For our purposes, we will illustrate setting up a straightforward A/B test in AdWords without going through the technical implementation of Website Optimizer to show how easy it is to start testing your website. Testing is not difficult, the hard part is determining what to test.

Creating A/B Landing Page Tests in AdWords

The first step, just like with ad copy testing, is to make sure that you are using the rotate campaign settings. You want each test to receive equal exposure. Next, choose two or three pages where you want to send traffic.

Finally, navigate to the ad group where you want to set up the test. Duplicate your existing ad copy a second or third time, depending on how many different pages you want to test. Then change the destination URLs of the new ads to send traffic to the new pages you want to test (Figure 15.26).

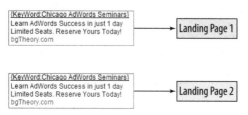

Figure 15.26 Use the same ad copy to send traffic to different pages.

Just as with ad copy testing, wait until you have enough data to obtain statistical significance by using chi-square or ANOVA in Excel, or the rules of thumb from the ad copy testing section earlier, "Rules of Thumb for Statistical Significance."

Make Sure Your Duplicate Pages Are Not Crawled

If you use the same content on multiple pages within your site, you can cause issues for your organic rankings. As Google will find two variations of the same content, they will choose which page to rank on your website. The focus of PPC landing pages should be conversions. If you also do SEO, you often need to change page elements based upon search engine ranking factors that might not increase conversion rates. Therefore, you might have multiple sets of similar pages on your website. One set for PPC and the other for SEO. If this happens on your website, use your robots.txt file to block your testing pages from being crawled by the organic spiders.

Once you have enough data, run a URL performance report (Figure 15.27) using at a minimum these data points:

Level of Detail

- Campaign
- Ad Group
- Destination URL

Performance Statistics

- Impressions
- Clicks

- CTR
- Cost
- Avg Position

Conversion Columns

- Conversions (1-per-click)
- Conv. Rate (1-per-click)
- Cost/Conv. (1-per-click)
- Conv. Value/Click
- Total Conv. Value

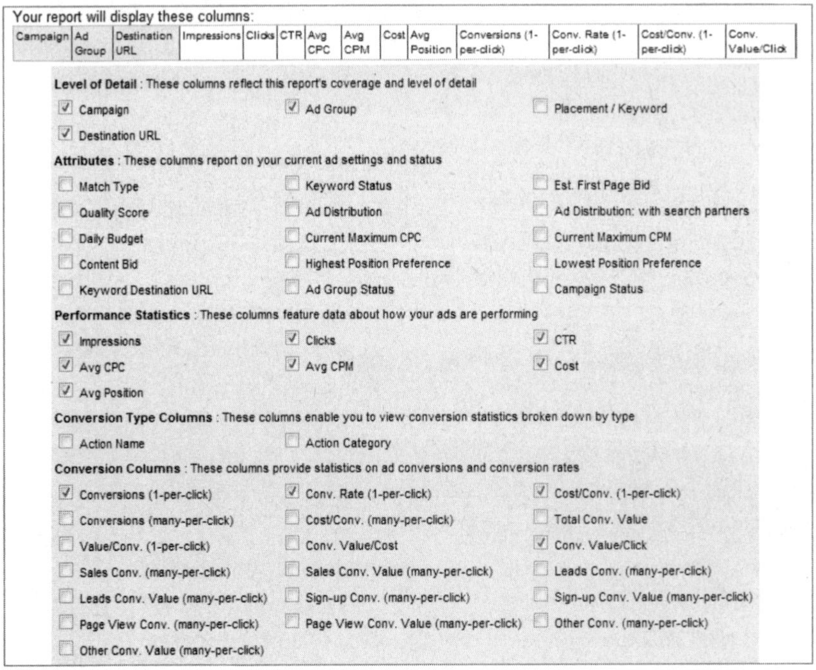

Figure 15.27 URL Performance Report

If you have multiple conversion types, then choose the various conversion actions you want to see performance data for to determine how well the page converted.

Examine the landing page metrics and compare those metrics to the goals you are trying to reach. There is no best landing page. If you want the most conversions, then the highest conversion rate is your best page. If you are looking for minimizing lead cost, then examine your lowest cost per conversion.

What is essential when running either ad copy or landing pages tests is that you do not combine search and content data. Figure 15.28 shows the results from a narrow theme site test.

If we were to combine all data regardless of whether the metrics came from search or content, it would appear that the PPC dedicated page would be the best page, as its ROI, value per click, cost per conversion, and conversion rate are all better numbers than the home page.

	A	B	C	D	E	H	I	J	K	L
		CPC	Impressions	Clicks	CTR	Conversion Rate	Cost Conversion	Revenue	Value Per Click	ROI
2	**All Networks**									
3	Home Page	$1.16	984,043	18,932	1.92%	8.73%	$13.34	$82,600	$4.36	375%
4	PPC Dedicated Page	$1.22	972,954	17,043	1.75%	10.70%	$11.42	$91,150	$5.35	438%
5										
6	**Search**									
7	Home Page	$2.23	43,565	4,065	9.33%	16.68%	$13.35	$33,900	$8.34	374%
8	PPC Dedicated Page	$1.90	40,785	4,251	10.42%	9.48%	$19.99	$20,150	$4.74	250%
9										
10	**Content**									
11	Home Page	$0.87	940,478	14,867	1.58%	6.55%	$13.34	$48,700	$3.28	375%
12	PPC Dedicated Page	$1.00	932,169	12,792	1.37%	11.10%	$8.99	$71,000	$5.55	556%

Figure 15.28 Narrow theme landing page test data

When someone is engaged in search, they have thought about the products or services associated with their search. They are somewhere within the buying funnel. In this case, we see that the home page led to a higher conversion rate than the PPC dedicated landing page.

The PPC dedicated landing page was a page that showcased a specific offer to the user. It had fewer navigation elements than the home page and did not explain multiple sides of the business. It had one call to action and explained only half the business. For the content network, the PPC dedicated landing page converted much better than the home page, which converted better for search users.

> **Note:** I conducted an informal survey of PPC experts on this experiment. Almost all of them thought the PPC landing page would do better. This result is the reason you test. Conventional wisdom is not always correct. Ideas will get you started thinking about layouts that will increase conversions. However, the data will give you conclusive results on which test result really is best for your company.

Testing Profit per Click and Profit per Impression

Which combination leads to higher profits?

- High CTR, many visitors, low conversion rate
- Low CTR, few visitors, high conversion rate

When you start to combine several metrics together, it can start to become overwhelming to determine which keyword, ad copy, and landing page combination leads to the highest profits for your company.

A searcher's query sets their expectations for the search results page. The ad copy on the search results page sets the expectation for the landing page. The landing page needs to be an extension of the ad copy and answer the searcher's initial question. Therefore, all of these elements affect each other. There is a way to boil down these various metrics to a single number that will tell you which combination is the most profitable.

This leads to my absolute favorite testing metrics: profit per click or profit per impression.

Every time your ad is shown on a search, you have a chance of a conversion. You chose a keyword. Someone searched for that keyword. Your ad was shown on a search page. You have a chance of converting that visitor. Therefore, you should measure how much profit you make on a search result every single time your ad is shown, even when it does not receive the click. This is known as profit per impression.

On the content network, you do not know the intent of the user. Some people are reading the articles, or the ad is well below the fold. In these cases, you should measure profit per click. However, when you use site targeting on the content network, as you are choosing specific sites on which you want your ad shown, you should measure profit per impression.

When we measure profit per click/impression, what we want to know is how ad copy and landing page combinations affect our total profits. Therefore, we will combine a landing page and an ad copy test together. To set up this test, follow these simple steps (Figure 15.29):

1. Write two pieces of ad copy.
2. Choose two landing pages.
3. Send ad copy 1 to landing page 1.
4. Duplicate ad copy 1 and send it to landing page 2.
5. Write ad copy 2 and send it to landing page 1.
6. Duplicate ad copy 2 and send it to landing page 2.

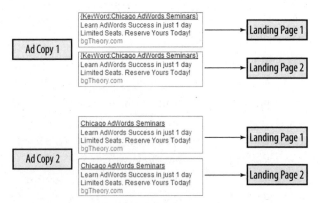

Figure 15.29 Profit per click ad group setup

Once the test is set up, let it accumulate the necessary data for you to make a decision. When you have enough data, run an ad performance report with the same data points as in the ad copy testing section earlier, "Measuring the Results of Your Ad Copy Test."

Export the report to a spreadsheet and add these three columns (Figure 15.30).

- Profit: Revenue – Cost (or other calculations you complete with margins)
- Profit per Impression: Impressions / Profit
- Profit per Click: Clicks / Profit

	A	B	C	D	E	F	G	H	I	J	K	L	M	N
1	Test Name		CPC	Impressions	Clicks	CTR	Cost	Conversions	Conversion Rate	Cost Conversion	Revenue	Profit	Profit Per Impression	Profit Per Cilck
2		Ad Copy 1												
3	Test 1	Landing Page 1	$0.73	376,023	22,034	5.86%	$16,032	1511	6.86%	$10.61	$75,550	$59,518	$0.16	$2.70
4	Test 2	Landing Page 2	$0.92	378,094	24,955	6.60%	$23,034	1823	7.31%	$12.64	$91,150	$68,116	$0.18	$2.73
5														
6		Ad Copy 2												
7	Test 3	Landing Page 1	$0.62	312,918	26,013	8.31%	$16,023	1103	4.24%	$14.53	$55,150	$39,127	$0.13	$1.50
8	Test 4	Landing Page 2	$1.16	369,447	18,991	5.14%	$22,034	1701	8.96%	$12.95	$85,050	$63,016	$0.17	$3.32

Figure 15.30 Profit per Click/Impression spreadsheet

In Figure 15.30, we can see that Test 2 has the highest profit per impression. This test does not have the highest CTR, conversion rate, or lowest cost per conversion. However, all the metrics combined lead to the most profitable user experience for either search or site targeting.

If we take this report to the extreme and look at total profit as if each combination received all the possible impressions (Figure 15.31), we can see how much profit each test combination would have received.

	A	B	C	D	E	F	G	H	I	J	K	L	M	N
1	Test Name		CPC	Impressions	Clicks	CTR	Cost	Conversions	Conversion Rate	Cost Conversion	Revenue	Profit	Profit Per Impression	Profit Per Cilck
2		Ad Copy 1												
3	Test 1	Landing Page 1	$0.73	1,436,482	84,174	5.86%	$61,245	5772	6.86%	$10.61	$288,616	$227,370	$0.16	$2.70
4	Test 2	Landing Page 2	$0.92	1,436,482	94,811	6.60%	$87,512	6926	7.31%	$12.64	$346,304	$258,791	$0.18	$2.73
5														
6		Ad Copy 2												
7	Test 3	Landing Page 1	$0.62	1,436,482	119,415	8.31%	$73,555	5063	4.24%	$14.53	$253,172	$179,616	$0.13	$1.50
8	Test 4	Landing Page 2	$1.16	1,436,482	73,841	5.14%	$85,672	6614	8.96%	$12.95	$330,691	$245,018	$0.17	$3.32

Figure 15.31 Extrapolated profit if each test received all available impressions.

Test 2 would have lead to $258,791 in revenue, which is $13,773 higher than the next most profitable combination, Test 4. Using profit per impression numbers is one the best ways to understand which testing combination leads to the highest profits.

The testing methodologies we have examined so far add new ad copy or landing pages to an ad group and split your traffic in half. If you have profitable ad groups right now, you are taking a lot of risk that the new combinations will lead to similar or higher profit margins than you already have. There is a way to lower your risk threshold when testing new ads or landing pages.

Lowering the Risk of Losing Profits While Testing

If you have an established ad group that has one ad and one landing page, and then you add either a new ad copy or landing page, you are putting half of your revenue in jeopardy. You will have to take some risks while testing; however, there is a way to lower the amount of profit you are putting at risk.

Instead of adding one new ad copy and hoping that the new one will perform as well or better than the established ad copy, first duplicate the existing ad copy several times. Wait for the ads to be approved by Google, and then add just one new test ad copy.

For instance, if you duplicate the existing ad copy three times and then have only one test ad (as shown in the following illustration), then the established ads will be served 75 percent of the time and the test ad 25 percent of the time. This will create a scenario where you are only putting 25 percent of your existing revenue at risk.

You can do the same risk mitigation for landing page testing. Duplicate the established ad copy several times and send all of those ads to your existing landing page where you know your profits. Then duplicate the ad one last time and only send the traffic from that single ad to the test page. If you only wanted to test 10 percent of the traffic, then you would have nine ads going to your established landing page and only one ad copy going to the test page.

Best Practices for Testing Techniques That Will Increase Profits

Testing ad copy and landing pages is essential to maximize the potential of your AdWords account. The most important thing with testing is to just start doing it. It is not difficult to test. Search behavior changes over time. Your competition will be changing their ads, landing pages, and offers. If you do not test ad copy and landing pages, you will never realize the full potential of your AdWords account or website.

By following the instructions in this chapter, you will be able to create both ad copy and landing page tests that will increase your profits and show you which of your marketing elements resonate best with your customers.

- When testing, make sure your campaign is set to rotate so all the ads receive equal exposure.

- Start by writing different types of ads, such as question, review, and information ads.

- Always filter your reports to see search only or content only data.

- When you have statistical significance, run an ad performance report and examine the data. Keep the best ad in your ad group. Examine the data from the losing ads to see if you can learn anything. Delete the losing ads, and then create new ads to continue the cycle of testing.

- On the content network, if you find that certain ads only perform better on specific sites, then use those ads in conjunction with placement targeting.

- When testing landing pages, first test where on your site you should send the traffic.

- Once you are certain where to send visitors on your website, create different layouts for your landing pages and test which one performs better.

- Use the URL performance report to see which page is best. You may see different pages perform best for a content network or a search network.

- If you are testing multiple metrics at once or are focused on profits, use profit per impression/click testing.

- If you have established ad groups, test a smaller percentage of your traffic to lessen the risk of losing profits.

When you first start testing, it is not uncommon to see dramatic changes. This is often because it is the first time you may have thought about how searchers view and interact with your ads and landing pages. Over time, your improvements will be smaller, yet every improvement continues to increase your profits—so never stop testing.

In this chapter, we used the ad performance report and the URL performance report to examine the data. AdWords offers 11 different reports. In the next chapter, we will dive into the reports to learn what type of data can be extracted from AdWords and the best uses of that data.

AdWords Reports: How to Extract Actionable Information

Your AdWords account will accumulate a variety of statistics that are available through the AdWords reporting interface. There are three steps to creating any report. The first is understanding what you need to know, the second is extracting the data from AdWords, and the third is analyzing the report. In this chapter, we will examine how to create a report, and then take a deep look into each of the reports and how to use them to improve your account's performance.

16

Chapter Contents

Choosing General AdWords Report Settings

Google allows you to extract a plethora of data about your AdWords account's performance. We will initially focus on how to run a report and the options for determining what metrics are included in the reports, and then we will examine each report type in detail and discuss its best uses.

To run a report, first navigate to the Reporting tab in your AdWords account (Figure 16.1). The report center will display your last 15 reports and any reporting templates you have created. Next, click on the Create A New Report link.

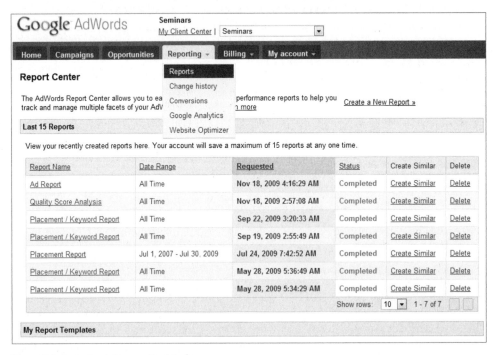

Figure 16.1 Navigating to the reporting interface

As you choose different reports, the available report settings will also change to match the type of report you are running. This section describes the settings that apply to all types of reports.

Report Settings

The report settings determine how the report will be displayed by both time and account structure. Choose the settings (Figure 16.2), explained as follows:

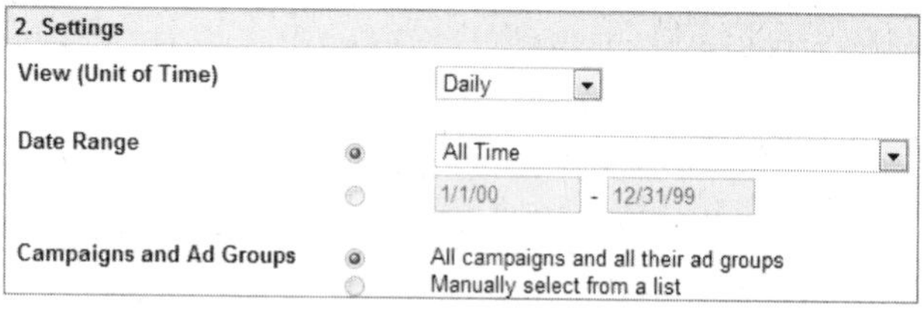

2. Settings		
View (Unit of Time)		Daily ▾
Date Range	⦿	All Time ▾
	○	1/1/00 - 12/31/99
Campaigns and Ad Groups	⦿	All campaigns and all their ad groups
	○	Manually select from a list

Figure 16.2 Choosing report settings

View (Unit of Time) Choose the time increment when you want to view the data. The default is summary data. Summary data does not break up your report by any time frame, but it includes each data point, such as a keyword or ad copy, on its own line. If you want to create trend charts in a spreadsheet, then viewing hourly, daily, weekly, or monthly data makes it easy to create charts from your reports.

> **Note:** Not all time frames are available for each report. If you are running a keyword/placement report, the smallest unit of time available is daily. If you are examining ad group data, then you can see hourly by day or hourly summarized. Therefore, if you wanted to see if you have conversion rate changes by hour of the day to determine if you want to use advanced ad scheduling, you will have to run an ad group or campaign report as this data is not available.

Date Range The date range option is straightforward. Choose the time frame for the report. Google has built-in options, such as last seven days, last business week, etc., or you can choose your own time frame.

Campaigns and Ad Groups Choose which campaigns or ad groups you want included in the reports. You can see data for a single ad group, multiple ad groups, entire campaigns, or your entire account. The default option is your entire account. Using naming conventions that allow you to easily identify an ad group's or campaign's purpose can help streamline your choices for choosing campaigns. For instance, ending campaigns with "- content" or "- search" indicates the campaign's network visibility. Within content campaigns, ending ad groups with "- images" or "- text ads" can let you see the types of ads running within the group.

After you have chosen how the information will be displayed, you can choose the data points you want included in the reports.

Advanced Report Settings

The advanced settings allow you to change the data available in your report as well as filter the data. Clicking the Add Or Remove Columns link will open up a list of all the variables you can see for the chosen report (Figure 16.3).

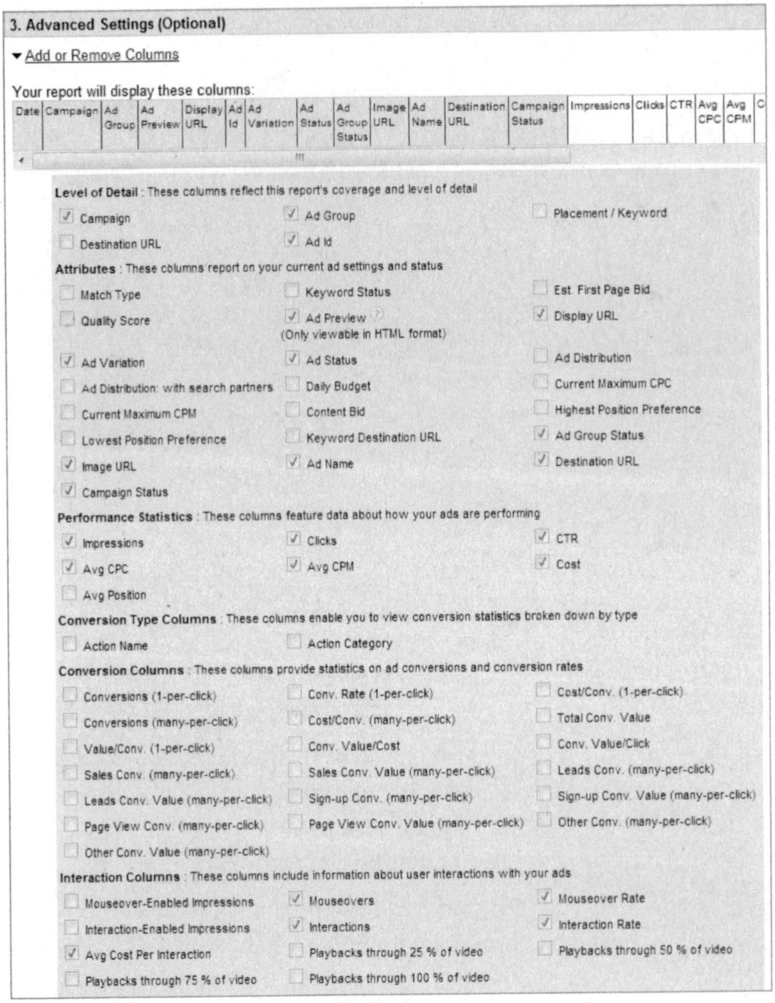

Figure 16.3 Adding or removing columns in reports

Above the options, you will see a list of columns that your report will display. The actual metrics are broken down into six sections:

Level of Detail The first set of options determines how granular you will see the data as it fits into your AdWords account. The most common selections are campaign and ad group. Some reports are only available at a campaign or ad group level. In cases where the data cannot be segmented to the ad group or keyword level, those options will not be displayed.

Attributes The attributes are the variables associated with the type of report you want to view. These items will vary the most between reports. If you are running a geographic performance report, many of the variables will be associated with geographies, such as city, metro, and region. If you are running a demographic performance report, your options will be age and gender.

> **Note:** Each time you add a new attribute, you are further segmenting the data, which can make it harder to analyze. For instance, if you run a geographic performance report including every single city, the stats for each city might be so small that you end up combining all the cities to see the statistics at the metro level. In cases like this, instead of seeing all the metrics by city, you might want to run the report only including the metro and not the city so that Google does the data combination for you. If you run a report and find that the data is too granular for you, removing a few attribute options can make the information easier to analyze.

Performance Statistics The performance statistics section correlates to your account's typical metrics, such as click-through rate, average cost per click, and so on. You will see these metrics for each attribute and level of detail combination you have chosen.

Conversion Type Columns These options are Action Name and Action Category and directly refer to the options you choose when you set up AdWords conversion tracking.

Conversion Columns The conversion columns will show you statistics that correlate the report type with your conversion activity. You can see cost per conversion, conversion rate, and other conversion metrics associated with each conversion type you are tracking.

AdWords shows two different metric options with each of the conversion types: many-per-click and 1-per-click. One-per-click is when someone clicked on your ad and only completed an action on your website within 30 days (the length of the AdWords conversion tracking cookie). Many-per-click is when someone completed more than one action on your website. If someone subscribes to a newsletter and contacts your company—hence conducting two actions on your website—that visitor would be a single 1-per-click conversion, but two many-per-click conversions.

Interaction Columns The last three sections, Historical Video Columns, Interaction Columns, and Local Business Ad Interaction Columns, are not shown with every report. If you are running a report that includes data from ads that a searcher can interact with, such as a video ad, then you will be able to see additional metrics for those ads such as how many people watched 25 percent of your video. If you are optimizing video ads or ads that people can interact with, these columns are useful to see which ads are engaging customers. If you are looking at keyword or text ad information, these columns are not applicable and will not appear in the report.

Filtering Your Reporting Data

The easiest way to narrow down the data you are working with is to set up filters. Filters allow you to determine what data is included or excluded from a report (Figure 16.4).

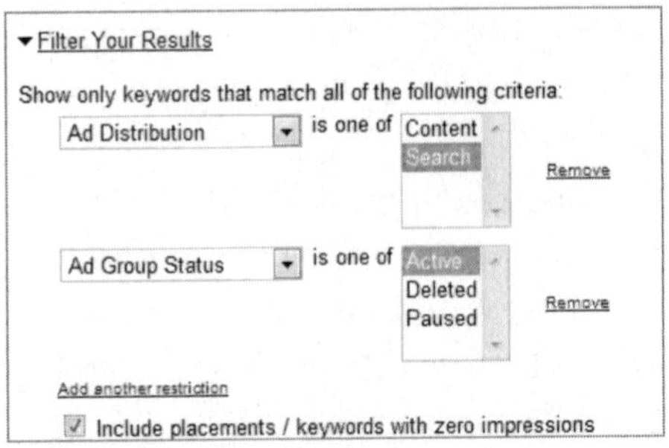

Figure 16.4 Filtering your data

The most common filter is to only view content or search data. As these two networks are different from each other, you should not combine the data when making optimization decisions. However, you can add additional filters based on a variety of metrics. For instance, if you are making keyword bid decisions, you might only want to see keywords that have accrued at least 100 clicks. If you are trying to track down all your disapproved keywords or ad copy, you can filter for only disapproved items. By filtering your data, you can include only the information necessary to help your analysis.

By default, AdWords only displays keywords that have received at least one impression. There is an optional check box that will include all keywords in a report regardless of impressions accrued.

Templates, Scheduling, and Automatically Emailing Reports

If you create a report and want to run that same report in the future, you can save it as a template (Figure 16.5). You can also set reports to be automatically run for you. If you look at keywords every single week, then schedule a weekly report. If you want to look at a quality score on a monthly basis, create a quality score report that is run every month.

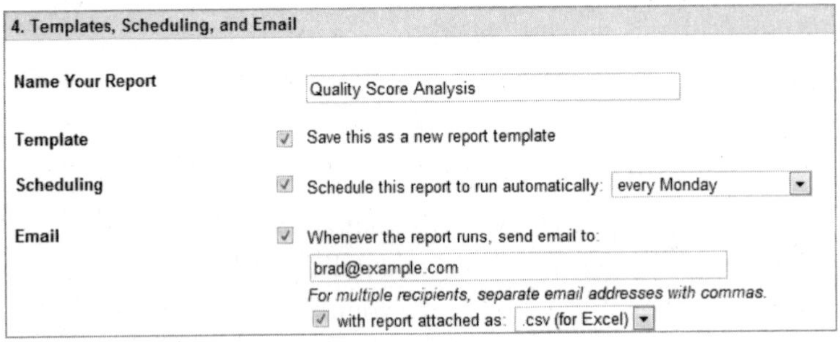

Figure 16.5 Saving and emailing reports

Finally, you can also have reports emailed directly to you. This makes it easier to receive the report in email, run your calculations, and then make changes in the AdWords editor. Using this method can be quicker than logging into the interface to receive your report and then trying to make changes in the interface. If your report is too large, often over 10MB, the report will not be attached in the email, but you will receive a notification that the report has been completed.

As discussed in Chapter 7 in the section "What to Do if Your Quality Score Drops," the quality score displayed is the quality score for your keyword when the report was run regardless of the time frame used to generate the report. Scheduling regular reports to be emailed to you can help in having archived reports so it is easier to determine when your quality score dropped and have a starting place for your investigation.

Using these various options, you can create reports that include specific information to make decisions in your account. Next, let us examine all of the reports and the best uses for each one.

Using Reports to Optimize Your Account

When you first navigate to the reporting screen, you will see a list of available reports (Figure 16.6). Each of these reports gives you different insights into your AdWords account.

1. Report Type

Choose a report from the following options: Learn more about report types

⊙	Placement / Keyword Performance	View performance data for keywords or placements you've specifically targeted.
○	Ad Performance	View performance data for each of your ads.
○	URL Performance	View performance data for each of your Destination URLs.
○	Ad Group Performance	View ad group performance data for one or more of your campaigns.
○	Campaign Performance	View performance data for your campaigns.
○	Account Performance	View performance data for your entire account.
○	Demographic Performance	View performance data for sites by demographic.
○	Geographic Performance	View performance data by geographic origin.
○	Search Query Performance	View performance data for search queries which triggered your ad and received clicks.
○	Placement Performance ⓘ	View performance data for content network sites where your ad has been shown.
○	Reach and Frequency Performance ⓘ	View reach and frequency performance data for your campaigns.

Figure 16.6 Available AdWords reports

Choosing the correct report to work from is important to ensure that you are making the best use of your valuable time in analyzing your account. With most of these reports, if you want to visualize the data utilizing conditional formatting, refer to Chapter 13's section "Revenue per Click" to color code your data so you can easily see what is making—or losing—you money.

Placement/Keyword Performance Report

If you want to see keyword information, this is the report you should start analyzing.

If you set bids for each keyword based on its returns, run this report and include keyword, match type, cost per conversion, value per click, and total revenue stats. Next, use the formulas in Chapter 13 in the section "Calculating Your Max CPC" to determine your new CPCs. Finally, input this data into a spreadsheet and use the AdWords Editor to upload your new CPCs.

If you have a significant number of keywords where the bid would have to be $0.00 based on your conversion metrics, you will have to choose to delete those keywords, set your own bid not based on conversion metrics, or move it to a budget optimizer campaign (see "Understanding Attribution Management" in Chapter 13).

Improving Your Quality Score If your quality score is under 7, you should continue to optimize your quality score. Run a keyword report and include the ad group, keyword, cost, and quality score columns. Then input the data into a pivot table and look for ad groups with low quality scores and high spends. This will help you find pockets of high opportunity areas to increase your quality score. For full details on this procedure, please see the Chapter 7 section "Increasing Your Quality Scores."

Determining What Keywords Are Not on Page 1 Some keywords may have limited impressions and low conversions because they are not on page 1. To quickly view what keywords are not on page 1, create a keyword report with the keyword, match type, first page bid, and max CPC columns. Then use conditional formatting to highlight keywords where the max CPC is below the first page bid. You may want to increase these CPCs so that the keywords receive enough impressions for you to make determinations about their effectiveness.

Ad Performance Report

The ad performance report will allow you to see metrics for each of your ads. If you are testing ad copy, this is the report you will want to use. When you run an ad performance report, in the Settings section of the reports you will be able to choose which ad types you want to be included in the report (Figure 16.7).

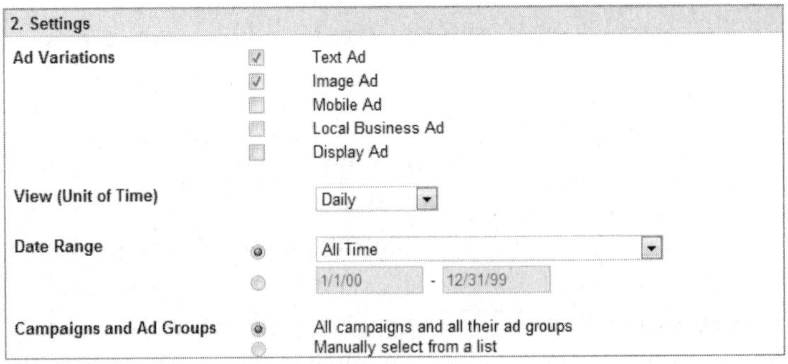

Figure 16.7 Choosing ad types

As it is common to see the best ad for search not being the same as your best ad for the content network, filter the data so that you are only viewing content or search data.

If your account does not accrue enough clicks per month for you to be able to test individual ads at the ad group level, and instead you used a tagline in several ads across your account, follow these steps to create the report necessary for you to analyze the data:

1. Create an ad group report that includes:

   Headline

   Description line 1

   Description line 2

   Display URL

   Impression

   Clicks

   Average CPC

   Cost

   Conversion rate

   Cost per conversion

2. Export the data to a spreadsheet.

3. Create a pivot table from the spreadsheet.

4. Choose your ad element (such as headline or description line 1) as your row element.

5. Add the metrics (impressions, clicks, etc.) as your values.

This will give you a pivot table that shows all of the metrics associated with an ad element, such as just description line 2 (Figure 16.8), so you can make decisions about which element of the ad copy is working best for your account.

While making decisions based on combining the data from various ads into a single report is not nearly as good as examining individual ad copy results within a single ad group, it is better than not testing at all.

The ad performance report allows you to see how ads are doing by ad group or campaign. However, it will not show you how an ad is doing on a specific placement. If there are placements where you are receiving a significant amount of high quality traffic and want to test different ads on those specific sites, then put just those sites, or even a single placement, in an ad group along with your test ads. This organization will allow you to create an ad performance report that only includes that specific ad group so you can see how multiple ads are performing on an individual placement.

Row Labels	Values Average of CTR	Average of Cost per Conversion	Average of Conversion Rate
AdWords Seminars for Success™	5.34%	$15.21	7.23%
Easy & Free Subscription Options	5.10%	$17.78	5.23%
Hosted by Brad 'eWhisper' Geddes	4.65%	$8.28	11.23%
Knowledge, Training, and Sales	2.12%	$16.90	9.23%
Learn AdWords Success	3.43%	$55.16	2.23%
Learn AdWords Success for Only $249	1.54%	$17.67	6.34%
Limited Seats. Reserve Yours Today!	4.45%	$25.11	2.23%
Limited space. Reserve seats now!	8.23%	$6.95	11.23%
Max your AdWords ROI for Only $249!	6.32%	$8.90	10.23%
Max your AdWords ROI.	2.23%	$7.78	17.23%
One Day Only. Register Online Now!	4.43%	$133.91	1.15%
Grand Total	**4.35%**	**$28.51**	**7.60%**

Figure 16.8 Pivot table for ad report

Find Underperforming Ads

Another use for this report is to find underperforming ads. Run an ad performance report for only the search network. Each report contains summary information where you can find your overall account's click-through rate, conversion rate, and cost per conversion. Then look to see which individual ads are below your account's norm.

Before you assume that these ads are underperforming compared to your account, always examine the keywords that are causing these ads to show. You will find instances where an ad group had more general keywords than other ad groups, in which case it is normal to see the CTR and conversion rate lower than the account's norm.

However, if the keywords are as specific as other ad groups, and those ads have lower conversion rates, then either the ad needs to be tested, or the landing page needs to be changed. Always look at the keyword or placement, ad copy, and landing page together when determining performance.

Find All Disapproved or Paused Ads

Within the ad performance report you can filter to see only disapproved ads or paused ads. If you have seasonal or month-end sales-based ads that you pause and resume on a regular basis, this report makes it easy to find all of your ads in a paused state.

In addition, if you have had several ads disapproved, you can filter only for disapproved ads so you know which ad groups need new ads.

URL Performance Report

The URL performance report allows you to see metrics for every single page you are sending traffic to within your AdWords account. If you are testing different landing pages, this is the report you should use to see which landing pages have the highest conversion rate.

You should note that you will see metrics for every destination URL even if they are different only through tracking parameters, such as those found in the Chapter 5 section "Step-by-Step Guide to Building Destination URLs." For instance, while these three links are the same page on a website, the URL performance report will show three different lines of data in your report:

Example.com?src=4

Example.com

Example.com?matchtype=exact&{keyword}

In this case, it is useful to strip off the tracking parameters and combine the data for each individual URL. Follow these steps to easily strip off the tracking links:

1. Copy the Destination URL column in Excel.
2. Paste the Destination URL column into Notepad (or any software that does not preserve Excel formatting).
3. Copy the Notepad file.
4. Create a new Excel sheet.
5. Paste the file into the new sheet.
6. Click on the clipboard icon that will appear next to your pasted information and choose Use Text Import Wizard.
7. Choose Delimited, then click Next.
8. Choose Other, and in the text box type in a question mark.
9. Click Finish.
10. You will now have a spreadsheet with your URL in one column and the tracking parameters in a second column.
11. Copy only the URL column and paste it into the original report in the Destination URL column.

While this appears to be a complicated process, after you do it once or twice you will find it takes less than 10 seconds to accomplish. Since you will now have the same URL on different rows, it is time to combine the data across all the rows. The easiest way to do this is to create a pivot table. In your Row Labels, show the destination URLs. In your Value column, choose the metrics you want to see, such as cost per conversion and conversion rate.

If you want to find underperforming landing pages, you can use the exact same steps as the ad copy analysis earlier; just substitute the destination URL for the ad copy information.

Ad Group Performance Report

Sometimes seeing keyword level information is data intensive and you might want to see a higher level of information. The ad group performance report is a good place to start.

Setting Ad Group Bids If you are setting ad group bids instead of keyword level bids for the search network, you can use this report just like the keyword report in running your max CPC calculations and then use the AdWords Editor to import the new bids into AdWords.

Setting Content Network Bids You cannot set keyword level bids for the content network, you can only set bids by placement or ad group. Therefore, when doing calculations for content network exposure, except for placement targeting, this is the report to run to determine your max content CPC. When using the report to determine content bids, make sure you filter the data so you are only seeing content information.

Viewing Conversion Rates by Hour The ad group performance report allows you to see performance statistics by hour, a unit of time that is not available in the keyword report. If you are doing analysis to see if you should use ad scheduling to change your bids on certain days or times of day, this report is a good place to start that analysis. In addition, if you find that only a handful of ad groups change performance by time of day, you might only move those ad groups to a new campaign and leave the others in the original campaign.

Campaign and Account Performance Reports

The campaign and account performance reports are almost identical. The only difference is that the campaign performance report lets you see your metrics at the campaign level, and the account performance report shows you metrics for your entire account at once.

As most of your decisions will be made at the ad group, placement, or keyword level, these reports would not be used often except that there are some performance statistics that are only shown at the campaign or account level (Figure 16.9).

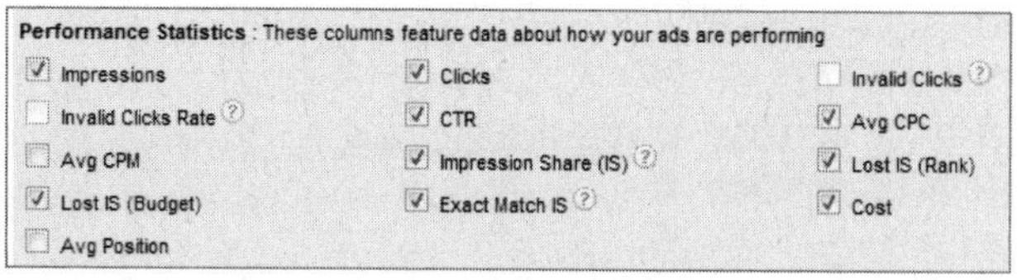

☑ Impressions   ☑ Clicks   ☐ Invalid Clicks ⓘ

☐ Invalid Clicks Rate ⓘ   ☑ CTR   ☑ Avg CPC

☐ Avg CPM   ☑ Impression Share (IS) ⓘ   ☑ Lost IS (Rank)

☑ Lost IS (Budget)   ☑ Exact Match IS ⓘ   ☑ Cost

☐ Avg Position

Figure 16.9 Performance statistics for campaign reports

Invalid Clicks Report Under the Performance Statistics section for both the campaign and account performance reports, there are two selections, Invalid Clicks and Invalid Clicks Rate, that will show you how many clicks you received for which you were not charged, and the percentage of total clicks that were not charged.

> **Note:** If you are trying to reconcile your analytics data with AdWords, this is a useful report to examine. Analytics systems include all visitors who made it to your website regardless of whether you were charged for that click or not. AdWords automatically discounts certain clicks from costing you money or accruing statistics within your account.

Impression Share Report Under the Performance Statistics section (Figure 16.9), there are data points called Lost (IS) Budget, Impression Share (IS), Exact Match IS, and Lost IS (Rank). If you choose all of these items and run a report, you will create an impression share report.

The impression share report (Figure 16.10) will show you how often your ads are being shown and reasons they are not being displayed. This information is only displayed for search; the content network is not included.

Impressions 794,787	Clicks 9,819	Impression Share (IS) 22.44%	Lost IS (Rank) 55.21%	Lost IS (Budget) 22.36%	Exact Match IS 34.85%	Cost $8,518.12	Avg Position 4.07

Campaign	Ad Distribution	Daily Budget	Impressions	Clicks	Impression Share (IS)	Lost IS (Rank)	Lost IS (Budget)	Exact Match IS	Cost	Avg Position
	Search Only	$10.00	794,787	9,819	22%	55%	22%	35%	$8,518.12	4.1

Show rows: 25 ▾   1 - 1 of 1   ◀ ▶

Figure 16.10 Impression share report

Impression Share (IS) is the percentage of times your ad was shown when it was eligible for the auction.

Lost IS (Rank) is the percentage of times your ad was not shown because your ad's position was below the number of ads displayed on a page.

Lost IS (Budget) is the percentage of times your ad was not shown because your budget was too low.

Exact Match IS is your impression share if all your keywords were set to exact match.

If you ever wonder how much an account could spend if you only increased the budget, the impression share report is the place to look.

Demographic Performance Report

This report will display your performance metrics, such as click-through rate or cost per conversion by age range, gender, and website. Demographic information is currently only available for some websites in the content network.

If you run this report and see very little demographic information, do not fret, it just means your ad is on sites that do not collect or do not share demographic information with Google. Generally, only social media sites collect and share this anonymous demographic data.

Note: If you run this report and see widely different conversion rates by demographics, you may want to use demographic bidding which can be found in Chapter 10 in the section "Setting Different Bids by Demographics." In addition, use the Google Ad Planner (Chapter 10 in the section "Google Ad Planner: Free Access to Expensive Data") to find other sites with similar demographics and content so you can placement target those similar websites.

Geographic Performance Report

The geographic performance report will allow you to see your metrics by country, region, metro, or city. In addition, you can see those metrics by content or search.

Run this report and examine the differences in your clicks and conversions by geography. If you find there are certain geographies that are not converting, you may want to create a separate campaign to show different messages to those areas. If you find there are geographies that are converting much higher than normal, you may want to create a campaign with a higher daily budget to reach just those areas.

This report can also give you a point of investigation for your website analysis. It is not uncommon for American companies to advertise in both the United States and Canada, only to find that their Canadian conversion rates are much lower. This is because many sites do not ship to Canada or accept non-U.S. billing addresses, yet these same companies still serve ads to Canada. By using this report to find areas where your conversions are lower than normal, you can find other errors that have nothing to do with AdWords.

One of the quality score factors is click-through rate in a specific geography. If you find that your CTR is much lower in a geographic region, your quality score for just that region may also be lower. In this case, you might want to exclude that geography or create a specific campaign with ad copy that speaks to that region to increase your CTR and visibility in that geography.

When trying to determine where people are clicking and buying, this is a good report to give you insight into the performance of various geographies and also to determine if you need to include, exclude, or change your geographic targeting options.

Search Query Performance Report

If you use broad or phrase match keywords, your ads will show for a variety of words that are not in your account. The search query report will show you what someone actually searched for that caused your ads to be displayed. If you use AdWords conversion tracking, you can see the conversion rate and cost per conversion for all of these keyword variations.

You should run this report regularly and look for two specific pieces of information:

Keywords That Spend Money But Do Not Convert With broad and phase match keywords, your ads will be shown on a variety of queries. Some of those variations will convert and others will not.

When you find variations that are spending money and not converting, you should first examine to see if the keyword is appropriate to that ad copy and landing page. If the keyword is not appropriate to that ad group, but is appropriate to another one, then add the keyword as a negative in the first ad group and as an actual keyword in the more appropriate ad group. Later, run a keyword report and either choose to keep that keyword in the more appropriate ad group, or delete the keyword altogether once it accumulates more data. As you still do not want this keyword shown in the first ad group, leave the negative keyword in place, or move the negative keyword to the campaign level so that none of the ad groups will show for that word.

If the search query is not appropriate to any ad group in your account, then add it as a negative keyword so that your ad will not be displayed for that search query again.

Keywords That Convert But Are Not in the Ad Group If you find there are words that are converting but are nowhere to be found in your ad group, add these variations as actual keywords so you can track their performance and set appropriate bids for each keyword.

Whenever you are conducting positive or negative keyword research, start with the search query report. Viewing actual search queries can give you insight into your customers and trigger new ideas for keywords.

Placement Performance Report

When optimizing for the content network, this is the best report to analyze. The placement performance report will show you metrics for each URL or domain where your ad is being displayed.

The Difference between the Placement Performance Report and the Placement/Keyword Performance Report

When viewing content information in the placement/keyword performance report, you can only see the domain where an ad was shown. You cannot view individual URLs. In the placement performance report, you *can* see the individual URLs where your ad is being displayed.

If you are optimizing managed placements, use the placement performance report. If you want to see a high level snapshot of your account, use the placement/keyword performance report. It is useful to segment the placement/keyword performance report to only see content data when viewing placement information.

With the placement performance report, you will have an additional Settings option (Figure 16.11) to choose Domain or URL. If you choose URL, you will see metrics for every URL where your ad was displayed. If you choose Domain, you will only see information for each domain and not the individual URLs. Perform the following two steps:

Figure 16.11 Placement performance report settings

1. The first step in optimizing the content network is to make sure your ad is being displayed on the correct types of pages. Therefore, run the report with the actual URLs included, and then click on the URLs and look at the pages where Google is placing your ads.

   • If the pages are correct, regardless of the performance metrics, then your keywords are creating appropriate themes and you do not need to adjust your keywords.

   • If the pages where your ads are being shown are not correct, you need to adjust your keywords so that you receive better placement.

   For more information on choosing content keywords, see Chapter 9 in the section "Choosing the Correct Words for Your Content Network Ad Group."

2. Run this report including only domains, or by putting the initial report into a pivot table and keying the metrics off of the domain:

- If you see domains that are not meeting your goals, block them with the Site and Category Exclusion tool.
- If you see domains that are meeting your goals, add them to a placements campaign and block them in the content-only campaign.

Note: When adding sites to a placements campaign, always check to see if there are subsections of a website available for placement and if so, look to see how your ads have done on the various subsections.

If you are seeing too many websites in this report and do not know where to start, utilize the filtering options and only look at websites that have sent you over a minimum amount of traffic, such as 200 or more clicks. By removing sites with low traffic from the report, you can create a report that only includes websites that have enough data for you to make decisions about blocking the site or turning it into a managed placement.

If you are using placement targeting, you can see your performance statistics in this report or in the placement/keyword performance report.

Reach and Frequency Performance Report

The reach and frequency performance report is only shown for CPM placement targeted ads. You can

- See the six-month cumulative frequency
- See the six-month cumulative reach for your ads
- Refine your report to a specific period

Reach and *frequency* are two common metrics for media campaigns and display ads that look to see how many people saw an ad and how often those people saw an ad, respectively.

With CPM, you are paying for impressions. Many CPM buys are on a set number of impressions. The lower your frequency cap, the less an individual person may see your message, but more total people will see your message for those impressions. Conversely, the more an individual person sees your message, the less total people will see your message.

There is a balance to be found in reinforcing your message to an individual person by having them see your ad multiple times vs. the total number of people you want to see your ad.

There is no magic number for frequency capping. Some websites are full of distractions, and any one ad might not be noticed, therefore you would want a higher frequency. Some ads are prominent, such as interstitials or large banners on a mostly text-based page, and therefore the frequency number can be lower.

 Note: It is recommended that you do set some frequency cap on your ads, even if it is as high as three per user per day, as that will help distribute your ad to more individuals.

If you find that your frequency is higher than you desire, you can set or adjust the frequency cap in your campaign settings.

Best Practices for Using AdWords Reports

Being able to extract actionable data from your account is essential to ongoing optimization. First determine the data you need, then examine the available reports.

By following the practices in this chapter, you should be able to create reports that give you the data necessary to make optimization decisions for your AdWords account.

- When you find custom reports that help you make decisions, save those reports as templates so you can easily re-create the same report.
- Schedule your favorite reports to be automatically created and emailed to you.
- Always segment the data so you are only viewing search data or content data. Never combine the two networks.
- When making keyword decisions, use the placement/keyword performance report. When optimizing for the content network, use the placement performance report.
- When running short on time, run an ad group report to find ad groups that are not meeting your goals. Then examine the keywords in just that ad group to determine new bid prices or move keywords into new ad groups with new ad copy.
- The URL performance report will show you weaknesses in your landing pages. Use this report to determine where you should be sending traffic.
- When you want to expand your keyword list or add negative keywords, start by analyzing the search query report.
- If the data you want to see is not available, try running a report that summarizes data at the next organizational point. For instance, conversion rates by hour are not available in a keyword report; therefore look to the next report, the ad group report, to find conversion rates by hour.
- If you need specific information that is not available, determine if there is another way to structure your account so you can retrieve that data. For example, if you wanted to see conversion rates by hour for a particular keyword, create an ad group with only that keyword. Now the ad group report will show you

conversion rates by hour for that particular keyword since it is the only keyword in that ad group.

You should regularly extract and analyze AdWords data so that you understand how your account is performing and what optimization steps you need to take to increase your account's effectiveness.

However, with so many options available in AdWords, it can be difficult to prioritize how often you should run reports and make decisions. In the final chapter, we will discuss the best places to spend your time so that you can continuously increase the success of your AdWords account.

Step by Step: Create and Monitor Your AdWords Account

17

Throughout the last 16 chapters, we have examined best practices, research, and optimization techniques. The amount of choices you have with AdWords is a dizzying array of possibilities. In this chapter, we will simplify the process of starting and managing AdWords by examining how to create and optimize your account step by step.

Much of the information in this chapter is contained in other chapters. This chapter consolidates the myriad information into a single place you can refer back to as you are optimizing your accounts.

Chapter Contents

Before You Create Your Account

It is easy with AdWords to start choosing keywords and writing ad copy, but do not start by getting caught up in the details. The time you spend doing keyword research can be wasted if you do not first lay out a plan based on your AdWords goals.

Follow this list of items you need to accomplish before working within your AdWords account.

List Your Marketing Goals The first step in creating a successful AdWords account is to determine your marketing goals. Goals are the reasons *why* you are advertising. If you do not have goals, it is impossible to tell if you are reaching your goals or wasting money. For a full recap of setting goals, please see "Setting Your Marketing Goals" in Chapter 13.

Always be as specific as possible. To make more money or to get more leads is not a goal. To increase your ROI from 200 percent to 240 percent or to receive 17 new leads a day from Miami are examples of well thought-out goals.

Set a priority for each goal. Do not list them as high, medium, and low. Instead, list them in order of importance. By making the hard choices of putting them in order to begin with, it is easier to determine budgets and account organization.

Keep in mind your AdWords campaign settings as you create these goals, as you may want to tailor your goals based on your potential exposure. For example, if you are selling insurance in Florida, you might have one goal for the state of Florida and another goal for Miami.

Determine Your Budgets Set a budget for every goal you listed. AdWords budgets are kept at the campaign level. The minimum campaign budget is $1 per day. Therefore, ensure that all of your goals can support a $30 per month spend.

Refine Your Starting Goals Based on Your Budget If you find that your budget is not high enough to support all of your goals, then you have two choices. One is to combine some goals. For instance, instead of having one goal for Florida and another for Miami, combine them into a single goal when you start. However, you should still plan to separate out these goals in the future. Periodically review and refine your initial goals.

The second option is to set a budget for each goal in descending order of importance. Once you have hit your maximum allowed spend, each goal without a budget will not be used for now (Figure 17.1). Review these goals in the future to see if you can allocate them some portion of the budget.

Determine Account Organization Once you have a list of goals and budgets, it is time to determine how to organize the campaigns in your account. See "Structuring Campaigns to Achieve Business Goals" in Chapter 14 for the in-depth details of account structure.

Install Conversion Tracking For every goal you want to track, set up conversion tracking. As the conversion tracking script is tied to the entire AdWords account, when you change your account structure, add or remove ad groups, or make other changes, the conversion tracking script will continue to work. See "AdWords Conversion Tracking Code" in Chapter 13 for details on creating and installing conversion tracking.

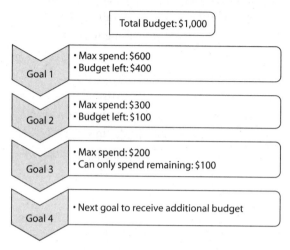

Total Budget: $1,000

Goal 1
- Max spend: $600
- Budget left: $400

Goal 2
- Max spend: $300
- Budget left: $100

Goal 3
- Max spend: $200
- Can only spend remaining: $100

Goal 4
- Next goal to receive additional budget

Figure 17.1 Allocating budget by goal importance

By installing conversion tracking before creating the account's details, you can determine if the site can support conversion tracking or if new pages need to be created. In addition, you will become more familiar with the content management system (CMS) of your website, which is necessary when choosing landing pages and keywords and determining testing methods. By determining if there are any issues before creating the account, you will save yourself from having to change all the landing pages if a new CMS is installed or new pages are created.

Please note: If you are using alternate conversions such as phone calls, create a method for tracking these conversions.

Install Analytics Finally, choose and install an analytics system. Google Analytics is a free analytics solution; however, based on your data needs you may require a more sophisticated system. The advantage of Google Analytics is that it is intimately tied to Google AdWords with a minimum amount of work.

After you have determined your goals, budgets, and installed tracking scripts, it is time to build the AdWords account.

Creating Campaigns

Once you have determined your account structure, it is time to create the campaigns. When creating the campaigns, we are going to examine the steps using the three types of campaigns we have discussed.

- Search only

- Content only (also called a discovery campaign)
- Placement campaign

Name each campaign appropriately so you can quickly see its purpose. Adding items such as geographic targeting, time of day targeting, search, content, or mobile to the name helps identify any one campaign. Some sample campaign names are:

- iPhone - California - Search Only
- Newsletter Subscriptions - Mobile - Search
- E-commerce Specials - USA - Content

If You Are Using the AdWords Editor

If you are planning on using the AdWords Editor to upload most of your keywords and ad copy, it is quicker to create all of the campaigns, ad groups, and keywords in the AdWords Editor and then upload all of the data at once.

If you want to use the interface to ensure that the campaign settings are correct, create the new campaigns in the interface and adjust the settings such as budget and geographic target. Next, download your account into the AdWords Editor. Then populate the ad groups, ad copy, and keywords into the editor using the bulk import functions. When you are done, upload the new data into your AdWords account.

Creating Search Campaigns

Search campaigns are only shown when someone does a search. These campaigns do not show up on the content network. Follow these steps to create your search campaigns.

Campaign Settings Start by determining all of the campaign's settings. These include budget, location targeting, devices (mobile or desktop), bidding options, and ad scheduling. In the network settings, choose Google search and search partners. These initial settings determine when, where, and how any ads within that campaign can be viewed (Figure 17.2).

Conduct Initial Keyword Research The purpose of doing some initial keyword research is to determine all of your themes, or ad groups. You do not need to find all of your keywords yet. Determine the various ways that people are searching for your products or services. Make a list of all your themes.

Focus on differentiating themes based on buying cycle, wide, informational, transactional, explicit, problem, symptom, product names, and branded keywords.

List Your Ad Groups From your initial keyword research, make a list of all the ad groups you want to create within your new campaign. By starting with ad groups, it will be easier to organize your keywords and ad copy. You ad group name is only used for organizational purposes. Therefore, use an ad group name that lets you easily identify the ad group's purpose.

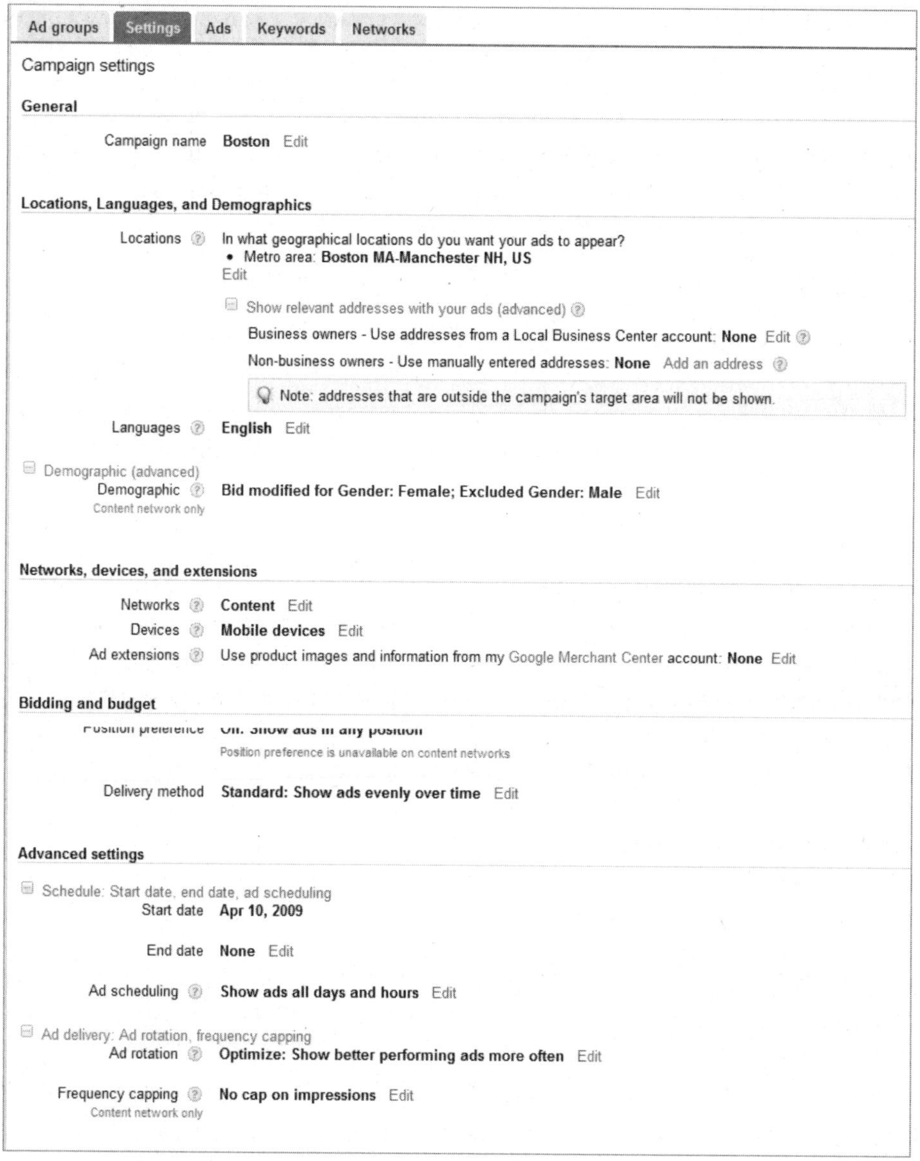

Figure 17.2 Available campaign settings

Choose Your Landing Pages For each ad group, choose the most appropriate landing page on your website. If you have two good landing pages for an ad group, first ask yourself if your ad groups are granular enough. You may need more granular ad groups. If you still have multiple landing pages for an ad group, make note of them so you can start testing different landing pages immediately.

If you are using a different landing page for each keyword, you should move this step into the keyword research phase.

Write One Targeted Ad per Ad Group For each ad group, write one highly targeted ad. When someone sees this ad, they should think that your specialty is selling the product or service the ad group provides. Ensure that the landing page you choose for the ad group shares the same intent as the ad copy. You may not use this ad once your account goes live. The ad is for organizational purposes.

While the ad shown in Figure 17.3 is not a great search ad, it is an excellent organizational ad. It segments businesses from consumers, separates Peachtree software from all other accounting software types, and is only for businesses in Denver.

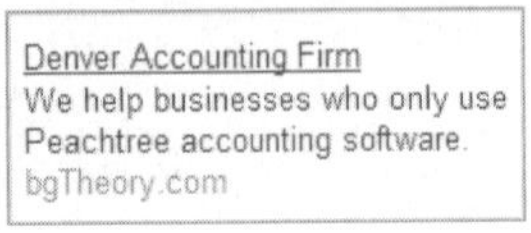

Denver Accounting Firm
We help businesses who only use
Peachtree accounting software.
bgTheory.com

Figure 17.3 Highly targeted ad copy

Start Your Keyword Research Conduct keyword research for every single ad group. As you choose a keyword for an ad group, look at the ad copy. If the ad copy accurately describes the keyword, it's in the correct ad group. If the ad copy does not describe the keyword, then put it in another ad group. You may find that you need to create additional ad groups.

Do not start with deep or long tail keywords. Few accounts should start with these types. Adding deep keywords is an optimization technique to use once you determine what words are leading to conversions.

Find Negative Keywords As you are conducting keyword research, whenever you find keywords that you do not want your ad to show for, add them as negative keywords. By starting with positive and negative keywords you can refine your ad display. If you are unsure if a keyword should be a negative, it can be useful to leave it out when you first start your account. Later on, you can use the Search Query report to see the metrics for these keywords and add them as negatives.

Determine Match Types As you do your keyword research, keep in mind the match types you will want to use. If you have a small budget, you will want to start with mostly exact and phrase match. If you have a larger budget, then start with more broad matches. It is okay to have the same keyword with different match types inside the same search campaign.

Write Ad Copy For each ad group, write at least two ads. By starting with at least two ads, you are starting the ad copy testing phase immediately. Since a brand new account does not have any metrics, there is no best or worst ad copy yet. If you have an established account, you should run an ad copy report to see what ads and taglines have been most effective so far and borrow those elements when writing your ad copy. If you have multiple landing pages for your ad group, then use the ad copy and landing page testing methodology found in "Testing Profit per Click and Profit per Impression" in Chapter 15. If you want, you can delete your initial ad that was created for organizational purposes.

Set Initial Bids Setting initial bids is difficult, as you have very few metrics to work from. The best way to set an initial bid is to estimate your conversion rate and profit per sale. Then use one of the bidding methodologies found in Chapter 13 to determine your initial CPC. If there are certain keywords that you think will do well regardless of initial bids, you could use the first page bid estimate to set bids. Be careful of using first page bids in competitive areas. You can easily lose a lot of money by overbidding to page 1 if the landing page or keyword does not convert as expected.

While it is okay for a keyword in different match types to appear twice in a search campaign, it is not okay for those keywords to have the same bid. The exact match version should have a higher bid than the phrase match. If you use broad match, that should be the lowest bid among the match types.

By following these steps, you should have a well organized beginning to a search campaign. You will need to refine your keywords, test ad copy, add negative keywords, and change bids over time to continuously optimize your campaigns.

Creating Content Campaigns

Content-only campaigns are only shown across the content network. As these campaigns are not triggered by individual keywords, but by the theme of the ad group, the setup is different than for search-only campaigns. It is okay if the same word appears in multiple ad groups within a content campaign. As individual keywords matter less than the theme of an ad group, you may have the same word in several ad groups.

In addition, you may have multiple ad groups with very similar keywords within a content campaign. Sometimes, subtle variations of keywords make a difference in where AdWords places your ad. The first step in content organization is finding what combinations of keywords are working. Therefore, feel free to have many closely related ad groups to see which one actually brings in returns.

Campaign Settings Start by determining all of the campaign's settings. These include budget, location targeting, devices (mobile or desktop), bidding options, and ad scheduling. If you want to use the CPM bidding option, make sure that only content network is selected before you choose your bidding option because the CPM bidding option is not displayed if the campaign is also shown on search. In the network settings, select Content Network, and Relevant Pages Across the Entire Network (Figure 17.4). These initial settings determine when, where, and how any ads within that campaign can be viewed.

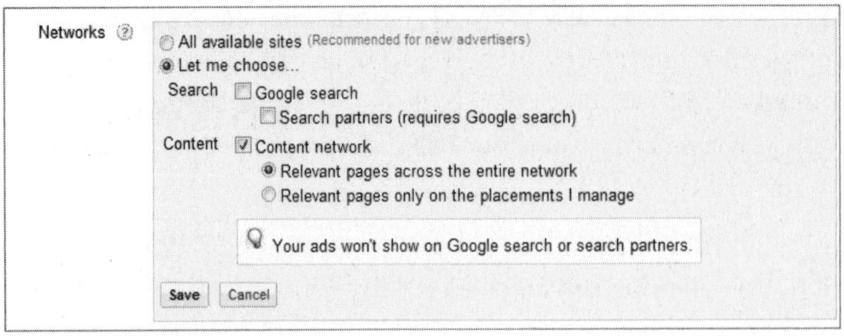

Figure 17.4 Campaign network settings

Find Web Pages Where You Want Your Ad Displayed Do some searches for your products or services and create a list of pages where you want your ad to be displayed. Examine the words used on that page or use a keyword density analyzer. If you are having a difficult time finding sites, use Google Ad Planner to help with your research or skip to the next step, "Play the Game Taboo."

If you find pages that closely resemble your products, but you do not want your ad to appear on those pages, determine what words are appearing on the page that you would want to use as negative keywords and add them to your list.

Play the Game Taboo For each product or service, play the game Taboo (see Chapter 9's section "Choosing the Correct Words for Your Content Network Ad Group" for details) and make a list of words. If there are words that you do not want to trigger your ads, add these as negative words.

Create Your Ad Groups For each list you have created by finding web pages or playing the game Taboo, make an ad group. A content ad group should contain anywhere from 1 to 12 words. Rarely will more than 12 be necessary. Please note that Google only uses 50 words at most to determine your ad group's theme, so never have more than 50 words in any content-only ad group. Match types do not matter for placing your ads. All of your keywords can be listed in broad match. Negative keywords are used in determining your placement. Therefore, add any appropriate negative keywords to each ad group.

When creating your ad group, name it something appropriate that describes the words inside the ad group. In addition, if you are using video only or image only ads within an ad group, it is a good idea to end the ad group name with the ad type for organizational reasons. For instance, "Verizon Cell Phone Plan - Video Ads" is a descriptive ad group name.

Create Your Ad Copy There are more ad formats available with the content network than with search. First determine what types of ads you want the ad group to have. While an ad group can contain a mixture of image, video, and text ads because content bids are only set at the ad group level, it can help to have ad groups that only show one ad type, as you may start bidding differently based on the ad that will be shown.

If you find that you want both image and text ads for the same keywords, you can duplicate the ad group and then have one ad group that is only image ads and another that only contains text ads.

When creating content ads, do not just think about your keywords; consider the pages that your ad will be shown on and that site's audience. As with search, start with two or more ads for each ad group.

Set Initial Bids Many times your content campaign will reach individuals not yet in the buying cycle. In these instances, your first conversion option may not be a sale, but instead another action to introduce someone to the buying funnel, such as a newsletter subscription or whitepaper download. In this instance, evaluate what you are willing to pay for someone to enter your buying funnel and your conversion rate to determine your starting bid. If you are trying to convert content clicks into sales, then use the same methodology as with search to determine your initial bids.

As there are more than a million sites in the content network, if in doubt about the initial bid, set a lower bid than you think is required. You can always raise your bid if you are not getting good placement, but you will never get your money for clicks returned if you overbid.

Following these steps will get you started creating content-only campaigns. Over time, you will have to measure results to block sites, change keywords within an ad group, and test new ad copy. One of the steps to optimizing content is to determine what sites are sending you good traffic and move those sites into a placement-only campaign.

Creating Placement-Only Campaigns

With placement-only campaigns, keywords can be used to refine your placement on an individual site; however, keywords are optional. You must choose each site where you want your ad to appear.

Campaign Settings As with both search and content campaigns, choose your initial settings such as budget and geography. In the network settings section, there are two options you want to choose. First, choose Content Network for your network reach. Under the Content section, choose Relevant Pages Only On The Placements I Manage (Figure 17.5). This is the setting that tells Google not to place your ad across the content network, but only on the specific sites you have chosen. If you are using CPM bidding for your placements, make sure you have unchecked Google Search and Search Partners before choosing CPM as your bidding methodology.

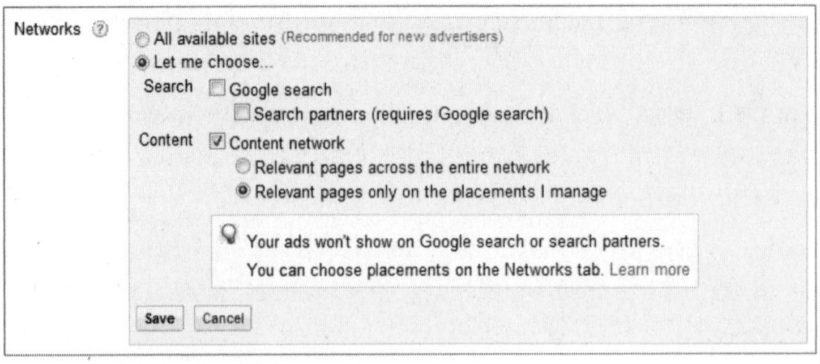

Networks ⑦ ○ All available sites (Recommended for new advertisers)
              ● Let me choose...
     Search   ☐ Google search
              ☐ Search partners (requires Google search)
     Content ☑ Content network
              ○ Relevant pages across the entire network
              ● Relevant pages only on the placements I manage

              💡 Your ads won't show on Google search or search partners.
                 You can choose placements on the Networks tab. Learn more

     [Save] [Cancel]

Figure 17.5 Only show ads on managed placements.

Ad Group Organization There are three reasons to make ad groups for placement campaigns. The first is if you are using enhanced campaigns that utilize both keywords and placements together. In this case, if a new placement needs to be refined with a set of keywords, you will only add placements to that ad group when you want those keywords to also control the ad's display.

For example, if you were Verizon attempting to market the Droid, you might have both ads in Figure 17.6 in your AdWords account. One of the ads compares the iPhone to the Droid. In this case, you would want iPhone-related keywords in the ad group so the ad shows up on pages that talk about the iPhone. The second ad talks mostly about Droid benefits; therefore, you would want a second ad group with more general keywords, such as "mobile phone" and "cell phone," to maximize the exposure of this ad on those placements. Both of these ad groups can have the same placements in them; it will be the keywords in the article that determine which ad is actually displayed.

Figure 17.6 Content network ads with different purposes

The second reason to create new ad groups is if you want different ads to be shown on different placements. In this case, if an existing ad group contains an ad you want to be shown on that placement, then add the placement to that ad group. If there is not an ad group with an ad you want to be shown, add the placement to a new ad group with the appropriate ad copy.

The third reason is if you are using different types of ad copy and want to set different bids for a placement based on the ad copy shown. This generally only applies if you are using both text ads and rich media ads, such as video or image, to target the same site. As you cannot set different bids for different ad copy, if you want to bid more for image or video ads than for text ads, you will have one ad group that contains text ads with a bid, and another ad group that has the same placements but uses rich media ads with a different bid.

Find Placements via the Placement Report If you are using the campaign organization discussed in "Organizing Your Content Campaigns" in Chapter 10, you will use the placement performance report to find sites doing well for you and add them to your placement campaign.

Find New Placements for Your Ads If you want to find highly relevant sites on which to place your ad, you need to do research to find them. There are two tools to use for finding new placements. The most robust tool is Google Ad Planner, discussed in "Google Ad Planner: Free Access to Expensive Data" in Chapter 10. The second tool is the placement tool, discussed in the Chapter 9 section, "Placement Targeting Tool." Using these two tools, along with the placement performance report, is the easiest way to find sites where you want your ad to be shown.

Create Ad Copy If you are using the placement performance report to find placements where you always want your ad to be shown, when you add the placement, copy the existing ad copy that should be displayed on the corresponding website.

If you are finding new placements, you can either write new ads or use the ad copy report to find which ads have been successful in your content campaigns. With placement-only campaigns, it is still useful to create multiple pieces of ad copy and test which one performs better.

Set Initial Bids If you are using the placement performance report to find placements for your placement targeted campaign, then you already know the corresponding metrics by placement, such as cost per acquisition, and can use the formulas from Chapter 13 to set your initial bids.

If you are adding new placements and have a content network campaign, then choose starting bids based on the data from similar types of placements.

If you do not have access to either set of data, you will have to choose a starting bid with little information. The steps will be the same as with the content campaign initial bid information discussed earlier. It is easy to raise and lower bids. Since it is easy to raise and lower bids, you should start with a lower bid, and if you are not receiving much exposure on a site, then raise the bid to see how that affects your exposure.

After you have created your initial campaigns, it is time to let the campaigns accumulate statistics. When the campaigns have data, it is time to optimize each campaign.

Optimizing Ongoing Campaigns

You will need to regularly run reports to determine how your campaigns are performing, and then make decisions on that data. In this section, we will examine optimization steps for each campaign type. In the next section, we will examine how often to run reports to create a comprehensive reporting schedule.

Optimizing Search Campaigns

The first step in optimizing search campaigns is to determine if you are going to bid at the keyword or ad group level. The most granular bid type, at the keyword level, gives you more control. However, it also takes more time to set keyword level bids. You may use a combination of both. For keywords that receive a significant amount of traffic, set keyword bids. For a set of keywords that receive little traffic, use ad group bids.

Making Bid Changes

Based on if you are using ad group level or keyword level bids, you will want to run the corresponding report. Use conditional formatting, found in "Revenue Per Click" in Chapter 13, to make a visual reference chart of your data (Figure 17.7). This will give you a high level look at how profitable or unprofitable the various keywords and ad group are. Next, use the formulas from Chapter 13 to adjust your bids.

Placement/ Keyword	Est. First Page Bid	Current Max CPC	Clicks	Avg CPC	Cost	Conversions	Value/ Click
Placement1		$0.35	8716	$0.32	$2,826.35	195	$1.96
Keyword1	$0.05	$0.50	8270	$0.65	$5,382.30	194	$1.37
Placement2		$0.35	6955	$0.31	$2,152.21	131	$0.51
Keyword2	$0.05	$0.50	3852	$0.95	$3,645.98	111	$0.49
Keyword3	$0.30	$0.35	3522	$0.27	$957.59	75	$0.31
Keyword4	$0.05	$0.50	1658	$0.53	$874.55	49	$0.29

Figure 17.7 Using conditional formatting to visualize the data

If you are making many bid changes, utilizing the AdWords Editor's import function can save you a significant amount of time.

The frequency of bid changes will be constrained by your technology and resources. If you are using automated bid systems, you may change bids daily. If you are using manual systems and you have other responsibilities besides AdWords, you might want to only change bids weekly.

If you find keywords that are not profitable, first examine the ad copy and landing pages to make sure they are appropriate. Make any adjustments as necessary. The second step is to examine the match type. If the unprofitable keywords are in broad or phrase match, you may want to look at the metrics in the search query report and change the match type to be more restrictive, such as exact match, to see how the keyword performs. If a keyword is not performing regardless of ad copy, landing page, and match type, then delete the keyword.

The logic just described assumes that you have unlimited budget if your keywords are profitable. However, that is rarely the case. If you are reaching your budget early in the day and cannot raise it, then delete the keywords that are not receiving conversions or have the highest cost per conversion. The other option is to lower your CPCs for all keywords. It is not uncommon to see an account that has a $100 daily budget and is spending $10 per click. This leads to only 10 clicks per day, and the budget is often depleted by noon. In this case, lowering your CPC to $5 might bring in 20 clicks at the same budget, or better yet, a $1 CPC for 100 clicks.

Conducting Additional Keyword Research

You will never find every keyword possible; there are just too many different ways that people search. However, you can continuously search for new words. There are three ways to keep conducting keyword research.

The first is by utilizing the search query report. This report will show you what someone actually searched for that triggered your ad. If you are using AdWords conversion tracking, you will also see the conversion rate and cost per conversion by each keyword variation. Run the search query report and look for keywords that are spending money and not in your account. If they are good keywords, then add them as actual keywords so you can set a bid. If the keyword is not leading to conversions, there are two steps to take. The first is to examine the associated ad copy and landing page. If the ad copy or landing page is not appropriate for that keyword, you may want to add that keyword to a different ad group that has a more appropriate landing page and ad copy to see if that keyword will be profitable under a different combination. If the ad copy and landing page are appropriate and the keyword is just not profitable, then delete the keyword and consider making it a negative keyword so your ad is no longer shown for that search.

The exception to deleting the keyword from your search campaigns is if you are also using a Budget Optimizer campaign to increase your exposure on early buy cycle keywords, as discussed in "Understanding Attribution Management" in Chapter 13. In the case of words that are not profitable but are leading to interaction on your website, delete these keywords from your current search campaign and place any appropriate ones into a Budget Optimizer campaign.

The second way to continuously conduct keyword research is to use the AdWords Keyword Tool site-spidering capability found in "Website Content: Jumpstarting Your Keyword List" in Chapter 3. If you are ever on a web page that discusses your products, use the site-spidering function to see if there are new keywords you do not have in your account yet.

The third method is to set aside time to conduct keyword research. Use the tools found in Chapter 3 and spend some time looking for new keywords.

Additional Optimization Techniques

Changing bids is the most common optimization. It is easy to become so focused on bidding that other types of optimization techniques are forgotten. There are other types of account analysis that should be performed on a regular basis.

Improving Quality Score Quality score is displayed at the keyword level. However, running a keyword report and examining all of the data can be time consuming. To use your time well, run a keyword report and then put the data in a pivot table, as discussed in "Increasing Your Quality Scores" in Chapter 7. Look for ad groups with low quality scores and high spends. Then work on the quality score for that ad group. Increasing the quality score in high spend, low quality score ad groups will lead to the largest gains for your account.

Test Ad Copy If you create at least two ads when you initially build a campaign, then you can start by measuring the results and refining your ad copy. To understand the metrics of your ad copy, run an ad performance report. Take the ad that performs the best and keep it. Examine the other ad copy to see if there are any outliers in the data where you can learn from other ad copy, then delete the underperforming ads. Create new ads for the ad group and continue testing. If you have well-established ad groups, you may only want the test ad to run a small percentage of the time. Refer to "Lowering the Risk of Losing Profits While Testing" in Chapter 15 to run limited tests.

Test Landing Pages You should continue testing landing page layouts and where you are sending traffic to increase conversion rates. Send traffic to different landing pages, and then run the URL performance report to see which landing pages are leading to the most profits. Keep the winning test, create new test variables, and continue testing. Small changes in conversion rates can lead to large changes in profits.

Budget Changes The easiest way to determine what you could have spent is by using the impression share report. The impression share report will tell you why your account did not accrue impressions. Combine this report with Google Trends or Google Insights for Search and you can learn to adjust your future budgets based on changes in search volume and lost impression share.

Trend Analysis for Ad Scheduling Analyze your data to determine if there are clear trends in your conversion rates or profit based on times of day or days of the week. If trends start to emerge, then you can use ad scheduling (see "Ad Scheduling: Automatically Changing Bids by Time Periods" in Chapter 13) to adjust your bids, or turn your campaigns on and off based on performance metrics.

Before deciding there is a trend, you should ensure that you have enough data to see a clear pattern. First, run an ad group performance report by hour. Next, run an ad group report by day of the week. Examine these two reports to see if there are clear trends. If there are, then use ad scheduling to adjust your bids.

Geographic Performance The geographic performance report allows you to see your performance in different geographic regions. Use this report to find underperforming areas. If there are geographies where your conversion rates are lower than normal, you will either want to exclude the area or create a campaign specific to that area. If you have areas where the conversion rates are higher than normal, you may want to create dedicated campaigns for that area to maximize your spend.

If your advertising reach is too big—for instance, any company advertising in every country with a $100 daily budget—then use Google Trends to find areas that are searching for your keywords, and limit your geography until you have the budget to start adding new areas.

While these techniques will get you started optimizing search campaigns, you should always be creative when trying to reach your target market. Whether it is running different ads by time of day for different geographies or using a single high value keyword in an ad group so you can test different ad copy with that keyword, there are many options available within AdWords if you know all of the settings. These steps to optimization should get you started, but they are not an ending point. You are only limited by a combination of your creativity and knowledge of AdWords.

Managing Budget Optimizer Campaigns

When you use the Budget Optimizer, also known as *focus on clicks bidding*, AdWords takes over your bidding and tries to maximize the clicks you are receiving for your keywords.

You can use the Budget Optimizer (Figure 17.8) in a search-only or content-only campaign. Therefore, your initial campaign setup is the same as when you are creating search or content campaigns.

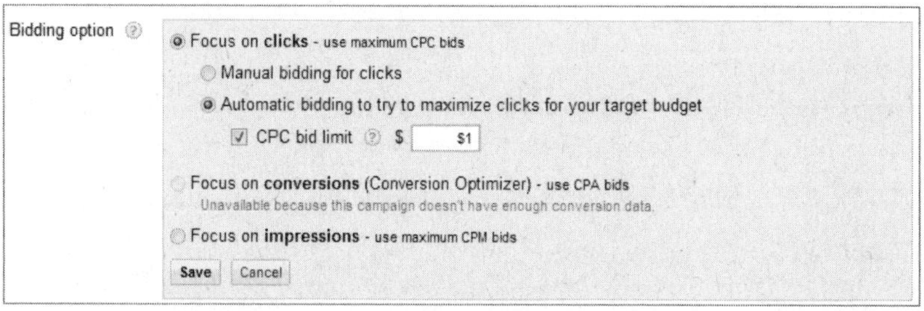

Bidding option ⓘ
- ⦿ Focus on **clicks** - use maximum CPC bids
  - ○ Manual bidding for clicks
  - ⦿ Automatic bidding to try to maximize clicks for your target budget
    - ☑ CPC bid limit ⓘ $ [$1]
- ○ Focus on **conversions** (Conversion Optimizer) - use CPA bids
  Unavailable because this campaign doesn't have enough conversion data.
- ○ Focus on **impressions** - use maximum CPM bids

[Save] [Cancel]

Figure 17.8 Choosing Focus On Clicks to enable the Budget Optimizer

When using the Budget Optimizer for search, you should ensure that each keyword is leading to page views, time on site, and low bounce rates. If a word in a Budget Optimizer campaign is not helping you reach your goals, that word should be deleted.

When using the Budget Optimizer for content campaigns, you will not see metrics by keyword, as all AdWords reports show content data at the ad group level. The success metrics for Budget Optimizer search and content campaigns are the same; however, for search you will examine keyword data and for content you will examine ad group data.

There are two ways of measuring Budget Optimizer campaign effectiveness. The first is to use the AdWords conversion tracker (Figure 17.9) and look at page views by keyword or ad group. However, as all keywords, ad copy, and landing pages share all conversion types within a campaign, you might not want to use every page view as a conversion to measure these campaigns' effectiveness. In this case, using Google Analytics or another analytics program to view this information is crucial. If a word or ad group starts to lead to conversions, you can move it back to your conversion optimizer or max CPC bidding campaigns to regain control over the keyword's visibility.

Conversion Tracking ▾ + Create a new action | Link your Analytics goals and transactions (2 unlinked) show: all | all but deleted

Delete | Edit Settings

	Action Name	Status	Tracking Purpose	Conversions (1-per-click) ▾	Conversions (many-per-click)
☐	Shopping Cart	Active	Purchase/Sale	221	395
☐	Contact	Active	Lead	122	147
☐	Pageview	Active	View of a key page	1021	10348

Figure 17.9 Tracking page views as a conversion

If the Budget Optimizer campaign is your only exposure campaign across all marketing channels, then examining the changes to brand searches and direct type in traffic can also give you an idea of any additional lift that this campaign is creating.

Optimizing Content Campaigns

The most exposure you can receive with AdWords is to run content campaigns, as the reach of the content network far exceeds that of search. However, with content campaigns there are steps you need to take to ensure that your ads are being placed correctly, and then you need to make sure your ads are being shown on those sites.

Ensure Your Ads Are Being Displayed Appropriately Once you have chosen keywords to create a theme for each ad group, your first optimization step is to make sure those ads are being shown on the correct sites. Run a placement performance report that shows the individual URLs where your ads are being displayed.

Click on the URLs in the report to see if the pages where your ads are being displayed are the types of pages where you want your ads. If they are not, then change the keywords in your ad group and repeat this step.

If the pages where your ads are being displayed are correct, it is time to move on to the next step, blocking websites.

Blocking Websites and Types of Content Examine the placement performance report. When you see sites that are not meeting your goals, use the site and category exclusion tool to block your ads from being shown on those sites.

Changing Content Bids Your bid for the content network is set at the ad group level. You cannot choose different bids by keyword. Therefore, when deciding what to bid on the content network, start by running an ad group performance report and segment the data to be content only.

If you are using the content network to bring sales into your company, and you are not necessarily using it as a discovery mechanism for finding placements, then you will want to set a bid based on your marketing goals. Take the data from the ad group report, and apply the same math from Chapter 13 to set your ad group level bids. The only difference is that you will not examine the bid for each keyword, you will examine the bid by ad group.

If you are using the content network as a discovery mechanism, you will still want to set a bid based on some performance metrics, but one of your goals will also be impressions and clicks for each ad group. If an ad group's bid is so low that it is not bringing in any impressions, you will never find new placements. Conversely, if your ad group is receiving so many clicks that you are quickly hitting your budget every day, then lower your ad group bids to receive more clicks at the same total budget.

Using Placements When you see a site that is meeting your goals, and you always want your ad to show on that site, you have two options.

You can add that site as a placement for that ad group. If you add a site as a placement, you can set a bid for that placement. Placement bids override ad group bids. Set a bid for that placement based on its performance.

The second option is to use a placement-only campaign. The advantage of using a placement-only campaign is that you can set a higher daily budget for the websites that are meeting your goals. In this case, block the website from the discovery campaign and add it to a placement-only campaign. The discovery campaign will be able to find new websites that meet your goals, and the placement campaign will be able to manage sites that are currently meeting your goals.

There will be times when you want to create a placement for a website, yet you cannot seem to add that site as a placement. A publisher can control if their website can be targeted specifically for placements. If the publisher does not allow this, then the only way for your ad to be shown on that site is through using the general content network with keywords.

Testing Ad Copy The content network reaches a large audience and is a good place to test ad copy to see which is performing best for you. Since the content network supports text, video, and image ads, you can conduct tests across different ad formats. Testing rich media ads in this manner is also useful before doing large CPM buys with websites directly.

When testing content network ad copy, run the ad performance report. With this report, you can segment out each ad type individually so that you only see video or image ads.

The content network has many options available. You can choose to display your ads based on keywords, placements, or placements and keywords, and then segment each ad group with different ad formats. Always keep in mind that the content network obeys your other campaign settings, such as ad scheduling or location targeting.

The just described steps will help you refine and optimize your content campaigns. However, keep your business goals in mind as you may want to use the content in unique ways that will cause you to use different optimization techniques.

Optimizing Placement Campaigns

Placement campaigns allow you to choose specific placements, either websites or sections of a website, where your ad will show. Because you are choosing a specific placement, your keywords are optional.

Placements Moved from Discovery Campaigns Do Not Perform If you run a placement performance report and find that the placements you found in your discovery campaign are no longer meeting your goals, do not immediately assume that the placement is no longer valid. First, examine these possibilities to see if you can regain the previous targeting.

Is different ad copy running on the new placement than what is in the discovery campaign? If yes, add the ad copy from the discovery content campaign. You may want to create a new ad group for just this placement and the new ad copy.

Did you add the placement, but not the keywords?

- While the placement might be the same, you could be shown on different pages of a placement if you did not move the keywords. Add the keywords from the discovery content ad group that found success on this placement.

- For narrow theme sites, you might not always move the keywords as the entire site could be relevant to your offer and using keywords may remove your ad from being shown to a targeted audience.

Use the placement tool to see if you can target a smaller section of the site. If you found success on the *New York Times* and added the entire site as a placement, your ad could easily be shown on a completely different section of such a large site. Your ad will convert differently when placed in the leisure section versus the business section. In this case, see if you can target a smaller section of the website.

Placements Added Directly Do Not Perform If you use the placement tool or Google Ad Planner to find websites, before assuming the websites do not convert, go through two steps. The first step is to test different ad copy. You might even test a couple of image ads and text ads to see if different ad copy performs. The second step is to add keywords to the ad group. Adding keywords is more appropriate for placements on large sites, but it can help refine your exposure on smaller sites as well.

Your Ad Is Not Being Shown on the Placement If your ad is not being displayed on a placement, there are two common reasons. The first is that your bid is too low. Raise your bid to see if your ad starts to be displayed. The second reason is publisher control. All website owners can filter certain ads from being shown on their sites. Just as advertisers have a category and site exclusion tool, the website owner has a similar tool. However, the advertisers are not notified if a publisher has rejected their ad or is not allowing your site to advertise on them directly.

When you combine placements, ad formats, keywords, ad scheduling, and geographic targeting, you have a lot of control exactly when your ad is displayed. Creating scenarios, as discussed in "Create Scenarios to Understand and Reach Your Targeting Audience" in Chapter 10, can help you put the correct message in front of your ideal audience at the proper time.

Optimizing CPM Campaigns

CPM bidding, also known as *focus on impressions*, is a bid type where you pay for an impression, not for a click. This bidding option is only available for a campaign that is only targeting the content network.

To create a CPM campaign, follow the earlier steps for creating a placement campaign or a content campaign. It is recommended that you start with only placements so you can choose each placement and become comfortable with the metrics. Bidding CPM for a keyword content campaign is possible, but you may waste a lot of money having your ads shown on inappropriate sites. CPM keyword bidding is not recommended for a beginner or anyone with a small budget.

With CPM campaigns, you are paying for the impression. The goal is often higher brand awareness or to introduce a new product. Since you are paying for an impression, not a click, you want every impression to count. Therefore, only use image or video ads when bidding CPM.

Reach and Frequency Performance Report The reach and frequency performance report will show you how many people saw your ad and how often they saw it over a certain time period. If your ad is being seen too often by the same people, change your frequency capping in the campaign settings.

Video Interaction Report If you are using video ads, your optimization goals should include how often a video is watched and how much of the video is being watched. Run an ad performance report to see these statistics. As AdWords video ads do not auto-play, the opening image is crucial to convince someone to watch your video. Testing the opening image to find which one leads to a higher play rate can drastically increase the success of a CPM campaign. It can be useful to test these images in a CPC campaign while you determine which image is best before moving to a CPM campaign.

Measuring Success for CPM Campaigns While you can get into complex measurements such as aided brand lift to measure your CPM campaigns, we will focus on some of the simpler ones to measure. The most common goals for online performance advertisers for CPM campaigns are to increase awareness and increase interaction with the website.

- Examine how many clicks you are receiving from the CPM ads.
- Examine the time on site and page views for those clicks.
- If using video, examine play rates and length of video viewed.
- While ads are running:
  - Examine changes in direct traffic.
  - Look for an increase in branded search keywords.
  - Analyze changes in CTR and conversion rates for your search ads.
  - Examine total conversions and sales.

These charts do not have to be complex; you can build a simple spreadsheet (Figure 17.10) that allows you to compare two time frames against each other.

	AdWords Only	AdWords & Display
Branded Searches	1211	1545
Conversion Rate	2.12%	2.45%
AdWords CTR	1.70%	1.70%
Total Site Visitors	212,083	302,423
Site Visitors from Display	0	12,089
Total Conversions	3605	5141
Total Sale $$	$90,135.28	$128,529.78
Cost of Display	0	$11,000
Cost of AdWords	$22,565	$21,872
Total Profit	$67,570.28	$95,657.78

Figure 17.10 A simple comparison of two time frames

With CPM ad buying, you often need to measure more than just the ad's metrics to determine success. It is not uncommon for a company to buy CPM ads and have the ads appear to be a failure. However, while those ads were running, the conversion rates of the search ads increased by 8 percent. In this case, examine the cost of the CPM ads versus the increase in revenue from the conversion rate lift to see if the ads are profitable.

Unless you have a sophisticated marketing department that understands how to measure success and failure of branding campaigns, judge the effectiveness of your CPM ads with metrics you can track.

Creating an Optimization Schedule

There are many ways to optimize campaigns based on your goals. With so many options available—from finding new exposure by expanding your placements to taking care of the money by setting bids—you need to create a structure that will help you continuously optimize and grow your account without feeling overwhelmed by the options.

We will walk through what a medium-sized account in a semi-competitive industry that is being run by an in-house person would do throughout the month to optimize their account.

If you are a small business, or AdWords is not your full-time job, then you may want to look at some of these reports less frequently. If you are a large account, you might want to break down these reports further so that you are only looking at a subset of data instead of the entire account. For instance, instead of examining the entire account daily, you might look at five campaigns on Monday and a different set of five on Tuesday. If you advertise in a competitive arena, you may want to look at some of these reports more often. However, the first step is to put together a time frame and what you want to see by each time frame.

Status Check: Every Day Run a campaign report that includes every campaign in your account. Look for changes in spend, profit, conversion rate, cost per conversion, and total conversions. What you are looking for are large changes from the norm. If you find changes, investigate the reason why. This is your daily AdWords check-in. You can also view this information in the AdWords Editor or the AdWords interface.

This will let you quickly see that your conversions dropped significantly and that it's because you had several ads disapproved. Or your content spend went up dramatically because your products were mentioned on CNN and people started looking for the products (in which case you might want to raise your budget).

Keyword Bids: Every Day or Week Decide how often you want to change bids, either daily or weekly. If you want to set bids weekly, then choose a day of the week, such as every Monday, to make these changes.

Run a keyword report that only includes search data. Use the formulas discussed in Chapter 13 to set your bids, add or remove keywords, or move them to a Budget Optimizer campaign.

Placement Bids: Every Day or Week As with keywords, choose how often you want to change placement bids. It is generally okay to change placement bids weekly and not to fret about them every single day. Run a placement performance report and then change the bids for your existing placements based on the formulas in Chapter 13. If you are changing your keywords bids each Monday, then run this report every Monday as well so you know that Mondays are bid change days.

How Often Should You Change Bids?

You will most likely not change every keyword, ad group, or placement bid every week. There will be some that need to be adjusted with new bids, and others will be fine with the current bid. Do not feel you constantly need to be changing bids if your account is doing well.

Most advertisers find that they need to change bids often in new campaigns to find the nice middle ground between exposure and conversions, and once it is found, the bid changes become more incremental in nature.

Quality Score Tuesdays Every Tuesday, work on quality score by using keyword reports and pivot tables. As quality score is not updated regularly in AdWords, keep track of the ad groups you have optimized for quality score. Leave those ad groups alone from a quality score standpoint for at least a week; often, two or three weeks allows time for AdWords to catch up to all your changes before you need to optimize the same ad groups again. If you are making landing page changes, it may take several weeks for those quality score changes to be reflected in your AdWords account.

New Keyword Wednesdays Every Wednesday, start by running a search query report. If keywords are not meeting your goals, then either make them negatives or put them in a new ad group with new ad copy.

If keywords are meeting your goals and are not in your account, add them as keywords. This is also the time to examine your match types. Technically the same keyword in broad and exact match is two different keywords. A unique keyword is both a keyword and match type combination.

Use the AdWords Keyword Tool and the SKTool to do some new keyword research. Another option is to bookmark pages throughout the week that discuss your products and services. On keyword Wednesday, use the site-spidering function of the AdWords Keyword Tool to spider those sites for new keywords.

If you have a small account, you may want to only do keywords research every other week or monthly. However, set aside a specific time each month to conduct keyword research and look for negative keywords.

Content Network Thursdays Every Thursday, run a placement performance report. If placements are not meeting your goals, block them in your campaign settings. If placements are meeting your goals, add them to a placement-only campaign.

If you are using demographic bidding, run the demographic bidding report each Thursday as well to see if you need to adjust your bids. If you are waiting to see if you have enough demographic data to set demographic bids, schedule a report to be sent to you monthly. You can then quickly examine it and determine whether to use demographic bids or delete the report and wait until next month.

Use the placement tool and Google Ad Planner to find new placements. If you are doing a minimal amount of placements, you may want to run these reports every other Thursday or once per month.

Testing Fridays You should always be testing. If you set up your ad groups with at least two pieces of ad copy, you always have testing data to analyze. There are two types of tests you should be running: ad copy and landing pages.

The first and third week of the month, run an ad copy report. Examine your ads to see if you have enough data to draw a conclusion about which ad is best for your account. For those ads, keep the best ad, examine the losers for any outliers, delete the losing ads, and then write a new ad so you are always testing.

If you have a large account and you are testing for both the content and search network, you might just look at search ads on the first Friday and your content ads on the third Friday.

The second and fourth week of the month, run a URL performance report to determine which landing pages are performing best for your goals. If you have conclusive data, then keep the best landing page and remove the other ones from your tests. If you do a limited amount of landing page testing, you might want to just look at a URL performance report the second week of the month, and then design new landing pages the fourth week of the month.

Trend Reporting: Monthly Each month, run a geographic performance report. Look for areas where you are not receiving good returns, then either write custom ads for those regions in a new campaign or exclude those regions from your campaigns.

Each month, examine your ad scheduling data by looking at conversion data by hour and day in both AdWords reports and your analytics systems. If there are changes to your conversion rates or cost per conversions, then change your ad scheduling settings.

Run an impression share report to see why you are losing impressions. This will give you a snapshot of your visibility for the previous month as well as ideas on how to increase your visibility.

Examine your demographic performance statistics to see if you want to set demographic bids or adjust your current demographic bids.

Use Google Trends and Google Insights for Search to see changes in your keyword trends so you can take advantage of seasonal behavior.

Creating a reporting schedule like this one for your account will help you keep track of what needs to be done each day or week and it will ensure that you are continuously optimizing the basics.

There are more metrics available in AdWords and analytics than we covered in this typical reporting schedule, as most companies do not need to see everything on a regular basis. For instance, the preceding schedule did not regularly examine conversion rates by position. As most companies' conversion rates do not vary by position, there is no need to constantly monitor those metrics where there are more important items to change. Some of these additional metrics you may want to examine on a quarterly basis.

If there are reports in this suggested schedule that are not applicable to you, just skip over them. If there are other metrics you do need to see on a regular basis, you can add them to your reporting schedule.

The best way to keep up with these reports is to put them in your calendar as recurring items. Then go into AdWords and set up the scheduling feature so these reports are run automatically.

It is also helpful to use a dedicated calendar for your AdWords account so you can keep track of notes, changes, and other reminders. For instance, if you are doing limited testing and do not want to look at test data every single week, instead of setting up recurring reports, add a note in your calendar that you started a test on this day, and then set a reminder to examine that data in one month so you do not forget to analyze the test results.

The more you customize your targeting, the more complex AdWords becomes to set up, monitor, and analyze. However, the system is flexible so that if you understand all of the settings and your company's goals, you can target users with unique and creative methods that will ultimately make your business more successful.

Best Practices for Creating and Managing Your AdWords Account

When creating and managing your AdWords account, first refer to the steps in this chapter. While each step seems simple, there are a large number of options for each step. When any one step involves making decisions that you are not yet comfortable making, refer back to the chapter where the options behind each step are fully explained.

By using the practices laid out in this chapter, you should be able to successfully create, organize, and optimize your AdWords account:

- The most important step in advertising successfully is first to determine the goals for your campaign.

- Once you understand the goals, you need to find a way of tracking your goals.

- Next, determine your campaign organization based on your goals and budget. When organizing your campaign, make sure you have search-only and content-only campaigns. Do not have campaigns shown on both networks.

- For each campaign, determine your ad groups before spending extensive time on keyword research. By determining your ad groups first, keyword research and ad group organization become more manageable.

- For each ad group, create keywords and ad copy. Make sure you include at least two ads in every new ad group so you can test ad copy.

- For search campaigns, use exact and phrase match keywords with small budgets or more control over ad serving. For larger budgets and for finding new keywords through the search query report, include some broad match keywords along with the other match types.

- When creating content campaigns, limit yourself to a handful of keywords, never more than 50. Do not worry about match types; they are ignored for the content network. Include any appropriate negative keywords, as AdWords does take these into account.

- For more control over the content network, use placement targeting so you know what websites will display your ads.

- Using a combination of keywords, content, and placement-only campaigns will help both maximize your exposure and control where your budget is being spent.

- Create profiles of your ideal customers and then use Google Ad Planner to find sites that house your target market.

- To properly optimize your campaigns, first create a reporting schedule. Set up a calendar with reminders for what you want to accomplish each day. Then schedule reports to be run and emailed to you automatically so you have data to work with each day and from which to make decisions.

AdWords allows you to be creative in reaching your target market. The system is flexible so that once you understand how ads are displayed, you can test the many variables discussed throughout this book to see which combination leads to the most profits for your account.

Following the advice in this book will help you create campaigns, choose keywords, write ad copy, design landing pages, and put your ad in front of your potential customers, which will help you succeed using Google AdWords.

The first ads were cave paintings created several millennia ago. The ancient Egyptians were the first to put ads on paper. The first ad to appear in a newspaper occurred in 1836. The first online clickable ad appeared in 1983. Google AdWords launched their first PPC product in 2002.

Google AdWords is still in its infancy. Many new features and targeting options will emerge over the coming years. By understanding how to use the advanced features of AdWords today, you will be able to take advantage of the new capabilities tomorrow.

Glossary

A

account performance report An AdWords report that displays metrics for the entire account.

ad extensions Expand ad copy with additional information such as business locations. This information is stored within the campaign settings.

ad group A collection of one or more ads and one or more keywords and/or placements.

ad group performance report An AdWords report that displays metrics for each ad group.

ad performance report An AdWords report that displays metrics for each ad copy.

ad preview tool An AdWords tool that allows you to see search results in various locations.

ad rank The position of an ad in a search result or on a content network page. Ad rank is determined by the formula: ad rank = (max cost per click) × (quality score).

ad scheduling Controls when an ad is shown by time of day or day of the week. The advanced version allows you to automatically change your max CPC by time of day or day of the week.

AdWords conversion tracking A free script offered by AdWords to track conversions on your website and view those metrics inside your AdWords account.

AdWords Editor A free downloadable desktop program created by Google that allows you to view and make changes to your AdWords account.

AdWords Keyword Tool A tool offered by Google that allows you to conduct keyword research and view metrics for each of those keywords.

automatic placements The placements where your ad is shown across the content network based on the keywords in that ad group.

average cost per click Also known as average CPC, the average amount paid for a click by any data point. If a keyword spends $100 and receives 100 clicks, the average cost per click is $1.

average position The average of all the positions where your ad is displayed. If your ad appears once in positions 1, 3, and 5, then your average position is 3.

B

B2B An acronym meaning business to business. It generally refers to businesses selling to other businesses.

B2C An acronym meaning business to consumer. It generally refers to businesses selling to consumers.

benefit An element of ad copy that showcases to a consumer a benefit of buying a product.

bid simulator A tool displayed for keywords that shows an estimate of impressions, clicks, and cost that the keyword would accrue if the maximum cost per click was changed.

broad match A keyword matching option that allows your keyword to show for misspellings and related words.

Budget Optimizer A bidding technique also known as "focus on clicks," where AdWords will bid for you in an attempt to maximize the number of clicks a campaign receives.

buying funnel The steps a consumer goes through before buying a product. The stages are: awareness, interest, learn, shop, and buy.

C

campaign A collection of ad groups. In AdWords, most of the options for controlling your ad's display are set at the campaign level and affect every ad group within that campaign.

campaign performance report An AdWords report that displays metrics for each campaign.

click A click occurs when someone sees your ad and then clicks on it.

click-through rate Also known as CTR, a calculation of the number of times your ad is clicked divided by the number of impressions that ad is displayed. If your ad has 100 impressions and 2 clicks, it has a 2 percent click-through rate.

conditional formatting A tool found in many spreadsheets, including Excel, that allows you to apply formats to cells or a range of cells based upon formulas or conditions in other cells.

content network A collection of sites that have partnered with Google to display AdWords ads. These ads are displayed based on the content of a page matching your keywords or chosen placements.

conversion A conversion occurs when a consumer conducts an action on your site that you deem valuable, such as subscribing to a newsletter, buying a product, or contacting your business.

Conversion Optimizer A bidding technique also known as "focus on conversions," where AdWords bids for you in an attempt to maximize the conversions a campaign receives.

conversion rate A formula derived from dividing the number of conversions a data point (keyword, placement, ad copy, etc.) receives by the number of clicks. If a keyword receives 100 clicks that lead to 2 conversions, that keyword has a 2 percent conversion rate.

cost per click How much a click costs. Related to average cost per click.

cost per conversion Also known as CPA or cost per action, the average amount it costs to receive conversions. The formula is total cost divided by total number of conversions. If an account spends $100 and receives 20 conversions, the cost per conversion is $5.

CPA See *cost per conversion*.

CPC See *cost per click*.

CPM An acronym for cost per thousand impressions.

CPM bidding Also known as "focus on impressions," this bidding technique is only available for content-only campaigns. With CPM bidding, you bid how much you are willing to pay each time your ad receives 1,000 impressions.

CTR See *click-through rate*.

D

daily budget The amount you are willing to spend on a campaign each day. Each campaign must have its own daily budget.

demographic bidding Demographic bidding allows you to automatically raise your max cost per click based on gender and age characteristics of the person viewing your ad.

demographic performance report An AdWords report that displays metrics based on demographic information, such as age and gender.

destination URL An aspect of ad copy that defines what page the user is taken to after they click on an ad.

Display Ad Builder A tool found inside an AdWords account that allows you to build different types of ads, such as video and image ads.

display URL An aspect of ad copy that allows the viewer to understand where they will be taken if they click on an ad.

DKI See *dynamic keyword insertion.*

dynamic keyword insertion A tool that allows you to automatically insert a keyword from your ad group into the ad copy.

E

enhanced content network A technique of using both placements and keywords in the same ad group to control where your ad is displayed on the content network.

exact match A keyword matching option that allows your keyword to show only when the search query matches your keyword exactly.

F

feature A term used in ad copy to explain an attribute or aspect of a product or service.

first page bid The minimum bid for a keyword to appear on page 1 for all geographies where the corresponding ad could be displayed.

frequency The average number of times a unique individual sees your ad in a certain time period. It is generally a measurement used for CPM ads.

frequency capping A campaign setting that allows you to cap the number of times an individual will see your ad in a given time frame. Frequency capping only applies to the content network.

G

geographic performance report An AdWords report that displays performance metrics for the geographies where your ads were displayed.

geo-qualified keyword Keywords that include geographic terms, such as "Chicago dentist" or "Arizona Insurance."

Google Ad Planner A research tool offered by Google that lets you see detailed statistics for websites and search for websites based on a variety of criteria.

Google AdWords Google's cost-per-click advertising platform.

Google AdWords Professional A certification offered by Google for those who meet certain requirements.

Google Analytics A Google tool that allows you to see detailed statistics for a website once you have installed a script on all the site's pages.

Google Local Business Center A website where one can input their local business information. This information can be connected to AdWords through ad extensions to display additional location information in the ad copy.

H

headline The top line of ad copy.

I

image ad An ad type that can be displayed across the content network that contains an image.

impression The number of times a data point (keyword, ad copy, etc.) is displayed.

impression share The percentage of times an ad is shown when it is eligible to be shown. This information is only available for search.

impression share report A campaign report that includes impression share metrics.

invalid clicks report A campaign report that includes information on the number of invalid clicks the campaign received.

K

keyword A single word or phrase inside an ad group that signals to AdWords that you would like an ad displayed when that word matches the search query. The match type is used in conjunction with a keyword to determine if your ad should be displayed for any given search query.

keyword content network Refers to a technique to show your ad on the content network based upon the keywords in an ad group.

keyword density analyzer A program that examines a page or set of pages and displays the frequency with which words and phrases appear on those pages.

keyword insertion See *dynamic keyword insertion*.

keyword match type Signals to AdWords how closely your keyword needs to be related to the search query before your ad can be displayed. The three options are broad, phrase, and exact.

L

landing page The page that is displayed after an ad is clicked.

landing page load time The length of time it takes for a page to load. This is a factor of quality score.

location extension An ad extension that is specific to a geographic location. This additional location information may be appended to ad text.

location targeting A campaign setting that allows you to choose where an ad will be displayed.

M

managed placements Placements specifically chosen by an advertiser and managed within an ad group.

match type See *keyword match type*.

max CPC Also known as maximum CPC, the bid set for a keyword, ad group, or placement and the most an advertiser will pay for a click.

max CPM Also known as maximum CPM, a bid set for a placement or ad group and the most an advertiser will pay for 1,000 impressions.

MCC See *My Client Center*.

mobile ad An ad type that shows on phones that do not have full HTML browsers.

multivariate testing A testing method that simultaneously tests several variables to determine which combination of variables is the best.

My Change History tool An AdWords tool that allows you to see what changes were made in an AdWords account.

My Client Center An administrative interface that allows you to connect, view, and manage multiple AdWords accounts from a single login.

N

navigational query A search query where the user's intent is to find a specific page on the Web.

negative keyword A keyword matching option that allows you to stop an ad from being displayed if the search query contains a listed negative keyword.

P

pay per click An advertising medium where the advertiser is only charged for each click that an ad accrues.

phrase match A keyword matching option that allows your keyword to show only when the search query contains that keyword. Additional words can appear before and/or after the search query.

pivot table A data summarization tool found in Excel and other spreadsheet programs.

placement Locations on the content network where an ad is displayed. A placement can be a domain, section of a website, or an individual ad unit within a website.

placement/keyword performance report An AdWords report that shows metrics for each keyword or placement where your ad is displayed. You can only see the domain where a placement is displayed, not the individual URL.

placement performance report An AdWords report that shows metrics for each placement where your ad is displayed. You can see individual URLs of the sites that display the ads.

position preference An AdWords feature that allows you to choose which position, or range of positions, in which you would like your ad to appear.

PPC See *pay per click*.

premium ads Ads that show above the natural search results at the top of a page.

profit per click The average amount of profit a data point (ad copy, keyword, etc.) receives each time it receives a click. If a keyword leads to $100 in profits on 50 clicks, each click leads to $2 in profit on average.

profit per impression The average amount of profit a data point (ad copy, keyword, etc.) receives each time it is displayed. If an ad copy receives 1,000 impressions that lead to $100 in sales, on average each impression is worth $0.10.

Q

quality score A measure of how relevant an ad copy, landing page, or keyword is. Quality score is used to determine your ad rank and whether an ad should be displayed.

R

reach The total number of unique users who see an ad over a given time period.

reach and frequency performance report A report that shows reach and frequency information for your ads on the content network.

return on investment (ROI) The ratio between how much is spent and revenue. To calculate ROI, divide revenue by spend. If an account spends $1 and makes $2, its ROI is 200 percent.

revenue per page view Also known as RPV, a measure of how much revenue each page view or 1,000 page views generate. Pertains to publishers who sell ad space on their sites.

rich media ads Ads that contain media types other than text, such as video or images.

ROI See *return on investment.*

RPV See *revenue per page view.*

S

search partners Websites that Google has partnered with to display Google search ads.

search query The words typed into a search engine by a user.

search query performance report An AdWords report that displays metrics based on the user's search query.

buying funnel See *buying funnel.*

site and category exclusion tool An AdWords tool that allows you to exclude ads being

shown on certain domains or certain types of content.

smart pricing The discounting system used by AdWords to determine what an advertiser should be charged for a click on the content network based upon how likely a site is to lead to a conversion.

spider A program that crawls the Web indexing content.

split testing Testing two variables against each other at one time to determine which leads to better performance.

T

transactional query A search query where the user is looking for a site on which to conduct a transaction.

U

URL performance report An AdWords report that displays metrics for each destination URL used within an account.

V

value per click An AdWords reporting metric that displays the average revenue that a click generates.

video ad An ad type that can be displayed across the content network that contains video.

Index

Note to the reader: Throughout this index **boldfaced** page numbers indicate primary discussions of a topic. *Italicized* page numbers indicate illustrations.

Special Offers